The Alchemy of Conquest

Writing the Early Americas

Anna Brickhouse and Kirsten Silva Gruesz, Editors

The Alchemy of Conquest
Science, Religion, and the Secrets of the New World

Ralph Bauer

University of Virginia Press
Charlottesville and London

University of Virginia Press
© 2019 by the Rector and Visitors of the University of Virginia
All rights reserved
Printed in the United States of America on acid-free paper

First published 2019

9 8 7 6 5 4 3 2 1

Library of Congress Cataloging-in-Publication Data

Names: Bauer, Ralph, author.
Title: The alchemy of conquest : science, religion, and the secrets of the New World / Ralph Bauer.
Description: Charlottesville : University of Virginia Press, 2019. | Series: Writing the early Americas | Includes bibliographical references and index.
Identifiers: LCCN 2018048205 (print) | LCCN 2018059506 (ebook) | ISBN 9780813942551 (ebook) | ISBN 9780813942544 (cloth : alk. paper) | ISBN 9780813942568 (pbk. : alk. paper)
Subjects: LCHS: America—Early accounts to 1600—History and criticism. | Alchemy—Early works to 1800—History and criticism. | America—Discovery and exploration.
Classification: LCC E141 (ebook) | LCC E141 .B25 2019 (print) | DDC 970.01—dc23
LC record available at https://lccn.loc.gov/2018048205

Cover art: "Nutrix eius terra est" (The Earth is his nurse). Emblema II. (In Michael Maier, *Atalanta fugiens* [1618]; courtesy of the Library of Congress); background: *Equatorial Jungle,* Henri Rousseau, 1909 (Shutterstock)

For Fredrika

What was America in 1492 but a Loose-Fish, in which Columbus struck the Spanish standard by way of waifing it for his royal master and mistress? What was Poland to the Czar? What Greece to the Turk? What India to England? What at last will Mexico be to the United States? All Loose-Fish. What are the Rights of Man and the Liberties of the World but Loose-Fish? . . . What is the great globe itself but a Loose-Fish?
 —Ishmael in Herman Melville, *Moby Dick*

The Brotherhood of American Explorers was established on April 17, 1492, the day that King Ferdinand and Queen Isabella consented to support the voyage of Christopher Columbus. Since then, according to promotional histories, the elitist organization has admitted to membership no more than nine brothers each year. The public notions held that the brothers were explorers to the nines; however, their perfections were not espoused from leather armchairs. The explorers were associated with political wealth, righteous patriotism, and covert activities on reservations and in Third World nations with deposits of uranium and other rare minerals.
 —Gerald Vizenor, *The Heirs of Columbus*

Contents

    List of Illustrations   xi

    Acknowledgments   xv

    Introduction: Alchemy and Apocalypse in Macondo   1

Part I. The Alchemy of Exception

  1 The Hermeneutics of Secrecy: Aristotle and Discovery   49

  2 Egyptian Gold: Alchemy and Crusade in the Later Middle Ages   75

  3 The Alchemy of Conversion: Ramón Llull's Chivalric Missionary Science   105

Part II. The Alchemy of Conquest

  4 The Secrets of the World: Christopher Columbus's Ecstatic Materialism   135

  5 The Llullian Renaissance and European Expansionism   184

  6 Physicians of the Soul: The Alchemy of Reduction and Ethno-demonology in Early America   213

Part III. Lucretius's New World

  7 Cannibal Heterotopias in the Sixteenth Century   267

  8 Homunculus americanus   290

  9 The Blood of the Dragon: Alchemy and New World *Materia Medica*   337

Part IV. The Alchemy of the White Legend

  10 Walter Raleigh's Legends: Black, Gold, and White   369

11	Things of Darkness: Alchemy, Ethno-demonology, and the Protestant Cant of Conquest	401
12	Eating Bacon: Alchemy and Cannibal Science	430
	Coda: Alexander von Humboldt, Alchemist of the Tropics	471
	Notes	487
	Index	625

Illustrations

Figure 1. Francis Bacon, frontispiece, *Instauratio magna* (1620) — 3

Figure 2. Andrés García de Céspedes, *Regimiento de nauegación* (1606) — 4

Figure 3. The serpent ouroboros (1618) — 17

Figure 4. Thomist natural law metaphysics — 52

Figure 5. Christ being hanged (Ullmann, *Buch der Heiligen Dreifaltigkeit*) — 86

Figure 6. Christ being killed (Ullmann, *Buch der Heiligen Dreifaltigkeit*) — 87

Figure 7. Woodcut depicting Arnald of Villanova (Hartmann Schedel, *Nuremberg Chronicle*) — 97

Figure 8. Christ being racked (Ullmann, *Buch der Heiligen Dreifaltigkeit*) — 101

Figure 9. Ramón Llull's "First Figure," showing the Nine Dignities — 118

Figure 10. The Llullian *Arbor scientiae* — 120

Figure 11. Columbus's signature, detail — 141

Figure 12. Columbus as Christ Bearer in Juan de la Cosa's *Mappa mundi* (1500), detail — 142

Figure 13. Table of lunar eclipses (1476) — 157

Figure 14. Heraldic symbol of the Crown of Aragon — 170

Figure 15. Dante's scheme of the universe, slightly modified (1855) — 176

Figure 16. "Nutrix eius terra est" (The Earth is his nurse) (1687) — 177

Figure 17. Missionary instructs Native Americans (1579) — 243

Figure 18. A mummy seen by André Thevet in Egypt (1554) — 273

xii   Illustrations

Figure 19. Native Americans executing prisoners of war (1558) — 283

Figure 20. Native Americans preparing a captive for ritual killing (1580) — 284

Figure 21. Brazlilian cannibalism (Theodor de Bry, 1593) — 287

Figure 22. Nicolás Monardes, "El Dragon" (1580) — 338

Figure 23. Nicolás Monardes, "El Dragon" (1580), detail — 339

Figure 24. Martin Schongauer, *Flight into Egypt,* woodcut — 352

Figure 25. Martin Schongauer, *Flight into Egypt,* woodcut, detail — 353

Figure 26. Nicolás Monardes, frontispiece to "Diálogo del hierro" (1574) — 356

Figure 27. Nicolás Monardes, frontispiece to "Diálogo del hierro," detail (1574) — 357

Figure 28. Dragon being slain (1687) — 386

Figure 29. "Taclla," Andean digging stick and symbol of *pachakuti* (1615) — 397

Figure 30. Passage of refracted light through a solid medium, according to Harriot's atomistic theory of matter — 405

Figure 31. Diagram of refraction as reflection — 406

Figure 32. John White, *The Flyer* — 410

Figure 33. Theodor de Bry, *The Coniuerer* (1590) — 411

Figure 34. Theodor de Bry, *Der Schwarzkünstler oder Zauberer* (1590) — 412

Figure 35. Sandro Botticelli, *Primavera,* with Hermes — 413

Figure 36. Sandro Botticelli, *Primavera,* detail: Hermes — 414

Figure 37. *Historia von D. Johann Fausten* (1587) — 416

Figure 38. Native Floridians worshipping a column decorated with the French royal coat of arms (1591) — 418

Figure 39. Theodor de Bry, frontispiece, *America,* pt. 3 (1593) — 420

Figure 40. Theodor de Bry, frontispiece, *America*, pt. 4. (1594)   421

Figure 41. John Smith, from *A map of Virginia vvith a description of the countrey, the commodities, people, government and religion* (1612)   426

Figure 42. Francis Bacon, frontispiece, *The Great Instauration* (1620), detail   431

Figure 43. The arrival of St. Bartholomew in pre-Columbian Peru (1615)   443

Figure 44. The Green and Red Lion (1618)   455

Figure 45. "Portavit eum ventus in ventre suo" (The wind carried him in his belly) (1618)   456

Figure 46. Theodor de Bry, "Their matter of prainge vvith Rattels abowt te fyer" (1590)   457

Figure 47. Alexander von Humboldt, chart showing mean temperature around the world as dependent on latitude, longitude, and altitude (1817)   476

Figure 48. Alexander von Humboldt's *Naturgemälde* of the Chimbarrazo (1805).   477

Acknowledgments

I would like to thank, first and foremost, Anna Brickhouse and Kirsten Silva Gruesz, the editors of the series in which this book appears, as well as Eric Brandt, Assistant Director and Editor in Chief at the University of Virginia (UVA) Press, and Ellen Satrom, Managing Editor of UVA Press, for their initial interest, as well as considerable support and patience with regard to the completion of this project. Special thanks go to the University of Virginia's Americas Center/Centro de las Américas for providing a generous publishing subvention that greatly helped with the publication of this book. I also want to thank the anonymous readers for UVA Press for their helpful comments and suggestions, as well as the UVA editorial board for their support. Thanks also to Susan Murray for her editorial work on the manuscript. I dedicate this book to Fredrika Teute for her long-standing leadership in expanding the horizons of early American studies generally, and for her generous support of my work, particularly, with her invaluable encouragement, advice, and critiques with regard to this book.

During the many years that this project has taken to complete, many friends as well as colleagues in my department, my university, and the profession at large have offered invaluable readings, advice, comments, and conversations on various earlier and partial iterations of this book. These friends and colleagues include Orlando Bentancor, Ruth Hill, Carles Pitarch, David Boruchoff, Surekha Davies, Marcy Norton, Allison Bigelow, Jessica Wolfe, Cynthia Radding, Jerry Passannante, Kellie Robertson, William Eamon, Harold Cook, Nicholas Popper, Holly Brewer, Richard Bell, Gordon Hutner, Nadine Zimmerli, Paul Mapp, Sandra Gustafson, Gordon Sayre, Luis Fernando Restrepo, Sara Castro-Klaren, Jaime Marroquín Arredondo, Ricardo Padrón, Hester Blum, Helmbrecht Breinig, Oliver Scheiding, Heike Paul, Günter Leypoldt, Jan Stievermann, Udo Hebel, James Delbourgo, Nicholas Dew, Nicholas Wey-Gómez, Zachary Matus, Tara Nummedal, Owen Stanwood, Hal Langfur, John Slater, Stephanie Kirk, Sarah Rivett, Santa Arias, Raul Marrero Fente, Timothy Bruno, Kelly Wisecup, Jason Payton, Steve Rojcewicz, Leon Jackson, Consolación Baranda, Robert Levine, David Shields, Vera Kutzinski, Ottmar Ette, Colin McEwan, Antonio Barrenechea, and Lukas Etter. Special thanks go hereby to James Dougal Fleming, who has read and commented on the entire manuscript. I could not be more grateful for his invaluable advice and comments. Special thanks also go to my colleague Andrea Frisch, from whom

I have learned a great deal in the course of several years of team-teaching a lecture course on early modern accounts of discovery and cultural encounter. This book is in many ways the product of our collaboration in teaching.

Thanks also go to the John Carter Brown Library (JCB) for granting me a long-term fellowship that was absolutely vital in the conception and research of this project. I am especially indebted for their intellectual and bibliographic resourcefulness to former director Norman Fiering, as well as to past and present members of the JCB staff and community, including Ken Ward, Leslie Tobias Olson, Susan Newberry, and Carol Delaney.

I also thank the English Department at the University of Maryland for its continuous support of my work and initiatives, providing me with research funds, leave, and research-assistant support over the years. With regard to this project, I want to express my special gratitude to the excellent research assistant who has worked with me on the intricacies of medieval Latin, Benjamin Turnbull, one of the most promising classicists of his generation.

Earlier versions of parts of this book have previously appeared in various journals and collections of essays. Specifically, earlier versions of a part of the introduction have appeared in a special issue of *Colonial Latin American Review* 26, no. 1 (March 2017); in the collection of essays *Turn of Events,* edited by Hester Blum (University of Pennsylvania Press, 2016), and in a special issue of *English Language Notes* (56, no. 2 [2018]), edited by Maria Windell. Parts of chapter 9 have appeared in *Medical Cultures in Early Modern Spain,* edited by José Pardo Tomás, Maria Luz López Terrada, and John Slater (Ashgate, 2014). Earlier versions of parts of chapter 10 appeared in *Science and Empire in the Atlantic World,* edited by James Delbourgo and Nicholas Dew (Routledge, 2007); in *Translating Nature: Cross-Cultural Histories of Early Modern Science,* edited by Jaime Marroquín Arredondo and Ralph Bauer (University of Pennsylvania Press, 2019); or are forthcoming in *The Routledge Companion to Colonial Latin America and the Caribbean (1492–1898),* edited by Santa Arias and Yolanda Martínez San-Miguel. And various early versions of parts of chapter 11 have appeared in *Coloniality, Religion, and the Law in the Early Iberian World,* edited by Santa Arias and Raul Marrero Fente (Vanderbilt University Press, 2014) and in *Religious Transformations in the Early Modern Americas,* edited by Sarah Rivett and Stephanie Kirk (University of Pennsylvania Press, 2014). Finally, various early versions of the coda have appeared in *The Eighteenth Century: Theory and Interpretation* or are forthcoming in a collection of essays in honor of Lois Parkinson Zamora and edited by John Ochoa and Monika Kaup. My thanks to the editors and readers of these earlier versions for their helpful comments.

Finally, I want to express my deepest gratitude to my wife, Grace Crussiah, for her love and companionship over the years. This work would not have been possible without her support and partnership.

The Alchemy of Conquest

INTRODUCTION

Alchemy and Apocalypse in Macondo

In Gabriel García Márquez's epochal novel *Cien años de soledad* (*One Hundred Years of Solitude*), the nineteenth-century South American patriarch José Arcadio Buendía and several of his fellow villagers set out from their newly founded town of Macondo in order to discover a passage to the Pacific Ocean. But instead of completing the age-old quest, they find, after many days of struggle, an enormous sixteenth-century Spanish galleon in the South American jungle: "Tilted slightly to the starboard, it had hanging from its intact masts the dirty rags of its sails in the midst of its rigging, which was adorned with orchids. The hull, covered with an armor of petrified barnacles and soft moss, was firmly fastened into a surface of stones. The whole structure seemed to occupy its own space, one of solitude and oblivion, protected from the vices of time and the habits of the birds. Inside, where the expeditionaries explored with careful intent, there was nothing but a thick forest of flowers."[1] The discovery of the galleon "broke José Arcadio Buendía's drive," for he considered it a "trick of whimsical fate to have searched for the sea without finding it, at the cost of countless sacrifices and suffering, and to have found it all of a sudden without looking for it, as it lay across his path like an insurmountable object." Realizing that the location he chose for founding Macondo is actually a peninsula, Buendía falls into a deep despair: "We're going to rot our lives away here," he cries out to his wife, Úrsula, "without receiving the benefits of science."[2]

Buendía's fascination with the wonders of modern science had first been incited by the arrival of an alchemist named Melchíades and his carnivalesque gypsy band in Macondo, which was then still a world so new that "many things lacked names and that in order to indicate them, it was necessary to point." But the scientific marvels that Melchíades brings—a magnet, a magnifying glass, a telescope, and even an entire alchemical laboratory—do not lead to the advancement of knowledge and social progress in Macondo; instead, they inflame the imaginations of the male members of the Buendía clan with futile quests for metallic transmutation; harebrained schemes of solar warfare; and vain attempts to find scientific proof for the existence of God. Generation after generation, the men of Macondo are trapped in a cycle of madness, solitude, and arrested development that ends a hundred years later with the dramatic realization of the last of Buendías, in the last paragraph of the novel, that Macondo's history and destruction had been scripted all along in an apocalyptic prophecy, written down in an enigmatic manuscript in the ancient Indo-European language of Sanskrit by the alchemist, chronicler, and prophet Melchíades. Thus, as Aureliano Buendías finally deciphers the manuscript, it is revealed that Macondo, "the city of mirrors (or mirages) would be wiped out by the wind and exiled from the memory of men at the precise moment when Aureliano Babilonia would finally finish deciphering the parchments, and that everything written on them was unrepeatable since time immemorial and forever more, because races condemned to a hundred years of solitude did not have a second opportunity on earth."[3]

This book might be described as an attempt to tell the literary and cultural history of Melchíades's alchemical manuscript, as well as to understand its apocalyptic power. The memorable image of the sixteenth-century Spanish galleon in García Márquez's novel shares a long tradition with the Melchíadean language of alchemy in the early modern historiography of the discovery of America. Perhaps the most iconic iteration of the former can be found on the frontispiece of the *Instauratio magna* (*The Great Instauration*, 1620), Francis Bacon's programmatic elaboration of a new method of scientific inquiry by inductive elimination that would come to define the so-called Scientific Revolution: a sixteenth-century galleon passing through the Pillars of Hercules into the pure realm of nature in the New World, leaving behind all tradition, politics, and culture in the Old. As is well-known now, Bacon's image was probably adapted from a Spanish manual on navigation, Andrés García de Céspedes's *Regimiento de nauegacion* (Madrid, 1606), which had presented on its title page a variation of the Habsburg coat of arms (see figs. 1 and 2).[4] For Bacon, the Habsburg topos of *plus ultra* (further beyond) seems to have captured his own idea of a new, reformed, or purified science that repudiated the old worlds of what he called "received philosophy"—the book-bound knowledge of Aristotelian Scholasticism. Although Bacon himself still had to employ all the arts of rhetoric to persuade his (largely indifferent) monarch of the benefits of his proposal for a state-sponsored science on an empiricist footing, by the end of the seventeenth century the European discovery of America had become a common allegory for the triumph of the experimental method in the so-called New Sciences among the Fellows of the newly founded Royal Society of London. Thus, the "chymist" Noah Biggs described his alchemical inquiry into the structure of matter as an "investigation into the America of nature."

> I praise God who hath been so bountifull to me, as to call me to the practice of Chymistry, out of the dregs of other Professions: Since Chymistry hath principles

Figure 1. Francis Bacon, frontispiece, *Instauratio magna* (1620). (Courtesy of the Library of Congress.)

Figure 2. Andrés García de Céspedes (1560–1608), *Regimiento de nauegacion q[ue] mando haser el rei nuestro señor por orden de su Conseio Real de las Indias a Andres Garcia de Cespedes* (Madrid: en casa de Iuan de la Cuesta, Año M.DCVI, 1606). (Courtesy of the John Carter Brown Library at Brown University.)

not drawn from fallacious reasonings, but such as are known by nature, & conspicuous by fire; and she prepareth the *Intellect* to penetrate, not the upper deck or *surface* of things, but the deep hold, the *concentrick* and *hidden* things of nature and maketh an investigation into the *America* of nature, farther then the whole *Heptarchy,* yea, then the whole Common-Wealth of sciences, all put together, and peirceth unto the utmost confines and profundities of reall truth.[5]

Biggs's peculiar phrase "the *America* of nature" suggests that, by the second half of the seventeenth century, the European discovery of America had become the *paradigm* of scientific discovery per se in the "New" or "Experimental Philosophy" as first theorized by Bacon and then implemented by the Royal Society—a paradigm of discovery predicated on the idea that "reall truth" is to be found by investigating not the "surface of things" but the "hidden things of nature."[6] In terms of Thomas Kuhn's famous formulation, we might say that it was in the wake of Bacon's New World paradigm of discovery that scientific change became itself *paradigmatic* in modern Western culture. By "paradigmatic" change, I mean Kuhn's sense of the term as a substitution or supersession of an older model of science by a newer one that makes an absolutist claim to truth in a larger metanarrative of scientific progress.[7] The modern structure of scientific change Kuhn described as a revolutionary "paradigm shift" stands in marked contrast with the early modern (or "Renaissance") pattern of scientific change during the sixteenth century, which Roland Greene has compared to a "palimpsest"—the overwriting of an older meaning of a word or concept (in his case, "invention") by an emerging new meaning, without the older one being erased, to the effect of a coexistence of several meanings that would seem to our modern minds to be anachronistic.[8] Whereas, arguably, the pattern of epistemic change Greene described still survives in the humanities today, paradigmatic change has governed the natural sciences from the eighteenth to the late twentieth century, when the debate about quantum physics and string theory signaled the "end of discovery" in the Baconian sense of the word.[9]

The White Legend

García Márquez's literary image of the European galleon entangled in (South) American nature defamiliarizes the triumphant narrative of scientific progress underwriting the Baconian paradigm of discovery, an apocalyptic narrative that had long been suspect from the "avant-garde" point of view of Latin America on scientific modernity. Indeed, Macondo's apocalyptic end in Melchíades's alchemical manuscript alerts us to some of the more dystopian legacies of Baconian science in its historical entanglements with the violence of European imperial expansionism and settler colonialism in the early modern period. One of these legacies came to a head in 2007, when the United Nations General Assembly adopted the long-anticipated Declaration on the Rights of Indigenous Peoples by a vote of 143:4. The four countries that voted in opposition to the Declaration were Australia, Canada, New Zealand, and the United States—all of them former British colonies. In the case of the

United States, this opposition was based on a long legal tradition that reaches back at least to the 1823 Supreme Court case *Johnson v. M'Intosh,* in which Chief Justice John Marshall ruled that private citizens (in this case, Johnson) could not purchase land from Native American nations because, by right of "preemption," the title to all Indian lands lawfully belonged to the federal government of the United States and that, therefore, the government held the exclusive right of conferring onto private citizens titles to Native American lands. The government's title to Indian land, Marshall explained, rested on what he called the "Doctrine of Discovery"—the principle "that discovery gave title to the government by whose subject, or by whose authority, it was made, against all other European governments, which title might be consummated by possession. . . . Discovery gave exclusive title to those who made it." The connection between "discovery" and "exclusive title" rested on a tradition in Roman law, according to which a *res* or *terra nullius* (a thing or land without an owner) belonged to whoever first finds it. But Marshall specifically invoked the examples of the Iberian empires in the Americas. "Spain did not rest her title solely on the grant of the Pope," he wrote. "Her discussions respecting boundary, with France, with Great Britain, and with the United States, all show that she placed it on the rights given by discovery." Marshall hereby perpetuated an Anglo-American legal fiction that sought to legitimate the Protestant territorial claims in the Americas vis-à-vis the claims previously made by other, Catholic European powers, not vis-à-vis indigenous claims to sovereignty in the New World. With regard to indigenous claims, he presumed that the question had been settled in the sixteenth century—that what he called the "doctrine" of discovery had been legitimated by the Spanish conquest of America.[10]

We do not usually think of discovery primarily in connection with indigenous rights, imperial conquest, and settler colonialism. In what Bruno Latour has called our modern "purified" science, discovery means not the expansion of one people's dominion at the expense of another but the extension of human knowledge into the realm of the unknown, into the realm of "nature."[11] Discovery comes hereby before conquest, and to the extent that conquests have often followed discoveries in history, they are seen as the result of a regrettable but avoidable aberration of the natural human propensity to want to discover new things. In fact, there is a hardy Anglo-American tradition that does not conceive of the British invasion and occupation of America as a conquest at all. Thus, Anglophone historians of America since the seventeenth century have preferred words such as "plantation," "settlement," and "colonization" to describe the English presence in America following its "discovery." The phrase "the conquest of America" hereby inevitably refers to sixteenth-century Spanish America, which appears as a temporary relapse into medievalism that seventeenth-century English colonists had been called on to rectify.[12] The Black Legend and the White Legend—the story of the inordinate cruelty of the Spanish conquest of America and the story of the English discovery of a virginal America respectively—thus became the two interdependent founding myths of Anglo-American settler colonialism. The founders of the United States are therein seen as the heirs not of Hernando Cortés the conqueror but of Christopher Columbus the discoverer.[13] Hence, in the United States, Columbus Day is celebrated but not Cortés Day, even though Columbus never came any closer than Cortés to a place that would later become a part of the United States. By contrast, the sixteenth-century Spanish conquest has appeared in the modern Anglo-American historical imagination as a sort of historical parenthesis within the "Age of Discovery"—the roughly two hundred years between Columbus's landfall and the publication of Isaac Newton's *Principia*.

According to the White Legend, it was an age when Western culture broke through the traditional confines of the book-bound circle of classical knowledge; liberated itself from the inherited religious superstitions of the medieval "Dark Ages"; and ushered forth the modern age of empiricism, progress, and even scientific "revolution." Columbus's first transatlantic journey is hereby seen as *the* watershed event that propelled Western culture on its distinctly modern path, a path that not only broke with its own medieval past but also set it apart from other, non-Western cultures in the world. Why, asked the popular American historian Daniel Boorstin, did not the Chinese, the Arabs, or the Indians discover America? The reason, in his view, was an essential difference in the history of humanity between those "solar" cultures that, like the modern West, prize innovation over tradition and those "lunar" cultures, like those founded by the Chinese, Arabs, or Indians, that prize tradition over innovation. "My hero is Man the Discoverer," he declared; "the world we now view from the literate West . . . had to be opened for us by countless Columbuses. . . . All the world is still an America."[14]

To be sure, few historians specializing today in the study of the early modern period, the early Americas, or the history of science still subscribe to Boorstin's heroic (and racist) account of "the discoverers" as the unambiguous heralds of universal human progress. Some historians have recently even described the disastrous demographic, ecological, and cultural consequences of Columbus's discovery for those who were discovered as an "American Holocaust."[15] More broadly, the Columbian Exchange following Europe's discovery of America has been seen as the beginning of the Anthropocene, the epoch in global history when "many geologically significant conditions and processes are profoundly altered by human activities."[16] Even the very idea of a European "discovery" of America in 1492 by Columbus has come under critical scrutiny. However, much of this debate has revolved around the question of who was "first" to discover America—the Norse, possibly even Phoenicians, Africans, and Chinese, not to mention Native Americans.[17] The question of discovery has become, in this school of thought, a mere question of perspective. In a classic statement characteristic of much modern scholarship on the question of discovery, Hans Selye writes: "Was America discovered by the Indians who were here from time immemorial, by the Norsemen who came in the tenth century, or by Christopher Columbus, who came in 1492? It is still being discovered now, every day, by anyone who drills a new well. . . . Discovery is always a matter of viewpoint and degree. Whenever we single out an individual as the discoverer of anything, we merely mean that for us he discovered it more than anyone else."[18] Selye's understanding of discovery as a "matter of viewpoint" is fundamentally flawed, however, for it presupposes not only that the various accounts of discovery (Native American, Norse, African, Chinese, European, etc.) constitute a single tradition but also that all these groups conceived of their presence in the Americas as the consequence of a "discovery." Yet, if surviving oral and textual traditions are an indication, most (if not all) Native American cultures conceived of their presence in the Americas as the result not of a "discovery" but, similar to Old World peoples, of various acts of genesis after which they have always been there.[19] And why should it be any different? While we know today by way of empirical science that *Homo sapiens* spread to Europe from Africa, few (if any) Europeans would think of their origin in terms of the "discovery of Europe" by Africans. In other words, the notion of a "prediscovery" of America—whether it was by Native Americans, Africans, Chinese, or Vikings—is based on a modern Western ideology that is hardly less Eurocentric than the claim that America was discovered by Columbus in 1492. The controversy about who was "first" has hereby merely reinforced a particularly hardy form of New World exceptionalism that still underwrote much of hemispheric American studies in the twentieth century. It is an exceptionalism that is predicated on the notion that, while most of the world simply *was,* America was *discovered.*

As the sociologist of science Augustine Brannigan has pointed out, the error of understanding discovery as a matter of viewpoint originates with the premise that ours "is a singular natural world which we know in common," unmediated and through empirical means.[20] In other words, its fallacy results from a particularly modern Western understanding of what it means to discover something, an understanding that the literary scholar James Dougal Fleming has called the "hermeneutics of discovery," which accords one particular ontology to the "thing" to be discovered.[21] It is this ontological notion of America as a "New World" that the Mexican philosopher of history Edmundo O'Gorman once called a "geographic hallucination" when asked to comment on Herbert Eugene Bolton's famous proposal that the Americas "have a common history."[22] In his own seminal works in hemispheric American studies, *La idea del descubrimiento de América* (1951) and *La invención de América* (1958), O'Gorman had therefore pursued a "hermeneutical" approach that built on the philosophical critiques of Martin Heidegger in order to argue that, before being able to discover something, one has first to hold or develop a *concept of its possibility*—a "fore-understanding" (*Vorverstehen*).[23] Hence, O'Gorman argued that before Europeans could "discover" America, they had first to *invent* the idea of a world with a fourth part—an idea that was impossible to conceive within the epistemic structure of traditional Christian cosmology, which acted as a sort of "cosmic jail" that committed its mental prisoners to the tripartite composition of the world on the doctrinal grounds that the *imago mundi* and its populations must be accounted for by the descendants of the three sons of Noah.[24] O'Gorman therefore challenged us to inquire not into the history of the discovery of America but into the history of "the *idea that America was discovered.*" Such a project would yield insights, he suggested, into "the historical nature of the New World and the meaning of its history" for modernity at large.[25]

More than a half century later, O'Gorman's critique still stands as an important reminder that the problem of discovery can never be approached as a question of positivist historiography but only as a question of intellectual history, philosophical hermeneutics, and literary tradition. Nevertheless, it is important to recognize some basic assumptions that O'Gorman's hermeneutical approach shared with Boorstin's positivist one. First, both proceeded from the assumption that there *was* a radical break in scientific mentality in the early modern period that allows us to speak of the "modern age," even though each would position Columbus on opposing sides of this great fissure. Thus, whereas for Boorstin, Columbus was the first of the moderns, for O'Gorman, he was the last of the ancients for having died believing (or at least insisting) that what he had reached was Asia. Second, both Boorstin and O'Gorman presumed that the European encounter with the New World was a decisive "event" from which this modern Western scientific culture emerged; that it was the hard "fact" of the European encounter with America itself over which medieval mentalities stumbled into modernity—that the discovery (or invention) of America was the *paradigm* of modern discovery per se. And finally, O'Gorman, like Boorstin, assumed that to "discover" something necessarily means to find something new and that "discovery" is therefore antithetical to "tradition." In short, O'Gorman eschewed the question of the historicity of the modern idea of discovery itself. Hence his argument that the history of the "invention of America" began not with Christopher Columbus but with Amerigo Vespucci—or whoever it was who wrote under his name the tract *Mundus novus,* published without place or date (though probably around 1504), therein declaring, "It is lawful to call it [the Indies] a new world because none of these countries were known to our ancestors, and to all who hear about them they will be entirely new."[26]

Although O'Gorman's critique of modern positivist historiography has been seminal in subsequent postcolonial and poststructuralist criticism in early American studies, its effect has been that the historical problem of the modern idea of discovery has largely been ceded to an often Eurocentric historiography and philosophy of science, while it has been all but ignored in (post)colonial and hemispheric American studies.[27] Thus, the word "discovery" has largely disappeared from the titles of scholarly books about early modern European expansionism in the Americas.[28] Instead, cultural and literary historians have preferred words such as "encounter" or "invention," rather than "discovery," in their titles, even though "invention" and "discovery" were still largely synonymous in the early modern period.[29] They have taken stock of the "darker side" of Boorstin's triumphant story of scientific progress, arguing that early modern forms of Western knowledge, such as humanist philology, cosmography, and historiography, served as the epistemic armature of empire with which Europeans colonized other, non-Western forms of knowledge, sign systems, conceptions of space, and cultural memory.[30] The very concept of the discovery seemed to be based on an erasure of indigenous subjects and knowledge that was rationalized by the claim that non-European peoples had no legitimate cultures, religions, or histories—that their knowledge didn't "count" because it was not recorded in alphabetical writing systems and because it was not Christian but superstitious or even diabolical. As the postcolonial critics Chris Tiffin and Alan Lawson have observed (in a different context), indigenous knowledge is invariably rendered invisible in the European discovery narrative. The Native must "know and yet not know," for the European can "discover" a place only if it is not already known. This paradox of modernity is resolved by "textualizing the event" in a way that renders Native knowledge pragmatic rather than conceptual and strategic. The Native has the "practical knowledge . . . but not the conceptual knowledge to see its 'true' significance."[31]

In this book, I revisit O'Gorman's critique of the modern Western idea of the discovery of America, but I wish to expand his original scope by asking how the European idea of the discovery of America became the paradigm of modern scientific discovery per se—of Boorstin's notion that, for the modern discoverer, "All the world is still an America." I hereby ask not how the Western notion of discovery rationalized conquest but what role the European conquest of America played in the history of the modern idea of discovery, particularly in the context of the Baconian idea of science as the "conquest of nature." Whereas recent work in the history of science has highlighted the sociological contexts that gave rise to the New Sciences in seventeenth-century Europe,[32] this book explores the intersections between the histories of science and geopolitics in the making of a modern paradigm of discovery in the age of European expansionism.[33] Moreover, whereas recent critical science studies have generally neglected the role that religion played in the history of scientific modernity, this book focuses on the language of alchemy in the early modern literature of discovery. I will argue that the Baconian paradigm of discovery has a *colonial* history that I call "the alchemy of conquest," a history in which conquest came before, not after, discovery;[34] for, I will argue, it was in large part the conquest of America that *legitimated* the modern idea of discovery by underwriting it with a salvific and even millenarian reason that forged an unprecedented synthesis of science, religion, and state power. An outgrowth of late medieval Aristotelianism, the language of alchemy operates in the early modern literature of discovery to mediate between innovation and tradition, the new and the known, natural philosophy and theology, as well as the material and the spiritual, by casting empiricist inquiry in strongly religious terms and the "discovery" of the secrets of nature in terms of divine revelations and the fulfillment of ancient prophecies.

When using the phrase "alchemy of conquest," I employ the term "alchemy" both literally and metaphorically: literally, because the modern empiricist concept of discovery has its epistemological roots in medieval alchemy—roots that are still evident in the verbal and visual language in which the narratives of the European discovery of America are cast; and metaphorically, because conquest, like alchemy, is what legitimated the (early) modern paradigm of discovery. When I say that it was the conquest of America that "forged" an unprecedented union between science, religion, and state power, I mean to invoke a number of premises on which my argument is based. First, I want to suggest that the modern paradigm of discovery was not a mere consequence of what has been called the "impact" of the New World upon the Old.[35] According to this historical narrative, the modern paradigm of discovery resulted ipso facto from the "event" of discovery itself, from an epistemic "shock" in the encounter with the unfamiliar and the new. This notion of a "shock of the unfamiliar" has been a dominant critical paradigm especially in New Historicist accounts of the literature of the European encounter with the Americas at least since Stephen Greenblatt's seminal *Marvelous Possessions: The Wonder of the New World* (1991). There, Greenblatt argued that the early European explorers of America, lacking a conceptual or philosophical language with which to absorb this "shock," resorted to a rhetoric of "wonder" that objectified, demonized, as well as ultimately commodified and appropriated the New World—its exotic plants, animals, and peoples—as "marvelous possessions." Greenblatt hereby conceived of the experience of "wonder" as a "rift" or "cracking apart of contextual understanding" that seems to "resist recuperation, containment, [and] ideological incorporation; it sits strangely apart from everything that gives coherence."[36] But, while it is true that the early explorers and natural historians frequently resorted to the language of the marvelous in the face of the new, they usually did not wonder for long before they began to philosophize, finding ready intellectual recourse when translating their experiences of "first encounter" in the experience of writing—an experience that may be called the "second encounter" with the New World.[37] For, as Anthony Grafton has reminded us, in the early modern period, the Western canon did not yet form a monolithic "grid" that rigidly imposed a uniform order on all new information but, rather, presented the discoverer with a remarkably elastic and eclectic "kaleidoscopic variety" of Aristotelian, Plinean, Epicurean, Neoplatonic, Hermetic, and Arabic textual traditions that was, in many ways, "perfectly suited" to handle the alleged epistemological "shock of discovery" through the "power of tradition."[38]

My second premise is that the modern paradigm of discovery is not a stable transhistorical category that was already available for the justification of conquest from the very beginning of European expansionism in the Americas (as Justice Marshall and many of his postcolonial critics have assumed). In the sixteenth century, the notion of "discovery" and the legal rights of possession attached to it in modern times (*res/terra nullius*) were not yet understood in the unequivocal terms of a European subject and a non-European object of knowledge. Thus, most sixteenth-century Europeans recognized that although the "Indies" were "new" to them, they were not new to Amerindians and that Amerindian knowledge of their world was entirely legitimate (though, as we will see, the early modern debate about the ontological status of Native Americans played an important part in the history of the modern paradigm of discovery). To most sixteenth- and seventeenth-century Europeans, the Americas ("the Indies of the West") were not so much new as they were *secret*. They were a secret that had been hidden from them until latter days but that had been known by *someone*. And yet, if by the nineteenth century, Justice Marshall could take for granted that the sixteenth-century Spanish conquest of America had established the "Doctrine of Discovery," it was because, in the course of a three-hundred-year process of intense intellectual labor and translation, a tradition of international law had evolved together with a particular paradigm of discovery in natural philosophy that delegitimated not only non-Western forms of knowledge but also the early modern European eclectic kaleidoscopic variety of knowledge traditions.

Third, by using the word "forged," I want to suggest that the empiricist epistemology that undergirds our modern notion of discovery did not emerge *ex nihilo* during the early modern period; rather, it had its roots in the late medieval Christian engagement with Islam, particularly in the medieval cultural nexus between crusade and the transmission of Aristotelian science, especially alchemy, into the Latin West during the thirteenth century. While the alchemical quests for the secrets of nature had remained a rather marginal enterprise in late medieval science—as a branch of meteorology surviving mainly as a technical art, practiced outside the courts and academies—it was only in the geopolitical context of European imperial expansionism in the New World during the sixteenth century that alchemy emerged as a prominent branch of natural philosophy—particularly in Neoplatonic "occult philosophy." It was now cultivated in the royal courts throughout Europe, and its hermeneutical, epistemological, and rhetorical models of discovery in terms of a "hunt" for the secrets of nature between and beyond the categories of Scholastic scientific reason became appropriated as instruments of power by the early modern imperial states, in institutions such as the Spanish *Consejo de Indias* (Council of the Indies) and *Casa de Contratación* (House of Trade), as well as the alchemical and botanical laboratories of Philip II's court at the Escorial.[39] In the context of the conquest of America, the secrets of nature were transformed into the secrets of state, and the alchemical seeker of natural secrets into the modern secretary.[40]

Finally, by using the word "forged" I mean to suggest that the prehistory of this modern hermeneutics of discovery often literally thrived on what we would today call literary forgeries—traditions of pseudonymous misattributions of alchemical texts and their empiricist epistemology to authorities renowned for their exceptional ancient wisdom or impeccable Christian piety (or both)—authorities such as Aristotle, Hermes Trismegistus, Geber, Albertus Magnus, Arnald of Villanova, or Ramón Llull. Although medieval Christian alchemy had roots in some of the authentic works of Aristotle that had entered the Latin West from the Arabic tradition during the twelfth and thirteenth centuries, it developed a tradition of "spiritualized materialism" in late medieval and early modern Europe that was Aristotelian in origin but distinct from the "mainstream" Scholastic Aristotelianism of Thomist (hylomorphic) metaphysics in ways that had important consequences for the history of the

European conquest of America and for the modern history of discovery. If this alchemical tradition lived largely in the shadows of these pseudo-authorities from medieval times up to the seventeenth century, the exposure of these forgeries by humanist philologists in the early modern period did little to stamp out its perennial appeal; on the contrary, by cutting it loose from its traditional ties to religious authority on which its legitimacy had traditionally depended, the humanists prepared its path for a new career in modern science.[41]

Convertibility, Reduction, and the State of Exception

In the third chapter of *Das Kapital*, in a section devoted to "the building of treasure" (*Schatzbilding*), Karl Marx cited Christopher Columbus's famous 1503 "Letter from Jamaica," in which the Admiral of the Ocean Sea exclaimed: "Gold is a wonderful thing! Whoever possesses it, is lord of all that he wants. By means of Gold, one can even bring souls to Paradise."[42] Marx saw the transformation of gold in the early modern period from a medium of exchange to a self-generating source of capital in surplus value of money as a form of alchemy that was intimately related to the history of conquest. Thus, he noted how the ancient Phoenicians, like the early modern Spanish conquerors in America, were in the habit of looting the Delphian temple treasures, melting down the sacred artworks made from precious metals, and remolding them into money coins.[43] Whereas for the Greeks, Marx argued, the temple treasures were "holy banks" (*heilige Banken*), for the Phoenicians, "the commercial nation *par excellence,* money was the transmuted form of everything" (*die entäußerte Gestalt aller Dinge*). Unlike the ancient Greeks, the ancient Phoenicians understood value in terms of the principle of *convertibility:* "As you cannot tell in money (*Geld*) what has been converted into it, everything is convertible, goods or not, into money. Everything can be sold and bought. Circulation becomes the great social crucible in which everything is captured and transformed into crystal money. Not even the bones of saints, and even less so the more delicate *res sacrosanctae extra commercium hominum* [sacred things, external to the trade of man], are able to resist this alchemy."[44] And yet, it was, of course none other than the Greek philosopher Aristotle who had famously written, in the *Nicomachean Ethics*, that "money measures all things."[45] Because it makes all things convertible, it has the name "money" (*nomisma*). But while in the *Nicomachean Ethics,* Aristotle writes that money "exists not by nature but by law (*nomos*) and it is in our power to change it and make it useless," elsewhere he writes that its principle of convertibility exists in nature, a "first" principle that he calls *archē:* "That of which all existing things consist and from which they first come to be and into which they finally pass away (the being, *ousía*, remaining but changing in its modification), this they say is the element and principle (*archē*) of all existing things, and therefore they think that nothing is generated or destroyed, as this kind of being is always preserved."[46] Scholars have struggled with the question of why the Greeks—a polytheistic culture—should have elaborated a monistic cosmogony. Drawing from mythology, psychoanalysis, as well as political and economic theory, Richard Seaford sees Aristotle's idea as the culmination of a philosophical tradition in cosmological monism beginning with the Milesians in the sixth century BC and elaborated in Hesiod's notion of the chaos in the *Theogony,* a monism that was shared also by other ancient Mediterranean and Middle Eastern cultures such as the Babylonians, the Hurrians, the Hittites, and Phoenicians. "The earliest state is envisaged as undifferentiated," Seaford writes, "whether as a dark chasm or (by implication) as sky and earth forming 'one shape'" before becoming separate.[47] This monistic cosmogony found its political expression in monarchy (i.e., Zeus's absolute rule). However, as political monarchy died out in Greek society, sociopolitical monism came to be defined as the "power of money, which, like monarchical power, is all-embracing, imposing a single, universal power on all things without destroying their diversity": "The transcendent power of monarchy had been projected onto the cosmos. The transcendent impersonal power of money, reified as a fact of nature, is projected onto the cosmos as a powerful transcendent substance. Unlike monarchy, money is *impersonal,* and is exchanged into, and the undifferentiated *equivalent* of, all things, each of which somehow embodies monetary value."[48]

This monism of money is predicated on the logic of two processes—*reduction* and *circulation* in liquid form. On the one hand, as Seaford notes, "everything—even the silver—is reduced in a sense to (pure) gold."[49] On the other hand, as Marx noted, "the continual circulation of the two antithetical metamorphoses of commodities, or the liquid exchange of sale and purchase, appears in the restless circulation of money, or its function as a *perpetuum mobile* of circulation." Thus, according to Marx, money "petrifies" into coagulated treasure as a sort of Philosophers' Stone in the merchant's alchemical opus. He is the "builder of treasures."[50]

Indeed, Marx's description of the money economy as a sort of alchemy predicated on a monistic logic of convertibility through reduction and circulation closely resembles the way in which late medieval alchemists understood the processes of metallic transmutation. One of the most famous of these alchemists makes a brief appearance also in García Márquez's *Cien años de soledad*—the Valencian physician Arnald of Villanova (1235–1311).[51] In the widely known alchemical tract *Rosarius philosophorum* (attributed to Arnald but most likely written after his death by a pseudo-Arnaldian alchemist before 1410), the Arnaldian explains that, while it is not possible to change one species of metal into another directly, metallic transmutation can be achieved through the alchemical regimen of "reduction" (*reductio*, a "leading back") through fire. In this violent regimen of fiery penitence, also called the *sol niger* (black sun), the substantial form of the metal is "killed" and the natural processes of elemental generations and corruptions that produced it are "reduced" (or reversed) to its "first matter" (*prima materia*) in the primal undifferentiated state of "chaos" (*in primam reductur materiam*). The idea of *prima materia* is based on an Aristotelian monistic conception of matter, the notion that an invisible, stable, and unchanging substratum exists beneath the constantly changing appearance of forms. In the monistic state, the elements can "circulate" freely, enabling the alchemist to recombine them and convert them into a different, more noble substance, in further alchemical regimens. This is known as the "work of circulation" (*opus circulatorium*), for "to change nature," the Arnaldian writes, "is nothing else but to rotate the elements in a circular fashion."[52] The contrary qualities of the four elements—air, fire, earth, water—present in every mixture are compared to warring enemies, each positioned at the extreme corners of the Aristotelian elemental square. In the *opus circulatorium*, however, these four contrary qualities are rebalanced into a new state of circular union and harmony, known as the "alchemical wedding," from which the "fifth element" and the Philosophers' Stone are born. As Lyndy Abraham writes: "During this circulation, the elements of earth, air, fire and water are separated by distillation and converted into each other to form the perfect unity, the fifth element. This conversion takes place by unifying the qualities that each element has in common: earth which is cold and dry may be united with water through the common quality of coldness since water is cold and moist (or fluid), water may be united with air through fluidity since air is hot and fluid, and air is united to fire through heat, since fire is hot and dry."[53] This conversion by rotation was often symbolized in alchemical iconography by the image of the *ouroboros*, the serpent which ingests its own tail, thus forming a circle (see fig. 3); but in medieval Christian alchemy, it also frequently appears in the form of various instruments of torture, such as the wheel and the rack (as we will see in chapter 2). The notion of "reduction" that makes possible this elemental circulation was first elaborated in the influential thirteenth-century alchemical tract *Summa perfectionis*, written by "Geber" (aka Paul of Taranto), who laid there the "materialist" foundation of all late medieval alchemical (i.e., non-Thomist) theory of matter as being corpuscular in structure, rather than continuous and homogeneous, a theory that would still be influential in the early modern period, most prominently in the concept of *reductio in pristinum statum* elaborated by the German alchemist Daniel Sennert (1572–1637), who, in turn, profoundly influenced Robert Boyle's "mechanical philosophy."[54]

From a Marxian point of view, then, the explosion of alchemy in the so-called Age of Discovery might be partially explained in terms of the socioeconomic changes of the Renaissance, especially in western Europe, which saw increased levels of urbanization and an unprecedented expansion of a money economy that began to loosen the old feudal social structures. The alchemical opus hereby reflects on a microcosmic scale the monistic logic of convertibility through reduction and circulation upon which the larger society and economy operate on a macrocosmic scale. However, as Marx also noted, early modern European culture was the heir not only of Phoenecian commercialism but also of Greek (especially stoic) philosophy, which "denounced money as subversive of the economical and moral order of things." Citing Athenaeus of Naucratis's *Deipnosophistae,* Marx writes that, in the stoic tradition, the money economy is seen through the analogy of pulling Pluto by the hair of his

Figure 3. The serpent ouroboros. Emblema XIV. (In Michael Maier, *Atalanta fugiens* [1618]. Source: *Secretioris naturæ secretorum scrutinium chymicum, per oculis et et intellectui accuratè accommodata, firguri cupro appositissimè incisa, ingeniosissima emblemata, hisque confines, & ad rem egregiè facientes sententias, doctissimaque item epigrammata, illustratus* [Francofurt Congress].)

head from the bowels of the earth; as a "greet[ing] gold as its Holy Grail, as the glittering incarnation of the very principle of its own life."[55] The late medieval and early modern treasure builder therefore feels a deep ambivalence about the monistic logic of reduction and circulation. Everything must be reduced to money and circulated, except for gold itself, which, as absolute value, must not be "transformed into a means of enjoyment." The treasure builder therefore "sacrifices his carnal lust to his gold fetish. He takes seriously the gospel of abstention. . . . Hard work, saving, and greed, are, therefore his three cardinal virtues, and to sell much and buy little the sum of his political economy."[56]

More recent scholarship on the cultural history of alchemy has followed up on Marx's sense that the explosion of alchemy in early modern Europe can partially be understood in socioeconomic terms. For example, the historian of science Pamela Smith, in her study of the seventeenth-century German alchemist Johann Joachim Becher, has argued that the increasing importance accorded to alchemy in the courts of early modern Europe can be understood in terms of alchemists' mediation between the immovable values of the landed nobility in the courts and the practices and movable values of the money economy of the commercial world. This is because, in medieval Christian alchemy, the operations of conversion through reduction and circulation had become deeply spiritualized through Christological analogies and attached to various strands of Christian messianism, millenarianism, as well as chivalric apostolic zeal and crusading militancy. Thus, alchemists such as Becher framed the "commercial projects in the traditional idiom and gesture of noble court culture and translated the commercial values into court culture."[57] Literary historian Karen Pinkus has further argued that early modern alchemy hereby generated a sort of "state of exception," functioning culturally to reconcile capitalist greed with Christian (especially Augustinian) spirituality and morality, where greed is seen as one of the cardinal vices: "Greed develops alongside money in history, and it must, therefore, be considered in relation to alchemy to the degree that alchemy is a production (of gold) and gold is money. Greed is precisely what is disavowed by those more 'spiritual' or philosophical forms of alchemy, and the typical early modern alchemical treatise includes disclaimers against the use of precious metals on the market."[58] If Pinkus was primarily interested in how the language of alchemy legitimated a state of exception in terms of early modern capitalist greed for wealth, in this book I will ask how alchemy legitimated a state of exception also with regard to another sort of greed in the context of early modern European expansionism. It is the kind of greed that St. Augustine, in the *Confessions,* had defined as *concupiscentia oculorum* (lust of the eyes), or "vain curiosity" (*vana curiositas*) about that which is hidden from us, the secret or the occult.[59] In other words, I am interested in how the language of alchemy transformed "vain curiosity" into Augustinian "just curiosity" (*iusta curiositas*) in the context of the conquest of America hereby theologically legitimating a Baconian paradigm of discovery that gave rise to scientific empiricism.[60] But, as we have seen, while the early modern period provided the socio- and geoeconomic contexts in which alchemy could become central to Western scientific culture in the context of European expansionism, the origins of the alchemical nexus between science, religion, and geopolitics inevitably take us back to the late medieval period, particularly to Scholastic Aristotelianism in the context of the "First Renaissance" of the thirteenth century and the Christian engagements with Islam. As we will see in the two subsequent chapters, the language of Western alchemy emerges in this context from the amalgamation of Christian messianism and millenarian prophecy with a (pseudo-)Aristotelian naturalism that had reentered the Latin West in translations from the Arabic since the twelfth century.

The Alchemy of New World Exceptionalism

Legitimating the scientific foray into the realm of the secret, the language of alchemy enabled a state of exception not only at the microcosmic scale ("the America of nature") but also at the macrocosmic scale—as a New World exceptionalism in international law (*terra nullius*). Although Giorgio Agamben, in his influential elaboration of the concept of the state of exception, was primarily concerned with totalitarian government in the modern nation-state—the *Ausnahmezustand,* or the suspension of constitutional law in modern states due to "global civil war"—its theological principle had already been elaborated by Thomas Aquinas (1225–1274) in his *Summa theologiae* in the context of his "theory of necessity." As Agamben explains, Aquinas's paradigm derived from Roman law in the concept of the *iustitium,* which means "standstill" or "suspension of the law."[61] It is significant, however, that Agamben's notion of the state of exception in reference to the modern state was adapted from the political theory of international law, particularly from the work of the twentieth-century political theorist Carl Schmitt. Schmitt argued that the modern state of exception found its first implementation not in modern totalitarian governments in Europe but in the "New World" of the European Age of Discovery. In fact, he saw the state of exception at the root of the (early) modern idea of discovery per se. It is necessary, he wrote, "to understand the new concept of discovery, with all its technical designations (such as *descobrimiento, découverte,* etc.) in its total historical and intellectual particularity"; for discovery is "not a timeless, universal, and normative concept; it is bound to a particular historical, even intellectual-historical situation: the 'Age of Discovery.'"62 In the context of early modern European expansionism, Schmitt argued, the state of exception manifested itself primarily in what he called "global linear thinking": "The struggle over land- and sea-appropriations of the New World began immediately after its discovery. . . . Lines were drawn to divide and distribute the whole earth. These were the first attempts to establish the dimensions and demarcations of a global spatial order."63 The most famous of these utopian lines was, of course, that stipulated in the bulls *Inter cetera,* promulgated by Alexander VI in the summer of 1493 in the aftermath of Columbus's first transatlantic voyage, demarcating Spanish from Portuguese titles in the Atlantic along a vertical line that ran, from pole to pole, 100 leagues west of the Azores and was later modified in the Treaty of Tordesillas (1494) assigning the eastern tip of South America to Portugal. Some thirty-five years after Tordesillas, Spain and Portugal entered into another treaty, the Treaty of Zaragoza (1529), which resolved competing claims in the Pacific, specifically with regard to the Molucca Islands. As Schmitt explained, this type of global line (*raya*) separated not Christian from non-Christian territories but the spheres of influence in the newly discovered territories in "the Indies" between two land-appropriating European (i.e., Christian) powers (in this case, Spain and Portugal) who both subscribed to a higher authority (in this case, the pope). Accordingly, they were "based on a consensus in international law concerning land-appropriation" by two powers who "recognized each other as equal parties to a treaty."64 These *rayas* were herein different from the "amity lines" that began to appear in the sixteenth century in treaties of truce between nonbelligerent European rival powers, especially Protestants and Catholics, competing for territory in the New World. However, while these treaties of amity obtained in Europe, they did not in the New World, which became an extralegal zone in which raids and skirmishes occurred outside the context of formal war. At these lines, "Europe ended and the 'New World' began" with regard to the law of nations. Beyond those amity lines was an "'overseas' zone in which, for want of any legal limits to war, only the law of the stronger applied." The characteristic feature of amity lines consisted in that, different from *rayas,* they "defined a sphere of conflict between contractual parties seeking to appropriate land, precisely because they lacked any common presupposition and authority. . . . Everything that occurred 'beyond the line' remained outside the legal, moral, and political values recognized on this side of the line. This was a tremendous *exoneration* of the internal European problematic. The significance in international law of the famous and notorious expression 'beyond the line' lies precisely in this exoneration."65 Thus, according to Schmitt, two basic types of "free spaces" emerged from early modern European expansionism as legal states of exception: one obtaining to the sea and one to the land of the New World. These "free spaces" challenged "all traditional intellectual and moral principles" that were normally accepted to obtain in Europe by Christian governments. Eventually, the seas would come to be viewed as common spaces, spaces that have never belonged to anyone and have never been occupied. The land of the New World would eventually become subject to the principle of "effective discovery," meaning occupation. It was a space imagined to exist in the prelegal "void" of dominion in natural law and the law of nations, the macroscopic analogue of the microscopic state of exception in the structure of matter according to Scholastic physics, in which the void was not permitted.[66]

But while the line of demarcation stipulated in *Inter cetera* and the Treaty of Tordesillas undoubtedly played an important role in this history of "global linear thinking," it did not create a "Doctrine of Discovery" with the stroke of a pen. Nor did such a doctrine as yet exist independently from Alexander's bulls of donation, as Marshall alleged when writing that Spain derived her title to the Americas not only from the papal donation but also by the "rights given by discovery." Although the Habsburg Emperor Charles V had asserted the notion of occupation as a ground for legal title as early as the negotiations leading up to the Treaty of Zaragoza, it was not formally theorized until one hundred years later—in that case, in order to challenge Iberian titles based on claims of "mere discovery"—by the Protestant jurist Hugo Grotius, who approached the question from the point of view of Roman and natural law. Thus, in *Mare liberum* (1609), Grotius argued that those who say that "those countries appertain unto them for a reward of the finding" are wrong, for "to find is not to see a thing with the eyes but to lay hold of it with the hands," hereby basing his argument on the classical (and mythical) Roman discoverer Gordianus, also known as "the Finder." "Whence the grammarians use the words *invenire* and *occupare* for words of one signification," Grotius argued, "and all the Latin tongue saith, 'we have found that which have gotten,' the contrary whereof is to lose."[67] Yet, despite Grotius's seventeenth-century theorization of international law, the notion of "occupation" as a legal ground for ownership never attained the status of a dogma that was universally accepted but was still in an "embryonic state" during the sixteenth and seventeenth centuries. It was not until the nineteenth century that occupation became the central feature in the debate about the so-called Doctrine of Discovery and could be invoked by Supreme Court Chief Justice John Marshall in his landmark decision *Johnson v. M'Intosh*.[68]

What was, then, the role that Alexander's bulls of donation played in the early modern history of the "Doctrine of Discovery" and the "global linear thinking" that Schmitt sees at the bottom of the geopolitical state of exception?

As the subsequent chapters here will suggest, the true significance of the bulls *Inter cetera* can be found in the fact that they were the last of their kind. As such, they did not come *ex nihilo* but as the final iteration in a long medieval tradition of similar bulls that had elaborated what Luis Weckmann-Muñoz has called the "*doctrina omni-insular,*" a hierocratic theory of dominion that entitled the pope to dispose as he wishes of newly discovered or conquered "islands" in the Mediterranean and the eastern Atlantic not yet occupied by a Christian lord.[69] The hierocratic tradition of *doctrina omni-insular* was rooted in an Augustinian conception of dominion as dependent on grace. During the later Middle Ages, it was further elaborated by canon lawyers into a theory that is known by the formula of *papa vicarius Christi*. Thus, the thirteenth-century Italian canonist Henry of Segusio (aka Hostiensis) explained that not only did all temporal dominion derive from God's original donation to Adam in the book of Genesis, but his Incarnation had voided all rights of dominion previously held by pagan lords. These rights had passed to Christ, who, as lord of the world both in a spiritual and temporal sense, passed them on to his successor St. Peter and the later popes. This hierocratic tradition of dominion was further elaborated in the fourteenth, fifteenth, and sixteenth centuries by such Irish and English canonists as William Fitzralph and John Wycliffe, as well as by such church reformers as Jan Hus and Martin Luther.[70]

Initially, in the absence of any challenges to the conquerors' common practice of taking possession of territories on behalf of the Iberian Crowns, the Alexandrine bulls were apparently considered to be sufficient legal ground for a Spanish claim to titles in the New World. Thus, in 1513, the principles of *Inter cetera* were adopted in the infamous *requerimiento,* a declaration authored by the jurist Juan López de Palacios Rubios that had to be read aloud to the American Indians before war could be waged on them and that informed them of Spain's title to the Americas by donation of the pope, who held authority over the entire world.[71] However, as the Catholic Monarchs were undoubtedly aware, the canon lawyers' hierocratic interpretation of dominion (*papa vicarius Christi*) had not gone unchallenged during the Middle Ages and would also not go unchallenged in the aftermath of the Alexandrine bulls. Already during the thirteenth century, the rise of Aristotelianism in the Latin West had resulted in a new understanding of dominion in terms not only of canon law but also of Roman and natural law. The medieval Scholastics hereby made a strict distinction between spiritual and temporal dominion, arguing that while the pope, as Christ's vicar, has spiritual dominion, temporal dominion originates not directly from God's grace but from God's law, which is manifest in the temporal world in natural and positive law. While natural law metaphysics would become the specialty of the Thomists, the distinction between natural and spiritual dominion had been accepted even by some of the popes in the later Middle Ages. Thus, Pope Innocent IV (1195–1254), himself a noted scholar of canon law writing even before Aquinas, addressed, in his commentaries on the Crusades, the question of whether or not pagans and infidels (in this case, Muslims) had the same natural rights as Christians to dominion. Innocent concluded that they did, since all men, regardless of their faith, possessed a natural right to property and self-government. However, while he argued that the Christian apostolic mission in itself is not a just cause for making war upon pagans and infidels, he insisted that the pope's spiritual responsibility over the entire world authorizes him to send missionaries to proselytize to non-Christian lands and, if necessary, protect these missionaries with the force of arms. This spiritual authority over the world belonged, however, to the pope alone.[72]

If the effect of Aristotelian Scholastic natural law theology during the later Middle Ages was a balance of power and authority between emperor and pope by assigning to the former temporal dominion strictly on the ground of natural law and to the latter purely spiritual dominion by divine law, the rise of metaphysical nominalism in the fourteenth century in primarily Franciscan circles (especially among the followers of William of Ockham) further challenged the hierocratic understanding of dominion of the canonists. Moreover, the Great Schism of the late fourteenth century, when there were two competing popes (one in Rome and one in Avignon) gave rise to the Conciliarist movement, which held that supreme authority in the church resided not with the pope but with the Ecumenical Council of the bishops. While this Conciliarist tradition was at the apex of its influence at the time of the Schism (1378–1414) at the University of Paris with such prominent nominalist theologians as Pierre d'Ailly and Jean Gerson, it would still play an important role in the debate about the rights of dominion in the Americas—in the commentaries, for example, of such influential early sixteenth-century theologians as John Mair.[73]

If the hierocratic canon law tradition alleging the pope's temporal dominion had already been undermined by late medieval Thomism and nominalism, it was further challenged when the fraudulence of the Donation of Constantine (upon which the tradition of the *doctrina omni-insular* was based) was proven by the Italian humanist Lorenzo Valla in 1440—some fifty years before Alexander issued his famous bulls *Inter cetera*. And even those canon lawyers who did not accept Valla's claim of fraudulence had to admit that the tradition of *doctrina omni-insular* had always referred to "islands" not ruled by a Christian lord. The applicability of a canon law tradition of dominion derived from the Donation of Constantine to the Americas would therefore be predicated on a hermeneutics of their discovery within a medieval *ontology of insularity*.[74] Although the donations of territories in Africa that previous popes had made to the Portuguese Crown already represented a certain stretch of this tradition, it could at least be argued that Constantine's donation to Pope Sylvester had pertained to "Italy"—which, if interpreted as the *Prefecture* of Italy, consisted of the three dioceses of Italy, Illyricum, and West Africa.[75] However, the artificial creation of a vertical line of demarcation in the middle of the Ocean Sea in *Inter cetera* and Tordesillas seemed to introduce a break in this medieval ontology that opened a space for what the Italian humanist Peter Martyr, working at the Spanish court as royal chronicler, would already in November 1493 call an *orbe novo*, a "new world," in which the temporal authority of the pope based on the Donation of Constantine could hardly be assumed.[76] As Miguel Batllori has suggested, the Catholic Monarchs therefore most likely never considered the significance of the Alexandrine bulls of donation as being anything more than subsidiary in their attempt to shore up their claims to titles in America. Nevertheless, they were a political gift gladly accepted in exchange for the many favors they had bestowed on the children of the Machiavellian Borgia pope from Valencia.[77]

When, during the second decade of the sixteenth century, the papal bulls increasingly became the subject of critical scrutiny by humanists in Spain and abroad—especially in the aftermath of highly public denunciations of the appalling abuses and cruelties committed by the Spanish conquerors—the Catholic Monarchs began to look for additional arguments that would underwrite their legal claim to titles in the New World. Thus, King Ferdinand appointed the Dominican friar Francisco de Vitoria (1483–1546), the future chair of theology at the University of Salamanca, to look into the question. A protracted debate ensued in Spain that outlasted King Ferdinand and carried over into the reign of King Charles I, who assumed the Spanish throne in 1516 and was elected Holy Roman Emperor as Charles V in 1519. In the 1520s and 1530s, Vitoria gave a series of lectures on the topic and concluded that, according to Thomist natural law, the papal bulls were not a sufficient basis for such territorial claims, since the pope had no jurisdiction over land and temporal possessions but only over souls. Moreover, Charles V, as Holy Roman Emperor, could claim no titles in the Americas based on the notion of universal imperium ("the lord of all the world") because the Roman Empire had never been universal even in the Old World, let alone extended to the New. Finally, even by the law of nations (*ius gentium*), Spain had no "title by right of discovery" (*in iure inuentionis*), because the "Indies" was not a land without an owner but had already been owned by the American Indians. Even though they may be barbarians, Vitoria argued, they held "natural legal rights as free and rational people," and the Spanish claim for first discovery of the Americas therefore *"provides no support for possession of these lands, any more than it would if they [the Indians] had discovered us."*[78]

I will return to Vitoria's arguments in more detail in a later chapter, but here it will suffice to suggest that, within his Thomist legal framework, the concept of discovery had no bearing on questions relating to Spanish rights of dominion in the Americas. Although the concept of *terra nullius* was patently a familiar one in the early modern period from the Roman law tradition—linking the act of finding something *(invenire)* with a right to take possession—its applicability to the America was not yet accepted norm. Yet, by the end of the period known as the European Age of Discovery—marking roughly the era of European settler colonialism and culminating with the establishment of settler-colonial nation-states from the sixteenth to the early nineteenth centuries—the idea that America was a "New World" that had been "discovered" by Europeans had come to underwrite a legal tradition—the so-called Doctrine of Discovery—according to which the overseas territories that Europeans had invaded and colonized were generally understood as a *terra nullius* or even a *vacuum domicilium*. While this latter concept has frequently been seen in modern scholarship as an appropriation of Roman law by early modern European imperialists attempting to justify their New World conquest in seminal Enlightenment texts such as John Locke's *Second Treatise of Government*, its use in fact solidified only by the nineteenth century, when American historians such as Peter Oliver and George Edward Ellis referred to it as the "accepted rule" by which colonial officials allegedly decided whether Indian lands could be appropriated. In other words, it took shape only in the course of a three-hundred-year history of European conquests and invasions in the Americas. However, Marshall's Doctrine of Discovery was not the "accepted rule" by which early modern European colonialism in the New World was legitimated; rather, its legitimation was the ideological *product* in which canon law, Roman law, and natural law had been amalgamated in an alchemy of conquest that shaped a modern hermeneutics of discovery during the three hundred years of European settler colonialism in the Americas.[79]

Nevertheless, there are several things about the Alexandrine bulls that are worth keeping in mind with regard to the early modern history of the state of exception: (1) the sly extension of a doctrine that had always pertained primarily to islands also to mainlands that could not possibly be conceived as being implied by the Donation of Constantine; thus, whereas the first or "secret" draft version of *Inter cetera (Inter cetera* I, written on May 3) speaks vaguely of "certain lands and islands" *(aliquas terras et insulas)*, the public revision *(Inter cetera* II, written on June 28 and antedated May 4) specifies "islands and mainlands" (*aliquas insulas et terras firmas*);⁸⁰ (2) the self-consciousness with which the bulls attempt to synthesize the hierocratic canon law theory of dominion with ideas borrowed from classical Aristotelianism and natural law, most prominently the notion of "barbarity" (*ac barbare nationes deprimantur*), a concept that is highly unusual in the canon law context; (3) the transfer of the papal apostolic mission of conversion to a temporal ruler (*et ad fidem ipsam reducantur*); and (4) the sheer scope of the concession resulting from its geographic open-endedness and vagueness. In the Spanish context, Alexander's cession of papal spiritual authority in the New World through *Inter cetera* led to the so-called *patronado*, created by yet another bull issued by Pope Julius II in 1508, by which the Spanish Crown was given the right to name bishops and other religious officials in the Americas. The effect was that from now on the Crown unified and commanded absolute authority, both religious and political, in advancing its ideological objectives beyond the line of demarcation.

The true significance of the bulls *Inter cetera* for the history of the state of exception thus lies not so much in the temporal dominion that they conferred but in the spiritual dominion that they relinquished. In effect, they ended the medieval balance of power and authority divided between temporal lords and the supreme pontiff, hereby putting an end to their own genre, a genre by which the pope had been able to use his spiritual authority in his temporal role as supranational arbiter in international territorial conflicts. Thus, when Spain and Portugal, in the following year of 1494, renegotiated the terms of *Inter cetera* at Tordesillas (moving the line of demarcation westward), the pope and his delegates had no seat at the table. True, previous popes also had, in the context of the Christian Reconquista, ceded their spiritual authority to temporal rulers, hereby offering rewards and incentives to undertake crusades of reconquest against Muslims. For example, in 1486, King Ferdinand had obtained a *patronado* from Pope Innocent VIII for the Kingdom of Granada, enabling him to appoint bishops and other religious authorities and to receive the tithes that would normally go to the church.⁸¹ But *Inter cetera* essentially transported this state of exception that had emerged in the context of crusade and the Reconquista onto a global scale. As the historian Pedro de Leturia has written, the effect of this unification of spiritual and temporal dominion was the "national expansion and the strengthening of royal power with the spiritual and missionary dream of the propagation of the gospel and the Church; the crusade of Granada is extended to the Indies."⁸² By ceding any future papal jurisdiction outside Europe to two temporal powers—the Spanish and Portuguese monarchies—the bulls *Inter cetera* not only abrogated the pope's spiritual authority over the New World but also invested the imperialist political aspirations of temporal monarchs with a spiritual and judicatory authority that had, during the Middle Ages, rested with the supreme pontiff alone. From now on, any military conflict outside Europe could potentially be defined as a crusade and holy war by quarrelling temporal rulers. Thus, as the eminent historian of canon law Manuel Giménez Fernández once argued, the most important consequence of the bulls *Inter cetera* was "the death of the medieval concept of the Christian Republic, ruled in the ultimate instance by the spiritual authority of the pontiff" and the inauguration of an "era of fratricidal nationalistic wars among European states," an era that would issue into early modern absolutism and modern totalitarianism, a particularly heinous phase of which Giménez Fernández was witnessing when writing these lines in Seville in 1944.[83]

In the chapters that follow, I focus on the role that the language of alchemy played in the late medieval origins and early American histories of Alexander's dual mission in *ac barbare nationes deprimantur* (to overthrow barbarous nations) and *ad fidem ipsam reducantur* (to "reduce" them to the faith) that the expanding monarchies inherited in the bulls *Inter cetera*. As we will see, the language of alchemy legitimated a new paradigm of discovery through a state of exception emerging from the mission not only of military crusade but also of spiritual conquest, especially of the missionary project of "reduction" in early American evangelical rhetoric and practice. The systematic relocation of Native American neophytes in artificially created towns known as *reducciones, doctrinas,* or (in colonial New England) "Praying Towns" in the early American apostolic context has long been compared to the twentieth-century concentration camp by modern historians of early America.[84] In a different context, the historian of Western esotericism Nicholas Goodrick-Clarke has shown the important role that the language of alchemy played in the conception of the modern concentration camp in Nazi Germany, where the symbol of the "black sun" (*sol niger*) for the alchemical regimen of reduction was adopted by a secret circle of initiates within the SS and presumably inspired their research of the perfect technology of genocide.[85] Likewise, the epistemic violence of the alchemical language of reduction in early American missionary projects illuminates the role that esoteric forms of spirituality played in rationalizing the scientific state of exception in ways that foreshadow more recent scientific dystopias. By placing the genealogy of the modern scientific distopias in a late medieval and early modern historical context, we can see the colonial dimension that I call "the alchemy of conquest" in the modern state of exception. If twentieth-century totalitarianism and the modern concentration camp represent some of the legacies of this early modern American exceptionalism, another legacy would be witnessed by Giménez Fernández the year after he penned his devastating critique of the Alexandrine bulls, when the United States dropped the first atomic bomb on Hiroshima on August 6, 1945.

The City of Mirrors

In the so-called Age of Discovery, both Old World international law and its New World states of exception developed together and interdependently. If Marshall's Doctrine of Discovery was still in an embryonic state in the sixteenth and seventeenth centuries, so was the legal regime of modern international law that would eventually obtain within Europe. The European conception of the New World hereby functioned as the experimental field for philosophical speculation during the Renaissance, particularly in the Christian reencounter with the ideas of its classical (i.e., pagan) past, many of which were profoundly un-Christian. In *Leviathan,* for example, Thomas Hobbes famously imagined man in the "state of nature"—not in the Thomist-Aristotelian tradition as a rational creature guided by universal moral principles imprinted by God's natural law (synderesis) but as an anarchic wild animal without moral or religious inhibitions ("homo homini lupus"). And for Hobbes, the paradigm of this anarchic state of nature from which the need for a monarchical legal regime emerges was, of course, America—the macrocosmic analogue of the microcosmic void, in which atoms collide at random.[86] Hobbes hereby reintroduced early modern Europe to the "materialist" (pre-Socratic) school of Thucydides and Democritus in political philosophy that had been suppressed as ethically problematic by the Stoic tradition in the Christian Middle Ages since the time of St. Augustine.[87] As we will see, however, Hobbes was not the first political philosopher to engage with pre-Socratic materialism in the experimental field of the New World in ways that were crucial for history of the modern paradigm of discovery both in modern science and international law. The history of this "New World" return of classical paganism to Renaissance Europe reaches back in early modern Spain to at least the so-called Great Debate (1550–51) between the Dominican friar Bartolomé de Las Casas and the Spanish humanist Juan Ginés de Sepúlveda over the latter's book *Democrates alter* (The Second Democritus) in which he invoked the pre-Socratic atomist in order to argue that the American Indians were not only a variety of Aristotle's "natural slave" but also only partially human (*humunculos*).

Michel Foucault has described these experimental New World spaces as "heterotopias," "other places'" in which the state of exception is transformed from theoretical speculation into political experiment.[88] Spaces of *otherness,* heterotopias are neither here nor there, simultaneously physical and mental, such as the space of a mirror, garden, cemetery, or (as we will see) the ventriloquizing minstrel mask of the American cannibal. Unlike utopias, which are not real and exist only in the human imagination, heterotopias are real places on the "outside" that exert "a sort of counteraction on the position that I occupy."[89] Despite the general Eurocentricity of his historical archive in *The Order of Things,* in this remarkable essay Foucault considered the role that European colonies played as heterotopias, as blueprints in the formation of the modern relationship between knowledge, power, and discipline the implementation of which were unimaginable within the feudal sociopolitical structures and human landscapes of late medieval and early modern Europe.[90] While the consequences of heterotopias may or may not be transgressive, Foucault suggested, their scope is always transcultural and their effect often transformative.[91] Foucault was hereby especially interested in the Jesuit reductions (or missionary towns) in eighteenth-century Paraguay as examples of the early modern heterotopia. As I suggested above, the early American history of reduction has an alchemical dimension that originates in the late medieval (i.e., Aristotelian) monistic idea of convertibility. But as we will see, in the early Americas, the idea of conversion as reduction did not originate with the Jesuits in seventeenth- or eighteenth-century Paraguay but with the Franciscans in the sixteenth-century Caribbean and New Spain (Mexico), many of whom were humanists trained during the revival of Llullism on the Iberian Peninsula of the Catholic reformer Cardinal Francisco Jiménez de Cisneros. The Franciscans' traditional primitivism, utopianism, reformism, and apocalyptic messianism, as well as their long tradition in alchemy, had a special role to play in the formation of the New World heterotopia of reduction. While late medieval Aristotelians (especially the Thomists) were busily elaborating a theory of the human subject in the universal concept of dominion as based on a natural law of the rights of property that left no "void" but applied to all sons and daughters of Adam regardless of their faith,[92] the Franciscans were theorizing a state of exception in the Scholastic understanding of the subject in their extreme rule of poverty. They hereby envisioned a state of freedom (or void) from rights and property in an edenic, prelegal existence before the postlapsarian division of dominium. Their utopia had been defeated when Pope John XXII (1249–1334) put an end to the protracted poverty controversy by decreeing, in the bull *Quum inter nonnullos* (1323), that there is no human subject without property—that even before the Fall, Adam had been given "dominium" of the earth by God; that even Jesus Christ and his apostles had dominium over the bread they ate; and that, likewise, so did the Franciscans own the things they used. But while the Franciscans had thus been forced to accept ownership by papal bull in the Old World, their missionary heterotopias in the New World held out the promise of realizing their medieval utopian dream in the "reduced" Amerindian neophyte, who was, childlike like St. Francis himself, without dominium. Thus, the metaphysical origins of the alchemy of conquest—the ontological "erasure" of the non-European subject in the European narrative of discovery—can be found in a Scholastic theory of dominium that generated its own state of exception in Franciscan nominalism and (later) humanist utopianism.[93] It is this ontological erasure of the non-European subject in the European narrative of discovery that dooms Macondo, the "city of mirrors," to its apocalyptic end in Melchíades's enigmatic alchemical manuscript.

The ethnographer of science Bruno Latour has provided a theoretical framework that illuminates the architecture of Melchíades's alchemical city of mirrors. According to Latour, the hegemony that the empirical sciences have attained in modern Western culture can be understood in terms of a dialectic between two ideological processes that he calls "purification" and "hybridization." Whereas purification separates nature from culture—mute things from speaking citizens, and objects from subjects—hybridization remixes them in cunning ways; that is, it redeploys "nature" in the realm of culture, and "culture" in the realm of nature. "Modernity," Latour proposes, is a sort of "Constitution" that renders the work of hybridization that assembles hybrids invisible, unthinkable, unrepresentable: "The modern Constitution allows the expanded proliferation of the hybrids whose existence, whose very possibility it denies." The more emphatically modern Western culture insists on purification and disavows hybridization, the more it actually proliferates hybrids. If the covert connections between purification and hybridization are exposed, as in the case of the recent postcolonial scrutiny of the "Doctrine of Discovery," modernity and all of its promises—progress, objectivity, historicism, and so on—vanish into thin air. (Hence, Latour's argument that "we have never been modern.")[94]

For the most part, Latour suggests, the moderns have been remarkably successful in their cunning duplicity of hiding the hybrids that purification spawns. In recent history, however, hybrids have proliferated to the point of creating a crisis in the modern project. While some of these recent historical developments have still been easily assigned to the modern notion of "progress" or its enemy ("declension")—the internet and the Iranian Revolution respectively, for example—others cannot unequivocally be assigned to either one—the atomic bomb or "surgical" drone strikes, for example. It is due to this crisis—resulting from proliferating hybrids mixing the "pure" realm of science with politics, ethics, and religion—that modernity has now been exposed to the possibility of ethnographic description: "Modernization consists in continually exiting from an obscure age that mingled the needs of society with scientific truth, in order to enter into a new age that will finally distinguish clearly what belongs to atemporal nature and what comes from humans, what depends on things and what belongs to signs. Modern temporality arises from a super-position of the difference between past and future with another difference, so much more important, between mediation and purification." Thus, the moderns want to have it both ways: they can "mobilize Nature at the heart of social relationships, even as they leave Nature infinitely remote from human beings; they are free to make and unmake their society, even as they render its laws ineluctable, necessary and absolute."[95]

Latour has provided here a useful conceptual tool for understanding the Baconian paradigm of discovery in terms of "purification" and "hybridization." He elaborates his notion of a "modern Constitution" in a celebrated critique of *Leviathan and the Airpump* (1985), Stephen Shapin's and Simon Schaefer's seminal sociohistorical study of the controversy between Robert Boyle and Thomas Hobbes during the English Civil War over the relationship between science and politics, as well as over the epistemological status of natural "facts" produced artificially by scientific experiments. In Latour's view, this controversy signals the beginning of the modern divide between scientific objects and political subjects: whereas Hobbes resorted to mathematical demonstration, Boyle employed empirical eyewitness testimonies of the "natural" effects artificially produced in his vacuum pump, which, he claimed, were "matters of fact" that spoke for themselves:

> The natural power that Boyle and his many scientific descendants defined in opposition to Hobbes, the power that allows mute objects to speak through the intermediary of loyal and disciplined scientific spokespersons, offer a significant guarantee: it is not men who make Nature; Nature has always existed and has always already been there; we are only discovering its secrets.... Boyle and his countless successors go on and on both constructing Nature artificially and stating that they are discovering; Hobbes and the newly defined citizens go on and on constructing the Leviathan by dint of calculation and social force, but they recruit more and more objects in order to make it last.[96]

Latour thus sees Boyle and Hobbes as the Founding Fathers of the modern Constitution consisting of natural objects to be discovered and political subjects who discover. But while he goes on to trace the history of the Great Divide between purification and hybridization forward through the modern Western philosophical tradition—from Kant to Hegel, Habermas, and Derrida—he fails to consider the colonial *prehistory* of the modern

Constitution, a prehistory of which we are reminded when considering that Boyle was not only the father of modern experimental science but also the son of a budding English colonial enterprise, serving as he did as the director of the East India Company and governor of the Society for Propagation of the Gospel in New England. Likewise, Hobbes was not only the father of modern political philosophy but also the heir to a long line of pre-Socratic thinking on the issue of war and peace that had returned to Renaissance Europe in the sixteenth-century Neo-Scholastic debate in Spain about the conquest of America.[97]

To be sure, Latour is not oblivious to the colonial dimension of the Great Divide between purification and hybridization: "Native Americans were not mistaken," he writes, "when they accused the Whites of having forked tongues. By separating the relations of political power from the relations of scientific reasoning, while continuing to shore up power with reason and reason with power, the moderns have always had two irons in the fire. They have become invincible." Thus, Latour argues that the separation of hybridization and purification is only one of the two Great Divides by which modernity legitimates itself—the "Internal Great Divide." The other—the "External Great Divide"—is that between the moderns ("Us"), who distinguish between nature and culture, and those premoderns ("Them") who do not. These premoderns include not only medieval but also all non-Western people.

> We [the moderns] are the only ones who differentiate absolutely between Nature and Culture, between Science and Society, whereas in our eyes all the others—whether they are Chinese or Amerindian, Azande or Barouya—cannot really separate what is knowledge from what is Society, what is sign from what is thing, what comes from Nature as it is from what their cultures require.... The internal partition between humans and nonhumans defines a second partition—an external one this time—through which the moderns have set themselves apart from the premoderns. For Them, Nature and Society, signs and things, are virtually coextensive. For Us they should never be.[98]

But while calling our attention here to a colonial dimension of the modern Constitution, Latour seems to suggest that the External was merely an exportation of the Internal Great Divide: "If Westerners had been content with trading and conquering, looting and dominating, they would not distinguish themselves radically from other tradespeople and conquerors. But no, they invented science, an activity totally distinct from conquest and trade, politics, and morality." He seems to assume, in other words, that the modern paradigm of discovery legitimated conquest, rather than conquest the modern paradigm of discovery.[99]

García Márquez's literary image of the sixteenth-century Spanish galleon entangled in South America's tropical nature challenges us to contemplate the role that the sixteenth-century Spanish conquest played in the formation of Latour's modern Constitution long before the invention of Robert Boyle's air-pump. Already by Bacon's time, García Márquez's literary image of the entanglement of nature and culture in the American tropics had become a common trope in the sixteenth-century literature of discovery. For example, it makes one of its earliest appearances in Peter Martyr's widely circulated *Decades,* originally written in Latin and later translated into English by the alchemist Richard Eden, who had published it as one of the first books about America to appear in the English language. Incidentally, Eden's translation is also one of the earliest texts published in English to use the sixteenth-century neologism "to entangle" (from "tangle," a species of seaweed).[100] "The currents of the sea there [in America] clash so violently," Eden wrote, that the Spanish ships become "entangled with whirlepooles."[101] And the quicksands are so powerful that they are called "vypers" by the Spaniards with good reason: "In them many shyppes are entangled, as the lycertes are implicate in the tayles of the vipers."[102] Whereas cunning Odysseus of old could choose between Scylla and Charybdis, becoming entangled in tropical America means being swallowed whole. But in the American tropics, nature not only entangles European means of transportation and progress but also revokes the European order of things. Thus, fish—which are supposed to live in water—still fly in the air, and the sea is "euery where entangeled with Ilandes: by reason whereof, the keeles of the shippes often tymes rased the sandes for shalownes of the water."[103] In Eden's tropical America, it seems, nature was still in a primordial state of Chaos, a *prima materia,* in which the four elements of nature were not yet fully separate. In Eden's translation, then, to "entangle" means to mingle, confuse, and circulate that which should be separate—the four elements, nature and culture, subjects and objects, past and present, time and space.

As we will see in chapter 4 of this book, the European idea of "the Indies" as a macrocosmic analogue to the alchemical crucible dates back in the literature of discovery at least to the writing of Christopher Columbus. But it is significant that, in García Márquez's novel, Melchíades the alchemist is associated not only with Columbus, the "first discoverer," but also (and primarily) with the so-called second discoverer of America—the nineteenth-century Prussian naturalist Alexander von Humboldt. If García Márquez hereby identifies the modern paradigm of discovery as a particularly *Protestant* ideological formation, he calls our attention to the role that religion, sectarianism, and interimperial rivalry has played in the alchemy of conquest.[104] I have already suggested earlier that the idea of an English "discovery" of America emerged during the early modern period as a "White Legend" that depended not only on the transmutation of indigenous subjects into objects but also on its counterpart—the Black Legend, the Protestant notion that the Spanish conquest of America was a historical parenthesis in the larger history of scientific discovery and in the history of modernity per se. The legacy of the Black Legend reached far beyond the early modern period and became, as Victor Navarro Brotóns and William Eamon have suggested, also a governing paradigm in the modern historiography of science.[105] In this modern historiographic tradition—much of it consisting of works written by northern European Protestant historians during the nineteenth and twentieth centuries—sixteenth-century Spanish science was often either entirely neglected or treated as paradigmatic of an "Old" science, whereas science in the British colonies was seen as paradigmatic of the "New" (i.e., Baconian) science.[106]

Navarro Brotón's and Eamon's critique of the expulsion of Catholic Spain and Spanish America from the history of scientific modernity by the early modern Black Legend and its modern legacy in the historiography, philosophy, and ethnography of science again finds a tragicomic literary anticipation in García Márquez's novel that brings into focus the epistemic violence of the White Legend of the English discovery of America. It is the passage where we first learn how Macondo came to be founded not on Colombia's bustling Caribbean coast, where it might have participated in early global modernity, but in the isolation of the South American jungle. It was the result of an originary traumatic encounter by Úrsula's Spanish American great-great-grandmother during the sixteenth century:

> When the Pirate Sir Francis Drake attacked Riohacha in the sixteenth century, Úrsula Iguarán's great-great-grandmother became so frightened with the ringing of alarm bells and the firing of cannons that she lost control of her nerves and sat down on a lighted stove. The burns changed her into a useless wife for the rest of her days. She could only sit on one side, cushioned by pillows, and something strange must have happened to her way of walking, for she never walked again in public. She gave up all kinds of social activity, obsessed with the notion that her body gave off a singed odor. Dawn would find her in the courtyard, for she did not dare fall asleep lest she dream of the English and their ferocious attack dogs as they came through the windows of her bedroom to submit her to shameful tortures with their red-hot irons. Her husband, an Aragonese merchant by whom

she had two children, spent half the value of his store on medicines and pastimes in an attempt to alleviate her terror. Finally he sold the business and took the family to live far from the sea in a settlement of peaceful Indians located in the foothills, where he built his wife a bedroom without windows so that the pirates of her dream would have no way to get in.

It was in that remote and hidden settlement of Indians that the Iguaráns first met the Buendías family and commenced a century-long cycle of interbreeding and incest that is associated with the clan's male tendencies toward madness: "Therefore, every time that Úrsula became exercised over her husband's mad ideas, she would leap back over three hundred years of fate and curse the day that Sir Francis Drake had attacked Riohacha. It was simply a way of giving herself some relief, because actually they were joined till death by a bond that was more solid that love: a common prick of conscience. They were cousins." The secret family history of incest invites the curse upon the two families that at the end of their crossed lines will stand a hybrid offspring—a child who will be born with the tail of a pig. In order to avoid the fulfillment of the curse, Úrsula refuses to consummate her marriage with José Arcadio. When his masculinity subsequently becomes the butt of a joke by Prudencio Aguilar—who offers this insult in revenge for having lost to José Arcadio in a cockfight—José Arcadio pierces his throat with a spear. However, the deceased offender begins to haunt the village every night in order to quench his pierced throat at the village well, and the Buendías family decides to embark on their quasi-biblical exodus that would end in the founding of Macondo.

As is well-known among Latin Americanists, besides Humboldt, another important source of inspiration for García Márquez's metahistorical novel was a contemporary of Francis Bacon and one of Latour's colonial precursors in the ethnographic description of the project of purification, who turned the anthropological gaze from "Them" to "Us" and thereby exposed the many hybrids that the modern project of purification proliferates. When the creole bureaucrat from Bogotá Juan Rodríguez Freyle (1566–1640) sat down in 1636 to write his gossipy picaresque history of the New Kingdom of Granada (roughly, present-day Colombia), he looked back at the first hundred years of a colonial society in South America that had sprung from the extraordinary violence and ordeals of conquest: three conquerors had arrived independently and more or less simultaneously in a quest to discover the legendary "El Dorado," the golden king whose empire was located, according to Native American lore, somewhere in the highlands of Bogotá. Significantly, Rodríguez Freyle therefore entitled his unofficial history of these events and the colonial society that emerged from it not (in keeping with most "official" histories of the day) "the discovery and conquest of...," but "The Conquest and Discovery of the New Kingdom of Granada" (*Conquista y descubrimiento del Nuevo Reino de Granada de las Indias Occidentales del Mar Océano*). America was conquered first, he suggests, and "discovered" only later, hereby anticipating the argument of this book by almost four hundred years. After providing a brief survey of the indigenous peoples and their wars before the arrival of the Spaniards, Rodríguez Freyle relates the Europeans' mad quest for the elusive El Dorado, as "the Spaniards made forays over the whole territory, uncovering its secrets," devising outlandish schemes that foreshadow the Buendías family's weapons of solar warfare, such as that of the conqueror Antonio de Sepúlveda, who drained a lake in order to recover the hidden gold:

> The persistent report that there was gold treasure to be found in all these lakes, and particularly in Guatavita, later led Antonio de Sepúlveda to come to an arrangement with His Majesty Philip II over draining it. He cut a first canal, that can still be seen, and affirmed that, as the level fell, he recovered gold to the value of over twelve thousand *pesos* merely from the shores. Long afterwards he tried draining it further at another spot, but without success, and in the end he wore himself out and died in poverty. Many others have tried their hand since and given up, for it is an interminable enterprise calling for vast expenditure of money and labour, in view of the depth of the lake and the amount of slime.

Our author confesses to having himself caught the golden bug when he once went with a Native guide on a treasure hunt for a golden alligator that was allegedly hidden in a nearby lake:

> One who had been a priest of the sanctuary guided me to the lake, but no sooner had we come within sight of it than he fell face downward on the ground, and nothing I could do would make him get up again or address another word to me. So I came away empty-handed, with all my expenses for nothing.... Great is the attraction of gold and silver that lures young and old alike and leaves them always wanting more.

The silent resistance of Rodríguez Freyle's guide to the golden alligator gives our narrator pause to ponder the modern project of discovery from the Native American point of view:

> The natives of these parts could well have spoken of the pre-conquest period as *their* golden age, of what came after as the age of iron, and of this present age as that of iron and steel. And what steel! For of all the earlier native population

there survive today only a few handfuls to be found in the district of Santa Fé [de Bogotá] and in that of Tunja, and even of these. . . . But no; it were better to keep silence.[107]

Keeping silent from this point onward about the disastrous consequences of the European discovery of gold for New Granada's indigenous population, Rodríguez Freyle turns his ethnographic gaze from the Native American cultures he has described in the early chapters of his book to the underbelly of colonial society, painting a devastating picture that offers a sharp contrast to the official histories written about the Spanish Empire by such prominent contemporary court historians as Antonio de Herrera y Tordesillas.

Not surprisingly, Rodríguez Freyle's text only circulated in manuscript throughout the viceregal period under the popular title "El carnero" (meaning "ram" or "sheep") until its first publication in Bogotá in 1859.[108] While there have been several interpretations of the significance of this popular title, the literary historian Roberto González Echevarría has maintained (citing archival work by Susan Herman) that "carnero. . . . is derived from *carnarium* and alludes by analogy to the place where discarded papers were thrown. 'Carnero' meant the wastepaper basket at the Santa Fe de Bogotá *audiencia,* the bin where the textual remnants of a variety of legal cases were discarded."[109] But, as González Echevarría points out, it is also an apt metaphor for the archive, the official storage space of state secrets, especially the secret information gathered by imperial officials and consulted by court historians such as Herrera y Tordesillas about the Spanish possessions in America. In other words, our colonial auto-ethnographer Rodríguez Freyle dug around colonial society's trash, left outside the official seat of the Spanish Empire in northern South America, in order to expose state secrets in the form of the many hybrids that the Habsburg's official imperial policy of purification had spawned and suppressed: the countless illegitimate "mestizo" offspring that had been proliferated by *limpieza de sangre* (blood purity) laws as well as the secret practices of "witchcraft" proliferated by the Inquisition. In the old days, Rodríguez Freyle writes, only good Catholics and "Old Christians" (i.e., Christians, like his parents, not recently converted from Judaism or Islam) could come to the Indies, as Spanish colonial policy was intent on keeping the Indians pure of European heresies. This law "was in effect for a long time. Nowadays anybody can come. It must have got lost."

One of the ironic consequences of *limpieza de sangre* was the spawning of an entirely new sort of hybridization that had to be concealed—hybridizations proliferated not by purified blood but by purified knowledge. Thus, Rodríguez Freyle relates the scandalous story a "young and pretty" wife from Bogotá who commits adultery while her husband is away on business in Spain. Finding herself pregnant and believing her husband's return to be imminent, she "took her problem to a friend, one Juana García, a freed negress." This Juana García "was something of a witch" who uses a water tub to conjure up images of the itinerant husband, showing him far from intent on returning home, in the amorous company of another lady in Santo Domingo. With her magic, Juana is even able to snatch a sleeve from the mistress's dress, which the young wife keeps for evidence with which later to blackmail her husband. Upon the latter's return some years later (after the wife's illegitimate child had been born and passed off as an adopted orphan), he is confronted with the piece of evidence snatched by magic. Wife and husband eventually reconcile, but poor Juana has the worst of it when the husband "took the sleeve and went off with it to the bishop.... and told him the whole story":[110]

> He [the bishop] being also chief inquisitor . . . called the wife before him and took from her a declaration, in which she confessed frankly to the incident of the tub of water. Juana García the negress likewise confessed everything.... Her statement implicated various other women, and report had it that quite a number were caught in the net, ladies of quality among them. In the end Jiménez de Quesada [the governor] himself waited on the bishop with other citizens of rank and besought him to quash the proceedings, saying that the kingdom was still in its infancy and they must not cast a slur on its fair name. Such was their insistence that the bishop gave way, refusing only to absolve Juana García. On her he imposed a penance that she stand on a raised platform in Santo Domingo church at the hour of high mass with a halter round her neck and a lighted candle in her hand. And there she lamented amid her sobs, "We were all in it, all of us, and I alone am made to pay!"[111]

Rodríguez Freyle's story of Juana García illuminates the colonial context—the colonial connection between Latour's Internal and External Great Divides that I call "the alchemy of conquest"—from which one particular hybrid emerged in the early modern project of purification: the hybrid of witchcraft emerging from the purification of magic. Of course, magic—the mixture of nature and culture—had a long tradition in medieval Europe, but its purification—its split into Christian knowledge and demonic superstition—was the project of the early modern science of demonology, in both its Reformation and Counter-Reformation varieties, that took place in the context of the increasingly intense European encounters with religious alterity since the thirteenth century. Thus, the year 1492 notoriously marked not only the European "discovery" of America but also the expulsion of the Jews from Spain and the completion of the Christians' so-called Reconquest of the Iberian Peninsula from the eight-hundred-year rule of Islam. As we will see in the chapters that follow, the three events—the Reconquest, expulsion, and discovery—had a long-standing nexus in late medieval and early modern alchemy. The expulsion and Reconquest gave rise to the purifying project of the Spanish Inquisition, whose purpose was to suppress the remainders of Islam and Judaism within Christian society on the peninsula. Similarly, the conquest of the New World promised to offer a purely Christian, a messianic, solution for procuring the technological and material means that would bring about a Reconquest of Jerusalem, a Catholic Christian world empire, a Reformation, a Scientific Revolution, an apocalypse.

The Alchemy of Conquest

The chapters that follow attempt to understand the sixteenth-century origins of Latour's modern Constitution in the confluence of science, religion, and state power in the conquest of America. They are presented in four parts. The chapters in part 1 provide an overview of the medieval background of this confluence in the fusion of Arabic-Aristotelian naturalism with apocalyptic prophecy, esoteric spirituality, and Christian church militancy in the context and aftermath of crusade. These chapters are intended to offer not a comprehensive history of medieval alchemy but a discussion of the role that alchemy played as an "experimental science" in legitimating scientific curiosity about the occult, which was regarded in Augustinian theology as impenetrable by providential design. Thus, chapter 1, "The Hermeneutics of Secrecy," begins with an overview of the late medieval ("Scholastic") coexistence of various forms of Aristotelianism resulting from the impact of Latin translations from the Arabic Aristotelian tradition during the twelfth and thirteenth centuries—mainly the Thomist *via antigua* and nominalist *via moderna* in Scholastic metaphysics from which Baconian inquiry emerged. By focusing on the Hermetic tradition, the chapter proceeds to theorize the epistemology and hermeneutics of the "secret" in alchemy and occult philosophy in the context of which the secret became increasingly distinct from the Scholastic marvel. In the interstice between the known and the unknown, between the old and the new, the late medieval and early modern secret offered a unique epistemological space of legitimate inquiry that functioned hermeneutically and rhetorically for the inscription of unfamiliar phenomena and occult causes. The language of alchemy hereby underwrote (early) modern curiosity with a spiritual and even millenarian telos, as well as with state power in sixteenth- and seventeenth-century baroque cameralism in the context of overseas imperial expansionism.

Chapter 2 turns to several influential late medieval alchemists more specifically in order to illustrate the synthesis of Scholastic "experimental science" with Christian apocalyptic messianism and church militancy. The alchemical works written by or attributed to Roger Bacon, Arnald of Villanova, and John of Rupescissa transformed the Aristotelian trade secret into a metaphysical secret of nature by synthesizing the technical language of alchemy with that of Christological passion. Pressing alchemy in the service of Christian church militancy—as the art of strengthening Christian bodies in preparation for the apocalyptic battles—alchemical texts such as Father Ullmann's *Buch der Heiligen Dreifaltigkeit* (Book of the Holy Trinity) employed the Augustinian rhetoric of "Egyptian Gold"—the theft of pagan knowledge justified by Christian apocalyptic ends. By focusing on the alchemical concept of "reduction," this chapter highlights the epistemic violence of alchemical transmutation described in the language of crusade and Christian passion. Similarly, chapter 3 focuses on the Majorcan polymath Ramón Llull, whose works, both authentic and spuriously attributed to him, fuse science and religion by enlisting Aristotelian inquiry in the service of Christian evangelical rhetoric. As this chapter shows, the famous *ars luliana* offered a seminal if idiosyncratic synthesis of Aristotelian inquiry with Neoplatonic natural theology that has been called a "frontier philosophy" for integrating Islamic, Jewish, and Christian elements. Moreover, his writings elaborated a unique synthesis of Aristotelian naturalism with a high medieval discourse of chivalric love, a mendicant evangelical ethos, and a Franciscan church militancy that would have a long-lasting and powerful legacy in the intellectual history of scientific discovery generally and of the European discovery of America particularly.

The chapters in part 2 turn to the literature of the Spanish discovery and conquest about the Americas. Thus, chapter 4 focuses on the writings of Christopher Columbus, particularly his later prophetic writings, which synthesize his curiosity about the secrets of the (new) world with a prophetic millenarianism into a rhetoric of "ecstatic materialism" that is strongly and directly indebted to the alchemical tradition of Arnald of Villanova and John of Rupescissa. Thus, the chapter traces Columbus's ideas about the redemptive power of gold to these late medieval alchemists, particularly his pseudo-Joachimite notion that a Spanish Last World emperor would redeem the Holy Sepulchre with gold brought from India and his cosmological ideas about the location and shape of the Earthly Paradise.

Chapters 5 and 6 turn to the early modern legacy of Ramón Llull—known as Llullism—in the literature of the discovery and conquest of America, as well as in the emergence of a modern proto-ethnographic curiosity about other (especially pagan) cultures. Thus, chapter 5 investigates the role that Llullism and Hermeticism played in the elaboration of an evangelical mission in the late medieval and early modern legal discourse of European expansionism in terms of an alchemical "reduction." In particular, the chapter focuses on the Llullian origins and connections of the canon law tradition of *papa vicarius Christi*, by which popes donated non-Christian territories to Christian lords, culminating with Pope Alexander VI's famous bulls *Inter cetera*. Chapter 6 investigates the intellectual debt of an emergent "missionary science" in sixteenth-century Spanish America to the Llullian encyclopedic and alchemical tradition by focusing on what I will call the "ethno-demonological" writings of several Franciscan and Jesuit missionaries working in New Spain and Peru (including Motolinía, Bernadino de Sahagún, Jerónimo de Mendieta, and José de Acosta). As this chapter shows, there is an intimate historical connection between the Franciscans' long tradition in alchemy and their unrivaled achievements in proto-empiricist modes of inquiry, as both derive from a conviction of the efficacy of human (or demonic) art vis-à-vis nature in the creation or corruption of substantial forms. This historical connection comes into focus with special clarity in Acosta's language of the alchemical wedding when describing the providential work of spiritual conquest as a "reduction."

As the chapters of part 2 suggest, the inquiry into the role that alchemy played in the literature of the discovery and (spiritual) conquest of America illuminates larger questions about the relationship between New World utopianism and the history of Western scientific modernity. With regard to sixteenth-century Franciscan New Spain, some scholars have emphasized the essentially "medieval" character of the New Spanish *doctrinas* and their literary representations, emphasizing, for example, the role that the Joachimite millenarian tradition played in the conception of their missionary enterprise. Others have insisted on the essentially "modern" (i.e., humanist) character of the sixteenth-century Franciscans in New Spain—emphasizing, for example, the role that the missionaries' ethnographic and natural history writings played in the rise of scientific empiricism in the early modern period.[112] Attending to the New Spanish Franciscans' adaptations of the late medieval Llullian alchemical tradition allows us to see beyond the medieval/modern binary and better to appreciate the important role that tradition plays in innovation. Specifically, by tracing the medieval alchemical roots of early American missionary utopias in the sixteenth century, we can see how the

New World came to function as a Christian humanist heterotopia for what has been called the "rational millennium" underlying the modern Baconian scientific project.[113]

From the point of view of such a *longue durée,* chapters 5 and 6—which deal with Llullism in the New World up to the sixteenth century—are intended to offer a "prehistory" of the various pansophic movements that arose in the Protestant Atlantic world during the seventeenth century and that played an important role in the so-called Scientific Revolution in England. The nexus between evangelical pansophism and the Scientific Revolution in the seventeenth-century Protestant context has been the subject of several important recent studies and is therefore not specifically dealt with here. Thus, in work that built on an early twentieth-century study by Robert Young, David Hill Scott and Sarah Rivett have each shown the crucial role that the seventeenth-century German-British polymath Samuel Hartlib (ca. 1600–1662) and the transatlantic Protestant pansophic circle of reformers gathered around him played in the conception and support of the Puritan missionary project in colonial New England.[114] While Rivett has shown the close interconnections between religion and Baconian science in seventeenth-century Puritan missionary discourse, Hill Scott also noted the Llullian background of one of the Hartlib Circle's most important intellectual forefathers in continental Europe—the German Calvinist reformer and encyclopedist Johan Heinrich Alsted (1588–1638), the teacher of the famous Protestant Czech reformer Jan Comenius.[115] Indeed, Alsted had been crucial in the translation of the early sixteenth-century humanist revival of medieval Llullism from a long tradition of Catholic (especially Franciscan) reformism into a Protestant context in several works, most importantly his 1612 edition of the influential early sixteenth-century Llullist work *Explanatio compendiosaque applicatio artis Raymundi Lulli* (Lyon, 1523).[116] While Hill Scott did not pursue this Llullian connection and was not specifically interested in alchemy, J. T. Young and William Newman had earlier shown the important role that alchemy (including pseudo-Llullian alchemy) played in the pansophic movement of the Hartlib Circle.[117] More recently, Walter Woodward has focused on the role that alchemy played also in the Hartlibian program of the governor of Connecticut John Winthrop II, a pansophic program that included economic projects such as salt- and ironworks as well as the Puritan missions to New England's Indians. Although my discussion of Llullism is informed by this body of work about the pansophic connections between the early American missionary project and the Scientific Revolution in the Protestant Atlantic world, I arrive at conclusions that are at variance with

Woodward's argument that alchemy had an irenic inspiration and effect in early American intercultural encounters and religious conflicts.[118]

The chapters in part 3 make a transition from the role that the language of alchemy played in the mendicant milieu during the conquest of America to the role that alchemy played in the humanist invention of discovery, particularly in the humanist critique of Scholastic (i.e., Thomist) Aristotelianism by positing the existence of "new" or multiple worlds. Thus, chapter 7, "Cannibal Heterotopias in the Sixteenth Century," investigates the so-called Return of Lucretius—the impact of Epicurean natural philosophy, especially of Democritan atomism, on Renaissance Europe—via a New World heterotopia of Brazilian cannibalism in seminal texts by Amerigo Vespucci, Thomas More, Jean de Léry, André Thevet, and Michel de Montaigne. As I argue, the Renaissance humanists' engagement with classical pagan natural philosophy was greatly facilitated through a rhetoric of "cannibal ventriloquism," where un-Christian but perennially powerful ideas such as pre-Socratic atomism were placed in the mouths of New World cannibals by European humanists who discovered an uncanny resemblance between Brazilian cannibal metaphysics and the sublimated forms of alchemical materialism evident in the common medieval and early modern European practice of medicinal cannibalism and the Catholic Eucharist.

Chapter 8 explores the geopolitical implications of this humanist cannibal heterotopia in the legal debates about the justness of the Spanish conquest of America between Dominican Thomists such as Francisco de Vitoria and Bartolomé de las Casas; Parisian nominalists such as John Mair; and humanists such as Paracelsus and Juan Ginés de Sepúlveda. The chapter begins with a reconsideration of the so-called Great Debate of 1550–51 between Las Casas and Sepúlveda from the point of view of multiple Aristotelian epistemologies that still coexisted during the sixteenth century, specifically the Thomist metaphysical realism of Las Casas and the nominalism of the humanist Aristotelian Sepúlveda. As I aim to show in this chapter, the debate between the two famous opponents can in part be understood in terms of their different understandings of Aristotle, derived from quite distinct intellectual traditions—the former from the Thomist tradition of Scholastic commentaries on Aristotle and the latter from the "modern" tradition of humanist scholarship on the Aristotelian corpus, particularly the *Politics*. I argue that there is an epistemological connection not only between the Thomists' general opposition to violent conquest and their adherence to Scholastic (hylomorphic) natural philosophy but also between the moderns' support of violent conquest and their embrace of alchemical (corpuscular) or pre-Socratic materialist (atomic) theory of matter. Whereas the former subscribed to a metaphysics of dominion as continuous, homogeneous, infinitely divisible, and governed by natural laws that functioned in concordance with universal reason, the latter were heirs to a Democritan materialist line of political philosophy that fused during the Renaissance with a Christian hierocratic conception of dominion, giving rise to an ontological distinction between the Christian republic on the one hand and barbarous nations that may or may not be part of God's original Creation. As I argue, it is this confluence between a humanist Aristotelianism with a Christian hierocratic conception of dominion that lies at the bottom of the early modern notion of the diabolic origins of the American Indians as a type of alchemical homunculus, a *homunculus americanus* descended not from Adam but, according to the Swiss alchemist Paracelsus, from "another Adam" created by demonic art in the New World and therefore exempt from God's original gift of dominion.

Chapter 9, "The Blood of the Dragon," turns to the impact of this humanist synthesis of medieval (i.e., Aristotelian) alchemy and classical natural philosophy on the inquiry into New World *materia medica* and natural history by secular imperial and mercantile authors, including Gonzalo Fernández de Oviedo y Valdés, Nicolás Monardes, and Juan de Cárdenas. As this chapter aims to show, all three natural historians attempted to purify the marvelously efficacious properties of American nature from its occult and diabolic knowledge and uses in Amerindian culture by recontextualizing American *materia medica* within a Christian framework. Whereas Oviedo hereby fuses the classical Plinean model of natural history with the language of Christian passion in the name of empire, Monardes imbues the curiosity about the American *materia medica* with the iconography of the alchemical "Dragon's Blood" for private profit. Finally, Cárdenas, like Acosta, employs the languages of ethnodemonology and alchemy in order to rationalize the conquest of America in terms of a penetration of its secret voids—the watery voids of New Spain and of the Western Hemisphere more broadly that explain its exceptional heat and humidity in which Amerindian bodies degenerate but Christian creole bodies thrive.

The chapters in part 4 explore the role that alchemy played in the translation of the literature of discovery and conquest of America from a Spanish (Catholic-Habsburg) into a Protestant context. Thus, chapter 10 explores the early modern origins of the "White Legend" of an English discovery of America by placing it in the context of both the "Black Legend" of the cruelty of the Spanish conquest and of the "Golden Legend" of the European quest for El Dorado. The chapter begins with a discussion of the translations prepared by the English alchemist Richard Eden of the works on natural history and cosmography by Sebastian Münster, Peter Martyr, and Fernández de Oviedo. The middle section focuses on the elaboration of an English discourse of discovery and conquest by John Dee. The main part of the chapter focuses on Walter Raleigh's *Discovery of the Beautiful Empire of Guiana* by exploring Raleigh's use of alchemical, Hermetic, and prophetic language from both European and indigenous traditions, particularly the European tradition of the alchemical wedding and the Inca tradition of *pachakuti*.

Chapter 11 explores the role of alchemical language in Thomas Harriot's *A Brief and True Report of the newfound lande of Virginia* and traces the dissemination of the idea of a Protestant discovery in the travel volumes published by the Calvinist engraver Theodor de Bry and his sons. The chapter ends with an exploration of the historical connections between ethno-demonology and New World exceptionalism in British America, in texts such as Cotton Mather's *Wonders of the Invisible World*. As these chapters show, the alchemical "corpuscular" or atomistic conception of matter rationalized the Protestant White Legend of the discovery and occupation of America in the fiction of a New World virginal "void" that had not yet been penetrated by Spanish conquerors and was therefore subject to the law of nations but saved itself for its "alchemical wedding" with the English discoverer. Thus, chapter 12, "Eating Bacon," explores how this purified "White Legend" of an English discovery of America informs Francis Bacon's influential conception of scientific discovery as the "conquest of nature." As I argue, Bacon's project in the reform of knowledge, as elaborated both in his tract of science fiction *New Atlantis* and in his theoretical works, can itself be understood as an act of epistemic cannibalism. Thus, Bacon's *Great Instauration* aims at a restoration of the ancient science of the pre-Socratics through a "philological alchemy" that is inspired by his dialogues not only with Montaigne but also with his heterotopic Other in "Of Cannibals" when devouring and digesting (even while suppressing), the textual tradition of the alchemists and that of the Spanish conquerors of America.

The coda returns to García Márquez by focusing on his critique of the (post-)Enlightenment traveler and natural philosopher Alexander von Humboldt, who has sometimes been called the "second discoverer" of America. Humboldt had begun his scientific career with forays into organic chemistry and metallurgy in the service of the Prussian cameralist state before turning his private scientific gaze upon South America. His later travel writings, like his early chemical experiments, aimed to make manifest the occult forces of nature that, Humboldt argued, reveal themselves more powerfully in the vexation (*Reizung*) of tropical climates. Translating the millenarian telos of the premodern alchemical opus into a transcendental aesthetic experience captured by the German concept of *Ruhe* (calm, solitude), the Humboldtian natural philosopher emerges from his South American travels as an "alchemist of the tropics" who relegitimates the alchemical construction of the occult for a modern bourgeois republic of science consisting of cosmopolitan, individual, and mobile "centers of calculation."

Part I

The Alchemy of Exception

1

The Hermeneutics of Secrecy
Aristotle and Discovery

In order to illustrate the problem, we may begin with semantics. In 1500 the meaning of the word "to discover" was not yet limited to the rather narrow modern sense of finding something new or previously unknown; rather, it could still have several meanings, some of which were synonymous with the verb "to invent" (from Latin *invenire,* to come upon, to find). According to the *Oxford English Dictionary* (*OED*), the early modern semantic field of the word "to discover" included the modern sense of "obtain[ing] sight or knowledge of (something previously unknown) for the first time;" but it also included several now obsolete or archaic meanings. For example, we find the now obsolete sense of "to manifest, exhibit, display (an attribute, quality, feeling, etc.)." We also find the now obsolete sense of "to explore" and to "bring to fuller knowledge" (i.e., of something that is already partially known). Finally, we find the (now archaic) sense of "reveal[ing]" or "uncover[ing]" something that had been hidden by something or someone, especially in the sense of exposing something that had been kept "secret." Lacking the oppositions between tradition and innovation, the known and the unknown, the early modern word "to discover" still had various meanings that we moderns would deem to be mutually exclusive. By the nineteenth century, it appears, the semantic field of the word "to discover" had completed a process of contraction toward the more exclusive and restrictive modern sense of finding by empirical means something new or previously unknown.[1]

The semantic change in the word "to discover" in English and other modern Western languages over the last five hundred years reflects a more fundamental epistemological transformation in scientific hermeneutics, in what it means to discover something. However, the roots of this modern transformation reach back to the later Middle Ages. For such early Christian church fathers and doctors as Clement, Origen, and Augustine, discovery meant primarily the finding of truth by means of divine revelation and Neoplatonic scriptural hermeneutics aimed at reconciling the New and Old Testaments. Since the twelfth century, however, discovery was in Europe increasingly understood in terms of the works of Aristotle, many of which had previously been unknown in the Latin West and become available only via translations from the Arabic in the context of the Christian Reconquest of southern Europe from Muslim domination.[2] For Aristotle, all inquiry began with sensory perception. In the first book of the *Metaphysics,* Aristotle writes: "By nature, all men long to know. An indication is their delight in the senses. For these, quite apart from their utility, are intrinsically delightful, and that through the eyes more than the others."[3] While historians of science now generally give due credit to the tremendous importance of medieval Aristotelianism—also known as the Thirteenth-Century Scientific Revolution—for the history of modern science,[4] one of the significant differences between the Thirteenth- and the Seventeenth-Century Scientific Revolution is that the former did not result in a "paradigm shift" (in the Kuhnian sense) in what it means to discover something, as the impact of Aristotelianism resulted in a variety of "Aristotelian" traditions that had previously led separate lives and even had distinct origins in the many works of Aristotle. Thus, in the *Topics,* Aristotle had elaborated a procedure of discovery as "invention" that was designed to serve as a guide in the choice of appropriate evidence and the most fruitful questions to ask in a variety of fields, including natural philosophy, ethics, politics, and rhetoric. However, when later elaborating more fully his system of logic in the *Organon,* especially in the *Prior* and the *Posterior Analytics,* Aristotle mainly focused on demonstration—the presentation of results in order to establish conclusions on the basis of accepted premises by syllogistic reason. In other words, the earlier emphasis on invention in the *Topics* had given way to a concern with demonstration in the *Organon.* The *Topics* subsequently played an important role in a continuous Western tradition of rhetoric, there being developed by Roman thinkers, most prominently Cicero and Quintilian, and later by Renaissance humanists such as Peter Ramus. By contrast, Aristotle's method of demonstration by syllogistic reason, as outlined in the *Organon,* became the dominant epistemology in medieval Scholastic natural philosophy.[5]

Many of the theologians of the Dominican Order—including Vincent of Beauvais, Albertus Magnus, Robert Kilwardby, and most of all, Thomas Aquinas—were on the forefront of elaborating this late medieval assimilation of Aristotelian natural philosophy in the Latin West that has come to be known as "Scholasticism," the synthesis between Aristotelian philosophy and Neoplatonic Christian theology. The "dogs of the lord" (as the Dominicans were known) had been newly founded in southern France in order to combat various brands of lay spirituality emerging from the impact of (Arabized) Aristotelian naturalism, especially the Albigensian Heresy, which had revived the old Manichean idea of the dual active principles of good and evil in the world that had already tempted St. Augustine.[6] Although the "Cathars" were defeated in a bloody crusade, the theological debate over how to reconcile Aristotle's pagan ideas with Christian Scripture continued. On the one end of the spectrum were the Christian followers of the twelfth-century Arab philosopher Averroës (aka Ibn Rushd), who had elaborated a synthesis between Aristotelian philosophy and Islamic theology. Ensconced in the arts faculties at the University of Paris, the Averroists insisted on a "double truth"—the notion that Aristotelian reason and the Christian faith were separate and ultimately irreconcilable epistemologies that had to be pursued in distinct disciplines. On the other end of the spectrum was the natural theology of such prominent Franciscan theologians as Roger Bacon (ca. 1219–1292), Bonaventure (1221–1274), John Duns Scotus (ca. 1265–1308), and William of Ockham (ca. 1280–1347). The central tenet of Franciscan natural theology was the concept of *reductio,* the "reduction" (or leading back) of all of the pagan liberal arts to the study of Christian Scripture (*reductio artium ad sacram scripturam*).[7]

Aquinas's influential compromise between the two extremes has come to be known as "Thomist" natural law metaphysics. According to the Thomists, the universe is governed by four realms of law—eternal law (the law by which God Himself acts); divine law (that which He revealed in the Bible and on which the church is founded); natural law (that which God implants in all men so that they should be able to understand his design and intention for the world); and human, or positive, law (that which men enact in order to govern themselves). Although the Thomists drew a distinction between these four realms, they did so in terms not of a separation but of a nested hierarchy in which human law was a subsection of natural law; natural law a subsection of divine law; and divine law a subsection of eternal law (see fig. 4). Because the four levels were congruous, eternal and divine laws were partially knowable insofar as men participated in them through their experience and natural reason. As Aquinas had put it in the *Summa,* "natural law is nothing else than the rational creature's participation of the eternal law."[8] Conversely, everything in the world happened on account of the first cause of eternal law, but it manifested itself through and was mediated by the secondary causes of natural law.

For the Thomists, natural law thus consisted of certain higher and universal principles that were *reflected* in the multiplicity of all positive human laws, regardless of culture and religion. Human societies and governments, whether Christian or pagan, originated from this innate principle of human nature. They were "perfect" insofar as they were in themselves complete, having evolved according to natural principles that are entirely independent from Christian revelation and Salvation history. The claim for a human participation in divine law was theologically grounded by the revelation in Genesis

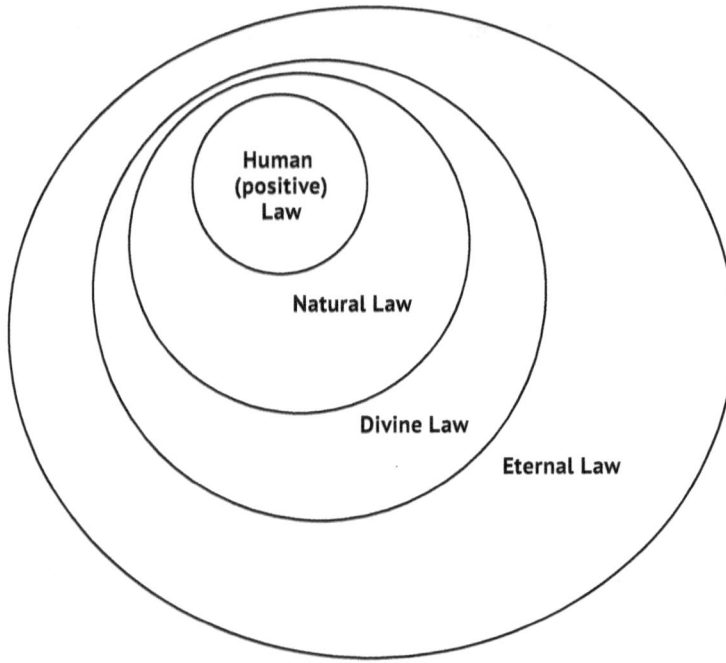

Figure 4. Thomist natural law metaphysics. (© the author.)

that Adam was created in God's own image and that all men descended from Adam. Although the biblical Fall had "wounded" (as Aquinas put it) men's direct experience of God, they retained a natural and innate tendency to want to know His truth. The Thomists referred to this innate tendency as "synderesis," meaning the principle in the moral consciousness of every human being which directs the agent to good and restrains him or her from evil. It is the human counterpart of animal "instinct" inhering in reason; for what all humans shared—and what distinguished them from other living things in Aristotelian natural philosophy, such as animals and plants—is that they have reason, or (as Aristotle understood it) a "rational soul."[9]

However, Thomist metaphysics never attained a paradigmatic status within late medieval Scholasticism but found itself in constant contest with various other ways of understanding the world. One of the major controversies that emerged from the attempt of reconciling Aristotelianism with Christianity during the late Middle Ages was the so-called *Wegestreit*, the conflict between the Thomists' *via antigua* of metaphysical realism and the Franciscans' *via moderna* of metaphysical nominalism. In essence, the controversy revolved around the question of whether or not abstract universals have "real" existence; that is, whether or not they were part of God's original Creation. Whereas the realists insisted that the original Creation consisted of particulars and universals, the nominalists held that reality consisted of particulars only and that universals are "but names"—the creations not of God but of man's (fallible) fancy—that have no "real" existence.[10] The Franciscans' *via moderna* of metaphysical nominalism was rooted in the extreme theological voluntarism of some of their most prominent thirteenth-century theologians, especially John Duns Scotus and William of Ockham, who insisted on the absolute sovereignty of the divine will. Thus, whereas the Thomists held that reality is the manifestation of the "second causes" of natural laws and principles that are intelligible to human reason and that are rarely broken by God's supernatural and direct intervention, the nominalists held that reality was the direct manifestation of the "first cause" of a divine will that was, by definition, inscrutable. By the end of the fourteenth century, Franciscan voluntarism had gained a position of dominance at the influential theology faculty at the University of Paris, with such prominent Conciliarists as Jean Gerson and Pierre d'Ailly.[11]

The controversy in Scholastic metaphysics between the adherents of the *via antiqua* and the *via moderna* held important implications for the history of discovery in natural philosophy. According to the Thomists' realist metaphysics, all reasonable men could begin with empirical observation and, by reasonable deduction (syllogism), arrive at metaphysical truth, as though ascending a ladder based on a foundation of experience and constructed of steps of reasonable deductions. The nominalists, by contrast, doubted the consistency between man's reason and metaphysics. As David Herlihy has put it, in the nominalist understanding, "the human intellect had not the power to penetrate the metaphysical structures of the universe. It could do no more than observe events as they flowed. Moreover, the omnipotent power of God meant in the last analysis that there could be no fixed natural order. God could change what He wanted, when He wanted. The nominalist looked on a universe dominated by arbitrary motions."[12] The upshot of this *via moderna* was threefold. Epistemologically, it disaggregated naturalist inquiry from metaphysics; politically, it shored up monarchical pretensions to power by likening God to an absolutist tyrant who had created the laws of nature but could break them at his pleasure at any moment; and legally, it undermined the centrality of natural law as a nexus between the human and the divine. As Heiko Oberman has explained, this shift in the terms of debate about the existence of universals had profound consequences for the history of science in the West in a decisive turn from the deductive to the inductive method during the early modern period in the sixteenth and seventeenth centuries.[13] As we will see in chapter 2, this background in nominalist metaphysics also helps to explain why, during the later Middle Ages since the thirteenth century, alchemy and apocalyptic expectancy flourished primarily in Franciscan circles.

While the nominalist opposition to the Thomist synthesis was registered already by thirteenth-century Franciscan contemporaries of Aquinas on theological and philosophical grounds, it gained momentum during subsequent historical events of cataclysmic crisis during the fourteenth century. The first one of these events came when Europe lost one-third of its population to the Black Death. In the face of apocalyptic catastrophe, the cause and course of which seemed utterly inscrutable, Aquinas's sublime sense of order was difficult to reconcile with lived reality. The second crisis came in form of the Great Papal Schism in 1378, in which two competing popes temporarily tore apart the Catholic Church. In the fifteenth century, a new generation of influential nominalist theologians such as Gabriel Biel laid the foundation for the sixteenth-century Protestant Reformation.[14] And while the sixteenth century saw a resurgence of Thomism at the influential University of Salamanca in such Dominican theologians as Francisco de Vitoria and Domingo de Soto, the nominalist tradition continued to flourish at the University of Paris with such prominent figures as Jacques Lefèvre d'Étaples and John Mair; as well as at Salamanca in the writings of Bartolomé de Castro and Antonio Coronel; and at the newly founded University of Alcalá de Henares with such formidable theologians as the Erasmian humanist Cardinal Jiménez de Cisneros.[15]

I will return to the historical connection between metaphysics, alchemy, and conquest in later chapters. As I will argue, it is no coincidence that many of the "moderns" such as Mair and Cisneros played an important role in the theological defense of violent conquest and the Spanish rights of discovery in the New World. Conversely, it is no coincidence that many of the Neo-Thomist proponents of realist metaphysics (such as Vitoria and De Soto) were generally (with some caveats) among the harshest critics of the Spanish conquest. Here, it will suffice to note that, while Aristotle's *Politics* played an important role in this metaphysical debate about conquest and the elaboration of a theory of the "rights'" of discovery in the early modern law of nations, his authority in natural philosophy came under intense scrutiny in the sixteenth-century literature of discovery, which proved many of his assumptions—such as the impossibility of life in the torrid zone—to be wrong.[16] However, the frequent attacks on "Aristotle" in sixteenth-century natural philosophy did not amount to a "revolution" that overturned the Aristotelian foundations of Western knowledge in general; rather, they further diversified the hermeneutics of discovery.[17] In response to these attacks, sixteenth-century Neo-Aristotelian philosophers and logicians such as Agosto Nifo and Jacopo Zabarella at Padua as well as Domingo de Soto at Salamanca attempted to salvage the syllogism by elaborating what is known as "regressus theory," a method for the discovery not of new facts but of the underlying causes of known facts. Regressus theory was based on the idea that one can discern the cause of a phenomenon from the effects it produces and then "regress," or go back, in the opposite direction from cause to effect, and so provide scientific demonstrations of the phenomenon being investigated. Thus, De Soto was famously able to demonstrate that, while the velocity of falling bodies is not constant but increases in the course of the fall, the *rate of acceleration* is regular and corresponds to laws apprehensible by mathematical reason—a natural principle that he called "uniformiter difformis." Regressus theory generally, and De Soto's investigations in physics particularly, had a profound impact on the history of sixteenth-century mechanics and astronomy, including Galileo's logic of discovery.[18]

The critics of syllogistic reasoning, by contrast, turned to the methods of discovery as they had been articulated in Aristotle's *Topics* (i.e., invention) and subsequently developed in the rhetorical tradition, giving birth to such early modern treatises on discovery as Polydore Vergil's *De inventoribus rerum* (1499). As a result, two intellectual strains evolved from the earlier Aristotelian notion of discovery as invention in the early modern period: first, a humanist "backlash" (exemplified by Ramus) that adopted the topics as the foundation for conceptualizing not only discovery in natural philosophy but also the process of human cognition in general as an assimilation of newly found things to the storehouse of knowledge built up since antiquity; and second, the "radical" strain as derived from Scholastic nominalist metaphysics and exemplified most prominently by Francis Bacon, who saw the crisis of syllogistic reason as an opportunity to replace traditional learning through a method of "inductive elimination."[19]

While the proponents of this radical strain retained some of the basic components of Aristotelian natural philosophy—such as the notions that discovery must begin with sensory perception and entail the making manifest of the causes of observable phenomena—they differed from the Scholastic defenders of Aristotle, as well as from his humanist critics, in three crucial ways. First, they rejected the book as a paradigm of discovery in natural philosophy, Scholastic or humanist, demanding that scientific inquiry begin not with scholarship but with direct observation of nature. In effect, they disaggregated the study of nature from other forms of philosophical inquiry both in its methods and aims. Second, in terms of its aims, they demanded that science have practical outcomes by expanding human control over the natural environment—leading to Bacon's famous formulation of discovery as a "conquest" of nature. And third, they radically enlarged the field of phenomena subject to scientific inquiry by disregarding Scholastic distinctions between what could and what could not be known. These distinctions included the Aristotelian borderline between "intrinsic" (naturally induced) and "extrinsic" (artificially induced) causes of change. Thus, Bacon argued that natural philosophy should concern itself not only with "natural" motions (such as a stone falling to the ground) but also with artificially induced motions produced by experiment (such as the propulsion of a cannon ball from a barrel). It was the status of these artificially produced "natural facts" that was famously at issue in the debate between Boyle and Hobbes.[20]

One of the consequences of the Baconian paradigm of discovery was the breakup of the sixteenth-century humanist concept of discovery as *inventio*. Only relatively recently has this modern distinction between discovery and invention become the subject of renewed scrutiny in seminal postmodernist work in the philosophy of science. As a result of this postmodern critique, philosophers of science now once again appreciate the important role that the imagination, creativity, and reason play not only in the arts and humanities but also in the process of scientific discovery. Thus, philosophers of science no longer distinguish between invention and discovery but between different modes of discovery—such as discovery by "exposure" or discovery by "generation."[21] Meanwhile, seminal twentieth-century statements in philosophical hermeneutics—from Martin Heidegger's *Being and Time* to Hans Georg Gadamer's *Truth and Method* and Luiz Costa Lima's *Control of the Imaginary*—have offered critiques of the modern paradigm of discovery from the point of view of the humanities.[22] These philosophical critiques of the modern paradigm of discovery have made it possible to subject it to a historical and ethnographic description.[23] As we will see in the next section, its most prominent feature is its relationship to secrecy.

From Marvel to Secret

In the *Metaphysics,* Aristotle argued that at the beginning of all philosophy is wonder. Men "wondered at those puzzles that were at hand, such as the affections of the moon and events connected with the sun and the stars and about the origins of the universe."[24] If wonder and knowledge have thus a longstanding connection in the Western tradition, one of the most distinctive features of this nexus in early modern times is, as Stephen Greenblatt has argued, its acquisitiveness, transforming "marvels" into "marvelous possessions" in the context of the European encounter with the Americas.[25] But equally significant is the modern attitude toward the occult; for, at the heart of the early modern concept of discovery is an assumption that truth is not manifest—that observable phenomena are a "cover" for something hidden—as well as an intentionality of making the hidden manifest. Peter Sloterdijk writes that, in order to describe the early modern idea of discovery, it is "indispensable to show the means of acquisition which guarantee that the cover concealing what was previously hidden is removed once and for all. Accordingly, whenever Europeans of the Renaissance spoke of discovery—*découverte, descubrimiento, Entdeckung*—they meant episodes of finding and the things found, but above all the means of making them known and keeping them."[26] A third distinctive feature of this (early) modern attitude toward the occult, Sloterdijk notes, is the crucial role played by human art in discovery. Whereas in the premodern understanding of discovery as revelation, the subject and agent of discovery was an omniscient God who uncovers supernaturally through grace what humans could never have uncovered by themselves, the modern concept of discovery is predicated on the notion of an "artificial uncoverability" through human intervention in nature. Initially, this modern idea of discovery as an "art" emerged in the Renaissance as the result of recording procedures of a geotechnical, hydrotechnical, ethnotechnical, and biotechnical kind. This connection between art and discovery led to the explosion of cartography in the early modern period, in the process of which the two-dimensional map (with its increasingly minute details) would ultimately relegate the globe (still the dominant medium of representation in the fifteenth century) to a mere decorative function.[27]

The early modern idea of discovery is thus predicated on the supposition that the truth is hidden from us; that it can be found by transforming the unseen to the seen, the undescribed to the described, and the unknown to the known through human art; and that what was hidden but is discovered by human art becomes the property of the artisan. With respect to (early) modern discovery, there is therefore an important distinction to be made between the "marvel" and the "secret." In premodern times, in both the Jewish and the early Christian traditions, marvels and secrets had been largely synonymous: they were divine mysteries that were unknown and unknowable by providential design—put before us in order to elicit, not curiosity but wonder, an emotional response that is supposed to lead to a contemplation of the divine.[28] In the late medieval (Scholastic-Aristotelian) context, secrets could pertain either to human secrets—trade secrets (such as the techniques of glassmaking or pigment manufacture)—or natural secrets.[29] Natural secrets were the occult qualities (such as magnetism) that could not be explained in the terms of the Aristotelian elemental qualities. In Scholastic Aristotelianism these occult qualities were therefore simply beyond the scope of science. They were *both unknown in fact and unknowable in principle*. By contrast, the central and defining feature of the early modern idea of the secret is that it is *unknown in fact but knowable in principle.*[30] Thus, when the Italian Renaissance polymath Girolamo Cardano (1501–1576) defined the secret in his *De secretis* (1562), he distinguished among three kinds of secrets, none of which entailed inexplicability: unknown phenomena that were still awaiting discovery; familiar phenomena whose causes were still awaiting discovery; and things that were known only by the initiated but not generally.[31] In Cardano's taxonomy of the secret, the principle of inexplicability has disappeared. Thus, as James Dougal Fleming has put it, the early modern "hermeneutics of discovery" are characterized by an "esoteric construction of the occult."[32] Whereas in Scholastic natural philosophy, occult qualities are "beyond the possibility of knowledge," the esoteric move is "to violate the scholastic conception (as it were) by embracing it."[33]

Moreover, like early modern perspectivist visual art, the early modern secret has a spatial dimension that the Scholastic marvel lacks. This spatiality becomes apparent if we consider the etymology of the English word "secret." Like its counterparts in Romance languages—the French *secret*, Portuguese *segredo*, Spanish and Italian *secreto*—it derives from the Latin *secretum*, the corresponding verb of which is *secenere*—to separate or make discrete, specifically as in a "place apart." In book 6 of Virgil's *Aeneid*, for example, the "secreta Sibyllae" refers to the "dark enormous cave" of the Sibyl that dwells on Hesperia, on the far western corner of the world.[34] Similarly, in his *Germania*, Tacitus refers to the remote areas of Germania as "secretiora Germaniae." At the root of the concept of the secret is thus the notion of something hidden from us by spatial distance, which acts as the concealing cover.[35] This notion of the secret as a spatial cover creates, as Hildegard Elizabeth Keller has written, "the possibility of a second world, next to the one that's manifest."[36] And Georg Simmel writes that a secret (*Geheimnis*) entails the "hiding of realities by positive or negative means." The "discoverer," in this sense, is one who straddles the boundary between the hidden and the manifest; he is a "messenger," a Hermes, a visionary, and a prophet who mediates between inside (the esoteric) and outside (the exoteric).[37] The discoverer of secrets thus acts as both a participant in and as messenger (*Hermeneut*) of the divine mystery. Thus, the Greek god Hermes was not only the god of commerce (as well as theft, music, and rhetoric) but also the guide of travelers across boundaries (especially those traveling to Hades). His statue was placed at crossroads in antiquity because he was constantly on the move. As Michel Serres notes, Hermes is the "philosopher of plural spaces."[38]

But Hermes was not only the guide of travelers across boundaries but also the protector of those boundaries. (Hence, we speak of something as "hermetically sealed"). Indeed, the early modern concept of the secret has both an "exoteric" and an "esoteric" quality; that is, there is an exoteric quality that invites the violation of the boundary and an esoteric quality that demands its protection (and assumption in the first place). In their three-volume collection *Geheimnis und Schleier* (Secret and veil), Aleida Assmann and Jan Assmann therefore posit three sorts of secrets: "substantial secrets" (*substantielle Geheimnisse*), which are by nature inscrutable; "strategic secrets" (*strategische Geheimnisse*), those which are deliberately kept secret by someone; and "constructive secrets" (*konstruktive Geheimnisse*), which provoke curiosity and intellectual penetration.[39] Because the constructive secret is a provocation, it is "not only the state of a thing that escapes from or reveals itself to knowledge," as Michel de Certeau has put it; it also "designates a play between actors. It circumscribes the terrain of strategic relations between the one trying to discover the secret and the one keeping it, or between the one who is supposed to know it and the one who is assumed not to know it (the 'vulgar')."[40] Because the modern secret both refuses meaning and invites discovery, Certeau further notes, it introduces an "erotic element into the field of knowledge"; it "impassions" it.[41]

The esoteric quality of the "strategic secret" is also evident in the spatial metaphor at the root of a related word—the Latin *arcanum*. In a chapter dealing with storage containers (*De vasis repositoriis*) in his *Etymologies* (10.9.2), Isidore of Seville (569–636) explains that a "strongbox" (*arca*) is so called because it "fends off" (*arcere*) and prohibits one from seeing inside. From this term also derives the "archive" (*arcivum*, i.e., *archivum*), a storage house of secrets from which the uninitiated and unauthorized are "fended off."[42] Finally, the esoteric quality of the early modern secret is evident in the Greek word for secret—*mysterium* (from Greek, *mysterion*, ritual initiation). This word originally referred to secret teachings and reminds of the closed eyes of those, like mystics, who separate themselves from the visible world (from Greek *myein*, "to close oneself"), resulting from their initiation into something that must be kept secret. Thus, in his translation of the New Testament into German, Martin Luther translated the Greek word *mysterion* as *Geheimnis* (secret). This German word and its adjective, *heimlich* (secret), have again at their root a spatial metaphor. Its Middle High German equivalent adjective, *heimelich* (as well as its nouns), demarcate that which is familiar, "homely" (as in what belongs inside the home, the private), as opposed to that which is outside the home, strange (*unheimlich*), foreign (*fremd*), or savage (*wild*).[43]

The consideration of the hermeneutics of secrecy thus provides an important insight into the spatial conception of the early modern idea of discovery.

On the one hand, it is predicated on the dual assumption that there is a boundary to what we *presently know* but not to what is *potentially knowable;* and, on the other, that which is potentially knowable is already known by *someone* ("secret" rather than "new"). The discovery of secrets is therefore distinctly "conquistadorial" in its spatial conception. Its artful operations demand a "cunning intelligence" that the ancient Greeks called "mêtis."[44] As William Eamon notes, Francis Bacon conceived of discovery as a "hunt" (*venatio*), hereby framing early modern scientific pursuits in the language and value systems of its courtly patrons: "The Renaissance princes quested passionately after natural 'secrets,' especially those pertaining to alchemy and magic."[45] Eamon further observes that an entirely new field of "secrets" emerged with Europe's overseas expansionism in the New World: "The 'search for secrets' in unknown regions of nature was an image that appeared in the period's scientific literature with monotonous regularity. The promise of revealing 'secrets' hidden even from the eyes of the ancients made excellent copy for works aimed at middle-class readers, whose curiosity about novelty was aroused by the revival of magic, the discovery of new worlds, and the revelation of new and bizarre natural phenomena."[46] Although he does not pursue the point, Eamon notes that Bacon's "conquistadorial attitudes" toward nature were "nourished by reports of the conquistadors themselves, conquistadors such as Hernándo Cortés."[47] Indeed, this conquistadorial attitude toward the "secrets of these parts" is a prominent feature of Cortés's letters to Charles V. For example, in his famous "Second Letter" (which was published in multiple languages throughout Europe), Cortés gave a description of the two great Mexican volcanoes, the Popocatépetl and the Iztaccíhuatl, that foreshadows Alexander von Humboldt's famous naturalist descriptions of New World volcanoes in the nineteenth century:

> Eight leagues from this city of Churultecal [Cholula] are two very high and very remarkable mountains; for at the end of August there is so much snow on top of them that nothing else can be seen, and from one of them, which is the higher, there appears often both by day and by night a great cloud of smoke as big as a house which goes straight as an arrow up into the clouds, and seems to come out with such force that even though there are very strong winds on top of the mountain they cannot turn it. Because I have always wished to render Your Highness very particular account of all the things of this land, I wished to know the explanation of this which seemed to me something of a miracle; so I sent ten of my companions, such as were qualified for such an undertaking, with some natives to guide them; and I urged them to attempt to climb the mountain and discover the secret of the smoke, whence it came, and how.[48]

Here we can see an example of how the European narrative of discovery often depends on the local knowledge of Native "guides," who must "know and yet not know," and whose knowledge is rendered merely "practical" but not "conceptual."[49] As we will see in subsequent chapters, this epistemic appropriation and recontextualization of Amerindian knowledge frequently underlies the European "discovery" not only of geographic knowledge but also of *materia medica* in some of the most significant scientific writings of the sixteenth century about the New World, including Bernadino de Sahagún's famous *Florentine Codex,* the so-called Badianus Manuscript (a collection of Nahua pharmacopeia), the *Relaciones geográficas,* and Francisco Hernández's *Rerum medicarum Novae Hispaniae thesaurus.*[50]

In the interstice between the known and the unknown, between the old and the new, the early modern secret thus offered a unique epistemological space of legitimate inquiry that functioned hermeneutically and rhetorically for the inscription of unfamiliar phenomena and occult causes. It is a space foreclosed upon by both our modern notion of discovery (predicated on the assumption that whatever is being discovered hasn't already legitimately been known by *someone*) and by Scholastic philosophy (predicated on the assumption that whatever is being discovered must be deducible from what is already known or otherwise be an error). Moreover, in its emphasis on the productive and providential role of human cognition and art, the early modern secret provided important epistemological venues not only for apprehending exotic or occult phenomena but also for the inscription of local, technical, and artisanal forms of knowledge. For this reason, historians of science have considered curiosity about the occult as the crucial feature of the New Sciences emerging during the early modern period. However, as we will see, there was an important medieval precedent in the history of alchemy. In the next chapter, I will consider the special role that Christian apocalypticism played in the transformation of medieval alchemy into a "state of exception" within the context of Scholastic attitudes toward the occult. But before I turn to alchemy proper, it will be necessary to reconsider the premodern relationship between scientific curiosity and religion more generally.

"Just" Curiosity (*Iusta Curiositas*): Science and Religion

Unlike the Black Legend of the Spanish conquest of America, the popular modern idea of the Middle Ages depends not on a geographical or sectarian divide (south/north, Catholic/Protestant) but on a chronological one—the notion of a radical historical break between premodern and modern scientific mentalities. This historical binary operates as what the medievalist literary historian Kellie Robertson has called a "gap" narrative, upon which the legitimacy of the idea of a modern age depends—from Friedrich Albert Lange's *History of Materialism and Criticism of Its Present Importance* to Hans Blumenberg's *The Legitimacy of the Modern Age* (published exactly one hundred years apart, in 1866 and 1966 respectively).[51] Like Lange before him, Blumenberg insisted on a radical discontinuity between premodern and modern scientific mentalities, especially with regard to what he called "the preponderance of theoretical curiosity in the modern age." The "legitimation of theoretical curiosity" during the Renaissance, he argued, was the "basic feature of the history of the beginning of the modern age."[52] And the central factor in the rise of a theoretical curiosity during the (early) modern age was, for Blumenberg, the changing role that religion played in natural philosophy. During the Middle Ages, man's curiosity was circumscribed by religion, especially the Augustinian theological interdiction on "vain curiosity" (*vana curiositas*). As St. Augustine (354–430) had explained in his *Confessions*, curiosity was one of the Christian vices, one of the three forms of concupiscence, namely that of the "lust of the eyes" (*concupiscentia oculorum*).[53] Not only was curiosity a vice; it was the first step into the cardinal sin of pride. This negative evaluation of curiosity did not, of course, originate with Augustine but was already evident in the stoic tradition of Western philosophy at least since Cicero, especially in his portrayal of Ulysses as the quintessential "*curiosus*"—somebody vainly "longing to know everything." In the subsequent Christian tradition, the interdiction of curiosity was, according to Blumenberg, especially severe when it came to the realm of the occult: "In the hiddenness of the *res obscurae* [obscure subjects] from human understanding, there lies a sort of natural prescription of the region to which the cognitive will should remain restricted by practical reason."[54] Hence, in Dante's Augustinian reinterpretation of Ulysses in the *Inferno*, we find the classic *curiosus* eternally tormented by flames in the Seventh Circle of Hell for having taken his ship crew beyond the Pillars of Hercules into the cosmological *secretum*.[55]

It is significant in this context that Blumenberg presented his argument explicitly as a critique of the so-called secularization thesis of the philosopher of history Karl Löwith, who had seen the central concepts of scientific modernity—especially that of scientific "progress"—as but secularized versions of medieval ideas, especially Christian apocalyptic eschatology.[56] Against Löwith, Blumenberg insisted on a radical break between the premodern and modern scientific mentalities. But despite this difference, the two philosophers shared one fundamental assumption: that the relationship between scientific curiosity and religion is an essentially antagonistic one and that religion, whether in form or content, had to be overcome before a theoretical curiosity could emerge. This assumption, however, has long drawn criticism from medievalists. Thus, Heiko Oberman pointed out that, while there were indeed areas in which medieval theologians such as Augustine saw Christianity as incompatible with curiosity (especially when it came to magic), the Christian tradition had not only a tradition of *vana curiositas* but also one of *iusta curiositas* (just curiosity)—a curiosity that is "not seen to be in contradiction with the faith, for it is a sort of curiosity that aims to further the faith."[57] Indeed, there is a long tradition reaching back at least to Paul's Epistle to the Romans of reading the visible works of Creation as a "sign" referring the Christian to his creator: "The invisible things of him from the creation of the world are clearly seen, being understood by the things that are made, even his eternal power and Godhead" (Rom. 1:20). St. Augustine himself had theorized this hermeneutic of reading the world in his *De doctrina christiana* by arguing that the proper use of the things of Creation is to understand them as signs of divine truth: "We must use this world," Augustine wrote, not to enjoy it but (citing from Rom. 1:20) "to discern 'the invisible attributes of God, which are understood through what has been made' or, in other words, to ascertain what is eternal and spiritual from corporeal and temporal things."[58]

Recent reassessments of the relationship between science and religion during later periods have lent support to Oberman's critique by showing how scientific inquiry in the West was often explicitly underwritten by religion. Stephen Gaukroger, for example, has argued that the "reasons commonly adduced for the success of a scientific culture in the West in the wake of the Scientific Revolution—its use of adversarial non-dogmatic argument, its ability to disassociate itself from religion, its technological benefits—are mistaken and cannot explain this success." Significantly, he begins his account of the emergence of a scientific culture in the West not in the seventeenth but in the thirteenth century, with a process that he calls the "Aristotelian amalgam"—the reintroduction of Aristotelian natural philosophy in the West. If science and religion had nevertheless remained in tension in the aftermath of this "first" (thirteenth-century) Scientific Revolution, Gaukroger argues, one of the distinctive features of the early modern Scientific Revolution of the seventeenth century is "that, unlike other earlier scientific programs and cultures, it is driven, often explicitly, by religious considerations: Christianity set the agenda for natural philosophy in many respects and projected it forward in a way quite different from that of any other scientific culture." It was, thus, the amalgamation—rather than the separation—of science and religion that set the stage for what Gaukroger sees as the "anomalous" path that Western scientific culture has taken since the seventeenth century, when the "traditional balance of interests" between cognitive practices characterizing premodern and non-Western societies was "replaced by a dominance of scientific concerns," while science itself experienced a rate of growth that is "pathological" by the standards of earlier cultures and no longer open to "refutation from outside."[59]

Although Gaukroger was not specifically concerned with alchemy, its history provides a good case of his larger point about the important role that religion has played in the history of modern science. Because of its explicitly religious, spiritual, and even apocalyptic overtones, alchemy was often treated as an embarrassment in the modern (i.e., nineteenth- and early twentieth-century) historiography of science—as a scientifically retrograde pursuit that had to be purged of its religious aspects before it could make a real contribution to the history of science as modern chemistry. However, more recently historians of science have left no doubt about the important contributions that medieval alchemy made to the history of modern science, in terms of both theories of matter and the history of scientific mentalities.[60] William Newman, for example, has traced the origins of modern atomic theory to the enormously influential medieval alchemical text *Summa perfectionis*, attributed during the medieval and early modern period to "Geber," the Latinized name for Jābir ibn Hayyān, the semi-fabulous eighth-century Arabic or Persian alchemist who is said to have written three thousand books. Today, we know that the *Summa perfectionis* was not actually a translation from the Arabic (as it purported to be) but a text originally composed in Latin by a thirteenth-century Franciscan friar, "Paul of Taranto," who was evidently familiar with Arabic alchemy and who is today known as "Pseudo-Geber." Although medieval alchemical texts such as the *Summa* were based on Aristotelian physics, Newman shows that they also elaborated an atomistic theory of mixture that was at odds with the Aristotelian conception of matter in terms of the four elements (air, fire, earth, and water).[61] Unlike the Epicurean (i.e., classical pagan) tradition of atomism, however, this medieval alchemical tradition was based not on philosophical speculation but on empirical experiment.

But the history of alchemy also illustrates why the Aristotelian amalgam did not create a "paradigm shift" (in the Kuhnian sense) in the thirteenth century. Until the sixteenth century, alchemy had remained a relatively marginal enterprise within the Scholastic paradigm of *scientia*, practiced outside the academies primarily as an artisanal pursuit, often fueled by a lay spirituality on the borders of religious orthodoxy that was theologically suspect and even banned at times by papal decree. In the religious, institutional, economic, and social context of the sixteenth century, by contrast, alchemy transformed from a marginal artisanal practice into an integral aspect of natural philosophy, especially in so-called occult philosophy. In the remainder of this chapter, I will outline some of the salient cultural factors, especially in respect to religion, that contributed to this change, including the historical intersection of alchemy with Renaissance Hermeticism, kabbalism, and Neoplatonism, as well as with baroque cameralism.

From Hermeticism to Occult Philosophy

One of the crucial events in the early modern relationship between science and religion was Marsilio Ficino's translation of the *Corpus Hermeticum* in 1463. Entitled *Poimandres* (*Poimander, Poemander*), it was a Latin translation of fourteen Greek manuscripts that had been brought to Florence from Constantinople (which had fallen to the Ottoman Turks ten years prior) by one of Cosimo de' Medici's agents and purported to contain the ancient wisdom of one Hermes (Mercurius) Trismegistus. Although Hermes Trismegistus had been venerated as a god in Hellenistic Alexandria during late antiquity—in a syncretic cult that had fused the Greek god Hermes with the Egyptian god Thoth (the god of writing and magic)—during the Christian Middle Ages he was believed to have been an actual person—an ancient sage who, though himself a pagan, had prophesied the coming of Jesus Christ. The text presented a mix of technical treatises on magic, alchemy, and astrology as well as philosophical books fusing Egyptian religion with Hellenistic philosophy.

Until Ficino's translation, only a small portion of the writings attributed to Hermes Trismegistus—mainly the *Asclepius*—had been known in the Latin West. In his *Divine Institutes,* Lactantius (ca. 240–ca. 320), one of the earliest Christian readers of the *Asclepius,* quoted copiously from both the Greek and Latin versions of the text circulating in the early centuries AD. Following Cicero, he explained that Hermes Trismegistus was one of five Mercuries known to antiquity—the killer of Argus who fled into Egypt and established laws and literature among the ancient Egyptians. "Though he was a man," Lactantius wrote, "he was so very old and so very learned in all manner of scholarship that his knowledge of many facts and skills gave him the extra name of Trismegistus [the Thrice Great]. He wrote books in great quantity which are relevant to knowledge of things divine; in them he asserts the supremacy of the one and only God most high, and calls him by the same titles that we do, 'lord and father.'"[62] As an advisor of Constantine I (the first Christian Roman emperor and himself a convert), Lactantius found the Hermetic writings useful for at least two reasons. First, they seemed to agree with Judeo-Christian ideas on many fundamental issues at stake in Lactantius's Christian apologetic writings against polytheism and especially against Epicureanism. Thus, unlike Epicurus, Hermes taught that "the world was made by divine providence" and that one god had created man out of mud: "He [Hermes] did not merely say that man was made in God's image," Lactantius wrote, "but tried also to explain the subtlety of the plan for the shaping of every individual limb of the human body."[63] Finally, and most importantly, according to Lactantius, Hermes had predicted the Incarnation, in the "son of God supreme and endowed with maximum power."[64] Lactantius quoted here from a Greek version of the *Asclepius* that had claimed that "The lord and maker of all things, whom we usually call God, created the second God visible and sensible ... and thought him fine and full of all good, he loved and cherished him as his only son."[65] Thus, according to Lactantius, Hermes had said "everything about God the father and much about the son which is contained in the divine secrets."[66]

Another reason why Lactantius found Hermeticism useful for his defense of Christianity—still a somewhat newfangled faith during Lactantius's time—was Hermes's presumed antiquity. For Lactantius, as well as for most medieval (and even early modern) authors, antiquity signaled authority. Today, the scholarly consensus is that the Hermetic Corpus originated in Alexandria as late as the early centuries AD—perhaps even only a century or so before Lactantius wrote his *Divine Institutes*. Indeed, some of the affinities that Lactantius perceived between the Hermetic and his own Christian ideas may have been the result of quite recent Jewish or early Christian influences on Alexandrian Hermeticism in the general cultural and religious syncretism of the early centuries AD. In other words, they had probably been gained in translation—a cultural translation of Jewish and early Christian ideas into Hellenistic Hermeticism and then back into Latin Christianity. However, Lactantius, based on the testimony of Cicero, assumed that Hermes had lived even before Moses's time, when he taught the Egyptians "laws and literature" (i.e., writing).[67] Some of Hermes's pronouncements on monotheism and "Christ" therefore seemed to be prophetic to Lactantius.[68]

Although St. Augustine, like Lactantius, also believed that Hermes had been an ancient prophet of the coming of Christianity, he adopted a darker view, arguing that Hermes had prophesied Christ not as a proto-Christian would have—with joy—but with the melancholy of a pagan lamenting the impending doom of his idols. In two sections devoted to Hermes in *The City of God*, Augustine cited from Apuleius's Latin translation of the *Asclepius*, which "seems to predict the present time, in which the Christian religion is overthrowing all lying figments [of idolatry] ... in order that the grace of the true Saviour may deliver men from those gods which man has made."[69] Nevertheless, Augustine acknowledged that, although Hermes seems to have deplored this Christian future, he had also confessed that the Egyptian forefathers "erred very far with respect to the knowledge of the gods" and thus "bears witness to Christianity by a kind of mournful prophecy."[70] For this reason, Augustine called Hermes a "wise man," but he doubted that Hermes was a true prophet who had been inspired by the Holy Spirit.[71] In fact, he wondered if Hermes may have been "compelled by divine influence, on the one hand, to reveal the past error of his forefathers, and by a diabolical influence, to bewail the future punishment of demons" on the other.[72] Augustine's comments on Hermes Trismegistus are characteristic of his general skepticism toward all things pagan—a skepticism that led to his struggles with Manicheanism, which he was finally able to overcome (ironically) only with the help of Plato.[73]

But despite Augustine's skepticism about Hermes, Lactantius had laid a firm foundation for the emergence of what Claudio Moreschini has called the "Hermes Christianus"—the long tradition of "intermingling of Hermetic piety and Christian thought" in the Latin Middle Ages and the early modern period. The apparent affinities between Hermeticism and Christianity gained in translation explain in part why Hermes was, for early Christians such as Lactantius, infinitely more acceptable than were Lucretius and the Epicureans when it came to naturalist inquiry and curiosity. That Lactantius was intimately familiar with Lucretius and the Epicurean tradition is quite patent in his frequent quotations from and references to the Roman poet. However, these invocations are invariably meant to excoriate the Epicureans, whose paganism had frequently resulted in "criminal and ungodly deeds." As far as Lactantius was concerned, Lucretius "had no truth to offer."[74] The church father hereby set the stage not only for a positive interpretation of Hermeticism in the Christian West but also for the thoroughly negative reception of Epicureanism throughout the Middle Ages. This condemnation of Epicureanism was, of course, unequivocally shared by Augustine, who accused the Epicureans of making themselves the "slaves of Pleasure, as of some imperious and disreputable woman."[75] While medieval philosophers continued to read Lucretius and engage with his Epicurean ideas in subterranean ways,[76] Epicurean philosophy posed too many challenges to the most foundational theological precepts of medieval Christianity. Among these challenges was not only the Epicureans' notion of pleasure (or the absence of bodily pain) as the purpose of life as well as their denial of an afterlife and of divine providence, but also their atomistic materialism, which flew in the face of the Christian concept of the Resurrection. It was only in the context of Renaissance humanism that Lucretius's Epicurean ideas reemerged openly in philosophical debate—and then (as we will see in chapter 7) largely by way of a "cannibal heterotopia" in sixteenth-century European proto-ethnographic accounts of Native Americans. While Epicureanism and pre-Socratic atomism ran afoul of the medieval Christian (Augustinian) interdiction on vain curiosity and of Scholastic metaphysics,

Christian Hermeticism provided medieval (pseudo-)Aristotelian alchemy with an alibi of *iusta curiositas*. Especially in the fifteenth century, influential theologians such as Nicholas of Cusa (1401–1464) sided with Lactantius rather than Augustine with respect to Hermeticism. In his *De docta ignorantia*, Nicholas invoked "Hermes Trismegistus" to prove why the only god—the Christian god who is the "totality of things"—has no other name than simply "God."[77]

This long medieval tradition in syncretist Christian Hermeticism from Lactantius to Cusa helps to explain the sensational success that greeted Ficino's 1463 translation of the *Corpus Hermeticum,* which went through eight incunabula editions and then twenty-two more editions before 1641.[78] As for Lactantius, so also for Ficino, the celebration of Hermeticism went hand in hand with a condemnation of Epicureanism. Although the young Ficino had initially flirted with Epicurean ideas after Lucretius's *De rerum natura* had become widely available in Gian Francesco Poggio Bracciolini's 1417 translation, he later retracted his early endorsement, instead defending the Platonic notion of the invincibility of the rational soul. Thus, in his *Platonic Theology* (1482), he labeled the "followers of Lucretius" as "cowards" who "declare war against its [the soul's] eternity."[79] By contrast, for Christian theologians such as Ficino, Hermeticism synthesized Neoplatonic Christian spirituality with the Aristotelian/alchemical interest in nature that had been gaining momentum in fifteenth-century Italy. Thus, Ficino's Hermes Trismegistus was primarily a spiritual alchemist, who received his knowledge not from experiment but directly from divine revelation. In his introduction to the *Poimandres,* the "Argumentum," Ficino wrote that Hermes "was the first among philosophers to move himself away from the company of natural philosophers and mathematicians toward the contemplation of the divine. . . . Yet there are things, which are above human nature, that we are unable to discover through human ingenuity. Therefore there is need of divine enlightenment so that we may look upon the sun itself by the sun's light."[80] Indeed, the technical and natural knowledge about alchemy, medicine, and astrology contained in the text is for Hermes but an entry into gnosis—the search for the knowledge of God, emphasizing the role of the soul in light of its astral and divine origins, thus synthesizing alchemy and magic with theosophy.

All the treatises included in Ficino's translation revolve around the same cast of characters: Hermes Trismegistus, his disciple Asclepius, as well as his two sons, Ammon and Tat. For example, the tract entitled "Mercurii Trismgestri *Clavis,* ad Tatium," a Platonic dialogue between Hermes and Tat, speaks of the "key" into the secrets of nature as a "gnosis" or gift to the magus as a divine revelation.[81] Ficino pointed out that Hermes, like Plato (but unlike Epicurus), preached the divine creation of the world and the suffusion of nature by divine essence and providence. Hermes was thus a forerunner of "Platonic Theology" more ancient than Plato himself: "The divine will, as Plato says in the *Timaeus,* is the beginning of all created things. We find the same view expressed time and again in Mercury Trismegistus. They both believe that the principle of the universe must have the most perfect mode of action: that He, who is the lord of all that is made, must through His will be the lord of all making, and by 'lord' I mean He who disposes by His free will."[82] If Hermes appeared to be the philosophical ancestor of Plato, Ficino also further elaborated the fusion of Hermetic and Judeo-Christian ideas begun by Lactantius. But whereas previous commentators had merely claimed that Hermes was at least as ancient as Moses, Ficino went one step further: In his *Platonic Theology,* he suggested that Hermes may actually have been "the same man as Moses." This identity explained, for Ficino, why Hermes articulated many central Platonic and Judeo-Christian ideas such as "a) that the world comes not from itself but from God; b) that God exceeds the world by an infinite interval—God who existed to infinity, one might say, before the world; c) that He produced the world from nothing by His infinite power; and d) that He moves it of His own free will, not from some necessity of nature. Mercurius Trismegistus has expounded this same origin of the world's generation even more plainly. It should not seem surprising to us that Mercurius knew such things if he was the same man as Moses."[83] In effect, Ficino fully integrated the pagan knowledge of Hermes into the history of Neoplatonic Christian typology and Scriptural hermeneutics.

The Hermetic tradition became one of the most important inspirations in the emergence of the syncretic Renaissance spiritual and intellectual movement known as "occult philosophy." Other sources of Renaissance occult philosophy include Neoplatonic astrology, natural magic, alchemy, Llullism, and Christian kabbala. I will discuss Llullism in more detail in chapters 3, 5, and 6. Christian kabbala, as elaborated most prominently by Giovanni Pico della Mirandola and Johann Reuchlin, refers to the early modern appropriation of the ancient Jewish tradition in the esoteric interpretation of the Bible based on the use of numbers and ciphers that was supposed to have been handed down orally from Moses himself. For his interest in kabbala, Pico had frequently found himself in trouble with church authorities throughout the 1480s, but his fortunes suddenly took a happy turn with the election of the Valencian cardinal Rodrigo de Borgia as Pope Alexander VI in 1492. Alexander was a great aficionado of Hermeticism, kabbala, Llullism, alchemy, astrology, and natural magic.[84] In an edict issued on June 18, 1492, he absolved Pico of heresy. A year later, he issued his famous bulls *Inter cetera* dividing the

New World of the Indies between Spain and Portugal. I will return to the connection between these two papal edicts in chapter 5, but here I want to conclude this section by underlining the importance of Pico's synthesis of occult philosophy for the impact it had on humanists throughout Europe. From Italy, it spread to France, Spain, and Germany, as well as England at the end of the sixteenth century. It profoundly influenced such famous occult philosophers and alchemists as Cornelius Agrippa von Nettesheim, Paracelsus, Giordano Bruno, and John Dee as well as such important Counter-Reformation polymaths as Eusebio Niremberg and Athanasius Kircher, who saw in occult philosophy a "*clavis universalis*" (universal key) to all knowledge. Most importantly, occult philosophy found powerful political allies, both on the Reformation and the Counter-Reformation side of the new sixteenth-century schism.[85]

The integration of Hermeticism and Christianity was further enhanced in the fifteenth and sixteenth centuries, in the wake of a general Egyptomania among Renaissance Neoplatonists, in which Ficino's Latin edition was expanded to include translations of three additional treatises derived from a fifth-century Greek compilation made by Joannes Stobaeus for a total of seventeen. These additional three treatises (as well as Ficino's original fourteenth) were the result of a careful selection of those Greek manuscripts that seemed particularly amenable to reconciliation with Christian doctrine and the omission of those with more obviously pagan overtones.[86] This careful editorial process of selection, translation, and integration with Judeo-Christian doctrines on the part of the Latin translators since Ficino ensured Hermes's perennial appeal in the early modern period, despite the fact that the alleged antiquity of the *Corpus Hermeticum* was disproven by the Jewish humanist Isaac Casaubon's *De rebus sacris et ecclesiasticis exercitationes XVI* (1614).[87] Although Casaubon dated the Hermetic texts only to the early centuries AD—when in fact they now seem to have originated in Hellenistic Alexandria—the authenticity and antiquity of Hermes's authorship was not generally discredited on the Continent until the eighteenth century. Moreover, after being brought to England from Italy by Giordano Bruno, the Hermetic tradition continued to exert a strong influence on sixteenth- and seventeenth-century English alchemists such as John Dee, Robert Fludd, George Starkey, and Elias Ashmole (one of the founding members of the Royal Society of London), as well as Puritan divines in New England such as John Winthrop Jr. (the governor of Connecticut and son of the governor of Massachusetts), and Cotton Mather, who designated Winthrop as New England's "Hermes Christianus" in his biography of Winthrop included in his *Magnalia Christi Americana* (1702).[88]

From Renaissance Magus to Baroque Secretary

Historians of Western esotericism have highlighted the social, political, and economic contexts that gave rise to occult philosophy during the European Renaissance. Thus, Nicholas Goodrick-Clarke observes that the "historical incidence and efflorescence of esoteric ideas" typically occurred in times "when the dominant worldview no longer commands general assent."[89] Similarly, in his social history of Jewish kabbalism in Renaissance Italy, Robert Bonfil has argued that the shift from Aristotelian philosophy to esoteric kabbala in the sixteenth century was caused by "the lack of religious certainty expressed by those who turned to philosophy with the aim of finding therein the answers to their existential problems as men and as Jews." An esoteric thought system such as kabbala was hereby able to provide a "corner stone of a popular movement" that provided the answers that the intellectual elites in the academies were unable to supply.[90]

This is an important insight that sheds light not only on the social function of esotericism across the ages but also on the important role that esotericism has played in the history of modern science. Frances Yates, in several seminal works published during the 1960s and 1970s, famously saw Renaissance occult philosophy as the origin of modern scientific empiricism, hereby building on Lynn Thorndike's earlier magisterial multivolume *History of Magic and Experimental Science,* published in the first part of the twentieth century.[91] During the 1980s, the so-called Yates thesis came in for sharp criticism by scholars who saw Renaissance occultism not as a catalyst of but as an obstacle to the rise of modern science, which (in their view) was all about openness and the reproducibility of experiment, not about secrecy.[92] However, scholars insisting on a clear-cut boundary between secrecy in Renaissance occult philosophy and openness in modern science fail to give due credit not only to the significant role that secrecy has played also in modern science (state-sponsored atomic science, for example) but also to the dialectic between the esoteric and the exoteric in early modern occult philosophy—the basic assumption that a significant part of reality is hidden from us on the one hand and the quest to "discover" it on the other. More recently, historians have given the Yates thesis a qualified but overall sympathetic reassessment by recognizing that one of the most important contributions of occult philosophy to the history of science during the early modern period lay precisely in its abandonment of the Scholastic attitude toward the occult. Thus, as John Henry has pointed out, occult philosophy initiated the gradual dissolution of the absolute boundary between Scholastic (Aristotelian) "manifest" and "occult" qualities, a dissolution that ultimately led to Bacon's "Tables of Instances," in which "Incidents involving heat (for Scholastics, a manifest quality) and incidents involving magnetism (an exemplary occult quality) were to be dealt with in the same way": as a question of science.[93]

By underwriting empirical inquiry into the occult with theological legitimacy, occult philosophy provided a rich hermeneutic recourse for the apprehension of what Thomas Kuhn called "para-normal" phenomena—i.e., phenomena that could not be explained within the epistemological structure of the "normal" sciences—in this case, Scholastic Aristotelianism.[94] Thus, the sixteenth-century Paracelsian alchemist Gerard Dorn wrote that "God does not want any secret to be so hidden, but that at any time it might be revealed and made manifest by man through magic."[95] Not bound by the limits of reason or authority, the magus of early modern occult philosophy refers the occult qualities directly to the transcendent. "The occult properties of things are not from the nature of the elements," Agrippa wrote in his *Three Books of Occult Philosophy*, "but infused from above, hid from our senses, and scarce at last known by our reason, which indeed come from the life, and the Spirit of the World, through the rays of the stars; and can not otherwise but by experience and conjecture be inquired into by us."[96]

As we will see in the next chapter, this idea of the magus's divine inspiration has its roots in the late medieval confluence of Aristotelian naturalism (especially alchemy) with the rise of a particular kind of lay spirituality that gave rise to the figure of the "Fool for God" and that set in motion ever-new cycles of ecclesiastic reforms. But here we can also see that the "secret" in occult philosophy is different not only from the Scholastic marvel but also from the mere "curiosity"—a category that emerged during the eighteenth century in the context of baroque cameralism.[97] While the penetration of the secret in early modern occult philosophy still required theological legitimation, the curiosity would develop into a largely secular notion that no longer requires divine sanction or arcane authority but is readily available for penetration by a scientific gaze authorized by the state. I will return to this development in the coda of this book, in reference to the famous (re-)discoverer of America Alexander von Humboldt. But the first step away from this theological justification of theoretical curiosity was already taken by sixteenth-century occult philosophers: unlike that of the medieval alchemist, the early modern occult philosophers derived their theological legitimation no longer *directly* from God through divine inspiration but from a secondary (Neoplatonic) source that Agrippa called "the light of naturall instinct" (*luminositas sensus naturae*).[98] Thus, the famous sixteenth-century Swiss alchemist and occult philosopher Paracelsus wrote that "when a man prophecies, he does not speak from the Devil, not from Satan, and not from the Holy Spirit, but he speaks from the innate spirit of the invisible body which teaches the *Magiam* and in which the *Magus* has his origin."[99]

As a result of these cultural and religious intersections in occult philosophy, the medieval tradition of alchemy was radically transformed in theory and practice, as well as in its status as a "science" within the order of Western knowledge. As William Newman writes, "Alchemy moved from a rather marginal position as a discipline concerned mainly with mineralogy, metallurgy, and the products of chemical technology to the center of the European stage, where it became the basis for a comprehensive theory of matter and the justification of a heterodox new medicine, occupying the best minds of the age."[100] This transformation took place in the broader context of European commercial and territorial expansionism, as well as the consolidation of early modern composite absolute monarchies and nation-states.[101] As a result, alchemy moved from the artisan workshop and the convent into the court. During the second part of the sixteenth century, the court of Philip II of Spain became one of the foremost sponsors of alchemy at his monastic retreat outside Madrid, the Escorial, where he employed scores of alchemists in laboratories established specifically in order to facilitate their experimental work.[102] At the same time, the courts of the Holy Roman Emperor Rudolf II at Prague and of King Stefan in Krakow became centers of alchemical experimentation that were were visited and admired by the two English Elizabethan occult philosophers and alchemists Edward Kelly and John Dee in the 1580s. In this context of state patronage, the works of such illustrious alchemists as Paracelsus began to circulate widely and freely throughout the German parts of the Habsburg Empire. With the expansion of print, a veritable flood of alchemical imprints, by both early modern and medieval authors, was inundating Europe by the end of the seventeenth century and became accessible to learned and popular readers, especially in predominantly Protestant areas such in Germany and the British Isles, but also (in a more subdued ways) in predominantly Catholic areas such as Spain and Italy.[103]

By the eighteenth century, alchemy would largely be purged of its religious contents and overtones but become, as chemistry, an integral discipline in the universities of continental Europe, especially in the context of the rise of cameralism, a state-sponsored "systematic science of administration that emerged and was codified," as Michael Dettelbach has explained, "in the curricula of... universities and academies" in the German and other areas of the Habsburg Empire—particularly with regard to the science of mining.[104] A *Staatswissenschaft* (state science), cameralism was a university curriculum that was still broadly humanist in scope but put the natural sciences at center stage and in the service of the state, with the aim of training bureaucrats (secretaries) for service in government administration. The origins of eighteenth-century cameralism, however, lay in the move of alchemy from the convent into the early modern courts. This move had already been anticipated by late medieval popes who employed the seekers for the secrets of nature as personal physicians since the thirteenth century.[105] We will return to some of these seekers in later chapters of this book, including the Valencian physician Arnald of Villanova and the Cypriot Lodovico Podocatharo, the former working for Pope Boniface VIII and the latter for Alexander VI. Nevertheless, while the history of "theoretical curiosity" about the occult did not begin in the early modern period but had an important precedent in medieval alchemy, it was in the social and institutional contexts of the fifteenth, sixteenth, and seventeenth centuries that secrecy came to occupy an important place in scientific inquiry. In the process, the secrets of nature were transformed into the secrets of state, and the alchemical seeker of natural secrets into the modern secretary.

2

Egyptian Gold
Alchemy and Crusade in the Later Middle Ages

> The treasures of the ancient Egyptians ... of silver and gold ... on leaving Egypt the people of Israel, ... surreptitiously claimed for themselves. ... [T]hey did this not on their own authority but at God's command. ... These treasures— ... which they did not create but dug, as it were, from the mines of providence, which is everywhere—which were used wickedly and harmfully in the service of demons must be removed by Christians, as they separate themselves in spirit from the wretched company of pagans, and applied to their true function, that of preaching the gospel.
>
> —St. Augustine, *De doctrina Christiana*

In his now classic 1956 study in comparative ancient mythology, *Forgerons et alchimistes* (*The Forge and the Crucible*), the ethnologist Mircea Eliade once argued that most religions have a deep connection with alchemy. Many ancient cultures shared the belief in the sacredness of metals and in the "ambivalent, eccentric and mysterious character of all mining and metallurgical operations."[1] In some cultures, metallurgical practices were therefore associated with rituals of human sacrifice, purification, and sexual taboos. The inner earth was considered to be sacred to spirits and deities. Still in the later Middle Ages of Christian Europe, religious ceremonies accompanied the opening of new mines. The makers of tools from various metals, smiths were often regarded as magicians, as they appeared to possess secret knowledge that allowed them to make things through art that were not natural. As a result, the art of metalworking developed an intricate language of symbols and code names (*Decknamen*) that further embellished its air of secrecy and cultivated "the idea of an active collaboration of man and nature, perhaps even the belief that man, by his own work, is capable of superseding the processes of nature."[2]

Even before Eliade published his anthropological account of the origins of alchemy, the Swiss psychoanalyst Carl Gustav Jung had argued in the 1930s that alchemy was profoundly spiritual in its roots. In a series of stunningly erudite studies, Jung compared the alchemical motifs and iconography in the Chinese, Indian, and Western traditions and found that they shared much of the same imagery even though they had apparently evolved independently from one another. Also, in the analyses of his patients' dreams, he noticed that they often contained the very imagery that he found in treatises on alchemy. Thus, he concluded that alchemy was not only the ancestor of modern chemistry and metallurgy but also "the forerunner of our modern psychology."[3] Alchemical symbols, Jung maintained, were representations of human archetypes that opened a window into what he called the "collective unconscious." Moreover, according to Jung, alchemy was itself therapeutic. Unlike in the modern chemical experiment, in alchemy there is no clear separation between subject and object: "The *artifex* accompanies his chemical work with a simultaneous mental operation which is performed by means of the imagination."[4] Crucial to this dual process is what Jung called "enigmatic speculation" and "projection": "While the artifex heats the chemical substance in the furnace he himself is morally undergoing the same fiery torment and purification. By projecting himself into the substance he has become unconsciously identical with it and suffers the same process."[5] Jung therefore evaluated the significance of the alchemical quest for transformation less in its perennially unsuccessful attempt of transmuting base metal into gold and more in its spiritual aspiration of psychic self-transformation. Like Eliade, he was hereby interested primarily in the soteriological functions of alchemy, particularly with respect to the Christian Eucharist.[6] Thus, the Christian Son of God was for him a sort of alchemical "paradigm of sublimation." One of the aims of alchemy was the attempt to "produce a *corpus subtile,* a transfigured and resurrected body, i.e. a body that was at the same time spirit."[7] But whereas the late medieval alchemists had used the iconography of the Eucharist to devise a "parallel transmutational rite in which their chemicals were changed in a manner comparable to the transubstantiation of the communion bread," such early modern alchemists as Paracelsus believed that, in the process of the opus, the alchemist was himself transmuted into the essence of Christ.[8]

Finally, Jung showed that much of alchemical iconography revolves around the theme of ambivalence and the transgression of boundaries, especially with regard to the boundaries between the material and the spiritual. For example, alchemical mercury—one of the two basic and most important substances in alchemy (next to sulfur)—is itself ambivalent: it is neither here nor there, eluding the conventional categories of science, morality, sexuality, and law. In respect to (Aristotelian) science, the metal mercury belonged to the element Earth but had the properties of the element Water. For this reason, alchemical Mercury was frequently represented as a hermaphroditic figure.[9] Also, in alchemical iconography, Mercury is often illuminated in yellow, a color that historically signifies ambivalence in Western culture. On the one hand, yellow is the color of light, illumination, enlightenment, and gold; on the other hand, it is also the color of death, decay, and excrement.[10] The color of liminality, yellow has been the preferred color of stigmatization in Western culture (the Yellow Star of David that Jews and the yellow clothes that prostitutes have been forced to wear since the Middle Ages, for example).[11] Other commonly occurring imagery and *Decknamen* transgressing the boundaries between the material and the spiritual in alchemy include those of animals, sometimes of enigmatic nature (the "green lion," the "dragon," the "unicorn"); celestial bodies (the "sun," the "black sun," the "moon"); naturally occurring things and substances (the "egg"); social types and rituals (the "king," the "wedding"); and religious, especially Christological, concepts (the "cross," "crucifixion," the "crucible").[12]

Jung's interpretation has been much criticized by historians of alchemy, who have dismissed his notion of "spiritual alchemy" as a nineteenth-century rebirth of Renaissance Neoplatonic obscurantism that occluded the very real, important, and positive contributions that medieval alchemy made to the history of modern science.[13] However, Jung would have agreed with these historians about the important role that alchemy played in the history of modern science. Thus, he wrote that in alchemy the "daemon of the scientific spirit compelled the forces of nature to serve man to an extent that had never been known before."[14] By privileging the authenticity of one's own experience of nature over the authenticity of tradition, alchemists "opened the way for the scientific investigation of nature and helped to emancipate natural science from the authority of tradition."[15] While Jung was admittedly not primarily interested in the particular historical and cultural contexts that made alchemy meaningful in human societies over the millennia, his alchemical studies remain valuable for my purposes precisely for alerting us to the important role that religion played in the history of science.

While religion is an aspect of the history of alchemy that has often been eschewed by modern historians of science, cultural and literary historians of alchemy have recently reasserted the "central" importance of religion for understanding the way in which alchemists "formed and communicated" their alchemical theories.[16] Following the lead of these scholars, this chapter explores how the language of apocalyptic prophecy merged with the technical and artisanal traditions of alchemy in the late medieval spiritual milieu of Franciscan Church militancy. In this Franciscan spiritual milieu, the curious gaze into the secrets of nature was transformed from a type of Augustinian "vain curiosity" into a "just curiosity," a curiosity legitimated by the aim of rejuvenating Christian bodies in their preparation for the apocalyptic battles of the Eschaton. In the context of apocalyptic church militancy, the Aristotelian trade secret was transformed into a metaphysical secret of nature where a proto-atomistic (i.e., corpuscular) theory of matter was born. Employing the logic of St. Augustine's well-known exegetical notion of the "Egyptian Gold" that the Israelites had received at "God's command . . . as it were, from the mines of providence,"[17] before their Exodus from Egypt, late medieval alchemists argued that in order to defeat the enemies of Christendom—Muslims, Jews, pagans, heretics, and even the Antichrist himself—the Christian church militant must appropriate their occult arts and technologies even if they appeared to violate traditional religious taboos. As Roger French and Andrew Cunningham have put it, to use pagan Greek philosophy was, for the Franciscan friars, "merely to obey God's own instructions. It was to 'spoil' (or despoil) the valuables of non-Christians for the benefit of Christians."[18] Thus, what St. Augustine had called the "sacred gift" of God to the Israelites of old was translated into the late Scholastic Franciscan context by the claim that pagan philosophy was a "maidservant" (as Roger Bacon put it) sent directly from God, who intervened into the normal order of things on behalf of his people in exceptional times of crisis.[19] Whereas St. Augustine's time of crisis (354–430) was the rapid disintegration of the (Christian) Roman Empire, in the late medieval period (ca. 1250–ca. 1450) this exceptional time of crisis—the state of exception—was one of religious conflicts with seemingly apocalyptic significance—the Reconquista of southern Europe; crusade within Europe and in the Holy Land; as well as the conversion of heretics and infidels.

After offering some basic background on the history of late medieval alchemy, this chapter explores the role that the idea of crusade played in the religious legitimation of alchemy. My first example will be drawn from near the end of the late medieval period, Father Ullmann's *Buch der Heiligen Dreifaltigkeit* (Book of the Holy Trinity), written in the early fifteenth century. One of the few medieval alchemical texts written in a European vernacular, it provides an apt illustration of the epistemic violence of alchemical apocalypticism in the analogy that Ullmann elaborates between the alchemical opus and the passion of Christ as well as in the articulation of a militant rationale for alchemy's role in holy war. From there, this chapter and the next will move back to the thirteenth and fourteenth centuries in order to offer a sketch of the historical role that the idea of crusade played in the alchemical amalgamation of Aristotelian naturalism with Christian revelation by focusing on a number of prominent late medieval authors of alchemical texts (both authentic and spurious) who would later play a prominent role in the literature of the conquest of America.

Alchemy, Apocalypse, and Crusade during the Later Middle Ages

Although China and India have long and rich traditions in alchemy, the roots of Western alchemy lie in the early centuries AD in Hellenistic Alexandria, where Aristotelianism flourished and fused with Persian and Egyptian traditions in metallurgy and spiritualism. In the eighth and ninth centuries, it was absorbed by the expanding Arabs, who transformed its practices and theories, adding, for example, the notion of the transmutatory "elixir" (or Philosophers' Stone), an agent that purportedly transformed any metal into gold by balancing its constituent elements. Alchemy entered the Latin West via translations from Arabic texts as a result of the increased contact with Islamic literary culture during a period of Christian reconquest in southern Europe. One of the most important events was hereby the Christian recapture of Toledo in 1086 by Alfonso VI ("The Brave") from the Moors, which subsequently resulted in the translation of scores of Aristotelian texts previously unknown in the West, including many (pseudo-) Aristotelian texts on alchemy. Much of this work was done in the so-called Toledo School of Translators under the patronage of Archbishop Ramon of Toledo (d. 1152) during the twelfth century and, during the thirteenth century, of Alfonso X, "The Wise" (1221–1284). The school drew many renowned scholars from all over Europe who produced an extensive Latin corpus of Arabic-Aristotelian natural philosophy, including the famous *Picatrix,* a Spanish and Latin translation of the eleventh-century Arabic text *Gayat-al-hakim* that became a source and inspiration for Latin Christian astrologers and alchemists, such as the Dominican Albertus Magnus and the Franciscan Roger Bacon.[20]

In medieval Christian Europe, alchemy was practiced primarily as a technical art that drew on the general principles of Aristotelian natural philosophy. Epistemologically, it was considered to be part of "meteorology," which is to say that it was concerned with things below the sphere of the moon; and within meteorology it concerned itself specifically with subterranean matter. A technical art, alchemy was regarded not as an academic branch of its own within natural philosophy but as a sort of applied science that explored the practical uses of fire in a number of artisanal fields. Although the attempt to find an artificial way to effect the transmutation of base metals into gold (chrysopoeia) was always a central goal of alchemy, its practitioners were engaged in a broad range of experimental activities, including metallurgical essaying, the refining of salts, the manufacture of dye, pigment, glass, and ceramics, artificial gemstones, incendiary weapons, as well as the brewing and distilling of drugs.[21]

In the course of their experimental activities, medieval alchemists elaborated a theory of matter that was based on Aristotelian physics but distinct from that in the "mainstream" (i.e., Thomist) Scholastic commentary tradition on Aristotle with regard to the understanding of matter and its relationship to form. At the root of Aristotelian physics are the two concepts of "first matter" (*prima materia*) and "substantial form," as well as the notion that every "substance" is a mixture of the four elements (Earth, Water, Air, Fire) and their distinct mixture of qualities (Hot, Cold, Wet, Dry), which are present in every substance to various "degrees" (First, Second, Third, and so on). First matter is the original and formless material of the universe in the state of primeval chaos; it is purely material, entirely passive, and shaped into a particular "substance" only as a result of being acted upon by the immaterial and preexisting "substantial forms" that underlie the species that we encounter in phenomenological reality. In the Thomist commentary tradition on Aristotle (mainly on the *Physics*), this interaction between passive matter and active form was understood in highly metaphysical terms. Thus, Thomas Aquinas had argued that a given substance can only receive its membership in a particular species from one single substantial form. This "teleological" relationship between form and matter in a given substance is known as hylomorphism, the principle that each substance is the product of passive matter being moved toward exactly one predetermined substantial form. Moreover, the Thomists believed that every substance is a mixture of the four elements that is entirely homogeneous, continuous, and infinitely divisible. This means that, when two substances formed a new mixture, the substantial form of each of the old mixtures was destroyed and a new substantial form was generated from the mixture.[22]

By contrast, the alchemists held that each substance can have not one but multiple substantial forms. William Newman has therefore called the alchemical understanding of the relationship between matter and form "pluralist," as opposed to the "unitist" understanding of that relationship by the Thomists.[23] Also, according to alchemical theory, matter is composed of individual corpuscular particles and pores that can interact with one another in mixtures that are neither homogeneous nor predetermined. As Newman explains, while this alchemical theory is "proto-atomistic" in certain ways, its tradition is different from that of the pre-Socratic atomists (Democritus and Leucippus), whose theory of the atom and the void was entirely philosophical (i.e., speculative) and reentered Europe during the Renaissance with the rediscovery of Lucretius's atomist poem *De rerum natura*.[24] While pre-Socratic atomism and medieval alchemical corpuscular theory coalesced in the seventeenth century in Baconian science, especially in the mechanical philosophy of Robert Boyle and Isaac Newton, medieval alchemical matter theory had not depended on pre-Socratic ideas but was rather conceived in reconciling Aristotelian physics with the observations of the processes taking place in the crucible. As a result, such medieval Christian alchemists as the thirteenth-century Franciscan Paul of Taranto (aka Pseudo-Geber) elaborated, in his influential tract *Summa perfectionis,* the theory of *minimae partes* or *minima naturalia* in adaptation from the writings of the eighth-century Persian alchemist Jābir ibn Hayyān (known in the Latin West as "Geber") and Averroës, the twelfth-century Islamic Aristotelian philosopher from Andalusia. Ultimately derived from the (probably spurious) book 4 of Aristotle's *Meteorology,* the theory of *minima naturalia* held that matter is composed of "smallest natural parts" that cannot be further divided without losing their essential form. The void was, in this tradition, not imagined as a vacuum of matter (as it was by the pre-Socratic atomists) but as "pores" in metallic substances that individual corpuscles of mercury could penetrate, hereby effecting metallic transmutation, in which the *minima naturalia* were not destroyed but retained their original identities and qualities.[25] As we shall see in later chapters, this alchemical conception of matter as composed of particles and pores had a profound influence on early modern narratives of the geographic discovery of America as a "New World" as well as on the missionaries' idea of religious conversion.

At the root of the alchemists' nonhylomorphic understanding of matter was their belief, tested in the laboratory, that art could not only equal but even surpass the products of nature. This belief was, again, fundamentally at odds with that of the Thomists, who, following the eleventh-century Persian Aristotelian philosopher Avicenna, argued that art could never equal nature's products and that humans did not have the capacity of transmuting the species of things through alchemy. When Avicenna's attack on alchemy was translated into Latin, it was erroneously attributed to Aristotle himself. Given Aristotle's formidable authority in the Middle Ages, this confusion led to a general skepticism about, and even animosity toward, the alchemists' belief in the possibility of transmutation by many of the Scholastics, especially the Thomists.[26] In 1317, Pope John XXII—the same pope who would later rule against Franciscan poverty—outlawed alchemy, in his decretal *Spondent quas non exhibent.*[27] Although the alchemists launched a counteroffensive against Avicenna's and the Thomists' attacks, the philosophical debate about the efficacy of alchemy henceforth assumed distinctly theological implications about the borderline between religious orthodoxy and heterodoxy.

Considering the prominent role that the Thomists traditionally played in the Inquisition, it is perhaps no surprise that alchemy largely thrived in the shadows of spurious textual traditions and pseudonymous authorship in the Latin West. This peculiarity of alchemical literature, however, had originated already in the Arabic tradition. For example, the *Tabula smaragdina* (Emerald table) was probably authored by an eighth-century Arab named Balinus but was attributed to "Hermes Trismegistus," the Alexandrine hybrid god fusing the Greek and Egyptian gods of writing, Hermes and Thoth respectively, and who came to be seen by medieval and early modern Christians as an ancient sage who had prophesied the Incarnation (as discussed in chapter 1). This tradition of pseudonymous attribution was later continued in the Latin West. This sort of "creative duplicity" in attributing alchemical tracts to authors of great authority or antiquity was virtually a constant feature of the alchemical tradition and facilitated its fusion with religious mysticism.[28]

Perhaps also as a partial result of the precarious theological and epistemological position that alchemy occupied in the scientific culture of the Middle Ages, the alchemists enveloped their theories of matter in prophetic spiritualism. This tradition, again, had originated already in many of the Arabic texts that were being translated into Latin from the twelfth century onward. Some of this religious mysticism was of Islamic origin (especially Ismailism); some of it of Hellenistic origin (especially Hermeticism); and some of it a mixture of the two.[29] Likewise, the thirteenth- and fourteenth-century Christian writers on alchemy fused its Aristotelian naturalism with the language of Christian passion, eschatology, and especially millenarian prophecy. As a result, millenarian prophecy was itself significantly transformed during the later Middle Ages. Thus, whereas Scriptural prophecy (especially the Revelations of John of Patmos and the book of Daniel) as well as high medieval millenarian prophecy (especially Joachimism) had categorically renounced worldly materialism in Christians as well as temporal ambitions for wealth and power, the alchemist prophets from the thirteenth century onward were keenly interested in the role that temporal means might play not only in the internal reformation of the church but also in its external struggles again the enemies of the faith.[30]

One of the consequences of this medieval intermingling between alchemy and Christian prophecy was that the apocalyptic tradition became attached to the Christian idea of crusade. Historians of Western apocalypticism have observed that, though the early crusades of the eleventh and twelfth centuries were significant for the unprecedented self-confidence that they manifested in Christian Europe's confrontation with an advancing Islam, they "did not comprise the expression of an apocalyptic impulse."[31] Conversely, the most important apocalyptic thinker of the High Middle Ages, Joachim of Fiore (ca. 1135–1202), had dismissed the idea that the crusades had any role to play in the coming of the Eschaton. Even though he was allegedly visited and consulted by Richard I ("the Lionheart") before the latter's departure for the Holy Land, the Calabrian abbot was "far from encouraging" about the Third Crusade.[32] By contrast, in the context of the thirteenth-century Scholastic nexus of alchemy, crusade, and Joachimite apocalyptic prophecy, there emerged a Christian messianism that was increasingly directed against non-Christians, especially Jews and Muslims. For Joachim himself, the Antichrist had been a false Christian rather than a renegade Jew. In fact, as Bernard McGinn has noted, Joachim's esoteric numerological apocalyptic chronology was most likely itself influenced by Jewish kabbala. "I think the time of forgiving them [the Jews] ... [and] of consolation and their conversion is here," Joachim had declared.[33] This relatively tolerant attitude toward other religions changed radically with the Scholastics, Thomas Aquinas being perhaps the most preeminent representative of a newly virulent anti-Semitism. As Arthur Williamson writes, "'Forgiving' the Jews was supplanted by expelling the Jews."[34] As we will see in more detail in chapter 4, the intellectual context in which Christopher Columbus would later bring his quests for the gold of India into connection with the expulsion of the Jews from Spain, as well as with the Christian reconquests of Granada and of Jerusalem from the Muslims, emerged from this thirteenth-century amalgamation of Scholastic naturalism, crusade, and Joachimite prophecy.

The mendicant orders played a crucial role in the formation of this late medieval nexus of pseudo-Aristotelian alchemy, apocalyptic prophecy, and crusade, despite the occasional attempts by bishops and popes to suppress and even outlaw the widespread practice of alchemy among their ranks.[35] Among the earliest and most famous alchemists of the thirteenth century was the Dominican bishop of Cologne Albertus Magnus (1193–1280). His immense knowledge about the secrets of nature had allegedly empowered him to make his garden bloom in the middle of winter; and he was even rumoured to have constructed an artificial man—a homunculus, who was then destroyed by one of Albertus's most brilliant students, Thomas Aquinas.[36] Although Thomas's wariness of his teacher's "promethean ambitions" set the stage for the general rejection of the Hermetic art in Dominican circles going forward, Albertus's homunculus would have an afterlife in sixteenth-century speculations about the ontology of Native Americans, especially among some Neoplatonists, such as Paracelsus, who were inclined to argue that America was a "new world" and its inhabitants not descendants of Adam (as we will see in chapter 8).[37]

But during the later Middle Ages, it was the Franciscans and their sympathizers who were the most fervent promoters of alchemy. As Lynn Thorndike once sardonically remarked, it is one of the "little ironies of history" that "the followers of St. Francis, the apostle of poverty, should have interested themselves in making gold."[38] This predilection for alchemy apparently began in the earliest days of the greyfriars, when Brother Elias, one of the companions of Francis, was deposed from the generalship of the order in 1239, partially for having dabbled in alchemy.[39] Nevertheless, alchemy continued to flourish among the Franciscan friars, especially in the spiritual and intellectual milieu of crusade and millenarian prophecy. Thus, many of the most renowned medieval alchemists of the thirteenth and fourteenth centuries, such as Roger Bacon, Sebastiano da Verona, Paul of Taranto, Bonaventura of Iseo, Arnald of Villanova, John of Rupescissa, and Ramón Llull, were either friars in the Franciscan Order or closely associated with it.[40] While artisanal alchemists had long maintained a tradition of secrecy in order to protect their trade secrets, in this Franciscan spiritual milieu the discovery of the secrets of alchemy became a messianic quest in an apocalyptic battle unfolding between Christianity and its enemies, including Muslims, Jews, degenerate Christians, and even the Antichrist himself.

One important example of this Franciscan tradition of spiritualized alchemy dates from the second decade of the fifteenth century, the *Buch der Heiligen Dreifaltigkeit* (Book of the Holy Trinity). It was written by a German Franciscan by the name of Father Ullmanus (Ullmann), who elaborated on the Passion, death, and Resurrection of Christ in the terminology and iconography of the alchemical regimen of the purification of metals. In characteristically Franciscan fashion, Ullmann's text attempts a "reduction" of Aristotelian naturalism to Christian doctrine through Augustinian Neoplatonic mysticism and his order's hardy (and often militant) devotion to Mary's divinity. Thus, Ullmann posits a correspondence between the seven sublunary metals, the seven planets, as well as the seven virtues and passions (or wounds) of Christ (gold/sun/purity/hands; silver/moon/charity/feet; quicksilver/mercury/holiness/head, and so on). The ultimate product of the alchemical opus, the Philosophers' Stone, unites all of these elemental qualities and Christian virtues. It has the power to convert base metals into gold; and those who consume it will be healed of all diseases and become invincible in battle. Ullmann offers detailed instructions for the use of alchemical substances, such as mercury, sulfur, vitriol, arsenic, ammoniac, mummy, and Virgin's Milk (*lac virginis*). However, in order to be successful, each alchemical operation must be performed at its appropriate, astrologically determined time.[41]

All of the book's technical information is pressed into the service of Christian salvific messianism. As Ullmann explains, his primary intention is spreading the Holy Faith through Christian teaching. Throughout, Ullmann's text and images emphasize the extraordinary violence that characterizes both the alchemical process in the crucible and the Passion of Christ on the cross. Just as the base metals have to be tortured and "mortified" (*mortifiziert*) by fire in the alchemical crucible before they can be transmuted into gold, so Christ had to suffer his passion and death before attaining his full divinity.⁴² In the process of elaborating this analogy between the metallic passions in the crucible and the bodily passions of Christ, the latter is subjected to modes of execution—such as hanging and decapitation—as well as forms of torture—such as breaking on the wheel and rack and burning by fire—that are never mentioned in the New Testament (see figs. 5 and 6, also 8 below). But all these non-Scriptural forms of torture and death in the *Buch* underline the allegorical character of Christ's Passion, known in alchemical literature as *amplificatio:*⁴³ they stand for the alchemical operation of the "calcination" or "reduction" of the old body of the metal to a powder from which the matter of the Philosophers' Stone will be distilled. Known as the "nigredo," it is the initial, black state of the alchemical opus in which the body of the impure metal is being "killed," putrefied, and dissolved into the *prima materia*, the original substance of Creation, so that it may be reborn in a new form.⁴⁴ Those who are converted through sympathetic participation in the redemptive alchemical opus will be able, as God's elect, to understand the book's mystical and allegorical language and, by following its alchemical instructions, succeed in producing gold and silver. But those who are not converted will be destroyed and will fall prey to the Antichrist, who, as God's incarnated nemesis, is the "root" (*wurczel*) of the seven deadly sins (*die siben totliche sunde*). Thus, toward the end of the book, the Manichean dualisms (good/evil, the faithful/heretics, the chaste/unchaste) culminate with the author calling for a Holy War against all those who resist the faith and remain unbelievers, especially Saracens (Muslims), Jews, heretics, and heathens.⁴⁵

The oldest alchemical tract in the German vernacular, the *Buch der Heiligen Dreifaltigkeit* survives in at least sixteen complete manuscripts and various fragments. The most important manuscript in the text's transmission history, now lost but attested to in various copies from the 1470s, was completed in 1433 at the Cadolzburg, a Hohenzollern castle outside Nuremberg, whose front gate prominently features a *Judensau* (Jewish sow), an anti-Semitic image common throughout late medieval Europe, of Jews in obscene contact with a large female pig, an unclean animal in Judaism. This anti-Semitic image provides an apt illustration of the militant milieu of Christian messianism in which the pagan art of alchemy was appropriated by Franciscans such as Ullmann.⁴⁶

Though one of the few alchemical treatises penned in a European vernacular by the early fifteenth century and not published in print until the twentieth century, Ullmann's text formed part of a long tradition of Franciscan alchemical literature going back to the thirteenth century, most of it written in Latin, that pressed the appropriation of alchemy into the service of Christian holy

86   The Alchemy of Exception

Figure 5. Christ being hanged. (In Father Ullmann, *Buch der Heiligen Dreifaltigkeit.* Image Hs 80061 © Germanisches Nationalmuseum, Nuremberg.)

war. This late medieval Christian tradition of alchemy promised not only the transmutation of base metals into the gold that would pay for the crusades against the enemies of the faith but also the alchemical production of the "quintessence" that would strengthen the bodies of the Christian warriors. As we will see in the remaining sections of this chapter, in this context of crusade and (re-)conquest, alchemy—originally the art of purifying metals—also became an important component in late medieval medicine, especially in the context of Franciscan natural theology.

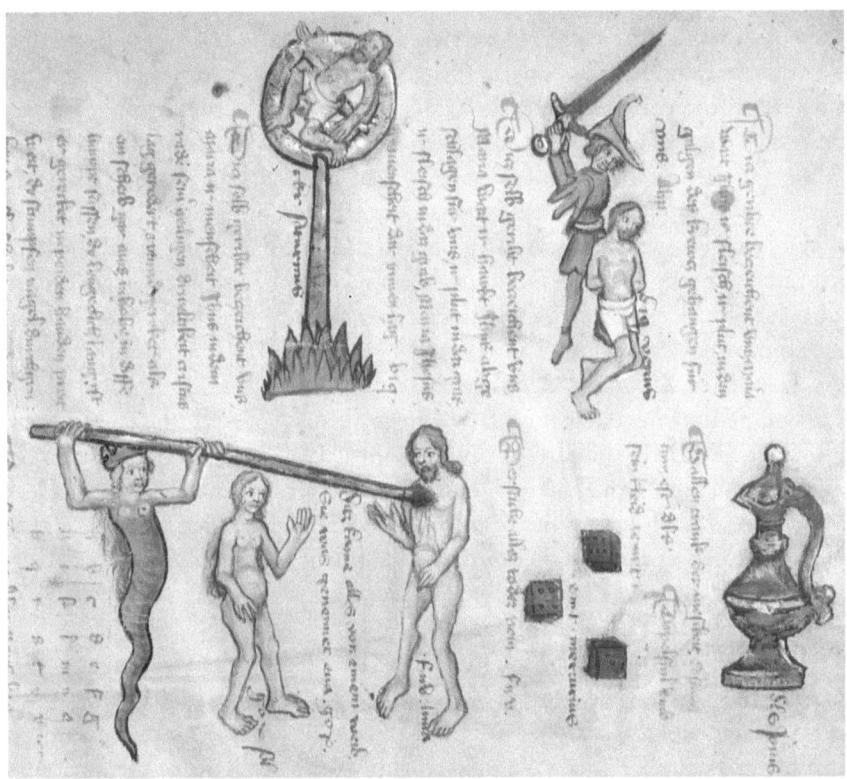

Figure 6. Christ being killed. (In Father Ullmann, *Buch der Heiligen Dreifaltigkeit*. Image Hs 80061 © Germanisches Nationalmuseum, Nuremberg.)

Doctor Mirabilis: Roger Bacon and the Tempered Christian Body

Perhaps the most famous among the early Franciscan men of learning was Roger Bacon (ca. 1220–ca. 1292), known in the popular literature of the Middle Ages and the early modern period as the "Doctor Mirabilis" for his reputation as a great magician, alchemist, wonder-worker, and even necromancer. Although Bacon was born into a prosperous English family, little is known about his youth or early education until he matriculated at Oxford University and later at the University of Paris. In the 1240s, he became the first professor at Paris to lecture on the scientific works of Aristotle, which had been banned from the curriculum several times during the early decades of the thirteenth century. In the 1250s, Bacon joined the Franciscan Order and came to the attention of Pope Clement IV for allegedly having written a great work of learning synthesizing the newly available Aristotelian corpus. Upon the pope's request to see the work (which was not finished and perhaps not even yet written), Bacon sent a hastily composed introduction and feverishly worked on the completion of the larger work, which subsequently came to be known as the *Opus maius* and which was then supplemented by the *Opus minus* and the *Opus tertium*. Bacon conceived of these three works as his great *summa* of all the sciences. In the *Opus maius,* Bacon provided a classification of the Scholastic sciences and their methods, including languages, mathematics, astronomy, optics, and moral philosophy. Also, he included a section on what he called "experimental sciences" (*scientia experimentalis*),[47] under the rubric of which he included alchemy. Due to his special attention to experimental science, Bacon has often been regarded as a medieval forerunner of his early modern namesake Francis Bacon in the history of scientific empiricism. However, already in the early twentieth century, Lynn Thorndike called into question the notion of Roger Bacon as "the first rebel against medieval scholasticism and the first prophet of modern science."[48] More recent historiography has largely confirmed Thorndike's assessment of Bacon as an essentially Scholastic thinker while also calling attention to some of the highly original and eccentric aspects of his thought.[49]

Although we know that Bacon conducted experiments with regard to a number of sciences such as optics, it is not clear whether he himself ever practiced alchemy, as the authorship of the greater part of the more than thirty medico-alchemical works attributed to him is spurious. One of the most important works among these, the *De retardatione accidentium senectutis* (*On Delaying the Misfortunes of Old Age*), was attributed to Arnald of Villanova and Ramón Llull during the later Middle Ages but since the fifteenth century also to Bacon, being published under his name in English translation in 1683 by Richard Browne.[50] Another text, the *Epistola de secretis operibus artis et naturae,* was also long considered to be spurious until William Newman's recent suggestion that it was either an authentic work of Bacon or written by somebody who was very familiar with his authentic scientific works, in light of its consistency with Bacon's treatments of alchemy in other works of undisputable authenticity, mainly in the *Opus tertium*. As Newman points out, if the *Epistola* is indeed an authentic work by Bacon, scholars will need to revise their long-standing idea of Bacon as a mere "armchair alchemist."[51]

I will return to some of Bacon's alchemical works more specifically in a moment, but his scientific works are generally important for my purposes because of their elaboration of a sustained theological defense of "experimental science" by synthesizing artisanal empiricism and (pseudo-)Aristotelian philosophy with a Christian hermeneutics of revelation. Thus, in the *Opus maius,* Bacon wrote: "There are two modes of acquiring knowledge, namely, by reasoning and experience. Reasoning draws a conclusion and makes us grant the conclusion, but does not make the conclusion certain, nor does it remove doubt so that the mind may rest on the intuition of truth, unless the mind discovers it by the path of experience.... He therefore who wishes to rejoice without doubt in regard to the truth underlying phenomena must know how to devote himself to experiment."[52] Compared to speculative science, experimental science is "the most useful" because "reasoning does not arrive at this truth" known from Scriptural revelation, but "experiment does." For this reason, experimental science is useful "not only to philosophy" but also (and more importantly) "to the knowledge of God, and for the direction of the whole world."[53] Excepting only moral philosophy, experimental science is the branch of knowledge that is most compatible with Christian theology, for it discovers the "spiritual meaning" that is hidden in both the book of Scripture and that of nature.[54]

Significantly, Bacon's notion of experimental science as elaborated in the *Opus maius* was based on the authority not of any of Aristotle's genuine works but of the pseudo-Aristotelian *Secretum secretorum* (Secret of secrets), a mid-twelfth-century Latin translation of a tenth-century Arabic treatise on a wide range of topics, including magic, alchemy, medicine, statecraft, and ethics.[55] Greatly impressed by the book after having studied it in 1247, Bacon went on to produce his own translation and edition, complete with an introduction and annotations. Whereas his early lectures seemed to suggest a rather conventional understanding of Aristotelian natural philosophy and even skepticism about the possibility of alchemical transmutation, he now became a firm believer in alchemy's efficacy and universal applicability.[56] Thus, in the *Opus tertium* Bacon explains that speculative alchemy (*alkimia speculativa*) treats of the Aristotelian ideas of the generation of things from the elements and animate bodies from the humors. "Practical alchemy" (*alkimia operativa et practica*), by contrast, teaches the manufacture of precious metals, medicines, and pigments. While Bacon's practical alchemist is essentially an artisan whose craft is learned from trade secrets passed down by technical literature and guild traditions, the Baconian experimental scientist is an alchemist of a higher order, an adept of the *Secret of Secrets* whose knowledge is gained not from tradition but from experiment aided by theoretical understanding and divine inspiration.[57]

As an "experimental science" (rather than a mere *techne*), alchemy can surpass even nature in the perfection of its creations. In the *Opus maius,* for example, Bacon offers the proposition that while high-carat gold occurs naturally and has always been produced artificially by conventional artisanal alchemists, the alchemist who practices the art as an "experimental science" will be able to make gold purer than has ever been known before. "There have always been a few who during their life have known this secret of alchemy," he writes, "and this science does not go beyond that. But experimental science by means of Aristotle's *Secret of Secrets* knows how to produce gold not only of twenty-four degrees but of thirty and forty degrees and of as many degrees as we desire."[58] Thus, in the course of Bacon's elaborations of "experimental science," the idea of the alchemical secret is transformed from its Aristotelian sense as an artisanal trade secret passed on by technical literature and oral traditions into a philosophical and metaphysical category as a secret of nature. What distinguishes the artisanal alchemist from the experimental alchemist is that the former's knowledge is derived from a *tradition* of human secret knowledge that has been subject to degeneration and corruption over the course of the centuries; by contrast, the knowledge of the experimental alchemist is derived from the mouth of "Aristotle" himself, who opens the original and ancient *Secret of Secrets* that derives not from men but from God and that is now accessible at last to Christians through Bacon's new Latin translation.

The Christian reader may wonder how Aristotle—a pagan—was privy to these divine truths revealed in the *Secret of Secrets*. Bacon's answer is that "Aristotle" may well have learned these divine secrets from an authority even greater and more ancient than himself—Hermes Trismegistus, the contemporary of Moses and pagan prophet of Christ. If that was the case, Bacon reasons, it would explain why "Aristotle" knew all about Adam and the Judeo-Christian Creation, a knowledge that he then passed on to the Arabs:

> Aristotle names Adam and Enoch, and therefore knew of the first man and the beginning of the world. Albumazar [the famous Muslim astrologer], moreover, in his book on Conjunctions, doing an excellent service for moral philosophy, assumes a first man, namely, Adam, and shows how long was the period from him to the deluge, and how long from the deluge to Christ, and how long from Christ to Mahomet, and how long from him to the foul law. Avicenna also explicitly assumes the creation.... Trismegistus also in his book on Deity says to Asclepius, "In the Creator are all things before he had created them," so that he is in agreement with John the Evangelist who says, "In himself was the life of which was made." Yet this Trismegistus lived near the time of Moses and Joshua, as Augustine states in his book on the City of God.[59]

Just as Hermes Trismegistus taught Aristotle the divine secrets of alchemy, and Aristotle passed them on to the Muslims, so can Aristotle's *Secret of Secrets* reveal the ancient secrets to the Christians. In effect, Bacon turned Aristotelianism into a branch of Hermeticism.

According to Bacon, the revelation of these ancient secrets to the Latin West comes at a critical and providentially appointed moment, as the church is about to engage in the apocalyptic battles that are foretold to inaugurate the End Times. Their technological application will afford the Christian church militant with the sorely needed youthful health and vigor as he marches against the enemies of the faith, especially the Muslims, whose long tradition in the secret art has put them at a strategic advantage. What's more, alchemy will provide the weapons in the church's apocalyptic struggle even against the Antichrist himself, who is, as the incarnation of Satan (a fallen angel), far superior to man in his knowledge of the secrets of nature and sure to use this cunning knowledge during his final struggles:[60] "And now the wonderful advantage derived from these three sciences in this world on behalf of the Church of God against the enemies of the faith is manifest, who should be destroyed rather by the discoveries of science than by the warlike arms of combatants. Antichrist will use these means freely and effectively, in order that he may crush and confound the power of this world."[61] Happily, "Aristotle's" *Secretum secretorum* teaches, through the example of Alexander the Great, how experimental science can be co-opted by the defenders of the faith and turned on the Antichrist and his minions. Thus, Alexander was able to defeat the numerically superior Persian forces of King Darius because he had on his side the great man of science Aristotle:

> Alexander conquered the world under the guidance of Aristotle and Callisthenes, who were his teachers in all knowledge. But Aristotle was his chief teacher; and it is easily apparent from what has been said how by the paths of knowledge Aristotle was able to hand over the world to Alexander. Moreover, the Church should consider the employment of these inventions against unbelievers and rebels, in order that it may spare Christian blood, and especially should it do so because of future perils in the times of Antichrist, which with the grace of God it would be easy to meet, if prelates and princes promoted study and investigated the secrets of nature and of art.[62]

Thus, the experimental science of alchemy is not only acceptable but also necessary for Bacon—not because it will enable the individual alchemist to enrich himself through the production of artificial gold but because it will be of great "advantage for the state."[63] For, what distinguishes the "experimental science" of alchemy from the conventional (artisanal) alchemy is that it not only turns the trade secrets of the art into metaphysical secrets of nature but also into the secrets of state. Thus, the "greatest nobility" of alchemy as an experimental science (as opposed to an artisanal practice) lies in its promise not of producing alchemical gold but of prolonging life.

> For this reason, Aristotle said to Alexander, "I wish to disclose the greatest secret," and it really is the greatest secret, for not only would it procure an advantage for the state and for everyone his desire because of the sufficiency of gold, but what is infinitely more, it would prolong life. For that medicine which would remove all the impurities and corruptions of a baser metal, so that it should become silver and purest gold, is thought by scientists to be able to remove the corruptions of the human body to such an extent that it would prolong life for many ages. This is the tempered body of elements.[64]

Whereas for other famous thirteenth-century alchemists such as Pseudo-Geber, alchemy was primarily an art of "curing" metals, the originality of the Baconian project lies in the expansion of the applicability of alchemy beyond its original purpose as an art of transmuting metals (chrysopoeia) into the field of medicine (spagyrics) for the production of the "tempered body of the elements"—a field that would have a long history extending into Renaissance Paracelsianism, New World utopianism, and the seventeenth-century Scientific Revolution.[65]

Bacon's idea that the experimental science of alchemy will be useful in medicine is rooted in his conviction that the lives of contemporary men are significantly shorter than were those of the biblical patriarchs, who, he believed, lived for a thousand years and even longer. This diminution of life spans was the result, he explained, of a general degeneration in the regimens not only of knowledge but also of health and morals since the times of the patriarchs: "The proper regimen of health, as far as a man can possess it, would prolong life beyond its common accidental limit, which man because of his folly does not protect for his own interest; and thus some have lived for many years beyond the common limit of life." Moreover, human life can be prolonged not only beyond its "accidental limit" by restoring a natural regimen of good health but also "much further" by use of a "special regimen" through alchemically produced medicines, which will reverse the cumulative effects of the many centuries of degeneration in health and allow men to enjoy the full natural life span set originally set by God.[66] Of special efficacy among these remedies is alchemically prepared potable and edible gold, the incorruptible substance of a perfect balance of elements and their qualities.[67]

Once again, the Muslims appear to have had the edge on the Christians in the art of the prolongation of life—which explained the historical fact that their heretical religion was able to make such enormous advances in recent centuries into Christian territories. Thus, Bacon cites the "Tegni" written by "Hali," who had asserted that "Those who have lived a long time have used medicines by which their life has been prolonged."[68] This "Tegni" was a (Latin) translation by Gerard of Cremona of an (Arabic) commentary on Galen's (originally Greek) *The Little Art of Medicine* (*Techne iatrike, Microtegni,* Lat. *Ars medica* and *Ars parva*) by the Egyptian physician Abu'l Hassan Ali ibn Ridwan Al-Misri (ca. 988–ca. 1061). While the classical medical authorities available in the Latin West such as Galen are silent on what those medicines are or how they are produced, "learned men devoted to experimental science" (such as "Aristotle" and "Hali") have observed the behavior and lives of animals that live a long life, such as "the stag, the eagle, and snake, and many other animals that prolong their life by natural action."[69] Bacon agrees with these men of experimental science that "God himself granted this power to brutes for the instruction of mortal mean": "Therefore they lay in wait for animals, in order that they might learn the powers of herbs, stones, metals, and other things, with which they improved their bodies in many apparently miraculous ways, just as we gather with utmost certainty from the books of Pliny, Solinus, Avicenna on Animals, Tullius on the Divine Nature, from the philosophy of Artephius, and from other books and various authors, and many people have had experience in this matter."[70] While Adam and the patriarchs still knew all these secret remedies of nature, much of this knowledge has been lost to contemporary Christians. However, the adept, especially the "saints and prophets" to whom these secrets are revealed by the spirit of divine wisdom, can still retrieve this knowledge through scientific experiment and thus "command[] the alchemist" to produce the medicine:[71]

> The experimenter, however, extends consideration to greater things and commands the alchemist that he prepare for him a body of equal complexion, in which all elements would be equal with respect to their virtues, and fire does not rule over him, as in choler and cholerics, nor air, as in sanguinity and sanguines, nor water, as in phlegm and phlegmatics, nor earth as in melancholy and melancholics, but this body is made up of equal humors: since it is possible for nature and art perfecting nature, because of the moderating grace of God. And this body cannot be corrupted in any way.[72]

Here Bacon explains that the panacea that "Hali" and other Arabs knew about from "Aristotle" is a miraculous "body of equal complexion" (*corpus equalis complexionis*) that the alchemist will produce with the instructions of the experimental scientist, a body that will cure disease and prolong lives.

But what is this "body of equal complexion"? At first sight, it would appear from Bacon's language in this passage that his understanding of human physiology was based on the conventional Galenic notion of health as a balance of the four humors or "complexions" (blood, phlegm, as well as black and yellow bile) and of disease as an imbalance of those humors and their mixture of the four qualities, which they, in turn, derived from their mixture of the four Aristotelian elements. Upon a closer look, however, it is clear that there is an important difference between Galenic and Baconian medicine: whereas Galenic medicine attempted to achieve bodily temperance by curing humoral imbalances through the introduction of qualitative opposites (i.e., heat cures diseases resulting from excessive cold), the remedies proposed by Bacon are based on the principle of achieving temperance through elemental sympathetic influence—the influence of a "body of equal complexion" that carries within it the principle of incorruptibility. This "equal complexion" does not mean that the body must have an equal amount of the four elements, but that it must have a balance according to the elements' "virtue and active power," considering that, say, fire is more active than earth.[73]

How does one know what this perfect balance is? And how does one obtain a body that has its characteristics? Unfortunately, as to the alchemical methods of producing this elixir or quintessence, Bacon remains rather vague. While in the *Opus minus,* he does discuss a general regimen for the production of the elixir, citing (pseudo-)Aristotle and (pseudo-)Avicenna, these prescriptions remain rather commonplace and overall so vague that efforts to correlate them with actual chemical processes are useless.[74] Bacon's theory of an alchemical medicine, proceeding as it did from the Galenic notion of the "complexions," does not offer a detailed explanation of matter and the exact causes and mechanics of its elemental, qualitative, or complexional transmutation. His alchemical theory still largely resorts to the mystical language of marvels and miracles, in which nature's occult powers, manifest in one body, can be transferred to other bodies, without offering a theory of the underlying causes of its marvelous effects.

Nevertheless, despite the lack of specifics, Bacon's alchemical theory is highly original in its conception of a universal panacea that can be used in medicine on human bodies. Thus, Bacon allows of three ways in which a body of equal complexion can be obtained. The first option—which is the simplest way (but also taxes patience)—is to wait until the Resurrection, when the universal conflagration will purify all bodies from their corruptions. The second option lies in the alchemical preparation of potable medicines from gold, which already contains within it the perfect complexional balance of incorruptibility. And third, this perfectly balanced substance contained in gold can also be distilled from other bodies with the help of alchemy. For example, a body of perfect complexional balance prolonging life can be distilled from substances taken from particularly long-lived animals, such as snakes. But the most suitable substance from which this perfect complexional balance can be alchemically distilled (other than gold) is blood; for it is the sanguine complexion that is most prevalent in youthful bodies. This notion of blood as a substance from which the body of equal balance is best distilled is based on the *Secret of Secrets,* which calls this substance the "Philosophers' Egg," and from Pseudo-Avicenna's *De anima,* which discusses how this "egg" is produced from blood.[75]

In later chapters, I will return to the importance of blood in alchemical theory, especially in so-called corpse medicine (or alchemical cannibalism). But here it must suffice to point out that, with regard to the origins of this miraculous principle of incorruptibility in gold, the Philosophers' Egg, and other bodies of equal complexion that may be distilled from blood, long-lived animals, and other bodies, Bacon has an original (though still mystical) explanation. In conventional Aristotelian physics, the substance with a perfect elemental balance was known as the "quintessence," or fifth essence—that is, an essence that contains a perfect mixture of the four Aristotelian elemental essences that constitute all matter in the sublunary realm. But in Aristotelian physics, the quintessence was thought to be confined to the celestial realm—a conclusion based on the observation that the stars (unlike sublunary matter) were never-changing and always regular in their motions (excepting only monstrous apparitions, such as comets). By contrast, Bacon explains in his *Opus tertium* that this celestial "elixir" (or quintessence) can also be harnessed on earth by being channeled into sublunary matter by astrological influence through the art of optics (or "perspective")—like a magnifying glass that channels the rays of the sun or a mirror that deflects their direction:

> When the excellent experimentor has prepared this body of equal complexion, he commands the astronomer to consider the rising of the beneficent stars above the horizon at a future time and the setting of the maleficent stars that that time, and he commands to the perspectivist that instruments be made with the aid of geometry that congregate the rays in which the equal body is put, so that, after it has received the wonderworking powers of the stars, it may wonderfully remove the defect of a [bad] regimen of life contracted from youth, and restore all that was lost, and retard the effects of old-age, and when they do come, mitigate them happily, so that life be prolonged marvelously.[76]

Just as the experimental scientist has "commanded" the artisanal alchemist to distill substances from various bodies, so he now "commands" the astronomer (or astrologer) to produce the relevant information about astral constellations and the perspective to build instruments that will channel the wonder-working rays of the stars into the sublunary substance.

In sum, although Lynn Thorndike may have had a point in maintaining that Bacon's contribution to the history of experimental science remained largely confined to the "recognition of experience as a criterion of truth and a promulgation of the phrase 'experimental science,'"[77] Bacon did play an important role in the history of alchemy by transforming an artisanal practice that jealously guarded its guild secrets in such mechanical arts as metallurgy or pigment preparation into an experimental "science," informed by (pseudo-) Aristotelian metaphysics and Christian revelation. His legitimation of alchemy as an experimental science transformed it from a pursuit of private gain in chrysopoeia to a noble pursuit for the benefit of state and church as spagyrics in the context of impending apocalyptic battles. His radical expansion of the alchemical field of application from metallurgy into medicine would prove highly consequential in the fourteenth century and the early modern period, especially in the resurgence of alchemy in the context of occult philosophy in the works of Paracelsus. Bacon's reading of pseudo-Aristotle's *Secretum secretorum* suggested that the discovery of natural secrets is not only legitimated but *necessitated* by their use ("the employment of these inventions") for the Christian cause in the apocalyptic battles of the Eschaton. The apocalyptic interpretation of alchemy effectively bypasses St. Augustine's censor of "vain curiosity" and a Christian moral tradition in which the natural secret is seen as providentially guarded.

The Alchemy of the Quintessence:
Arnald of Villanova and John of Rupescissa

If Bacon's alchemico-astrological theory of the quintessence had remained someone vague on the physics of transmutation, subsequent writers further developed both his alchemical theory of the prolongation of life and its theological legitimation in militant Christian apocalypticism. While some of these works were still spuriously attributed to Bacon, during the second part of the thirteenth century his tradition was already rivaled by that of another important figure in the history of late medieval alchemy: the Valencian physician Arnald of Villanova (ca. 1235–1311). Although Arnald was not, like Bacon, a friar, he also had close ties to the Franciscan Order; and although he is not widely remembered today except among specialists, his fame spread far and wide throughout western Europe during the late medieval and the early modern periods. In the *Nuremberg Chronicle* (1493), for example, he is portrayed as an eminent medical scholar with a paradigmatic book in his hands (see fig. 7). Today, the National Library in Paris owns more than a hundred editions of his collected or single works published from the fifteenth to the eighteenth centuries, as well as at least an equal number of late medieval manuscripts. A prolific author, Arnald also edited and translated from the Arabic into Latin many of the foundational texts of late medieval medicine by authorities such as Galen, Avicenna, Al-Kindi, and Hippocrates. He served as the personal physician to several kings and popes; and it was largely due to his affiliation that the academy at Montpellier became the center of medical learning in late medieval Europe.[78]

Arnald's best-known medical works, such as the *De conservanda iuventute et retardanda senectute* and *De humido radicali,* are concerned with the conservation of youthful vigor essential for Christian victory in the apocalyptic battles expected to unfold at the end of time. Indeed, late in his life, Arnald acquired considerable notoriety also as an apocalyptic prophet, having

Figure 7. Woodcut depicting Arnald of Villanova. (In Hartmann Schedel, *Lib[er] cronicarum, cu[m] figuris et ymagi[ni]bus ab inicio mu[n]di* [*Nuremberg Chronicle*] [Nuremberg: Anton Koberger, July 12, 1493]. Courtesy of the Library of Congress.)

composed numerous heterodox chiliastic tracts in which he excoriated the church for its worldly corruptions and predicted the imminent advent of the Antichrist. However, despite his fame as a physician, he had no academic credentials in theology and Scriptural exegesis; and he was severely censored by the faculty of theology at Paris, dominated by Dominicans, who even had him imprisoned on charge of heresy after he had circulated some of his apocalyptic writings while serving as a delegate of the Crown of Aragon on a diplomatic mission. He was eventually released only after retracting the offending passages and after Pope Boniface VIII (whom he had previously cured of a kidney stone) had interceded on his behalf. As soon as he was released from prison, he retracted the retraction, and his prophetic writings were posthumously condemned by the Council of Tarragon in 1316.[79]

Modern historical scholarship on Arnald has often been fragmented, with historians of science studying his medical writings and historians of religion his eschatology.[80] However, for Arnald himself, there was a deep connection between medicine and eschatology, as the bodily ailments of man were but symptoms of a more general disintegration of the world. Medicine had therefore not only a physical but also a spiritual dimension, and medical diagnosis was for him a microcosmic form of eschatology. The larger objective of his medical practice was the universal renovation, reformation, and rejuvenation of man. In this regard, the Arnaldian physician is Christ-like, and he is frequently compared in Arnald's medical corpus not only to Christ but also to a priest, confessor, and preacher, while the patient is compared to a sinner. Unlike in Aristotelian metaphysics, where the soul is the substantial form of bodily matter, in Arnald's works the soul is represented *by* the body. As Joseph Ziegler, the foremost authority on Arnald's medical writings, observes, the basis of his medicine is the "belief in the existence of a perfect correspondence between body and soul."[81] Whereas in the Augustinian understanding the relationship between body and soul is that of an opposition between decay and renewal, between the City of Man and the City of God, in the Arnaldian medical works, there is a complex web of connections between body and soul predicated on the notion of companionship and partnership: "The soul needs the body as the craftman (*artifex*) needs his tools, as form needs matter."[82]

In light of the close connections between medicine and religion in Arnald's authentic writings, it is not surprising that many works of alchemy were attributed to him in the late medieval and early modern period.[83] As with Bacon, so also with Arnald, there has been much confusion among modern historians about which—if any—of the alchemical works attributed to him were actually written by him, as there is much continuity and conceptual fluidity between the two corpuses. Thus, both Arnald's medical and alchemical works similarly discuss the production of artificial medicines and their applications in the prolongation of life in an apocalyptic context. However, most historians today distinguish between his authentic medical works and the spurious alchemical ones on the basis that the former offer a plethora of artificially produced remedies (based on the assumption that each specific ailment required its own specific medicine), while the latter continue to develop the Baconian theory of the elixir, the quintessence, or the Philosophers' Stone as a universal panacea for all ailments, while also dealing in metallic transmutation.[84] Some of the most famous alchemical writings that were attributed to him include the *Tractatus parabolicus,* the *Rosarius philosophorum,* the *Novum lumen,* the *Flos florum,* and the *Speculum alchemiae.* These works are important for both the development of alchemical theory and the history of the cultural nexus of science, militant Christianity, and apocalyptic prophecy. Thus, in the *Tractatus parabolicus* (ca. 1305), a pseudo-Arnaldian book of alchemical aphorisms that was perhaps written even before his death in 1311,[85] the Arnaldian develops an extensive amplification on the similarities between the alchemically produced elixir and the life of Christ. "Christ was the example of all things," he writes, "and our elixir can be understood according to the conception, generation, nativity, and passion of Christ, and can be compared to Christ in regard to the sayings of the prophets."[86]

Of special interest for the history of the experimental sciences and the theory of alchemical transmutation is the *Rosarius philosophorum,* which was composed sometime between 1311 and 1410.[87] There, the Arnaldian explains that there is "only one Philosophers' Stone" and, for the alchemist to discover the method of producing it, it is "necessary . . . [to] have steadfast determination in his work."[88] Because the alchemy of the Philosophers' Stone is not an artisanal but a philosophical endeavor, it is not sufficient for the alchemist merely to put into practice the recipes and secrets he might read about in alchemical trade literature (including the *Rosarius*). Rather, he must discover this secret for himself during the arduous work of alchemical experimentation: "Let no one assume that he can attend to that work of his by using only this method [of ours], since our craft is not perfect in many ways, for our approach is only one among many. For there is only one stone, only one remedy, to which nothing extraneous was added, nor was anything subtracted, except those things that were removed because they were superfluous."[89] With regard to the production of efficacious medicine, the Arnaldian explains that the alchemist must "gather those things in nature that are especially suitable for the body." It is therefore necessary "that medicine itself is suitable to those things present in nature and that it corresponds especially to those things that exist within the profound unknown: that it [medicine] completes whatever has been diminished by perfecting it."[90]

Significantly, the Arnaldian also offers a theory of the physics of alchemical transmutation. According to Aristotle's *Meteorology*, he writes, it is not possible to change one "species" of metal into another directly, because each has undergone its own distinct processes of generation and corruption. For example, the species of silver (*argenti*), which is silverness (*argenteitas*), cannot be changed into the species of gold (*auri*), which is goldness (*aureitas*), and vice versa. However, while it is not possible to convert one metal into another *directly*, transmutation is possible when subjecting metals to the alchemical *regimen* of the Philosophers' Stone that consists of four basic operations (1) dissolving (*solvere*); (2) washing (*abluere*); (3) reducing (*reducere*); and (4) fixing (*figere*). In the introduction of this book, I already discussed the special significance of the third *regimen*, "reduction," in alchemical transmutation. The Arnaldian of the *Rosarius* explains that "the philosophical work consists of dissolving the [Philosophers'] stone in its mercury, so that it is reduced to its prime matter."[91] "Reducing" means making dry what is moist (*reducere humidum in siccum*); to "wax, to fatten or impregnate, to make subtle" (*incerare, impinguare vel impraegnare, subtiliare*). Likewise, the Arnaldian explains, before one metal can be transformed into another, each species of metal must first be "reduced" to the "prime matter" (*prima materia*) that all metals share, which is *argentum vivum*.[92] This alchemical "reduction" into *argentum vivum* is like a "changing of nature in its first roots" (*in suam primam radicem*).[93] In alchemical iconography, this process of reduction is frequently compared to the turning of a great rack or wheel—the so-called Philosophical Wheel—on which the quarrelling elements are symbolized by Man-Christ, who is violently "tortured" in a passion (see fig. 8). In the *Rosarius*, his body is converted "into spirit and spirit into body until each is able to mingle together; or unite in the chemical wedding to form a new perfect being, the philosopher stone."[94]

The Arnaldian Philosophers' Stone, like that of Roger Bacon, can "cure" not only imperfect metals by transmuting them into gold and silver but also rejuvenate human bodies by reversing their natural corruptions:

> [Besides curing metals] it [the Philosophers' Stone] also holds an effective virtue—greater than all other physicians' medicines for curing every ailment, whether they are caused by heat or by cold, it maintains good heath, it enhances physical and mental fortitude. It turns the old into young, and it expels every

Figure 8. Christ being racked. (In Father Ullmann, *Buch der Heiligen Dreifaltigkeit*. Image Hs 80061 © Germanisches Nationalmuseum, Nuremberg.)

infirmity. It prevents poison from reaching the heart, moistens the arteries, breaks down congestion in the lungs, heals ulcers; it purifies the blood and purges obstructions to the soul in the spirit's breathing, and it preserves these things in constant purity.[95]

Moreover, these alchemical operations apply not only to the inanimate but also to the animate world, meaning those parts of creation that have a "soul" (in the Aristotelian sense) that animate it, whether it be the vegetable soul that animates all living creatures; the sensitive soul that animates animals and humans; or the rational, or highest, soul that animates human beings. As we will see in chapter 6, this Arnaldian analogical understanding of "soul" in terms of Aristotelian elemental theory and the possibility of its alchemical "reduction" to *prima materia* is also at the root of the sixteenth-century Franciscan millenarian understanding of conversion in the New World.

Perhaps because of Arnald's heterodox credentials in being persecuted by the academic theologians at Paris, as well as because of his spiritualized understanding of medicine, his writings—medical, alchemical, and apocalyptic—appealed especially to members of the Spiritual branch of the Franciscan Order. The most important Franciscan follower of Arnald was John of Rupescissa (1310–1362), probably of Catalan extraction, who had joined the Franciscans sometime in the 1340s after having studied at the University of Toulouse. He became associated with the Franciscan convent of Aurillac but soon attracted the wrath of the church authorities for his heterodox prophetic writings, as well as for his patent inclinations toward the Spiritual branch, incessantly demanding that the Franciscan Order return to its original apostolic poverty and publicly lambasting ecclesiastic authorities for living lives of wealth and power. First incarcerated in 1345, he would spend most of his life in either provincial or papal prisons, where he put his time to use in writing dozens of ever-more-inflammatory tracts on the imminent End Times. Also, he produced numerous important alchemical works, including the *De quinta essencia* (1351/52) and the *Liber lucis* (probably 1354).[96]

I will return to John's prophetic writings in chapter 4, but here I would like to focus on the significance of his contribution to alchemical theory, which rests on his elaboration of the Baconian idea of the quintessence and its production by means of the alcoholic distillation. It is first elaborated in the tract *The Consideration of the Fifth Essence,* which today survives in more than one hundred manuscripts, and is divided into two parts ("books"). The first book contains twelve canons (fifteen in some manuscripts) dealing with alchemical theory, and the second book contains twenty remedies, including applications of the elixirs to various diseases and infirmities, such as old age, palsy, leprosy, and melancholy. It also offers an extended discussion of astrology in which John explains that people born under the sign of Saturn are susceptible to melancholy and the vexing by demons. However, the power of quintessence is such that it frees men from demons, especially when extracted from gold and pearls. Although he concedes, with Bacon and other Christian alchemists, that it is not possible for art to achieve human immortality, he believed that alchemy can prolong health and vitality.[97]

The first book is concerned primarily with alchemical theory, as derived from Aristotelian and pseudo-Aristotelian physics. Like Bacon's, John's theory of the quintessence still proceeds from a basically Aristotelian division between the sublunary and the superlunary realms of the cosmos. As discussed earlier, according to Aristotelian physics, the quintessence was the dominant element of the superlunary region of the stars, which were perfect and unchanging, not being subject to the processes of generation and corruption. By contrast, the sublunary region is predominantly made up of the four imperfect elements and therefore subject to constant change and corruption. As Bacon had done before him, John argues that, while pure quintessence is the dominant element of the superlunary world, it is also present (albeit in inferior form) in the sublunary realm. However, John's alchemical theory departed from Bacon's in two important ways. First, whereas Bacon had regarded blood as the ideal substance for distilling the quintessence, for John, it was the alcoholic substance of alchemical *aqua ardens* (burning water). This quintessence is a sort of "bridge" connecting the (perfect) superlunary and the (imperfect) sublunary realms. But, second, whereas Bacon had still subscribed to the classical Aristotelian notion that the quintessence was naturally confined to the superlunary realm and could be channeled into sublunary matter in an alchemical process that mobilized occult astrological sympathies that were analogous to the supernatural Resurrection, John understood the quintessence as a substance that naturally pervades the entire cosmos and could therefore be produced from any terrestrial matter, independent of astrological influence. As we will see in chapter 3, this is a development that must be seen in light of the complicated relationship that John's alchemical theory had with pseudo-Llullism, a tradition that fused (pseudo-)Aristotelian elemental theory with the Neoplatonic notion of a chain of divine dignities that connects all of creation and that would ultimately dissolve the Aristotelian ontological distinction between the supra- and the sublunary realms. Thus, John's alchemical *aqua ardens* is not ordinary alcohol but a purified spirit that can be alchemically distilled, mainly from wine but also from blood, flesh, eggs, and other organic matter, as well as from gold and other precious metals. Once it is freed from its mixture and distilled into purified form, it has miraculous efficacy in medicine and alchemical transmutation.[98]

Like Bacon's and Arnald's, John's particular alchemical quest was aimed not so much at attaining wealth through the transmutation of metals as it was at effecting health, youth, vigor, and a long life by staving off natural corruption and putrefaction, especially in the Christian missionaries and crusaders who will participate in the battles of the End Times. "First of all, I considered ages to come, which were predicted by Christ in the Gospels," he wrote in his *Book of Light*,

> namely the tribulations at the time of the Antichrist, under whom the Roman Church shall be tormented and have all her worldly riches despoiled by tyrants.... On account of this, for the sake of liberating the chosen people of

> God, to whom it is granted to know the ministry of God and the magistracy of truth, I wish to speak of the work of the magical Philosophers' Stone without lofty speech. My intention is to be helpful to the good of the holy Roman Church and briefly to explain the whole truth about the Stone.[99]

Thus, while Roger Bacon had provided a theological defense of alchemy as an "experimental science" and translated into a Christian context the Arabic notion of the alchemical elixir as a universal cure not only for metals but also human bodies, both Arnald of Villanova and John of Rupescissa made important contributions to the development of alchemical theory by elaborating the notions of alchemical reduction to the *prima materia* and the theory of a quintessence that can be alchemically distilled from sublunary matter. For all three, the ultimate purpose of alchemy was the strengthening and rejuvenation of Christian bodies in the context of holy war and the apocalyptic battles that would inaugurate the end of time. As we will see in subsequent chapters, their legacy would still exert a strong influence during the so-called Age of Discovery in the early modern period, especially in the cultural context of the conquest of America and the missionary attempt to convert pagan souls to Christianity. First, however, I will turn, in the next chapter, to the intimate connection between science and religion in the missionary enterprise already during late medieval times, particularly in the writings by and attributed to the Mallorcan polymath Ramón Llull.

3

The Alchemy of Conversion
Ramón Llull's Chivalric Missionary Science

> I have discovered a new kind of knowledge whereby one may learn the truth and destroy falsehood. Saracens, Tartars, and Jews, along with many in error shall be baptized by means of the knowledge God has granted me.
> —Ramón Llull, *Song of Ramon*

For Roger Bacon, Arnald of Villanova, and John of Rupescissa, the main purpose of alchemy was to aid the triumph of Christianity in the apocalyptic battles inaugurating the Eschaton. However, in the late medieval and early modern period up to the seventeenth century, alchemy also became an important factor in the history of Christian evangelism in the works attributed to the remarkable figure of the Majorcan polymath, Arabist, Franciscan tertiary, and missionary Ramón Lull (ca. 1232–1316). The son of a nobleman from Barcelona who had participated in the conquest of Majorca by Jaime I of Aragon from its Muslim rulers in 1229, Llull had spent his early years at the royal court at Palma living, by his own account, a rather dissolute life as a troubadour, writing poems of chivalric love, and pursuing married women. In his twenties, he married Blanca Picany, with whom he had two children, Domènec and Magdalena (though this did apparently not prevent him from chasing other women). At age thirty, he had a conversion experience after a series of visions in which the crucified Christ appeared to him at night, suspended in midair. Deeply impressed by this experience, Llull decided that he must dedicate his life to the service of God by converting infidels or by dying a martyr's death in the attempt of doing so. For this purpose, he vowed to write a book—"the best in the world," he said, "against the errors of the unbelievers."[1] After hearing a sermon on the life of St. Francis, he purchased a Muslim slave to teach him Arabic. He sold all of his possessions, made some financial provisions for his family, and abandoned his former life in order to devote himself entirely to the service of God. He embarked on a rigorous course of study, encompassing Latin, rhetoric, logic, the Arabic language and philosophy, as well as the Islamic religion and Judaism. After nine years of intense study and spiritual seeking, God finally revealed to him, during solitary prayer on Mount Randa (in Majorca), the "form and method" of his book.² From this revelation was born his famous "Art," the *ars luliana* of evangelical rhetoric and logic for the discovery of truth, which he elaborated in not one but more than 260 works, some of which he originally wrote in Arabic.³

Most of these books were composed while Llull was traveling throughout the Mediterranean, northern Africa, and Armenia, in order to persuade kings and popes to establish academies for the training of Christian missionaries in Arabic and Asian languages. Not discouraged by the general lack of material support for his enterprise from Christian men of influence and power, he founded, in 1276, his own missionary academy at the Monastery of Miramar in Valldemossa, Majorca, where he trained Franciscan missionaries for their work in Muslim kingdoms. When this project folded several years later, Llull decided to go to the Muslim kingdoms himself in order to put the magic of his Art into action. He went on a total of three apostolic missions to northern Africa, during which he debated with Muslim clerics and preached in the streets of Tunis. When these attempts also yielded few results (and after he had twice been discreetly dispatched on a ship back to Europe by local officials), Llull began to write tracts urging the launch of another crusade, in order to force Muslims to listen to his apostolic message. His death in 1315, after his last mission to Tunis, is the stuff of legend, to which I will return in chapter 5.

Although Llull never wrote on alchemy except to discredit it, he is an important figure in the history of the Hermetic art because of the more than one hundred works of alchemy that were attributed to him spuriously and that were believed to be his authentic works during the late medieval and early modern period. As we will see in later chapters, this fusion of pseudo-Llullian alchemical works with the authentic *ars luliana* into the tradition known as "Llullism" played an important role in the history of the *idea* of the discovery of America as a paradigm in modern science and international law. In this chapter, I offer some background on the medieval missionary mystic from Majorca and explore his idiosyncratic fusion of science with religion—a fusion that helps partially explain why so many works of alchemy were spuriously attributed to him after his death. I call this peculiar fusion the "chivalric missionary science" of the *ars luliana,* a system of natural theology that synthesized the high medieval discourses of chivalric love and Neoplatonic mysticism with a late medieval Aristotelian naturalism and mendicant missionary zeal. While the chivalric motif in Franciscan evangelicalism originated already with St. Francis himself—who is said to have taken his name for his love of the French troubadour tradition—Llull's prolific writings integrated St. Francis's tradition in chivalric missionary ethos with Bonaventure's tradition in natural theology and the new Scholastic Aristotelianism. As we will see in subsequent chapters, Llull's missionary science would still have a strong influence during the sixteenth century in the (spiritual) conquest of America.

Ramón Llull and the Mendicant Movement

During Llull's lifetime, his native island of Majorca, like many other parts of southern Europe, had only recently been conquered from the Moors and still had a large Muslim population. Missionary work among this population was encouraged by Christian rulers, especially at the court of Aragon, which had been at the forefront of Christian expansionism into Moorish territories on the Spanish Peninsula and the Balearic Islands.[4] However, unlike in the early modern period, during the later Middle Ages, church and state did not yet take an active role in the missionary enterprise, Llull's lifelong efforts notwithstanding. Nor did church and state usually play an important role in the persecution of religious minorities. Although the Fourth Lateran Council in 1215 inaugurated a gradual shift toward religious bigotry and surveillance—by introducing special dress codes for Muslims and Jews or barring Jews from holding certain public offices, for example—church and state generally remained a force for tolerance and even protection of religious minorities. There were political, economic, and theological reasons for this relative tolerance. One was the eschatological justification that the Jews were not to be converted until the final days before the Second Coming, in order to serve as an exemplum and reminder to Christians of the fate and condition of unbelievers. According to St. Augustine's *The City of God,* the Jews should be preserved in their state of uprootedness and dispersal in which they had lived since the Roman destruction of the temple "to bear this testimony, so that the Church of Christ has everywhere increased."[5]

By the same token, the Christian wars of the Reconquista against Muslims in southern Europe were crusades waged over territories, not souls. In fact, the Muslim populations in the reconquered territories were usually guaranteed the right to continue the practice of their religion by the conquering Christian princes, and in some territories they coexisted for centuries with Christians and Jews. Even within the church, it rarely occurred to any popes, bishops, or secular priests to expend much effort on converting the conquered Muslim population, the majority of whom lived in subjection to their new Christian lords and performed agricultural or other sorts of menial labor, most of them as free peasants but some also as slaves. For the most part, Muslims in the reconquered territories were thought to be irredeemably "hardened" in their errors and incapable of conversion. Even as late as the surrender of the Emirate of Granada in 1492, the Catholic kings assured the defeated Moorish ruler, Abu Abdallah Muhammad XII, that he and his subjects could remain in the country and keep their religion, property, and customs. Unlike the Jews, who were given a choice to convert or be expelled that same year of 1492, the unconverted Muslim (*mudéjar*) population in Spain was generally tolerated in the various kingdoms of the Iberian Peninsula (with the exception of Portugal, where they were expelled in 1497). However, forced conversions of *mudejares* were becoming more frequent in the first part of the sixteenth century; and by the second half, virtually all *mudejares* had been either converted or expelled; finally, even those who had converted (*moriscos*) were officially expelled from Spanish territories beginning in 1609, albeit with uneven results.[6]

To the extent that there were any concerted efforts to convert nonbelievers to Christianity during the later Middle Ages, the task had fallen exclusively on the friars of the mendicant orders, mainly the Franciscans (founded in 1209), the Dominicans (founded in 1216), and the Augustinians (founded in 1244). The mendicant orders had been created as a response to a number of challenges that the church had to face in the early thirteenth century, including the increased contact with nonbelievers, both within and without the political borders of Christian Europe, in the context of the Reconquista and long-distance trade. But a more significant challenge was the rise of various forms of mystical lay spirituality within European Christendom, such as the Cathar heresy in southern France. These spiritual movements were expressions of the social and economic transformations that resulted from increasing urbanization and the growth of the third estate that loosened the structures of feudal society. The mendicant orders made it their mission to respond to these challenges by intervening into lay society. The friars' primary task had therefore been to work "in the world"; and their theater of action was typically the city, where they lived an itinerant and active life in poverty, preaching and modeling the Christian life in a society increasingly in motion.[7]

From the beginning of the mendicant movement, the Franciscans had taken the leading role with regard to the missionary efforts outside Christian Europe. While Francis of Assisi had traveled to Muslim territories in Africa (reportedly converting the sultan of Egypt, Melek-al-Kamil), others, such as William of Rubruck, Giovanni da Montecorvino, and Giovanni Carpini, traveled as far as China. But while these efforts produced a modest corpus of missionary travel literature and a more substantial corpus of hagiography and martyrology that speaks of millions of baptisms purchased with gruesome passions, the Franciscans' actual effectiveness in converting nonbelievers outside Europe is an open question. Recent research suggests that most of the Franciscans who worked outside Europe ministered primarily to Christians living in non-Catholic lands, such as European merchants, soldiers, and slaves living and working in Muslim lands, or minority non-European and non-Catholic Christian groups, such as Orthodox in Greece, Copts in Africa, or Jacobites in India.[8]

Although the vow of poverty applied to all the mendicant orders, it had been especially central to the apostolic mission and primitivist ethos of the Franciscans. However, almost from the beginning, the order had been beleaguered by controversies over this issue. As the order grew rapidly in the thirteenth century, different factions arose who disagreed in their interpretations of St. Francis's original rule. Was a convent allowed to own property, such as books? Did the mendicant friars own their garb, or even the food they consumed? Questions such as these had sparked endless debates during the thirteenth, fourteenth, and fifteenth centuries that consistently gave rise to ever-new reformist movements whose members chastised the order's leadership for having become too worldly, beginning with the Spiritual movement during the fourteenth century and still continuing in the sixteenth century with the Cisnerean reforms of the Observant branch, from which the majority of the Franciscan missionaries working in the Americas originated.[9]

If the Franciscans' specialty was the missionary work outside Christian territories, the Dominicans' foremost mission was the protection of Catholic orthodoxy within Christian Europe. Their primary focus had hereby been on the Christian laity and the Jewish population, especially on the Iberian Peninsula, where Jews had often held prominent government positions at both Muslim and Christian courts in economic administration and medicine.[10] The Dominicans therefore saw themselves primarily as educators rather than as missionaries. As the spiritual and intellectual heirs of St. Dominic, the "Soldiers Against Heresy" played an important role in the Inquisition and in Scholastic institutions, priding themselves on the many doctors, professors, archbishops, and popes that had sprung from their ranks. To the extent that the Dominican friars involved themselves in the conversion of Muslims in Reconquista Europe, they attempted to apply the methods used in the struggle against heresy and the conversion of Jews. However, the conversion of Muslims presented somewhat different problems. Among these was a linguistic problem, as Latin was the only language being taught at the universities. Under the leadership of Ramón de Penyafort (ca. 1175–1275) in Aragon, the Dominicans were among the first to implement the study of Arabic in the academy.[11]

Another problem was methodological: the Cathars were Christians who accepted the authority of the Bible (despite the unorthodox interpretation that was deemed heretical by the Catholic Church); and the Jews accepted at least the authority of the Old Testament. By contrast, Islam, though an

Abrahamic monotheistic religion that accepted Jesus of Nazareth as a prophet, did not share any sacred texts with Judaism and Christianity. This dilemma led to a shift in emphasis in thirteenth-century missionology away from a reliance on biblical and ecclesiastic authorities and toward argumentation by natural reason as derived from the writings of Aristotle, who enjoyed considerable prestige in Arabic literature and philosophy. Although ecclesiastic authorities were initially suspicious of the philosopher's pagan wisdom, by the end of the thirteenth century, his works were required reading at most of the major universities. One of the systems of evangelical logic that emerged from this shift was that elaborated in the *Summa contra Gentiles,* written by Thomas Aquinas at the University of Paris upon Penyafort's instigation in 1269.[12] Another influential missionary work to emerge from Penyafort's leadership was the *Pugio fidei adversus mauros et iudaeos* (1278), written by the Catalan Dominican Ramón Martí. The third system was that of Ramón Llull, who had been specifically advised by Penyafort *not* to come to Paris for academic study but to begin his training on the cultural, linguistic, and religious frontiers of his native Majorca.[13]

Perhaps partially as a result of heeding Penyafort's advice, Llull's intellectual and spiritual life, as well as his evangelical ethos and rhetoric, developed a character very different from those of Aquinas and Martí. On the one hand, whereas Aquinas personified the Scholastic life in the medieval university, Llull was almost constantly on the road, tirelessly crisscrossing the Mediterranean world as a missionary, activist, and lobbyist for his evangelical cause; and whereas the literary works of the "Doctor Angelicus" stand out for their intellectual subtlety and unimpeachable academic rigor, the system of the "Doctor Illuminatus" (as Llull is known) is unique for its idiosyncratic autodidacticism, intellectual charisma, and zealous lay spirituality.[14] On the other hand, whereas Martí's method was to employ Aristotelian logic and rhetoric in order to prove the falseness of the Jewish and Muslim faiths, Llull attempted to prove scientifically not only the falseness of those religions but also the truth of the Christian faith.[15] What's more, he intended to furnish such a scientific proof by using a system of logic that partially derived from Arabic philosophy itself. For its method of interfaith dialogue, Llull's Art has been dubbed a "frontier philosophy"—a logical system not only of rhetoric but also of transcultural metaphysics that began with the experience of God's Creation in nature and proceeded by way of argument through syllogistic reason and analogy.[16] This was no mean task, considering the patent irrationality of some of the basic tenets that distinguish Christianity from both Islam and Judaism, such as the Incarnation or the Holy Trinity. Ideas as irrational and yet so central to medieval Christianity as the claim that the Virgin Mary was the mother of God (proclaimed at the Councils of Ephesus in 431 and Chalcedon in 451) not only stretched medieval Christian imaginations but also elicited reactions from Muslim and Jewish religious scholars that ranged from indignation to laughter.[17]

One of Llull's earliest works is a verse compendium on the *Logic* of the Arabic philosopher al-Ghazali, the *Compendium logicae algazelis* (1271), originally written in Arabic by Llull and later translated into Latin. Also among his early works is an encyclopedic volume about the Creation, entitled the *Libre de contemplació en Déu* (1273; The book of contemplations), which has been called "one of the most extraordinary books of the Middle Ages."[18] The work contains in gestation some of the ideas that would later become the cornerstones of his own "Art"—ideas such as the dynamic activity of the divine dignities and their pervasion of all of nature. It is a cosmological idea that is broadly Augustinian in its roots but was probably more immediately inspired by the *De divisione naturae*, written by the ninth-century Irish Neoplatonist theologian John Scotus Erigena (815–ca. 877).[19] However, according to the *Vita coaetania* (a sort of autobiography as told to the friars of the monastery of Vauvert in Paris in 1311), it was not until the divine revelation on Mount Randa that he conceived of the "form and method" of his Art. The first work that resulted from this revelation was the *Ars compendiosa inveniendi veritatem* (1274; The brief art for the discovery of truth), with multiple expositions of its applications to various disciplines to follow throughout the second part of the 1270s. The second cycle of the Art began in 1283, with the *Ars demonstrativa* (The art of proof) and its various applications, which were written throughout the 1280s. The third cycle of the Art (the so-called Ternary Phase) began in 1290 with the completion of the *Ars inventiva veritatis* (The art for the discovery of truth), which again was followed by multiple applications and culminated with the *Ars brevis* (1308) and the *Ars generalis ultima* (1308).[20]

The "Fool for God": Ramón Llull's Evangelical Ethos

Although Llull joined the Franciscans as a tertiary, he never became a friar living in full subjection to the order's rule and serving as a priest in the office of ministry. Possibly, he found the demands of regular order and office unsuitable to his independent, restless, entrepreneurial, and charismatic spirit. Upon the encouragement by Penyafort, Llull had initially intended to join the Dominicans. According to his *Vita*, a star and a voice revealed to him that "in this [i.e., the Dominican] order you can be saved." Yet, Llull is impatient with the procrastinations and hesitations with which he is treated by the Dominican friars. Then, he "remembered that the Franciscans had accepted the

Art which God had given him on the mountain much more willingly than the above-mentioned Dominicans. Whereupon, hoping that said Franciscans would promote the Art more efficaciously for the honor of our Lord Jesus Christ and for the good of the Church, he thought that he would leave the Dominicans and enter the Franciscan order."[21] At first, Ramón seems affirmed in his decision when "there appeared next to him, as if hanging on the wall, a band or cord like those that the Franciscans wear around their waists." But then he is thrown into consternation when the same star that he had seen earlier in the Dominican convent reappears to threaten him: "Did I not tell you that you could only be saved in the Dominican Order? Be careful what you do!" He falls into a deep despair upon deliberating his dismal choices: "Ramon, therefore, considering that on the one hand he would be damned unless he remained with the Dominicans, while on the other hand his Art and books would be lost unless he remained with the Franciscans, chose (which was most admirable of him) his own eternal damnation rather than the loss of the Art which he knew he had received from God for the salvation of the many and especially for the honor of God himself."[22] This anecdote exemplifies several late medieval ideas that are central to Llull's evangelical ethos. First, it illustrates his conviction that he had received his Art directly by divine intervention for a higher and special mystical purpose that eluded man's comprehension. Second, it illustrates his belief that the purpose of all natural knowledge, such as the knowledge of the stars (i.e., astrology), is to illuminate the divine presence in creation and the supremacy of the divine will for human salvation. And third, the passage exemplifies the idea of the "Fool for God," a trope that emerged from late medieval lay spirituality in the tradition of *idiotas*, the humble "divine jongleurs" (*ioculatres Dei*).[23] Llull had elaborated this chivalric ethos in the dozens of literary works written in the vernacular Catalan, where he imagined his Art in apostolic action.[24] These include an apologetic work, *The Book of the Gentile and the Three Wise Men* (1274); a treatise on knighthood; a catechism addressed to his son, the *Doctrina pueril* (1282); and two didactic novels, *Blanquerna* (1283) and *Felix: or, the Book of Wonders* (1288). While the latter novel is a mixture between a medieval quest romance and scholastic encyclopedia, the former is a Christian utopia exemplifying eremitic and apostolic life that also includes two shorter devotional works, the *Book of the Lover and the Beloved* and *The Art of Contemplation*.

Among the early works in which Llull synthesizes the language of chivalry with the language of Christian evangelism is the *Book of Knighthood and Chivalry* (ca. 1276)—first translated into English by William Caxton in the fifteenth century and perhaps among the most influential handbooks of chivalry of the later Middle Ages. It presents a typically Llullian narrative frame in which an aging knight, after having won glory in many victorious tournaments, retires from the vanities of the world into hermitage in a forest, a *locus amoenus* complete with fair meadows, refreshing springs that quench his thirst, and shady trees whose fruits sustain the eremitic hero as he spends his final days in the contemplation of God.[25] On one of those days, a squire turns up who has lost his way while traveling to a royal court in order to be elevated to knighthood. Scandalized by his discovery that the young squire seems to know nothing about the rules of chivalry, the aged hermit-knight presents him with a book and sends him on his way. Having arrived at the court, the squire shares the book with the king and all the assembled noblemen, whose devotions to the rules of knighthood are hereby regenerated. The remainder of the tract is a presentation of the contents of the book of knighthood, divided into chapters devoted to the traditional topics of chivalry—charity, loyalty, truth, justice, and verity, as well as the duties of sports (i.e., tournaments) to keep themselves valiant, the responsibility to protect lords and peasants, as well as damsels, and so on. Interspersed are some lessons that shed light on Llull's own career as a troubadour-turned-missionary and reformer. Among these is the idea that "the knowledge of [chivalry] should be put into books, that the art is known and read in such a manner as other sciences have been read, that the son of knights learn first the knowledge that pertains to the order after they have been squires."[26] In other words, Llull demands that young noblemen receive a rigorous training and apprenticeship as squires in the art of chivalry before being elevated as knights. It is a "great wrong ... to the order of knighthood," Llull writes, "that it is not a written science and read in schools, like the other sciences."[27] Rather than assuming that chivalry is knowledge that runs in the blood resulting from birth, Llull demands that it be made a science. What's more, knighthood is an *office,* meaning that a knight who does not perform his duties is a knight in name only, not worth the title and in fact "more vile than the smith or the carpenter, who does their office."[28] Finally, the nobility of the office of the knight in the world is matched only by that of the office of the "clerk" (cleric), especially the missionary, "and therefore the greatest friendship should be in this world between clerks and knights." Thus, Llull's *Book of Knighthood* elaborates an analogy between the knight and missionary in which Christian evangelism is defined in the distinctly masculine language of chivalric office and honor.

Llull's ethos of chivalric evangelism is further developed in his semi-autobiographical novel *Blanquerna* (ca. 1283), which features an eponymous hero who is torn between the life of the Christian hermit, who would abandon the world, and the life of the missionary, who would reform it. As a young man, Blanquerna leaves his loving Christian parents, Evast and Aloma, for the life of a hermit, "so that he would fain depart to contemplate God in rustic places and in regions uninhabited by man."[29] When the occasion arises, however, he changes course during his solitary itinerancies to become an ecclesiastic reformer and even ascends to the Holy See to become the sort of pope that Llull himself hoped for throughout his life—a pope committed to ecclesiastical reform and to the evangelical missions to unbelievers. In his endeavors, he is assisted by a "wise fool," not coincidentally named "Ramón the Fool," who advises Blanquerna in the reformation of the church.[30]

Before his ultimate return to the life of a hermit, Blanquerna encountered, during one of his pilgrimages in the forest, three allegorical figures: two sisters named Faith and Truth, and their brother, named Understanding. A despondent Faith explains that she and her sister have just returned from the land of the Saracens, where they failed to convert any infidels to Christianity. However, Faith vows to return for a second try, this time aided by her brother, Understanding, "that he may visit those people from whom I come, and demonstrate to them by necessary reasons the fourteen articles of the faith; for the time has come when they will not receive the authority of the saints; and there are now no miracles such as those of old whereby they that knew not me nor my sister were enlightened. And since the people require arguments and necessary demonstrations, I go to my brother, who has power, by the virtue of God, to prove the fourteen articles."[31] Assuming the role of Devil's Advocate (and that of Llull's critics), Blanquerna objects by pointing out that Faith's efficacy would seem to be compromised if her articles had to be demonstrated by Understanding, as "Faith enlightened to believe even against Understanding." But Faith (speaking for Llull) counters that faith, while important, is secondary to the knowledge and love of God. In the end, she explains, knowledge through understanding will exalt knowledge through faith, as understanding is not an end to itself but instrumental to a knowledge by faith. Hence, Faith and Truth turn to Understanding, who explains Llull's credo that "unbelievers demand necessary demonstrations and reasons, and refuse credence to aught beside. It is time for us to go, and make use of the science which we have; for, if we use it not as we ought, in honouring Him from Whom we have it, we act against conscience and against that which we know, and we desire not to have the merit and the glory which we can have if we use our knowledge."[32] Referring to Llull's own Art, Understanding announces, "We have a new method of argument with the unbelievers, by showing them the *Brief Art of Finding Truth;* and, when they have learned this, we shall be enabled to confound them by this art and by its beginnings."[33]

The final chapters of the novel consist of two shorter devotional works that illustrate the spiritual state of mind at which the hero has arrived at the end of his journey. One of them, the *Book of the Lover and the Beloved,* is an assembly of 366 short, often lyrical paragraphs that translate the chivalric ideal of unrequited temporal love for a woman—which Llull had been in the habit of celebrating as a young troubadour—into the selfless love of a Christian (the lover) of God (the beloved). Modern literary scholars have been intrigued by the homoerotic imagery of some of the text's passages, as well as about the source of the basic motif of the "fool for God" and its ecstatically sensual variations (including the theme of "drunken" fool), especially in light of what Llull tells us about his source:[34]

> When Blanquerna was thinking in this way, he remembered how when he was pope a Saracen once told him that the Muslims have various holy men. The most esteemed among these or any others are some people called Sufis. They offer words of love and brief *exempla* that inspire a person to great devotion. Their words require exposition, and thanks to the exposition the Intellect rises higher, which develops it and spurs the Will to devotion. After considering this, Blanquerna proposed to make a book in this manner.[35]

This passage illustrates that Llull, despite his missionary zeal, had a profound appreciation for the subtleties of Arabic philosophy, the aesthetic beauty of the Arabic language, art and poetry, as well as for the mystical spirituality of certain branches of Islam. For Llull, these were cultural elements that could be repurposed and harnessed for the evangelical mission and that made Saracens eminently convertible.

The purpose of Llull's art was to serve as an intellectual instrument for the peaceful realization of the perennial medieval dream of a universal Christian empire, the *reductio omnium ad unum*.[36] This goal of peaceful conversion through "necessary reason" is most vividly illustrated by Llull's most important apologetic work, the *Book of the Gentile and the Three Wise Men,* written in Majorca in the early 1270s. It is a work of narrative fiction in which a Gentile (i.e., pagan) who is ignorant of the three Abrahamic religions but who has a basic understanding of philosophy wanders through an allegorical shadowy forest suffering spiritual distress upon contemplating his mortality until he comes to a sunlit meadow where he encounters three wise men—one Christian, one Muslim, and one Jew—engaged in respectful discussion in the shade of some trees. The Gentile asks them to provide proof of the existence of God and the truth of the Resurrection. By the end of the first book, the Gentile is convinced of the existence of God and the afterlife but falls into still further confusion when learning that each of the wise men belongs to a different faith. The subsequent three books of the work consist of dialogues between the Gentile and the representative of each of the three monotheistic religions, who take turns in attempting to persuade the Gentile of the superior truth of his religion, while the other two remain silent. The epilogue presents the Gentile's nondenominational prayer of thanksgiving, after which the three wise men take their leave not wishing to know which religion the Gentile has chosen. But although the book closes open-ended in this regard, it is clear that Llull intended the reader to come away from the disputation convinced by "necessary reasons" that the Christian had the superior arguments and that the Gentile will choose his religion.[37]

Llull does not specify who exactly this Gentile is. However, it is likely that he envisioned a Tartar, or Mongol. As already pointed out, in the thirteenth century, several Franciscans had visited China and had written accounts of their journeys with detailed, if at times embellished, descriptions of their culture.[38] Llull also wrote about the Mongols—for example in his *Liber super psalmum "Quicumque vult,"* or *Llibre del Tartar*.[39] Also, in his novel *Felix: or the Book of Wonders,* there is a thinly veiled autobiographical passage in which "a man who had long labored for the good of the Roman Church" came to Paris and spoke to the king of France about sending missionaries with translations of the *Ars demonstrativa* to the "Tartars to preach to them and show them the Art."[40] Similarly, in the novel *Blanquerna,* the eponymous hero-pope sent thirty Tartars who had learned Latin and were converted to the Christian religion together with five friars to the court of the Khan. They "came before the great Khan, and preached the faith of the Christians, and converted many people in his Court, and they turned the great Khan from the error wherein he lived and made him to doubt it; and after a time, by process of this doubt, he came to everlasting life."[41] As one modern critic has pointed out, Llull imagined the conversion of pagans (or Gentiles) such as the Tartars as a kind of "competitive forum for logical disputation between monotheistic religions" and viewed pagans not only as prospective converts but also as potential allies in the contest of the three monotheistic religions of the Mediterranean world against one another—a contest that would come to a showdown at the end of times.[42]

In the same vein, the novel *Blanquerna* also betrays an interest in India. Thus, Llull wrote that the last act performed by Blanquerna as pope, before he retreated into hermitage, was to send an apostolic mission to India:

> It came to pass one day that two messengers from the king of India came to the Pope, beseeching him to give them students to learn their language. So the Pope [Blanquerna] sent immediately to the Cardinal of Tu Solus Altissimus, and commanded him to procure that which the king of India besought of him; for the

producing thereof accorded with his office. The Cardinal made treaty, and procured that which the Pope commanded him. Great was the benefit and good was the example that resulted from the office of the Cardinal. And because the Pope and the Cardinals did their utmost to serve in the offices which they had taken upon themselves, God gave them blessing, and to their works fulfilment, and made them to be pleasing to men.[43]

Thus, Llull's vernacular works elaborate an evangelical ethos that synthesized the high medieval languages of eremeticism and chivalry with late medieval mendicant missionary zeal and Aristotelian rationalism, attempting to reconcile faith, truth, and understanding in the Neoplatonic motif of the "Fool for God." At the core of his missionary science is the study of non-Western languages, the philosophical and metaphysical categories of other religions, as well as the logical method of argumentation based on syllogistic reason, analogy, and the experience of creation. Before turning to Llull's legacy of an alchemist in the many pseudo-alchemical works attributed him, it is necessary to take a closer look at the basic ideas of the authentic *ars luliana,* especially its application to medicine.

The Art of Conversion

The *ars luliana* was predicated on an extreme metaphysical realism that presumed a mystical grammar underlying both the order of nature and the rational categories available to the human mind. Intended to provide scientific proof of the truth of the Christian religion, it proceeded not from the authority of biblical Scripture but from Aristotelian natural philosophy and logic, as well as Neoplatonic metaphysics. Building on certain precepts that were shared by Christianity, Judaism, and Islam—all cultures of the letter and the book—Llull's Art relied heavily on the use of alphabetical symbols to represent the "Nine Dignities" of God that pervaded man and the natural world. Geometrical figures arranged the letters into columns and wheels that may be rotated, combined, or otherwise manipulated, thus functioning as a sort of "thinking machine" that has been seen as a medieval forerunner of the (early) modern computational systems of Gottfried Wilhelm Leibniz (who was a fervent Llullian) and Alan Turing.[44] In the course of its various iterations, Llull elaborated countless applications of his Art to just about any scientific topic under the sun, including law, rhetoric, memory, astrology, optics, mathematics, navigation, and medicine.[45]

At the core of Llull's system of logic were the transcendental Neoplatonic principles (*absoluta*) shared by Judaism, Islam, and Christianity about the

Figure 9. Ramón Llull's "First Figure," showing the Nine Dignities. (In *Ars brevis*, eighteenth century. Palma de Mallorca BP MS998. Digital version Biblioteca Virtual del Patrimonio Bibliográfico. Courtesy of Ministerio de Educación, Cultura y Deporte, Spain.)

nature of God from which all knowledge could be deduced by way of symbolic logic, as well as by comparison and analogy. These absolute principles were the Divine Attributes (or Dignities) and their various correlatives or predicates. In the original iteration of the Art, the *Ars compendiosa inveniendi veritatem* (Short art for the discovery of truth), Llull posited sixteen Dignities; but in the final, simplified version, the *Ars generalis ultima*, there were only nine: Goodness, Greatness, Eternity, Power, Wisdom, Will, Virtue, Truth, and Glory. For Llull, these Dignities were the active powers that pervade, to varying degree, the entire Aristotelian scale of being, connecting, as through a chain, all of the material and immaterial creation from the stars and angels all the way down to the four elements. Llull's Art arranges these dignities in a circular "First Figure" (Prima Figura), identified by the letter "A," in which each Dignity is assigned a further distinct alphabetical letter: Goodness [Bonitas] = B; Greatness [Magnitudo] = C; Duration [Duratio] = D; Power [Potestas] = E; Wisdom [Sapientia] = F; Will [Voluntas] = G; Virtue [Virtus] = H; Truth [Veritas] = I; and Glory [Gloria] = K (see fig. 9). The letter "A" represents a trinity, namely Essence (essentia), Unity (unitas), and Perfection (perfectio). Similarly, the nine correlatives (*relata*) are also assigned alphabetical letters and arranged in a geometric figure, identified by the letter "T," consisting of three triangles that form another circle. They are Difference (Differentia = B); Concordance (Concordantia = C); Contrariety (Contrarietas = D); Beginning (Principium = E), Middle (Medium = F); End

(Finis = G); Majority (Majoritas = H); Equality (Aequalitas = I); and Minority (Minoritas = K) (see fig. 9). These Dignities and Correlatives arranged in geometrical figures are supplemented by two tables with sets of "questions" (quaestiones) and "subjects" (subjecta) about which the Art generates knowledge, namely the Divine World (Deus = B); the Angelic World (Angelus = C); the Celestial World (Coelum = D); the Human World (Homo = E); the Imagination (Imaginativa = F); the Animal World (Sensitiva = G); the Vegetable World (Vegetativa = H); the Elemental World (Elementativa = I); and the Arts and Sciences (Instrumentativa = K). Thus, in the *Ars demonstrativa* of 1283, Llull explained the application of his Art to natural philosophy as a tool for unlocking all secrets of nature:

> Whoever has become skilled in the use of the Art and follows its principles, according to the doctrine given above, will know how, with the help of A to discover the secrets of nature, and he will have knowledge of A S T V X Y Z, as well as of how to devise and compile books. Moreover, he will know how to find out whether there is error in ancient sciences, and whether those who discovered them did so with true doctrine or devised them in accordance with natural sense; for this Art will give him rule and doctrine by which to know whether in some way they erred out of ignorance, and it will make their science more loved in those aspects in which their intellects did not deviate from the path of truth.[46]

Through the rotation and combination of its geometric figures, the Art can discover a solution for virtually any problem. The countless applications that Llull wrote to each new phase of his Art translate these mathematical combinations into prose, typically resulting in rather formulaic exercises that fill thousands of pages.[47]

In order to illustrate the notion of a fundamental unity of human knowledge and its correspondence to the structure of the cosmos for a nonacademic audience, Llull introduced into his Art the famous metaphor of the tree—with its roots, trunk, branches, leaves, and fruits—in a tract written in Rome in 1295, the *Arbor scientiae* (The tree of knowledge). The eighteen roots of the tree represent the nine transcendent principles and the nine relative principles, which correspond to the Nine Dignities and Nine Correlatives of the Art, the foundation of a unified pansophy about creation. The sixteen branches of the tree correspond to the various *subjecta* of the Art, each bearing a fruit with a label (*vegetalis, sensualis, imaginalis,* and so on) (see fig. 10). As Mary Franklin Brown has written, Llull's metaphor of the tree of knowledge would become the "paradigm of encyclopedism" in the late Scholastic encyclopedic tradition and would still be further elaborated during the sixteenth and seventeenth centuries by Descartes and Bacon. The objective of the Llullian "book about everything" was the "exhaustive coverage, the ordered presentation of material, the dissemination of knowledge beyond traditionally learned circles, and the conversion of souls."[48]

Figure 10. The Llullian *Arbor scientiae*. (In *Raymvndi Lvllii maioricensis opvs nvperrime recognitvm reuisum et correctum* [Lyon: ex officina Ioannis Pillehotte, 1535]. Courtesy of Universidad Complutense, Madrid.)

While the Art has thus applications to virtually all fields of Scholastic knowledge, its overriding purpose for Llull always remained its service as an aid to the missionary in the conversion of unbelievers and to prove, by rational means, the truth of the Christian faith. Whereas St. Francis had, according to hagiographic tradition, converted Muslims through living example that aroused admiration for Christian piety and charity, Llull's intention was to convert through intellectual arguments, respectful dialogue, and "necessary reasons."[49] Although the art is patently based on the principles of Aristotelian science, Llull rejected some of Aristotle's basic tenets, such as the ontological separation between the supra- and sublunar world, between the spiritual and the material, and between the creator and creation, all of which are joined through the Neoplatonic chain of the divine Dignitites and their Correlates. Llull's system was hereby strongly indebted to the Franciscan tradition of natural theology, especially Bonaventure's notion of *reductio artium ad theologiam*.[50] Like Bonaventure, Llull also utterly rejected the Averroist notion of a "double-truth"—which held that reason and faith be treated as separate realms—then dominant among the theology faculty at the University of Paris, with whom Llull was at war throughout his life. But Llull also rejected Thomist natural law metaphysics, which (as we saw) attempted a compromise between the Franciscans' notion of *reductio* and the Parisian Averroists' "double-truth" through a nested hierarchy of laws—divine law, natural law, and human law.

Metaphor and Medicine

Llull's Art aims to convert unbelievers to Christianity not only through the visual art of symbolic logic and rational demonstration but also by way of analogy. He often described this analogical mode of argumentation as "metaphor," which he defines as "one thing signifying another."[51] Interestingly, his most elaborate treatment of metaphor appears in a book on medicine, the *Principles of Medicine* (1273). In the Second "Distinction" (or part) of that work, he included a section that deals with "fever, urine, pulse, and metaphor." He explains that urine, pulse, and appetite are all "metaphors" in the sense that they are accidents, examples, and signs by which the causes of diseases such as fever can be diagnosed and accidents of health can be revealed. By grasping the metaphorical dimension of medicine, human understanding is enhanced not only in the realm of medicine itself but also in all the other arts, such as theology and natural philosophy. As an example he offers the classic case of magnetism: "You see a magnet attract iron, but do you know why it does so? Because in a magnet earth is closer to its simplicity than in any other species, and iron contains more earth than any other element, and this is why the earth in the iron is impelled towards its simple nature in the magnet."[52] Once readers have understood that principle, they can understand the relationship between scammony and choler through analogy—or, as Llull puts it "metaphorically": For "the choler existing in your body in excessive quantity is impelled towards the scammony which you have drunk, and the scammony is impelled towards the choler."[53] Thus, he concludes, "if by means of iron and the magnet you can understand this simile, then you know how to lift up your understanding by means of metaphor. . . . As a result of what you understand in medicine, you can, by the use of metaphor, understand that in theology virtue accords with the midpoint between two extremes, and vice with the extreme."[54] In Distinction Ten of *Principles,* he further theorizes metaphor as "a method for uplifting the intellect in this as well as in other arts, for metaphor gives the intellect the power to understand, since at one and the same time it turns on several different species." Through metaphor, what is said in the art about medicine, "the reader can understand other things that have to do with the sciences of theology, law, and nature, as well as with other sciences by which the intellect is uplifted to understand."[55]

In order to make sense of the assertion that the metaphorical system of the Art enables the use of medico-pharmaceutical theory in illuminating theological truth, it is important to remember that Llull uses the word "metaphor" not in the modern sense of an arbitrary invention of similitude between two things through language but a metaphysically "real" similitude based on the notion that the entire elemental world is pervaded by the divine principles, to a greater or lesser degree, depending on where on the scale of creation a thing or being is located (i.e., at what "distance" it is from God). Thus, celestial things are higher on the scale of creation than are sublunary things. This pervasion is the effect of the act of creation, in which God imprinted himself on the world like a seal upon wax: "The seal which imprints the similitudes of its letters on the wax pours its influence into the similitudes (*similitudines influit*) which are not of the essence of the seal. For the seal does not put anything of its essence into the wax; for the letters which are on the seal are of its essence and do not leave it."[56] If these imprints constitute the "proper" qualities of every natural thing, it also has what Llull calls "appropriated" qualities, which can be either "common" (i.e., not particular to a thing) or "specific" (i.e., particular to a thing). As Joseph Ziegler has noted, Llull's thought is, in this respect, closely related to that of his contemporary Arnald of Villanova, whom he had met in 1308. But Llull went even further than Arnald in arguing that "medicine's metaphorical dimension fashioned it into an important instrument for deciphering divine truths."[57] Thus, in the epilogue to his preaching guide, *Ars abbreviate praedicandi,* Llull wrote, "It is a book to which law, natural philosophy, medicine and the liberal and mechanical arts could be applied."[58] In order to be effective, preaching must be done in a "knowledgeable way" (*scire predicare scientifice*), moving in subject matter up and down the entire chain of creation, even to include examples from profane wisdom.

The encyclopedic conception of knowledge in preaching necessary for the art of conversion also informs his catechistical works, such as the *Doctrina pueril,* which Llull had written for juveniles. It is addressed to "my beloved son," though this must probably be understood in a generic sense, as it is a common formula that can frequently be found in the Solomonic Proverbs and in the Hermetic tradition. The book is divided into two parts. The first sixty-seven chapters are strictly catechistical in nature, including the Articles of the Faith, the Ten Commandments, and deadly sins, and so on. The hundred chapters comprising the second part, however, are encyclopedic in nature, treating such subjects as law, the liberal and mechanical arts, as well as the soul, the body, and the seven ages. However, this text also puts into perspective the project of Llull's art of peaceful persuasion illustrated by the *Book of the Gentile and the Three Wise Men.* Thus, in chapter 83, which deals with the conversion of infidels, he writes that "conversion means to lead infidels to the path of truth." For this purpose, one needs "three things: power, wisdom, and will."[59] He especially recommends beginning the effort to convert infidels with the forcible conversion of their children:

> Beloved Son, the will of God gives you the power to convert infidels. And because it is a good thing to convert an infidel according to the goodness, justice, mercy, empathy, and magnanimity, the divine will must will it. Because God wills it, He has given power to the pope and the cardinals and all of his prelates and priests in form of riches, servants, and wise men who have the necessary knowledge. There are many Jews and Saracens in Christian dominions who have no knowledge of the catholic faith, despite the fact that the Christians have the power to force the children of the infidels to learn the faith, so that they would know it. Through this knowledge, they would understand that they are in error, whereby they would in turn be converted and perhaps convert others. A prelate or lord who does not undertake this [the forcible conversion of children] because he is afraid that the infidels might quit his lands loves his worldly possessions more than the honor of God and the salvation of his fellow men.[60]

As can be seen from this passage, Llull's apparent ideal of respectful interfaith dialogue should not be mistaken as evidence of religious tolerance. In modern scholarship, he has sometimes been seen as a "pacifist," due to the fact that his Art was designed to convert by the force not of arms but of reason.[61] However, for Llull, military conquest and religious coercion were not in contradiction with Christian conversion; rather, they were complementary. Gentiles, Jews, and Muslims were afflicted by the disease of unbelief that will lead them into damnation, whether they were willing to accept it or not; and only conversion, by whatever means, to the true faith could cure and save them. If conversion did not succeed in those territories controlled by Christians, Llull advocated expulsion.[62] For Llull, both the *modo bellandi* and the *modo convertendi* were hereby necessary and integral to the *ordinatio* that would bring about the unification and salvation of the world.[63] The Christian militancy of Llull's missionary project increasingly came to the fore in his calls for a new crusade in his later tracts, such as *Liber de fine* (1305) and in the *Liber de acquisitione Terrae Sanctae* (1309). In these writings, the utopian optimism that characterized his earlier works, both in his fictional and scientific writings, gives way to disillusioned alarm and prophetic apocalypticism. We will return to one of these works—the *Liber de civitate mundi* (1314)—in chapter 5, in the context of the canon law tradition of *papa vicarius Christi,* by which popes donated non-Christian territories to Christian lords. As we will see in the final section of this chapter, it is this prophetic apocalypticism, as well as his chivalric ethos as a missionary, and the combinatory logic of his art that made Llull the perfect "auctoritas" to whom to attribute works of alchemy that would become enormously influential in the Llullian renaissance during European age of expansionism.

Pseudo-Llullism: The Llullification of Alchemy and the Alchemification of the *Ars luliana*

The historical Llull, it appears, did not practice alchemy; he wrote no treatises specifically on the subject; and those of his writings that dealt with metals caution against alchemy. For example, in book 6 of his *Felix: or the Book of Wonders,* which is written in form of a dialogue between "a philosopher" and the young protagonist named Felix who had been sent out into the world by his father so that he would "wonder[] at the wonders of the world" and "inquire[] about whatever he did not understand,"[64] the philosopher explains that transmutation is impossible to achieve by artificial means, "for nature needs all her powers to do it."[65] From this, it is patent that the historical Llull, like Thomas Aquinas, did not think that human art could equal or surpass nature in effecting change. But despite the historical Llull's disavowal, a large corpus of alchemical writings was attributed to him spuriously after his death, beginning with the famous *Testamentum* (1332), originally written in Catalan and translated into Latin in the fifteenth century. The author did not identify himself as Llull and is still unknown today. Some of the Catalan manuscripts contain an epilogue in which the author claims that the *Testamentum* was composed in St. Katherine's Church, opposite the Tower of London, during the reign of an "Edward of Woodstock" in the year 1332, while some Latin versions add that the text was translated from the Catalan in the Priory of St. Bartholomew in London in 1443.[66] In light of the patent inaccuracy of much of the historical information contained in the epilogue, it is altogether unlikely that the *Testamentum* was actually composed in England. But whatever the location of its composition, its author was evidently familiar with Llull's authentic works, as he explicitly refers to some of them and makes use of figures and alphabetical symbols that are similar (though not identical) to those devised by Llull.[67] He also identifies himself as the author of two other fourteenth-century alchemical works, the *Liber de intentione alchimistarum* and the *Liber lapidarii* (both of which were later also attributed to Llull); and he refers to Arnald of Villanova as the author of the *Rosarius*.[68] From this, Michela Pereira, the foremost authority on the pseudo-Llullian alchemical tradition, has concluded that the author of the *Testamentum* must have been an experienced alchemist, possibly a physician at the medical faculty of Montpellier, where Arnald's writings were introduced into the curriculum in 1309.[69]

Although there are considerable textual variations across the numerous extant manuscript traditions and print editions, Pereira, in her introduction to a modern edition of the *Testamentum*, concludes that the original manuscript must have contained four parts: *Theoria, Practica;* the *Liber mercuriorum* (Book of mercury); and the *Practica de furnis*.[70] In the first part, the author elaborates on the natural principles underlying alchemy: the temperaments of the four Aristotelian elements; the processes of corruption in the sublunary world resulting from wrong mixtures; and the alchemical theory and preparation of a universal medicine—the elixir, fifth essence, or Philosophers' Stone—as a cure for all ills; its division and dissolution into mercury and sulfur; and so on. The author hereby follows the scheme of Roger Bacon but also makes two significant deviations from Bacon's tradition that reflect the distinctly Llullian influence that I have already mentioned in the last chapter with regard to John of Rupescissa, who probably borrowed some of the alchemical theory elaborated in his *Consideration of the Fifth Essence* (composed in 1356) from the author of the *Testamentum* (1332). The first deviation pertains to the theory of the quintessence: in the Llullian's (and John's) alchemical theory, the realm of the quintessence is no longer confined to the superlunary world but pervades the entire cosmos, though existing in a form less pure in the sublunary world, where it is mixed with the corrupted four elements. This concept of an all-pervasive quintessence seems to derive from the historical Llull's Neoplatonic notion of the divine Dignities pervading all of creation. Lynn Thorndike has called the absorption of this idea by alchemical theory the "Llullification" of alchemy in the course of the fourteenth century.[71] This Llullification of alchemy had important implications for the history of science. As we have seen, during the Middle Ages, alchemy had primarily been a technical art belonging to the branch of meteorology and was therefore confined to the Aristotelian sublunary world. By contrast, Llullian alchemy held out the possibility that the laws of physics applied equally to the entire cosmos, hereby pointing to a way beyond the Aristotelian ontological separation between the sub- and superlunary spheres, ultimately leading to the fusion between alchemy and astrology in Neoplatonic occult philosophy during the early modern period. The idea of one principle ruling the entire cosmos was also crucial to the pre-Socratic notion of an atomistic structure of matter. But whereas the pre-Socratics thought that atoms were eternal (and that "nothing came from nothing") and that their collisions and combinations were random (by "mere chance"), medieval pseudo-Aristotelian Christian alchemists such as the Pseudo-Llull of the *Testamentum* subscribed to the metaphysical notion that the quintessence was originally created by God "de nihilo" and divided into three different levels or grades of purity.[72] The purest level was reserved for the angels; next came the heavens, stars, and planets; and the lowest level of purity was given to the sublunary world. An analogous gradation of purity applies to the elemental world, which is divided by the Creator into a five-level hierarchy. The purest level is called the "quintessence of the elements" (*quintam substanciam elementorum*) which is followed, in descending order, by fire, air, water, and earth. Originally, the four elements all contained the same admixture of quintessence, but resulting from the Fall, they have been corrupted and will continue to degenerate until Judgment Day, when only the quintessence will survive the universal conflagration.[73] But despite its lower level of purity there, quintessence is present in sublunary matter, including human bodies, and can be extracted (or separated) by way of alchemical distillation.

From this theory of the quintessence emerges in the *Testamentum* a radically expanded conception of alchemy itself, which is reflected in the practical part of the text. As the author explains on the first page of *Practica,* alchemy is "a hidden part of natural philosophy, very necessary, and a basic art which cannot be learned by just anyone. It teaches us how to change all precious stones by returning them [*reducere*] to their true balance of qualities; how to bring human bodies to their healthiest condition; and how to transmute all metals into the true sun and the true moon [i.e., gold and silver] by means of a unique body, a universal medicine, to which all particular medicines are reduced."[74]

Whereas for Bacon and Arnald the value of alchemy had inhered primarily in its medical applications to the human body—specifically, the prolongation of life—the author of the *Testamentum* postulates the quintessence's universal efficacy for the curing not only of human diseases but also of the corruption of metals and gems, as well as of all organic matter.[75] What's more, the quintessence can pass on its perfection to every being simply through contact. The regenerative process is the same throughout creation, the author explains, and can be effected through the four basic alchemical operations or regimens (*regiminis*): dissolving, washing, coagulating, and fixing. In Llullian fashion, each operation and substance is assigned an alphabetical letter that functions as a mnemonic device. For example, "A" stands for dissolving; "B" stands for common mercury; "C" for saltpeter; "D" for vitriol; and so on. Using these figures, the author offers detailed instructions on how to produce the elixirs of mercury and medicinal waters curing all diseases; how to dissolve pearls into a paste from which larger and more precious pearls can be artificially made; as well as how to use vinegar, ferments, and salts in the alchemical opus.

The foundation of the entire pseudo-Llullian alchemical corpus, the *Testamentum* is an important text in the history of alchemy at large, transforming the secret art into a comprehensive philosophical system for the perfection of nature, including but not limited to the human body. But despite (or perhaps because of) the author's innovations, subsequent Llullian alchemists writing during the first part of the fourteenth century found it necessary to emphasize the connections between the *Testamentum* and the alchemical traditions of Arnald and Bacon. Thus, in the *Ars operativa medica,* a "Raymond" claims to present two treatises that have been given to him under secret seal from a "King Robert," who had in turn received them from Arnald. Also, this Raymond claims that he had himself learned many alchemical secrets from Arnald directly.[76] Thus, the *Ars operativa* is a compilation of four brief treatises on the medicinal virtues and applications of the *aqua medicinales* produced in the distillation of spirits, in the tradition of Arnald. Similarly, in another early fourteenth-century alchemical text that is presented as the *Codicillus* to the *Testamentum,* the author explained that Llull was converted, late in his life, to a belief in alchemy by Arnald, hereby apparently attempting to account for the explicit skepticism about alchemy in Llull's authentic writings.[77] The author claims to be the same person who had written the *Testamentum,* as well as the *Liber de intentione alchimistarum*. This claim seems plausible in light of certain similarities between the *Testamentum* and the *Codicillus*: like the author of the *Testamentum* (and unlike the author of the *Ars operativa*), the author of the *Codicillus* does not identify himself as Llull but makes use of figures, tables, and alphabets that are reminiscent of Llull's Art; also, like the *Testamentum,* the *Codicillus* posits a correspondence between the human body (microcosm) and the world at large (the macrocosm) and even develops an analogy between human generation and the four-stage alchemical process. More so than the *Testamentum,* however, the *Codicillus* emphasizes the spiritual dimension of alchemy. Thus, the author writes, "And as Jesus Christ, of the house of David, assumed human nature for the liberation and salvation of mankind, who, for Adam's transgression, were in the bonds of sin, so will that which has been wrongfully defiled by one thing be absolved by its contrary; it will be cleaned and delivered from that stain."[78] The *Codicillus* may be one of the earliest texts to elaborate the analogy between the saving grace of Jesus Christ and the miraculous effects of alchemical Philosophers' Stone—an analogy that would become an increasingly prominent feature of the alchemical tradition in the course of the fourteenth century (as we have already seen in the example of Ullmann). Also, the author further refines the *Testamentum*'s theory of the quintessence by explaining that the first matter (*prima materia*) of Genesis consisted in fact of divine mercury, of which the "fifth essence" was a lower form. It is this divine mercury that causes the vitality and activity of each material body and can be alchemically extracted in order to transform and perfect other bodies.[79] Finally, the author also introduces the important motif of the divine inspiration of the alchemist, whose discovery of the secrets of nature are the result of divine revelation. As we have seen, this late medieval motif of the "Fool for God" was already a commonplace in the authentic Llullian corpus. It would have a long tradition in the history of alchemy that culminates in the sixteenth century with Paracelsus's notion of "Elias Artista," his name for the Prophet Elijah cum alchemical adept who will return to prepare the world for the Second Coming.[80]

Although the author of the *Testamentum* and the *Codicillus* was clearly familiar with the alchemical writings attributed to Bacon and Arnald, his notion of an admixture of quintessence in the four sublunary elements developed in the early Llullian alchemical tracts marks an important innovation in alchemical theory. He hereby also parts ways with the tradition of John of Rupescissa, perhaps the most important alchemist of the fourteenth century, who saw the quintessence as entirely separate from the terrestrial elements. Nevertheless, during the second part of the fourteenth century, another Llullian author attempted a synthesis of the alchemy of John of Rupescissa, based on the distillation of wine, with the elemental theory of the *Testamentum* in the tract *Liber de secretis naturae seu de quinta essencia.* Consistent with the Llullian motif of the "Fool for God," the author begins the tract by introducing a despondent Llull walking in deserted places and lamenting that the world scorns the travails he has suffered for the progress of the Christian faith and even derides him as a crazy person.[81] Then, however, he meets a Benedictine monk who praises his "great wisdom" (*magna scientia*) and his great art that has converted many infidels. The monk encourages Llull to write down the alchemical secrets that he has unlocked through his Art of logic. The epilogue returns to this theme, after a *Tertia distinctio* of "questions" (*questiones*) has explained the use of the Llullian system of combinatory logic for the discovery of alchemical secrets. Thus, the monk expresses his admiration for the alchemical book that Llull has written but scolds him for expressing skepticism in his writings about the possibility of alchemical transmutation.[82]

Whereas Rupescissa was concerned primarily with the medicinal application of the quintessence, the author of the *Liber* elaborates the theory of transmutation as found in the *Testamentum* and the *Codicillus*. He is also the first author explicitly to ascribe the *Testamentum* to Ramón Llull, which has led historians to see the *Liber* as the starting point of the pseudo-Llullian tradition proper. Although the *Liber* is clearly influenced by Rupescissa's *De consideratione quinta essentia,* it would eventually supersede it, and Rupescissa's ideas would become ascribed to Llull.[83] Like the author of the *Testamentum* (and unlike Rupescissa), the author of the *Liber* regarded the quintessence as a perfectly balanced mixture of the four elements. Thus, he largely replaces Rupescissca's references to *caelum* (the superlunary realm) with references to blood (*menstruum*) and "our mercury" (*noster Mercurius*) as the first agent of alchemical transmutation. Nevertheless, the author followed Rupescissa's compositional model in dividing his text into three "books" that explain the alcoholic distillation of the quintessence and its various applications, including the curing of illnesses such as leprosy, paralysis, and fevers, as well as the transmutation of metals and stones. In accordance with the Llullian tradition, the author of the *Liber* explains alchemical operations and principles in the symbolic terms of an alphabetical code, which functions as a mnemonic device that is supposed to enable the alchemist to discover the secrets of nature. In addition, the text also includes a prologue and an epilogue, each of which is presented in the form of a dialogue in the Llullian style of the *Arbor scientiae* and explains the consistency between Llullian natural theology and alchemy.

As Pereira has observed, the Llullian Art and the dynamic conception of nature underlying its philosophy probably appealed to fourteenth-century alchemists because it offered a coherent system opening "the possibility of thinking" what alchemists attempted to make real: "the dynamics of the elements at the very first level of creation, *chaos,* which could be identified with first matter."[84] Indeed, here lies an important point of convergence between Llull's authentic natural philosophy and that of the alchemists who wrote under his name. Despite his skepticism about the possibility of alchemical transmutation, Llull shared with the alchemists the Aristotelian notion that all things, animate and inanimate, originated from an elemental first matter (*prima materia*), the chaos, from which all species and individual forms proceed through a continual process of separation and composition. This concept of first matter, which Llull had elaborated in his *Liber chaos* (ca. 1286), was of crucial importance for the alchemical idea of transmutation. As we have already seen in chapter 2, according to this idea, transmutation was not a *direct* change of one substance into another but a multistep process that included a *reduction,* or "leading back," of a given substance to the first degree of chaos through an alchemical operation that reverses the natural processes, enabling the alchemist to start the process anew according to his design through the artificial imitation and manipulation of natural separation and composition through art. This remains a constant feature of virtually all the alchemical texts attributed to Llull. All of these works made various extraordinary claims for the art of alchemy, but the central idea was the notion of the "elixir," or Philosophers' Stone, an agent of transmutation that perfected metals, cured diseases, and prolonged Christian lives.

A second important point of convergence between Llull's authentic works and the pseudo-Llullian alchemical corpus is that both placed science fully in the service of evangelization and religious messianism. And like the alchemical texts attributed to Joachim of Fiore, those attributed to Llull were hereby frequently apocalyptic in character. By the sixteenth century, the legend of Llull the alchemist missionary would take on many additional fanciful embellishments. According to one version recorded in the sixteenth century by the Venetian Ettore Ausonio (ca. 1520–ca. 1570), Llull had been converted from his early skepticism about alchemy into a believer by Arnald of Villanova during an accidental meeting in Rome. While Arnald taught Llull the technical aspects of alchemy, Llull, as a great magus, natural philosopher, and prophet, taught Arnald the theoretical understanding of the art of transmutation, which had been divinely revealed to him during a stay in Athens, when he came across a book with seven seals written by King Solomon. The result of this professional exchange between the artisan Arnald and the magus Llull was that alchemy became a true "science," meaning that it combined practice with theory. The divine origin of Llullian alchemy, Ausonio argued, equates it to a latter-day revelation that even sheds new light on the meaning of some of the mysterious passages of Scripture, such as the one concerning the heavenly Jerusalem. Renowned for such perfect knowledge, Llull is invited to England by an "Abbot Cremer," whose (equally spurious) "testament," the *Testamentum Cremeri,* was allegedly the original source of this portion of the story related by Ausonio. Once arrived in England, Llull performed alchemical transmutations for a "King Edward," who had promised that he would use the gold Llull produced for the launch of another crusade to reconquer Jerusalem. However, the duplicitous and power-hungry English king used the alchemical gold instead to start yet another war with France and had Llull imprisoned when he registered his protest.[85]

As we saw, the historical Llull had also advocated for crusade in his later life, despite the ostensibly irenic method of his art of conversion based on Aristotelian empiricism and syllogistic reason, as well as a Neoplatonic metaphysics of correspondences. However, pseudo-Llullian alchemists gradually dissolved the realist metaphysics and deductive logic on which Llull's original Neoplatonic system depended. Whereas Bacon, Arnald, and John of Rupescissa had devised alchemical formulas intended to strengthen Christian bodies in the apocalyptic battles of the final days, the Renaissance Llullians conceived of their art as salvific in analogy to the passion of Christ in evangelical and educational projects that were equally apocalyptic in inspiration. We may conclude this chapter, then, by amending Lynn Thorndike's assessment of the significance of pseudo-Llullism for the history of science in terms of the "Llullification" of alchemy. In chapter 2, we have seen how alchemical theory of matter differed from Thomist hylomorphism: whereas the Thomists presumed that all matter will receive its predetermined substantial form naturally—guided by the forces of natural laws—alchemical theory of matter presumed that the natural process of the formation of matter into the substantial forms that God intended at Creation has been corrupted by sin. As a result, there were, in the postlapsarian world, not one but multiple substantial forms toward which matter moved naturally. Worse, since human reason is similarly subject to the processes of corruption, man cannot even distinguish any longer between the substantial forms originally created by God and those produced by the Devil's illusionary counterfeits and fabrications. In this chapter, we traced the twofold and bidirectional consequences of the confluence between the *ars luliana* of converting souls and the alchemy of converting material substances in the fourteenth and fifteenth centuries for the history of Scholastic metaphysics and the history of science. On the one hand, the "Llullification" of alchemy turned a technical art of meteorology into a universal natural philosophy explaining all cosmic (sub- and superlunary) phenomena according to the same principles. On the other hand, the "alchemification" of the *ars luliana* fused Llull's original metaphysical system—predicated on a staunchly Neoplatonic realism—with a Franciscan tradition of metaphysical nominalism that emerged with the attacks on Thomism by William of

Ockham in the early fourteenth century and would become increasingly dominant in the faculty of theology at Paris for the coming century. As we will see, this coalescence between Llullism, pseudo-Llullian alchemy, and Franciscan metaphysical nominalism would have important consequences for the rise of a missionary science in the sixteenth century in the context of the European spiritual conquest of America.

Part II

The Alchemy of Conquest

4

The Secrets of the World
Christopher Columbus's Ecstatic Materialism

> Gold is most excellent.... Gold constitutes treasure, and he who possesses it may do what he will in the world,... and may so attain as to bring souls to Paradise.
> —Christopher Columbus, "Letter from Jamaica," July 7, 1503

A Key to the Secrets of the World

Marooned off a beach in Jamaica, his ships ruined by worms and termites, his crew decimated by Indian raids, disease, and three hurricanes, a desperate Christopher Columbus penned, on July 7 1503, a letter to the Catholic Monarchs in which he lamented the string of ordeals and disasters that had befallen him during his fourth and final transatlantic voyage. He relates how, at one particularly desperate moment of the journey off the coast of Panama the previous May, he had climbed the top mast of his ship and fallen asleep there "in a high fever and in a state of great exhaustion," when he heard a voice exhorting him in the following manner:

> "O fool and slow to believe and to serve your God, the God of all! What more did He for Moses or for His servant David? Since you were born, ever has He had you in His most watchful care. When He saw you of an age with which He was content, He caused your name to sound marvelously in the land. The Indies, which are so rich a part of the world, He gave you for your own; you have divided them as it pleased you, and He enabled you to do this. Of the barriers of the Ocean Sea, which were closed with such mighty chains, He gave you the key; and you were obeyed in many lands and among the Christians you have gained honorable fame. What did He more for the people of Israel when He brought them out of Egypt? Or for David, whom from a shepherd He made to be king in Judea?"

"I heard all this," Columbus continued, "as if I were in a trance [*ansí amorteçido*], but I had no answer to give to words so true, but could only weep for my errors. He, whoever he was, who spoke to me, ended saying: 'Fear not; have trust; all these tribulations are written upon marble and are not without cause.'"[1]

Who was it that spoke to Columbus in May 1503, placing him in line with Moses and David as well as revealing to him the providential significance of his art of navigation as a "key" to the "mighty chains" of the ocean sea unlocking the riches of the Indies? Columbus's modern biographers and most historians of the European discovery of America have generally eschewed this question, embarrassed as they were by the great discoverer's apparent descent into religious mysticism and perhaps even madness in his final years. Foundational modern scholarship such as Samuel Eliot Morison's landmark biography *Admiral of the Ocean Sea* (1942) and popular media such as Ridley Scott's Hollywood movie *1492: The Conquest of Paradise* (1992) alike have portrayed a Columbus committed to scientific empiricism, progress, and secular Enlightenment, a "modern" man who stood opposed to the "medieval" Scholasticism and religious fanaticism of his age. Similarly, more recent revisionist accounts of Columbus's enterprise have failed to take seriously the role that prophecy and religion played in his writings and in the history of the European discovery of America more generally. From the seminal and erudite studies of Edmundo O'Gorman in the 1950s and 1960s to Stephen Greenblatt's brilliant New Historicist reading in *Marvelous Possessions* as well as some of the sharp indictments by Kirkpatrick Sale and David Stannard in the 1990s, revisionist historiography has either dismissed Columbus's religious mysticism as an inconsequential vestige of medievalism or explained it away as a mere rhetorical strategy of a hard-nosed businessman, shameless self-promoter, and ruthless exploiter attempting to appeal to his zealous audience, the Catholic Monarchs, Ferdinand and Isabella.[2]

Historians of medieval religion and Christian eschatology, by contrast, have long taken seriously Columbus's prophetic mysticism. Scholars such as Marcel Bataillon, James Phelan, Alain Milhou, Pauline Moffitt Watts, Margarita Zamora, James Romm, and Valerie Flint have left little doubt about the important role that Scriptural prophecy, Old Testament geography, and medieval millenarianism played in the conception of Columbus's enterprise of "reaching east by going west." As these scholars have shown, it is a mistake to dismiss Columbus's expressions of religious mysticism as a mere rhetorical ruse. Messianic, apostolic, and chiliastic ideas were rampant in the age of European discovery and expansionism, pervading not only Columbus's official correspondence with the Catholic Monarchs and the court but also his private readings, evident in the marginalia he left in his books, many of which are preserved in the magnificent library begun by his son Hernando and today located in the Biblioteca Capitular y Colombina, adjacent to the cathedral of Seville. Owing to this body of scholarship, we now have a clear sense of Columbus's profound conviction that his discovery of a route to "India" would lay the groundwork for the universal conversion of all people, the Christian recovery of Jerusalem, as well as the advent and eventual defeat of the Antichrist, the Second Coming of Christ, and the apocalypse. Thus, Moffitt Watts has convincingly argued that it was Columbus's "personal spirituality or the spirituality of his age [that] inspired him to undertake his voyages of discovery."[3]

But what sort of spirituality was it that could make a connection between the Second Coming of Christ and voyages of discovery in a hunt for riches, gold, and spices? After all, Christian Scriptures, as well as the church fathers and doctors, taught that this world was vain, and Christian millenarian movements during the High Middle Ages had been inspired by a radical protest against the church's corruption by worldliness and wealth, by a primitivist yearning for a return to an otherworldly spirituality and to the ideal of apostolic poverty exemplified by the life of Jesus Christ and the early church fathers. And how is it that, after being marginalized for centuries by Augustinian theology, radical traditions of millenarian prophecy could be mobilized for the cause of the acquisition of wealth, empire, and natural knowledge in the European age of discovery and expansionism? Although historians of religion have provided an important corrective to the general neglect of the spiritual dimensions of the European discovery of America long prevailing in the historiography about Columbus, they have fallen short of interrogating the epistemological and historical connections between religious prophecy and scientific discovery in the age of European expansionism. As a result, we are still left, by and large, with two Columbuses, both of whom are anachronisms: the "modern" and forward-looking Columbus familiar from the historiography of scientific discovery and the "medieval" and backward-looking Columbus familiar from the historiography of religion.

In order to discern the early modern relationship between prophecy and discovery, it is necessary to leave behind the purported oppositions between tradition and innovation, between the medieval and the modern, and attend to the way in which scientific innovations are enabled through hermeneutical practices of living traditions.[4] Significantly, Columbus invokes, in the same letter written from Jamaica, the most important millenarian and fervent advocate of apostolic poverty and monastic asceticism of the Middle Ages—the twelfth-century Calabrian monk Joachim of Fiore, who allegedly had prophesied that the Christian to reconquer Jerusalem and Mt. Zion would "come from Spain."[5] This Christian from Spain, Columbus proposed, was none other than his patron, King Ferdinand of Aragon, who would be enabled to reconquer

Jerusalem by the riches gained from the "enterprise of the Indies." While historians have long taken this reference as evidence of the "Joachimite roots" of Columbus's eschatological ideas, today we know that Joachim of Fiore never said that a Christian from Spain would restore the Holy Sepulchre to Christendom. This prophecy has been traced back not to the twelfth-century Calabrian mystic but to the thirteenth-century Valencian physician-turned-prophet Arnald of Villanova (1235?–1311), specifically to his *Tractatus de mysterio cymbalorum* (ca. 1300), a collection of millenarian prophecies about the Antichrist, his defeat, and the Second Coming that circulated widely among the Spanish Franciscans with whom Columbus associated. Although the prophecy about a Spanish messiah king restoring the Holy Land had indeed become attributed to Joachim of Fiore in this tradition since the mid-fourteenth-century commentaries by the Franciscan Spiritual John of Rupescissa, the fact that Columbus's knowledge of Joachimite prophecy was evidently mediated by the pseudo-Joachimite tradition of Arnald of Villanova and John of Rupescissa is significant, I would submit, as it suggests a little-noted prophetic context for understanding the voice heard by Columbus in 1503 and the spirituality of European expansionism more generally. For John of Rupescissa and Arnald of Villanova were discoverers not only of the secrets of Scripture but also of the secrets of nature; that is, they were renowned authorities not only on Christian eschatology but also on alchemy.

To be sure, the metaphor of the "key" had a long history in Neoplatonic Christian Scriptural exegesis (*clavis Scripturae sacrae*), in particular a tradition of millenarian exegesis that interpreted the "key of David" offered by Christ to the Sixth Church of Philadelphia in Revelation 3:7 as the key that would "open the door" to the hidden meaning of Scripture. But it was the writings of these late medieval alchemists that had synthesized the Christian millenarian tradition with (pseudo-)Aristotelian naturalism as it had been translated by the Hermetic tradition from the Arabic, thus providing a theological context in which early modern transoceanic exploration would be underwritten by apocalyptic significance.

In this chapter, I want to take seriously the question of who the prophet was who spoke to Columbus in 1503, revealing to him the providential role of his art of navigation as key to the riches of the world. I will argue that the spirituality of Christopher Columbus—and that of the European discovery and conquest of America more generally—is profoundly indebted not only to Judeo-Christian Scriptural or Joachimite prophecies proper but also to a late medieval tradition of what I will call "ecstatic materialism," a materialism underwritten by late medieval Christian spirituality that had derived from alchemy, particularly the (often pseudonymous) traditions of Villanova,

Rupescissa, as well as Roger Bacon and Ramón Llull. "Ecstasy" was, as Robert Lerner has shown, a rhetorical stance that pervaded much of the late medieval tradition in millenarian prophecy, especially that of Franciscan and lay prophets and who saw themselves in the tradition of Joachim of Fiore's notion of "spiritual intelligence." In this late medieval tradition, a "Fool for God" announced his (and also often her) illumination based on the notion that the "gift" of divine insight was "showered most copiously on the humble" (shepherds, fishers, and merchants, often semi-literate or illiterate in Latin).[6] But whereas the biblical prophets and early Christian chiliasts had seen their roles in Redemption history primarily as passive witnesses in the unfolding of the cosmic drama that would culminate in the destruction of worldly wealth and power, these late medieval/early modern alchemists saw themselves and their art as God's instruments and even active agents in the advent of the Eschaton: they would provide the apocalyptic Christian with the militant means of defeating the Antichrist and his minions, hereby preparing the ground for the Second Coming of Christ through the recapture of the Holy Sepulchre and the conversion of all peoples to Christianity. In this process, they had thoroughly synthesized Aristotelian naturalist inquiry and an empiricist hermeneutics of discovery with a Christian sense of apocalypse. While the pseudo-Joachimite tradition of alchemical prophecy provided hereby the apocalyptic and spiritual fuel for the scientific project of the prolongation of youthful life, the (pseudo-) Llullist tradition had forged (as we will see in chapter 5) a connection between alchemy, the Christian missionary enterprise, and the proto-ethnographic inquiry into non-Christian cultures and religions.[7]

Prophecy and Discovery in the *Book of Prophecies*

We can find much of the immediate context for the voice that Columbus reported hearing in his trance of 1503 in his *Book of Prophecies,* a collection of biblical texts and *auctoritates* drawn from the church fathers and doctors, as well as from late medieval theologians and scholars that he compiled with the help of the Carthusian monk Gaspar Gorricio. The materials collected there were chosen by these two men because they seemed to shed prophetic light on the theological and eschatological significance of the "enterprise of the Indies" in the broad scheme of salvation history. Columbus had begun working on this collection shortly after he returned in disgrace and in chains from his third voyage in 1500. No doubt this literary project was in part conceived as an effort to redeem himself in the eyes of the Catholic Monarchs, after having been indicted for abuses and mismanagement as governor of Hispaniola. But many of the materials collected there reflect his readings going back more than a decade, even before the embarkation on this first transatlantic voyage. Thus, some of the excerpts originate with annotations he had made during the 1480s in his copy of the *Historia rerum ubique gestarum* (pub. 1477) by Aeneas Sylvius Piccolomini (1405–1464), also known as Pope Pius II, who offered a digest of classical geography and Christian eschatology, as well as calls for another crusade in the Holy Land. Most intriguingly, it included an anecdote about "Indians" (Homines de Catayo) who had supposedly been shipwrecked off the coast of Galway in Ireland—suggesting to Columbus that the distance between Europe and Asia was quite short.[8]

Columbus sent a first draft of the *Book of Prophecies*, written partially in his own hand and partially in the hand of an anonymous "Italian scribe," to Gorricio, who added to it and returned it in 1502, in time for Columbus's embarkation on his fourth and final voyage. Columbus had the manuscript in his possession—probably still adding to it—at the time when he reported hearing the mysterious voice in his "Letter from Jamaica" to the Catholic Monarchs. It has been suggested that he intended to use these materials for a lengthy apocalyptic epic poem he was planning to write about his discoveries for the Catholic Monarchs but died before he was able to realize it.[9] However that may be, the manuscript of the *Book of Prophecies* was later completed by his son Hernando, who had accompanied his father on the last voyage as a thirteen-year-old boy. It is today preserved at the Biblioteca Colombina in the handwritings of the four men, though it was not published until the late nineteenth century.[10]

Although Columbus had no formal training in theology, there can be no doubt that the New Testament was one of the primary inspirations of his religiosity, especially of his apostolic messianism, eschatological expectancy, and the typological hermeneutics of reading Scripture that he probably learned from Gorricio's commentaries. Since his return from the first transatlantic voyage early in 1493, he had cultivated the notorious habit of signing his letters "Xpo Ferens," or the "Christ Bearer"—which is the Graeco-Latin form of his given name (Christoforo—Christophorus)—with a pyramidal arrangement of letters on the top (fig. 11).[11] Columbus's idea of himself as a pastoral "Christ Bearer" would later be popularized by Juan de la Cosa, the owner and captain of the *Santa Maria* (Columbus's flagship on this first voyage), who became a prominent cartographer. In his famous *Mappa mundi* of 1500, the first world map to incorporate the Americas, de la Cosa depicted an image of an itinerant Columbus carrying an apostolic staff in his hand and Christ on his shoulders (see fig. 12). Columbus never explained the significance of these letters in any of the surviving documents, and they have been the subject of much speculation by historians. Morison, for example, suggested that the initials of the first

Figure 11. Columbus's signature, detail. (Reproduced in Paul Lacroix, *Science and Literature in the Middle Ages and at the Period of the Renaissance* [London: Bickers and Son, 1877], 291.)

two lines may be expanded to read "Servus Sum Alitissimi Salvatoris" (Servant I am of the Most High Savior) and the third line as "Christ, Mary, and Joseph." Milhou, by contrast, read the final line as "Xpoforus—Maria—Yonnaes," the latter being the Latin form of John the Baptist, who had a substantial devotional following in fifteenth-century Italy.[12]

Whatever the intended meaning of these letters, it is patent that Columbus attached profound Christological significance to his name. Indeed, upon a first reading, the rebuke of the voice he reported hearing in his "Letter from Jamaica" seems to echo that of Jesus Christ himself. According to Luke 24:25–26, Jesus had, after his Crucifixion, rejoined in disguise his remaining eleven disciples, traveling downcast along the Road to Emmaus, and chastised them for their feeble faith: "O foolish and slow of heart to believe in all things, Which the prophets have spoken. Ought not Christ to have suffered these things and so, to enter into his glory?"[13] The *Book of Prophecies* suggests the special role that the Gospel of John played in Columbus's discovery of this Christological significance, including this passage from John 10 (14–16), which we find excerpted there: "I am the good shepherd; I know my sheep, and they know me. . . . I have other sheep who are not of this fold, and I must bring them, and they will hear my voice and there will be one fold and one shepherd."[14]

If the Gospel of John had provided the primary apostolic subtext for Columbus's literary representations of himself and his enterprise of the Indies in the *Book of Prophecies,* the excerpts from the last book of the New Testament, the "Revelation" or "Apocalypse" of John of Patmos (believed to be the same person as John the Evangelist in the fifteenth century), place Columbus's

Figure 12. Columbus as *Christum ferens* (Christ Bearer). (Detail in Juan de la Cosa's *Mappa mundi* [1500]. Reproduced from R. H. Major, ed., *Select Letters of Christopher Columbus* [London, 1870].)

role as a *Christum ferens* in a distinctly eschatological context. Indeed, Columbus's experience of a vision and a voice as recorded in his "Letter from Jamaica" is distinctly reminiscent of Revelation 1:9–10: "I, John, your brother and your partner in tribulation and in the kingdom and patience in Christ Jesus, was in the island which is called Patmos, for the word of God and for the testimony of Jesus. I was in the spirit on the Lord's day and heard behind me a great voice, as of a trumpet."[15]

On the one hand, the excerpts from John's Apocalypse in the *Book of Prophecies* place the recently discovered *"insulis maris"* (islands of the sea) in a typological relation to John's island of Patmos and Columbus himself in an analogous position to John as a prophet and witness of Christ. Thus, Columbus chose to excerpt verse 9, the moment when John's Apocalypse speaks in the first-person singular for the first time.[16] Similarly, the subsequent excerpts from the Apocalypse are concerned with the prophetic significance of the "islands" of the sea: "Every mountain and island has been moved from its place" (Apoc. 6); "Every island fled, and the mountains were not found" (Apoc. 16). On the other hand, Columbus's discoveries of a multitude of new islands in the ocean sea present a first step toward the fulfillment of John's chiliastic prophecy, in Revelation 21:1, of the coming of a "new heaven and a new earth" before the end of times in which "the unjust will not be able to live."[17] According to John's Apocalypse (20:4), there will be a time on earth when the human suffering and toil caused by Original Sin will be reversed by the Second Coming, when Satan will be bound for a thousand years during Christ's reign on earth, before his final uprising, the Last Judgment, and the end of the world: "And I saw seats. And they sat upon them: and judgment was given unto them. And the souls of them that were beheaded for the testimony of Jesus and for the word of God and who had not adored the beast nor his image nor received his character on their foreheads or in their hands. And they lived and reigned with Christ a thousand years."[18]

Finally, the excerpts from John's Apocalypse in the *Book of Prophecies* provide an important context also for Columbus's and Gorricio's late medieval/early modern hermeneutics of discovery, particularly regarding the analogy they saw between discovery through empirical experience and discovery through prophetic revelation. The idea of discovery in Columbus's project of "reaching East by going West" has been notoriously confusing, at least from a modern point of view.[19] On the one hand, Columbus's proposal for the discovery of a westerly route to the East was based on reasonable (though, as it turns out, false) deductions about the size of the earth from scientific authorities, including Roger Bacon, Pierre d'Ailly, and Aeneas Sylvius Piccolomini. From this point of view, Columbus's travels were an exercise in scientific "discovery" in the sense of a demonstration or making manifest that which could reasonably be deduced to be true based on the knowledge derived from tradition. Similarly, the East that he proposed to reach was already known to him and to Europeans (albeit anachronistically) from books such as Marco Polo's *Travels* and Mandeville's *Travels*. Thus, during his first transatlantic crossing, he thought he had landed on some islands off the coast of China and incessantly looked for signs of the great civilization of the Grand Khan known from the descriptions of medieval European travelers. As is well known, Columbus would die believing (or least insisting) that what he had found was not a new part of the world, hitherto unknown to Europeans, but a new way of reaching the other side of the Old World. In no sense of the word could any of the places he was *looking to find*—India, Cathay, Cipango—be construed as a "new" world, let alone a *terra nullius* (in Roman law, a land without an owner). The Grand Khan known from medieval travelers, though a pagan who had allegedly requested a papal mission to learn about Christianity, was doubtlessly the legitimate lord whose line had ruled for many centuries and who held undisputed rights of dominion. In fact, throughout the later Middle Ages, European hopes of a military triumph over a superior, advanced, and advancing world of Islam rested on the fantasy of an alliance with the even more powerful Mongol Empire of the Far East.

Yet, on the other hand, the *Capitulations of Santa Fe,* the contract that the Catholic Monarchs entered into with Columbus in the camp city set outside the recently fallen Moorish city of Granada in April 1492, "give[s] and grant[s]" to the latter "what he has discovered in the Ocean Seas and will discover on the voyage that now, with the help of God, he is to make on the same seas," further appointing him "admiral on all those islands and mainland discovered or acquired by his command and expertise in the Ocean Seas during his lifetime and, after his death, by his heirs and successor one after the other in perpetuity."[20] The odd distinction between "what he has discovered" and what he "will discover" in this document—drafted some four months before his embarkation on his first voyage—as well as the perplexing absence of any reference to Asia, have given rise to endless speculations about a "prediscovery"— the idea that Columbus had some secret foreknowledge of the existence of a hitherto unknown fourth part of the world, resulting either from one of his own voyages or from the voyage of some legendary "anonymous pilot" who, the story goes, discovered America after being blown off course in the eastern Atlantic and who imparted the news of his discovery to Columbus just before dying at the latter's house. A more plausible explanation is, perhaps, that of historians who have argued that the ambiguity of the Capitulations of Santa Fe was intentional, calculated to confound Portuguese spies.[21] While this is certainly possible, it is also important to keep in mind the semantic and epistemological openness (or ambiguity, from a modern point of view) in the idea of discovery in the fifteenth century. While ultimately hoping to make contact with the known civilizations of the East for the purpose of trade and military alliance, Columbus and the Catholic Monarchs also expected to find hitherto unknown islands on the way, which would be "discovered" only in the course of historical experience. Modern conspiracy theories positing that the rhetoric of discovery in the prediscovery documents are evidence of some prior knowledge of the existence of a fourth continent on the part of Columbus are the result of an anachronistic imposition of a modern hermeneutics of discovery upon the fifteenth century—a hermeneutics that was then only in the making. Columbus's later writings about his voyages of discovery—although they never relinquish the idea that he had found a way to Asia—provide a unique glimpse into the role that prophecy played in this epistemological formation in the context of the conquest of America.

Margarita Zamora has noted the conspicuous absence of any religious motives in the prediscovery documents, suggesting that, for the Catholic Monarchs, the commercial aspects of Columbus's project were of primary interest.[22] By contrast, the so-called "Proem" of Columbus's *Diario* from the first voyage suggests an interest of placing his project in a religious and spiritual context by bringing it into connection with the recently completed Reconquista. In the same year that the Jews were expelled from Spain and the last bastion of Islam fell at Granada, "Your Highnesses ... resolved to send me, Christopher Columbus, to the said regions of India to see the said princes and the peoples and lands and determine the nature of them and of all other things, and the measures to be taken to convert them to our holy faith; and you ordered that I should not go by land to the East, which is the customary route, but by way of the West."[23] As Zamora has pointed out, the "Proem" was not part of the original *Diario* but added later by the Dominican friar Bartolomé de las Casas (our only source) from another (and most likely now lost) letter that Columbus had written to the Catholic Monarchs before embarking on his first voyage. By the time Columbus and Gorricio composed the *Book of Prophecies* with the benefit of hindsight, the discovery of many hitherto unknown islands with millions of people who, though probably located somewhere on the way or close to China or India, were apparently not the subjects of any Christian or pagan lord known from textual traditions, had assumed providential significance the meaning of which could be found only in Scriptural prophecy. For Columbus and Gorricio, empirical discovery through historical experience and prophetic revelation are fundamentally similar in the sense that they are not based on a demonstration or "making manifest" of something that is already knowable by syllogistic reason or "science" (*scientia*); rather, both are predicated on an esoteric construction of the occult, on the idea of a providential penetration of something that is hidden, occult, and "secret." Gorricio's commentary on John's Apocalypse explains what the "Apostle [*sic*]" meant by the word "revealed" [*manifestatam*] by quoting from 2 Timothy 1:9–10: "'Not according to *our works,* but according to his purpose and grace, which was given to us through Jesus Christ an eternity ago, and now has been revealed through the coming of our Savior.' He [John] refers to the grace as given, when as yet the ones to whom it would be given did not exist, because in God's arrangement of events that which would take place in its own future time had already happened, therefore the Apostle says it has been 'revealed.'"[24]

Historical experiences that seem new to man's limited vision—bound as it is by time and space—are not new at all from the point of view of God's omniscient providence, where they have "already happened." Because they "already happened" (in the mind of God), future events still unknown from historical experience and unknowable through human reason can be known through the divinely inspired prophecies recorded in Scripture. In other words, Scriptural prophecies can serve as a sort of shortcut to knowledge of God's plan that would otherwise be revealed only gradually and slowly through historical experience. But because Scriptural prophecies are notoriously cryptic, they require a "key" in order to unlock their meaning. By the same logic, the meaning of any new empirical discovery defying scientific reason or tradition can be discovered in terms of a fulfillment of scriptural prophecy whose occult meaning has been revealed by historical experience. Both prophetic exegesis and new discoveries through empirical experience are thus similarly an "unravelling" of the mysteries of God's inscrutable purpose that remain ever elusive to the "science" of demonstration based on human understanding of natural law.

The model for Gorricio's typological reading was, of course, the Neoplatonist exegesis of St. Augustine, whose writings are excerpted and commentated copiously throughout the *Book of Prophecies*.[25] Just as latter-day historical experience is the fulfillment of New Testament prophecy, so were the historical events recorded in the New Testament Gospels the fulfillment of Old Testament prophecy. The significance of the historical experience of the discovery of a new route to India and, on the way, of millions of unconverted people in the *Book of Prophecy* derives thus in large part from a rather conventional Christian typological reading of the Old Testament, which rests on the Neoplatonist proposition that Scripture has a "double meaning" and that everything in the Old Testament is a prefiguration of what comes to its fulfillment in the New: "It must be kept in mind," Gorricio writes, "that Sacred Scripture often has a double literal meaning: events in the Old Testament prefigure events in the New Testament. . . . Therefore, when in the Old Testament it is said that something has been fulfilled in an Old Testament person and it is more truly and completely fulfilled in the New Testament, there exists a double literal meaning: a primary meaning and another more fundamental sense related."[26]

Thus, it appears from the *Book of Prophecies* that the New Testament and Augustinian Neoplatonic exegesis had provided Columbus and Gorricio with a model not only for their universalist, providentialist, and salvific interpretation of Columbus as a *Christum ferens* but also for a hermeneutics of discovery—a hermeneutics not in terms of making manifest through syllogistic reason or *scientia* but in terms of historical experience understood as the fulfillment of prophetic revelation of a world of things "hidden" from human view and reason. In this hermeneutical tradition, the "double" meaning of Scripture was presumed to be occult but providentially "discovered" by way of the "key" of a divinely inspired insight, prophetic gift, or gradual revelation by historical experience that may seem new in man's limited vision but that has always "already happened" in the mind of God.

Yet, there remains a stark dissonance between the evangelical and prophetic voices of the New Testament proper and the voice heard by Columbus in his head in 1503. The John of the Apocalypse is a passive witness whose role is limited to that of a scribe who is instructed to "write" to the bishops of Ephesus, Smyrna, Pergamus, and Thyatira: "Write therefore the things which thou hast seen: and which are: and which must be done hereafter" (1:19). Apart from acting as a witness, John himself plays no role in Redemption history, let alone in the unlocking of the "New Heaven and New Earth." He does not go to Patmos in order to find this New Heaven and New Earth or to assuage his curiosity; rather, he is already there and terrified once he experiences the vision of Jesus Christ: "And when I had seen him, I fell at his feet as dead. And he laid his right hand upon me, saying: Fear not. I am the First and the Last" (1:17).

By the same token, while the metaphor of the "key" does occur in John's Revelations and the New Testament more broadly, it never appears there in the sense in which it was used by the voice heard by Columbus. Rather, it is used there invariably in the sense of locking away evil, death, and hell. Thus, in Revelation 1:18, Jesus speaks of holding the "keys of death and Hell" (*claves mortis et inferni*) and Revelation 20:1 speaks of an angel coming down from heaven, having the "key to the bottomless pit," in which he will lock away the Devil at the end of days. Luke 11:52 also refers to Scripture as the "key" to the knowledge of God; and Matthew 16:19 speaks of the "keys to the kingdom of heaven." But nowhere does the New Testament promise Christians a key to so "rich a part of the world," as does the voice heard by Columbus, let alone a "key" to the secrets of *this* world. Yet, these are precisely the terms in which Columbus described his enterprise in another letter to the Catholic Monarchs that he never sent but later included in his *Book of Prophecies*. The "art" of the mariner, he wrote there, creates a "curiosity about the secrets of the world" that had inspired his enterprises for more than forty years.[27]

New Testament prophecy proper thus provided an unquestionably important but ultimately incomplete context for explaining the voice heard by Columbus in 1503. If we turn to Old Testament prophecy in search of a source of the metaphor of Columbus's art of navigation as a "key" with which to unlock the "chains" of the secrets of the world, the first place to look would be the prophet Isaiah—the source also for John of Patmos's prophecy of a "New

Heaven and a New Earth" in the Apocalypse. In a letter to Juana de la Torre, the nurse of crown prince Don Juan, Columbus wrote, "Of the new heaven and earth which our Lord made, when Saint John was writing the Apocalypse, after what was spoken by the mouth of Isaiah, He made me the messenger, and showed me where it lay."[28] And in the letter to the Catholic Monarchs included in the *Book of Prophecies,* Columbus wrote, "For the voyage to the Indies neither intelligence nor mathematics nor world maps were of any use to me; it was the fulfillment of Isaiah's prophecy."[29] Indeed, later in the *Book of Prophecies,* we find the metaphor of the chain in the following excerpt from Isaiah 25: "On this mountain the Lord of hosts will make for all the peoples a feast of fatty meats, a feast of wines, etc. And on this mountain he will destroy the image of chains restraining the peoples and the web spun over all of the nations."[30] Another excerpt, from Isaiah 22:22, also employs the metaphor of the key.[31] But, again, it is here hardly used in the sense used by the prophet heard by Columbus; rather, it is "the key of the house of David" to all the Gentiles before the end of the world, not a key to the riches or the secrets of the world.[32]

The invocation of "so rich a part of the world" by the voice Columbus reported in his "Letter from Jamaica" seems reminiscent not so much of Isaiah as of the book of Kings, as well as Chronicles, which tell of King Solomon and the gold of Ophir. Indeed, later in the letter, Columbus specifically refers to the book of Kings, asserting that the place from which Solomon's ships obtained this gold is the same as "Veragua," the place on the Central American *tierra firme* on which he landed during his Fourth Voyage.

> To Solomon on one journey they brought six hundred and sixty-six quintals of gold, besides that which the merchants and sailors brought, and besides that which was paid in Arabia. From this gold, he made two hundred lances and three hundred shields, and he made the covering that was above them of massive gold and adorned with precious stones. Josephus writes this in his chronicle of the Antiquities; in the book of Chronicles, and in the book of Kings, there is an account of this. Josephus holds that this gold was obtained in the Aurea. If it were so, I declare that those mines of the Aurea are one and the same as these of Veragua, which, as I have said above, extend westward twenty days' journey, and are at the same distance from the Pole as from the Equator. Solomon bought all that gold, precious stones, and silver, and you may command it to be collected there, if you wish. David, in his will, left three thousand quintals of gold of the Indies to Solomon to aid in building the Temple, and, according to Josephus, it was from these same lands.[33]

In the *Book of Prophecies*, the excerpt from 3 Kings, chapter 9 (which deals with the reign of King Solomon) is followed by a commentary on Ophir that sheds light on the fluid nature of the biblical prophetic tradition to which Columbus had recourse: "This is the name of a province in India in which there are gold mines inhabited by lions and the most savage beasts, . . . [N]o one dares to approach these mines unless his ship is holding close to the shoreline as a refuge. Then the sailors, estimating the hour at which these beasts withdraw, rapidly disembark and throw the soil dug up by the claws of the lions into their ship and depart. Later this soil is put into the furnace, so that the impurities are consumed and removed by fire and pure gold remains."[34] Passages such as this one about the biblical Ophir or Tarshish in the *Book of Prophecies* have led some scholars to argue that the "Hebrew Bible should be counted among the ancient texts that informed the discovery of the Americas" and others even to speculate that Columbus may have had some Jewish ancestry.[35] While most historians today reject the latter claim, Columbus did indeed identify the islands he discovered with the biblical Ophir; and though there can be no doubt about the importance of Old Testament geography in the conception of Columbus's project, the curious detail about the purification of the gold of Ophir by fire reminds us that the Bible, as it was read by Columbus, was not an "ancient text" but a living tradition in the world of late medieval Scholasticism, before the advent of humanist philology that would introduce the modern antithesis between tradition and discovery. This particular excerpt, for example, is taken not from any passages in Scripture proper but from the popular late medieval commentary of the famous Franciscan theologian and exegete Nicholas of Lyra (ca. 1270–1349), included in the *Biblia sacra cum glosa ordinaria et interlineari*, which was published in two separate editions in 1492 and 1498, one of which was most likely the text used by Columbus and Gorricio as a source when compiling the materials collected in the *Book of Prophecies*.[36]

Thus, while much of the scholarship on the European encounter with the New World has focused on the notion of an alleged "shock of discovery"—an epistemological dialectic between textual tradition and empiricist innovation—the late medieval Scholastic tradition of biblical commentary on which Columbus and his contemporaries drew in order to make sense of their world was in fact not devoid of the flexibility, versatility, and indeed spuriousness that Europeans such as the Jesuit José de Acosta and many more recent humanists would later come to attribute to non-European oral or nonalphabetical traditions. Like nonalphabetical traditions, the late medieval European biblical tradition had its "ancient texts," but it continually renewed these ancient texts in multiple adaptations through commentaries, hereby performing an important cultural function of ensuring continuity not unlike that performed by oral traditions in non-Western cultures. In order to appreciate the importance of the "power of tradition" in Europe's Age of Discovery, it will be necessary to place Columbus's excerpt from Nicholas of Lyra's gloss about claws of lions, furnaces, and purification by fire in the context of a closer look at the late medieval nexus of millenarianism and science, particularly with regard to alchemy.[37]

Apocalypse and Discovery

If Columbus's understanding of biblical geography was heavily mediated by late medieval textual traditions (in particular biblical commentary), so was his understanding of salvation history, especially his notions about the apocalypse as it relates, in his mind, to his enterprise of the Indies. As we've seen, there can be little doubt about the importance of Christian Scripture proper, and especially of John's Apocalypse, as a foundational source of information about the Eschaton for Columbus and his contemporaries. Besides John's Apocalypse, the New Testament contains apocalyptic references in 2 Thessalonians, Matthew 24, and Acts, most of which are excerpted and commentated in the *Book of Prophecies*. But of special importance for the history of Christian millenarianism in the West was the Old Testament's book of Daniel and its fourth-century AD commentary by St. Jerome for giving clues as to calculating eschatological chronologies. The *Book of Prophecies* contains several excerpts from Daniel, including this one from Daniel 12: "At that time Michael will rise up, a great leader who defends the children of your people," along with the marginal commentary that "This chapter deals with the end of the world."[38] Daniel 12:11 contains the prophecy that "from the time that the daily sacrifice shall be taken away, and the abomination that maketh desolate set up, there shall be a thousand two hundred and ninety days." Perplexingly, however, Daniel 12:12 states that "Blessed is he that waiteth, and cometh to the thousand three hundred and five and thirty days." In his commentary on Daniel, St. Jerome had explained that these numbers (1,290 and 1,335) related to the advent and defeat of the Antichrist and the Last Judgment respectively but was left to account for the surplus forty-five days that the prophet Daniel had left between these two eschatological events. Although this extra time was usually seen as a period of penance in the early commentaries, beginning in the twelfth century, it was also frequently interpreted, as Robert Lerner has shown, as a final period of "the refreshment of the saints," a period that would see the general amelioration of the world in its final days—the conversion of the Jews and heathens, church reform, and spiritual revelations. Thus, the book of Daniel and the commentary by Jerome had laid the most important Old Testament foundation for virtually all subsequent millenarian speculations in the Latin West, as the "forty-five days" had opened up the possibility of a temporal gap between the coming of Isaiah's "New Heaven and the New Earth" and the end of this world. In effect, this small chronological inconsistency in Old Testament eschatology, together with John's millenarian prophecy in the Apocalypse, had provided the two Scriptural cornerstones on which prophetic schemes about the millennial reign of Christ on earth could be mounted, holding out the possibility of the betterment and progress of a fallen and vain world, and even a return of the Earthly Paradise.[39]

The growth of these Christian millenarian schemes during the early centuries AD had in part depended on a typological Neoplatonic exegesis of the Old Testament, in which Redemption history was seen to parallel the account of Creation week in Genesis, so that each day of Creation would represent one millennium in the history of the world. This idea was based on a passage in 2 Peter 3:8, according to which "One day is with the Lord as a thousand years." According to this analogy, regular history was expected to end in its six-thousandth year, with a thousand years of repose representing God's rest on the seventh day. Eusebius (263–339) and later Bede (672–735) had calculated that Christ's birth happened 5,199 years after Creation. In AD 400, St. Augustine, in *De catechizandis rudibus* (On the catechizing of the uninstructed), had divided world history from Creation to the end into seven ages, hereby inadvertently lending future support to millenarian speculations he meant to suppress. Nevertheless, on the whole, St. Augustine dealt a serious blow to millenarian speculations in the Christian West by digging a deep theological trench between the City of God and the City of Man. For Augustine, historical time was the monotonous, unchanging, hopeless, and bleak existence of postlapsarian man. With the birth of Christ, history had entered its sixth and final phase, but relief or even redemption could be hoped for only after the passing of the temporal world. Meanwhile, all human activity was the result of vile and vain interests punctuated only by occasional moments of transcendence in contemplations of God's creation. In book 10 of *The City of God*, he emphatically rejected the notion that each of his seven ages could be equated with a thousand years or the eschatological notion of a refreshment of the saints during the last ages of earthly existence. Attempting to detract from the proliferating millenarian interpretations of John's Apocalypse of his age, particularly of the passage, "They shall be priests of God and of Christ, and shall reign with Him a thousand years," he wrote:

> Those who, on the strength of this passage, have suspected that the first resurrection is future and bodily, have been moved, among other things, specially by the number of a thousand years, as if it were a fit thing that the saints should thus enjoy a kind of Sabbath-rest during that period, a holy leisure after the labours of the six thousand years since man was created, and was on account of his great sin dismissed from the blessedness of paradise into the woes of this mortal life, so that thus, as it is written, "One day is with the Lord as a thousand years, and a thousand years as one day," there should follow on the completion of six thousand years, as of six days, a kind of seventh-day Sabbath in the succeeding thousand years; and that it is for this purpose the saints rise, viz. to celebrate this Sabbath. And this opinion would not be objectionable, if it were believed that the joys of the saints in that Sabbath shall be spiritual, and consequent on the presence of God; for I myself, too, once held this opinion. But, as they assert that those who then rise again shall enjoy the leisure of immoderate carnal banquets, furnished with an amount of meat and drink such as not only to shock the feeling of the temperate, but even to surpass the measure of credulity itself, such assertions can be believed only by the carnal. They who do believe them are called by the spiritual Chiliasts, which we may literally reproduce by the name Millenarians.[40]

By postponing the end to a distant future in their world chronologies, the early church doctors such as St. Augustine attempted to deflate the apocalyptic fervor that had been rampant during the early centuries of the Christian era. With regard to John's revelation of a thousand-year reign of Christ, the official position of the Roman church was that the millennium had already begun and Christ's reign on earth was realized through the pope. The idea that the millennium was yet to come in an earthly, temporal, and carnal future beyond the church was seen as dangerous and subversive, being officially declared heretical at the Council of Ephesus in the fifth century. Augustine himself had argued that John's "thousand years" must be understood figuratively and in two ways: "either because these things happen in the sixth thousand of years or sixth millennium (the latter of which is now passing), as if during the sixth day, which is to be followed by a Sabbath which has no evening, the endless rest of the saints . . . or he used the thousand years as an equivalent for the whole duration of this world, employing the number of perfection to mark the fullness of time."[41]

But unsurprisingly, not all medieval commentators on eschatology shared the Latin church doctors' wariness of millenarian schemes. Nor did all writers on the apocalypse accept Eusebius's and Bede's chronology that Christ's birth happened 5,199 years after the Creation of the world. When the "6,000th" year after Creation came and went—roughly in the year AD 800, according to Eusebius's reckoning—some writers quietly pushed back the millennium to the 7,000th year. Thus, despite St. Augustine's formidable medieval antimillenarian theological tradition, chiliastic beliefs survived into the High Middle Ages and into the fifteenth century. However, the particular articulation of Columbus's historicized millenarianism—specifically his ideas about the chronology of the Eschaton and the active role that human agents such as himself would play therein—depended also on a number of medieval prophetic traditions that were either not at all, or not exclusively and directly, derived from the Bible and the Latin church doctors; rather, they had originated on the fringes of religious orthodoxy and often by way of translations from Greek, Syriac, and Arabic during the High Middle Ages.

There were two medieval traditions, in particular, that mitigated the pessimistic outlook of St. Augustine on temporal existence, holding out more hopeful, "chiliastic" notions of the end. Not coincidentally, the older one of these two was originally of eastern Christian provenance and had long been ascribed to Methodius, the fourth-century Greek bishop of Olympus, martyred under the Roman emperor Diocletian in Chalcis. Entitled the *Apocalypse*, it purported to be a vision received by Methodius but was, in fact, authored by an anonymous seventh-century Syriac writer, today known as Pseudo-Methodius. The *Apocalypse* of Pseudo-Methodius drew on the fourth-century Tiburtine Sibyl, a prophecy of the advent of a Last World emperor, the "king of the Greeks or Romans," who would vanquish the enemies of Christianity and whose reign would usher in a period of peace before the final onslaught of the Antichrist. The Antichrist would be assisted by the race of Gog and Magog (mentioned in John's Apocalypse), who had been contained in Asia beyond the Caspian Mountains by Alexander the Great during his Eastern conquests but who would break loose into the world during the End Times. The *Apocalypse* was still very influential during the fifteenth century, being published in several editions, including one instigated by the German Franciscan Johann Meder that was published in Basel in 1498 by the German humanist Sebastian Brant, author *A Ship of Fools* (1494), a satire which contained the earliest mention of the New World in all of European poetry. By the fifteenth century, however, the apocalyptic tradition of Pseudo-Methodius had become fully mediated by late Scholastic Latin commentaries and editions (many of them spurious) that reflected shifting political concerns of the age. Thus, Pseudo-Methodius's *Apocalypse* had originally associated the enemies of Christianity defeated by the Last World Emperor with the "Ishmaelites." While the Ishmaelites were still in the thirteenth century interpreted to be the Tartars (or Mongols), who had recently invaded eastern Europe, by the fifteenth century—especially in the aftermath of the Ottoman conquest of Constantinople in 1453—a more common interpretation was that the enemies of Christianity vanquished by the Last World emperor were the Muslims.[42]

Moreover, by the fifteenth century, the tradition of Pseudo-Methodius's *Apocalypse* had become entangled with another prophetic tradition that had grown into the most influential millenarian movement in the Latin West during the later Middle Ages. Known as Joachimism, its origins were attributed to the twelfth-century Cistercian abbot from Calabria Joachim of Fiore (d. 1202). It is this Joachim whom Columbus invoked in the "Letter to the Sovereigns" of 1501 (included in the *Book of Prophecies*) when writing that "the Calabrian abbot Joachim said that whoever was to rebuild the temple on Mount Zion would come from Spain."[43] Joachim had regarded himself not as a prophet but as an exegete with special, divinely inspired insights into the hidden meanings of Scripture, particularly the Apocalypse of John. Thus, in his *Exposition on the Apocalypse,* Joachim wrote that the exegesis of John's prophecy was "the key of things past, the knowledge of things to come; the opening of what is sealed; the uncovering of what is hidden." The discovery of these hidden things, he believed, could be achieved by way of numbers, specifically by apprehending the mysterious course of Redemption history in terms of numerical patterns of twos, threes, and sevens. Thus, building on St. Augustine's chronology, he posited that all of history was composed of seven ages. His own lifetime, he believed, was near the end of the sixth age, which would usher in the seventh age that would be like that of a Sabbath or time of repose. However, whereas the Eastern or "Sibylline" traditions had foretold the advent of better things *before* the coming of the Antichrist, Joachim and his followers put them *after* this event. Thus, he believed that the Antichrist either had appeared already in the historical person of Saladin (the sultan of Egypt and Syria who had conquered Jerusalem in 1187) or would appear within the next two generations (by ca. 1260) before the seventh age, the Age of Peace, would arrive. Also unlike the apocalyptic writers of the Sibylline tradition, Joachim believed that the crucial agent in the Eschaton was not a Last World emperor but a newly emergent angelic pope. Finally, what distinguished Joachimite millenarianism from earlier traditions was that he superimposed on the conventional chronology of seven "ages" that of three "states," each representing an aspect of the

Trinity: those of the Father, the Son, and the Holy Spirit. The "third state" of the Holy Spirit, which corresponded to the seventh "age," was marked by the emergence of "the order of monks" (*ordo monachorum*), a new sort of "spiritual men" (*viri spiritualis*) who would live in peace as the earthly vanguard of redeemed humanity and have greater insights into divine things than any men living in previous states, conceiving in gestation a progressivist theory of history that would later prove highly influential in Western culture. These spiritual men would participate in the apocalypse not merely as witnesses of the final defeat of the Antichrist but as active participants in the battle against him. Therefore, they needed to prepare themselves for the final onslaught by whatever means possible.[44]

Thus, in the medieval traditions of both Pseudo-Methodius and Joachim, ancient Judeo-Christian Scriptural apocalypse had acquired human actors with a sense of historical mission, a call to arms in the name of apocalyptic ends, though for Pseudo-Methodius this human agency was represented by the Last World emperor (and thus the state), whereas in the Joachimite tradition it was represented by otherworldly monastic "spiritual men." The tradition of Pseudo-Methodius would prove important, as we shall later see, in the early modern period of European imperial expansionism. More immediately, the Joachimite tradition proved influential mainly in the rise of the mendicant orders in the thirteenth century, who left the monastery for the city because they considered it their mission to intervene in Redemption history through preaching and proselytizing. However, the more radical reformist followers of Joachim were also prone to heresy and persecution by the mainstream church, especially those associated with the Spiritual branch of the Franciscan Order. Moreover, whereas Joachim's "spiritual men" were still preparing themselves for the battles of the End Time through contemplation, his Franciscan followers during the thirteenth and fourteenth centuries increasingly welcomed also the arts and sciences into their arsenal of apocalyptic preparations. The result of this fusion was, as David Noble has written, that "technology now became at the same time eschatology" in the late medieval and early modern period. The crucial factor in this development was the reentry of classical science into the Latin West through translations from the Arabic, undertaken in the context of the Christian reconquest of southern Europe since the twelfth century. In the process, Judeo-Christian millenarianism became entangled with naturalist inquiry, in particular Neoplatonic astrology and (pseudo-)Aristotelian alchemy. Before I turn to the language of alchemical prophecy in Columbus's writings, it will first be necessary to discuss the role that the related discourse of astrology played in his hermeneutics of discovery.[45]

Astrology and Discovery

After his first landfall in the Caribbean, Columbus cultivated the notorious habit of renaming geographical places, presumably an act of linguistic expansionism of the religious and political world of Spain. Thus, he renamed an island "San Salvador" (the Holy Savior) that he knew the Natives called "Guanahaní," and he renamed an island "Isla Juana" (for Prince Juan of Asturias) that he knew already had the name "Cubá."[46] Similarly, he renamed the rivers on the islands he discovered in the course of his first voyage. But the names he assigned to rivers are derived from a different discourse. Thus, he renamed a river he came across on Monday, October 29, "río de la Luna" (River of the Moon); a river he came across on Tuesday, October 30, "río de Mares" (River of Mars); and a river he came across on Sunday, November 11, "río del Sol" (River of the Sun).[47] As Juan Gil has pointed out, Columbus's schema of naming rivers in the New World according to the days of the week is derived not from biblical or political language but from the "most ancient concepts of astrology." Similarly, building on Gil's observations, Evelina Gužauskytė has shown that the principle of many of Columbus's place-names originated in the Neoplatonic convergence of astrology and alchemy during the Renaissance.[48]

Indeed, in the *Book of Prophecies,* Columbus stated that God had endowed him with a special talent for astrology.[49] He owned and annotated printed copies of such popular treatises on astrology as the *Ephemerides astrologicae* and the *Alchmanac perpetuum* by the Nuremberg scholar Regiomontanus, the *Tabule tabularum celestius motuus* by the Jewish scholar Abraham Zacut, as well as various astrological manuscripts. Today, the Biblioteca Colombina owns 258 late medieval and early modern astrological treatises, 107 printed before 1500—142 in Italian, 108 in Latin, 4 in French, one in Spanish and one in Catalan, though the vast majority of these titles was purchased after Columbus's death by his son Hernando.[50] In the biography of his father, Hernando relates an incident when Columbus's knowledge of the heavens saved the day while he was in desperate straits off the beach in Jamaica. After some of his men had abused and killed several Natives, Columbus was informed that the "Indians" were refusing to barter for any more of the desperately needed food and even threatened war. He had in his possession a copy of a 1474 edition of Regiomontanus's *Calendarium,* which included diagrams and tables of calculations for eclipses for thirty years in advance, including the days and hours on which they would occur (Nuremberg time) as well as how long they would last (see fig. 13). From this book, Columbus learned that there would be a lunar eclipse on the evening of February 29 of that year (a leap year) and was able roughly to calculate the time of its beginning by adding several hours or so to make up for the time difference between central Europe and the West Indies. On the day of the predicted lunar eclipse, he summoned the Native leaders from the surrounding area to a conference and announced that "we were Christians and believed in God, who lived in the heavens and whose subjects we were, and who cherished the good and punished the wicked."[51] This God was very angry with the Indians, he explained, because he "saw how little they cared to bring us food in exchange for what we paid them and for our trade-goods." As proof of God's anger, Columbus warned, there would be a sign

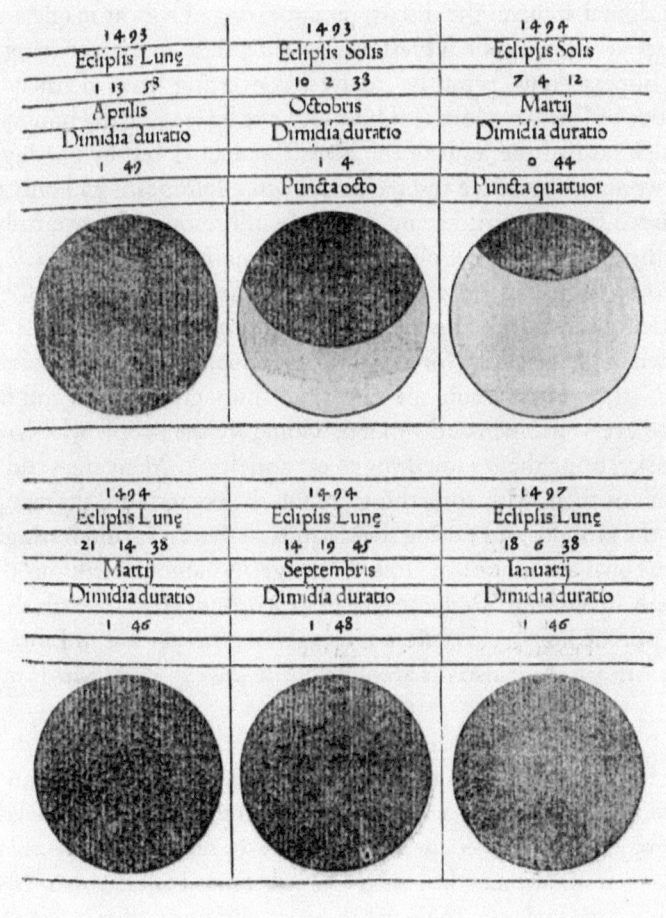

Figure 13. Table of eclipses. (In Johannes Regiomontanus, *Calendarium* [Venetiis: Bernardus Pictor, Petrus Loeslein et Erhardus Ratdolt, 1476]. Image courtesy of HathiTrust Digital Library.)

in the heavens. Initially, his threat made little impression on the Natives but when at nightfall the moon rose blood-red, they returned in terror, offering provisions and imploring Columbus to intercede with his god to assuage his wrath. Columbus promised he would do so, and soon the moon reappeared in its accustomed silvery brightness, to the relief of the grateful and henceforward more cooperative Indians.[52]

This story—first told by Columbus's son Hernando and later repeated by Las Casas as well as many historians since—has become one of the most iconic moments in the history of the European colonial encounter with the New World, one that would be reenacted in countless later iterations in the European colonial archive: the discoverer appearing as a great magician-wizard and messenger of the gods, a Hermes-like *Christum ferens* overawing simpleminded, superstitious, primitive natives, converting them neither through the practice of Christian love and humility nor by feeding the hungry or curing the sick (as had the Jesus of the New Testament), but by putting on display the wonders of science and technology that Europeans had only recently appropriated from the Turks and Arabs. It still resonated powerfully in the modern historiography on Columbus, from John Boyd Thacher's *Christopher Columbus* to Morison's *Admiral of the Ocean Sea* and beyond.[53] Columbus had himself given rise to this Hermeticist topos in his "Diario" of the first voyage, when, in his entry for October 14, 1492, he wrote that several Caribbean Natives, upon seeing the European ships, greeted him and his crew, calling "to everyone, men and women, 'Come see the people who have come from the sky; bring them something to eat and drink.' Many men and women came, each of them with something, giving thanks to God, throwing themselves to the ground, and raising their hands to the sky."[54] Interestingly, however, in his own account of the fourth voyage, Columbus mentions the lunar eclipse only in passing: "In the year '94 I sailed 24 degrees towards the east in a period of nine hours; . . . there was an eclipse; the sun was in Libra and the moon in Aries."[55] And also his account in the *Book of Prophecies* is unusually sober:

> While I was in the Indies on the island of Jamaica in the port called Santa Gloria, which is almost in the center of the island in the northern part, there was an eclipse of the moon. Because it began before the sun had set, I was able only to make note of the time when the moon had returned to brightness. This was accurately registered: two and one-half hours after sunset, that is, exactly five hourglasses. The difference from the middle of the island of Jamaica in the Indies to the island of Calis in Spain is seven hours and fifteen minutes, so that in Calis the sun sets earlier than in Jamaica by seven hours and fifteen minutes. Refer to

the Almanac. In the port of Santa Gloria in Jamaica the polestar rises eighteen degrees when the guards are in the arm."[56]

Morison notes that this passage in the *Book of Prophecies* represented "one of the best latitude observations on record for the early years of the sixteenth century," its method looking forward to the eventual solution of the perpetual problem of determining longitude later in the century and other future scientific progress.[57]

Perhaps Columbus's reticence in relating the story of the lunar eclipse (if it is indeed factual) can be explained by the ethos of Christian penitence that he increasingly adopted in his later writings. But it is also important to note the context in which this apparently modern and forward-looking scientific observation occurs in the *Book of Prophecies.* There, it is bookended, on the back, by excerpts from the New Testament Gospels of Luke, Matthew, and John, including chapter 10 ("I am the good shepherd..."); and, on the front, by another, similar observation of a lunar eclipse on the eastern tip of Hispaniola, in September of that year (including the measurement of the temporal difference of five and a half hours between the phenomena as recorded by experience on that island and as expected by science on the Portuguese island of St. Vincent) and, more importantly, by an excerpt from book 7 of Seneca's tragedy *Medea:* "During the last years of the world, / the time will come in which Oceanus / will loosen the bounds, and a huge landmass will appear; Tiphys will discover new worlds, and Thule will no longer be the most remote land."[58] For Columbus, the discovery of the latitude of the West Indies by way of astronomy was significant less because it resolved a perpetual problem in the science of cosmography and the art of oceanic navigation than because it fulfilled, in his mind, ancient prophecies about the emergence of a new world that would inaugurate the end of the world.

The curious mix of Christian eschatology and classical pagan prophecy that flank Columbus's astronomic observations about latitude in the *Book of Prophecies* alerts us, then, to yet another overtone in the prophetic voice he recorded hearing in a trance in 1503, revealing to him the providential significance of his art of navigation as a key that would unlock the "bounds" (*atamientos*) of the ocean sea, the riches of the Indies, and the secrets of world—that of Neoplatonic astrology. He writes that on his way from Puerto Gordo to Veragua, he put into harbor, for he "did not dare to await the opposition of Saturn, so tossed about on a dangerous coast, since that generally bring storms or heavy weather."[59] He was convinced that his entire ill-fated fourth voyage—as well as much of the fourth and last "Age" of his life—stood under the fearful sign of Saturn. According to his reckoning, the power of the stars had governed his life and his project of discovery in patterns of sevens: Thus, at Age 28 (4 × 7), he first arrived in Spain to offer his services but then went to Portugal for 14 years (2 × 7); after his return to Spain, he petitioned the Catholic Monarchs for seven years; and he discovered Hispaniola at Age 49 (7 × 7); upon his return from his first transatlantic voyage, he promised the Catholic Monarchs to bring enough gold for the reconquest of Jerusalem in seven years.[60]

Modern readers of Columbus have often dismissed Columbus's patent belief in astrology as yet more evidence of his gradual descent into mysticism, superstition, and even madness during his later years. However, in the fifteenth century, astrology was, as Laura Ackerman Smoller has written, regarded as "the most rational of science." Since Ptolomy, astrology was considered to be an integral part of mathematical astronomy in Neoplatonic philosophy. Whereas astronomy predicted the movements of celestial objects, astrology theorized their influence upon the terrestrial world, which was understood to be linked to the stars through a series of occult correspondences and sympathies between the sub- and superlunary worlds, as well as between the microcosm of the human body and the macrocosm of the stars.[61]

It is significant in this context that Columbus claims to have experienced the mystical voice off the coast of Jamaica while being "as though in a trance" (*así amortecido*), and in a "high fever and [being] in a state of great exhaustion." On the one hand, the passage invokes a long literary tradition in the Platonic association of Saturn and "inspired madness" (*furor divinus*), which is the source of genius and the special gift of prophecy. Thus, in Plato's dialogue *Phaedrus,* Socrates had taken issue with the notion that "madness were simply an evil," for there is "also a madness which is the special gift of heaven, and the source of the chiefest blessings among men. For prophecy is a madness, and the prophetess at Delphi and the priestesses of Dodona, when out of their senses, have conferred great benefits on Hellas, both in public and private life, but when in their sense few or none. And I might tell you how the Sibyl and other persons, who have had the gift of prophecy, have told the future of many a one and guided them aright."[62] Saturnalian frenzy, Socrates continues, is the dominant complexion not only of prophets but also of poets. This Platonic idea of inspired Saturnalian frenzy enjoyed renewed popularity in the fifteenth century, after having been passed down by Neoplatonists such as Plotinus from late antiquity to medieval Arab astrologers such as Al-Kindi and then translated into the Latin West since the thirteenth century by the scholars employed by King Alfonso the Wise in his Toledo School of Translators, who produced the so-called Alfonsine Tables, which had a wide diffusion throughout Europe and were cited by Columbus twice in his *Book of Prophecies*.⁶³ Columbus probably had this tradition in mind when newly fashioning himself not only as a collector of prophecies but also as an aspiring poet of the apocalyptic epic that he may have planned to write on the basis of the materials in the *Book of Prophecies*.⁶⁴

On the other hand, Columbus's dream vision invokes the astrological tradition reaching back to the famous "Problem XXX, I," long attributed to Aristotle but probably written by Theophrastus (ca. 371–ca. 287 BC), which posited a physiological basis for the mental state of melancholia in the predominance of the humor of black bile, a condition believed to be induced by the influence of the planet Saturn and the cause not only of pathological sadness but also of great genius as well as (in Aristotle's *Eudemian Ethics*) prophetic insight and speculative thinking. "The action of black bile being variable," the author of Problem XXX writes, "melancholics are variable, for the black bile becomes very hot and very cold.... Since it is possible for this variable mixture to be well tempered and well adjusted in a certain respect... therefore all melancholy persons are out of the ordinary, not owing to illness, but to their natural disposition."⁶⁵ Other influential writers of classical antiquity who had discussed the connection between the melancholic humoral complexion and the prophetic gift include Cicero, who in his *De divinatione* distinguished between "furor"—direct and natural inspiration (especially in dreams)—and the superstitious augurs or interpreters of omens; and Plutarch, who in his *De defectu oraculorum* rejects the common opinion that, since melancholics dream and phantasize a lot, they often hit upon truth by chance. The idea that those under the sign of Saturn were therefore plagued by melancholia and were also gifted with unusually profound knowledge and insight into things hidden from other, happier zodiacs, was reintroduced to the Christian West through the Latin translations from Arabic texts by John of Seville (Johannes Hispalensis) in Alfonso the Wise's School of Translators at Toledo.⁶⁶

The reintroduction of Neoplatonic-Arabic astrology had important consequences for the late medieval understanding not only of the human physiological and psychological complexion but also of history, and in particular for eschatology. Columbus reveals some of his own direct sources for his eschatological chronology in a dramatic statement in the unsent letter to the Catholic Monarchs included in the *Book of Prophecies:* "Holy Scripture attests in the Old Testament, through the mouths of the prophets, and in the New Testament, through our redemptor Jesus Christ, that this world will end. The signs of when this must happen are described by Matthew and Mark and Luke, and the prophets frequently predicted the event. St. Augustine said that the world would end in the seventh millennium after its Creation; the holy theologians agree with him, in particular, the cardinal Pierre d'Ailly in Statement XI and in other passages."[67]

Historians of the European discovery of America have long been aware of the important role that the French cardinal Pierre d'Ailly (1351–1420) played as a mediator of multiple and multifaceted traditions of knowledge in the conception of Columbus's project. Thus, d'Ailly's *Imago mundi*, together with certain letters that Columbus may have received from the Florentine physician and cosmographer Paolo Toscanelli and Piccolomini's *Historia rerum ubique gestarum*, had suggested to him not only that the western ocean was not as vast as most cosmographers believed—and therefore could be traversed in an effort to reach Asia—but also that the inhabitable parts of the earth were much more extensive than many believed, including also the "torrid zone," which Aristotle had held to be uninhabitable. But whereas historians of the European discovery have hereby focused on d'Ailly's cosmographic works annotated by Columbus, particularly chapter 8 of *Imago mundi*, "De quantitate terrae habitabilis," historians of religion have also alerted us to the crucial role that d'Ailly's astrological and eschatological writings played in the conception of Columbus's enterprise. Columbus's heavily annotated copy of the writings of d'Ailly, today preserved in the Biblioteca Colombina, was an anthology printed by Johann von Paderborn in 1483 in Louvain under the title *Tractatus de imagine mundi et varia ejusdem auctoris et Joannis Geronis opuscula*. It contained not only his cosmographical work, the *Imago mundi*, but also several apocalyptic tracts, including the *Tractatus de legibus et sectis contra superstíciosos astronomos*, the *Tractatus de Concordia astronomice veritatis cum theologia*, the *Tractatus de Concordia astronomice veritatis et narrationis hystorice*, the *Elucidarium astronomice concordie cum theologia et hystorica veritate*, the *Apologetica defensio astronomice veritatis*, the *Secunda apologetica defensio astronomice veritatis*, and the *Tractatus de Concordia discordantium astronoorum*. D'Ailly, a theologian with a strong nominalist bent then popular at the University of Paris, had written these works in defense of astrology in the context of a theological debate with his student Jean Gerson about the legitimacy of that science in dating events mentioned in Scriptural prophecy about the end of the world. While d'Ailly conceded, in accordance with his nominalist metaphysics, that the human art of astrology could not predict the timing of the end of the world—which would depend on a supernatural act of the inscrutable divine will that does not adhere to regular natural laws—he did insist that the coming of the Antichrist, a creature and hence part of nature, could be predicted. To be sure, at the end of the fourteenth century and the beginning of the fifteenth, recent European history had given ample occasions for apocalyptic speculation. But the immediate context of d'Ailly's apocalyptic writings was the Great Schism (1378–1414) that divided Christianity, pitting first two and then three rival popes and their followers against each other, each group perceiving in the rival group the arrival of the Antichrist. D'Ailly had played a prominent role in this conflict as well as in its final resolution at the Council of Constance, and most of his apocalyptic works were written during the years leading up to it. In his later years, he backed away from some of his claims about the imminence of the apocalypse but not about the legitimacy of astrology for forecasting events of the future.[68]

Reading d'Ailly several decades later, Columbus heavily annotated these apocalyptic works and marked passages to be transcribed by the "Italian scribe" into the *Book of Prophecies*. He encountered there many of the notions on which his own eschatological speculations would come to be founded. Few of these ideas, however, were original or particular to d'Ailly; rather, Columbus found in the works of the French cardinal a great digest of the many and varied apocalyptic traditions circulating in western Europe during the fourteenth and fifteenth centuries, including those of Pseudo-Methodius and Joachim of Fiore. Thus, in the *Book of Prophecies*, we find an excerpt from chapter 61 from d'Ailly's *De concordia astronomice veritates et narrationis historice*, which summarizes what "Methodius the Martyr [*sic*]" had "spoken about the coming of the Antichrist." Among the events that would precede the coming of the Antichrist, d'Ailly had listed a great "discord" (*dissentio*) among Christians; the subjugation of many kingdoms to Roman rule; the rising up of the Jews ("the sons of Israel" [*filii Israel*]) against Roman authority; the capture of the Promised Land and other victories by the Saracens ("the sons of Ishmael" [*filii Ysmael*]) because of the sins of the Jews; as well as the coming of many evils and iniquities, including sodomy. But then, suddenly, "tribulation will fall upon them [the Saracens] and the king of the Greeks or of the Romans will come forth in fury from the Ethiopian Sea and descend upon the inhabitants of the promised land" issuing into a time of "great peace and tranquility upon the earth, unlike any other, the ultimate peace marking the end of the world."[69]

If d'Ailly was Columbus's source of information for Pseudo-Methodius's prophecy about the advent of the Antichrist and his defeat by an emergent Last World emperor, the French cardinal's digests had also provided the rationale for calculating apocalyptic chronology by way of astrology. Thus, in the letter to the Catholic Monarchs included in the *Book of Prophecies*, Columbus cites d'Ailly's assessment of the calculation offered in the Alfonsine Tables that "From the creation of the world or from Adam until the coming of Our Lord Jesus Christ there are 5,343 years and 318 days"—2,242 years from the

Creation to the Flood and 3,101 years from the Flood to Christ. Moreover, Columbus specifically invoked "the cardinal Pierre d'Ailly" who had written, he says, "at length about the end of the religion of Mohammad and the coming of the Antichrist in his treatise.... [H]e discusses, particularly in the last nine chapters, what many astronomers have said about the ten revolutions of Saturn."[70] From these sources, Columbus comes to the stunning conclusion that "only 155 years remain of the 7,000 years in which, according to the authorities cited above, the world must come to an end."[71]

It is evident from the passages excerpted from d'Ailly in the *Book of Prophecies* that Columbus assumed that all of d'Ailly's astrological prophecies were ultimately of Arab provenance, whose secrets had been revealed to Christians in translations undertaken in territories recently reconquered by Christendom in southern Europe. In the "Letter to the Sovereigns" about his fourth voyage included in the *Book of Prophecies,* he specifically invokes the tables purportedly compiled in the thirteenth century by Alfonso the Wise's School of Translators at Toledo, which were based on the works of Arabic astrologers and accompanied by "canons" written by John of Saxony in the early fourteenth century explaining their use. D'Ailly had consulted these tables along with the canons, as well as a twelfth-century translation by John of Seville of the works of the Arabic astronomer al-Qabisi, known in the Latin West as Alchabitius.[72]

But perhaps the single-most important source of Columbus's calculation of apocalyptic chronology was the astrological tradition that d'Ailly had attributed to the tract *De magnis coniunctionibus,* a Latin translation of the astrological works by the ninth-century Arab scholar Abu Ma'shar (787–886), known in the Latin West as Albumasar. As was the case with his knowledge of al-Qabisi, d'Ailly's knowledge of Albumasar was only secondhand, however. Indeed, it has been known since the publication of Alexander von Humboldt's *Examen critique de l'histoire de la géographie du nouveau continent* (1836) that d'Ailly's primary source for Albumasar's astrology was the *Opus maius* (completed 1267) of the English Franciscan polymath Roger Bacon, particularly part 4, which was devoted to the science of mathematics. This part of the *Opus maius* also offered a discussion of geography that patently inspired Columbus as he encountered it in d'Ailly's *Imago mundi.* Thus, Bacon had written: "It is clear to us that beneath the tropics the Ethiopians are subject to the heat. Therefore it appears that the region beneath the equinoctial circle is the hottest of all; just as is commonly supposed. But without doubt Ptolemy maintains in the book before mentioned that that region is temperate in comparison with the tropics."[73]

Similarly, the passages from d'Ailly's *Tractatus de legibus et sectis contra supersticiosos astronomos* that Columbus had selected for transcription were taken almost verbatim from Bacon's discussion of Albumasar's astrology in the *Opus maius*. What Columbus encountered there was therefore a Christianized version (as mediated by Bacon and d'Ailly) of Albumasar's theory of the Great Conjunctions, one of the most influential among the various astrological conjunction theories that circulated during the later Middle Ages and the early modern period. According to this tradition, there was a correspondence between events on earth and celestial events, such as the great conjunctions of Saturn and Jupiter occurring at intervals of roughly 240 and 960 years. Thus, the duration of the world was assumed to correspond with the amount of time it takes for a complete revolution of each of the eight planetary spheres, calculated to be a total of 36,000 years. Because the planetary movements and conjunctions can be predicted by mathematical reason, it was possible also to predict terrestrial events that will come to pass in the future before the completion of the 36,000 years, as they also correspond to the movement of the planets. Thus, every planet has a certain quality that makes itself felt on earth and whose movements and conjunctions with other planets are connected to various aspects of human history. Jupiter, for example, is one of the two "benevolent and fortunate" planets and rules over the histories of faiths and religions in the world, called "laws" or "sects." Each of the other planets signifies a particular world religion, and its conjunction with Jupiter announces the ascendancy of that particular religion in history. For example, Jupiter's conjunction with Saturn signified the ascendancy of the Jews; the conjuction with Mars, that of the Chaldeans; the conjunction with the sun, that of the Egyptians; the conjunction with Venus, that of the Saracens; the conjunction with Mercury, that of the Christians; and the conjunction with the moon, that of the Antichrist, which was the final ascendancy before the Second Coming.[74]

In the passages of *De magnis coniunctionibus* summarized by Bacon and then annotated by Columbus in his copy of d'Ailly, Albumasar had predicted that the Muslim faith would last only 693 years after its founding by the Prophet Mohammed. D'Ailly, writing in the early fifteenth century, lamented in his *Tractatus de legibus et sectis contra supersticiosos astronomos* that, despite the invasion of Baghdad and the death of the caliph at the hands of the Tartars, Albumasar's chronology was obviously off, given the fact that the Saracen faith was alive and well—that "the perditious religion has not yet been destroyed"; but he predicted that its destruction would soon come to pass, if not at the hands of the Tartars, then at the hands of the Christians. Columbus annotated these passages in his copy of d'Ailly: "Saracens will be destroyed by Tartars or by Christians. Tartars will destroy the kingdom of Baghdad and the caliph."[75] In addition, in the *Book of Prophecies,* he included an instruction to the Italian scribe for transcription of his "Note about the destruction of the law of Mohammed" in his copy of d'Ailly next to an excerpt from chapter 4 of the *Tractatus* in which d'Ailly discussed the basis for Albumasar's astrological prophecies about the destruction of Mohammedan domination after 693 years.[76] Thus, the destruction of the Saracens will be a sign that the apocalypse is imminent because, according to (d'Ailly's) Albumasar, "after Muslim domination no other religion will come except the rule of the Antichrist."[77]

It is not clear whether Columbus was aware of the fact that, when he was reading d'Ailly, he was in fact often reading Bacon. Historians have long assumed that Columbus did not know of Bacon's existence, but that is clearly inaccurate, given the fact that Columbus refers to him by name in one of his postils to d'Ailly's *Elucidarium astronomice concordie cum theologica et historica veritate,* where he noted that "Bacon writes to Pope Clement that the world was doubtlessly created in the full moon of October."[78] In light of the fact that many of the passages annotated by Columbus in the works of d'Ailly actually came from Bacon's book on mathematics in the *Opus maius,* historians such as Moffit Watts and, more recently, Nicolás Wey-Gómez have persuasively argued that Bacon (as mediated by d'Ailly) must be considered to be an important interlocutor for Columbus's cosmographical ideas (especially his belief, contradicting Aristotle, that the "torrid zone" was not uninhabitable but fecund) as well as for his notions about the eschatological significance of his discoveries.[79] In addition, it would appear that Columbus was indebted to Bacon's tradition in mathematical cosmology for his esoteric hermeneutics of discovery. According to Bacon, mathematics is the "gate and key" not only to all the other "human sciences, but in that which is divine"; they were discovered "at the beginning of the world ... [and have] always been used by all the saints and sages more than all other sciences."[80] They are the key to the knowledge of "celestial things," the heavens, as well as to "things that are lower," as "celestial things are the causes of terrestrial."[81] Moreover, according to Bacon, mathematics is of great value to the Christian church militant. Thus, anticipating, by some six hundred years, José Arcadio Buendía's harebrained scheme of applying a magnifying glass for solar warfare in Gabriel García Márquez's *One Hundred Years of Solitude,* Bacon explains that the science of perspective would make it possible to construct a giant mirror that can bundle the rays of the sun and set ablaze the Infidel forces.[82]

Yet, while Hernando Colón and many subsequent biographers of Columbus and historians of the discovery of America have painted an image of

Columbus as a man of great learning—Hernando even (falsely) claimed that his father had studied at the University of Pavia—hereby emphasizing the importance that the liberal arts of mathematics and astrology played in his enterprise of discovery, this is not how Columbus portrayed himself in his own writings, especially his later ones. There, in language that echoes the medieval tradition of the "Fool for God," Columbus fashioned himself as a simple sailor, as an artisan whose art of navigation had inspired him with a curiosity about the secrets of the world and hereby fulfilled ancient prophecies. Thus, in the "Letter to the Sovereigns" included in his *Book of Prophecies,* he wrote that in his discovery of a route to the "Indies" neither "intelligence nor mathematics nor world maps were of any use to me." Rather, it was simply "the fulfillment of Isaiah's prophecy."[83] The rational science of mathematics, astronomy, and astrology were not, then, what unlocked the mighty chains of the Ocean Sea in Columbus's mind. He proudly owns the scornful judgment of him by the schoolmen of Salamanca "as an uneducated man, an uninformed sailor, and ordinary person, etc."[84] by pointing out that the gift of prophecy through revelation "operates . . . not only in the wise, but in the ignorant as well."[85] In its distinctly artisanal ethos, Columbus's hermeneutics of discovery was inspired, I would submit, less by Bacon's tradition of astrology and mathematics than by another branch of science on which Bacon had elaborated in the *Opus maius:* In chapter 1, part 6, he dealt with "Experimental Science" (*scientia experimentalis),* in particular the experimental science of alchemy. As we will see in the next section, it is primarily the late medieval tradition of alchemical prophecy that informs not only Columbus's notion that the "excellence" of gold can bring souls to paradise but also his idea that the Last World emperor who was to rebuild the temple on Mount Zion "would come from Spain."

Alchemy, Apocalypse, Discovery

The prophecy of a Last World emperor redeeming the Holy Sepulchre appears three times in the Columbian corpus, and each time it is attributed to Joachim of Fiore. Thus, we find it twice in the *Book of Prophecies* and once in the "Letter from Jamaica," where Columbus wrote that "Jerusalem and Mount Sion are to be rebuilt by the hand of a Christian; who this is to be, God declares by the mouth of his prophet in the fourteenth Psalm. Abbot Joachin said that he was to come from Spain."[86] However, it is clear that Columbus's familiarity with Joachimite prophecy was based not on any direct knowledge of Joachim's authentic writings but on various interlocutors. We know that Columbus had been familiar with the name of Joachim of Fiore at least since the 1480s, when he encountered it while reading d'Ailly's *Imago mundi.* In his own personal copy of the *Imago mundi,* Columbus had added the postil "Joachim abbas Calabrus" next to a passage in the tract *Concordia astronomice veritatis et narrationis hystorice* that dealt with a prophecy that Joachim had allegedly made in Messina, Sicily, in 1190 to Phillip Augustus II of France and Richard I ("The Lionheart") of England, before the two kings embarked on the Third Crusade.[87] In the *Book of Prophecies,* Columbus excerpted a lengthy passage from d'Ailly's *Concordia* that explained that Joachim had predicted that the two kings "would have little success" in their crusade, for "the time of positive progress had not yet come."[88] However, there is no mention in d'Ailly of a future liberator of the Holy Sepulchre; nor is it there alleged that such a liberator would come from Spain. Apparently, the rather discouraging prophecy that Joachim had made in 1190 with regard to the reconquest of Jerusalem (still to be found in d'Ailly) had been reinterpreted in the course of the fifteenth century to mean that now the time was right and that the king to fulfill the messianic mission would come from Spain.

The *Book of Prophecies* provides a few clues about the geopolitical history of this fifteenth-century innovation of the Joachimite millenarian tradition. In a section subtitled "De futuro: In novissimi," intended to include prophecies relating to the last days of history, Gorricio had transcribed a passage from a "letter of the Genoese envoys to the rulers of Spain who were received in Barcelona in 1492[:] 'With respect and good cause, I state, most magnificent rulers, that greater things are in store for you, for we read that Joachim, abbot of Calabria, predicted that someone from Spain would recover the wealth of Zion."[89] That letter, today lost, had been presented (actually in 1493) by two Genoese ambassadors, Francesco Marchesi and Antonio Grimaldi, as part of their mission on behalf of the Genoese republic to congratulate the Catholic Monarchs on their recently successful completion of the seven-hundred-year-long Christian struggle against the Moors on the Iberian Peninsula. The envoy continued a long tradition of close diplomatic ties between the Kingdom of Aragon and the republic of Genoa as well as of a shared anti-Islamic crusading spirit that had recently been rekindled in Genoa resulting from the fall of Constantinople to the Ottoman Turks in 1453. The city-state of Genoa (Columbus's birthplace) had a special ax to grind in these events, as it had maintained a thriving commercial colony in the city on the Bosporus—the most famous remnant of which, the Galata Tower, can still be admired today—and its four hundred soldiers under Giovanni Guistiniani (whose family knew the Columbus family) were among the last to surrender to the overbearing might of Mehmed II's army.[90]

But the close anti-Islamic geopolitical ties between Ferdinand's Aragon and Columbus's Genoa reach back even further than this in history. Thanks to the pioneering works of James Phelan, José Pou y Marti, and Alain Milhou, we know today that the prophecy, attributed by Columbus and his fellow Genoese to Joachim of Fiore, of a "Spanish" Last World emperor to redeem Jerusalem originated not with the Italian abbot but with the Valencian physician and famed alchemist-turned-prophet Arnald of Villanova (ca. 1235–1311), who had been active in Genoa and, in fact, died in a shipwreck before its coast during a diplomatic mission there.[91] As we saw in chapter 2, Arnald had been a famous author of works of medicine, including alchemy, although many of the alchemical tracts that were attributed to him during the late Middle Ages and early modern period are today known to be spurious. In his later years he also became increasingly preoccupied with apocalyptic prophecies. Arnald's apocalyptic writings offered a synthesis of several traditions that included that of Western Christian Joachimite millenarianism and the Eastern Christian/Sibylline tradition of Pseudo-Methodius's Last World emperor ("the king of the Romans or of the Greeks"). Thus, in the tract *De tempore adventus Antichristi,* he rejected the argument of the astrologers that the end of the world must coincide with the completion of the revolution of the eighth sphere after a total 36,000 years, as the end of the world, like its beginning, was a supernatural event that would not depend on the regular laws of nature and therefore could not be calculated by way of mathematics or human reason. However, Arnald also argued that the injunction of Acts 1:7 ("Non est vestrum nosse tempora . . .") applied only to the end of the world and Judgment Day but not to the advent of the Antichrist, and that biblical revelations provided clues as to the time line of this apocalyptic event. Taking cues from Jewish exegesis on the book of Daniel, Arnald proposed that the 1,290 days said in Daniel 12:11 to pass between "the taking away of the daily sacrifice" and "the setting up of the abomination that makes desolate" must be interpreted allegorically as 1,290 years separating the end of the Jewish worship in Jerusalem and the beginning of the reign of the Antichrist. Given that the Temple in Jerusalem was destroyed in AD 75, the projected year of the advent of the Antichrist must be 1365. This event would be preceded by the unification of the Latin and Greek Churches as well as the defeat of the Saracens.[92]

When he was publicly criticized by the faculty of theology at the University of Paris, who considered him unqualified in matters of biblical exegesis, he doubled down by writing a new tract, entitled *De cymbalis ecclesiae* (Of church bells), while residing at Sgurgola (outside Rome) in service to Pope Boniface VIII in the fall of 1301. In this tract, he reiterated his earlier claims and defended himself against the attacks by pointing out that prophetic visions are often imparted upon simple and uneducated persons. Thus, in a section beginning "Vae mundo in centum annis" (woe to the world in one hundred years), he reported how a mysterious prophet—"an almost illiterate man, who breathed entirely for the exaltation of the faith" (*virum fere illiteratum, quie totus ad exaltationem fidei suspirabat*)—had a revelation of the future that he, in a miraculous fit of ecstasy, wrote down in "eloquent Latin," though he could not himself understand its meaning.[93] All the Christian countries around the Mediterranean—starting from Syria, Greece, and Sicily, moving west—would be chastised. The Christian cities of Tripoli and Akon would be devastated by the Saracens and remain in a desert condition; Spain would be torn apart by Muslim treachery and Christian discord. Then, however, a new messianic hero would emerge, a "novus David," also called a "Western Bat" (*vespertilionis occidui*) who would reduce "adulterous Greece" (i.e., the Eastern Church) to the true (i.e., Roman) faith (the "house of the bride") and "repair the ark of Zion." Thus, "adulterous Greece [i.e., the Eastern Church] will suffer a new pillage and thanks to the Bat of the West will be brought back into the House of the Bride."[94]

This late medieval salvific Batman (*vespertilio scinifes*) will expel the Moors from Spain ("devour the Spanish mosquitoes"), conquer Africa, and humble the people of Egypt. All of this, however, is merely a prelude to the coming of the Antichrist, who will "separate the sons of Jerusalem from the sons of Babylon" before his final defeat for eternity.[95] The rather strange image of a Spanish redeemer king as a western "bat" (*vespertilio* in Latin, *murciélago* in Spanish) is probably derived from the heraldic animal in the coat of arms of the Crown of Aragon (including Arnald's birthplace, Valencia, as well as Catalonia and the Balearic Islands), where it typically appears above the crown over the shield to represent the winged dragon that had traditionally crowned the helmet of the kings of Aragon (see fig. 14).[96]

Figure 14. Heraldic symbol of the Crown of Aragon. (Courtesy of Wikimedia Commons.)

Although there is no evidence that Columbus was directly familiar with Arnald or his corpus—he never mentions him specifically—the writings attributed to Arnald circulated widely in the fifteenth century. For example, the tract containing the prophecy of a Spanish redeemer of the Holy Sepulchre, *De mysterio cymbalorum,* was cited by Pico de la Mirandola in his *De rerum praenotione,* where he wrote that two hundred years had passed since the prophecies of Arnald about the arrival of the Antichrist had not been fulfilled.[97] They were particularly well-known in Genoa, where Arnald had been on a diplomatic mission before his death, which would explain why his prophecy was cited in the letter of the Genoese ambassadors to King Ferdinand. And they circulated widely in the Kingdom of Aragon and in Spain more generally.[98] Especially his figure of a Western *vespertilio* who would take back the Holy Land had become a common trope in Aragonese court historiography, such as Juan Unay's *Libro de los grandes hechos,* as well as romances and ballads celebrating King Ferdinand.[99]

If the language of Arnaldian millenarian and messianic prophecy was patently circulating in the late fifteenth-century western Mediterranean, Arnald was also renowned for his scientific writings, as we have seen in chapter 2. Diego Álvarez Chanca, physician-in-ordinary to the Catholic Monarchs who had attended their first-born child, Princess Isabella, and who subsequently became the official physician on and chronicler of Columbus's second transatlantic voyage, wrote a treatise after his return from Hispaniola to Spain entitled *Comentum novum in parabolis divi Arnaldi de Villanova,* which was published in Seville in 1514. It was a (critical) commentary on *De conservanda juventute et retardanda senectute,* a tract that Arnald had written for Robert of Naples, in which he discusses the recovery of youth by use of a certain miraculous root, though he withheld more specific instructions on its use, for it was "a great secret, known to only a few."[100] Bartolomé de las Casas, one of Columbus's first biographers, was patently familiar with Arnald's medical and naturalistic corpus, presuming in his account of Columbus's third voyage in his *Historia de las Indias* that one of Columbus's sources on the "natural secrets relating to the nurturing or production of pearls" in the Indies was "Arnoldo."[101]

While Arnald had been first to elaborate the idea that a Spanish redeemer king, a "Western Bat," was soon to be revealed in order to take back the Holy Land, he had not mentioned Joachim of Fiore in this context, although he was doubtlessly familiar with the abbot's prophetic tradition. In "Vae mundo in centum annis," the anonymous prophet is simply identified as "an almost illiterate man, who breathed entirely for the exaltation of the faith." The attribution to Joachim was added not by Arnald but by one of his fourteenth-century readers and commentators, the Franciscan alchemist and prophet John of Rupescissa. In his 1354 commentary of "Ve mundo" entitled *Breviloquium de oneribus orbis,* he had identified the "almost illiterate man" to be Joachim of Fiore, presenting Arnald's prophecy with the declaration that "Sequitur expositio prophetie Joachim abbatis de oneribus orbis" (here follows a prophetic exposition by the abbot Joachim about the tribulations of the world).[102]

While Columbus's letters from his third and fourth transatlantic voyages, as well as the letter from the Genoese ambassadors presented to the Catholic Monarchs in 1493 and excerpted by Gorricio in the *Book of Prophecies,* provide evidence that Arnaldian prophecies, as mediated by the Franciscan alchemist John of Rupescisssa, were circulating in the western Mediterranean in the 1490s and early 1500s, Columbus had most likely encountered the (pseudo-)Arnaldian corpus already well before his first voyage, through his associations with Spanish Franciscans, with whom he had a very close relationship throughout his life. According to the chronicler Andrés Bernáldez, who witnessed Columbus's return from his second voyage, he even occasionally appeared in public dressed in a Franciscan habit.[103] Arnald's tradition would certainly have been familiar to the Franciscan friars of La Rábida, one of the centers of Franciscan learning in fifteenth-century Spain, where Columbus stayed before his embarkation on his first voyage, after he had received considerable support from the friars there.[104]

There has been some controversy about the question of when Columbus first came into contact with the Franciscans at La Rábida. His son and biographer, Hernando Colón, wrote that Columbus's first stay at La Rábida coincided with his first arrival in Spain early in 1485, after his proposal to reach India via a western route had been rejected at the Portuguese court and he had secretly crossed into Spain, first landing at the port of Palos.[105] According to Hernando, his father had left his first son, Diego, only a boy then, with the friars at La Rábida while he was presenting his proposal to the Catholic Monarchs, then in residence at Córdoba and in preparation for the final assault on the Moorish kingdom of Granada. Some later historians, such as Navarrete in the nineteenth century and Rumeu de Armas in the early twentieth, have argued that Columbus's stay at La Rábida did not occur until 1491, the year before his embarkation on his first transatlantic voyage.[106] However that may be, there is no doubt that the friars of La Rábida played an important role in both the inception and the final success of Columbus's attempt to gain support for his proposal at the court of the Catholic Monarchs. When, in 1491, Columbus's proposal was finally rejected after prolonged deliberations by the so-called Talavera Commission (a group of scholars who had been charged with studying his proposal), he returned to La Rábida with the intention of taking his proposal to France. However, Hernando writes, "God, who would not permit his plan to be thwarted, caused the head of the house, Fray Juan Pérez, to form such a strong friendship with the admiral and think so highly of his enterprise that he was distressed by his decision and what Spain would lose as a result."[107] According to Hernando, it was Pérez, formerly the confessor of Queen Isabella, who accompanied Columbus back to the royal court, now in residence at the military camp of Santa Fe in the final stage of the siege on Granada, and who finally persuaded the queen to reconsider Columbus's proposal. The other Franciscan from La Rábida who is explicitly acknowledged by Columbus himself, was Antonio de Marchena. Thus, in the letter from the second voyage that is now lost but quoted in Las Casas's *Historia de las Indias*, Columbus wrote: "As your majesties are aware, I spent a total of seven years at your court petitioning for your support in this matter. During all that time, there came forward no pilot, mariner, or philosopher, nor any man versed in some other discipline, who did not declare my enterprise to be founded on sand. The only person to offer any support apart from that vouchsafed me by the Almighty, was Brother Antonio de Marchena."[108] Later, Las Casas continues, Columbus goes on to remark in his letter that "everybody treated my project with scorn, save, as noted earlier, for Brother Antonio de Marchena, etc." Las Casas remarks that he was never able to ascertain to which order Marchena belonged, though he imagined that he was of the Order of St. Francis, because "ever since he was created admiral, Christopher Columbus had an especial devotion to that order."[109] Although our knowledge about the person of Marchena is still scanty today, we know that he had been a missionary on the Canary Islands and that he was a renowned man of science, famous especially for his knowledge of astronomy and astrology, being referred to in contemporary sources as "*el fraile estrólogo.*"[110]

The milieu of this Franciscan environment at La Rábida provides the cultural context for much of Columbus's blending of science with prophecy, as well as material with spiritual concerns, in his later travel writings about the New World. The millenarian traditions that Columbus attributes to the various scriptural sources, such as the book of Daniel and John's Apocalypse, as well as to high medieval authorities such as Joachim of Fiore and Methodius were thoroughly mediated by late medieval alchemists, who had infused these apocalyptic traditions with what I have called an "ecstatic materialism," to the effect of holding out the promise of the rejuvenation and invigoration of Christian bodies and coffers, setting the stage for a Christian triumph in the apocalyptic showdowns at the end of days. While there can thus be no doubt that Columbus's quest for gold can in part be understood in his Christian millenarian militancy, it is important to appreciate the full range of connotations—both material and spiritual—that gold held in the fifteenth-century scientific and religious imagination. As José Luis de Pando Villarroya has pointed out, gold was precious not simply because of its scarcity and economic use-value, but because it was seen to have inherent transformative and magical power within the scientific-religious mentality of the early modern period in general and in the alchemical imagination in particular.[111] As we will see in the final section of this chapter, Columbus's belief in the redemptive power of gold, evident in all of his travel writings from the New World but especially in the letter from his third voyage, is derived from this late medieval nexus between prophecy and alchemy.

Virgin's Milk and the Crucible of the Tropics

Although Columbus's third voyage had been intended as a resupply mission for the colony on Hispaniola, he deliberately veered south on his return to the Indies rather than heading straight for the Greater Antilles. This decision brought him to the Island of Trinidad, the continental shores of South America, and the mouth of the Orinoco River. His letter from the third voyage has become notorious due mainly to the cosmological speculations to which this journey gave rise. "Each time I sailed from Spain to the Indies," he wrote there, "I found that when I reached a point a hundred leagues west of the Azores, the heavens, the stars, the temperature of the air and the waters of the sea abruptly changed. I very carefully verified these observations, and found that, on passing this line from north to south the compass needle, which had previously pointed north-east, turned a whole quarter of the wind to the north-west. It was as if the seas sloped upward on this line."[112] Based on his sense that he was sailing not only westward and southward but also "upward," he takes issue with Ptolemy and other cosmographers who had maintained that the earth was a perfect sphere: The earth is "not round," he wrote, but "the shape of a pear, which is round everywhere except at the stalk, where it juts out a long way; or that it is like a round ball, on part of the which is something like a woman's nipple."[113] This "nipple" (*teta*) was for him nothing else than the Earthly Paradise, which he thought to be located below the equator. Indeed, he reasoned, the enormous quantity of fresh water dumped into the ocean by the Orinoco River could not possibly spring from an island. Rather, the Orinoco must be one of the four rivers flowing from a new part of the world containing Mount Purgatory:

I have already told what I have learnt about this hemisphere and its shape, and I believe that, if I pass below the Equator, on reaching these higher regions I shall find a much cooler climate and a greater difference in the stars and waters. Not that I believe it possible to sail to the extreme summit or that it is covered by water, or that it is even possible to go there. For I believe that the earthly Paradise fits here, which no one can enter except by God's leave. I believe that this land which your Highnesses have commanded me to discover is very great, and that there are many other lands in the south of which there have never been reports. I do not hold that the earthly Paradise has the form of a rugged mountain, as it is shown in pictures, but that it lies at the summit of what I have described as the stalk of a pear, and that by gradually approaching it one begins, while still at a great distance, to climb towards it. As I have said, I do not believe that anyone can ascend to the top. I do believe, however, that, distant though it is, these waters may flow from there to this place which I have reached, and form this lake. All this provides great evidence of the earthly Paradise, because the situation agrees with the beliefs of those holy and wise theologians and all the signs strongly accord with this idea. For I have never read or heard of such a quantity of fresh water flowing so close to the salt and flowing into it, and the very temperate climate provides a further confirmation.[114]

As modern scholars have long been aware, this image of the Earthly Paradise as the world's "stalk" or "nipple" recalls the universe of Dante's *Divine Comedy*, which depicts the Southern Hemisphere on the top and which had revived for the Christian world the ancient idea of the hills of the gods and the antipodal mountains (see fig. 15). Columbus may have been familiar with the *Libro de Conoscimiento*, a fourteenth-century travel account by an anonymous Franciscan who located the Earthly Paradise in the south, somewhere beyond the kingdom of Prester John, which the author located in Africa ("Nubia and Etiopia"). There the author claims to have visited the capital of Prester John's kingdom in "Malsa" and inquired about the location of the Earthly Paradise. Some "wise men" told him that it was located on top of a high mountain,

> so high that they came near to the circuit of the moon. No man has been able to see it all, for of twenty men who went, not more than three ever saw it, and that they had never heard tell of any man who had ascended he mountain. There are men who say that they saw it from the east, and others that they saw it from the west. They say that when the sun is in Gemini they see it to the south, and when the sun is in Capricorn they see it from the east. They further told me that these mountains were surrounded by very deep seas, and that from the water of those seas come four

rivers which are the largest in the world. They call them Tigris, Eufrates, Gion, and Fixcion. These four rivers irrigate all Nubia and Etiopia. The waters which descend by these rivers make so great a noise that . . . all the men who live near it are deaf, and cannot hear each other owing to the great noise of the waters. In all the time the sun in those mountains is there day and night either on one side or the other. This is because half those mountains are over the horizon, and the other half are over the horizon, so that, on the top of the mountains, it is never either cold nor dark, nor hot nor dry, nor moist, but an equable temperature. All things, whether animal or vegetable, can never decay nor die. They told me many other secrets of the stars both as regards judgments and magical virtues, also concerning herbs, plants, and minerals, and I saw several marvelous things. The Greeks call this place Ortodoxis, and the Jews Ganheden, and the Latins Paradiso Terrenal, because there is always good temperature.[115]

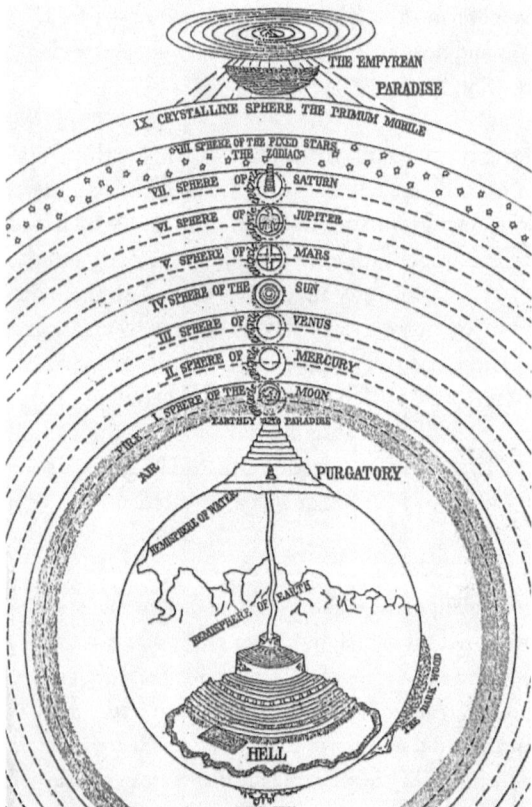

Figure 15. Dante's scheme of the universe, slightly modified. (From Michelangelo Caetani, duca de Sermoneta, *La materia della Divina commedia de Dante Allighieri dichiarata in VI tavole*, Monte Cassino, 1855, in *Studies in the History and Method of Science*, ed. Charles Singer [Oxford, UK: Clarendon, 1917], 1:31.)

The author's cosmology is clearly Aristotelian, with the superlunary world being composed of the perfect mixture of the four elements (the quintessence) that prevents the corruption occurring in the imperfect mixtures of the sublunary world. Of course, in Aristotle's cosmology there was no passage (no Earthly Paradise) that would bridge the gulf between the two spheres, as our Christian author suggests here (clearly influenced by Neoplatonism).

However, a more specific context for the animism of Columbus's *imago mundi* of the world as a pear and a woman's breast can be found in Neoplatonic Christian alchemical literature, particularly in the common analogy between the figures of Maria and of Natura (fig. 16). As we saw, in the alchemical cosmology of John of Rupescissa, man does not have to go to the stars via the Earthly Paradise in order to retrieve the quintessence, as it can be alchemically distilled from the imperfect mixtures of sublunary nature. In this tradition,

Figure 16. "Nutrix eius terra est" (The Earth is his nurse). Emblema II. (In Michael Maier, *Atalanta fugiens* [1618]. Source: *Secretioris naturæ secretorum scrutinium chymicum, per oculis et et intellectui accuratè accommodata, firguri cupro appositissimè incisa, ingeniosissima emblemata, hisque confines, & ad rem egregiè facientes sententias, doctissimaque item epigrammata, illustratus* [Francofurti: Impensis Georgii Heinrici Oehrlingii . . . , 1687]. Courtesy of the Library of Congress.)

Mary is the Christian version of a fountain nymph, the Romans' "black goddess of the earth," Flora, to whom fountains were frequently dedicated in pre-Christian times. The comparison between Mount Purgatory (with its four rivers flowing from Eden) to the female nipple, in particular, recalls the motif of *lac virginis,* or Virgin's Milk, which in the Christian alchemical corpus symbolizes the transforming mercurial waters of the philosophers that are often described as the "blessed Water," the "elixir" of the wise that the alchemists believed could be obtained in the alchemical dissolution of litharge in vinegar and alkaline salt.

The tradition of *lac virginis* had been an especially prominent feature of the Arnaldian alchemical corpus, as mediated by John of Rupescissa. This alchemical tradition was primarily concerned not with the transmutation of base metals into gold (chrysopoeia) but with medical alchemy by way of distillation of natural substances (spagyrics) that would promote health, vigor, youth, and a long life by staving off corruption and putrefaction. As we saw in chapter 2, the general idea of the alchemical production of a medicinal elixir of youthfulness and health seems to be derived from alchemical texts attributed to Roger Bacon, but John calls this elixir the "Quinta Essentia," a "fifth essence" or "quintessence." This quintessence would enable evangelical men and church militants to perform their work even in their old age, when they are increasingly susceptible to melancholy—a proposition that surely would have appealed to an aging Columbus, who saw himself as suffering under the sign of Saturn. As John explained in the ninth canon (in part 1) of *Consideration of the Fifth Essence,* one of the products of the alchemical reduction of mercury sublimate as a source of the quintessence is a water called *lac virginis:* "Take mercury sublimate with vitriol and common salt, but better is its fifth essence. Take sal ammoniac nine or ten time sublimated, mix them together and grind diligently and spread on a slab of marble and put at night in quiet and serene air or in a cold cellar. And there it will be converted into a water which is of so great virtue that if one small drop falls thrice on your hand it will immediately perforate it and similarly if it falls on a lace of copper or iron."[116] Similarly, in his shorter *Book of Light,* he describes the use of *lac virginis* in a seven-step process of producing the Philosophers' Stone. This process involves the production of philosophical sulfur (sulfuric acid) from vitriol Roman. This is not common sulfur, he explains, but an invisible "Spirit of Sulfur." When mixed with saltpeter and sal ammoniac—a process that is known as "expressing the milk of the virgin"—it produces *lac virginis,* or virgin's milk, a substance as white as snow that is so powerful that one drop of it will whiten a heated metal plate within and without. Finally, this *lac virginis* is reduced to powder through calcination whereby it attains its red color (from the mercury sublimate). It is, finally, from this red powder that the Philosophers' Stone is created.[117]

John explains that the use of *lac virginis* in the creation of the Philosophers' Stone was not known to the Islamic alchemists "Geber" and "Avicenna" but was originally revealed only to the "Christian" adepts—Hermes Trismegistus and Arnald of Villanova. The latter, in particular, had elaborated on the significance of the analogy between the alchemical opus and the Passion of Christ in his *Rosarius,* an alchemical tract attributed to Arnald since the fourteenth century. But, John explains, while these previous Christian alchemists had concealed the method of producing this miraculous substance lest it get in the hands of unworthy men, the imminent advent of the Antichrist now demanded the revelation of this secret to the Christian church militant, for it will provide the remedy for the afflicted elect. Despite Pope John XXII's 1317 decree forbidding the practice of alchemy, *De crimine falsi titulus VI,* he therefore decided to break with the tradition of alchemical secrecy only, he explains, because of the exceptional demands of his times, in which the prophesied despoliation of the church will need these alchemical remedies in order to prevail in the face of the coming tribulations.[118]

If Columbus had indeed derived not only the figure of the "Western Bat" (redeeming the Holy Sepulchre) but also the image of the Earthly Paradise as the world's "nipple" from a tradition attributed to Arnald of Villanova by John of Rupescissa, then we can better understand his hermeneutics of discovery in its dual material and spiritual terms: enabled by his mechanical "art" of navigation, Columbus's journey was an analogue to the alchemist's opus; his geographical forays into the terra incognita south of the equator were an epistemological analogue to the alchemists' forays into the occult "secrets of nature"; and the earth's tropical regions were the macrocosmic analogue to the microcosmic crucible, where the power of fire ennobles the world's corruptible substances and forces the secrets of nature to be revealed. The image of *lac virginis* sheds light, then, on the significance of the language of late medieval/early modern alchemy in the European literature of the discovery of the New World: whereas many of the Scholastic authorities had claimed, following Aristotle, that the "torrid zone" was a desolate and impenetrable wasteland—and hence of no interest to questions of natural philosophy—Columbus and many subsequent historians of the conquest of America built on a late medieval tradition of Roger Bacon, Albertus Magnus, Arnald of Villanova, Ramón Llull, John of Rupescissa, and other Christian (pseudo-)alchemists who subscribed to an esoteric construction of the occult that held out the possibility of multiple worlds beyond the microcosmic and macrocosmic Pillars of Hercules that were extraordinarily fecund and productive.[119]

More specifically, a consideration of the Arnaldian alchemical tradition of *lac virginis* in this context sheds light on Columbus's rather enigmatic claim for the redemptive power of gold with which he seems so obsessed in much of his travel writings about America. "Gold is most excellent," he wrote from the fourth voyage; "Gold constitutes treasure, and he who possesses it may do what he will in the world, and, God willing, may so attain as to bring souls to Paradise."[120] His assertion of the redemptive efficacy of gold drew on alchemical connections between a given metal, its corresponding star, and the human constitution that stood under its influence. Thus, the color of the metal gold connected it to the golden glow of the sun, and that of silver to the moon and their astrological influences. His thinking seems here particularly indebted to Albertus Magnus, who had, in his *De mineralibus et lapidibus,* conceived of the inquiry into the hidden realms of nature on both the macro- and the microcosmological level in analogous terms and whose writings provided a rich rhetorical recourse in the literature of the discovery of America. Thus, Bartolomé de las Casas, in his account of Columbus's third voyage in his *Historia de las Indias,* veers from his steady attempt to demonstrate Columbus's providential mission as a Christ Bearer to the New World by embarking on a scientific excursion explaining how pearls are engendered—"something," he writes, "that I do not feel will be disagreeable to the readers": "At certain times of the year—when they have the inclination and appetite to conceive—they go on to the shore and open themselves. And there they await the dew from the sky, almost as if they are awaiting and desiring a husband. They take in the dew, from which they conceive and become pregnant. And thus they produce their children, which are the pearls, or *margaritas,* depending on the quality of the dew. If it is pure, white pearls are born. If it is cloudy, brown or dark ones come about."[121] Besides "Arnoldo," Las Casas mentions as his sources Pliny, Megasthenes, Solinus, Isidor of Seville, and Albertus Magnus. There are some modern authors, Las Casas continues, who argue that this theory of how pearls are engendered is fabulous. In order to refute them, he cites book 1, chapters 7–9 of Albertus Magnus's *De mineralibus et lapidibus* and explains that "the stars in their quantity and their luster, location, and movement, move and order the world, including things of any material and location that are engendered and decay. The potential of the stars is infused and flows to where each engendered thing is produced and receives this potential almost as a woman's uterus, or 'mother,' as women say, receives the formative potential of the embryo."[122] However, the stars' generative potential is not identical everywhere, Las Casas continues, "nor does it exist in the same quantity everywhere," which is evident in the fact that "some places produce lions and not elephants, and other elephants and not lions." Likewise, "some produce gold and others silver," while yet others produce pearls and precious stones.[123]

Similarly, Columbus's notion of the tropics as a macrocosmic analogue of the microcosmic alchemical crucible (as far as we are able to tell from Las Casas's paraphrases of Columbus's travel writings) inspire his curiosity not only about gold and pearls but also about the vegetable, animal, and human world. Thus, the ethnographic descriptions in Columbus's *Diario* of the Natives teem with imagery that evokes not only fecundity and plenty but also prelapsarian youthfulness and vigor: "They go as naked as their mothers bore them, even the women, though I only saw one girl, and she was very young. All those I did see were young men, none of them more than thirty years old. They were well built, with handsome bodies and fine features."[124] If the alchemists applied their gehennical fires in order to reverse the bodily infirmities and corruption of old age and death introduced by the Fall, the geographical journey to the tropics similarly holds out the promise of a return to prelapsarian existence of eternal youth, a "Fountain of Youth" springing from the *lac virginis* of tropical nature.

Columbus's alchemical/spagyrical imagination about the miraculous efficacy of tropical nature manifests itself not only in his notion of the "growth" of redemptive gold and precious stones but also in his belief in the miraculous power of exotic herbs and spices, which can be expected to be far superior to those grown in more northern regions. Thus, in his entry of Friday, October 19, Columbus wrote in his *Diario:* "I believe that there are on the islands many plants and trees which would be of great value in Spain as dyes and medicinal spices, but I do not recognize them, which I much regret. When I came to this cape such a fine sweet aroma of flowers or trees came from the land that it was the most delightful thing in the world."[125] While he does not recognize the majority of the herbs and spices he finds, instilling him with a characteristic curiosity and yearning to learn their secret uses, he believes he will find valuable spices known to grow in India, especially cinnamon, nutmeg, and pepper, the latter of which was known in the early sixteenth century as "black gold" because its price was actually higher than that of gold by the time it reached the cities of western Europe via the trade routes from Asia.[126]

Columbus's s spagyrical interest in the medicinal qualities of herbs and spices is evident also in the postils with remedies that he inserted into his books, such as Pliny's *Natural History* and Piccolomini's *Historia rerum ubique gestarum.* While some of these remedies, such as the description of the medicinal use of parsley as a diuretic, are derived from natural history, others are clearly of an alchemical nature. For example, he explains the use of the dust of sulfur, dissolved with ammoniac and arsenic.[127] While his descriptions of the application of poisonous arsenic in the concoction of a "white" medicinal substance when mixed with salt and vinegar—have perplexed his modern editors, I would suggest that they provide clear evidence of Columbus's familiarity not only with Arnaldian millenarian prophecy but also spagyrical alchemy.

Although none of Columbus's authentic writings (nor Las Casas's paraphrases of his writings) were published in the sixteenth century, many subsequent sixteenth-century writers about the European conquest of America participated in the same alchemical tradition of Roger Bacon, Albertus Magnus, Arnald of Villanova, Ramón Llull, and John of Rupescissa when arguing that the New World's mineral wealth held out a special promise for both physical renewal and spiritual transformation. As the sixteenth-century German cosmographer Sebastian Münster would later write, those regions that are closest to the sun are more likely to "grow" gold.[128] It was no coincidence that the earth's regions richest in minerals are also the most remote and populated by the most primitive people; rather it was divinely planned, as God had "hidden" it in secret places so that it would be found out by those chosen and initiated in the occult arts.

As Michael Nerlich has argued, the language of magic in early modern literature generally must be seen in the context of the social decline of the knightly class and the loss of the "real meaning of knighthood," as commercial adventure stood in increasingly defiant opposition to the courtly ideology of adventure. Whenever possible, therefore, commercial adventures would have to be cloaked in the forms of courtly ideology itself in order to be persuasive to the aristocracy. While the aristocratic world of the courts became increasingly aware of its dependence on the mobile world of commerce and trade as well as on the empirical knowledge on which this world functioned, the bourgeoisie began to "imitate the nobility" and its aristocratic values. Tales of magic hereby obviated the difficult explanation of economic interconnections and allowed for a transcendental justification of emerging bourgeois economic relations.[129] Similarly, the language of alchemy in the literature of European discovery of America synthesized the renewed interest in the material world during the Renaissance (already evident in the travel accounts of Marco Polo about China) with the mysticism of recovering esoteric and arcane knowledge, as well as the Christian messianism of the crusades, hereby lending a strongly transcendent, spiritual, and "magical" character to the early modern "hunt" for gold and silver, as well as exotic spices, drugs, and even slaves. In Columbus's *Book of Prophecies,* the alchemical hunt for the secrets of the New World—and indeed the emergence of the very *idea* of a new world (as opposed to the old world of Asia)—finds its literary figuration in an early modern, Christianized version of the pagan myth of Jason and the Argonauts and their hunt for the Golden Fleece, a hunt that becomes, as Antoine Faivre has shown, increasingly interpreted as an allegory of the alchemical opus since the founding of the Order of the Golden Fleece by Philip the Good of Burgundy in 1430.[130] To be sure, it is unlikely that, as has been suggested, Columbus could have aspired to membership in this order (which was restricted to knights). However, as we have seen, he does compare his expedition to that of the Argonauts and himself to Tiphys, Jason's pilot and guide on his mythical voyage. Thus, below his excerpt from book 7 or Seneca's Medea (quoted above), he glosses: "During the last years of the world, the time will come in which the Ocean sea will loosen the bounds and a large landmass will appear. A new sailor like the one named Tiphys who was the guide of Jason, will discover a new world, and Thule will no longer be the most remote land."[131] The navigator's oceanic journey beyond the Pillars of Hercules, like the alchemist's forays into the secrets of nature, will result not only in the magus's personal fame and material wealth but also in universal spiritual transformation and the triumph of the Christian church militant against the Antichrist, preparing the stage of the Second Coming of Christ. The language of the occult in the texts written by the early explorers and conquerors of exotic New Worlds such as Columbus, I would suggest, functioned in ways similar to those observed by Nerlich about the courtly magicians patronized or entertained by the landed aristocracy. The tales neither of traveling merchants nor of crusading knights in the traditional sense, their accounts about the sixteenth-century quests for New Worlds recast the mystical frames that the alchemists had been forging for centuries, holding out the promise not only of material transformation (or "ex-change") in trade and plunder but also of spiritual transformation and renewal in the act of penetrating the secrets of the world.

5

The Llullian Renaissance and European Expansionism

> Wherefore, as becomes Catholic kings and princes, after earnest consideration of all matters, especially of the exaltation and spread of the Catholic faith, as was the fashion of your ancestors, kings of renowned memory, you have purposed with the favor of divine clemency to subject the said mainlands and islands with their residents and inhabitants and to reduce them to our Catholic faith [ad fidem Catholicam reducere proposuistis].
> —The bull *Inter cetera,* May 3, 1493

> "If Matthew, Mark, Luke, and John are waiting for me on that nearby beach, I'm screwed."
> —Christopher Columbus in *El arpa y la sombra,* by Alejo Carpentier,

On August 14, 1314, the Franciscan tertiary, missionary, Arabist, and logician extraordinaire from the island of Majorca Ramón Llull (ca. 1232–1315) embarked, at some eighty years of age, on his third and final mission to Tunis in order to convert "Saracens" (Muslims) to the Christian faith. What exactly happened to Llull on his last apostolic journey is the stuff of legend. While most historians today believe that he returned to Majorca and died there peacefully shortly after, according to one tradition that originates in the fifteenth century, he was martyred by being stoned in the streets of Bugia (Béjaïa, today in eastern Algeria) by a crowd enraged at his bold public proclamations of the falseness of the Muslim faith. Still alive but mortally wounded, the story goes, he was brought on board a ship belonging to two Genoese merchants who intended to return his broken body to his native island of Majorca. In his dying hour, Llull revealed to the two merchants the existence of another continent hitherto unknown beyond the western Ocean Sea, the future discovery of which by a Christian would result in the salvation of millions of pagan souls. One of these merchants was named Stephen Columbus, an ancestor of Christopher Columbus, who passed down Llull's secret in a family tradition that would inspire his famous descendent to fulfill Llull's prophecy 150 years later.¹

In chapter 3 of this book, I discussed Ramón Llull's "alchemy of conversion"—his peculiar mix of a chivalric missionary ethos as a "Fool for God" with that of the Aristotelian scientist; his remarkable logical system, the *ars luliana,* for the discovery of truth; and the extensive alchemical corpus that was spuriously attributed to him after his death. I return to Llull in this chapter because the legend of his foreknowledge of the existence of America calls attention to the role that his extremely wide-ranging and multifaceted intellectual and spiritual tradition—known as "Llullism"—played, *not* in the history of the European discovery of America (as the legend claimed), but in the history of the *idea* that America was discovered. Still in the eighteenth century, the Cistercian professor at the University of Majorca Antonio Raimundo Pascual explained that Llull had hypothesized the existence of another, hitherto unknown, continent on the western shores of the Atlantic Ocean (*un continente que de acá no vemos ni conocemos*) as early as 1287, in a tract entitled *Quaestiones per artem demonstrativum solubiles.*² As a result of Llull's death on Stephen Columbus's ship, Pascual continued, the Columbus family had inherited the sage's books and had always harbored a special affection and devotion for his teachings.³ For Pascual, this long-standing connection between Llull and the Columbus family provides the clue to the question of why Christopher had set out in 1492 to discover the New World. The Llullian connection disproved once and for all the insidious allegations—made since the sixteenth century by court historians such as Gonzalo Fernández de Oviedo y Valdés—that Columbus had received his foreknowledge of the existence of America from some "anonymous sailor" who had divulged his secret before dying in the discoverer's house after surviving a shipwreck.⁴ Such allegations, Pascual wrote, were "fabulous and invented in order to diminish the merit of that hero [i.e., Columbus]."⁵ In fact, Pascual's Columbus, who was a great scholar of "Latin, mathematics, geometry, cosmography, and astronomy," had come to his conclusion from a close study of Llull's books in the family library. While the rest of the world had forgotten about Ramón Llull in the general ignorance prevailing during the Dark Ages, Columbus became the legitimate heir to a scientific tradition about the existence of a New World that had begun with "the Blessed Ramon Llull, the only original author of such an idea."⁶ In short, Pascual's Columbus was a Llullian, and his discovery of America the fruit of Llull's Art of discovering truth.⁷

Although the story was part of a propaganda campaign for the Majorcan missionary's canonization that began in the fifteenth century and ultimately resulted in his beatification by Pope Pius IX in 1858, it would be a mistake to dismiss Pascual's story about Llull's foreknowledge of America as a mere footnote in the intellectual history of discovery. While Llull is today remembered primarily among students of medieval Catalan literature as well as historians of Western esotericism, during the late medieval and early modern period, Llull's works were enormously influential, being widely disseminated throughout Europe in hundreds of manuscripts, as well as in thirty-two incunabula and 148 print editions published by 1600. Although it is unlikely that the real Columbus knew about Llull's geographic theories, it is indeed possible (and even likely) that the admiral was generally familiar with the name of the famous Majorcan missionary and perhaps even with some of the writings attributed to him. After all (as Pascual didn't fail to point out), Llull had spent significant periods of time in Columbus's native city of Genoa, and it was from there that he had embarked on his first mission to Tunis in 1297.[8] Also, some of the spurious works attributed to Llull were actually based on the writings of the fourteenth-century Franciscan alchemist John of Rupescissa—the same author who had cultivated Arnald of Villanova's notion of a Spanish *vespertilio sanifex* that would inspire Columbus's association between his voyages and the reconquest of the Holy Land, which (as we saw in the previous chapter) may have reached Columbus via the Franciscan friars at La Rábida.[9] Today, the Biblioteca Capitular y Colombina in Seville does indeed preserve several early print editions and medieval manuscripts of authentic Llullian works, such as the *Tractatus astronomiae,* the *Ars brevis,* and the *Ars inventiva veritatis,* but these were purchased only by Columbus's son Hernando in the early sixteenth century.[10]

Nevertheless, Hernando Colón's collection of Llullian works is significant, as it points to what we might call a "Llullian renaissance" that was under way in Italy, Spain, France, and Germany during the European Age of Discovery and Expansionism. Although Llull's ideas had been received with skepticism by the Averroist theologians at the University of Paris during his own lifetime, he had upon his death many followers at the renowned faculty of medicine at the Sorbonne, including Pierre Lacepierre of Limoges and Thomas Le Myésier of Arras, who copied and commentated his works. And even though Llull was attacked by the prominent Parisian nominalists Pierre d'Ailly and Peter Gerson in the late fourteenth century, he continued to have many important followers including such famous physicians and theologians as Raymond of Sabunde at Toulouse and the bishop and vicar-general Nicholas of Cusa.[11] The late fifteenth and the sixteenth centuries saw a veritable explosion of interest in his works among such Italian Neoplatonists as Marsilio Ficino, Giovanni Pico de la Mirandola, and Giordano Bruno; among humanists at the University of Paris such as Jacques Lefèvre d'Étaples (ca. 1455–1536), his student

Charles de Bovelles (1479–1553), and Bernardo de Lavinheta (d. ca. 1530); as well as among such northern European "occult philosophers" as Cornelius of Agrippa and John Dee. In post-Tridentine Spain, Llull's followers were legion at the court of Philip II, including not only the monarch himself but also Juan de Herrera, the famous architect of the Escorial and author of *Tratado del cuerpo cúbico conforme a los principios de R. Llull*.[12] During the seventeenth century, Llullism would inspire not only such renowned Counter-Reformation theologians as Athanasius Kircher and Eusebio Niremberg but also such English Protestant theologians as John Donne; alchemists such as George Starkey; as well as the men of science associated with the Royal Society of London, including Robert Boyle, Elias Ashmole, and Sir Isaac Newton. Meanwhile, on the Continent, Gottfried Wilhelm Leibniz became one of the most influential Llullians in the history of modern science, forging a crucial link between Llull's medieval *ars combinatoria* and modern computational theory.[13] In sum, it would not be an exaggeration to maintain, with Frances Yates, that Llullism was, in its various strands, "one of the major forces of the Renaissance,"[14] when Llull's original, late medieval art of conversion developed into a veritably encyclopedic "clavis universalis,'" a key to all knowledge.[15]

Finally, Pascual's transformation of Columbus into a Llullian illuminates also the important role that Christian evangelism has played in legitimating the modern European expansionism. As we saw in chapter 4, the apostolic mission was indeed one (though not the only one) of the reasons why Columbus claimed that God had given him, the "Xpo Ferens," a key to the secrets of the world in the form of his art of navigation for reaching the East by going west and perhaps even to "a New Heaven and a New Earth" in the South. However, for Columbus the apostolic mission of his enterprise appears to have been largely an afterthought (or a work in progress), and he continued to see the ultimate spiritual significance of his enterprise in the East, particularly in the Christian reconquest of the Holy Land. The Capitulations of Santa Fe—the Catholic Monarchs' original set of instructions and concessions to Columbus before the first voyage—had made no mention of any apostolic significance of Columbus's project. This changed drastically after the admiral's return in April 1493, when Pope Alexander VI's famous bull of donation redefined Columbus's western mercantile project as an apostolic mission that he described with the momentous phrase *"ad fidem Catholicam reducere"* (to reduce [the Indians] to the Catholic faith).[16] Responding to this revision, the Catholic Monarchs sent along a number of missionaries on Columbus's fleet embarking from Cádiz on September 25, 1493, for the second Atlantic crossing. The reason for this was stated unequivocally in the new set of instructions to Columbus that now explained the significance of the discovery in terms of the apostolic mission in the yet unidentified islands and mainlands in the West: "Because it pleased God our Lord in his great mercy to grant the discovery of those islands and mainlands to the King and Queen..., [we] order and charge said admiral... that by every means and ways possible he should try to persuade the inhabitants of said islands and mainlands to be converted to our holy Catholic faith."[17] Thus, Spain's claim to a monopoly of access to the "Indies of the West" would come to rest exclusively on an apostolic mission for at least two hundred years to come. Still in 1680, under the reign of Carlos II, the *Recopilación de Leyes de Indias* [Compendium of the Laws of the Indies] specified that the foundation of Spain's claim to dominion in the Americas was the mission to bring "to the body of the holy Roman Catholic faith the innumerable peoples and nations who inhabit the Western Indies."[18]

This chapter attempts to elucidate the evangelical hermeneutics of conversion underlying the phrase "ad fidem Catholicam reducere" in the famous bulls *Inter cetera*. The Latin verb *reducere* derived from the root *reduco* ("lead back," "bring back," "restore"), and its use has a long history in hierocratic canon law theories of "dominion" as elaborated in the tradition of *papa vicarius Christi*, especially in the late medieval tradition of papal bulls of donation that Luis Weckmann-Muñoz has called *doctrina omni-insular*.[19] But it is used here for the first time in reference to a particularly *Spanish* apostolic mission to the American Indians. As such, its use would initially be adopted also in the Spanish language (*reducir*) in early modern missionary discourse in the early Americas. However, in the early modern period, the word acquired several new meanings in Spanish that it had lacked in Latin, including that of "to subdue," "to conquer," "to persuade," and "to reorder." In addition, in sixteenth-century Spanish missionary discourse, its late medieval hermeneutics of conversion was translated into a particular *methodology* of conversion in terms of the physical relocation, concentration, and catechization of the American Indian neophytes in so-called *reducciones, doctrinas,* or *hospitales*.[20] In this chapter and the next, I will argue that the origin and transformation of the concept of reduction from a late medieval *hermeneutics* to an early modern *methodology* of conversion can be understood in the context of the history of Llullism, especially in the history of the (pseudo-)Llullian relationship between medicine, alchemy, and conversion. In particular, I investigate the early modern legacies of the medieval missionary polymath in the context of the Llullian renaissance that was being nurtured and patronized in imperial Spain by the powerful figure of Cardinal Francisco Jiménez de Cisneros. While this chapter offers some of the historical background on the role that Llullism played in the justification of late medieval and early modern European expansionism, the next chapter will turn to an analysis of the language of alchemy in several sixteenth-century missionary writings about their evangelical work.

Ad fidem Catholicam reducere: Llullism and *Inter cetera*

Despite Llull's fame during the early modern period, Llullism had a complicated history in late medieval Europe. This is due to the fact that Llull's works, like those of Arnald of Villanova, had often been the subject of significant theological controversy, resulting in their repeated placement on the Index of banned books by the Inquisition, which was traditionally dominated by the Dominicans. Among the regular clergy, Llull had always been most influential with the Franciscans but had consistently met with opposition by the Dominicans, who (correctly) perceived Llullism as a threat to Thomist natural law metaphysics. Llull's works hereby became a flashpoint in more fundamental theological disputes between the two orders. For example, in 1376, the Aragonese Dominican Inquisitor Nicholas Eymerich (ca. 1320–1399), an avowed enemy of Llullism, had Llull's works banned after producing a papal bull entitled *Conservationi puritatis,* allegedly issued by Pope Gregory XI, that declared Llull's works to be heretical.[21] Although Eymerich's presentation of the document as a papal bull was later exposed as a forgery, controversy about the orthodoxy of Llullian ideas lingered throughout the later Middle Ages and into the sixteenth century. One of the theological issues over which the Llullists frequently clashed with the Thomists was the question of whether or not Christ would still have come into the world had man not fallen in Original Sin. Whereas the Thomists (beginning with Aquinas) argued that Christ would not have, Llull and the Scotists argued that he still would have.[22] To the modern mind, such questions have the ring of proverbial "Scholastic" hair-splitting, but such technical theological distinctions often had profound implications for the metaphysical relationship between the divine will and natural law, as well as for the political relationship between the temporal power of the church and that of civil authorities. On a most basic level, the Thomists objected to Llullism not only because of Llull's claim of being able to discover scientific proof of the truth of the Christian religion but also because of his tendency toward a mystical lay spirituality, as well as his frequent use of the vernacular (mainly Catalan) in discussing matters of theology.[23] Moreover, the central tenet of Llullism was the belief that any effective evangelical rhetoric would need to be informed by the missionary's systematic study and thorough understanding of the ontological and linguistic categories by which a convert apprehended the phenomena of God's creation. As we saw in chapter 3, in the example of Llull's *The Gentile and the Three Wise Men*, Llull's method of ostensible interfaith "dialogue" (despite its ultimately monological nature) involved an engagement with ideas that could have heretical effects among Christians, who were, traditionally, the primary target of Dominican preaching. Yet another reason why Llullian works frequently ended up on the Index was that many theologically problematic works, including works of alchemy, had spuriously appeared under his name. As we saw in chapter 2, the Dominicans (again starting with Aquinas) had traditionally been skeptical about and even hostile toward alchemy, which flourished primarily in Franciscan circles. Thus, still in the sixteenth century, Llullian works were placed on the Index (in 1557 and 1559). At the Council of Trent (1545–63), some of Llull's admirers effected their removal from the Index, but in the 1570s, they appeared there again until their final removal in 1590 as a result of the personal intervention by King Philip II, who was a great patron of Llullism.[24]

It is no coincidence that early modern political rulers with absolutist aspirations such as Philip frequently sided with the Llullians rather than with the Thomists, for whom all temporal dominion had a strictly natural, not a supernatural, origin. Indeed, if Llullism became "one of major forces of the Renaissance," it is arguably in part due to its absolutist political implications in enabling a theocratic legitimation of civil authority against Thomist-Aristotelian natural law metaphysics. Nevertheless, due to the uncertain status of their orthodoxy still during the sixteenth century, Llull's works had to be used with caution. Even some of the most important Llullists of the fifteenth century, such as Nicholas of Cusa and Raymond Sabunde, never cited Llull openly.[25] Similarly, we rarely find Llull's name mentioned in the works written by the American missionaries, despite the fact that we know that Llullian and pseudo-Lullian works found their way into New Spanish libraries and were read, used, and quoted there without attribution.[26] For example, as Linda Báez Rubí has shown, the American-born Franciscan missionary Diego de Valadés incorporated, virtually verbatim, an early sixteenth-century pseudo-Llullian work, *In rhetoricam isagoge* (1515). Yet, in his *Rhetorica Christiana*, Llull is not listed in the table of authorities cited by Valadés or mentioned anywhere in the text. Báez Rubí's analysis suggests that the Llullian tradition often influenced the works of the New Spanish Franciscans not only clandestinely but also indirectly—not from any of the medieval works written by or attributed to Llull but from early modern Llullist works written by several influential Renaissance humanists working at universities and courts in Italy, Spain, and France who thoroughly mediated the Llullian medieval tradition with Renaissance Neoplatonic currents as well as the pseudo-Llullian alchemical tradition.[27] For the historian of Llullism, both in Europe and in America, this phenomenon creates the interesting methodological and hermeneutical problem that Llullian ideas and concepts are often used and developed by late medieval and early modern writers but attributed to other, less controversial authors, such as St. Augustine, Bonaventure, or Duns Scotus.

Due to the uncertain orthodoxy of the writings attributed to Llull, the Llullian renaissance of the late fifteenth and early sixteenth centuries is more conspicuous in courtly and academic settings than it is in mendicant ones. Llullism had especially strong support at the Crown of Aragon, under the reigns of King Pedro IV (1319–1387) and his successor, King Juan I (1350–1396), who sent Bishop Eymerich into exile over his continued opposition to Llullism. In the fourteenth century, the Crown of Aragon—then a composite monarchy comprising Aragon, Catalonia, Valencia, and Majorca—was one of the most formidable powers in Europe, and the Aragonese monarchs strongly supported a homegrown culture of learning that gave rise to what the eminent Catalan intellectual historian Miguel Batllori has called a distinctly "Catalan-Aragonese Humanism."[28] The patronage of Llullism by the Aragonese monarchs was in this context not limited to the protection of Llullians and the suppression of their enemies but also involved the active promotion of Llullian science in the academies. Thus, in 1393 King Juan I oversaw the creation of the Escuela Luliana in Barcelona, which would be committed, he wrote, to "studying and lecturing the art and philosophical doctrine of the great Catalan philosopher Ramon Llull."[29] During the fifteenth century, the Llullian renaissance spread from Barcelona to other academic centers of the new humanist learning, including Bologna and Paris. Meanwhile, the strong support that Llullism had traditionally enjoyed at the Aragonese court had also carried over into Castile after the marriage of Ferdinand and Isabella in 1469. Ferdinand's authorization in 1483 for the creation of a new academy for Llullian studies at Palma de Mallorca, the Estudio General Luliano, set the stage for the Llullian renaissance in the greater Spains. Its first chair was the Catalan priest Pedro Daguí (1435–1500), the royal chaplain of the Catholic Monarchs.[30] In 1482, Daguí had published his influential compendium on Llull's Art, the *Ianua artis magistri Raymundi Lull*, in Barcelona. Soon enough, however, the book was denounced for heresy by the Dominican inquisitor of Majorca, Guillermo Caselles, after a theological controversy had been reignited by an incident in which some Llullists in Aragon had publicly criticized an inscription at a Dominican church relating to the relationship between Original Sin and the Incarnation. Daguí, being in the cross fire of this renewed controversy, was summoned to Rome by Pope Sixtus IV in order to defend himself against the charge before a commission.[31] However, the pope (himself a Franciscan with a Scotist bent and wary that the campaign begun by Caselles against Daguí was part of a Dominican conspiracy against Scotist theology) appointed to the commission six theologians sympathetic toward Llullism and Scotism, including two other Franciscans and two known Llullists from Spain, Fernando de Cordova and Jaume Conill, the vicar-general at the Archdiocese of Valencia.[32] Unsurprisingly, Daguí was exonerated by the commission and his book republished in Rome in 1485 by the printer Eucharius Silber, who had earlier that year also printed Llull's *Ars brevis,* probably upon instigation by Daguí. The Roman edition of *Ianua artis magistri Raymundi Lull* included the commission's report affirming its orthodoxy,[33] and it was subsequently republished in at least five additional editions that appeared in major intellectual centers, including Paris, Valencia, and Seville by 1500. Daguí went on to publish several other Llullian works, including the *Formalitates breves in artem Raimundi Lulli* (1491) and the *Tractatus de differentia* (1500).[34]

One of the judges whom Pope Sixtus had appointed to the commission investigating Daguí in 1485 was Jaume Conill, the vicar-general of the Archdiocese of Valencia, one of the centers of Llullism in the Crown of Aragon, besides Barcelona and Palma. The Llullian circle around Conill included his superior, the Cardinal of Valencia, Rodrigo de Borgia (or Borja), and the Majorcan humanist Esperandéu Espanyol.[35] The former would soon be elected pope and ascend the throne of St. Peter under his chosen regnal name of "Alexander VI," in August 1492; and the latter would become the teacher of one of Rodrigo's many illegitimate children, Cesare Borgia. While it can hardly be claimed that Rodrigo attempted to imitate Llull's asceticism and eremiticism (given his notoriously flamboyant and lascivious lifestyle before and after he was elected pope), he had a noted interest in Llullism.[36] This interest must, however, be seen in the context of his ideological attempt to cultivate his own personal mythology as a Spanish (especially Catalan-Aragonese) occupant of the supreme pontiff's throne in Rome. Thus, Rodrigo maintained close ties with King Ferdinand, both before and after his election. The letters that passed between them were all written in Catalan; and while Rodrigo dealt in Latin for church business and in Italian for local Vatican politics, the official language spoken at the Borgia papal court in Rome was Catalan.[37] Although Rodrigo had received his education in Bologna, he remained a great champion of Catalan-Aragonese humanism and a supporter of Aragonese political ambitions (at least during his early years as pope). No doubt, his display of Aragonese patriotism and partisanship was in part driven by his Machiavellian personal ambitions, especially when it came to advancing the prospects of his children. Already as cardinal of Valencia, Rodrigo had taken full advantage of his good political relations with the Spanish monarchs—before anointing them later as the "Catholic Monarchs" (probably in 1496). Thus,

King Ferdinand had permitted Rodrigo de Borgia to add to the bishopric of Valencia those of Cartagena (1482) and Majorca (1489). Also, in 1485, Ferdinand had invested Rodrigo's oldest son, Pedro Luis, with the duchy of Gandia, near Valencia, thereby elevating him to one of the most important members of the Aragonese nobility. After Rodrigo's election to the papal throne, Ferdinand nominated Rodrigo's son Caesar Borgia as the new bishop of Valencia.[38]

Rodrigo's choice of the regnal name "Alexander" may seem peculiar in the context of his professed Catalan-Aragonese patriotism. But it was actually a continuation of a Borgia dynastic tradition that had cultivated the idea of a "Hellenistic" origin of the Valencian family in particular and of the Crown of Aragon in general. As we saw in chapter 4, the idea of a "Greek" lineage had been an important element in Aragonese patriotism at least since the fourteenth century, with Arnald of Villanova's claim that the king of Aragon, as the Last World emperor, was "the king of the Romans or of the Greeks." Rodrigo's uncle, Alfonso de Borgia, had chosen the Greek name "Calixtus" (the beautiful) when he was elected as pope in 1455. Similarly, Rodrigo, as Pope Alexander VI, created the special mythology that his election as the pope from the "Hellenistic" Crown of Aragon signaled the rightful return of the "true" ruler to Rome, whose ancient paganism had betrayed the heritage of Greek civilization, which instead lived on in Hellenistic Alexandria. As Pope Alexander, Rodrigo's self-mythologization hereby revolved around the Borgia family crest, the bull, by which he traced his Valencian lineage back to the ancient Egyptians, in particular to the bovine cult around the Egyptian god Osiris, under whose wise guidance Hermes Trismegistus, the alleged contemporary of Moses, gave the Egyptians their ancient culture of learning at Alexandria. For Alexander, Hellenistic-Egypt, and Alexandria especially, was the cradle of civilization and true religion. For, like other Christian Hermeticists, Alexander saw Hermeticism as being proto-Christian—the religion of Hermes, contemporary of Moses and the prophet of Christ. Hermeticism was the *prisca theologia* from which all religions sprang but whose promise was fulfilled only in Christianity.[39] Hence, Alexander was a great sponsor not only of Llullism but also of Hermeticism, Neoplatonism, Egyptology, hieroglyphology, kabbala, astrology, alchemy, and natural magic.[40] This Hermeticism intermingled in his personal mythology with the Christian iconography of the Virgin Mary, for whose mystical cult he, like Llull, harbored a special affection as the Mother of God and patron saint of Christian Reconquista, crusade, and conversion.[41] The Llullism of the Catalan-Aragonese renaissance thus functioned in the ideological context of the Borgia papacy to synthesize the Christian crusading ethos of the Reconquista with the Neoplatonism and Hermeticism of the Italian Renaissance.

Not surprisingly, later Protestant commentators saw nothing proto-Christian in Pope Alexander's Hermeticism. For example, the English collector of travel literature and Anglican minister Samuel Purchas sarcastically punned on the homonym "bull" in English by comparing the Alexandrian cult of the "bull" with the magic of his "bull" *Inter cetera,* in which he had decreed that Spain was the exclusive recipient of the right of access to the Americas based on its exclusive mission to the Indians "*ad fidem Catholicam reducere.*"

> And what right then had the Pope to propound that Method in his Bull, Vobis subjiere & ad fidem Catholicam reducere? Is any thing more free, then to believe? Else if Ethnikes had beene to be compelled to enter into the Church (for it is otherwise with the Children of the Kingdome) hee would have sent Captains, Conquerors, Alexanders . . . not Fishermen, Tent-makers, Publicans, as Sheepe amongst Wolves, not Wolves amongst Sheepe. . . . And if I should shew out of [Bartolomé de las] Casas, a Spanish Bishop in those parts, the executions of this Bull, you would say, that the Brazen Bull of Phalaris, the Monster-Bull of Minos, the fire-breathing Bull subdued by Hercules, the Jewes Behemoth, and those of Aegypt were but Calves to this Pope Alexander. . . . It is no marvell that this Bull hath begotten such brutish Christians in America.[42]

Most likely, however, the "bull" Alexander was not responsible for the phrase "*ad fidem Catholicam reducere*" in the bull *Inter cetera,* as Purchas assumed. There are a total of five bulls relating to the Columbian discoveries, and the phrase appears only in the two bulls that began (after the introductory salutations) with the phrase "inter cetera" and are hence so called.[43] The earlier one of these two bulls (*Inter cetera* I) was written and dated May 3, 1493; and the second one (*Inter cetera* II) was dated May 4 but not actually written until June 28. Very close to the original, it was a revision that had been prepared in response to the dissatisfaction expressed by the Spanish Monarchs and Columbus with the vagueness in language of the original donation. The changes reflect the results of the intense negotiations that had ensued between Barcelona and Rome after the dispatch of the first version of May 3. It was only the revision (*Inter cetera* II) that introduced the famous line of demarcation one hundred leagues west of the Azores, and historians have surmised that the idea most likely originated with none other than Christopher Columbus, who in his letter from the third voyage, seems bent on naturalizing this artificial line by writing that every time during his journeys to the Indies when he reached "a point a hundred leagues west of the Azores the heavens, the stars, the temperature of the air and the waters of the sea abruptly changed" and that, from that point onward to the Indies, the seas "sloped upward on this line."[44] While the second version (*Inter cetera* II) was issued as an official and public bull from the office of the papal Chancellery (as was customary), the first ("draft") version had been dispatched to the Catholic Monarchs as a secret brief from the Apostolic Chamber. Although the original versions of these bulls are not preserved, Manuel Giménez Fernández has studied the various extant copies and concluded that the first ("draft") version was written not by Alexander but by the head secretary of the Apostolic Chamber, Lodovico Podocatharo, who appears as one of the signatories ("L. Podocatharus") on both *Inter cetera* I and *Inter cetera* II.[45]

Who was this "L. Podocatharus"? Surprisingly little is known about his life (?–ca. 1508). What we do know is that he was a Cypriot physician, a member of the Greek diaspora who had fled his native Nicosia after the Ottoman conquest of Constantinople in 1453. One of Alexander's closest associates, he apparently had a reputation already as a man of science and as a seeker of the secrets of nature when Alexander appointed him as the chief secretary of the Apostolic Chamber, as well as his personal physician. A friend and supporter of Giovanni Pico de la Mirandola, he had edited multiple recent translations of Aristotle from the Greek into Latin in the 1470s and 1480s, most notably the *De animalibus*.[46] A scholar of Asian languages, he had also served as rector of the University of Padua and was appointed as regent of the University of Rome by Alexander. He became an influential figure in the church, due in part to his close connection to Alexander, being appointed bishop of Capaccio (1483), cardinal of St Agatha (1500), and archbishop of Benevento (1504). After Alexander's death in 1503, he only barely missed his chance of becoming pope during the election that resulted in the papacy of Pius III.[47] Before serving Alexander, Lodovico had also served as the personal physician of Pope Innocent VIII, who, according to legend, was treated with "corpse medicine" after falling seriously ill in July 1492 and dying shortly thereafter. This medicine involved the use of human blood, an alchemical practice that had become widespread in the context of fifteenth-century Renaissance Egyptomania, but the history of which goes back (as we have seen) to the alchemical writings of Roger Bacon, who believed that human blood was an excellent source for distilling the miraculously efficacious quintessence. According to the legend of the "vampire pope," Innocent was administered the blood taken from three boys (who died in the process).[48]

Most likely, as secretary of the Apostolic Chamber, Podocatharo had researched and written the draft of *Inter cetera* I (presumably in consultation with the recently elected pope), according to the customary formulas that had been established in the tradition of the many bulls of this type by which previous popes had donated islands and lands in the eastern Atlantic and in Africa to the Portuguese, some of which also began with the unremarkable phrase *inter cetera* (among other [works]). For example, in 1456, Pope Calixtus III (aka Alfonso de Borgia), had issued a bull *Inter cetera* in which he confirmed the terms granted the year before by Pope Nicholas V in *Romanus pontifex* to the Portuguese and conferred upon Prince Henry, governor of the Portuguese military Order of Christ, all the lands in Africa "from Capes Bojador and Nam through the whole of Guinea and beyond its southern shore all the way to the Indians."[49] In the tradition of these previous bulls of donation, Podocatharo would also have found the phrase "*ad fidem Catholicam reducere,*" where it (or some version of it) had frequently been used since the thirteenth century, especially in the context of the tradition of the bulls of donation that Weckmann-Muñoz has called *doctrina omni-insular*. As pointed out earlier, in classical Latin the word *reducere* had simply meant "to return" (i.e., somebody or something to an earlier state), "to lead back" or "bring back" as well as to "withdraw." However, its use in the sense of "to convert" (i.e., "leading back to the true faith") during the Middle Ages appears to have been rather particular to the discourse of canon law and papal bulls.[50] For example, in the Bull *Romanus pontifex* (1455), Nicholas V wrote that Prince Henry had traveled to "the most remote and undiscovered places ... to bring [back] into the bosom of the faith the perfidious enemies of him and of the life-giving Cross" (*ad ipsius fidei gremium reduce*).[51] Initially, however, the verb *reducere* in the sense of "to convert" was used primarily in reference to heretics and schismatics. Thus, in 1302, Pope Boniface VIII (Arnald of Villanova's patron) had used the word in this sense in his bull *Unam Sanctam* ("One Holy Church"), promulgated in the context of his confrontation with King Philip IV of France over the church's rights to collect tithes in France. Invoking the principle of *papa vicarius Christi* in order to claim the pope's universal primacy over temporal lords and his right to collect tithes, he threatened Philip with excommunication for heresy and asserted that there is no salvation outside the church and that all heretics must be "reduced" to the supreme dominion of the church.[52] Also, four years later, in 1306, Pope Clement V, in *In superne preeminentia,* describes the Greek Orthodox Christians as schismatics who should be "reduced" to the orthodox faith (*ad fidem reduci valeat orthodoxam*).[53]

The technical use of the Latin verb *reducere* in the sense of *convertere* seems plausible enough in the Bonifacian context of heretics and in the Clementian context of schismatics. However, the usage in the context of an apostolic mission to unbelievers (infidels) in both *Romanus pontifex* and *Inter cetera* seems peculiar. Although it would be a difficult task to establish definitively the origin of this usage in reference to infidels, its use in this context has a particularly Llullian flavor, considering Llull's monistic theory that the three major religions of medieval Europe—Judaism, Christianity, and Islam—shared certain basic common roots in the Divine Dignities that suffuse the Platonic chain of creation from the Creator all the way down to the Aristotelian elements—common roots to which each metaphysical system could be logically reduced and rebuilt by correct logic to arrive at the universal truth of the Christian faith. Indeed, the use of the phrase *ad fidem Catholicam reducere* in the context of the conversion of unbelievers does frequently appear in the writings of Ramón Llull, especially in his later apocalyptic writings in which he openly called for crusade as a fallback solution if attempts at peaceful conversion were not successful. For example, in his *Liber de civitate mundi* (1314), which he wrote late in his life in Messina shortly before embarking on his final trip to Africa, he laments the general indifference and complacency on the part of the church and Christian princes, who preside over a fallen and corrupt "worldly city" from which Justice has fled. When "Justice" returns to the "city" with the seven Virtues to call on Llull that he return to the Curia and courts in order to present his apocalyptic book of warning, "so that they will have knowledge and fear of God's justice," Ramón excuses himself, explaining that

> he had gone to the Curia several times and also to Christian princes and told them that the Faith would be exalted all over the world; and he wrote books in which he showed the manner in which the entire world could be redeemed, but it has all been in vain. And several times, he was [even] ridiculed, abused, and called a phantasticus. And so Ramón excused himself and said that he would go to the lands of the Saracens and see if he could convert those same Saracens to the Holy Catholic Faith [*ad fidem sanctam Catholicam reducere*].[54]

The reference to being called a "phantasticus" (a crazy person) relates to an incident that had happened three years earlier, in September 1311, when Llull was ridiculed by a cleric to whom he had explained his militant apostolic agenda while traveling from Paris to Vienne (south of Lyon), in order to attend the Ecumenical Council of the Roman Church, which was held there in 1311–12. The insult must have stung, after Llull's ideas had again been rejected by the theologians at the University of Paris during his second visit there. During his stay at the Council of Vienne, Llull wrote several books in which he responded to his critics, including the *Disputatio Petri clerici et Raymundi phantastici,* in which he defiantly took ownership of the token "phantasticus" in an imaginary dialogue with the priest who had ridiculed him. Also, he elaborated most succinctly his theory of the "two swords" that would bring about the reformation of the world—the crusader's material sword of steel and the rhetorical sword of the missionary's knowledge and devotion. With the combination of these two swords, Llull proposed, the church would be able to "reduce all infidels to the path of truth" (*omnes infideles ad uiam reducere ueritatis*): "First, the pope should send wise and learned men who are prepared to die to the Saracens, Turks and Tartars, to show the infidels their errors and to open up for them the truth of the Holy Catholic faith, so that they might come to the holy cleansing of regeneration. If they resist, the pope should apply the secular sword against them. This is both licit and required, and he who is against it in any way is crazy and culpable."[55] During the Ecumenical Council at Vienne, Llull presented his proposal formally before Pope Clement V. Entitled *Petitio Raymundi in concilio general ad acquirendam Terra Sancta* and structured into ten *ordinatione* (rules), the proposal called for the establishment of three seminaries for the teaching of Eastern languages to future missionaries, which would be based in Rome, Paris, and Toledo. Also, he called for the training of knights to conquer the Holy Land and for the writing of books against Averroism. With regard to the missionaries, they should follow the example of Spain, where "many Jews and also Saracens have been subjected by the Christians," who preach to the Jews on Saturdays and to the Saracens on Fridays, hereby "reducing them to inference and reason" (*reducantur ad syllogismos et an intelligibile*).[56]

The synod decided to support the first of these three proposals but rejected the other two. Worse for Llull, at the same council, Pope Clement condemned the Knight Templars, resulting in the seizure of their assets and the burning at the stake of many of their leaders, including the Master of the Temple in Nicosia, who had hosted Llull during his visit in Cyprus ten years earlier. While, in 1312, Llull could at least celebrate a partial victory in the synod's decision to realize his old vision of language seminaries for missionaries, nothing had come of the plan by the time a frustrated Llull sat down two years later to pen his *Liber de civitate mundi,* where he announced his decision, at age eighty-two, to go on one more apostolic mission to Africa. Indeed, nothing would come of the plan for almost two hundred more years, until it was finally realized by the Franciscans in their *doctrinas* in the Americas.

In the Llullian context of *Liber de civitate mundi,* the use of the verb *reducere* for *convertere* refers, of course, to Muslims, whose religion can be apprehended, from a Christian point of view, as a sort of "heresy" in the sense that, historically, Islam, like Christianity, is an offshoot from the trunk of Abrahamic religions but originated later than Christianity. From this point of view, its usage could also be explained in the context of Calixtus III's bull *Inter cetera* (1456) which also pertained to the conversion of "Saracens" (or Arabs) in regions lying south of Cape Bojador and "all the way to the

Indians."⁵⁷ But in what sense can the "Indians" referred to in the Alexandrine bull *Inter cetera* be "brought back" to Christianity? After all, they presumably lived, theologically speaking, not in "vincible" but in "invincible" ignorance of Christ. This is to say that, unlike Muslims or Jews, they had never come into contact with Christianity and their ignorance was therefore not sinful. This distinction was made abundantly clear in Thomas Aquinas's *Summa*:

> Wherefore through negligence, ignorance of what one is bound to know, is a sin; whereas it is not imputed as a sin to man, if he fails to know what he is unable to know. Consequently ignorance of such like things is called "invincible," because it cannot be overcome by study. For this reason such like ignorance, not being voluntary, since it is not in our power to be rid of it, is not a sin: wherefore it is evident that no invincible ignorance is a sin. On the other hand, vincible ignorance is a sin, if it be about matters one is bound to know; but not, if it be about things one is not bound to know.⁵⁸

Aquinas's distinction would play an important role in the disputations of the Thomist natural law theorists about the justness of the conquest of America (as we will see in chapter 8). As we saw in chapter 3, Llull also had an interest in the conversion of pagans ("gentiles"), mainly the Tartars and the Indians. But, as far as I am aware, he never proposed to "reduce" them to the Catholic faith.

One clue to this extension of Llull's "Abrahamic" paradigm of conversion as a "reduction" to the *prima scientia* of God to peoples other than the Jews, Christians, and Muslims in the *papa vicarius Christi* tradition can be found in Nicholas's bull *Romanus pontifex* (1455). There, Nicholas explained that what was meant by "all the way to the Indians" was "as far as to the Indians who are said to worship the name of Christ" (*usque ad Indos qui Christi nomen colere dicuntur*).⁵⁹ Nicholas appears to refer here to the legend of Prester John (Iohannes Presbyter), a fabulous Christian king of Greek extraction who was believed to rule over a marvelous kingdom located in "India." The legend had emerged during the twelfth century, when, on May 5, 1122, Pope Calixtus II (1119–24) allegedly held an audience with a certain patriarch from the Indies named John. He reportedly informed the pope about a certain eastern city named "Hulna," the site of the apostle Thomas's tomb, from which a miraculous balsam is extracted that cures every person who visited on the day of the apostle's anniversary. Shortly therafter, a letter entitled *Epistola presbiteri Johannis* (The letter of Prester John, ca. 1170) was circulated purporting to be addressed to Emperor Manuel of Byzantium from a Christian king named Prester John, who claimed to be a "Thomas Christian" (a disciple of Thomas, the "Apostole of India"). In the letter, Prester John describes his marvelous kingdom and expresses his wish to make contact with Western Christendom in order to fight the common Muslim foe.[60] The author hereby appears to have been inspired by a story he had read in Otto of Freising's *Chronica sive historia de duabus civitatibus* (Chronicle or history of the two cities, 1145), where the Austrian bishop reports on a meeting he had with the Latin bishop Hugh of Jabala, who told him about "a certain John, priest and king," a Nestorian Christian who lived beyond Persia and had just defeated two Turkish princes. However, the descriptions of Prester John's kingdom in *Epistola presbiteri Johannis* are derived from the tradition of the so-called Alexander Romance, the *Historia Alexandri Magni*, which dates back in its Latin tradition to the tenth century and to the fourth century AD in its earlier Greek varieties.[61] Like the pseudo-Aristotelian *Secretum secretorum*, it tells the story of the Asian exploits of Alexander the Great, patron and beneficiary of the arts and sciences. But unlike the *Secretum secretorum*, which had entered the Latin West from the Arabic, the Alexander Romance, being of early Christian provenance, mixed the history of Alexander and its Hellenistic mythology with elements from Judeo-Christian traditions, especially the Greek and Syriac apocalyptic traditions of John of Patmos and Pseudo-Methodius. Thus, Alexander fights not only Amazon woman warriors but also the cannibalistic armies of Gog and Magog, whom he locks up behind a wall that he erects especially for this purpose in central Asia. Allegedly, in 1177 Pope Alexander III, standing on the Rialto Bridge in Venice, dictated a letter in reply to this eastern Christian potentate and sent his own physician to find the fabulous kingdom in India.[62]

In the thirteenth century, the story of Prester John became the specialty of Franciscan apostolic utopianism, especially in travel accounts written by several Franciscan missionaries who had visited China, such as Giovanni da Plano Carpini and William of Rubruck. There, Prester John became a synthetic figure—the spiritual heir of Thomas the Apostle, the military heir of Alexander the Great, and the scientific heir of Alexander's magus, Aristotle. Thus, in his *The History of the Mongols*, Carpini relates a story, clearly inspired by the Alexander Romance, in which it is not Alexander but Prester John who employs Aristotelian pyrotechnics ("Greek fire") in warfare. When a Tartar ruler with a superior army attacked "the Christians who live in Greater India," Carpini writes:

> The king of that country, who is commonly called Bishop John, met him with his army. He made copper dummies of men, put them on horseback with fire inside them, and a man behind with bellows. The Indians advanced against the Tartars with many such dummies and prepared horses and when they had come to the battleground they placed these horses next to one another. The men who were

behind put I do not know what on the fire which was in these figures and pumped hard with the bellows. Because of this the enemy's men and horses were burned by Greek fire, and the air was polluted with smoke, and then the Indians shot arrows at the Tartars and wounded and killed many and they drove them in confusion from their borders. We have not heard that the Tartars ever went back.[63]

This story later patently inspired Roger Bacon's proposals for the military applications of alchemy, as well as his idea of using the magnifying glass for solar warfare—an idea, as we have seen, that would still resonate with the nineteenth-century men of Macondo in García Márquez's *One Hundred Years of Solitude*. In his *Opus maius*, Bacon located the kingdom of Prester John in "Black Cathay," by which he presumably meant a region south of China, or "India."[64] In the fourteenth century, Marco Polo, impressed by the technological advancement of the Mongol Empire but unable to find any trace of Prester John's kingdom, gathered that the Christian king must have been vanquished by the Mongol emperor Genghis Khan at last but that certain provinces in the Mongol Empire were "of the lineage of Prester John."[65] Alexander's Aristotelian scientific tradition had thus been passed on to the Mongol emperor, but the Apostle Thomas's Christian tradition must have fallen prey to the human tendency toward idolatry. While it became the mission of medieval Christian Europe to "reduce" the Mongols and Indians to the true faith from which they strayed, in India still today the followers of Thomas (Mar Thoma) hold that this Apostle of India was buried outside Chennai (Madras) after having founded the first continuous Christian tradition in India in the early centuries AD—long before the arrival of the Portuguese in 1498.[66]

Francisco Jiménez de Cisneros and the Llullian Renaissance

Even though by the second decade of the sixteenth century, it had become increasingly patent that the lands discovered by Columbus were neither India nor China, their relationship to Greater Asia remained far from certain, and missionaries found traces of "St. Thomas the Apostle" from Mexico to Peru throughout the sixteenth century.[67] If the Llullian language of reduction had provided an important source of missionary zeal and hermeneutics in the medieval canon law tradition of *papa vicarius Christi*, to which Alexander VI's bulls *Inter cetera* were heir, the revival of Llullism during the Renaissance by Spanish humanists was an important catalyst for translating the Llullian hermeneutics of conversion into missionary programs, methods, and practices in the peninsular academies and on the colonial frontiers. A crucial aspect of the Llullian revival during the early sixteenth century was hereby the fusion of Llull's *ars* of evangelical rhetoric with the pseudo-Llullian alchemical corpus. For example, in 1506, the Cistercian Jacob Janer, one of Daguí's students, published his *Ars metaphysicalis naturalis ordinis* with the official approbation of Conill (the late Pope Alexander's vicar-general during his time as cardinal of Valencia).[68] Janer provided there an explanation of the Llullian Art; asserted the authenticity of Llull's martyrdom in Tunis; and offered a synthesis of several pseudo-Llullian alchemical works, presenting them as being authentic works of Llull.[69] The first printing of these alchemical manuscripts occurred in 1514, when they appeared in Venice together with the medical and alchemical works of Giamatteo Ferrari da Grado, Maimonides, Arnaldus of Villanova, and John of Rupescissa in a volume entitled *De secretis naturae*, which went through multiple editions in the sixteenth century. This volume also contained the prefatory dialogue between Llull and the Benedictine monk from the *Liber de secretis naturae* but not the *Tertia distinctio* and the concluding dialogue between Llull and the monk (discussed in chapter 3).[70]

While the Crown of Aragon—especially Palma de Majorca, Valencia, and Barcelona—had been the most important center of the Llullian renaissance on the Iberian Peninsula during the last two decades of the fifteenth century, during the early sixteenth century, its center of gravity shifted to Castile under the formidable patronage of the powerful figure of Francisco Jiménez de Cisneros (1436–1517). In 1492, Cisneros became the confessor of Queen Isabella; also in 1492 archbishop of Toledo; and in 1507 grand inquisitor and cardinal. He was twice regent of Spain, once after Isabella's death in 1504 and a second time after Ferdinand's death in 1516. The great reformer of the Spanish church and the universities, Cisneros was an ardent admirer of Llull, especially of the medieval missionary's commitment to an eremetic and austere lifestyle, his Scotist theology, and militant missionary zeal. As Joseph Pérez, one of Cisneros's modern biographers, has remarked, Llull and Cisneros were remarkably similar in their intellectual and spiritual disposition; however, Cisneros surpassed his medieval hero in a sense, disposing as he did of the considerable political power and influence that Llull had lacked two hundred years earlier. Both shared the same utopia: one Catholic faith, united by one church and one universal Christian empire.[71] But what Llull had created in ideas—written down in hundreds of theoretical books on encyclopedic logic, evangelical rhetoric, and metaphysics, as well as utopian fictions—Cisneros converted into reality. Thus, with the conquest of Oran, led by Pedro Navarro on his behalf in 1509, Cisneros waged the African crusade that Llull had called for two hundred years earlier. Cisneros reformed the convents of the Observant Franciscans in Spain and established the academies for the linguistic instruction in non-European languages for which Llull had petitioned popes and princes in vain.[72]

But for Cisneros, there was ultimately no theater of action better suited for realizing Llull's Christian utopia than the Americas. In 1500, he founded the University of Alcalá de Henares, northeast of Madrid, where many of the missionaries that would come to the New World were given a humanist training—not in the Italian (i.e., classicist) Renaissance tradition of Lorenzo Valla but in the Christian humanist tradition of Erasmus and Llull. Thus, he promoted the study of languages others than Latin and Greek—specifically Arabic and Chaldean—a project that culminated, with the help of the Spanish humanist Antonio de Nebrija, in the production of the famous Alcalá Polyglot Bible, printed in Latin, Greek, Hebrew, and Chaldean fonts and completed in 1517. Llullism hereby occupied a central place in the Cisnerean vision. At Alcalá, he implemented a chair for Llullian studies and began a library at the College of Ildefonso that would include more than seventy Llullian works. He also had several Llullian works reissued in print, including the *Book of the Lover and the Beloved*.[73]

The first appointed chair of Llullian philosophy and theology at Alcalá was the Majorcan Llullist Nicolás de Pax, the author of one of the two influential early sixteenth-century biographies of Llull, the *Illuminati Doctoris et Martyris Raymundi Lulli* (1519);[74] he redacted a new version of the *Vita coaetania*, and copied, edited, and translated many of Llull's manuscripts and books, including the novel *Félix*, originally written in Catalan, which he rendered into Latin as *Liber de mirabilibus orbis*.[75] The Llullian circle around Cisneros also included the humanist Alfonso de Proaza, the editor of Garci Rodríguez de Montalvo's chivalric novel *Las Sergas de Esplandián* (1510) and Fernando de Rojas's famous *La celestina* (1514).[76] Together with Pax and with the support of Cisneros, Proaza edited and published Llull's *Art of the Discovery of Truth* (1515),[77] in addition to several other Llullian works, including the *Raymundi Lulij . . . De noua logica, de correllatiuis, necnon [et] de ascensu [et] descensu intellectus* (1512) and the *Carmen endecasyllabum in laudem Artis Raymundi Lulli*, which accompanied the publication of Janer's *Liber artis metaphysicalis*.[78]

The Llullian renaissance in Cisnerean Spain did not happen in isolation but had deep connections to the resurgence of Llullism also in other centers of learning, most notably the University of Paris. Already in 1499, the famous French humanist Jacques Lefèvre d'Étaples (ca. 1455–1536) had published an edition of Llull's writings, the *Disputatio clerici et Raymundi Phantatici aut Phantasticus* (1499); and in 1505 he edited Llull's novel *Blanquerna* for print. Lefèvre's interest in Llull had been inspired by Italian Neoplatonism, kabbalism, and Hermeticism, especially by his connection to Marsilio Ficino

(1433–1499) and Pico della Mirandola (1463–1491), the latter of whom he had met in 1492.[79] Lefèvre's connection with Italian Neoplatonism resulted in a tract about magic, the *Magia naturalis* (1493), and an edition of the *Corpus Hermeticum*, the *Mercurii Trismegisti liber de potestate et sapientia dei* (1499).[80] Although the *Magia naturalis* was condemned by the faculty of theology at Paris and was never printed during his lifetime, Lefèvre's interest in Hermeticism explains why he was attracted to the mystical aspects of Llull's works. Lefèvre's student Charles de Bovelles (1479–1553) continued the revival of interest in Llullian metaphysics, theology, ecclesiastical reformism, missionary zeal, and crusading spirit at Paris. In 1506, Bovelles visited Toledo, where he was hosted in the archbishop's palace by Cisneros, and some historians have speculated that the exchanges with Bovelles played an important role in Cisneros's decision to initiate the military campaign that led to the Spanish conquest of Oran.[81] Like Cisneros, Bovelles was attracted to the eschatological schemes that had been an important aspect of the Llullian tradition, in which Christian conquests and conversion of pagan and infidel lands, together with the reformation of the church, paved the road for the Second Coming. Both the *Vita coaetanea*, which was circulating in manuscript in Paris at the time, and Lefèvre's 1505 edition of *Blanquerna*, hereby conveyed to Bovelles the Llullian ideal of the scholarly missionary saint that informed his biography of Llull, the *Epistola in vitam Raymundi Lulli* (1511). Thus, Bovelles wrote that Llull "had been able to insert into his works the light of knowledge given not by men but by God, and had over forty years established means of composing and writing. For his mind showed the stamp of God himself."[82] One of the copies of this book—the first biography of Llull to be printed—found its way into the library of Fray Juan de Zumárraga, the first archbishop of Mexico and cofounder of the Colegio Imperial de Santa Cruz de Tlatelolco, the Franciscan academy in Mexico founded for the instruction of the native Mexica nobility's children in grammar, Latin, Spanish, rhetoric, the classics, and natural philosophy. Zumárraga's utopian and millenarian conception of the Franciscan missionary enterprise in New Spain was patently inspired in part by the medieval example of Llull as mediated by Bovelles.[83]

It is no coincidence that, of all of Llull's writings that were available at Paris, Lefèvre would chose to edit and publish the Christian utopia *Blanquerna* and the *Disputatio Clerici et Raymundi Phantatici aut Phantasticus*. As we saw in chapter 3, in *Blanquerna* the Llullian protagonist was a Christian hermit turned pope in order to realize the church reforms, the evangelical initiatives, and the crusades that Llull had called for in vain. One of Llull's medieval themes on which the Christian humanists Cisneros, Lefèvre, and Bovelles focused was the incessant call for a Christian crusade against Islam. This crusading spirit had been rekindled during the Renaissance by the Ottoman conquest of Constantinople in 1453, and the Greek diaspora to the Latin West that ensued as a result of it—a diaspora that also brought back the Hermetic and the Epicurean tradition into the Latin West, whose intellectual culture was dominated during the fifteenth century by Scholastic Aristotelianism and Ciceronian humanism. As Richard Tuck has shown, more so than the Thomist Scholastics, it was the Christian humanists who were on the forefront during the Renaissance in elaborating an aggressive theory of war based on the idea of a "Christian republic" that must strike out in unison against Islam. Originating in Cicero's theory of preemptive war, this Renaissance humanist tradition in Christian militancy had a broad array of followers that included Llullians such as Cisneros, Lefèvre, and Bovelles, as well as Christian humanists such as Erasmus and Juan Luis Vives; humanist Aristotelians such as Agostino Nifo and the Spanish theologian and philosopher Juan Ginés de Sepúlveda; and Protestants such as Alberico Gentili.[84]

Besides Cisneros, Lefèvre, and Bovelles, another important Llullian interlocutor who exerted an important influence on the missionary enterprise in America was the Franciscan Conventual Bernardo de Lavinheta (d. ca. 1530). Most likely of Catalan extraction, Lavinheta belonged to the Franciscan convent of St. Bonaventure in Lyon. After completing his studies in Toulouse, he taught at various universities in France, Spain, the Netherlands, and Germany. Before moving to the University of Paris, he had lectured on Llull at the University of Salamanca, where such famous Franciscan missionaries as Bernadino de Sahagún would be trained for their mission in America.[85] While teaching at Salamanca, Lavinheta composed two disputations on Parisian nominalism and edited several Llullian works. In 1516, he also published a new and corrected edition of Daguí's *Janua artis Lulli*.[86] After his return from Salamanca, he became the first holder of the Chair of Llullian Studies at the Sorbonne, instituted by Lefèvre d'Étaples.

Lavinheta's own major work in the Llullian tradition, the *Explanatio compendiosaque applicatio artis Raymundi Lulli* was published in Lyon in 1523. It followed Janer in providing an encyclopedic synthesis of Llullian and pseudo-Llullian works, as well as applications to various fields of knowledge. As Lavinheta wrote, his compendium on Llull's Art offered an "introduction to all faculties, not only speculative—that is, physics, mathematics, metaphysics, theology—but also ethics, preaching, mechanical arts, and even medicine, as well as canon and civil law." It treats of "all the articles of the faith most highly and profoundly."[87] At the beginning of this work, he included an illustration of a "Tree of the Sciences" that is very similar to Llull's original. "There is a necessity," he wrote, "for a general art that contains all the common principles, basic ones and necessary ones, through which the principles of the other sciences can be proved and examined. The multiplicity of the sciences and the brevity of life force man to seek such a universal instrument of knowledge, the possibility of which is based on the universality of its objective and in which human understanding is empowering."[88] The work is divided into nine parts, each of which treats topics as diverse as grammar, rhetoric, logic, physics, mathematics, medicine, metaphysics, theology, ethics, and jurisprudence. Of particular interest for my purposes here is book 8, which is devoted to medicine, the liberal arts (both trivium and quadrivium), as well as the mechanical arts. On the subject of alchemy, Lavinheta relies on several pseudo-Llullian works, including the *Testamentum,* and a tract on alchemical medicine entitled the *Raymundi artes operativam medicina,* the latter of which he reproduces verbatim albeit with some odd modifications. Thus, the author identifies himself as "Raymundus Hylerde," but in the margins he is glossed by Lavinheta as the "Doctor Illuminatus."[89] As Wolfram Platzeck, the modern editor of the work, has noted, such an identification of the two Raymonds is patently erroneous, but neither the identity of Raymund of Lérica nor the independent existence of the text from which Lavinheta allegedly copied has been established.[90] Other prominent alchemical works that are partially copied there include John of Rupescissa's *De consideration quintae essentiae,* which contain the secrets of the "Aqua ardens" and the "Quinta essentia" as well as other highly secret methods of producing medicine for the cure of all diseases by way of the alchemical distillation of various medicinal herbs with alcohol.[91] Lavinheta's *Explanatio* represents the humanist culmination of the encyclopedic-alchemical tradition of Llullism that would become one of the cornerstones of Renaissance occult philosophy later elaborated by Cornelius Agrippa and Giordano Bruno.[92] More immediately, through his connection to Cisneros and his tenure at Salamanca, Lavinheta was also of great importance for the missionary enterprise in America. His *Explanatio* was published in 1523, the year before the famous "first twelve" Franciscan missionaries departed for New Spain under the leadership of their provincial, Martín de Valencia.

But even before the publication of Lavinheta's *Explanatio,* one of his students, who identifies himself as Remigius Rufo Candidus of Aquitaine, had published, in 1515, the two tracts *In rhetoricam isagoge* and *Oratio excemplaris* pseudonymously under Llull's name, with Rufo supposedly acting as editor. Both were treatments of Llull's logic as an art of encyclopedic discourse. Thus, in the preface, the book is described as a "very clear mirror of all the sciences" (*nicidisimo speculo ominium disciplinarum*) as the orator should "have knowledge of everything," and be able to master "the whole world of the sciences, which has been called the 'encyclopedia.'"[93] In accordance with the Llullian formula, Rufo incorporates elements of the pseudo-Llullian alchemical medical tradition and opens with a metaphor that defines the art of rhetoric as the "Alchemy of words." However, Rufo is not literally interested in alchemical transmutation but in alchemy as a metaphor for the transformative healing power of evangelical rhetoric in the work of conversion. Thus, he writes, "God, with your help and your mercy here begins the art of rhetoric, which is called the alchemy of words. Light comes into darkness. For, He who hides in darkness emerges on the mountain summit engulfed in smoke and fog (Exodus 19). Those who want to learn the system of rhetoric will have it available to them, so as to reach it in silence. Hence the Pythagorean silence."[94] The references to a "Pythagorean silence" and to him "who hides in darkness [and] emerges on the mountain summit engulfed in smoke and fog" relate to the notion (in the book of Exodus) that God is hidden in a cloud but "revealed" not through words but through signs, the secrets of his creation. The preacher thus acts as a *hermeneut* who translates this revelation through natural signs into words.

Báez Rubí has suggested that the phrase "alchemy of words" (*alchemia verborum*) may derive from the kabbalistic tradition, where alchemy (the combination of the elements) frequently corresponds metaphorically to rhetoric (the combination of words).[95] Indeed, a connection between Llullism and kabbala in *In rhetoricam isagoge* is possible by way of the work of Giovanni Pico della Mirandola (1463–94). After his *Conclusiones sive theses DCCCC* (*900 Theses*, 1496) had been banned as heretical by Pope Innocent VIII in 1487, the famous Italian humanist and Hermeticist fled to France and was absolved in 1492 by the newly elected Pope Alexander VI. After his absolution, Pico went on to publish his *Apologia tredecim questionum* (1496), where he attempted an adaptation and synthesis of Jewish kabbala, Llull's combinatory system of logic, natural magic, and Hermeticism. He saw himself as the first Christian to reveal the secrets of the kabbala, though he acknowledged certain similarities with the Llullian Art, which may itself already have been influenced by kabbala in the thirteenth century.[96] Also, Pico's Neoplatonic astrological "natural magic," which he had elaborated in his *900 Theses*, had most likely been inspired directly by the Llullian notion of the divine chain of Dignities suffusing all of creation, hereby connecting the sub- and supralunary worlds that had been seen as separate in mainstream Scholastic Aristotelian science: whereas the sublunary world was ever subject to elemental change and corruption, the supralunary world of the stars was seen as perfect and unchanging. By contrast, the Llullian (and later occultist) idea of a correspondence between sublunary matter (such as metals) and the stars laid the foundation for a merging of alchemy and astrology in Neoplatonic occult philosophy that held wide-ranging implications for the history of science.[97]

While it is therefore possible that Pico's kabbalistic interpretation of Llull's Art was a source of Rufo's phrase "alchemy of words" in *In rhetoricam isagoge,* a perhaps more immediate context can be found in the (pseudo-)Llullian medico-alchemical tradition itself, as it had originated with Llull's own *Principles of Medicine* and become "alchemized" in such fourteenth-century pseudo-Llullian tracts on medical alchemy as the *Raymundi artes operativam medicina,* and was finally integrated during the Llullian renaissance by early modern encyclopedists such as Janer and Lavinheta (Rufo's teacher). As we saw, medical alchemy functions in this tradition to illuminate "metaphorically" other fields of knowledge, hereby facilitating not only the *discovery* of occult truths (as in Pico's Christian kabbala) but also a *transformation,* particularly the conversion of unbelievers through an encyclopedic art of preaching that begins with the human experience of God's creation. In accordance with this tradition, the author of *In rhetoricam isagoge* rehearses the "subjects" of the Llullian Art moving up and down the Neoplatonic chain of creation, following the model of Llull's own *De conversione subjiecti et praedicati et Medii: I. De ordinatione, II. De Deo, III. De angelo, IV. De caelo, V. De homine; VI. De imaginative, VII. De sensitive, VIII. De vegetative, IX. De elementativa, X. De subiecto artificiato.*[98] In this tradition, the operations of Llull's art of rhetoric, like the art of alchemy, are not natural but *artificial,* designed to reverse the regular corruptive course of nature by "reducing" the elements to an earlier state of *pristinum statum.* As we will see, the notion of preaching as an "alchemy of words" in *In rhetoricam isagoge* provides an important context for understanding how the sixteenth-century Franciscan missionaries in the Americas conceived of the metaphysics of their work, particularly of the role of preaching in the process of conversion.

Llullism in Early America

Although a history of Llullism in the early Americas remains to be written, the existing scholarship on the earliest evangelical missions allows for at least a preliminary sketch that will provide the historical context for my analysis of some of the missionary writings in the next chapter. Thus, historians have noted the Llullian inspiration of the fourteenth- and fifteenth-century missionaries working in the Canary Islands, where they were based in the diocese of Telde on Gran Canaria. Many of the missionaries active there originated from Majorca and displayed a distinctly Llullian commitment to missionary training in non-Western languages and a reliance on arguments derived natural philosophy and reason rather than Scriptural authority. Thus, Antonio Rumeu de Armas observed that the legacy of Llull's missionary ethos and method was the "principal engine" of the evangelical endeavors of the priests and missionaries who had arrived in Gran Canaria from the diocese of Palma de Majorca in the 1340s, which was then governed by the local bishop Antonio Colell, an admirer of Llull's proselytizing spirit.[99] In 1342, twelve Guanches had been captured in a raid on Gran Canaria in 1342 and brought to Palma de Majorca, where they were catechized and baptized and where they taught the local friars their language before they returned in the company of the friars as collaborators in the evangelical mission.[100]

As I have pointed out above, it is also possible that Christopher Columbus was generally familiar with the legacy of the Majorcan missionary, given his close connection to the Franciscans and especially to the convent of La Rábida in Palos. After Columbus's return from his first transatlantic voyage and the promulgation of the first *Inter cetera* bull on May 3, 1493, Pope Alexander issued, on June 25, the second bull in the series, entitled *Piis fidelium,* in which he appointed the first apostolic vicar-general of the Indies.[101] The person that was chosen (most likely upon recommendation of King Ferdinand and Cisneros) was the Aragonese priest and avid Llullist Bernardo Boyl (also Bernat Boil or Buil [1444–1506]).[102] We know about Boyl's Llullian inspirations from the correspondence that he carried on as abbot of Montserrat with the Majorcan humanist and Llullist Arnaldo Descós before his departure for the Indies, as well as with Cisneros thereafter.[103] But while Boyl became, upon arrival in Hispaniola, the first priest to celebrate a Christian mass in America, he soon had a falling out with Columbus over the admiral's practice of enslaving Indians, and he returned to Spain after only one year. Due to the short duration of his stay, his achievements as a missionary received a mixed report later in the sixteenth century from the Franciscan historian Jerónimo de Mendieta.[104] However, his status as the "first apostle of the New World" was solidified in the early seventeenth century, when he became the protagonist of the widely disseminated *Nova typis transacta navgatio,* written by the German Benedictine monk Caspar Plautius (aka Honorius Philoponus) and illustrated by the famous engraver Wolfgang Kilian. There, however, Boyl appeared in the tradition not of Llull but of another famous apostle—the Irish Saint Brendan the Navigator, and his legendary discovery of the "Isle of the Blessed," or "Saint Brendan's Island," which had been believed to be located in the Atlantic Ocean since the ninth century. It appears in several late medieval maps, including the Ebstorf Map (1270), the Hereford *mappa mundi* (1300); and it was still in 1492 depicted on Martin Behaim's famous world globe.[105]

Also on board of Columbus's second expedition were several Franciscans and the Jeronimite friar Ramón Pané. We know the identities of at least two of the Franciscans. They were Juan de la Deule and Juan de Cosin (or de Tisin), both lay brothers from the chapter at Florenze (in France) who had come to Barcelona after having been chosen for the mission by their vicar-general, Olivier Maillard.[106] The hermit friar Pané was instructed by the admiral to live among the Natives of Hispaniola in order to learn their language, convert them to Christianity, as well as to "discover and understand of the beliefs and idolatries of the Indians, and of how they worship their gods."[107] Based on his ethnographic studies, Pané composed an account that is not only the first text written on American soil in a European language but also the earliest European ethnographic description of Amerindian cultures and religions, as well as the only direct surviving source about the cultural beliefs of the Taínos. Pané hereby initiated the translation of Llull's medieval project of the study of non-Western languages and non-Christian religions for the purpose of conversion in an American context, giving rise to the early American genre of missionary ethnography—the descriptions of Native American cultural and religious practices written with the explicit aim of gathering cultural and linguistic information that would be useful to missionaries in their attempts to "extirpate idolatry"; descriptions that are today, ironically, our best ethnohistorical sources about pre- and post-Columbian Amerindian cultures.[108]

While Pané drops out of the historical record after the delivery of his manuscript to Columbus in 1500, Boyl had returned to Spain in 1494 and filed charges at court against the admiral. Although King Ferdinand ruled in Columbus's favor, the occasion marks the decline of the admiral's courtly fortunes, ultimately leading to his replacement as governor of Hispaniola in 1500 by Francisco de Bobadilla. On board of Bobadilla's fleet arrived several more Franciscan friars, including Juan de Robles, who had owned and studied the works of Llull and Arnald of Villanova before his departure.[109] Like many of the missionaries who would arrive in the Indies in subsequent decades, Robles was the intellectual product of the Llullist revival that was under way in late fifteenth- and early sixteenth-century Spain in the context of the humanist educational reforms implemented by Cisneros. By 1500, several additional Franciscan priests had arrived in Hispaniola, including Francisco Ruiz, Juan de Trasierra, and Rodrigo Perez—"all of them," writes the sixteenth-century biographer Alvar Gómez de Castro, "intimate associates of Cisneros and sons of the Province of Castile."[110] Their letters back to Cisneros provide harrowing accounts of disease, starvation, and destruction on Hispaniola and the Greater Antilles.[111] In 1502, seventeen more Franciscan priests and friars arrived on the fleet of the new governor, Nicolás de Ovando, under the leadership of Fray Alonso de Espinar, who founded the first two Franciscan convents. By 1505, there were enough Franciscans on Hispaniola to found the first Providence in America, the Province of the Holy Cross, which included also Haiti, Cuba, and Jamaica. Its first provincial would be Pedro de Mexía, who arrived in Hispaniola in 1507 or 1508 as a recent graduate from Cisneros's new university at Alcalá.[112]

In the aftermath of Vasco Núñez de Balboa's expedition to Darien in 1510, Juan Ponce de León's expedition to La Florida in 1513, and Hernando Cortés's conquest of Mexico in 1521, Spanish proselytizing efforts shifted in focus from the Caribbean basin to the newly created settlements on *tierra firme*. Cisneros had died in 1517, but his branch of Llullism continued to play an important role in the missionary enterprises of the 1520s. In his letters from Mexico to Charles V, Cortés had repeatedly implored the emperor to provide the "means whereby the natives of these parts may be more speedily converted and instructed in Our Holy Catholic Faith."[113] At first Cortés had requested that a bishop with his usual entourage be sent to Mexico but then changed his mind—"because," he wrote, "if we have bishops and other dignitaries, they will only follow the customs which, for our sins, they pursue these days, of squandering the goods of the Church on pomp and ceremony," setting a bad example for the Indians and discrediting the faith. In his "Fourth Letter to the Emperor," he therefore requested that missionaries from the mendicant orders be charged with the task of conversion, specifically representatives "from the Order of St. Francis and the other from the Order of St. Dominic."[114]

Up to the time of Tenochtitlán's final fall to Cortés's forces in 1521, there was only a very small number of missionaries in the Valley of Mexico, including the Mercedarian Bartolomé de Olmedo, who proselytized some of the lords of Tlaxcala and Texcoco, as well as two Franciscans, Fray Pedro Melgarejo and Fray Diego Altamirano. In 1523, three Flemish Franciscans arrived in Mexico, Johann van den Auwera, Johan Dekkers, and Pedro de Gante (aka Peter of Ghent), who may have been an illegitimate son to the family of the Emperor Charles V. Gante and his fellow Flemish Franciscans worked by the authority of the emperor but without apostolic license from the pope. Meanwhile, already in 1521, Pope Leo X, in the bull *Alias felicis,* had put two Franciscans in charge of leading such a papal mission. One of them, Francisco de los Ángeles (aka Francisco de Quiñones), had been educated as a page for Cisneros before entering the Franciscan friary of Santa Maria de los Ángeles at Alcalá. The other one was a Flemish Franciscan, Juan Clapión, the emperor's confessor. After Pope Leo died that year, the new pope, Adrian VI, issued a new bull, *Exponi nobis fecisti* (1522), addressed to Charles V, confirming the provisions of Leo's bull and authorizing the Franciscans and other mendicant orders to undertake the conversion of the Indians wherever there was no bishop within reach of a two-days' journey. However, after Clapión's unexpected death and Quiñones's appointment as commissary general of the Franciscan Order north of the Alps, the latter recommended the minister provincial of the Custody of San Gabriel, Martín de Valencia, from the provincial convent of Santa Maria de Berrocal.[115] The Franciscan missionaries from San Gabriel were practitioners of an extreme asceticism in the tradition of Pedro de Villacreces (1350–1422), Pedro de Alcántara (1499–1562), and Fray Juan de Guadalupe (d. 1505), the spiritual founder of the Descalced (barefoot) Movement, which was the latest radical outgrowth of the Observant branch of the Friars Minor. The Observants had recommitted themselves to their order's original ideals of strict apostolic poverty and total devotion to the service to God, which, many of them felt, had been diluted by the main branch of the order, the Conventuals.[116]

Finally, on May 13, 1524, the famous "first twelve" Franciscan apostles disembarked at Veracruz under the leadership of their superior, Martín de Valencia. They made their uphill journey on bare feet to the Mexican *altiplano* and, on June 17, made a carefully choreographed entry at Mexico/Tenochtitlán before a curious crowd of Native onlookers. Years later, Bernal Díaz del Castillo wrote:

> When Cortés knew that the Friars were approaching, he dismounted from his horse, as did all of us, and when we met the reverent friars the first to fall on his knees before Fray Martín de Valencia and to kiss his hands was Cortés himself, and the Friar would not permit it, so he kissed his garments and those of all the other ecclesiastics and so did nearly all the captains and soldiers who were present and Guatemoc and the Mexican chieftains. When Guatemoc and the other caciques saw Cortés go down on his knees to kiss hands they were greatly astonished, and when they saw that the friars were barefoot and thin and their garments ragged, and that they had no horses but came on foot and were very jaundiced looking, and [then] turned to Cortés, whom they looked on as an Idol or one of their Gods, on his knees before the friars, all the Indians from that time forward followed his example, and now when friars arrive they give them a reception and pay them reverence in the way I have described.[117]

Two years later, in 1526, the Franciscans were followed by a mission of twelve Dominicans, who arrived under the leadership of Fray Tomás Ortíz; and the first mission of Augustinians arrived in 1533. The so-called "spiritual conquest" of Mexico had begun.[118]

6

Physicians of the Soul
The Alchemy of Reduction and Ethno-demonology in Early America

> The physician cannot conscientiously apply medicine to the sick person without first learning... the cause of the disease. Likewise, the preachers and confessors, who are the physicians of souls, must have practical knowledge of the spiritual medicines and diseases in order to provide spiritual cures.
> —Bernadino de Sahagún,
> *Historia universal de las cosas de la Nueva España*

> God can work in all metals, and transmute all metals: he can make a moral man, a Christian; and a superstitious Christian, a sincere Christian: a papist, a protestant; and a dissolute protestant, a holy man, by... preaching.
> —John Donne, *Sermons*

In the previous chapter, I explored the role that the language of Llullian evangelical rhetoric played in late medieval and early modern European expansionism, particularly in the canon law tradition of *papa vicarius Christi*, in which the pope was licenced to confer spiritual dominion upon temporal rulers charged with the conversion of infidels. I also investigated the crucial role that the "Llullian renaissance" played in the educational reforms implemented in early modern Spain under the leadership of Cardinal Francisco Jiménez de Cisneros in the religious orders and universities from which missionaries would come to the Americas. Finally, I considered the confluence of the Llullian evangelical tradition with pseudo-Llullian alchemy in Christian humanist encyclopedic rhetoric as an "alchemy of words" in the early sixteenth century. In this chapter, I will turn to the role that the Llullian renaissance played in what Robert Ricard once called the "spiritual conquest" of America.[1] In fact, it was Ricard who, in his seminal book *The Spiritual Conquest of Mexico* (1933), provided the first impetus for this line of inquiry by noting the similarities between Llull's *Doctrina pueril* and the *Doctrina christiana breve traduzida en lengua Mexicana,* the first catechism written in New Spain both in Spanish and Nahuatl by the Franciscan Fray Alonso de Molina.[2] As Ricard pointed out, Molina's more famous *Vocabulario en lengua castellana y Mexicana* (1555)—the first printed Nahuatl-Spanish dictionary—may also be seen as the belated fruit of Llull's medieval program of training Franciscan missionaries in non-European languages, which had languished throughout the later Middle Ages.[3] In Cisnerean Spain, Molina's Nahuatl dictionary had been anticipated by Pedro de Alcalá's Arabic dictionary, the *Vocabulista arauigo en letra castellana* (Granada, 1505), written for the missionaries working among Spain's *morisco* and *mudéjar* populations.[4] Ricard did not follow up on the possibility of a deeper connection between the Llullian renaissance in Europe and the missionary enterprises in America; and subsequent scholarship on Molina has remained inconclusive in this regard.[5] More recently, however, several pioneering studies by Mauricio Beuchot, Linda Báez Rubí, Rodolfo Fernández, and others have shown the profound impact of Llullian evangelical rhetoric—especially the Llullian art of memory—on several prominent Franciscans working in sixteenth-century New Spain.[6]

Following the lead of these scholars, I investigate in this chapter the role that Llullism played in early American missionary discourse. However, my focus and approach here will be different from theirs, for I am specifically interested not in the art of memory but in the role that the (pseudo-)Llullian language of spagyra (medical alchemy) played in the early American missionaries' hermeneutics and methodology of conversion. As we have seen in previous chapters, while Llull himself did not practice or write about alchemy, by the sixteenth century he had been spuriously credited with an entire corpus of more than 140 alchemical texts that merged elements of his authentic art of conversion with alchemical theory and practice. The Franciscans had hereby played a key role in what I have called the "alchemification" of the *ars luliana*—the fusion of Llull's system of evangelical rhetoric, combinatory logic, and Neoplatonic metaphysics with Roger Bacon's Franciscan tradition of *scientia experimentalis,* in which alchemy had always been understood primarily as the art of rejuvenating Christian bodies. While modern scholarship on Llull generally distinguishes between his authentic writings and the pseudo-Llullian alchemical corpus, during the late medieval and early modern period, the two corpuses bled seamlessly into each other. The pseudo-Llullian alchemical works therefore constitute an important and integral aspect of the history of early modern Llullism—the legacy of the "Doctor Illuminatus" not only as a Christian missionary, martyr, and logician but also as a great alchemist.

In this chapter, I explore the role that pseudo-Llullian alchemy played both in the early American missionaries' hermeneutics and methodology of conversion in terms of "reduction," as well as in the rise of a "missionary science"—an encyclopedic discourse that involved the empirical study and description of Native American religions and cultures, as well as the study of the natural environment of the New World.[7] While this missionary science has often been seen as the early modern forerunner of modern anthropology, I argue that it must more properly be understood as what I want to call "ethno-demonology"—a forensic inquisitorial discourse that laid the methodological foundations for (but is not identical with) modern ethnography. My initial focus here will be on the sixteenth-century Franciscans in New Spain within the broader context of the mendicant movement. Thus, I contrast the Franciscans' "alchemical" approach with the Dominicans' "hylomorphic" approach to conversion. Finally, I also consider the influence of the alchemical approach beyond the mendicant orders, specifically on the Jesuits, who arrived in the Americas during the second part of the century. Although none of the missionaries I am concerned with here practiced or wrote about alchemy per se (as far as we know), the close analogical relationship between ministering and medicine—between spiritual and physical healing—in the Llullian tradition gave rise to an autoptic epistemology that transformed the late medieval encyclopedic tradition into an empirical ethno-demonology in the service of the evangelical enterprise. In the following section of this chapter, I consider how the Franciscans' understanding of religious conversion in terms of alchemical reduction and transmutation illuminates the ambivalent character of their missionary enterprise in its dialectic between iconoclastic violence and proto-ethnographic curiosity. In the middle sections, I explore the transformation of the concept of "reduction" from a hermeneutics into a methodology of conversion in the heterotopian Franciscan *doctrinas* (also called *reducciones*) of New Spain. Next, I focus on the work of the Franciscan missionary Bernadino de Sahagún in order to consider the coalescence of ethno-demonology with the Llullian encyclopedic tradition of the "alchemy of words." In the last section, I focus on the writings of the famous Jesuit missionary and historian of Peru, José de Acosta, specifically on his elaboration of the spiritual conquest in terms of the "alchemical wedding" in the context of the so-called Reducción General undertaken in the Andes by viceroy Francisco de Toledo beginning in 1569.

The Alchemy of Conversion

Historians of religion have offered various explanations for the rise of the mendicant movement in the thirteenth century. According to one socioeconomic account, the mendicant style of living and preaching in the city reflected the values as well as the language of mobility and adventure of the emergent bourgeoisie but elaborated the idea of a more "noble" Christian commerce by offering the Gospel without monetary exchange. The mandate of a life in poverty hereby served as an exemplary warning against the dangers of a growing money economy and those who dealt in it.[8] As we saw in the introduction of this book, Marxian historians of science have offered similar socioeconomic explanations for the rise of alchemy in the Latin West during the thirteenth century. Like the mendicant orders, alchemy emerged in the context of a late medieval cash nexus on the principle that I have called the "logic of convertibility through reduction and circulation." Here, I wish to highlight another historical dimension of this principle of convertibility as manifest in the simultaneous rise of alchemy, the mendicant movement, and Christian evangelism during the thirteenth century: the impact of Scholastic Aristotelianism on the late medieval and early modern hermeneutics of religious conversion.

As historians of religion have pointed out, the idea of conversion is not a constant in the history of Christianity, as its meaning is always contingent on cultural and social contexts.[9] However, a distinction may be drawn between two basic meanings of conversion. In the Augustinian tradition, conversion was seen primarily as a Christian's spiritual growth, beginning with the sacrament of baptism and coming to fruition in salvation. This type of conversion experience pertains to somebody who already is, at least nominally, a believer and who is "being lifted from a lower to a higher level of spiritual harmony."[10] This notion of conversion as a self-transformation is at the root of high medieval monasticism and eremeticism. As Mark Johnston writes, "The condition of this vocation might involve complete isolation in a wilderness hermitage, inclosure as an anchorite (often in cells built within the walls of a church or town), living quietly near a religious house, or seclusion in one's own home." Called *conversio,* this state of seclusion was common among widows and retired couples, "all done with varying degrees of official recognition or adherence to a formal religious rule."[11] Self-transformation in this state of *conversio* was seen not as a natural but as a mystical and supernatural process that required a Christian's preparation but ultimately depended on divine, not human, intervention.

The other sense of conversion pertains to the replacement of one belief system by another. Before the mendicant movement of the later Middle Ages, this type of conversion typically occured as a top-down process, beginning with a ruler's official adoption of a new faith and its subsequent imposition as a state religion. The paradigmatic case is that of Constantine's conversion and the implementation of Christianity as the official religion of the Roman Empire. If, in the course of the thirteenth century, conversion came increasingly to be understood in terms of an evangelical mission from the bottom up—i.e., the conversion of heretics, infidels (mainly Jews and Muslims), and pagans among the laity—this shift reflects the impact of an Aristotelian metaphysics that presumed the dynamic mutability and *convertibility* of God's creation through human art.[12] This new hermeneutics of conversion was articulated with great urgency in the bull *Cum hora undecima* (1235), in which Pope Gregory IX authorized missionary friars to preach to and convert pagans, infidels, and heretics. It was further elaborated in the Disputation of Tortosa, which convened over a period of some twenty months beginning in 1413 and explained that the Scripture could be used "like an apothecary" in curing Jews of their infidelity.[13] If this metaphysical idea of the convertibility of creation is at the epistemic root of what Jonathan Boyarin has called the late medieval "incorporating society," it first manifested itself primarily in unprecedented levels of religious intolerance (i.e., coerced conversions and expulsions) within Christian Europe.[14]

As Karl Morrison has pointed out, in the Scholastic (Aristotelian) context of the later Middle Ages, *conversio* (as a transformation of others) was originally an "artist's idea"; it was "a metaphor taken into the language of religion from that of arts and crafts. Something of the original, and not the religious (or metaphorical), sense still survives when the word *conversion* is used to describe, for example, chemical and metallurgical change."[15] Morrison's analysis of the artisinal (and materialist) origins of the concept of religious conversion in an Aristotelian context sheds light on the mendicants' traditional interests in both missionology and alchemy: both evangelical rhetoric and alchemy emerged in this context from the promethean idea that the essential nature of substances and forms in God's creation could (or even should) be changed through the intervention of human art—whether it be a material transformation through "alchemy tried in the fire" or a spiritual transformation through the art of evangelical rhetoric, the "alchemy of words."[16]

When I say that both mendicant evangelical rhetoric and alchemy were predicated on an "Aristotelian" metaphysics of convertibility, I should clarify that late medieval and early modern Aristotelianism was not one coherent tradition but had several strands.[17] As we saw in the initial chapters of this book, the Thomists had traditionally been skeptical about the possibility of alchemical transmutation and conceived of the process of religious conversion in ways that were fundamentally different from those of the Franciscans. In *The Matter of Empire,* Orlando Bentancor has focused on the important role that Thomist-Aristotelian metaphysics played in the sixteenth-century formation of a Spanish imperialist ideology of colonial exploitation and evangelization as elaborated by the so-called Second Scholastics at the University of

Salamanca—mainly the Dominicans Francisco de Vitoria, Domingo de Soto, and Melchor Cano, as well as (later) the Jesuits Luis de Molina and Francisco Suárez. In particular, Bentancor focuses on the Aristotelian principle of hylomorphism, the operations of immaterial active forms that move imperfect passive matter toward an ever-higher and more perfect form in the universal hierarchy of creation until it reaches its one "substantial form" intended by God during Creation. Building on Heidegger's critique of the Western metaphysical tradition, Bentancor argues that Aristotelian hylomorphism can be described in terms of its "metaphysical instrumentalism," as lower forms exist merely for the benefit of higher forms.[18] Although this Aristotelian metaphysical instrumentalism had been introduced into the Latin West by Thomas Aquinas in the thirteenth century, it had remained "virtual" throughout the later Middle Ages until it was developed into a full-fledged imperialist ideology by the Second Scholastics at the University of Salamanca in the sixteenth century and "actualized" in America in the colonial and protocapitalist exploitation of its human and natural resources, especially through mining.[19] Moreover, according to Bentancor, this metaphysical instrumentalism informs not only early modern Spanish attitudes toward New World nature but also toward Native American peoples, whose lack of Christianity and civility was seen as an analogue to the Aristotelian shapeless matter destined by nature to be moved to a proper form by a (godlike) Christian European colonizer. Thus, in this Thomist intellectual milieu, conversion is understood in terms of an Aristotelian metaphysics of *formation,* in which the European missionary appears as an analogue to an artisan—such as a sculptor working bronze into a statue—who molds pagan shapeless matter into Christian forms.[20]

This is an important insight for understanding the Aristotelian roots of the origins of the mendicant concept of conversion and its legacies in the Americas. However, we must remember that Thomist hylomorphic natural law metaphysics was not universally accepted by Scholastic theologians. In fact, it was consistently attacked by Scotists, Llullists, and nominalists, who offered "Scholastic" syntheses of classical and Arabic Aristotelian with medieval Christian (i.e., Augustinian Neoplatonic) thought alternative to that of Aquinas.[21] Hylomorphism is less helpful for understanding the missionologies of the early modern Franciscans, who typically described their work of conversion in analogy not to that of a sculptor molding prime matter into perfect form—in terms of *formation*—but to that of a physician restoring healthy bodies and souls through a *re-formation* of corrupted matter. Thus, the famous Franciscan missionary Bernadino de Sahagún famously opened his monumental *Historia universal de las cosas de la Nueva España* (Universal history of the things of New Spain) by arguing that, just as "the physician cannot conscientiously apply medicine to the sick person without first learning... the cause of the disease," so the preachers and confessors, "who are the physicians of souls [*médicos . . . de las almas*], must have practical knowledge of the spiritual medicines and diseases in order to provide spiritual cures."[22] For this reason, Sahagún explained, "it is necessary to know how they [the Indians] practiced... their idolatry, for, due to our lack of knowledge of this, they perform many idolatrous things in our presence without our understanding."[23] In the process of inquiring into the hidden secrets of New Spain's indigenous languages, cultures, and religions, Sahagún discovered not only elements of diabolic perversion but also elements of angelic beauty that could be harnessed for the work of conversion.

The analogy that Franciscan missionaries such as Sahagún saw between spiritual and physical healing is not surprising, as caring for the sick had long been an integral aspect of Franciscan education since the creation of the order in the early thirteenth century.[24] Indeed, spiritual and physical healing had been closely associated in Christianity even since the early centuries AD, when the Gospels of the New Testament were written. The analogy was later adopted by St. Augustine, who, in book 1 of his *Doctrina christiana,* compared the Word of God (i.e., the Bible) to a sort of "medical care": God's care has "taken it upon itself to heal and restore sinners by the same methods."[25] This analogy was later echoed by Pope Gregory the Great (d. 604) in his treatise *Cura pastoralis* (591).[26] However, unlike the healings performed by the Jesus Christ of the Gospels or the early church fathers, the late medieval Franciscans did not understand the task of healing as the supernatural work of divine miracles that would naturally unfold upon the opening of Scripture to infidels; rather, their healing was the work of human art and science, often including rhetoric and alchemy. As Joseph Ziegler has pointed out, it was in this Franciscan spiritual milieu that preachers adopted the concept of a "physician-patient relationship" from the pagan philosophers who had called themselves "physicians of the soul." They "employed the traditional image of Christ or God the Physician, and reinforced it with medical imagery of the nature of sin and analogies between the physical and the mystical body."[27] As we have seen in chapters 3 and 5, the analogy between the physician and the missionary preacher had special currency in the Llullian tradition, beginning with Llull's authentic writings, most notably the *Principles of Medicine* (1274), and culminating in the concept of an "alchemy of words" in early modern pseudo-Llullian works such as Remigius Rufo Candidus's *In rhetoricam isagoge*.[28] It was in this context that the analogy was adopted by Franciscan missionaries in New Spain such as Sahagún and Andrés de Olmos, the latter of whom proposed, in his *Tratado de hechicerías y sortilegios* (1553), that the "spiritual physicians" should apply their missionary rhetoric as the "medicines to cure" indigenous superstitions.[29]

Attending to the distinct intellectual traditions that each of the mendicant orders had cultivated in late medieval Europe is helpful for understanding the diverse approaches they took to their missionary work in the early Americas, as well as the distinct literary records that they produced. Ricard distinguished between two principal attitudes among Christian missionaries toward pagan civilizations and religions: *"tabula rasa"* and "opportunistic preparation." The latter, Ricard explained, is based on the assumption that "any people, however decadent its beliefs and institutions, is not totally in error and sin, for hidden among the most backward is at least a modicum of truth and an obscure aspiration toward light and perfection.... Thus the neophyte will not be obliged to break entirely with his former life, and will be allowed to retrain that part of his traditions which is naturally good and true."[30] Ricard saw the prevalence of this approach as a relatively recent phenomenon in missionary history (since the nineteenth century). However, it might be argued that "opportunistic preparation" is already evident in the attitudes of many sixteenth-century mendicants, especially among Dominicans such as the famous defender of Indians' rights Bartolomé de las Casas. Strongly influenced by Thomist natural law metaphysics, Las Casas viewed Native Americans' paganism as a sort of *praeparatio evangelica* for their conversion and salvation, in analogy to the ancient Roman paganism that had served as a preparation for the triumph of the Christian Gospel in Europe.[31] According to the *via antigua* of Thomist realist natural law metaphysics, God's providence unfolded through a regular and natural process of secondary causes in which human reason participated; for, as Aquinas had explained, natural law is nothing but the "participation in eternal law through reason" by man.[32] Thus, the missionologies of such sixteenth-century Dominicans as Las Casas, as well as Antonio de Montesinos or Tomás Ortiz, were strongly indebted to the Thomist concept of *synderesis,* the natural capacity of rational men to apprehend first principles and their natural tendency toward the one true God. For Thomists such as Las Casas, there was an essential concordance between nature and grace, and they therefore understood salvation as a *perfection* of human nature.[33] This Thomist tradition of synderesis would later become an important part also of the Jesuits' intellectual inheritance, especially in the wake of their fusion of Neo-Thomist natural law metaphysics with the Hermetic tradition during the seventeenth century, in the works of Eusebio Niremberg and Athanasius Kircher.[34] Still in the early eighteenth century, Joseph-François Lafitau, a prominent Jesuit missionary working in New France, argued that all pagan religions, including that of the Wyandot (Hurons) among whom he worked, were but a faint memory of the true and only religion—i.e., the Judeo-Christian one—as is evident by their similarities and structural symmetries. "One cannot deny this resemblance and conformity," he wrote. "We find, for example, vestiges of the mystery of the Very Holy Trinity in the mysteries of Isis, in the works of Plato, in the religions of the East and West Indies, Japan and Mexico. . . . Augustine and many other Church Fathers have thought that they saw in Plato's works quite clear knowledge of the mystery of the Very Holy Trinity. This philosopher had gained this knowledge from the works of Mercury Trismegistes." And to illustrate his point, he adds that "nothing more greatly resembles the Caduceus of Mercury" than does the Huron peace pipe.[35]

By contrast, according to Ricard, missionaries working according to the model of *tabula rasa* consider everything about Native culture to be completely corrupt: religious, political, and social institutions, as well as souls and spirits. Native religions are condemned "*en bloc.*" Hence, everything that existed before the coming of the missionaries must be completely destroyed, and the neophyte must make a clean break with his or her former environment and life before Christianity can take root.[36] While Ricard saw the notion of *tabula rasa* as the prevalent attitude among the Franciscans during the sixteenth, seventeenth, and eighteenth centuries, more recently historians have pointed out that the Franciscans did not categorically reject all aspects of Native culture but attempted to "remove the deceptions of the devil in order that the Indians might re-appropriate . . . that knowledge of the true God."[37] Indeed, while the sixteenth-century Franciscans in the Americas are today infamous for their violent campaigns of iconoclasm and extirpation, they are also, paradoxically, renowned for their meticulous proto-ethnographic descriptions, which involved the collaboration of Native informants, artists, and authors. Unrivalled in the sixteenth century as sources of ethnohistorical knowledge, they often demonstrated a genuine curiosity about and even aesthetic appreciation of Native cultural forms, the beauty of which could be harnessed for the purpose of the evangelical mission. Just as the physician must cure—not kill—the patient, so the missionary, the physician of the soul, must heal—not destroy—Native spirituality. For example, in the *Psalmodia Christiana* (Christian psalmody [1583]), the only one of his works that was published during his life, Sahagún used popular Nahua song traditions—originally composed in honor of the multiple Mexica deities—as a foundation of catechizing the Indian neophytes in the concepts of the Christian religions. Although the aesthetic qualities of this sort of mixture of Nahua and Christian cultural forms have been a subject of debate, it is patent that Sahagún appreciated the beauty of Nahua song and poetry, despite their diabolical perversion and misdirection in pre-Hispanic religious rites.[38] As such, the Franciscans' methodology of conversion provided the foundation for a process of cultural *mestizaje* in sixteenth-century viceregal New Spain that is manifest in the rich record of visual art, material artifacts, and architectural remnants of the missionary towns.[39]

George Baudot and others have explained the Franciscans' extraordinary ethnographic curiosity and productivity in terms of the singular apocalyptic fervor that they brought to bear on their task of conversion and the extirpation of idolatry. Baudot hereby emphasized the impact of the millenarian schemes of Joachim of Fiore (1130–1202) upon the followers of the radical reformer Juan de Guadalupe at the Franciscan Custody of the Holy Gospel in Extremadura, whence the "first twelve" originated.[40] However, while there can be little doubt that the early Franciscans in New Spain had a keen sense of apocalyptic urgency, not all apocalyptic prophecies that circulated in the sixteenth century were specifically "millenarian" in theory or Joachmite in origin.[41] As we have seen in chapter 4, some of the ideas attributed to Joachim during the fifteenth century had actually originated with the separate tradition of Pseudo-Methodius. Other ideas originated only with later writers, especially among the Spiritual Franciscans, and were spuriously attributed to Joachim. Thus, in the course of the later Middle Ages, Joachim's original "millenarian" schemes were transformed and adapted for new purposes. For example, his notion of the emergence of a "spiritual state" at the end of times was perhaps still reflected in the New Spanish Franciscans' insistence that the "Indian Church" they had erected in America was the only true church, superceding that of the secular episcopacy. However, the most characteristic element of the "Joachimite" tradition of millenarian prophecy—the intricate division of history into seven "ages"—largely dissipated. Also, the mendicants attributed new ideas to Joachim that would have seemed quite alien to the Calabrian abbot. For example, as we also saw, Joachim had no great interest in either crusade or the conversion of infidels. Although he did believe that the Jews would be converted in the final days, his reformist zeal was entirely monastic, directed inward and toward the reform of a corrupt temporal church brought about by spiritual men in an "order of monks" (*ordo monachorum*). Finally, as we also saw, Joachim considered himself to be a biblical exegete, an interpreter of John's Apocalypse through numerology, not a discoverer of natural or preternatural (especially diabolic) secrets through proto-ethnographic empirical inquiry. Although Baudot also noted the important role that John of Rupescissa's fourteenth-century apocalyptic writings played in the transmission of Joachimite prophecy into the sixteenth century, he failed to consider the alchemical nature of many of John's prophecies.[42] Thus, in order properly to understand the "Joachimite" inspiration of the early New Spanish Franciscans' missionary zeal and ethnographic curiosity about Native American cultures, it is necessary to place their apocalypticism in the context of late medieval and early modern Aristotelianism, especially that of alchemical prophecy.

As I want to suggest here, the apparent paradox of the Franciscan spiritual conquest—violent iconoclasm and extirpation on the one hand; admiration for Native forms of cultural expression and their use in missionary work on the other—can be illuminated in terms of the mendicants' Aristotelian understanding of matter and form. But it is not Thomist metaphysical hylomorphism but the (pseudo-)Aristotelian alchemical theory of material mixture that underlies the logic of Franciscan conversion in terms of cultural and religious *mestizaje*. The Franciscans saw Native spirituality not as an undifferentiated matter that had to be formed; rather, they saw it as its own *substantial form* that had to be *reduced* to its *prima materia* in order to be *re*-formed. Moreover, in their alchemical understanding of matter, the Franciscans viewed the "substance" of Native spirituality not as homogeneous and continuous—as a "*bloc*" (as Ricard put it)—but as a *compound*, in analogy to an elemental mixture of discontinuous cultural *particulars* (or particles) that could be reduced, rebalanced, and reformed into a new mixture. In short, their understanding of Native spirituality was not Thomist (hylomorphic) but alchemical (corpuscular) in its materialist conception. As we saw in chapter 2, whereas in Thomist metaphysics, the "form" of a substance is destroyed in the process of conversion (such as glass into sand), in alchemical matter theory, the "smallest part" (*minima naturalia*) survives and retains its elemental qualities in the new mixture. As I will argue here, the Franciscans saw many *minima naturalia* in Native culture and religion that were worth preserving in the new mixture of a perfect Christian form, the "spiritual gold" of salvation. However, the work of this conversion, like alchemical transmutation in the crucible, was a potentially violent process of penitence that gave rise to the genre of ethno-demonology, based on a quasi-inquisitorial forensic epistemology of information gathering that would become the model for modern ethnography in its methodology (though not in its aim) of studying other cultures.[43]

The Devil in the Matter: Alchemy and the Birth of Ethno-demonology

Attending to the multiplicity of "Aristotelian" intellectual traditions in late medieval Scholasticism is helpful for understanding why the European evangelical enterprise in the Americas was not a monolithic endeavor but consisted of diverse approaches and responses to Native American (i.e., "pagan") religions on the part of the various groups of missionaries in the Americas. Even though most mendicants working in the New World were in concert in their condemnations of the abuses of the Indians at the hands of *encomenderos* or royal officials, there was significant disagreement as to the justness of the initial military conquest and the use of coercion in the work of conversion. On the one hand, Dominicans such as Las Casas unequivocally rejected, in his 1534 tract *De unico vocationis modo* (The only way), the use of coercion in missionary work. Admittedly, Las Casas represents an extreme case, but his positions were, in fact, deeply rooted in Thomist metaphysics and widely shared by more orthodox confriars among the Dominicans, such as Domingo de Soto and Francisco de Vitoria (as we will see in chapter 8). On the other hand, most of the Franciscans, following in the Llullian tradition of Cisneros, were staunch supporters of military conquest. And while they preferred conversion by peaceful means wherever possible, they did not shy away from the use of coercion in their evangelical work, especially with regard to the conversion of Native children against the will of their parents.[44] Thus, as the Franciscan friar Toribio de Benavente, one of the "first twelve," wrote in his "Letter to the Emperor Charles V" of January 22, 1555, "it is fitting that the holy gospel be preached throughout these lands and those who do not willingly wish to listen to the gospel of Jesus Christ, be forced to do so; for here that old proverb is applicable: 'better good by force than bad by one's will.'"[45] These philosophical differences could sometimes result in open controversy, as in the famous case involving Toribio de Benavente and Las Casas, the former of whom launched, in the same letter to the emperor, a virulent attack on the Dominican defender of the Indians, offering a staunch defense of the military conquest.[46]

In part, this difference between Franciscan and Dominican approaches to conversion in the New World can be explained in terms of the distinct theological hermeneutics through which the friars had interpreted paganism during the later Middle Ages. More so than the Dominicans, the Franciscans had traditionally attributed significant agency to the Devil in the world. As Fernando Cervantes has argued, the Franciscans' almost Manichean obsession with diabolism in the New World was a consequence of their long tradition of metaphysical nominalism, which had been elaborated in the attacks on Thomism during the fourteenth century by John Duns Scotus and William of Ockham and which regained currency during the Reformation and Counter-Reformation during the sixteenth century. Unlike the Thomist adherents to metaphysical realism, the Franciscan nominalists emphasized the incongruence between postlapsarian natural reason and divine grace. Thus, Cervantes argues that the nominalists conceived of salvation not as a *perfection* but as a *breaking* of human nature, which had been utterly corrupted by the Devil.[47] While it was, of course, the Dominicans who played the more prominent role in the Inquisition, they had traditionally been concerned primarily with heresy and crypto-Judaism. The Thomists also played a prominent role in the history of demonology and witch hunts in late medieval and early modern Europe (Heinrich Kramer and Jacob Sprenger, the authors of the famous *Malleus maleficarum* [1487], for example, were both Dominicans); but, as Cervantes explains, the Thomists interpreted witchcraft primarily as a social crime (malefice), whereas the Franciscans, influenced by the metaphysical nominalism of Duns Scotus and Ockham, interpreted witchcraft as idolatry—a crime against God.[48] Indeed, there can be little doubt that the Franciscans' preoccupation with the power of the Devil (or his incarnation, the Antichrist) was an important factor in their long tradition of Christian militancy. This militancy was evident during the sixteenth century in the Franciscans' campaigns of "extirpation," iconoclasm, and even genocide. An infamous example is the campaign that was instigated in the town of Maní in Yucatán in 1562 by Diego de Landa and documented in his own *Relación de las cosas de Yucatán* (ca. 1566). Known today as the "Franciscan terror," the campaign resulted in the burning of hundreds of Maya codices, the torture of 4,500 Indians, and even in 157 deaths, including 13 suicides, according to some reports.[49] Another prominent example of the Franciscan militancy is the so-called Indian Inquisition that disciplined the Native neophytes between 1536 and 1543 under the leadership of Fray Juan de Zumárraga, the first archbishop of New Spain, who ordered the burning not only of all the royal archives of Texcoco but also of a native lord named Don Carlos, on account of the latter's continual practice of polygamy.[50]

The Franciscan preoccupation with the Devil was also an important impetus of their empirical and proto-ethnographic interest in Native American cultures and religions. For example, Fray Andrés de Olmos is famous for having written some of the earliest linguistic treatises on Nahuatl, the *Arte para aprender la lengua mexicana* (1547) and the *Vocabulario en lengua mexicana* (1547); but of equal significance is his work on ethno-demonology, starting with the (now lost) *Tratado de antigüedades mexicanas* (completed ca. 1540), its (also lost) summary, the *Sumario,* and culminating with the *Tratado de hechicerías y sortilegios* (1553). These texts provided some of the earliest alphabetical accounts of pre-Hispanic Nahua origin myths, deities, cosmological ideas, dynastic histories, educational and social institutions, as well as religious cults, including ritual cannibalism, human sacrifice, and flaying.[51] According to the late sixteenth-century Franciscan historian Jerónimo de Mendieta, Olmos had been commissioned as early as 1533 by the president of the second royal *audiencia,* Bishop Sebastián Ramírez de Fuenleal, to "compile in a book the antiquities of these Indians" so that they would be identifiable to the Franciscan missionaries still inexpert in Nahua language and culture.[52] As Baudot has pointed out, Fuenleal's charge can in many ways be seen as the "birth certificate" of missionary ethnography in New Spain.⁵³ Most likely, Olmos was chosen for such a task because of his previous experience in Spain. Before they arrived together in Mexico in 1528, Olmos and Zumárraga had collaborated in a witch-hunting campaign in the Basque country, where the two, together with the Franciscan Inquisitor Friar Martín de Castañega, had employed some of the same forensic methods of prosecution and information gathering that Olmos would later employ in his ethno-demonological studies in New Spain. These included the use of interrogations, questionnaires, and interviews of local informants. In fact, scholarship has shown the close dependence of Olmos's *Tratado de hechicerías y sortilegios* upon the tract produced by Castañega about Basque witchcraft, the *Tratado de las supersticiones y hechizerias* (1529). The protoscientific empiricism of the Franciscans' ethno-demonological studies in America has thus deep roots in the inquisitorial prosecution in witchcraft; and the Franciscans' campaign of "extirpation" of idolatry in the New World was hereby modeled on the quasi-medical practice of exorcism. For this reason, the Franciscan missionaries had to "examine," as Cecelia Frost has written, "like physicians engaged in the healing of the sick, all manifestations of the demonic cult."⁵⁴ However, Olmos also introduced significant modfications to Castañega's Spanish model in response to the specifically local circumstances in New Spain.⁵⁵ Thus, he conducted close studies of Nahua pictographic codices and enlisted the expertise of Native informants chosen from among the Native elders who had survived the trauma of the conquest. These informants supplied not only memories and oral traditions about pre-Hispanic life and religious practices but also crucial assistance in Olmos's systematic transcription of the pictographic content of the pre-Hispanic codices into alphabetized Nahuatl.⁵⁶

In light of Cervantes's argument about the incongruence between human nature and salvation in the Franciscan metaphysical tradition, we may posit that, in Franciscan metaphysics, the work of conversion was understood not as a *natural* process at all (as it was in Thomist hylomorphic metaphysics) but as an *artificial* operation that potentially entailed the application of significant amounts of epistemic violence and coercion.⁵⁷ In other words, the Franciscans understood conversion not in terms of Aristotelian processes of formation but in (pseudo-) Aristotelian terms of alchemical transmutation, especially of spagyric healing in the tradition of Roger Bacon's experimental science. As we have seen in chapter 3, the history of the nominalist attack on Thomist metaphysics during the fourteenth and fifteenth centuries was intimately related to the history of alchemical theories of matter, in particular to what I have called the "alchemification" of the Llullian Art of conversion. This nominalist alchemification of Llullism still had important implications during the sixteenth century for the way in which the Cisnerean Franciscans understood the relationship between art and nature as well as the power of the Devil in the world, especially in America.

Indeed, the medieval Franciscans' particular understanding of the relationship between art and nature had been at the root of their traditional interest in both alchemy and diabolism from the beginning.[58] Whereas Thomist hylomorphism was predicated on the assumption that every material substance will *naturally* attain (in due course) the one substantial form ordained by God, the Franciscans held that the Devil's art of counterfeit had sufficiently corrupted material substances so that they would no longer attain their originally intended substantial forms without the intervention of art. Significantly, as William Newman has shown, the Scholastic controversy about the possibilities of alchemical transmutation emerged in the thirteenth century precisely in the context of theological disputes about the limits of demonic power. Thus, Aquinas, following the eleventh-century Persian philosopher Avicenna, held that while art, both human and demonic, can imitate nature, its products can never be the same as those produced by nature. Aquinas therefore disputed that humans could transmute the species of things alchemically, arguing, for example, that while alchemical gold may *look like* gold, it isn't *real* gold. Bonaventure, by contrast, argued that the gold produced by the alchemists was just as real as that produced by nature. Though the alchemists, like the Devil, cannot be creators (like God), they can "administer agents to patients in the same way as demons: they do not act in a purely artificial fashion, but employ their art to lead nature to an end that it would otherwise fail to attain."[59] Moreover, whereas the adherents of both hylomorphic and alchemical theory of matter assumed that all substances were elemental mixtures that were subject to change due to the natural processes of generation and corruption, the Thomists argued that in the process of natural transmutation the original substantial form is utterly destroyed. Consequently, if air is transmuted into water and then back into air, it would not be the *same* air as before but *new* air freshly produced from the water.[60] By contrast, in alchemical corpuscular theory of matter, the "smallest parts" did not lose their identity in the process of transmutation but continued to exist and interact in a different mixture. Finally, whereas Aquinas held that every substance only has one substantial form—the one originally created by God—Franciscans such as Bonaventure held that every substance in the postlapsarian world has multiple possible substantial forms, due to the Devil's art of counterfeit. Thus, for the Thomists, every species of metal, such as "lead," was gold in the making by the natural processes of generation and corruption; by contrast, for the Franciscans, the power of the diabolic art was manifest not only in the natural processes of material corruption but also in the counterfeit of immaterial substantial forms. This counterfeit may well have made highly corrupted "lead" its own substantial form among the metals. If so, "lead" was at the end of its own natural process of generation and corruption, from which it would never naturally become gold without being first "reduced" to its *prima materia,* in which its elemental corruptions are reversed. For the Franciscans, alchemical transmutation of things was therefore not only possible; it was *necessary* in order to reverse the demonic corruptions that prevented matter from attaining the substantial form God had intended during Creation.[61]

This peculiarly Franciscan understanding of the relationship between art and nature during the later Middle Ages sheds light on the important role that Llullism played in Franciscan missionology in the early Americas, especially in the (pseudo-)Llullian evangelical rhetoric of the "Alchemy of Words" that I discussed in chapter 5. Although the Llullian Art had originally been predicated on a strong Neoplatonic metaphysical realism and an ideal of conversion by dialogue and scientific demonstration, it was fully committed to militant crusade and coercive conversion when peaceful dialogue was not effective. Similarly, the sixteenth-century Franciscans in America stressed the importance of intercultural dialogue, but, as Louise Burkhart has observed, their "ultimate goal was to silence indigenous voices, to resolve dialogue into monologue, to replace cultural diversity with conformity."[62] Indeed, it is arguably in the attitude toward violent conquest and coercive evangelization that the early modern adherents of Llullism are most reliably distinguished from its Thomist opponents, who were strongly committed to a natural law metaphysics that grounded all knowledge and civil authority in natural law, not the divine will.[63]

One interesting sixteenth-century intellectual descendant of Llull's interfaith dialogue in *The Book of the Gentile and the Three Wise Men* (1274) is in this regard Bernadino de Sahagún's *Libro de los Colloquios* (1564), a literary semi-imaginary reenactment, written in both Nahuatl and Spanish, of the earliest dialogues between the "first twelve" Franciscan missionaries who had arrived in 1524 and several Nahua lords. Of course, whereas Llull's dialogue was ultimately a contest among Christians, Muslims, and Jews for Gentile souls, Sahagún's dialogue is between Christians and "Gentiles" (i.e., pagans). Thus, whereas the Franciscans in the *Colloquios* argue that the Christian god is the only true one, the Nahua lords contend that, while the Christian god may be true, so are the Mexica gods.[64] Also, whereas in Llull's dialogue the epistemic violence of imposing one universal monotheistic truth on pagans remains implicit (presumably, the Gentile will convert to the "correct" religion as a result of the Christian's superior rhetorical art), in Sahagún's text the historical "fact" of the Spanish conquest is the most persuasive argument for the truth of the Christian faith. Thus, the missionaries explain to the Nahua lords that their idolatrous religion has angered God, who has sent the Spaniards in order to "punish and afflict" them.[65] As Viviana Díaz Balsera has noted, this passage is a "paradigmatic moment of epistemic violence recurrent in the Spanish colonialist discourse in the Americas," for the "framing of the conquest as punishment cancels out all possible political arguments about lawful military self-defense, the right to demand subjection to Charles V, and even the (convenient) rationale of the *requerimiento*."[66] The conquest, however, represents not God's vindictive but his corrective and salvific punishment, which has softened recalcitrant pagan hearts, making them receptive to the Christian message. The *Colloquios* hereby present the Franciscans' efforts at conversion in terms of the art of medicine and Nahua religion in terms of bodily disease, pollution, and corruption. Thus, in the Nahuatl version of the texts, the missionaries are said to have been sent to Mexico in order to show the Nahuas "how to cool the heart of He by Whom All live, so He will not completely destroy you."[67] Mexica religious images are described as a form of "witchcraft, ... very black, very dirty ... they vomited on people."[68] As Díaz Balsera writes, "Epidemics, disease, deforminities, and any form of physical suffering were deemed to be the consequence of infringements on the established natural order and balance of forces."[69] In drawing connections between physical and spiritual healing, the Franciscan missionaries could hereby utilize Nahua ideas. Thus, Mendieta writes that the Mexica believed that "an essential part of medicine" was the "cast[ing] out sin from their souls for the health of the body."[70] However, as the translation of these concepts into the Nahuatl idiom also shows ("how to cool the heart"), the conversion process entailed not only the Christianization of the Nahuas but also, to some extent, "the Nahuatization of Christianity."[71]

One consequence of the Franciscans' spagyric understanding of conversion was their view of their evangelical work in America not as a civilizing mission in the sense of a cultural Hispanization but as a renovation of or return to an earlier, more primitive state of Christian spiritual life that had been lost in Europe by worldly corruption but could be reborn in the New World.[72] Even in the very idolatry that they were trying to eradicate from Nahua culture, the Franciscans found a seed (or particle) of Native spirituality that they thought worth preserving. Thus, according to many of the Franciscan missionary writers, the Indians are, despite their idolatry, exemplary in their exceptional religious zeal and devotion. For example, Mendieta asserted, "It is true that no nation or people have been discovered in the world better disposed and prepared for salvation (if they are helped to) than the natives of this

New Spain."[73] In their extraordinary promise, the Indians even surpass most Spanish Christians, who "are unfortunately not prepared to do for Jesus Christ one-hundredth part of what they did for our common enemy, the devil. Christians should be put to shame by the zeal displayed by these heathens of inferior ability and by the fact that in their time of idolatry they observed, as far as moral and social behavior goes, better customs and rules than they do now as Christians and under our control."[74] As can be seen in Mendieta's comment, the Mexicans' religious "zeal" can be understood independently from its object of devotion (the Devil) and thus be repurposed in the work of Christian conversion. Also, civility—good "customs and rules"—does not depend on Christianity; nor does Christianity necessarily prevent barbarity. Yet, the idea of native spirituality and culture as a composite mixture of particulars—rather than as a homogeneous mass whose form was entirely destroyed in the process of conversion—also heightened the Franciscans' anxiety about the possibility that, even in the new mixture of native Christianity, the Devil might still be hiding in the new, hybridized forms. If, on occasion, he was discovered in secret places, the friars' response was all the more violent.[75]

Still, the early Franciscan missionaries in America typically saw in the Indian neophyte a unique potential for realizing St. Francis's primitivist ideal of a Christian life in apostolic poverty, a utopian ideal of life on earth without property and rights that had been theorized in the thirteenth century by Peter John Olivi (1248–1281), but the realization of which the Franciscans had been denied in Europe, after being forced to accept by papal decree that there was no descendent of Adam without property and rights.[76] Many of the young Franciscan friars who had received an excellent humanist training in the new curricula introduced into Spain during the Cisnerian reforms before embarking for the New World must have been profoundly impressed by the earliest accounts of the New World, in which such humanist explorers, chroniclers, and utopists as Amerigo Vespucci, Peter Martyr, and Thomas More claimed that there was a "New World" where people lived without private property. Thus, Peter Martyr wrote in his history of Columbus's voyages in the first book of his *Decades of the New World:* "It is proven that amongst them the land belongs to everybody, just as does the sun or the water. They know no difference between *meum* and *tuum,* that is the source of all evils."[77] Many of the Franciscans, upon their arrival in the Americas, continued to nurture the fantasy that the "poor" Indians who had been reduced to abjection by the cataclysmic events of the conquest were in fact *reduced* to an Edenic state of poverty that had turned them into willing fellow travelers in a common journey back to the prelapsarian world. Thus, Fray Toribio de Benavente (who embraced his Nahuatl nickname "Motolinía," meaning "he is poor"), wrote in his *Historia de los indios de la Nueva España*, that when the Indians were asked why "they loved them [the Franciscans] and were beloved by them," they answered "because they go about poorly dressed and barefooted like us."[78] The Indians, Motolinía explained, "have almost none of those obstacles to prevent their achieving salvation which we Spaniards have and by which we are kept down, for their life is content with very little, so little, in fact, that they have scarcely enough to clothe and feed themselves.... They are extremely patient and long-suffering, as gentle as sheep.... They are humble and obedient to all, either willingly or of necessity, and they know only how to serve and work."[79] Although Las Casas also described the Indians as "gentle sheep" (*ovejas mansas*) in his *Brevíssima relación,* he argued that the Native lords, despite their paganism, had held rightful dominion of their lands and property, and that they had unlawfully been "reduced" to horrible slavery by the infernal tyranny of the Spaniards.[80] By contrast, Franciscans such as Motolonía celebrated a postconquest world of Indian neophytes who had been reduced to a utopian state without property and rights.

In Motolinía's providentialist and typological historical scheme, the violent conquest of Mexico was one of "ten plagues" (*diez plagas*), analogous to those with which God had smitten the Egyptians of old in the book of Exodus.[81] However, the "Israelites" in Motolinía's typological retelling of the book of Exodus are not the Europeans (as the reader of Anglo American colonial literature might expect) but the *Indians* who leave their former allegorical ("Egyptian") land of idolatry after God had "chastened" (*castigó*) them for their former ways and from which they are being healed by the Franciscans missionaries in the new promised land of the Christian Indian church.[82] The disease, however, started long before the plague with Mexica idolatry, which infected not only Nahua spirituality but all aspects of culture and even the natural environment. Thus, Motolinía marvels how, before the Indians' conversion, the land, like the Indian souls, resembled an inferno, with Popocatépetl, one of the two great volcanos in the valley of Mexico, continuously spewing sulfur and ash. All of this ceased, Motolinía writes, "after 1528, a fact much commented upon by both Spaniards and Indians. Some claimed that it was the mouth of hell."[83]

For many of the Franciscan historians of the spiritual conquest, the military conquest was therefore a manifestation not of God's natural law (which includes the law of nations) but of his immediate supernatural will, facilitated by his exceptional gifts to his Christian messiahs of "Egyptian gold"—the pagan arts of alchemy, navigation, metallurgy, and pyrotechnical warfare that would prepare the path for the conversions inaugurating the apocalyptic battles of the final days. As we saw in chapter 4, this voluntarist interpretation of history had already inspired Christopher Columbus, who thereby seemed influenced primarily by the Parisian nominalist and voluntarist Pierre d'Ailly. This tradition of voluntarism also frequently underwrote the narratives of conquest as told by the conquerors themselves. For example, in his "Second Letter" to the Emperor Charles V, Hernando Cortés reports that several natural signs were interpreted by his men as an ill omen about the prospects of his enterprise to conquer Mexico: "When we had rested somewhat, I went out one night, after inspecting the first watch, with a hundred foot soldiers, our Indian allies and the horsemen; and one league from the camp five of the horses fell and would go no further, so I sent them back. And although all those who were with me in my company urged me to return, for it was an evil omen, I continued on my way secure in the belief that God is more powerful than Nature."[84] The "fact'" of the conquest thus becomes a voluntarist argument against Thomist metaphysics, natural law, and the law of nations. Similarly, reflecting on a century of Franciscan missionary activities in the Americas, Mendieta wrote that the discovery and conquest had never been "a purely human enterprise, no fortuitous escapade, but all arranged by Divine Providence." First, God had "selected Columbus as his instrument for setting in motion of the discovery and the paving of the passage to the New World"; next, He had "selected Hernán Cortés as his agent, and all this for the purpose of the conversion of the untold millions of natives."[85] As we saw in chapter 4, the Dominican Las Casas agreed with the first part of Mendieta's story (about Columbus), but he vehemently disagreed with the second part (about Cortés). For Las Casas, the military conquest was antithetical to the fulfillment of the providential history of salvation inaugurated by the discovery and had betrayed Spain's mission in the New World, starting even with Columbus. By contrast, for Mendieta discovery and conquest were part of the same continuous story of salvation. In fact, he went so far as to anoint Cortés a "new Moses," whose conquest alone gave meaning to Columbus's discovery. For Mendieta, as for Llull 250 years earlier, military conquest and spiritual conquest represented the "two swords" that would prepare the world for the apocalyptic Second Coming.

As for Motolinía, so also for Mendieta, the exodus that was led by this New World Moses was not that of a European migration to the New World but the exodus of the very Indians whom he had conquered, an exodus from the tyrannical dominion of Satan into the Franciscan Promised Land of salvation in the final days of the world before the advent of the expected apocalyptic battles:[86]

> In the year of Cortés's birth, 1485, they [the Aztecs] celebrated most solemnly, in the city of Mexico, the dedication of their principal temple and its idols. On this

occasion they sacrificed 80,400 human beings. You can see that the clamor of so many souls and that so much blood spilled, and offence against the Creator, was sufficient cause for God to say: "I have surely seen the afflictions of my people" (Exodus III). God wished to send somebody in His name to remedy such great evil, appointing one like Moses in Egypt. Cortés was born in the very year and even on the first day of that great massacre, and this is a definite sign and evidence of Cortés's election.[87]

Just as Moses fearlessly confronted Pharaoh, so did Cortés, "with a boldness looking like the utmost madness" that was out of character with his usual shrewdness (but reminiscent of Llull's "Fool for God"), embark with his four hundred Christians upon the conquest of a mighty Aztec empire (Mendieta downplayed the crucial role that Cortés's Tlaxcalan allies hereby played); just as Moses stammered and was given the gift to speak Pharaoh's language in front of him, so was Cortés ignorant of the language of the Aztecs but given translators in the persons of the Indian woman Doña Marina and the redeemed Spanish captive Jerónimo de Aguilar, a Franciscan friar. (Mention of the other Spanish captive among the Maya, Gonzalo Guerrero, who chose not to return, is discreetly omitted.)[88]

As the *sanifex* of the New World, Cortés represents in Mendieta's narrative a sort of Anti-Luther in a time of exceptional spiritual crisis. For, just as the Old World Luther was leading millions of European Christians into heresy and damnation, so did the New World Anti-Luther bring millions of idolaters into the Christian fold. And to make the analogy more persuasive, Mendieta even claimed (wrongly) that Cortés was born in the same year not only when thousands of Aztecs were sacrificed to the Devil but also when Martin Luther was born. In light of this, the unlikely success of Cortés's small band against the enormous Aztec army—a success that seemed to defy the laws of nature—is a sure sign of God's direct intervention into human history, a manifestation of the divine will that puts into abeyance natural law accessible to human reason:

> This simply must lead us to the conviction and conclusion that God, without a doubt, had specifically elected Cortés and had appointed this courageous captain as his instrument to open the door and the path for preachers of the Gospel in the New World, as well as to compensate the Holy Catholic Church with the conversion of so many souls for the great losses caused and damage done by that accursed Luther to ancient Christianity at about the same time. It follows that while one part was lost, another was gained. It is surely a miracle that in the same year as Luther was born in Eisleben, a town in Saxony, Hernán Cortés was born in Medellín, a city of Spain. Luther was born to disturb the world and to

place under the banner of Satan many of the faithful, whose fathers and grandfathers had been Catholics for ever so many years. By contrast, Cortés sowed the seed of a church of an infinite multitude of nations who for centuries had been in the power of Satan, enmeshed in vice and blinded by idolatry. In the very year of 1519 Luther began to corrupt the Gospel among Christians, while Cortés spread it in his loyal and sincere manner among nations who had never before been aware of it or heard the message of Christ.[89]

For Mendieta, the conquest of America was akin to an "opening of the door" into an occult realm of the world that had been providentially hidden by the Devil but the penetration of which was justified by a messianic purpose in the apocalyptic battle between the forces of Christ and the Antichrist.[90] Insofar as Cortés's conquest had resulted in a "river of blood" among his Indian Israelites (as Las Casas had put it), it was the sacrificial and penitential blood that was shed for the Indians' physical and spiritual salvation from their bondage to the Devil. And it was the Franciscans' art and science that had set the apocalyptic story of discovery and conquest into motion. While Santiago and the Virgin Mary, the patron saints of the Reconquista, did assist in its unfolding,[91] the story began with "Juan Pérez de Marchena [sic]," the friar at La Rábida, who had supported Columbus before his first transatlantic voyage:[92]

> Humanist and cosmographer as he was.... the friar took an enormous risk, for though he knew more than Ptolemy, he showed great courage in supporting a theory, suggested to him by a lost foreigner [*hombre perdido*] who had wandered from kingdom to kingdom and backing a person everybody regarded as mad. We are driven to the conclusion that this modest friar and inspired and devout man, was much more than just a cosmographer, he arrived at the certainty of new lands and people, as yet unknown, not by means of his human science but as a result of divine revelation.[93]

Mendieta's messianist interpretation of the spiritual conquest of America brings into focus yet another consequence of the difference between the Franciscans' alchemical and the Dominicans' hylomorphic understanding of matter with regard to natural law and the rights of conquest. According to Dominican theologians, the American Indians were "pagans" and therefore fundamentally different from Muslims, who (like the Jews) lived in "vincible" ignorance of Christ, which is to say that they had been in contact with Christians for centuries and that their rejection of Christianity was therefore willful and sinful. By contrast, the American Indians' ignorance of Christ was "invincible" (and therefore not sinful). Whereas this distinction was critical in the

Dominicans' general rejection of violent conquest on the basis of natural law (as we will see in chapter 8), the Franciscans generally tended to see the conquest in America as continuous with the project of Reconquista—of returning formerly Christian lands in Europe under the rule of Muslims to the "fold" of the Catholic faith.[94] For Franciscans, the Dominican argument about vincible versus invincible and sinful versus sinless ignorance was largely a nominal distinction without a difference, for both originated in the same cause, which is the pervasive diabolic corruption of nature (including human natural reason) leading man from his or her *prima scientia* of the true creator into error. "We know that this prince of darkness," wrote Mendieta, "wishing to hide from men the light of the Holy Trinity (which is the foundation of evangelical law), ordered three strikes and raised three flags of deceived and perverted people, which the church has continuously been fighting since its first inception. These are the Jewish perfidy, the Muslim falsehood, and the idolatrous blindness."[95] For Franciscans such as Mendieta, pagans are infidels not essentially different from Muslims and Jews, who, as the descendants of Adam, Noah, and Abraham, had knowledge of their true creator before falling victim to the Devil's art of counterfeit and being expelled from Paradise. In this sense, the conversion of the three groups, though requiring distinct methods, is fundamentally similar in nature: all must be "reduced" to the *prima scientia* of God, which began not with Peter but with Adam, Noah, and Abraham.[96] It is precisely in terms of the "alchemical" (i.e., monist) extension of Llull's "Abrahamic" paradigm of conversion as a *reductio* to include pagans—which we observed in chapter 5 with regard to the canon law tradition of *papa vicarius Christi* of the fifteenth century—in which Mendieta also understands the American mission. Thus, he writes:

> The pre-eminence or prerogative granted to the blessed monarchs of Castile by God Almighty in return for their zeal for the faith, resembles that conceded to the patriarch Abraham, by which he was assured that his lineage would be blessed by all nations. The blessing conferred upon Abraham's descendants was further expanded with the arrival of the Son of God in this world, who was born of the Virgin and descended, in direct time, from the great patriarch. He came to bring about the redemption of the human race, a task in which he succeeded by the sacrifice of His own precious blood. This blessing has not been granted and transferred to the New World and the countless nations discovered therein. . . . It follows that the title Abraham has among the Hebrews, who call him "Father of the Faith" (and so St Paul called him), could with complete justification be applied by the Indians to our Catholic Monarchs, for it was a result of their zeal and care that the Holy Catholic faith became rooted in Western parts. It follows that we

may well call them "parents" of the many nations and millions of souls, generated by holy baptism.⁹⁷

Thus, according to Mendieta, the Christian missionaries in America have "reduced" the Indians to the patrimony of Abraham, which had been expanded by Jesus Christ to the nations of the Old World but not to those of the New World until the final days. It is in the terms of this monist understanding of salvation history that Mendieta explains the meaning of the phrase in Alexander VI's bulls *Inter cetera:* after Columbus had "discovered in the Ocean sea certain islands and mainlands, populated by many infidels, which had until this time been neither seen nor discovered by anyone," the pope had charged the Catholic Monarchs with the task of "subjecting the said lands and people in order to reduce them to the confession of the Holy Catholic Faith" (*sujetar las dichas tierras y gentes para reducirlas á la confesión de la santa fe católica*).⁹⁸ Later, Mendieta explains, when Pope Leo X issued, on April 25, 1521, his bull *Alias felicis* to Fray Juan Clapión and Fray Francisco de los Ángeles (aka Quiñones) authorizing the papal mission of the "first ten" to New Spain, it was done with the purpose of "reducing mankind to the knowledge and now path of salvation" (*humanum genus ad cognitionis et salvationis semitas reducere*).⁹⁹ When Clapión died and Quiñones was appointed commissary general of the Franciscan Order, Fray Martín de Valencia from the Custody of San Gabriel was chosen as the heir of the evangelical mission to seek the "reduction to the fold of the Militant Church of both believers and unbelievers" (*de reducir al gremio de la Iglesia militante, así los fieles como los infieles*).¹⁰⁰ Mendieta is translating here from the "Obediencia" that Quiñonez wrote, in Latin, on October 4, 1523, to Valencia, charging the twelve apostles of Mexico to "reduce to the fold of the militant church, both believers and unbelievers" in New Spain (*ad gremium militantis Ecclesie tam fideles quam infideles cognabatur [sic] reducere*).¹⁰¹

As we can see from Mendieta's translation from the Latin into Spanish, the technical usage of the Latin verb *reducere* in the sense of "to convert" in the canon law tradition of *papa vicarius Christi* was also adopted in early modern Spanish-language missionary discourse by Franciscans in the New World. However, as Las Casas's usage ("reducing to slavery") suggests, in early modern Spanish, the word also became increasingly associated with conquest and subjection—a connotation that it lacked in the original Latin, where the two concepts—military subjection and religious conversion—usually appeared not far from one another but were conceptually separate.¹⁰² In order to illuminate this semantic history in early modern Spanish, it is instructive to investigate the usage of this verb in early American missionology more closely.

The Alchemy of Reduction

During the sixteenth century, the verb *reducere* continued to be used in Franciscan (and later Jesuit) missionologies in the technical sense of "to convert," as it was inherited from the late medieval canon law tradition. For example, in the "Preface to the Studious and Christian Reader" of his *Rhetorica christiana* (Perugia, 1579), the American-born (some say *mestizo*) missionary Fray Diego de Valadés wrote, "As the saying goes, you must take the path of good people, which is the correction of man's errors and returning them to the right path" (*in viam reducere*).[103] Similarly, Fray Juan de Focher's (Latin) *Itinerarium Catholicum* (which Valadés edited and published in Seville in 1574 after Focher's death), included a chapter on the method of conversion that is entitled "The Method of Reducing the Unbelievers" (De modo servando in reducendis infidelibus).[104] There Focher wrote, "In order to outline a norm for the ministers of the church to follow in the reduction of the barbarians, I thought that there is nothing better than what has been observed for many years, by mandate and authority of the pope and the king, by the religious mendicants and especially by the Franciscans."[105] Focher, who was educated at the University of Paris during the Llullian renaissance in Europe, explains that in order to convert the Indians, the missionaries should first attract them with "affability, making manifest the true God in words and works," before attempting to "reduce" them to the faith. However, in Focher's (and Valadés's) *Itinerarium Catholicum,* the verb (and also the noun, *reductio*) also had another technical meaning. Thus, Focher explains that, once the Indians' friendship has been secured, they should be "concentrated, forming towns and cities" especially created for this purpose.[106] For, as long as they live in their native state, dispersed in the mountains, they will return (like dogs) to the "vomit" of their paganism. In the towns, the Indians will be catechized and learn to sing, play musical instruments, read, write, and become expert in the mechanical arts. In the process, the Indians will be "liberated" from the "tyrannical slavery" of the Devil.[107]

Thus, as suggested by Focher's missionology—the first of its kind written in the Americas—the papal mission of *ad fidem Catholicam reducere* was translated on the ground into the implementation of Indian resettlement into specially constructed missionary towns. This practice had actually begun as early as the 1520s in the Caribbean, particularly in the first Franciscan Province in America, the Province of the Holy Cross, headquartered on Hispaniola. There, however, the idea of resettlement was not yet called "reduction" but rather "experience" (*experiencia*) and "miners" (*mineros*).[108] Thus, the first provincial, Pedro de Mexía, a graduate from Cisnero's new university at Alcalá, wrote in 1517 a *parecer* (opinion), in which he proposed a remedy to the widely reported abuses of Indians by their encomenderos by introducing an experiment in reform. In what he called an *experiencia,* the Indians would be taken out of the spiritual care of their lay encomenderos and placed into the care of the missionaries in specially created towns. The encomenderos would be compensated for the loss of labor with black slaves from Africa.[109] This reform project provided the blueprint for the Indian towns that would later come to be called *congregaciones, doctrinas,* and *reducciones,* established in New Spain by the Franciscans and also by some secular clergy, such as Vasco de Quiroga (who called them *hospitales*), as well as in South America by both Franciscans such as Luis de Bolaños and (later) Jesuits.[110] Whereas the early missionary towns established by Bartolomé de las Casas in Venezuela had mixed Spanish colonists with indigenous peoples, the model of these heterotopian reductions was predicated on the idea of concentrating and isolating the neophytes from all corruptive influences.[111] Thus, in 1546, the church council of prelates in New Spain determined that the Indians should be "reduced in towns and not live scattered and dispersed throughout the ranges and forests."[112] By the end of the decade, the idea was adopted as official policy by the Council of the Indies. In 1551, Charles V issued a royal decree (*cédula*) that codified the link between conversion and relocation:

> It has always been the aim to impose with great care and particular attention the best means possible so that the Indians may be instructed in the Holy Catholic Faith and Evangelical law, and for this to be done with the greatest ability our Council of the Indies was called together various times [as well as] other Priests and the Prelates of New Spain to meet by order of the Emperor Charles [and] who with the desire to succeed in the service of God and ours, resolved that the Indians be concentrated [*reducidos*] into towns, and [and] not live dispersed and isolated among the mountains and hills depriving themselves completely of temporal and spiritual benefits.[113]

In order to understand the translation of the particular *hermeneutics* of conversion as "reduction" into a *method* of conversion through spatial relocation and concentration, it is instructive to consider some of the other meanings of the Latin root *reduco* and the Spanish verb *reducir*. With regard to the latter, Tom Cummins has observed that it "was conceptually greater than the physical concentration of previously dispersed individuals into a physically more restricted space. *Reducir* implies a sense of ordering according to a universal, preexisting structure.... [It] was the process of bringing into being a more perfect state. Christianity was at the metaphysical center of this colonial

Physicians of the Soul   239

ordering process."¹¹⁴ Accordingly, as Cummins also points out, another context in which the early modern Spanish verb *reducir* was frequently used is that of grammar. Cummins cites, for example, the famous Spanish humanist Antonio de Nebrija, who wrote that his Spanish grammar (1492)—the first of its kind—would "reduce" the artifice of the Spanish vernacular to the Latin rules underlying it.¹¹⁵ In this sense, the verb was especially common in the grammars and vocabularies of indigenous languages produced by the missionaries in America, whose humanist *arte* "reduced" Native American languages without indigenous alphabetical scripts to the rules of the Latin alphabet and grammar. As Cummins notes, in the context of this new linguistics: "Such an understanding of *reducir* and *reducción* was not an innocent revelation. It restored a lost unity brought about by the building of the Tower of Babel and the dispersal of nations and tongues. The biblical multiplicity of languages and nations ... was ... the cause of idolatry. The capacity to bring languages hitherto unknown to each other into harmony restored a once lost unity. That Christianity could therefore be preached as result of this reunification would mean a final end to idolatry."¹¹⁶ Although all three mendicant orders, as well as the Jesuits later, made important contributions to this new form of linguistics, it was, again, the Franciscans who had taken the lead. In New Spain, they stand out among the religious orders in the sheer volume of instructional linguistic treatises about Native American languages that they produced.¹¹⁷ Although the flood of publications of this technical literature ebbed in the 1560s (when the first laws against books of Native language instruction are passed by imperial authorities), this body of works represents one of the main and earliest genres of colonial American literature—the "art" of reducing non-Western languages to the rules of written grammars and dictionaries.¹¹⁸

In order to illuminate the connection between the Franciscans' projects of spatial "reduction" and concentration on the one hand and of the intellectual "reduction" of their languages to the art of grammar on the other, it is furthermore useful to consider missionologies such as Focher's *Itinerarium* and Valadés's *Rhetorica Christiana* in the context of the Llullian tradition of medical discourse, particularly of Remigius Rufo's (pseudo-Llullian) notion of evangelical rhetoric as the "alchemy of words" in *In rhetoricam isagoge*—the text that was partially reproduced by Valadés in his own missionology.¹¹⁹ As we saw in chapter 5, Rufo's analogy between alchemy and evangelical rhetoric built on a long Llullian tradition in which spiritual and physical healing had a "metaphorical" relationship that had first been elaborated by Llull in his *Principles of Medicine* (1273). This metaphorical relationship was, as Ziegler has shown, one of the hallmarks of the Arnaldian and Llullian tradition of medical discourse.¹²⁰ In general medicine, the word *reductio* meant the intervention by the arts of medicine in "reshaping" the body (i.e., to "reduce" a broken bone back in its intended place).[121] It was in this medical sense of *ad pristinum statum reducta* that late medieval preachers had developed the idea of themselves as "physicians of the soul."[122] Moreover, as we have already seen, in pseudo-Llullian alchemy, *reducere* meant to return substantial forms to their *prima materia* in one of the four basic operations of the alchemical regimen of transmutation also known as the *sol niger* (black sun)—the "killing" of the metal (or other substance containing the quintessence) in a violent opus of fiery penitence.[123] Thus, in the *Testamentum,* the Llullian wrote that alchemy is "an occult part of philosophy, the most necessary, a basic art which cannot be learned by just anyone. Alchemy teaches how to change all precious stones until they achieve the true balancing of qualities; how to bring human bodies to their healthiest condition; and how to transmute all metals into the true Sun (gold) and true Moon (silver), by means of a unique body, universal, to which all particular medicines are reduced (ad quod omnes medicinae particulares reductae sunt)."[124] In this alchemical sense, the use of the verb *reducere* was still common during the early modern Llullian renaissance in the (pseudo-)Llullian medical-alchemical tradition of the *Medicina operativa* that was being taught by Bernardo de Lavinheta at Salamanca and Paris and that he later incorporated in his encyclopedic *Explanatio* (1523).[125] A few years after Lavinheta, the Swiss alchemist Paracelsus would use the word *reducere* in the sense of "to restore a metal to the unchanged or metallic state." Paracelsus's source was the pseudo-Llullian tradition—in fact, the very definition of alchemy in the Llullian *Testamentum.*[126] As we will see in the next section of this chapter, the pseudo-Llullian alchemical tradition informed not only the Franciscans' project of spatial and linguistic reduction but also their encyclopedic projects in missionary ethnography and natural history in the New World.

The Alchemy of Words

Due to their mission of intervening into lay society, one of the features that distinguished all of the mendicants from their monastic counterparts was their emphasis on preaching, confessing, and ministering.[127] By the sixteenth century, the mendicants had become specialists in the art rhetoric, taking advantage of the humanists' recovery of classical models. The most famous theoretician of rhetoric in sixteenth-century Spain was the Dominican Luis de Granada (1504–1588), who had written several treatises on preaching, including the *Ecclesiasticae rhetoricae* (1576), which was based, like most sixteenth-century manuals on rhetoric, on Cicero's classical treatise, *De inventione*, as well as on the (medieval) pseudo-Ciceronian *Ad herennium*. It attempted to synthesize the Christian message with the classical rhetorical tradition, especially Cicero's model of the orator combining both eloquence and wisdom. Written in the spirit of the Counter-Reformation and in the wake of the Council of Trent (1545–63), its main purpose was to instruct preachers in the best methods of persuading the adherents of the Protestant heresy to return to the fold of the church.[128] Although preaching had traditionally been an integral part of the propagation of the Gospel, and although this tradition had been preserved throughout the Middle Ages among the mendicant orders, its importance had been overshadowed by the administration of the liturgy among the secular clergy. In the context of the Protestant challenge, however, church authorities reemphasized the importance of rhetorical skills among all clergy, regular and secular.[129] Granada's treatise on ecclesiastic rhetoric specifically answered the Council's renewed call for "institutionalizing preaching," as Anne Cruz and Elizabeth Perry have written, "as a means of rhetorically controlling the people and of disseminating social propaganda that encouraged the status quo. In its attempt to regularize oratory, the church formulated a religious discourse intended to instruct, entertain, and persuade."[130] In response to this mandate, Granada's *Ecclesiasticae rhetoricae* focused on the conventional Ciceronian topoi in the study of rhetoric—invention, amplification, disposition, and elocution.

But while manuals based on classical rhetoric would serve for the assistance of preachers addressing a European audience, they were utterly inadequate for the tasks of a missionary addressing a non-Christian audience, especially in the Americas. Similarly, despite the excellent humanistic training that the early mendicants who arrived in New Spain in the 1520s and 1530s had received in Spain under the Cisnearean reforms, nothing could quite prepare them for the challenges they faced in the Americas.[131] As already pointed out, the first obstacle was of a linguistic nature. How should they communicate with the Indians whom they were supposed to convert? There was significant debate in the sixteenth century about which language should be used in the missionary work. Some argued that the instructional language should be Spanish or even Latin, fearing that the subtleties of the Christian faith—such as the Trinity—would get lost in translation into indigenous languages and that language and religion are too closely intertwined. Others, however (including most Franciscans), insisted that in order to be effective, the missionaries had to meet the Indians on their own ground on the level not only of language but also of ontology. While the latter position prevailed early on, one problem in addressing the Indians in their own languages was the staggering diversity of indigenous languages even within one region. Although the Aztec Empire had spread its language, Nahuatl, around Mesoamerica, only a small elite in the provinces of the old empire was conversant in it. The vast majority of the people comprising the newly conquered Spanish territories that would comprise the viceroyalty of New Spain spoke only their local languages, such as Otomí or Tarascan. In both New Spain and Peru, the friars therefore promoted the indigenous language spoken in the former political centers of power—Nahuatl and Quechua—as the lingua franca for catechization. In the aftermath of the Council of Trent, however, the authorities in the church, and especially in the Inquisition, became increasingly wary of the use of *any* vernacular in theology, especially when it concerned translations from Scripture.

Besides the study of indigenous languages by "reducing" them to the rules of grammar, the Franciscan missionaries also inaugurated the close ethnological inquiry into Native cultures and religions. As pointed out earlier, this ethnological interest was partially inspired by the Franciscans' preoccupation with the role that the Devil played in Indian spiritual and material culture. But the missionaries were hereby looking not only for those elements that they must extirpate and eliminate but also for those that they could use and exploit in their catechization. As we saw in chapter 5, this is a practice that had already begun in the Caribbean with Ramón Pané's description of the Tainos and ultimately has roots in the thirteenth century, especially with Ramón Llull's and Ramón Martí's missionologies. But the Franciscans in New Spain implemented this ethnographic project on a new scale of rigor and systematization. Not only did the Franciscans in New Spain preach to the Indians in their native languages, but they also used concepts, categories, and media that were borrowed from Native cultures. One pioneer in this regard was the Franciscan priest Jacobo de Testera, who devised a medium for teaching the catechism that made use of Nahua glyphs.[132] Another pioneer was the Flemish Franciscan Pedro de Gante, who had already arrived in 1523, one year in advance of the *doce*. A pioneer in the use of music in missionology, he set up the first European academy for training Native Americans, the convent school of San José de los Naturales, where he trained the first generation of American-born—indigenous, mestizo, and creole—missionaries. He also composed catechisms in Nahuatl that made use of Mexica pictographic media traditions.[133] Among his students was Valadés, who would later use pictographic media that drew on both Mexica and European traditions when preaching in front of his Native congregations (see fig. 17).[134] In order to be effective as a preacher in the Americas, Valadés argued, it is necessary to conduct close studies of Native religions, cultures, and media traditions. Missionaries unfamiliar with Native religion and rites, he explained, are destined for failure, for they are like the "blind leading the blind."[135] The preacher must

Figure 17. A missionary instructs Native Americans using graphic depictions of the Passion; a monk holds an hourglass on the steps of the pulpit. "Ad sensus aptat coelestia dona magister, Aridaq eloquij pectora fonte rigat." (In Diego de Valadés, *Rhetorica christiana ad concionandi, et orandi usum accommodata* . . . [Perugia: Pietro Giacopo Petrucci, 1579]. Courtesy of the John Carter Brown Library at Brown University.)

therefore not only know about sacred things but must also draw from all of nature, including profane things, just as a doctor can obtain medicines from low things, such as reptiles. Thus, in his Preface to the Pope Gregory, Valadés wrote:

> I think that the teaching of the disciplines is above all for our own benefit. Not only that most noble and proper, which despises all literary adornment and all dispute and which is confined to the beauty of salvation and intellectual things but also those profane things, which many Christians despise and look upon with evil eyes as treacherous and fallacious and apart from God. Thus, we know that fire, food, iron, and other things are neither useful nor harmful by themselves, but with respect to their use; what's more, just as we obtain medicine from reptiles for our health, so also with respect to them, which provide us with material for investigation and contemplation. But when we are dragged toward the devils, error, and even to the depth of perdition, then we despise them. Because although these things in no way affords us piety, we still choose the better from worse and hereby fortify our expression.[136]

As Linda Báez-Rubí has shown, the organization of "things," both sacred and profane, in Valadés's *Rhetorica christiana* follows closely the order of the Llullian *subiecta* and *praedicata*.[137] These are the Divine World, the Angelic World, the Celestial World, the Human World, the Imagination, the Animal World, the Vegetable World, the Elemental World, and the Arts and Sciences. These nine rubrics are called the "subjects" or the "matter." As Valadés explains: "In the consideration of these divine subjects we find all the instruments that give notice of God. Nevertheless, he remains the beginning, the middle, and the end, and all obey him, whose goodness is manifest in all the *praedicata*. There are nine *praedicata*: goodness [*bonitas*], greatness [*magnituda*], duration [*duratio*], power [*potestas*], wisdom [*sapientia*], will [*voluntas*], virtue [*virtus*], truth [*veritas*], and glory [*Gloria*]. They are called *praedicata* because they qualify the *subiecta*."[138] The *praedicata* are the instruments of God, for they represent the hierarchy of all of creation, as though organized on a scale (*scala*): "The preacher must ascend and descend this scale," Valadés writes, "from the highest to the lowest, and from the lowest to the highest."[139] The ascent from the lowest to the highest begins with empirical reality, including minerals, plants, and animals, and moves up the scale to the heavens. As Báez Rubí notes, however, Valadés does away with Llull's alphabetical and geometric figures, using instead "pictorial figures" that he deemed more appropriate for most of his Indian neophytes, for whom alphabetical signs were alien.[140] Thus, based on the "alchemy of words" of the *ars luliana*, Franciscan missionaries such as Valadés provided a blueprint for the encyclopedic study of Native cultures, religions, and natural histories of America.

Valadés's *Rhetorica christiana* was, of course, primarily intended as an art of memory designed for the "discovery" of topics in preaching—discovery in the sense of "invention" in the tradition of *Aristotle's Topics*. Nevertheless, the arrangement of his materials according to the Llullian *subiecta* on a Neoplatonic chain of creation illuminates the encyclopedic form also of many of the proto-ethnographic projects that grew out of the Franciscan missionary effort in sixteenth-century New Spain. For example, Báez Rubí has pointed to the possibility of a Llullian influence on Motolinía and his *Historia de los indios de la Nueva España*.[141] As we saw earlier, other important sixteenth-century Franciscan ethnographic histories include Andrés de Olmos's *Tratado de hechicerías y sortilegios*. Like Valadés's work, these missionary tracts present the reader with a great amount of historical, ethnological, and naturalist material intended to aid the missionary effort. But unlike Valadés's *Rhetorica*, Olmos's *Tratado* was not explicitly written as a guide for preaching, and the ethnological materials it contains are not the *subiecta* of rhetoric; this is to say that they serve for the purpose not of the "discovery" (invention) of topics drawn from a world that is manifest to all sensitive and rational creatures but of the *dis-covery* (the uncovering) of that which is secret—the hidden traces of idolatry in neophyte Christian practices. It is this difference that modern historians have often seen as a marker of a "transition to modernity." As Walden Browne has observed, whereas the medieval interpreter ultimately "reduces all knowledge of the cosmos to divine revelation, the modern interpreter sees him or herself as an observer who is eccentric to, or at a distance from, the world and, therefore, as someone who must actively participate in the production of knowledge by heavily relying on such human . . . tools as reason and experience."[142] As such, ethno-demonology shared its hermeneutics of discovery with late medieval and early modern alchemy. This is to say that the hermeneutics of discovery in both alchemy and ethno-demonology is predicated on the notion of an "autoptic" knowledge in the nominalist tradition of late medieval medical discourse, a knowledge that is based on empirical information intended for the diagnosis of sickness for the purpose of healing, both physical and spiritual.[143] As Stuart Clark has explained, autopsia in demonological discourse is predicated on a "a kind of ocularcentrism. . . . in which the twin traditions stemming from the perceptual preferences of the Greeks [i.e., Aristotle] and the religious teachings of St. Augustine combined to give the eyes priority over the other sense."[144] As we will see in the next section, the autoptic hermeneutic of discovery in (ethno-) demonology, medicine, and alchemy coalesced with the Llullian tradition of encyclopedism in a comprehensive "missionary science" during the second part of the sixteenth century.

Bernadino de Sahagún and the History of All Things

In 1536, the Franciscans officially opened the Colegio de Santa Cruz de Tlatelolco, an academy of higher education in the liberal arts for the purpose of preparing the children of the Native nobility for entry into the university. The location of the Colegio had been chosen because Tlatelolco had in pre-Hispanic times been the site of a famous Mexica *calmecac,* a quasi-monastic temple establishment for the education of the the Nahua elites, including the last legitimate Mexica ruler, Cuauhtémoc.[145] As Bernadino de Sahagún, one of the teachers at Tlatelolco, explained, the idea of the Colegio was in part inspired by the Mexica concept of the *calmecac:* "Since we found that in their ancient republic the boys and girls were brought up in their temples, and there they were disciplined and taught the culture of their gods and subjection to the republic, we took their style of bringing up the boys in our houses and they slept in the house that was built for them next to ours."[146] The Franciscans' knowledge about the "style" and function of pre-Hispanic education at the *calmecac* at Tlatelolco was one of the fruits of the ethnographic and linguistic research by Olmos.[147] While the Franciscans had initially intended for the students of the Colegio to become missionaries themselves, the plan was later thwarted when the Mexican church decided to ban neophytes from entering the priesthood.[148] Worse, from the 1550s to the 1590s, in the aftermath of the Council of Trent, the church gradually began to suppress the proselytizing in Native American languages, against the fierce but eventually futile opposition on the part of the mendicants against the Crown's and the bishops' policy of Hispanization. When the university was finally established (in 1551–53), no chairs were devoted to the study of indigenous languages and cultures. After the 1560s, the Colegio was afflicted by a number of problems, including a decline in financial support.[149]

Nevertheless, for about thirty years, the Colegio de Santa Cruz de Tlatelolco represented the crown jewel of Franciscan achievements in missionary education. Although it was not officially inaugurated until January 6, 1536, the Colegio had been in operation since 1533, when it was created upon the initiative of the president of the royal Audiencia and former bishop of Santo Domingo, Sebastián Ramírez de Fuenleal, and the bishop of Mexico, Juan de Zumárraga. There, the missionaries trained "trilingualists," Native scholars competent in Nahuatl, Latin, and Spanish. Among its distinguished teachers were Olmos and Molina as well as Francisco de Las Navas. However, the most accomplished sixteenth-century scholar at Tlatelolco was Sahagún. He had arrived in New Spain in 1529, after graduating from the University of Salamanca, where he would certainly have encountered the *ars luliana,* which was being taught there by Lavinheta when Sahagún matriculated in 1516.[150] With regard to his methodology, Sahagún was a true pioneer in the history of empirical and collaborative research, hereby synthesizing Llull's encyclopedic method with pseudo-Llullian medical empiricism and Olmos's interest in ethno-demonology. In his collection of ethnographic and naturalist information, he engaged several Native collaborators who had been educated at Tlatelolco. Under his leadership, the Colegio became a center not only of linguistic but also of ethnological study, including the inquiry into Native *materia medica,* a topic of special interest to Sahagún.[151] For example, the Native scholars produced the famous *Libellus de medicinalibus indorum herbis* (Little book of the medicinal herbs of the Indies, 1552), a unique treatise on Mexican *materia medica* written in Nahuatl by Martín de la Cruz and translated into Latin by Juan Badiano (hence now also known as the Badianus Manuscript). The book inspired the later investigations of the royal *protomédico* Francisco Hernández, which resulted in his *Historia de las plantas de Nueva España* (ca. 1577).[152] Although Hernández's *Historia de las plantas* remained in manuscript during his lifetime, it enjoyed significant dissemination throughout Europe and influenced seventeenth-century men of science associated with the Scientific Revolution, such as Galileo Galilei, John Ray, Francis Willughby, and Fabio Colonna, who published a Latin version of it in 1651 for the Accademia dei Lincei in Rome.[153]

The linguistic, humanistic, and ethnological scholarship undertaken at the Franciscan college at Tlatelolco culminated with the monumental *Historia universal de las cosas de la Nueva España.* As Sahagún explains in the prologue to the work, its purpose was to assist future missionaries in their attempts at "indoctrination, the propagation and perpetuation of the Christianization of these natives of this New Spain, and as a help to the workers and ministers who indoctrinate them."[154] Although the majority of the Indians in the Central Valley of Mexico had been baptized by the late 1540s, when Sahagun began this project, he was horrified to discover, during his many years of experience as a missionary, that "the sins of idolatry, idolatrous rituals, idolatrous superstitions, auguries, abuses, and idolatrous ceremonies are not yet completely lost."[155] Worse, he lamented, most of the early missionaries, being ignorant of the old beliefs and rituals, were unable to detect them when disguised as Christian rituals by the deceptive Natives. Motolinía's triumphant celebration of millions of converts had been based on an illusion, whereas in reality the Indians had continued to worship their ancient idols in Christian disguise.

Thus, in the prologue to his *Arte adivinatoria* (The art of divination), Sahagún wrote that the Indians "turn up in public to receive the sacraments and to celebrate the festivals of Christians, while on the inside they have not renounced their gods as gods, serving them secretly by offering sacrifices and holding festivals whenever the missionary work permits secrecy."[156] The ethnological and linguistic research that informed his book would therefore function like a "dragnet" (*red barredera*) or a "sieve" (*cedaço*), he wrote in the prologue to the *Historia,* "to bring to light all the words of this language with their exact and metaphorical meaning."[157] In other words, the book was intended as a sort of diagnostic manual that would enable missionaries to discover the idolatrous elements in Nahua Christian rituals that would otherwise remain hidden from them. Thus, while Sahagún has often been hailed by modern scholars as a pioneer of modern anthropology, Jesús Bustamante García has convincingly argued that he should more properly seen as an "inquisitor."[158] Indeed, if Sahagún's method reveals the forensic roots of modern empirical ethnography, his work can be understood in terms of the distinct genre of missionary writing that I have called "ethno-demonology."

After having received the original commission to write such a book in 1557 from Francisco de Toral, the Provincial of the Franciscan Order in New Spain, Sahagún made an "outline or summary [*minuta o memoria*] in Spanish of all the topics to be considered."[159] The following year, after having decided on the topics that should be considered, he took his *memoria* to the village of Tepepulco (today called Tepeapulco, in the state of Hidalgo) in order to commence his ethnographic fieldwork. He was hereby assisted by several of the Native trilingualists whom he had trained at the Colegio de Santa Cruz in Tlatelolco. Among these Native collaborators was Antonio Valeriano, Sahagún's most accomplished student and the alleged author of the *Nican Mopohua,* the account of the miraculous appearance of the Virgin of Guadalupe to the Indian Juan Diego in 1531 (though this authorship has been disputed).[160] Also involved were Alonso Vegerano; Martín Jacobita, who later became the rector of the Colegio; and Pedro de San Buenaventura.[161] Having arrived at Tepepulco, Sahagún assembled the local nobility, including a man christened as Diego de Mendoza, "of great distinction and talent, very expert in all things courtly, military, governmental, and even idolatrous."[162] He explained his purpose to the town leaders and requested their collaboration. After a day of deliberation, the leaders agreed to Sahagún's proposal and assigned him several leading elders who would serve as cultural informants and provide answers to his questions about the proposed subjects. "With these leaders and grammarians," Sahagún wrote ("grammarians" referring to his trilinguists), "I conferred many days, close to two years, following the sequence of the outline which I had prepared."¹⁶³ Thus, the work was truly a collaborative effort that involved not only Sahagún but also a host of Nahua informants and trilinguist scholars who can rightfully be called the coauthors of the *Historia universal*.¹⁶⁴

The *minuta* or *memoria* that Sahagún brought along to Tepepulco in 1558 is the first documented stage of the *Historia universal* that would be completed some twenty years later, when, in 1580, Fray Rodrigo de Sequera, the Franciscan commissary general, took a manuscript of the work to Spain. That manuscript would be known as the Florentine Codex, due to the fact that it came into the possession of the Medici family in the 1580s and has since then been preserved at the Laurentian Library in Florence. Meanwhile, Sahagún kept on working on the book all the way up to his death in 1590, but the Florentine Codex remains the most complete version of the work.¹⁶⁵ It consists of the pictographs provided by the informants pertaining to the subjects and questions that Sahagún supplied; the alphabetical Nahuatl commentaries prepared by Sahagún's trilinguist assistants based on the oral explications of the images by the informants; and Spanish translations (sometimes only summaries or paraphrases). Textual scholarship has shown the significant transformation that the work underwent in the course of the twenty years. Thus, whereas the early version only contains the pictographs and alphabetical texts in Nahuatl that are basically glosses on the primary pictographic content, in the Florentine Codex the alphabetical texts, both Nahuatl and Spanish, have assumed—presumably in accommodation of a European readership—a central place, while the pictographic content functioned more or less in an ancillary fashion as illustrations.¹⁶⁶ Also, the original *memoria* that Sahagún distributed had only five headings: the first two chapters deal with "divine things"—one on the gods and one on angelic beings (both celestial and infernal); two chapters on human things (one about rule and one about social life) and one about things of nature and the earth (animals, plants, minerals, metals, etc.). By contrast, the Florentine Codex that was taken to Europe in 1580 is divided into twelve books: I: Mexica Gods; II: Religion (calendar, holidays and ceremonies, sacrifices, etc.); III: Sacred History (i.e., the origins of Nahua gods); IV: knowledge of the stars (astrology, etc); V: natural magic (omens and prophecies derived from animals, such as birds); VI: human knowledge (rhetoric, moral philosophy, theology); natural philosophy (sun, moon, stars, the four elements of the sublunary world); VIII: politics (kings and lords); IX: commerce (merchants); X: common people; XI: natural things (animals, birds, fish, snakes, trees, stones, metals); and XII: the history of the conquest.¹⁶⁷

Various theories have been offered with regard to the rhetorical models that may have inspired Sahagún's organization of "things." Ángel Maria Garibay

Kintana, for example, has shown the influence of Pliny's *Natural History* on book 11 of the *Historia universal*.[168] Jesús Bustamente García has called attention to the influence of St. Augustine's *Of Christian Doctrine* and *The City of God*.[169] For his part, Donald Robertson has argued that the organization of materials in Sahagún's work is indebted to the medieval encyclopedic tradition, particularly to that of the seventh-century *Etymologies* of Isidore of Seville and the *De proprietatibus rerum* of Bartholomaeus Anglicus.[170] This apparent debt to a thirteenth-century encyclopedia led Robertson to conclude that the *Historia universal* is essentially backward-looking and "medieval" in its form.[171] Finally, Walden Browne has considered the *Historia universal* in the context of Scholastic hermeneutics and metaphysics, particularly in light of the late medieval genre of the *summa* and its method of *manifestatio*. According to Browne, this method of logical demonstration, by which Thomas Aquinas's *Summa* attempted to bridge Christian faith and Aristotelian reason, breaks down in Sahagún's attempt to integrate the Nahua's radical cultural alterity within the Scholastic universalist structure of knowledge—a breakdown that, Browne argues, positions the *Historia universal* as a transitional text on the eve of modernity.[172]

While all these interpretations offer important insights for understanding the design of Sahagún's history, they run the risk of underestimating the considerable continuities between late medieval and early modern structures of knowledge. As we have seen, the challenge to Thomist realist metaphysics did not begin in the sixteenth century but originated already in medieval Franciscan nominalism. The continuity between late medieval and early modern models for Sahagún's encyclopedism is nowhere as evident as it is in the much more immediate influence of early modern (i.e., alchemified) Llullism that was thriving in the sixteenth century in the works of such Renaissance humanists as Lavinheta, who revived and repurposed Llull's medieval Neoplatonism in their attacks on "Scholastic" Aristotelianism.[173] The "modernity" of the humanists' encyclopedias inheres precisely in their debt to the "medieval" Llullian rejection not only of the Scholastic practice of *compilatio* and citation of authorities but also of the Aristotelian separation between science and religion, especially between natural description and spiritual exegesis. When Sahagún distinguishes himself as an author from all those Scholastic writers who avail themselves of authorities—because "I have lacked all of these foundations in order to authorize what I have written in these twelve books"—he stands in a long line of medieval encyclopedists who had employed a similar authorial stance. Mary Franklin-Brown has helpfully characterized the Scholastic Aristotelian encyclopedia as "horizontal" and the Neoplatonic Llullian tradition as "vertical" in this regard. The former, she writes, "found its purpose in running over the surfaces of things, detailing their properties and describing their natures." The Llullian tradition, by contrast, is distinguished by its tendency toward a "participatory symbolism" that limits "to an absolute minimum any contact with the surface of things, by transcending them almost immediately, with the result that his [Llull's] encyclopedia unfolds... as a repeated demonstration of a single meaning." This single meaning is the manifestation of God's Dignities in His creation, the visible unfolding of salvation history, and the demonstration of divine truths in the work of evangelization. Thus, whereas the Scholastic authors "seemed to feel some anxiety about indulging their *curiositas*," the Llullians turned scientific inquiry into a branch of "spiritual exegesis."[174]

These continuities illuminate the important role that Sahagún's work in missionary ethnography and natural history would play as a model in the development of subsequent early modern scientific projects, such as in the works of Hernández, as well as in those of the royal chronicler Juan López de Velasco, and the Jesuit historian José de Acosta, inquiring into the secrets of American nature and cultures.[175] For Sahagún, the interrelationship between secrecy and discovery is of providential design. Thus, he writes, "It is certainly a matter of great wonderment that, for so many centuries, our Lord God has concealed a forest (*selva*) of so many idolatrous peoples whose luxuriant fruits only the demon harvested and holds hoarded in the infernal fire."[176] And in the prologue to book 12 of the *Historia* (which deals with the conquest from the Nahua point of view), Sahagún wrote:

> When these lands (which are beneath the Torrid Zone and Equinoctial line) were discovered, many truths were discovered that before were hidden. One of these was that previously everyone thought that all this land beneath the Torrid Zone was uninhabitable as far as the Antarctic Pole; and now we see with our eyes that all the aforementioned is densely populated. In the same way it was affirmed that the Southern Star would never be seen; and now we see that the North Star serves navigators until the Equinoctial line, and from there onward the Southern Star serves those who sail toward it. So too was it affirmed, until now, that the Ocean Sea (which extends westward, with respect to Spain) had neither boundary nor end; and now we see that, departing from San Lucar toward the Canary Islands, a very broad ocean gulf stretches to the island of Santo Domingo; and from here in New Spain, one embarks in the port of Acapulco, where there is another gulf, as large as that mentioned above, across which they go to the Philippines, guided in half this journey by the North Star, and in the other by the Southern Cross.[177]

As did most other sixteenth-century Franciscan historians of America, Sahagún hereby assigns a providentialist significance to Cortés's military conquest, which opened "a path" [*camino*] and a "door" [*puerta*] through the "wall [*muro*] with which this infidelity was enclosed and immured . . . so that Preachers of the Holy Gospel might enter to preach the Catholic Faith to this most miserable people, who were for so long subject to the servitude of so innumerable idolatrous rites, and so many and so great sins, with which they were enwrapped, and by which they condemned themselves."[178] Although Sahagún lamented (more so than Motolinía) the terrible consequences of the conquest on the Nahuas' society and culture—which, he said, had reduced them to a shadow of what they had been before—the violence of the conquest was yet a necessary evil that made them receptive to the Christian life and message. The violence of the conquest opened a "door" into the "wall" behind which satanic idolatries had been hidden away from Christian eyes. "Whatever it may be that they were in times past," he wrote, "we now see through experience."[179]

As sons of Adam and heirs of his Original Sin, the Indians still retain a faint memory of the first knowledge of God. However, because of their lack of alphabetical Scripture and the Devil's perversion of human knowledge, it has been corrupted and degenerated into idolatry. Thus, Sahagún reports that the ancient traditions of the Nahuas relate how their ancestors arrived from the north, from the direction of Florida, and landed in Panuco, which means "the place where those who crossed the waters arrived."[180] They came in search of the Terrestrial Paradise, located on a high mountain, from which Adam had been expelled, which they call "'Tamoanchan,' which means 'We seek our home.'" In looking for the Terrestrial Paradise on a high mountain in the south, Sahagún observes, the Indians were not mistaken, "for it is the opinion of the writers that it is below the equinoctial line. Nor did they err in thinking it is some very high mountain, for the writers say so: that the terrestrial paradise is below the equinoctial line and that it is a very high mountain, that its summit reaches near to the moon. It seems that they or their ancestors possessed some oracle regarding this subject, either from God, or the demon, or from the tradition of the elders."[181] These similarities between the Mexica and Christian sacred histories prove to Sahagún that "it is most certain all these people are our brothers, stemming from the stock of Adam, as do we. They are our neighbors whom we are obliged to love, even as we love ourselves."[182] However, for Sahagún, these similarities were the sign not of a natural tendency of rational creatures to tend toward the true God but of a diabolic corruption of spirit and matter that must not be cultivated but has to be reduced before spiritual healing can occur. Thus, in the reductions the Indians are taught "all the crafts and they practice them. They are also capable in learning all the liberal arts and sacred theology." The experience of the conquest has proven their ability to endure penitent hardship: "How strong they are in enduring the hardships of hunger, thirst, cold and sleeplessness! How willing and ready they are to undertake all kinds of dangerous missions! They are no less capable of our Christianity; besides, they have been duly indoctrinated."[183]

Despite (or because of) the impressive accomplishment of Sahagún and his students in missionary ethnography, not all of his contemporaries appreciated his efforts. Some of his fellow brethren deemed it imprudent to record, describe, and hereby memorialize idolatrous practices that should be conferred to the dust bins of history. While these critical voices had been there from the beginning of Sahagún's project, the situation took a turn for the worse for Sahagún in the general climate of retrenchment and paranoia in the aftermath of the Council of Trent. Not only did the authorities in church and state attempt to suppress the use of Nahuatl in the missionary effort and insisted on the Hispanification of the Indian neophytes, but they also began to scrutinize Sahagún's ethnographic studies, wary that they might actually facilitate a nefarious relapse into or a rebirth of idolatry among the Indians. In 1570, the Provincial Superior Alonso de Escalona had Sahagún's papers confiscated and distributed among theologians throughout New Spain so that they could give their opinion as to the project's merits and prudence. Although Sahagún was eventually able to retrieve most of his papers, in 1577, King Philip, who had been aware of the project for some time, ordered the immediate confiscation and dispatch of Sahagún's ethnographic works to the Council of the Indies and forbade their printing or circulation in New Spain.[184] Although Sahagún complied by surrendering several of his manuscripts, he continued his work with the support of Sequera. The more he learned about Nahua culture in the course of his ethnographic studies, the more he grew doubtful about the success of the missionaries in their attempts to extirpate ancient idolatries and to implant Christianity in Mexico. But regardless of whether or not his history of all things in New Spain achieved their intended evangelical purpose, it provided a methodological and rhetorical blueprint for the European scientific discovery of American flora, fauna, and culture.

José de Acosta's Alchemical Wedding

In this last section of this chapter, I would like to consider the history of Llullism in the early Americas beyond the missionary writings of the Franciscans. Specifically, I will turn to the enormously influential *Historia natural y moral* (1590), written by the Jesuit missionary José de Acosta (1540–1600). The son of a *converso* family of merchants, Acosta had been educated at Alcalá de Henares before coming to the Americas as a missionary. He arrived in Peru in 1571, the year before the last male descendant of the Inca line, Tupak Amaru Inca, would be publicly executed on the main square of Cusco. The execution of the Inca was the work of the iron fist with which the new viceroy, Francisco de Toledo, ruled in Peru, implementing drastic reforms of the viceregal state's administration and of the system of rotational Indian labor known as *mita,* all of which had the effect of considerably consolidating Spanish hegemony and control over the Indians and revitalizing Peru's silver production by making available a cheap and compulsory work force after the high-quality and easily accessible ores had been depleted. As part of this reform program, Toledo had ordered, in 1569, the so-called Reducción General, the coercive resettlement of millions of Indians from their villages in the central Andes to artificially created towns (*reducciones*) that were laid out in a uniform grid (*traza*) with a plaza and a mission church at their centers. After the completion of the resettlement, the original villages of the Indians were to be destroyed. As Jeremy Ravi Mumford writes, the ambition of the resettlement project "anticipated state projects of the twentieth century, from Tanzanian model villages to Soviet collectivization." And although Ravi Mumford does not use the word "concentration camps" and resists the term "ethnocide" (because the resettlement relied partially on the collaboration of the Native elites and built on pre-Andean models of the coercive *mita* system), other historians have not minced words.[185] As Ravi Mumford goes on to point out, missionary ethnography had been central in the conception and execution of the project of reduction also in Peru. "Missionary priests studied indigenous cultures as an aid to evangelization, and the Spanish crown sent questionnaires to local officials on subjects such as native tribute systems. Those investigations shaped the General Resettlement of Indians."[186]

Acosta's presence in Peru overlapped with the implementation of this program, and his missionary research and writings are deeply implicated in these events. Upon his arrival in Peru, the young Jesuit quickly rose to a position of prominence in the viceregal state and church. The following year, he was appointed as president of the Jesuit College in Lima and the year after that as provincial of the Jesuits in Peru. He also became affiliated with the University of San Marcos, where he would participate in the Third Provincial Council of Lima in 1581. In these functions, Acosta became a close associate of the viceroy, but they eventually had a falling out, and he returned to Spain in 1587, after a brief sojourn in Mexico. Back in Spain, he became an advisor of Philip II and his delegate to the Vatican in Rome.[187]

Before coming to Peru, when he was still a student at Alcalá, Acosta had received the sort of eclectic education that was the legacy of the Cisnerean educational reforms during the early sixteenth century and that became the hallmark also of Jesuit education, synthesizing the major currents of the sixteenth-century Catholic world, including Neo-Thomism, Christian humanism, as well as Franciscan nominalism, Neoplatonism, and Llullism.[188] Acosta's works are notable for the degree to which they reflect this intellectual eclecticism, synthesizing these various, often conflicting and rivalling, currents into a coherent Counter-Reformation epistemology. One measure of Acosta's success as an author of natural history, philosophy, as well as theology and missionology in America is that, unlike the majority of the Franciscan writers discussed above, who ran afoul of the inquisitorial censors, Acosta was able to publish several of his works during his lifetime.[189] In 1581, he published in Lima a Latin work that appeared in two parts, the *De natura Novi Orbis* and the *De promulgatione Evangelii apud Barbaros, sive De Procuranda*. While the former was a natural history, the latter was a tract on missionology. The two should be published together, he said, because the natural history would serve as a sort of introduction to his tract on missionlogy. According to Acosta, one could not begin the work of conversion without first studying the Native peoples and their world.[190] Also during his tenure in Peru, he published a biography of a fellow Jesuit missionary, Bartolomé Lorenzo, as well as several catechisms.[191] Back in Spain, he republished the earlier Latin work on natural history and missiology, which appeared in two editions in 1588 and 1589, both in Salamanca.[192] Also in 1590, he published in Seville the work for which he is best known, the *Historia natural y moral de las Indias*. Parts of the *Historia* were based on the earlier, Latin natural history; other parts he had written anew for the Spanish publication; and yet others had been adapted from the Jesuit Juan de Tovar's missionary ethnography about New Spain, which in turn were indebted to the *Historia de las Indias de Nueva España,* written by the Dominican friar Diego Durán.[193] The *Historia natural y moral* would become enormously influential, being translated in short order into multiple languages, including English, French, Dutch, and German. As we will see in later chapters, it had a significant influence also on many of the English writers on New World expansionism and science, including Francis Bacon.

The *Historia natural y moral* is a voluminous work of encyclopedic scope in the tradition of missionary science established by the Franciscans. However, whereas the encyclopedic works of Sahagún and Valadés were organized along the principle of a single Platonic chain that connected all of creation, Acosta's materials, as his title suggests, are divided into two major subject matters—the "natural" and the "moral" history of America. Despite this formal distinction in the title, however, the book is formally structured not into two distinct parts but presented in a continuous sequence of seven books, each of which are divided into several chapters. Thus, the first four books are concerned with the natural history of the New World in chapters that are arranged, in the Franciscan tradition, in the order of the Neoplatonic chain, beginning with the description of the heavens and moving from there down the scale of creation to the climate and winds, bodies of water and land, including minerals and metals. The final three books, by contrast, are concerned with Native American religion and history, both in Peru and in New Spain. Thus, whereas in the histories of Sahagún and Valadés, the description of Native American society, culture, and religion formed part of the uninterrupted scale of creation and appeared there—in accordance with its proper place in the universal hierarchy—below the heavens and the angels but above the animals, Acosta excludes Native American culture and history from this Neoplatonic chain and instead treats them after the natural history as a separate subject. This deviation in structure is significant, as it reflects a distinctly "viceregal" ontology of America, its nature, resources, and people: whereas the encyclopedic histories of Motolinía, Valadés, Sahagún, and Mendieta were church histories of a *Franciscan* New Spain—a utopian world that consisted of missionaries and their Indian neophytes—Acosta's history is distinctly imperialist in outlook, where the Indians are only one sector of a larger viceregal society; where the natural world exists separately from Native American cultures and religions; and where the New World's natural resources (including Indian labor) exist for the benefit of the viceregal and monarchical state. As we will see later, in this organization of his book Acosta draws not only from the Llullian school of the missionary scientists I discussed above but also on the classical Plinean school of imperial natural historians such as Gonzalo Fernández de Oviedo y Valdés.

As Antonio Barrera, Andrés Prieto, and others have shown, Acosta's natural history is informed by a strongly empiricist spirit, in his descriptions of both Amerindian religions and New World nature.[194] Fernando Cervantes and Jorge Cañizares-Esguerra have added that Acosta hereby follows the rhetorical model of Franciscan ethnographers such as Motolinía and Sahagún in justifying this curiosity in paganism by presenting Native American religions as a form of idolatry and diabolism that must be exposed in order to be destroyed.[195] Finally, Anthony Pagden and Ivonne del Valle have each demonstrated how Acosta elaborates in his description of Native American history, culture, and religion a universal taxonomy of comparative ethnology that presents a four-tier hierarchy of "barbarism" in which each culture is categorized based on its writings technology. Thus, the Chinese (who use hieroglyphs) are above the Incas (who use *quipu,* or multicolored knotted strings), who are above the Chichimecs (who have no writing system), and so on.[196]

Acosta hereby draws not on the Neoplatonic model of the Franciscans but, as Orlando Bentancor has shown, on the language of early modern Aristotelianism, both on the late Scholastic Aristotelianism of the so-called School of Salamanca and especially on the humanist Aristotelianism of classicists such as Juan Ginés de Sepúlveda (to whom I will return in chapter 8 of this book).[197]

Bearing in mind Acosta's intellectual eclecticism, my particular interest here is in book 4, which deals with metals, minerals, plants, and animals. In chapter 12, Acosta wrote that "God's wisdom created metals for medicine and for defence and for adornment and as instruments of men's activities."[198] Medicine is, of course, one of those "men's activities," and Acosta saw a medicinal, salvific, and even providential significance in the discovery and exploitation of America's mineral wealth. After calculating the total revenue that the Crown had collected from American gold and silver by the time he wrote, he marvels:

> How great is the power that the Divine Majesty has graciously placed in the hands of the kings of Spain, heaping so many crowns and realms upon them that through Heaven's special favor the East and West Indies have been joined, circling the world with their power. We must believe that this has occurred through the special providence of God, for the good of those people who live so far distant from their head, who is the pope of Rome, vicar Christ of our Lord, and also for the defense of the Catholic Faith itself and the Roman Church in these parts, where the truth is so much resisted and persecuted by heretics.[199]

Just as the sacred gift of alchemy had aided the Christians in their struggle against infidels and the Antichrist during the later Middle Ages, so the conquest of America has yielded the gold that has aided the Spanish monarchs in their apocalyptic battles against the modern enemies of the faith, especially the Protestants of Europe. But for Acosta, Spanish greed for gold is justified not only by the military might it purchased in the mission to defeat Old World heretics but also by Spain's original apostolic mission in America, anchored in Pope Alexander's bulls *Inter cetera*. Thus, Acosta wrote that "God placed the greatest abundance of mines [where] this would invite men to seek those lands and hold them, and in this way to communicate their religion of the true God to those who did not know them." And to put it more poetically, he compares God to "a father with an ugly daughter [whom he] gives a large dowry to marry her; and this is what God did with that difficult land, giving it much wealth in mines so that by this means he would find someone who wanted it."[200] As for the medieval alchemists, so also for Acosta, the *concupiscentia* for gold is justified as an instrument for God's transcendent plan for universal salvation—in this case, Spanish greed for New World gold by bringing Christianity to the New World on the heels of greedy conquerors, prospectors, and adventurers.

At first sight, the allegory of the conquest of America as a marriage between an American bride and a Spanish groom recalls the wedding imagery of the Song of Songs of the Old Testament; but it has a long tradition also in Christianity in the motif of the mystical marriage of the church father in the union of the soul with Christ the Logos. It was also a frequent metaphor for spiritual union in Alexandrian Hermeticism and early medieval Christian Neoplatonism.[201] However, Acosta's materialist language of imperfect brides and material dowries in precious metals seems unusual (almost perverse) in this context. As I want to suggest, a more immediate context for this analogy can be found in the language of the alchemical wedding, the "fiery" unification of sulfur and mercury. Indeed, Acosta himself invokes this context by comparing the conversion of souls to the purification of silver. Thus, after giving a detailed account of Andean mining technology in Potosí, he reflects on

> what Scripture says of just men, "colabit eos, et purgabit quasi argentum," he shall purify them, and refine them as silver. And I thought of what it says elsewhere, "sicut argentum purgatum terrae, purgatum septuplum," as silver purged from the earth, refined seven times. To purify silver, and refine it and cleanse it of the earth and clay where it occurs, they purge it seven times, for indeed it is done seven times; that is, many and many times is silver tormented until it is left pure and fine. So it is with the Word of the Lord, and just so will the souls destined to partake of his divine purity be refined.[202]

Orlando Bentancor has argued that Acosta's analogy between the work of conversion and the purification of silver ore is based on a Thomist Aristotelian metaphysics of hylomorphism—the principle that immaterial active substantial forms operate on passive matter. "Natural law and mining are isomorphic," Bentancor writes, "because they share the same hylomorphic and teleological structure based on the principle of natural subordination of matter to form and means to an end."[203] According to Bentancor, this Aristotelian hylomorphic principle informs Acosta's understanding not only of the work of mining but also of the work of conversion. Especially the Spanish practice of the refinement of silver ore through the use of mercury is "analogous to the 'refinement'" of Amerindian habits, wherein the accidental is corrected and conducted through evangelization and administration.[204] However, if Acosta's understanding of the work of conversion indeed draws on the language of Scholastic Aristotelianism, it is significant that the Jesuit missionary historian elaborates this analogy in a comparison of conversion not to the refinement of silver in general but to the quite specific practice of the use of fire in the amalgamation of ore with mercury. It is a process, Acosta writes, in which silver is "tormented until it is left pure and fine." This is also the context of the passage that he quotes from Psalms 11:7: "eloquia Domini eloquia munda argentum igne probatum separatum a terra colatum septuplum eloquia Domini eloquia casta argentum igne examinatum probatum terrae purgatum septuplum (The words of the Lord are pure words: as silver tried by the fire, purged from the earth, refined seven times)."[205] In short, Acosta compares spiritual conversion not to the hylomorphic process of natural material formation but to the artificial process of the alchemical trial by fire, mercury, and salt.

As Tara Nummedal has shown, the purification of silver ore with mercury, fire, and salt had been developed in theory and practice in the Habsburg Empire in the sixteenth century, in such works as Georgius Agricola's *De re metallica* (On metals, published posthumously in 1556).[206] This technology derived from an alchemical tradition reaching back in the Latin West at least to Albertus Magnus (Aquinas's teacher) but that was not specifically "Thomist" in any sense of the word. It was "Aristotelian" in a medieval but not in a modern sense, which is to say that this tradition heavily relied upon many pseudo-Aristotelian works of Arabic or late medieval Latin provenance that included even alchemical works spuriously attributed to Thomas Aquinas (an avowed enemy of alchemy), such as the fourteenth-century *De essentiis essentiarum (On the Essence of Essences)*.[207] The technique of mercury amalgamation was introduced in Mexico in the 1550s and in the Andes in the 1570s, leading to an enormous spike in the production and export of American silver. Thus, silver export to Spain from America increased by more than thirty-fold in sixty years—from 86 metric tons in the 1530s to 1,118 in the 1570s and to 2,707 in the 1590s. Whereas before the introduction of the alchemical method, it had been impossible to extract silver from low-grade ore, the alchemical purification of ore with mercury and salt greatly improved the efficiency, facilitating the extraction of silver in low-grade ore that would previously have been lost.[208]

This alchemical technique in the purification of silver mightily impressed Acosta as a quasi-magical process and also informs his hermeneutics of religious conversion, as is evident in his account of the mixture between silver and mercury in the furnace. In order to illustrate this, it will be necessary to quote at length Acosta's extended description of this process. In the quote below, I place in italics some of the key words that I want to focus on in my subsequent analysis.

Before the invention of furnaces, the ore was *kneaded* with quicksilver many times and oft, in great troughs, and they made round balls like mud balls and left them for several days and *kneaded* them again and again until they knew that the quicksilver was *thoroughly mixed into the silver.* This took twenty days or more, and nine days at the very least. *Later, because the desire for profit is a spur,* it was discovered that *fire was useful to shorten* the time and caused the quicksilver to *incorporate with the silver* more quickly; and so they built furnaces with large receptacles in which the ore is placed *with salt and quicksilver,* and a slow fire is built in certain vaults made for the purpose, so that within the space of five or six days, the *quicksilver absorbs the silver.* When they see that the quicksilver has done its work, which is *to absorb all the silver whether it be much or little, leaving none behind, but, like a sponge, taking the silver into itself and separating it from the dirt and lead and copper* that is found with it, they then uncover it and take it out and separate it from the quicksilver, which is done in the following manner: the ore is placed in barrels of water, where it is turned with paddles or waterwheels, turning the ore round and round *as if dissolving it or making mustard.* The dross or lees emerge in the water that runs away, and the silver and quicksilver, because they are heavier, settle on the bottom of the barrel. The ore that remains resembles sand, and they take it out and wash it again in large troughs or barrels of water, and there the rest of the dross is washed away, leaving the silver and quicksilver behind.... When the silver and quicksilver are clean and begin to shine because the dross and earth have been removed, they take all the ore and turn it out on a cloth, squeezing it very hard; and so all the quicksilver that is not incorporated into the silver runs out, and what is left is a ball of silver and quicksilver, just as the harder parts of almonds are left when they are pressed to make oil; and after the remaining ball is thoroughly pressed only a sixth of it is silver, and the other five-sixth mercury. So that, if a sixty-pound ball is left, ten pounds of it are silver and fifty are of mercury. Out of these balls they make pinecone shapes like sugarloaves, hollow inside and usually weighing a hundred pounds; then, to separate the silver from the mercury, they place them in a hot fire and cover them with an earthenware vessel made like the molds used for sugarloaves. These have the form of a hood, and they cover them with coal and light the fires. Then the quicksilver escapes in the form of vapour, and when it touches the clay hood it thickens and distils, like the steam of a covered pot, and all the quicksilver that is distilled is carried through *a tube like an alembic and recovered, leaving only the silver, which is the same in form and size but is five parts less in weight.* Rather, it is *wrinkled and spongy,* which is a remarkable thing to see; from two of these cones, they make a bar of silver weighing sixty-five or sixty-six marks, and in this form, it is taken to be assayed and stamped and the royal fifth deducted.[209]

On the one hand, this quote shows that Acosta's understanding of the purification of silver ore is thoroughly Aristotelian. Also, the description of the purification of silver ore *before* the introduction of the furnace seems entirely hylomorphic—the "kneading" of the silver ore/quicksilver compound in "great troughs," making it into "round balls like mud," all of which takes a long time, and much of the silver in the lower-grade ore will be entirely lost in this process. However, on the other hand, the passage also shows that Acosta's understanding is Aristotelian not entirely in the hylomorphic tradition of Thomist metaphysics as based on Aristotle's *Physics* and *De caelo* but also alchemical in the tradition of the pseudo-Aristotelian book 4 of the *Meteorology*, which had elaborated a theory of elemental mixture different from that developed in the Thomist tradition. As we saw in chapter 2 of this book, both traditions accepted the Aristotelian doctrines of the permanence of matter; the impossibility of two bodies occupying the same space at the same time; and the necessity of contact between the mover and that being moved in order to affect change.[210] However, as we also saw, whereas in the Thomist tradition, matter was understood to be homogeneous and continuous, in the alchemical tradition, the structure of matter was understood to be porous and corpuscular, composed of *minima naturalia*. Acosta's description of the mixture between silver and mercury under fiery duress as an "incorporation" or "absorption" of silver in the ore by mercury, which is "*like a sponge,* taking the silver into itself and separating it from the dirt and lead and copper that is found with it," clearly shows that his understanding of matter was not Thomist (i.e., continuous, homogeneous, hylomorphic, and "unitist" with regard to substantial forms) but alchemical (i.e., corpuscular, nonhylomorphic, and "pluralist" with regard to matter's substantial forms).[211]

Moreover, this difference in the conception of matter also implied a difference in the understanding of elemental mixture: as we saw earlier, in Thomist physics, a true mixture results from the recombination of the elements into a perfectly homogeneous new substance, in which the elemental qualities of the old mixture are destroyed.[212] By contrast, in the alchemical understanding of mixture, the elemental qualities of the *minima naturalia* in the new mixture are the *same* as in the old mixture, because they are the same particles. If, therefore, air is converted into water and then again back into air, one would get exactly the *same amount* of air with which one started—a theory that the Thomists denied.[213] Although this theory originates in Latin alchemy with Pseudo-Geber's *Summa,* definitive proof of the theory would be provided only in the early seventeenth century by the Flemish alchemist Jan Baptist van Helmont (1580–1644) in the form of weight measurements of transmuted substances in the alchemical production of glass. Remarkably, as we can see in the quote above from Acosta, it is a phenomenon already familiar from the observation of the purification of silver in the Andes decades before Helmont conducted his measurements. Thus, in his description of the separation of the silver and the mercury, Acosta writes that the proportion of silver and quicksilver that went into the mixture of the two is the same that came out of it—five to one. It is *"the same in form and size but is five parts less in weight."* Moreover, it is *"wrinkled and spongy."*

While my distinction between the two Aristotelian traditions—Thomist and alchemical—in approaching Acosta may seem like a latter-day case of pedantic Scholastic hairsplitting, I would point out that it helps to clarify Acosta's understanding of Native American religions, the nature of the missionary work as theorized in *De procuranda,* as well as his general position on the rights of conquest. Thus, as Bentancor observes, while Acosta, in *De procuranda,* sides with the Thomists such as Vitoria and Las Casas on many issues, when it comes to the question of violence and coercion in missionary work, he sides with the nominalists and humanists such as Mair and Sepúlveda. While he distances himself from colonial abuses and wanton cruelties, Bentancor writes, Acosta "nevertheless defends the necessity of violence, both direct and indirect, throughout *De procuranda.* This violence is defended as the means of subordinating the barbarous and intransigent inhabitant of the New World to a natural order organized toward the realization of the common good."[214] Whereas, in the Thomist tradition, conversion is understood as a natural process—a process of matter moving toward its substantial forms that may be sped up by but is not dependent on human art—in the alchemical tradition, it is understood in artificial terms of reduction, a process that, like the application of fire in the alchemical crucible, licenses and even necessitates substantial epistemic violence. Without reduction, many souls, like the silver contained in low-grade ore, would be lost forever.

As we will see in subsequent chapters, the distinction between the Thomist (i.e., unitist) understanding of matter and of conversion as a hylomorphic (i.e., natural) process on the one hand and the alchemical (pluralist, corpuscular) understanding of matter and of conversion as an artificial process on the other, helps to clarify not only the various sixteenth-century philosophical positions on the question of the justness of conquest but also on the various metaphysical interpretations of Native American religions. On the one hand, the "unitism" of the Thomists' metaphysical realism led to an apprehension of Native American religions in terms of synderesis—the metaphysical notion that all mankind is one in reason and therefore *by nature* inclined to seek the true creator. Just as all metals will seek and eventually attain their "true" substantial form of gold in the natural hylomorphic process, so will pagans eventually become Christians, and their souls "spiritual gold," in the course of time. In this Thomist hermeneutics, Native Americans were merely "behind" the Christians on their natural path to salvation, just as lead is "behind" silver in its natural process of becoming gold. On the other hand, the "pluralism" of the Franciscans' metaphysical nominalism led to an apprehension of Native American religions as a form of diabolic perversion. If the hylomorphic processes of nature are allowed to run their course, Native American idolaters will never arrive at salvation because human reason has been corrupted by demonic counterfeits—by a sort of diabolic hylomorphism. Idolaters are like lead that will never become gold naturally because metals have not one but a plurality of substantial forms. The conversion of lead into gold requires the active intervention of art—an art to counteract the art of the Devil. While it is not possible to convert an idolater into a Christian directly—just as it is not possible to convert lead directly into gold—idolaters, like lead, have to be "reduced" to a state of *pristinum statum* before they can be purified and become Christians. As we will see, it is Acosta's alchemical understanding of the purification of silver by "torture" that would, in the seventeenth century, lead to an overturn of his Thomist notion of the purification of silver by "kneading" in the so-called Scientific Revolution.

Acosta's allegory of America as the ugly bride with a rich dowry of silver for a Spanish husband may thus in part be read as the macrocosmic analogue of the alchemical wedding, the "fiery" unification of sulfur and mercury. As Lyndy Abraham notes, the motif of the alchemical wedding is in fact older than the mystical wedding of the Christian church fathers, which is itself based on classical pre-Christian Greek traditions in alchemy. In alchemical literature, the wedding involved a significant "strife" between the warring elements before the "peace" that follows from the rebalancing of their opposite qualities and the harmonious state resulting from the unification. This strife involved not only an extraordinary amount of violence but even death: "The emblems of the chemical wedding almost always include symbols of death which overshadow the coniunctio. . . . The death at the wedding symbolizes the extinction of the earlier differentiated state before union, and also powerfully conveys the alacrity with which the festive moment of the coagula or wedding is transformed into the lamentation of the solve or death."[215] Considering the close interconnections that Tara Nummedal has shown between the histories of mining, metallurgy, medicine, and alchemy in early modern Europe, it is perhaps not surprising to encounter the marriage motif in Acosta's writings as an allegory of the European conquest of America. As we have seen, the medieval alchemical wedding resulted in the Philosophers' Stone that transforms all things into gold by mere touch, not in purified silver to be turned into money coins. Also, accounts of the alchemical wedding typically imagined that mercury "killed" the other metal with which it reacted in the alembic by penetrating its pores and dissolving it into the *prima materia*. Thus, in the *Rosarius,* Arnald wrote that mercury is "the water that kills and revives.... It is the water which dissolves and congeals."[216] Significantly, the process in which Acosta imagines this alchemical reaction is the other way around: the mercury absorbs the silver into its pores ("like a sponge") in a proportion of five to one. While this explanation seemed perhaps more plausible to Acosta in light of the technical realities of industrial mercury amalgamation in sixteenth-century mining metallurgy, it also corresponds more closely to the way in which he imagines the evangelical process of conversion through reduction: the unpurified "ore" of Indian souls is "incorporated" into the salvific body of the church to be purified there for use in the imperial state and economy.

Acosta's allegory of the conquest as a marriage between America and Europe and the spoils of conquest as a dowry would become a recurrent trope in the literature of discovery and conquest. It was still used in the seventeenth century, for example, by the Jesuit missionary and historian of northwestern Mexico Andrés Pérez de Ribas. "God, in His highest providence (as someone else cleverly said)," Pérez de Ribas wrote (clearly referring to Acosta), "gave this silver to these impoverished and barbarous peoples as a dowry, to attract civilized Christians who would enter into friendship and peace with these fierce people, who were accustomed to feeding on the flesh of those who were not of their nation."[217] As Pérez de Ribas explains, at the time when the holy apostles were preaching in Europe, "the people of the New World did not exist, or if they did, *it was as if they did not.* At least that is what the ancient historians supposed, for they did not believe that such nations could exist hidden away somewhere in a new world; nor was there any way of finding them for many, many centuries and thousands of years; nor was there any point of entry to these regions; nor any tracks left by those first conquerors and captains whom the Son of God had sent throughout the entire world. God reserved for our time and for the sons of our Company the conquest of these peoples who did not exist and had never been heard of; and the Lord Himself opened the door for their entry."[218] As we will see in subsequent chapters, in both Spanish and British America, Acosta's and Pérez de Ribas's sexualized language of *coniunctio* derived from the motif of the alchemical wedding and, elaborated by the missionary science, would have a long afterlife as a full-fledged colonialist ideology in which America appears as a porous compound of particulars and voids (or pores) that are ready and willing for penetration by the European discoverer and colonist.

Part III

Lucretius's New World

7

Cannibal Heterotopias in the Sixteenth Century

In the previous three chapters, I explored the role that the language of late medieval alchemy—in particular in the traditions of Roger Bacon, Arnald of Villanova, John of Rupescissa, and (pseudo-)Ramon Llull—played in the literature of the discovery of America, especially in the context of the Franciscan spiritual and intellectual milieu that had originated in the Crown of Aragon in the fifteenth century. In this chapter, I shift focus to the legacy of the man for whom America came to be named—Amerigo Vespucci. I will place his writings—or rather those attributed to him (probably spuriously)—in the intellectual milieu of Italian Renaissance humanism, as the various strands of late medieval Scholastic Aristotelianism (including alchemy) encountered classical (pagan) philosophy, especially the atomism of the pre-Socratics as it was passed by the tradition of the Roman poet Lucretius. Whereas this chapter investigates the role that this epistemological encounter in sixteenth-century New World travel narratives and utopias played in the history of the idea of discovery in modern science, the subsequent chapter will consider the geopolitical consequences of this encounter for the history of international law.

The philosopher of science Michel Serres once wrote that "it so happens that Western science has consistently *not* chosen Lucretius." And by that choice, Serres averred, Western science has "opted for war and plagues, for brawls, blood, and bodies burnt at the stake. Western science, Heraclitus to Hiroshima, has only known martial nature."[1] Yet, historians and literary critics alike have long insisted on the importance of the "return" of the classical Roman poet to Europe during the Renaissance, after his tradition had languished in the shadows of literary history throughout of the Middle Ages.[2] Stephen Greenblatt, for example, in *The Swerve,* argued that the "world became modern" in 1417, when Poggio Bracciolini rediscovered Lucretius's *De rerum natura* (ca. 55 BC), the Latin pagan verse manifesto espousing Epicurean materialism, which held that the soul dies with the body but atoms are eternal; that the purpose of human life is temporal pleasure, which is to say the simple pleasures of nature and the avoidance of misery and pain; and that the gods don't give a farthing about ordinary mortals, since "nothing at any time detracts from their peace of mind."[3] Our universe is composed of multiple worlds, Lucretius taught, in which everything generates by pure chance, as the result of indifferent atoms randomly colliding and occasionally transforming bodies from one form to the next in a nature that is constantly changing and perpetually in motion: "The atoms themselves collided spontaneously and fortuitously, clashing together blindly, unsuccessfully, and ineffectually in a multitude of ways, until at last those atoms coalesced which, when suddenly dashed together, could always form the foundations of mighty fabrics, of earth, sea, and sky, and the family of living creatures. So I insist that you must acknowledge the existence elsewhere of other aggregations of matter similar to this world of ours which the ether hugs in a greedy embrace."[4]

These were profoundly un-Christian propositions that would become the target of a long tradition of condemnations by the Christian church fathers and doctors—from Lactantius to Augustine, Thomas Aquinas and beyond—who chastised the vanities of the temporal world, especially of the vice of "vain curiosity" (*vana curiositas*) that Epicureanism seemed to espouse.[5] Moreover, Lucretius's Epicurean ideas flew in the face of not only the Christian notions of the immortality of the soul, of God's omnipotent providence, as well as of the Judeo-Christian belief in the Creation and Judgment Day, but also of Scholastic hylomorphic metaphysics, which insisted on the primacy of form over matter.

In light of this, it comes as no surprise that the "return of Lucretius" to Christian Europe during the Renaissance should have taken some highly circuitous and subterranean paths during the fifteenth and sixteenth centuries. Thus, the circulation of the manuscript of *De rerum natura* remained extremely limited during the first two decades following Poggio's announcement of his "discovery" in 1417. And even during the second half of the fifteenth century, the intellectual engagement with Epicureanism often took place in the form of what Greenblatt has called a "dialogic disavowal"—in Platonic dialogues where un-Christian ideas are proposed in a sort of ventriloquism by a foolish advocate of Epicureanism only to be refuted by a stalwart defender of Christian orthodoxy.[6] Nevertheless, by the early seventeenth century, Epicurean materialism would come to play a prominent role in Francis Bacon's and Pierre Gassendi's reforms of natural philosophy that would lead to the so-called Scientific Revolution.[7] What has not been sufficiently appreciated in the recent accounts of the "return" of Lucretius to Renaissance Europe is the crucial role that the European colonial encounter with and conquest of the Americas in the sixteenth century played in Renaissance Europe's reencounter with its own pagan past. The alchemy of conquest—the colonial history of scientific modernity—is the "missing link," I would argue, that illuminates the apparent paradox between Serres's view that Western science has "consistently not chosen Lucretius" and Greenblatt's view that the "world became modern" with the return of Lucretius to Renaissance Europe.

The encounter with the cultures of the Americas from the late fifteenth century onward presented European travelers, missionaries, and historians with a radical alterity that challenged some of their most fundamental metaphysical and ontological concepts about what constitutes the "world," "nature," and "natural law" while also providing an experimental field for age-old philosophical and theological speculation. Was private property "natural" to man, as the Neo-Aristotelian Thomists and the medieval church had held? Or was it only the result of the biblical Fall, as some of their Franciscan nominalist (and later humanist) adversaries argued? Did postlapsarian man, created in the image of God, retain some of her prelapsarian divinity in the capacity for reason or was natural reason hopelessly corrupt unless assisted by Christian revelation? Does Christian salvation heal "wounded" postlapsarian human nature, or must salvation break it? The European encounter with a "New World" promised to hold empirical answers to many of such old theological questions and philosophical speculations. But arguably, there was nothing that fascinated (and horrified) Europeans more than the New World cultural practice of anthropophagy, or cannibalism.

In the wake of the postcolonial studies movement in the 1980s, there has been no shortage of scholarship on European representations of New World cannibalism as a "colonial discourse" constructing modern Western selves and others. But, as I want to suggest in this chapter, the topos of New World cannibalism provided not only the discursive space for marking social boundaries and cultural identities in Early Modern empires but also for the philosophical engagement and experimentation with nonhylomorphic metaphysical theories of matter that had, in medieval times, been largely confined to alchemy, especially in the long alchemical tradition of corpse medicine. As I will argue here, the European rediscovery of classical natural philosophy—especially pagan materialist atomism—during the Renaissance was largely facilitated by the rhetorical foil of the "cannibal heterotopia" that emerged in sixteenth-century Europe in the context of the conquest of America.[8] It is in the context of the "uncanny" encounter between Old World and New World cannibalism during the sixteenth century that Lucretian materialism returned to Renaissance Europe—*not* as a classically Epicurean (pagan) enjoyment of nature but as a Christian, penitential, and alchemical *conquest* of nature in the natural philosophy of the so-called Scientific Revolution.

Cannibal Metaphysics

While early modern Europeans were familiar with the idea of "anthropophagy" (man-eating) from classical Greek mythology, the modern word "cannibal" originates only with Christopher Columbus's logbook account of his first transatlantic voyage to the Americas. There, he reports being told by some of the "Indians" he encounters of the existence of a certain hostile and man-eating nation called "caniba" or "cariba," thus giving birth not only to the modern word "cannibal" but also to that of the "Caribbean."[9] But while Columbus does not report ever having witnessed any actual acts of cannibalism, the first European who claimed in print to have seen firsthand evidence of the practice was a writer who was (or claimed to be) the Florentine banker and traveler Amerigo Vespucci. In the tract *Mundus novus*, published under dubious circumstances in 1503, the author announced not only that had he seen firsthand evidence of cannibalism but also that the lands discovered by Columbus were not part of Asia but a "New World"—because, he wrote, "none of these countries were known to our ancestors and to all who hear about them they will be entirely new."[10] The tract offered an account of Vespucci's third voyage, to Brazil, on board a Portuguese ship and indulged in sensational descriptions of a Brazilian society that had no private property, no kings, no religion, and no laws—"each man his own master." Most remarkably, Brazilians (most likely from the Tupi-Guarani ethnic group) are in the *habitus* of eating their enemies and even their own kin. "Together with other kinds of meat, human flesh is common fare among them," the Vespuccian informs his readers, "because one father was known to have eaten his children and wife, and I myself met and spoke with a man who was said to have eaten more than three hundred human bodies; and I also stayed twenty-seven days in a certain city in which I saw salted human flesh hanging from house-beams, much as we hang up bacon and pork."[11]

Modern scholars have struggled to come to terms with the meaning of early modern European representations of New World cannibalism such as this one. While some have dismissed European accounts of New World cannibalism as a mere "man-eating myth"—a colonialist fantasy invented in order to justify violent conquest—more recently anthropological scholarship has reconsidered early modern accounts of New World cannibalism as more or less reliable ethnographic descriptions of actual cultural practices. However, unlike early modern ethnography, this modern scholarship suggests that anthropophagy, far from being anthropologically abnormal, is in evidence in many cultures, albeit in more or less sublimated forms as rituals of bodily incorporation and transformation, such as that of the Eucharist in Western Christendom.[12]

Much of this postmodern perspective on the cannibalistic origins of the Eucharist has been informed by Sigmund Freud's classic account of primeval neurosis. According to Freud, monotheistic religion is the product of a sublimation of a primeval murder and devouring of a father by his sons who, both hating and loving, sublimate their act of cannibalism first in the form of totemic rituals and, later, in the sacrament of the Holy Eucharist.[13] As Slavoj Žižek explains Freud's account, "Murdering and consuming the father apotheosizes him, in the sense that his function becomes transcendentalized, rather than located in a particular set of individuals and contingent circumstances."[14] In a more historicist vein, Caroline Walker Bynum has argued that the ritual of the Eucharist is a sort of "transcendent cannibalism," an "eating that does not consume," that has its origins in the early Christian trauma of the Roman circus. Universal human cultural rituals of incorporation and trans-*formation* thus found a quite particular articulation as a ritual of trans-*substantiation* in the Christian West. "The fact that we are what we eat—that we become Christ by consuming Christ, but Christ can never be consumed—guarantees that our consumption by beasts ... is *not* destruction."[15]

But even on a more basic level of sublimation, "cannibalism" has always been an integral part of Western culture. As Richard Sugg has pointed out, in the Roman circus it was not only Christians who died by being devoured by wild beasts but also gladiators, whose bleeding (but still strong) bodies were dragged from the public arena (Lat. for "sand") to more private spaces. There, they were awaited by physicians eager not to stem the gush of blood from their deadly wounds but to administer the flow into the mouths of desperate sufferers of epilepsy and other strange diseases, who hoped to be cured by the miraculous medicine of blood from these "living cups."[16] As pointed out in chapter 5 of this book, it was a tradition that was still alive and well in 1492, the year when Pope Innocent VIII fell ill and was allegedly administered the blood of three young boys. However, during the later Middle Ages, this diet of medicinal "vampirism" had also been enriched (so to speak) by the medicinal use of human flesh. As Karl Dannenfeldt has pointed out, the practice of corpse medicine in the West has its roots in the belief in the miraculous medicinal efficacy of "mummy" (lat. *mumia*). The word itself actually derives from the name given to bituminous materials derived from black rock-asphalt (or pissasphalt) from the region of Darabjerd in Persia that was believed by the Arabs to have therapeutic properties in curing broken limbs and as an antidote to poison. The local name for this rock-asphalt was "mumiya" (from mum, wax), which is the origin of the Latin word *mumia* and the English word "mummy." This word came to be associated with corpse medicine because pissasphalt was believed to be one of the substances used by the ancient

Egyptians in embalming their deceased in order to stave off the process of bodily decomposition. Although in the Arabic tradition, "mumiya" was always distinguished from the bodies embalmed therewith, in the course of translation from the Arabic to the Latin, "mumia" became associated with the mixture of the embalmment (including pissasphalt and also other natural extracts from plants, such as aloe) and the bodily tissues and fluids that were treated with it. Thus, in the twelfth century, the translator of Arabic scientific texts at the Toledo School, Gerard of Cremona, explained in a translation from the works of "Rhazes" (the tenth-century Persian polymath Zakariya al-Razi) that *mumia* is "the substance found in the land where bodies are buried with aloes by which the liquid of the dead, mixed with the aloes, is transformed and it is similar to marine pitch."[17]

Although the medicinal use of mummified flesh originated in medieval Europe as early as the tenth century, it was during the general Egyptomania that accompanied the rise of Neoplatonic Hermeticism and Paracelsianism during the Renaissance that the practice became common and widespread in European courts. Still in the sixteenth century, European apothecaries explained that mumia was "an exudation from corpses, obtained in this fashion: when the man dies they remove his intestines, lungs, etc. and throw in myrrh and aloes; then they sew up the corpse and put it in a sepulcher with holes. This mixture with the moisture of the body drips out and is collected. This liquor is called mummy."[18] One of the sixteenth-century experimenters with mummy was the Franciscan cosmographer André Thevet (?–1590), who had traveled in the Levant and Egypt. He explained that mumia was harvested from Egyptian tombs, where two-thousand-year-old bodies could be found still well preserved (see fig. 18). On the advice of a Jewish physician who was expert in its medicinal application, Thevet took some mumia but subsequently suffered from a stomachache and a "fetid breath."[19] Presumably, this experience explains his later reactions to news of Brazilian cannibalism (to which we will return shortly.)

So lucrative had the trade in Egyptian mummy become by the fifteenth century that the majority of the Egyptian tombs had been robbed not only of their gold but also of their ancient mummies, which were being traded for twenty-five gold pieces per hundredweight. As a result, other sources of mumia were found, often of questionable provenance. One convenient source came from travelers who had expired more recently in sandstorms in the African desert, as their bodies had already been dried by the sun and required little additional processing. Another source came from counterfeits, such as camel meat that was fraudulently sold as human mummy. But gradually the main source of the mummy that was sold in Alexandria to the insatiable European

Figure 18. A mummy seen by André Thevet in Egypt. (In André Thevet, *Cosmographie de Levant, par F. André Theuet d'Angovlesme* [Lyon: Jean Tournes et Guil. Gazeau, 1554]. Courtesy of the Library of Congress.)

Christians came from the sun-dried bodies of people who had died of diseases (such as leprosy, smallpox, or the plague) or from the bodies of murdered slaves and executed convicts. One sixteenth-century writer, a physician to the king of Navarre, reports meeting a Jewish merchant with a thriving business of trading in mummy in Alexandria. The merchant "marveled that the Christians, so daintily mouthed, could eat the bodies of the dead."[20]

During the sixteenth century, the alchemical use of mummy saw a further boom in Europe in the wake of the influence of the Swiss-German physician and occult philosopher Theophrastus Bombastus von Hohenheim, aka Paracelsus (d. 1541), who not only prescribed the traditional Egyptian *mumia* for ingestion but also theorized that mummy, like human blood, was an especially good source for the alchemical distillation of the quintessence, or the balsam. He argued that miraculous healing power inhered not only in the bodies of Christ and the saints but in all of nature, especially in the human body, which, as a microcosm, partakes in the perfection of the stars through occult astrological influence, like a magnet that attracts metal. In fact, he suggested that the most efficacious mummy comes from "the body of a man who did not die a natural death but rather died an unnatural death with a healthy body and without sickness."[21] Preferable were hereby the relatively fresh bodies (not older than a day or a night) of criminals who were "hanged, thrust-through, or broken on the wheel."[22] Also acceptable were bodies of men who had died by drowning or burning. For his part, the German Paracelsian Oswald Crollius opined that a violent death was an absolute prerequisite for producing good mummy. The ideal kind, he explained, would come from a red-haired man, roughly twenty-four years old, who had been hanged, broken on the wheel, or thrust through; exposed to air for a day and a night; and then cut into small pieces or slices, sprinkled with a little powder of myrrh and aloes, then soaked in spirits of wine, dried, soaked again, and dried. All of this would produce mummy that smelled like smoked flesh and was the best source for distilling the quintessence.[23] In Frankfurt, three varieties of mumia were sold at the fairs: mumia arabus (mumia from tombs); mumia arabis vulgaris (common mummy); and mumia graecorum (Greek mummy, from pissasphalt).[24] As we will see, at the time Frankfurt was also the center of operation for the De Bry printing house, which publicized images of New World cannibalism throughout Europe. Paracelsus's alchemical corpse medicine was still popular during the seventeenth century among his numerous followers such as Robert Fludd in England and Edward Taylor in New England.[25] But even some of those seventeenth-century natural philosophers of the so-called Scientific Revolution—who ostensibly disavowed Paracelsus and alchemy—were firm believers in the efficacy of mummy. Thus, the English natural philosopher Francis Bacon wrote, "Mumy hath great force in Staunching of Bloud; which, as it may be ascribed to the mixture of Balmes, that are glutinous; so it may also partake of a secret Propriety; in that the Bloud draweth mans Flesh."[26] And the "father" of modern mechanical philosophy, Robert Boyle, praised mummy as "one of the useful medicines commended and given by our physicians for falls and bruises, and in other cases too."[27]

To be sure, there were also critical voices in early modern Europe about the medicinal and alchemical use of human blood and mummy. These critics blamed not only the (pagan) Romans and the Hellenistic Alexandrians for such barbaric practices but also their intellectual ancestors, the Greeks. Thus, the sixteenth-century English physician Thomas Moffett (d. 1604) wrote that the "Grecians" "were as bold and impious as the Romans, tasting of every inward and outward part of man's body, not leaving the nails unprosecuted.... Let Democritus dream and comment, that some diseases are best cured with anointing the blood of strangers and malefactors, others with the blood of our friends and kinsfolks; let Miletus cure sore eyes with men's galls; Artemon the falling sickness with dead men's skulls; Antheus convulsions with pills made of dead men's brains; Apollonius bad gums with dead men's teeth."[28] Moffett's association of medicinal cannibalism with the pre-Socratic atomistic philosophy of Democritus is significant, and I will return to this connection momentarily. But the discussion above should suffice to remind us that the ingestion of human bodily materials was far from unfamiliar in Western culture during the European Age of Discovery and the cultural encounters in the Americas.

Once we let go of the Western fiction of the exceptionalism of New World cannibalism, we can begin to reread colonial ethnography as lessons in transcultural *philosophy* and dialogues about the metaphysics of universal rites of transformation as transubstantiation. As recent work in transcultural philosophy and metaphysics by Eduardo Viveiros de Castro (on Brazil), James Maffie (on Mexico), and others has suggested, sixteenth-century ethnographies about America can serve as the historical records of the intercultural dialogues that occurred during the early modern period between Western "mono-naturalism" and Amerindian "multi-naturalism" in their respective understandings of bodily incorporation and material transformation.[29] Indeed, while there can be no doubt that European representations of Amerindian cannibalism rationalized violent conquest, Viveiros de Castro sheds light on the question of why the practice and representation of cannibalism would elicit such violent responses in the Western Christian tradition. For, reports of New World "everyday" practices of culinary cannibalism presented a challenge to one of the most fundamental ideas of Western metaphysics for which medieval Christian corpse medicine in alchemy had created a state of exception: the Christian doctrine of the Resurrection. It is a doctrine that had had a long history in Christian apologetics and that had been put on trial in spectacles of the Roman circus that were especially staged to provide visible proof of its foolishness. Thus, the early Patristic writers and church fathers conceived of the Resurrection as a sort of reassemblage of bodies, like the "remolding of a vessel."[30] If God was able to create human bodies, they argued, He surely would be able to reunite the original substance of a decayed body, regardless of how mutilated, disintegrated, and widely dispersed it had become as a result of gruesome martyrdoms. As St. Augustine wrote in *The City of God,* "Far be it from us to fear that the omnipotence of the Creator cannot, for the resuscitation and reanimation of our bodies, recall all the portions which have been consumed by beasts or fire, or have been dissolved into dust or ashes, or have decomposed into water, or evaporated into the air. Far from us be the thought, that anything which escapes our observation in any most hidden recess of nature either evades the knowledge or transcends the power of the Creator of all things."[31] However, as St. Augustine also recognized, cannibalism represented hereby the "most difficult" question of all to the doctrine of Resurrection: "To whom, in the resurrection, will belong the flesh of a dead man which has become the flesh of a living man? For if someone, famishing for want and pressed with hunger, use human flesh as food—an extremity not unknown... —can it be contended, with any show of reason, that all the flesh eaten has been evacuated, and that none of it has been assimilated to the substance of the eater though the very emaciation which existed before, and has now disappeared, sufficiently indicates what large deficiencies have been filled up with this food?" St. Augustine contrives an answer that would hardly have been convincing to his pagan contemporaries: he argues that human flesh consumed by another human because of hunger, though temporarily sustaining the eater's body through digestion, eventually "finds its way into the air by evaporation, whence ... God Almighty can recall it. That flesh, therefore shall be restored to the man in whom it first became human flesh. For it must be looked upon as borrowed by the other person, and like a pecuniary loan, must be returned to the lender."[32] If this would still appear to create an overall deficit of substance, the problem will be resolved when God, during Resurrection, will also restore the substance that the famished eater had lost through "evaporation." Thus, in Resurrection, each body will attain its true and "ideal" form, even if that form was never attained in the temporal world due to premature death, and even if it has long been lost due to aging. In other words, in St. Augustine's Neoplatonic understanding, there is a divine economy of matter in the world that allocates to each body an ordained substance that is unchangeably its own "dominium" (so to speak) from the moment it becomes human flesh from digestion of those parts of creation given to man as his dominium by God. As a bodily dominium, its substance can pass, as a temporary possession, to another human body, but it can never be transformed into another body's property, or dominium. Here we can see, then, the reason why late medieval and early modern doctors and patients preferred the blood and flesh of executed convicts in corpse medicine. Presumably, they would be resurrected, as living symbols of human sin, as some sort of zombie to suffer the pains of hell, while the Christians in grace will enter heaven in the resurrected substantial form of Adam, as God created him.

New World Epicureanism

It is instructive, in this context of Christian anxieties about bodily consumption, to observe the philosophical context that the Vespuccian's travel narratives aim to construct for understanding the Brazilians' cannibalism. Their lives are entirely lived, he claims, for no other purpose than temporal pleasure. Thus, their women, "being very lustful, make their husbands' members swell to such thickness that they look ugly and misshapen; this they accomplish with a certain device they have and by bites from certain poisonous animals. Because of this, many men lose their members, which rot through neglect, and they are left eunuchs." Generally, "They take as many wives as they wish, and son may couple with mother, brother with sister, cousin with cousin, and in general men with women as they chance to meet. They dissolve marriage as often as they please, observing no order in any of these matters.... What more can I say? They live according to nature, and might be called Epicureans rather than Stoics."[33] Similarly, in his letter to Pier Soderini, gonfaloniere of the Republic of Florence, published in late 1505 or early 1506, the Vespuccian writes, "We do not encounter among these peoples any who had a religion, nor can they be called Moors or Jews, and are worse than heathens, because we never saw them perform any sacrifice, nor did they have any house of prayer: I judge their life to be Epicurean."[34]

The Vespuccian's characterization of the Brazilians as "worse than heathens" (i.e., atheists) and "Epicureans rather than Stoics" is highly significant for the connotations it would have held for the early sixteenth-century Florentine reader. Thus, in *De voluptate* (Of pleasure, 1431), the humanist Lorenzo Valla had presented a dialogue between an advocate of Christian Stoicism and an advocate of Epicureanism in which the latter is ostensibly refuted by the former but defends his arguments so valiantly and persuasively that he clearly emerges as the winner of the dialogue. By the 1440s, copies of both the manuscript of *De rerum natura* and of Traversari's *Life of Epicurus* were circulating in the humanist community of Florence.[35] But, predictably, in the following decades, Epicurean ideas were publicly reviled by the guardians of Christian orthodoxy. In light of this, few dared quoting Lucretius publicly, let alone approvingly. One exception was the young Marsilio Ficino, but even he later retracted his initial endorsement of Lucretian Epicureanism. Defending the Platonic notion of the invincibility of the rational soul in his *Platonic Theology* (1482), Ficino labeled as "cowards" those "followers of Lucretius" who "declare war against its [the soul's] eternity."[36] Those followers again became the target of public criticism during the 1490s, when the Dominican friar and then regent of the city-state Girolamo Savonarola condemned Epicurus as one of those pagan philosophers who "looked at the natural world and said the maddest things about these natural things that you ever heard," including the idea that the world was composed of atoms, by which he meant "those tiny little bodies that fly through the air and can be seen through a shaft of light when they enter the window."[37] In 1497, Savonarola's supporters instigated the archetypal "Bonfire of the Vanities"—the burning of sinful objects such as cosmetics, arts, and books, including copies of Lucretius. In 1516, the poem would officially be banned from being read in schools by the Florentine Synod.[38]

Nevertheless, the text of Lucretius's poem was already circulating in multiple printed editions that had been published in cities throughout Europe, including the Venice edition of 1500 that appeared three years before the publication of *Mundus novus*. No doubt, in the context of this culture war, the Vespuccian's addressee (and Vespucci's sponsor), Lorenzo di Pierfanceso de Medici, who was known for his liberal views as well as his love of poetry and the arts, would have been amused and pleased by the Vespuccian's claim that the Brazilian Natives were Epicureans who go about naked without shame and own no private property. Even though the Vespuccian maligned them as heathen cannibals, their lifestyle implicitly raised the heretical question of whether the Brazilians were perhaps not the descendants of Adam and the heirs of his Original Sin, echoing the Epicurean idea (also attacked by Savonarola) of the possibility of multiple worlds. Indeed, the very existence of "a continent in those southern regions that is inhabited by more numerous peoples and animals than in our Europe, or Asia, or Africa" seemed to lend support to the Epicurean challenge to the book of Genesis and was perhaps calculated to tweak the noses of Lorenzo's enemies, the followers of the religious zealot Savonarola (who had died in 1498).[39] As we will see in chapter 8, only several decades later, Renaissance occult philosophers such as Paracelsus would make precisely such heretical propositions as the notion that the American Indians were not the descendants of Adam.

While the Vespuccian's characterization of Brazilians as "Epicureans rather than Stoics" would have been associated with Valla's dialogue *De voluptate,* his description of cannibalism in this context is, of course, a caricature of Epicureanism, for there are no references to cannibalism either in *De voluptate* or in *De rerum natura*. In his New World ethnographic account, Brazilian cannibalism becomes the extreme conclusion of an Epicurean (pagan) atomism that denies the integrity of the individual human body by insisting on the primacy of matter beyond the destruction of form. Thus, if Valla had mediated his patent interest in Epicureanism in a rhetorical strategy of "dialogic disavowal," we can discern a related but somewhat different rhetorical strategy in the Vespuccian's travel accounts: he engages in a cannibal ventriloquism in which Epicureanism appears stylized as the philosophy of the New World. In effect, the New World becomes a platform for openly experimenting with ancient pagan ideas about materialism, curiosity, and the pleasures of nature, a heterotopia at a safe distance from the author himself.

Yet, the Vespuccian, as a writer, was clearly conscious of his own seduction by Epicureanism when indulging in sensationalist descriptions of "savage" Brazilian mores. He is amazed that, despite the practice of cannibalism, the land is extremely populous. The multitude of people and the vastness of the land—unheard of by ancients or moderns alike—remind him of the Apocalypse of John (of Patmos), who foretells the coming of a "New Heaven and a New Earth" in the final days of the world, a prophecy that had repeatedly been invoked by Columbus. The Vespuccian's invocation might (and should) have placed his "discovery" of a "New World" in the context of Christian salvation history. Indeed, this was precisely the context in which Columbus had attempted to tell the story of his own voyages of discovery, even signing his name "Xpō Ferrens" (the "Christ Bearer"), hereby punning on his name "Christoforo."[40] The Vespuccian, too, in the so-called Ridolfi Fragment, briefly and loosely quotes from Revelation 7:9—"I saw so many 'that no one can enumerate them.'"[41] But whereas a few verses later, in Revelation 7:16, John would have offered the Vespuccian the opportunity to put his voyages of discovery into a Christian providentialist and apostolic context—"They shall no more hunger nor thirst: neither shall the sun fall on them, nor any heat"—the Vespuccian refuses his readers this religious edification and instead treats them to sensationalist ethnographic descriptions of Tupi cannibalism. Thus, at the beginning of his "Soderini" letter, he apologizes that his account of the New World is "written in a barbarous style well beneath any standard of humane discourse."[42] By "barbarous" style, the Vespuccian referred to the plain (or "proto-scientific") style of his ethnographic descriptions, whose language was as "naked" as his barbarian objects and which seemed utterly gratuitous and voyeuristic, eliciting his readers' curiosity for mere pleasure's sake but failing to edify them with religious allegory or moral lessons. Clearly, the Vespuccian was aware that his account was beyond the pale of what St. Augustine and the Christian church doctors would have considered to be "just curiosity"—a kind of curiosity licensed only by serving the progress of the Christian faith and Redemption history. Thus, he is uneasily reminded of "Our poet Dante," particularly the "26th chapter of the *Inferno,* where he treats of the death of Ulysses"—the Greek hero who had been regarded as the quintessential *curiosus* in the stoic tradition of Western philosophy at least since Cicero.[43]

Dante's Greek hero has another early modern reincarnation as a New World traveler in the character of Raphael Hythlodaeus (meaning a "purveyor of nonsense") in Thomas More's *Utopia*. The reader first meets Raphael at a gathering of a group of men—a cardinal, a lawyer, as well as a character called Thomas More and his friend Peter Giles—over dinner. The political society of the island called Utopia that Raphael described was notable, to be sure, for its resemblance to Plato's Republic. Thus, the Utopians reject private property and live entirely for the commonwealth. But in its relationship to the material things of this world, the Utopians' philosophy was less Platonic than it was Epicurean.[44] Thus, the Utopians' main purpose in life is not that of moral edification by seeking ideal and transcendent truths, we learn, but that of natural pleasure: "The Utopians . . . regard the enjoyment of life—that is pleasure—as the natural object of all human efforts, and natural, as they define it, is synonymous with virtuous."[45] The Utopians are no base hedonists, however. Following the philosophical teachings of Epicurus, they strictly distinguish between "foolish" or extravagant pleasures and simple, "true," or "natural" pleasures: "Pleasure they define as any state or activity, physical or mental, which is naturally enjoyable. The operative word is *naturally*. According to them, we're impelled by reason as well as an instinct to enjoy ourselves in any natural way which doesn't hurt other people, interfere with greater pleasures, or cause unpleasant after-effects."[46] They divide pleasure into two categories, physical and mental. The mental pleasures include also the pursuit of knowledge, particularly "the satisfaction that one gets from understanding something, or from contemplating truth."[47]

The complex narrative structure of *Utopia* in its exploration of these ancient pagan ideas is suggestive of the circuitous ways in which Epicureanism had reentered Renaissance Europe. Significantly, Raphael is said to have discovered the island of Utopia on a voyage to the New World aboard the ship of Amerigo Vespucci. If Vespucci's mouthpieces of Epicurean philosophy had been New World cannibals—the "objects" of his ethnographic descriptions at a safe distance from himself, the describing subject—More's Epicureans came cloaked in the garb of the ancient wisdom of the "divine" Plato, whose spiritualism had provided one of the theological foundations of the New Testament (especially for the idea of a "Holy Spirit") and whose philosophical system had further been Christianized by St. Augustine. Like the Vespuccian's cannibals, More's Epicureans were pagans; but, unlike the Brazilians, they were also citizens of a highly developed "Platonic" republic, in which the spiritualism of the proto-Christian Greek philosopher sublimated what may appear to be an Epicurean indulgence in pleasure. Moreover, More's Utopians, while embracing some of Lucretius's Epicurean ideas—most importantly, the lack of private property and the idea that the purpose of life is the pursuit of pleasure as well as the avoidance of pain and misery—they also dispense with its most central metaphysical tenet—atomistic materialism. Thus, More's Utopians have strict laws punishing with slavery anyone who questions the existence of divine providence or of the afterlife. In effect, More's *Utopia* "sanitized" Epicurean ideas for his Christian reader on his otherworldly island. Finally, More's engagement with Epicureanism was carefully mediated by the intricate literary form of his text, which kept Epicurean practices and beliefs at a safe distance—thrice removed—from the author himself: they were reportedly practiced by a remote culture in a place called "nowhere," visited and seen only by a traveler whose last name means Nonsense, who relates his travels to a group of characters, one of whom happens to be named More but who is clearly distinct from the author. More's *Utopia* thus further elaborated and stylized the ventriloquism of Vespucci's letter; but whereas the Vespuccian had suggested that Epicureanism was still alive in "other spaces"—the remote corners of the world among people living in a state of nature—More parodied Vespucci's "barbarous" account in a purely philosophical speculation about a classical and ideal world that was in every way different from Europe. In other words, whereas the Vespuccian made a claim that there really was a "New Word"—the existence of which had been proved by "my last voyage"—and that other worlds are not only possible but real, More's choice of literary form of fantastic parody disavowed such a possibility, suggesting that Vespucci's New World was but a "noplace" and that the Vespuccis of the world were but a particular brand of "purveyors of nonsense." Both espoused a certain humanist primitivism, but the difference between the Vespuccian's "barbarous" style and More's witty metafiction would prove momentous during the course of the sixteenth century: while the Vespuccian's rhetorical strategy of managing Epicureanism points in the direction of the Baconian rhetorical ideal of an indexical referentialism devoid of irony and parody, More's rhetorical strategy points in the direction of the emergent modern novel—from Rabelais to Swift and beyond—the most characteristic feature of which is, as Mikhail Bakhtin has argued, its parodic polyphony—the capacity of representing worldviews other than those held by its author through multiple levels of narrative layering.[48]

Transcultural Cannibal Metaphysics

If the Vespuccian was the first to forge a connection between Old World classical pagan natural philosophy (especially Epicurean atomism), and New World cannibalism, another "philosophical" reader of New World cannibalism seduced by Epicureanism was Michel de Montaigne. Montaigne's profound interest in Epicureanism is evident from his annotations in his personal copy of Denys Lambin's 1564 edition of *De rerum natura* (recovered only in 1987). There, Montaigne toys with the Epicurean idea of the primacy of matter over form, specifically with the idea that the atoms of which he himself is composed will survive and, possibly, give birth to another Montaigne, if chance has it (rather than fate or providence permit): "Since the movements of the atoms are so varied, it is not unbelievable that the atoms once came together, or will come together again in the future, so that another Montaigne be born."[49] What Montaigne meant here by "another Montaigne" was not a *reincarnation* of his spirit or eternal soul but a *transformation* of the atoms constituting his present body. In his published *Essays,* Montaigne is more guarded in his engagement with Lucretian/Epicurean atomism. He invokes Epicurean atomism in multiple places but mainly in a metaphorical sense. He explicitly quotes from *De rerum natura* only in his essay "Of Coaches," and none of these excerpts deal with atomism.[50] The essay in which he offers the most direct engagement with Lucretian/Epicurean atomism is, significantly,

"Of Cannibals"—the essay in which he also confronts most explicitly the philosophical questions raised by the New World.

Originally published eight years before "Of Coaches," "Of Cannibals" begins with an account of Pyrrhus, who, during his military campaign in Italy, encountered the armies of Rome. Contrary to his ethnocentric Greek ideas about the "barbarity" of all non-Greek-speaking people, Pyrrhus is impressed by the well-ordered manner of the Roman army. Montaigne takes this reflection as an occasion for entering into a meditation on the relativity of Christian ideas about civility and barbarism. His own primary examples are the reviled New World savages. Montaigne wonders how Europeans can habitually allege the barbarity of the Americans and yet "should be so blind to our own" in Europe, especially in light of the savagery that had resulted from the confessional wars in France: "I consider it more barbarous to eat a man alive than to eat him dead; to tear by rack and torture a body still full of feeling, to roast it by degrees, and then give it to be trampled and eaten by dogs and swine—a practice which we have not only read about but seen within recent memory, not between ancient enemies, but between neighbours and fellow-citizens and, what is worse, under the cloak of piety and religion."[51] Similar to the character of Raphael Hythloday, the Vespuccian traveler in Thomas More's *Utopia*, Montaigne indicts the depravities of Europe by comparing them unfavorably with the "original naturalness" of the New World, hereby anticipating Rousseau's rhetorical figure of the noble savage as social critic. "The very words denoting lying, treason, deceit, greed, envy, slander, and forgiveness," Montaigne writes, "have never been heard" in the Americas.[52] Toward the end of the essay, Montaigne appears as an ethnographer recording the words of a certain "ballad" allegedly in his possession in which a Brazilian cannibal who had himself been captured and was about to be eaten by his enemies "tauntingly invites his captors to come boldly forward, every one of them, and dine off him, for they will then be eating their own fathers and grandfathers, who have served as food and nourishment to his body": "'These muscles,' he says, 'this flesh, and these veins are yours, poor fools that you are! Can you not see that the substance of your ancestors' limbs is still in them? Taste them carefully, and you will find the flavor is that of your own flesh.'" Here, Montaigne observes with patent delight, is a "shaft of wit that by no means savours of barbarism": The Brazilian cannibal's speech betrays a perfect understanding of Epicurean metaphysics—that "Since the movements of the atoms are so varied, it is not unbelievable that the atoms once come together, or will come together again in the future," so that another cannibal be born.[53]

Although Montaigne claims that he knew about Brazilian cultural mores from an eyewitness who stayed at his house—"a man who had lived ten or twelve years in that other world" and who was a "plain, simple fellow" and of the type that are "likely to give true testimony"—and that he therefore had no need to "inquire what the cosmographers say about it,"[54] it is clear that this passage was inspired by several sixteenth-century accounts published by Frenchmen who had written about the Tupinamba in Brazil, including the French Franciscan and experimentor with alchemical mummy André Thevet, as well as the Huguenot missionary Jean de Léry (see figs. 19 and 20). Thus, in his lavishly illustrated *Les singularitez de la France Antarctique* (1557), Thevet reports a "song" sung by a Tupi prisoner who is about to be eaten: "The Margageas, our friends, are good people, strong and powerful in war; they have taken and eaten a great number of our enemies, and they will also eat me when it will please them. But I have killed and eaten the parents and friends of him, to whom I am a prisoner."[55] Even more striking are Jean de Léry's accounts of cannibalism not only among the Tupinamba but also among some French

Figure 19. Native Americans executing prisoners of war. "Commes ces Barbares font mourir leurs ennemis, qu'ils ont pris en guerre, & les mangent." (In Andre Thevet, *Les singularitez de la France Antarctique autrement nommée Amerique* [Paris: Chez les heritiers de Maurice de la Porte, au Clos Bruneau, à l'ensiegne S. Claude, 1558]. Courtesy of the John Carter Brown Library at Brown University.)

Figure 20. Native Americans preparing a captive for ritual killing. "Comments les Ameriquains traittent leurs prisonniers prins en guerre, & les ceremonies qu'ils obseruent tant à les tuer qu'à les manger." (In Jean de Léry, [*Histoire d'un voyage fait en la terre du Bresil*] *Histoire d'vn voyage faict en la terre du Bresil* [1580]. Courtesy of the John Carter Brown Library at Brown University.)

("Norman") interpreters who had lived in Brazil for some eight years and were "leading the lives of atheists, not only pollut[ing] themselves by all sort of lewd and base behavior among the women and girls . . . but some of them, surpassing the savages in inhumanity, even boasted in my hearing of having killed and eaten prisoners."[56]

Modern literary critics have generally seen the interest of both Léry and Montaigne in practices of cannibalism in the context of the confessional wars raging in France at the time, specifically in reference to the controversy about the Catholic Eucharist.[57] This certainly holds partially true for the Huguenot Léry, who draws an explicit analogy between Brazilian cannibals and French Catholics, comparing the "savagery" of the former favorably to that of the latter. However, Montaigne's comment about the "shaft of wit" in the cannibal's ballad—which "by no means savours of barbarism"—seems to suggest a different reading of American cannibalism. What was at stake for Montaigne in this passage, I would argue, was not primarily a sectarian conflict over Catholic trans-substantiation versus Protestant con-substantiation but a more fundamental metaphysical challenge of Christian notions of the body by the pagan (Lucretian) atomist notion of trans-*formation.* Not only did Lucretian atomism deny that the nature of matter can be changed by divine intervention or miracle; it also asserted the continued existence and identity of matter beyond the destruction of its form as eternal atoms (here, as the transformation of bodily matter from the form of the captors' ancestors, to that of the captive, to that of the captors).

If Thevet and Léry were indeed the sources of Montaigne's anecdote (as they doubtlessly were), it is striking how Montaigne's retelling of this incident changes the cultural significance of Tupi cannibalism. Both Thevet and Léry, despite their sectarian differences, are in agreement that, with the exception of the old women (who "have an amazing appetite for human flesh"), the Tupis' cannibalism is not a form of nutrition: "for although all of them confess human flesh to be wonderfully good and delicate, nonetheless it is more out of vengeance than for the taste."[58] Indeed, in Thevet and Léry, cannibalism is an act of revenge that entails a ritualized sense of honor and dignified stoicism. Thus, in Thevet, the victim explains that he is at peace with the fact that he is about to be eaten by the Tupinamba because he has previously also eaten some of their parents and friends; and he is comforted by the thought that most likely he will himself be avenged when his own people will capture and eat his captors in the future. Similarly, Léry explicitly compares the stoicism of one of the Tupinambas' victims about to be eaten to the Roman general and consul Marcus Atilius Regulus, who voluntarily returned into Carthaginian captivity to be tortured to death but vowed to be avenged by the Roman Republic: "'Very well,' replies the [Tupinambas'] prisoner (as resolved to be slain for his nation as Regulus was steadfast in enduring death for his Roman Republic), 'my kinsmen will avenge me in turn.'" For Thevet and Léry, Brazilian stoicism in the face of cannibalism was an expression of civic virtue and of the belief in a higher justice beyond the violations of the physical body. Though in itself reprehensible, cannibalism, as an act of revenge, was intelligible as a primitive expression of a universal code of honor, possibly analogous to the *point d'honneur* in feudal France.[59]

If most sixteenth-century European travelers interpreted New World cannibalism as an act of revenge based on their own cultural norms and codes, modern anthropologists have increasingly unsettled our understanding of the cultural meanings of cannibalism in Tupi-Guarani society. While some have seen cannibalism motivated by a religious desire to ingest the victim's vital sources with his or her flesh, Alfred Métraux, Florestan Fernandes, and most recently Eduardo Viveiros de Castro have each argued that Tupi-Guarani cannibalism must be understood as an attempt not so much to appropriate the enemy's vital spirit as to *re*-appropriate the substance of the kinsman whom the victim has eaten. Whereas Florestan Fernandes still remained somewhat beholden to the Western idea of revenge when reading Tupi cannibalism as an act of "restoration of the collective we" after it had been violated by an enemy,

Viveiros de Castro has argued that, "rather than a juridical system based on a restorative vendetta," Tupinamba cannibalism must be understood in the context of a metaphysics of "ontological predation," in which the self is always defined in relation to an enemy. That is, unlike the Western Christian (i.e., Augustinian-Neoplatonic) notion of the body—predicated on the notion of an ideal form—the Tupinamba's notion of the body was one of "perpetual disequilibrium"; it was part of a world in perpetual motion in which acts of predation were seen not as a state of exception—"wrongs" that had to be "avenged"—but a norm realized in constant warfare.[60] Thus, captives marked for being eaten often lived with their captors for months and even years; they were well treated, given women as mates; and they were called "brothers-in-law." Upon their death, their killers adopted their names, just as the victim had adopted the names of those kin he had previously killed. Hence, Viveiros de Castro concludes, Tupinamba cannibalism was essentially "an incorporation of enmity that sought immortality—for the eaters and the eaten."[61]

While this is not exactly the same idea as Montaigne's notion of the immortality of atoms—which may "come together again in the future, so that another Montaigne be born"—his interpretation of the accounts he read in Léry and Thevet similarly recognizes the fundamental challenge that Tupinamba cannibalism poses to Western Christian metaphysics, especially when it comes to the relationship between form and matter, as well as to the Christian doctrine of the Resurrection. Not unlike a postmodern anthropologist, Montaigne took the ethnographic accounts he had read as an occasion for engaging in intercultural philosophy on metaphysics, as a contest between static/idealist and dynamic/fluid understandings of form.[62] These are savage practices, indeed, Montaigne conceded in reference to the Brazilians' cannibalism. And "Compared with us [they, the Brazilian cannibals] are savages indeed. They must be so, indubitably, if we are not, for there is an amazing difference between their characters and ours." But in light of his exposition of the manly virtues of his New World savages and his own savage critique of European "civilization," the Epicurean interpretation of Tupinamba cannibalism is calculated to leave the reader ambivalent and unsettled about Christian norms of civility and barbarity.[63]

The topos of New World cannibalism was further developed during the final decade of the sixteenth century in several highly sensationalist publications released by the printing house of the Calvinist engraver Theodor de Bry in Frankfurt, in particular part 3 of his spectacularly successful series *Americae* (see fig. 21). Published for the first time in 1593 in both Latin and German, part 3 dealt with Brazil and reproduced the accounts of Léry as well as that of

Cannibal Heterotopias 287

Figure 21. Theodor de Bry, Brazilian cannibalism. (In Theodor de Bry, *America*, pt. 3 [Frankfurt, 1593]. Courtesy of the Library of Congress.)

the German traveler Hans Staden, both of which were richly embellished by copperplate engravings. Modern readers have long seen de Bry's visual representation of Tupinamba cannibalism as more or less a continuation of Lery's anti-Catholic propaganda intended to provide a pretext for Protestant colonial projects in the New World. More recently, however, Michiel van Groesen has demonstrated how De Bry's edition of the text in fact systematically excised Léry's anti-Catholic polemic in the Latin edition. The German edition stayed rather faithful to its French source text—the 1585 edition of Léry's travel account, in which the Huguenot had generalized the critique of European barbarism while also emphasizing his sympathy for Tupinamba culture by comparing it favorably with European culture. Regarding de Bry's engravings, van Groesen points to the strongly allegorical nature of de Bry's images, which are intended, he argues, to emphasize not so much sectarian difference between Protestants and Catholics but the contrast between pagans and Christians.[64] Indeed, as Andrea Frisch has noted, de Bry's highly graphic images of Tupinamba cannibalism undercut and often blatantly contradicted

Léry's sympathetic interpretation of Tupinamba culture that they supposedly illustrate, giving the De Bry edition an entirely different character from his French source text: whereas in the French edition overseen by Léry, the woodcuts are mere illustrations, secondary to the alphabetical text, in the De Bry edition the hierarchical relationship between alphabetical and graphic text is reversed, privileging the image. In addition, de Bry's images give Tupinamba cannibalism an unequivocally negative connotation that is at odds with Léry's interpretation. Whereas in Léry the account of cannibalism occurs in the context of his discussion of Tupinamba warfare—suggesting that it is a ritual of revenge that was characterized by a certain dignity and stoicism—de Bry's engravings focus on the ferocity and barbarism of the act of cannibalism as a mundane aspect of Tupinamba diet. Thus, the image of random human body parts being roasted on a grill is inserted into a passage where Léry actually discusses Tupinamba cooking and eating habits, particularly the grilling of fish.[65] Perhaps this choice of pairing the human victim of cannibalism with fish was not coincidental, as the fish is, of course, a Christian symbol for the Eucharistic body of Christ, the *Ichthys*. But regardless of whether or not the connection between cannibalism and fish in the De Bry edition of Léry was meant to invoke the Eucharist, it is noteworthy that the horror of the passage is entirely divorced from any ritual or cultural context and given expression by the visible outrage on the face of an onlooking European inserted into the scene. Indeed, in de Bry's strongly Calvinist interpretation, there can be no honor, nobility, or wisdom in Tupinamba cannibalism; for him, all non-Christian knowledge is, by definition, a diabolical perversion. To be sure, de Bry's reading could hereby not be further apart from Montaigne's. Nevertheless, even though de Bry's interpretation divests Tupinamba cannibalism of all ritualistic contexts, it is closer to Montaigne's reading of cannibalism than it is to Léry's insofar as both Montaigne and de Bry understand cannibalism as a transformation of bodily matter in digestion.

As we will see in subsequent chapters, the sixteenth-century "heterotopic" debate about New World cannibalism had important repercussions for the history of discovery, both in international law and in science. In the seventeenth century, Lucretian atomism continued to be a prominent topic of discussion in a new genre that we might call an early version of science fiction. Works such as Tomasso Campanella's *City of of Sun* (1602), Francis Bacon's *The New Atlantis* (1627), John Wilkins's *Discovery of a World in the Moon* (1638), Cyrano de Bergerac's *States and Empires of the Moon* (1657), and Christiaan Huygens's *Cosmotheoros* (1698) were not utopias (no-places) but heterotopias, "other spaces" in which atomism gradually became Christianized by sublimating New World cannibalism through the language of alchemy. But, as we will see in the next chapter, the alchemical state of exception to Christian morality facilitated not only the return of the pagan atomism of Democritus and Lucretius to early modern Europe but also the erasure of the (Native) American subject from the law of nations.

8

Homunculus americanus

> This thing of darkness
> I Acknowledge mine
> —Prospero in William Shakespeare's *The Tempest*

In the last chapter, I explored how the Americas functioned as a scientific heterotopia in the humanist engagement with the pre-Socratic atomism of Democritus, Epicurus, and Lucretius through a discourse about New World cannibalism. In this chapter I turn to the geopolitical implications of this heterotopian engagement in the context of the various strands of neo-Aristotelianism through the prism of which jurists and theologians interpreted the Spanish conquest of America as well as the return of ancient pagan philosophy to Renaissance Europe. The collision between these various strands of early modern Aristotelianism came to a head in the so-called Great Debate that was inaugurated in Valladolid in August 1550 before a *junta* of fourteen theologians and members of the Royal Council of the Indies about the question of the justness of the Spanish conquest of America, the nature of the American Indians, and the legitimacy of Spanish claims to possession in the New World. On one side of the debate was the Dominican friar Bartolomé de las Casas (d. 1566), famous today as the defender of the human rights of the American Indians; on the other side was the Spanish humanist Juan Ginés de Sepúlveda (1494–1573), who represented the interests of the conquerors. The immediate reason why Emperor Charles V had decided to convene this debate was a controversy that had arisen over a book Sepúlveda had written in 1545, in which he had fashioned himself as a "Second Democritus." Entitled *Democrates alter de justis belli causis apud Indios* (*A Second Democritus: On the Just Causes of the War with the Indians*), it was a dialogue that advanced the arguments that the Spanish conquest of America had not only been *justified* as a punishment of the Indians' violations of natural law (such as cannibalism, human sacrifice, and idolatry), but that it had also been *necessary* in order to convert them to Christianity. Moreover, Sepúlveda argued, the American Indians were like the natural slaves (*natura servi*) discussed by Aristotle in his *Politics,* who were by nature destined to be ruled by superior men, such as the Spaniards. In fact, Sepúlveda suggested that the American Indians are not truly human men (*humani*) at all but "*humunculos* [little men], in whom you will barely find the vestiges of humanity."[1]

When Sepúlveda's petition for a license to publish his book was denied by the Royal Council of the Indies in 1547, some of his allies at the court persuaded the emperor to issue a *cédula* referring the case to the Royal Council of Castile for reconsideration. However, as the book touched on issues of religion, the Council of Castile decided to refer the book for inspection to some of the leading theologians at the Universities of Salamanca and Alcalá de Henares.[2] Meanwhile, Las Casas, having just returned from the Americas and learned of Sepúlveda's efforts, lobbied vigorously against the publication of the manuscript. When the theologians in the academies (probably under the sway of Las Casas) also determined that the manuscript should not be published, Sepúlveda sent it to some friends in Rome, complete with an approbation by one of his principal Spanish allies, the bishop of Segovia. Upon learning that a summary version of Sepúlveda's book had been published in Rome,[3] the emperor issued another edict ordering its confiscation in Spain and forbidding its translation into Castilian. Sepúlveda promptly produced just such a Castilian translation (now lost), so that "it could be read not only by scholars but also by the common folk who don't know Latin."[4] In order to counter its effects, Las Casas wrote a 550-page Latin treatise, the *Argumentum apologiae*, of which he also seems to have prepared a Spanish summary (also now lost).[5] Finally, in order to put the case to rest once and for all, the emperor ordered the hearing of the two great antagonists to be staged at the Council of Castile in Valladolid. Although the affair has come to be known as the "Great Debate" of Valladolid, the two men never actually faced one another in the same room; rather, each read his own statement to the judges. Thus, Sepúlveda took three hours to summarize the arguments he had already presented in his dialogue and summary. For his turn, Las Casas read his entire *Apologética* (which took five days), in which he argued that Native Americans were free human agents; that violent means could never be justified by the ends of Christian conversion; and that the Spanish conquest had been an unjust war.[6]

Although no official royal judgment was rendered in the matter, two years later the Sevillian printer Sebastián Trujillo published a pamphlet, entitled *Aqui se contiene una disputa, o controversia*, that provided a summary of the debate by the president of the *junta*, the Dominican friar Domingo de Soto (1494–1560), as well as Sepúlveda's and Las Casas's responses. De Soto was a prominent theologian at the University of Salamanca who had served as the confessor of Charles V and as the emperor's representative at the Council of Trent. After having completed his studies at the University of Paris and having taught at Alcalá de Henares, De Soto had joined a cadre of prominent scholars at Salamanca that included the renowned theologian and jurist Francisco de Vitoria (1483–1546). Together, De Soto and Vitoria founded what has come to be known as the "School of Salamanca" or the school of the "Second Scholastics," which would eventually also include such famous Neo-Scholastics as Luis de Molina (1535–1500) and Francisco Suárez (1548–1617). While, collectively, the School is famous in modern historiography for laying the philosophical foundations of what would evolve into modern international law during the nineteenth century, their intellectual legacy with regard to the history of sixteenth-century Spanish imperialist expansionism, European colonialism, and indigenous rights in the Americas has been the subject of debate in modern historiography.[7] Much of this debate has hereby revolved around the evaluation of the School's Neo-Scholastic Aristotelianism in a sixteenth-century context. While some historians writing during the 1950s and 1960s have seen the School's Neo-Thomism as the forerunner of modern human rights discourse and Catholic liberation theology confronting capitalist exploitation of humans and natural environments,[8] more recently historians have seen the intellectual legacy of Thomism in a more critical light. Thus, historians in this latter group have argued that, despite the Second Scholastics' criticisms of the *abuses* of the conquest, their Neo-Thomist theology was not only essentially complicit with Spanish imperialist ideology but even "the origin of the contemporary reduction of nature to technologically disposable materials."[9]

In this chapter, I revisit the debate about the philosophy underwriting the Spanish conquest of America in the context of the multiple traditions of "Aristotelianism" to which the early sixteenth century was heir.[10] I will argue that, within this broader intellectual spectrum of sixteenth-century Aristotelianisms, the School's Neo-Scholastic philosophy offered a relatively tempered and "conservative" approach to conquest and colonial exploitation vis-à-vis that of the "moderns," such as the humanist Sepúlveda in Spain as well as the Scottish theologian John Mair and the French Llullian humanist Jacques Lefèvre d'Étaples in Paris. Although, at the beginning of the sixteenth century, none of these intellectual traditions was predestined to triumph two hundred years later, it was arguably the repudiation of Neo-Thomist metaphysics—not its rise—that prepared the theological path for the ascendancy of the modern paradigm of discovery in both science and international law since the seventeenth century.[11] During the sixteenth century, these multiple intellectual traditions and confluences contributed, actively or passively, to the emergence of not one but several sets of ideas about Spanish imperialism, its role in history, as well as of America's natural resources and human populations within it. For example, as we will see in this chapter, while Sepúlveda eclectically drew on several of these traditions in his *Democrates alter,* his particular argument that the American Indians were not lawful lords of their lands because they were "humunculos" was "Aristotelian" insofar as it was based on a medieval tradition postulating the possibility of artificially generated life that was attributed to the thirteenth-century physician Arnald of Villanova and passed down in alchemical works some of which were spuriously attributed to "Thomas" (i.e., Aquinas) during the fourteenth century. This tradition ultimately culminated with the *De homunculis* (1529–32) written by Sepúlveda's contemporary, the Swiss alchemist Philippus Aureolus Theophrastus Bombastus von Hohenheim, aka Paracelsus. But while the possibility of the artificial creation of life is an idea the history of which indeed reaches back to Aristotle, it was utterly rejected by the Thomists, who had, over the centuries, produced a distinctively Christianized hermeneutics of "Aristotle" that was quite at odds not only with the (pseudo-) Aristotelian-Arabic tradition of the medieval alchemists but also with the "pagan" Aristotle exposed by the Renaissance humanist philologists. As we saw in chapter 6, the preoccupation with demonic power had a long tradition in Franciscan metaphysics. However, for the Franciscan missionaries, there was no question that the American Indians were the descendants of Adam and, thus, the progeny of God's original creation. The Indians' religion was diabolic not because they were the minions but rather because they were the *victims* of the Devil's demonic art of counterfeit. By contrast, in the context of sixteenth-century occult philosophy, the idea of the American Indians' artificial origins was born in works of Christian humanists such as Sepúlveda's *Democrates alter.* From there, it was only a small (though still heretical) step for Paracelsus's claim, in his *Astronomia magna,* that the American Indians, who had recently been discovered, were the descendants not of Adam but of "another Adam," a creature of nature's spontaneous creations or of demonic art.

The Second Scholastics and the Rights of Dominion

The history of the public controversy about the justness of the Spanish conquest and claims to titles of possession in America leading up to the debate at Valladolid is well known and can be summarized rather briefly here.[12] By most accounts, it began on the island of Hispaniola on the fourth Sunday of Advent, December 21, 1511, when the newly arrived Dominican friar Antonio de Montesinos preached a sermon in which he excoriated the Spanish conquerors and colonists for the abuses of the Indians whom they held in encomienda. A feudal tenure system that had originated in the reconquest of

Spain from the Moors by which conquerors who had served in a just war were entitled to exact tribute and labor from a certain number of the conquered population in exchange for assuming responsibility of their conversion, the encomienda had been introduced into the Caribbean in 1503, after the enslavement of Indians had been outlawed by an edict of Queen Isabella the Catholic.[13] The encomienda was not a system of slavery that entailed property rights in either land or the persons held in encomienda by an encomendero. It had, in fact, been implemented as a more benign alternative to enslavement. Though obliged to provide labor and tribute, Indians held in encomienda were legally free imperial subjects, and sixteenth-century documents make a strict distinction between *indios esclavos* and *indios encomendados*.[14] Nevertheless, the system of coercive rotational labor of the encomienda system had led to several rebellions and a catastrophic collapse of the indigenous population, hereby compounding the effects of European and African diseases into the Caribbean.[15]

Among Montesinos's audience was the secular priest Bartolomé de las Casas, who, after having himself been an encomendero, appears to have had a conversion experience that would later lead him to join the Dominican order in 1513 and become the most vociferous advocate for the rights of the American Indians and the harshest critics of the Spanish colonial system in America. It was largely due to Las Casas's tireless political and literary activities, as well as substantial legal acumen, that the Crown promulgated the so-called New Laws in 1542, which implemented stricter protections of the Indians and stipulated that any encomienda should revert to the Crown after the death of the holder (a clause doubtlessly intended not only to afford greater protection for the Indians but also to reallocate the spoils of conquest and colonial administrative control from the original conquerors and their descendants toward Crown bureaucrats sent to the Americas).[16]

Although neither Montesinos nor Las Casas had initially questioned the legitimacy of the Spanish monarchy's claim to titles in the New World per se—they were rather concerned with the conquerors' abuses of Spanish rule—the Crown began its attempts to shore up its claims to sovereignty and property rights in America vis-à-vis critics of the Alexandrine bulls both at home and abroad.[17] As early as the 1510s, King Ferdinand had charged a number of jurists and theologians at the University of Salamanca to examine the question of Spanish dominion in the Americas from a legal and theological perspective. Initially this consultation with the academics had amounted to rather perfunctory efforts on the part of the Crown to secure legal cover against the critics. Thus, in 1512, the Crown had promulgated the Laws of Burgos, which codified the practice of the encomienda while also attempting to curb some of its worst abuses. In 1513, the Laws of Valladolid established certain protections for indigenous workers. But they had little measurable effect in ameliorating the actual social and demographic situation of the Native population living in encomienda; nor did they address the illegal practice of enslavement, which continued unabated despite its official abrogation. Worse, in 1513, the Crown promulgated the so-called *requerimiento,* a document drafted by Juan López de Palacios Rubios (1450–1524), a canon lawyer at Salamanca, that was to be read out aloud to any pagans in America before war could be made on them. The text informed the Indians (in Latin) that the document's carrier acted on behalf of the Spanish monarchy, who were the rightful lords over the Indians' lands by virtue of the donation of Pope Alexander VI, successor of St. Peter and God's representative on earth, and that it was the Indians' duty to accept Christianity and Spanish rule peacefully or else face violent conquest. Las Casas lambasted the *requerimiento* in his copy of the text, writing in the margins "absurd," "false," and "heretical" next to passages in which Palacios Rubios claimed that any civil jurisdiction held by pagans and infidels were illegitimate; that the pope had authority over the entire world; and that pagan lords became legitimate only once they accepted the authority of the church.[18]

Las Casas was not alone in his criticism of the Spanish Crown, especially among the international leadership of the Dominican order. Thus, in 1517, after listening to an account of the affairs in the Indies by a Spanish Dominican following King Ferdinand's death the year before, the Italian master general of the order in Rome, Thomas Cajetan (1469–1534), asked, "And do you doubt that your king is in hell"?[19] Encouraged by the authority, influence, and support of mounting critical voices such as Cajetan's, Las Casas published, in 1534, his *De unico vocationis modo,* in which he argued that "the only way" of conversion was by peaceful means. In 1537, Pope Paul III issued the bull *Sublimis Deus,* which proclaimed that "the Indians are truly men and they are not only capable of understanding the Catholic faith, but, according to our information, they desire exceedingly to receive." Referring to Alexander's earlier *Inter cetera* bulls and their hierocratic interpretations, Pope Paul continued, "Whatever may have been said or may be said to the contrary notwithstanding, the said Indians and all other people who may later be discovered by Christians are by no means to be deprived of their liberty."[20] Meanwhile, the theologians and jurists at Salamanca had been debating the issue. The most important statements that they produced on the topic were De Soto's *relectio* "De dominio" (1534) and Vitoria's "De indis" (1539), both of which discussed the status (in Vitoria's words) "of these barbarians in the New World, commonly called Indians, who came under the power of the Spaniards some forty years ago, having been previously unknown to our world."[21]

Francisco de Vitoria and the Metaphysics of Dominion

Much of the modern historiographic debate about the role that the School of Salamanca played in the history of Spanish imperialism in the Americas has been focused on Francisco de Vitoria's famous treatise "De indis," due to the apparent ambiguities of the position he takes there with regard to the legal status of the American Indians.[22] On the one hand, Vitoria considers, in the first part, the question "whether these barbarians, before the arrival of the Spaniards, had true dominion, public and private."[23] He considers several arguments to the contrary (allegations of the Indians' sinfulness, paganism, violations of natural law, and lack of rationality) only to reject them all, concluding that "the barbarians undoubtedly possessed as true dominion, both public and private, as any Christian."[24] Similarly, in part 2, Vitoria considers arguments that have been used to make claims to Spanish titles in the New World and concludes that these arguments were invalid and therefore "unjust titles." These unjust titles include (1) the Habsburgs' claim to universal empire; (2) the right of the pope, as temporal representative of God, to donate pagan dominions to Christian lords; (3) the right of discovery as derived from Roman law; (4) the Indians' refusal to receive Christ by peaceful means; (5) the justness of the conquest as punishment of Amerindian mortal sins; (6) their free acceptance of Spanish dominion; and (7) their subjection by divine intervention (as the Canaanites had been subjected by the Jews). Again refuting these arguments one by one, Vitoria points out that the Roman Empire has never been universal in its expanse, not in ancient times and especially not now, considering the newly discovered parts of the world. Also, the pope's bulls of donation had no legal standing, as "Our Lord Jesus Christ had no temporal dominion (*dominium*) . . . [and therefore] much less so does the pope, who is His vicar."[25] Nor did the Roman law *Ferae bestiae* (in Justinian's *Institutes*) give Castile a "title by right of discovery" in America, considering that the lands were neither unoccupied nor deserted upon the arrival of Spaniards but lawfully held by the Indians.[26] Furthermore, the Spaniards' Christian duty to evangelize does not grant just titles to take someone else's possessions, especially not by the force of arms. Nor were the American Indians subject to punishment for their sins, as they were not infidels guilty of "vincible" (sinful) ignorance but pagans who had lived in "invincible ignorance" of Christ (i.e., an ignorance not of their fault). Even if many Indians have freely accepted the Christian faith, this does not justify taking possession of their lands. Finally, there is no indication that God had directly intervened in the conquest of America, as he had in biblical times, by way of miracles.

On the other hand, in the third and final part of "De indis," Vitoria offered a theory consisting of seven *potential* just titles by which the Indians "*could have*"—and presumably still could—come under control of the Spaniards.[27] These include (1) Spanish natural rights to travel and trade, as well as (2) to proselytize; (3) the right to protect converts from forceful reconversion by an infidel lord; (4) the pope's right to replace an infidel with a Christian lord once a large number of the population has been converted; (5) the right to protect innocents from acts of tyranny perpetrated by an infidel lord; (6) voluntary acceptance of Christian rule; and (7) the protection of allies and friends. To these seven "just titles," Vitoria added an eighth "possible title," which concerns the question of the "mental incapacity of the barbarians" to govern themselves in a rational way.[28] In other words, Vitoria here considered the possibility that Spanish dominion in the New World could be legitimated if the American Indians were "natural slaves," as discussed by Aristotle. As we will see, this last point would become a central issue later in Sepúlveda's defense of the conquest in his *Democrates alter* in 1545 and in the debate of Valladolid in 1550–51.

Due to Vitoria's consideration of natural slavery as a possible justification of Spanish titles in the Americas, scholars of Latin American history and literature have sometimes seen his position as being more or less consistent with the imperialist arguments later advanced by Sepúlveda.[29] But while there can be little doubt that Sepúlveda pushed open the rhetorical back door left unlocked by Vitoria in the third part of "De indis," it would be a mistake to evaluate the Dominican theologian's treatment of natural slavery in the 1530s merely through the lens of its later exploitation (and even perversion) by Sepúlveda during the 1540s. In order to see Vitoria's discussion of natural slavery in its proper context, it is first of all necessary to consider "De indis" in light of the generic conventions of the Scholastic *relectio* (literally a "rereading") in which it was presented. As Prime Professor of Theology at Salamanca, Vitoria produced two categories of texts: on the one hand, his "lectures" were basically continuous commentaries on Thomas Aquinas's *Summa theologiae* and Peter Lombard's *Sentences,* in the tradition of Aquinas's own commentaries on Aristotle; on the other hand, his *relectiones* were longer and more formal investigations of a particular problem that had emerged in the course of the regular lectures and that had some immediate political or social significance. The subject treated in the *relectio* "De indis," for example, had arisen from a lecture he had originally given in 1534–35 on the issue of the evangelization of unbelievers in Thomas Aquinas's *Summa theologiae,* in which Vitoria had also considered the question of whether or not it is lawful to convert children against the will of their Jewish and Muslim parents (and in which he categorically concluded that it is not).

As Vitoria did not publish anything during his lifetime, most of his lectures and *relectiones* survive only in form of notes and transcriptions undertaken by his students.[30] From these surviving documents, it is apparent that his *relectiones* were presented in the Scholastic form of dialectical disputations, meaning the formalistic method of posing a question (*quaestio*); the consideration of propositions and objections answering the question in the negative; the consideration of answers or replies to those objections; and finally the conclusion by weighing the opposing arguments based on experience, authority, and syllogistic reasoning. It is important to keep in mind this dialectical procedure when reading Vitoria's *relectiones* because much of his discussion consists of the development of speculative arguments and positions that are not necessarily his own but rigorously follow, as an intellectual exercise, particular syllogistic chains leading to conclusions that ultimately stand to be refuted (or "answered"). Also, this method associates him with a certain "old school" of Scholastic theological writing that was increasingly being rejected (and even ridiculed) by many of the "modern" theologians, especially those embracing the new humanist learning on both sides of the emerging sectarian divide.[31]

In terms of Aristotelian rhetorical theory, Vitoria's arguments in "De indies" roughly fall into three categories—judicial (making arguments about past actions); demonstrative (making arguments about present actions); and deliberative (making arguments about future actions). Thus, he employs judicial rhetoric in Question 1, where he establishes that the Indians had lawful dominion over their territories and of their possessions at the time of the Spanish arrival in the New World. He employs demonstrative rhetoric in Question 2, where he refutes the a posteriori justifications of the Spanish conquest and claims to titles by certain contemporary jurists and theologians whom he does not name ("Some, I know not who, say . . .").[32] And, in Question 3, he employs deliberative rhetoric with regard to hypothetical (and possible future) scenarios and conditions for just Spanish titles not yet realized. Vitoria himself drew attention to these rhetorical distinctions, writing that "not all theological disputations are of the deliberative kind. Frequently, they are *demonstrative*—that is, undertaken not to argue about the truth, but to explain it."[33] Accordingly, he applies demonstrative rhetoric when "explain[ing]" the truth that is already known (i.e., titles of dominion and natural rights that can or cannot be derived from natural law); and he employs deliberative rhetoric when "argu[ing] about the truth" in order to discover what is not certain, as not yet based on experience or established by syllogistic reason: whether there hypothetically still *might* be just titles for Spain in the New World.

Some historians have speculated that Vitoria's consideration of the possibility of just Spanish titles in America may have been added by him under pressure when he delivered his lecture in late 1538 or early 1539. According to this interpretation, his equivocations served as a sort of rhetorical balancing act, after some of his previous lectures at Salamanca—such as *On the Power of the Church* (which had questioned the legitimacy of papal grants of temporal dominion, such as the *Inter cetera* bulls)—had already created some controversy that reached beyond the halls of the university.[34] Indeed, several months after Vitoria had delivered "De indis," on November 10, 1539, the emperor explicitly ordered the professors at Salamanca to refrain from any further discussions of "our right to the Indies, the islands and lands of the ocean sea" and all existing academic writings on the subject to be surrendered to his councilors for inspection.[35] Generally, there can be little doubt that Vitoria understood his academic *relectio* to be relevant to a current debate about imperial politics. Indeed, the issue of Vitoria's ethos as a professor of theology involving himself in matters of politics is the very first *quaestio* that he addresses in the introduction of "De indis." He considers there several possible objections from those who might argue that theologians like him have no "warrant to question or censure the conduct of government in the Indies." His answer, supported by quotes from Aristotle's *Nicomachean Ethics,* is that it behooves those in political power to consult "experts" and "wise men" when there are doubts in questions of politics, law, religion, or ethics.[36] The analogy he offers here in establishing his ethos is telling: he compares those in political power (i.e., the emperor) to a man who is uncertain whether or not he is legally married to a particular woman. Unsure whether or not it is lawful for him to consummate the marriage under such circumstances, the man consults the expert theologians (as King Ferdinand had done in 1513 with regard to his rights in the Indies). Although the experts' answer is an "emphatic negative," the man proceeds to consummate the marriage anyway on his own authority, citing his love for the woman. "Now in this case the man certainly commits a sin," Vitoria writes, "even if it is in fact lawful, because he is acting willfully against conscience. It must be so, because in matters which concern salvation there is an obligation to believe those whom the Church has appointed as teachers, and in cases of doubt their verdict is law."[37] By "acting willfully against conscience," Vitoria means that the man's ignorance about whether or not he is allowed to consummate the marriage in such circumstances is no longer invincible. The man's actions may or may not have been lawful (depending on whether he was indeed legally married); but they were not sinful as long as his ignorance was still invincible. However, having been instructed to abstain, his "conscience" was changed and his ignorance become vincible. Therefore, his act is now sinful regardless, even if it later turns out that he was legally married. As can be seen here, the logic behind Vitoria's argument is that truth is not to be found through experiment in the realm of uncertainty. Dominion may justify conquest, but conquest can never justify dominion. Any a posteriori justification of conquest may be pragmatic philosophy, but it is not moral theology leading to metaphysical truth.[38]

As can also be seen here, as a piece of political rhetoric, "De indis" is carefully crafted for the benefit of Charles and his councilors when considered in the context of imperial politics during the late 1530s, when the Habsburg monarchy was engaged in an attempt to consolidate administrative control over the conquered territories by rolling back some of the privileges that his predecessors, the Catholic Monarchs, had earlier granted to the conquerors. Thus, Vitoria established, by way of judicial rhetoric (under Question 1), that the Spanish conquest *as it had happened in history* was unjust—especially when one hears of "bloody massacres and of innocent individuals pillaged of their possessions and dominions";[39] by way of demonstrative rhetoric, he establishes (under Question 2) that the a posteriori arguments cited in justification of the conquest are invalid and that, therefore, the conquerors' existing titles are illegitimate. Finally, by way of deliberative rhetoric, he offers a speculative theory (under Question 3), in which the emperor's claim to titles in the New World could still be justified provided there is a new legal regime under which the Indies will henceforth pass under Spanish dominion. This new legal regime would seem to have arrived three years after Vitoria had delivered his lecture at Salamanca, with the promulgation of the "New Laws" of 1542, which stripped the conquerors' rights to pass down their neofeudal privileges to their descendants, hereby permanently codifying the patrimonialist structure of the Spanish Empire in America.[40]

However, if the tripartite structure of "De indis" can in part be understood in terms of this imperial political context on the eve of the promulgation of the New Laws, it is important to note that Vitoria approached questions of politics and law (meaning human or positive law) primarily as a theologian. That is, issues of imperial politics were for him not independent from but subordinate to the science of theology. He therefore treated questions of positive law within a metaphysical frame of reference that included the law of nations as a subset of natural and divine law. As such, Vitoria's particular arguments about the politics of empire must be seen in the broader European context of a theological debate about the rights of dominion, especially in the context of his engagements with the implications that Parisian nominalism as well as German Lutheranism held for monarchical power. Unlike Las Casas, Vitoria was concerned with the "affairs of the Indies" not primarily because he harbored a special empathy for the plight of the Indians (whom he doubtlessly considered to be barbarians) but because their case had significant implications for natural law metaphysics—in particular his theory, elaborated more directly in "On Civil Power" and "On the Power of the Church," that all rights were natural and proceed from God's law, not from His grace. Vitoria understood very keenly that in a legal regime in which Europeans are able to argue that American Indians have no rights of dominion because they are sinners or pagans, such "modern heretics" as Luther will be able to argue that European princes who are (or are perceived to be) in a state of sin can legitimately be deposed by those who are (or claim to be) visible saints.[41]

The theory of dominion as dependent on grace was not, of course, original to Luther or Calvin but had a long history in medieval theology. In "De indis," Vitoria singles out for special criticism the fourteenth-century Irish "bishop of Armagh" Richard Fitzralph and the Oxford theologian John Wycliffe, the latter of whom held that "no one is a civil master while he is in a state of mortal sin."[42] In fact, both Fitzralph and Wycliffe built on the papalist legal thought of Augustinian theologians such as Giles of Rome (Ægidius Romanus) and William of Cremona, who were instrumental in elaborating the hierocratic theory of *papa vicarius Christi,* which underwrote the late medieval tradition of papal bulls of donation that Luis Weckmann-Muñoz has called *doctrina omni-insular.*[43] However, whereas Giles and William had elaborated this theory in order to shore up the papacy's claim to temporal dominion, Fitzralph insisted that dominion by grace is not reserved to ecclesiastic leaders (such as the pope) but is granted directly by God also to secular rulers living in grace. Wycliffe even went so far as to argue that righteous secular rulers could confiscate ecclesiastical property held by unrighteous clergy.[44] Another reformer mentioned by Vitoria who would espouse this theory is the Czech theologian Jan Hus. But despite the universal condemnation of the hierocratic theory of dominion (and Hus's execution at the Council of Constance in 1415), it survived in the fifteenth century in the works of the German theologian Conrad Summenhart before being embraced by the sixteenth-century Protestant reformers.

As Vitoria observes, if one accepts these theologians' premise that temporal dominion is founded in grace, one could indeed argue that "the barbarians were not true masters because they were continually in a state of mortal sin." But, he objects, the question had already been settled by the Council of Constance: "Mortal sin is no impediment to the civil right of ownership, nor to true dominion."[45] With regard to the former (civil right of ownership), Vitoria points out that, if sinners had no right to the food they must eat to sustain themselves, they would be compelled to steal, which would trap them in a cycle of sin and therefore cannot be in accordance with either natural or divine law. Both civil and natural dominions are gifts from God to man, regardless of sin. With regard to natural dominion, this can be seen in the Bible, which includes multiple examples of rulers who are notorious sinners, such as Solomon and Ahab, as well as occasional sinners, such as Saul and David. The reason for this is that even sinners are created in the image of God, which is the Old Testament foundation for all dominion, reaffirmed in the New Testament by Matthew 5:45: "For the Lord maketh his sun to rise on the evil and the good, and sendeth rain on the just and on the unjust."[46] Thus, Vitoria explains that while both the right to ownership and the right to rule are codified in positive law or custom, they originate in natural law by which man participates in divine and eternal law.

One of the reasons why Luther's shadow looms so large over Vitoria's writings about the affair of the Indies is that the German reformer had not only resuscitated Wycliff's hierocratic theory of dominion but also synthesized it with the *via moderna* of Ockhamian nominalism, as it had been further developed by the early fifteenth-century Conciliarists at Paris, Jean Gerson and Pierre d'Ailly, whom Vitoria disparagingly called the *neoterici* (modernists).[47] Although Luther came to embrace the centrality of grace as a result of his quarrels with the doctrine of free will espoused by both the Parisian nominalists and Erasmian humanists, Vitoria was keenly aware that it was the soil of precisely those two latter traditions that had nurtured Luther's heretical ideas.[48] Of course, in the fourteenth century, Fitzralph and Wycliff had elaborated the hierocratic idea of the origin of dominion *against* Ockhamian nominalism in the context of the Franciscan poverty controversy. In the medieval context of almost constant competition for power between the pope and the emperor, the two Augustinian traditions had often been at political loggerheads, with the former being founded in a metaphysical realism that usually undergirded arguments intended to strengthen the authority of the pope, while the latter had lent itself to arguments in favor of secular authority. Whereas in the former tradition, there was no just dominion except in divine law, in the latter, dominion was entirely independent from it.[49] It was precisely to avoid this radical bifurcation that Aquinas's natural law metaphysics had been devised in the thirteenth century—as a "middle way" between Bonaventure's natural theology and the Averroists' "double truth." In the fourteenth century, both radical solutions reemerged in the hierocratic conception of dominion as elaborated by Fitzralph and Wycliffe on the one hand and Gerson's and Ailly's nominalism on the other, both similarly presenting an "Augustinian" challenge to Thomist-Aristotelian natural law metaphysics. In the hands of the Parisian Conciliarists d'Ailly and Gerson, nominalist metaphysics was adapted to arguments limiting the power of the pope vis-à-vis the church council. They argued that the church was not like a monarchy, ruled by the Roman pontiff alone, but a mixed polity, including also aristocratic and democratic elements.⁵⁰

However, already the Parisian Conciliarists, while influenced by Ockhamian nominalism, had begun to synthesize the hierocratic conception of dominion that would later be adopted by the Protestants. Thus, d'Ailly fundamentally agreed with Fitzralph that true dominion proceeds from God only and must be founded in grace. In his *Questio de legitimo dominio,* d'Ailly wrote that "just as by the gift of God, Christ-made-man is Lord-Creator of all things, so without the gift of Christ, no other man may wield just *dominium* . . . just as every secondary cause is contingent upon the first cause, so from the first and supreme *dominium* is derived every secondary *dominium.*"⁵¹ While both the hierocrats and the nominalists agreed that just dominion is grounded not in nature but in divine grace, the difference between the two traditions rested on a rather subtle distinction in what is meant by "grace." Thus, the late medieval papalists and the early modern Protestants interpreted grace to be *gratia gratum faciens,* that is "created" and "justifying" grace (i.e., God's supernatural gift to some already in the act of creation that will be "visible" or manifest in the recipient's abstinence from committing mortal sins). Civil dominion held by a ruler not in grace or, worse, living in mortal sin was therefore a perversion of the divine order. By contrast, for d'Ailly and Gerson grace was an "uncreated" grace. Dominion by grace was therefore a *concession* of the divine will (*gratia gratis data*) to a temporal ruler for mere temporal ends that was independent of the ruler's spiritual estate.⁵² Whereas for Fitzralph and Wycliffe, dominion by grace proceeded from God's ordained powers, for the nominalists it proceeded from the absolute powers of an inscrutable divine will, which did not preclude the temporal rule of sinful Christians and even non-Christians. According to the nominalists, no ruler—Christian or infidel, regenerate or reprobate—therefore had a higher "right" to dominion except by human laws. These human laws, however, were upheld only by God's will, not by His law, and could therefore be abrogated at any moment and without need of justification. Thus, while both traditions constituted an attack on Thomist metaphysics by holding that natural law had no relevance in the justification of dominion, they did so for opposite reasons: the nominalists held that natural law did not exist apart from divine law, which was unknowable except through revelation and experience; the hierocrats, by contrast, held that natural law did not exist apart from human law, which was fallen unless assisted by grace.⁵³

Vitoria was keenly aware that the Lutheran heresy was ultimately a radical outgrowth not only of the papalists' hierocratic conception of dominion but also of the nominalist attack on Thomist natural law metaphysics by the Parisian *neoterici* in this regard. He was deeply wary of the dangerous implications that this attack on Thomist natural law metaphysics held for both monarchical and papal authority. This wariness must be seen as one of the principal reasons why Vitoria, after having been exposed to (and apparently flirted with) nominalism during his studies at Paris, recoiled into a staunch Thomism after his return to Spain in 1522. As Vitoria was watching, during his last years in Paris, the Protestant revolt unfolding in the aftermath of Luther's posting his ninety-five theses on the door of the Wittenberg Castle church in 1517, it must have demonstrated to him that Parisian nominalism was a slippery slope and that Thomism was the best line of defense against the Protestant challenge.[54]

In his lectures and *relecciones,* he therefore misses no chance to attack not only Wycliffe, Fitzralph, Hus, and Summenhart but also the *neoterici,* both of previous centuries—most notably Duns Scotus, Gerson, and d'Ailly—as well as of his own days, some of whom he had encountered during his days at Paris. Thus, in his *relectio* "On the Power of the Church," he chides Gerson for his "erroneous opinion that the pope is not empowered to punish all sins against the natural law by sentence of excommunication, but only those sins which are directly against the Gospel, such as those which concern the sacraments or the faith." This, Vitoria objects, is "contradicted by Paul in 1 Cor. 5, where he excommunicates those guilty of incest."[55] In his lecture on the *Summa* II–II.10.8, which deals with the evangelization of unbelievers (from which the *relectio* "De indis" emerged), he attacks both Duns Scotus and his fifteenth-century follower, the German theologian Gabriel Biel for their position that "a prince may forcibly convert pagans who live in his own kingdom."[56] And in his lecture on the *Summa* I–II.100, he attacks the nominalist notion, expressed by d'Ailly, Ockham, and Biel, that God could at any time dispense with the laws he had laid down in the Ten Commandments—a notion that implied that right and wrong, good and evil had no independent existence outside of God's will.[57] During the very years in which John Calvin was at work on his *Institutes of the Christian Religion* (1534), Vitoria already understood that at the end of the nominalist *via moderna* stood the destruction of monarchy, the church as he knew it, and of Christian morality itself.[58]

Vitoria and Natural Slavery

When considering Vitoria's arguments about Indian and Spanish rights of dominion in the New World within the context of this wider debate about the metaphysics of dominion in the Old World, it is easy to see why the notion of natural slavery did not overall occupy a very prominent place in "De indis." It is mentioned twice, once in the conclusion to Question 1, only in order to be refuted as an objection to his argument that the American Indians "undoubtedly possessed true dominion" before the arrival of the Spaniards; and a second time at the very end of Question 3, where its appearance is notable for its logical inconsistency with the seven points about potential just titles preceding it. I say "logical inconsistency" because the previous seven points all treated the question of Spanish rights of dominion in the New World in the context of natural law, in particular the law of nations and just war theory (i.e., titles 1, 2, 5, 7), as well as canon law (titles 3, 4, 6). Title 8, by contrast, deals not with natural law, the law of nations, or just war theory at all. Instead, it considers the possibility of deriving a Spanish title of dominion not from the discourses of law or theology but from an entirely different discourse, namely that of "philosophy," particularly the theory of natural slavery derived from classical (i.e., pagan) Aristotelianism:

> There is one further title which may be mentioned for the sake of the argument, though certainly not asserted with confidence; it may strike some as legitimate, though I myself do not dare either to affirm or condemn it out of hand. It is this: these barbarians, though not totally mad . . . , are nevertheless so close to being mad, that they are unsuited to setting up or administering a commonwealth both legitimate and ordered in human and civil terms. . . . It might therefore be argued that for their own benefit the princes of Spain might take over their administration, and set up urban officers and governors on their behalf, or even give them a new master, so long as this could be proved to be in their interest. . . . But I say this, as I have already made clear, merely for the sake of argument; and even then, with the limitation that only applies if everything is done for the benefit and good of the barbarian, and not merely for the profit of the Spaniards.[59]

The highly tentative and speculative manner in which Vitoria presents this deliberative argument is noteworthy. Unlike in his treatment of the first seven "just titles," here he does not come to a conclusion as to whether or not a just title for Spanish dominion in America could be claimed on the basis of natural slavery or whether the concept could even be applied to the American Indians. And even *if* the answer were to be found to be affirmative, the justness of such a title would still depend on the implementation of a regime that is mutually agreed upon by Indians and Spaniards alike and has beneficial outcomes for both. Most importantly, even though he does consider the possibility that natural slavery might constitute a just title for Spanish dominion in the New World, nowhere does Vitoria say or suggest that natural slavery is a just cause for waging war. All of this—as well as the fact that natural slavery is not mentioned in any of his other writings—suggests that Vitoria's discussion of the notion of natural slavery in the context of the question of Spanish rights of dominion in America may well have been an afterthought in "De indis" in which he tackled a rather newfangled idea about which he was quite uncertain.

As is well known by now, Vitoria had probably first encountered this idea in the writings of the Scottish theologian John Mair, the "chief" of the nominalist school of the College of Montaigu at the University of Paris.[60] Vitoria had studied there under Pierre Crockert, a Flemish student of Mair's who was at first taken with his teacher's Ockhamian nominalism before fully realigning himself with the Thomist revival.[61] In 1519, in his commentary on book 2 of Peter Lombard's *Sentences,* Mair had explained:

> This nation [of the Indians] lives like beasts on either side of the equator; and beneath the poles there are wild men as Ptolemy says in his *Quadrapertito* [Tetrabiblos] And this has now been found by experience, wherefore the first person to occupy them, justly rules over them; for they are by nature slaves. To clarify: in the third and fourth chapters of the first book of the *Politics,* the Philosopher [Aristotle] says that some men are manifestly slaves by nature [and] others by nature free; and in some men it is determined that there is such a thing and that they should benefit from it. And it is just that one man should be a slave and another free, and it is fitting that one man should rule and another obey, for the quality of leadership is also inherent in the natural master. Therefore, Aristotle, in the first chapter of that book says that the Greeks should rule the barbarians.[62]

As Anthony Pagden has noted in his important discussion of the history of the concept of natural slavery in the conquest of America, the originality of this argument inheres in Mair's invocation of a classical pagan authority (Aristotle) on subjects (the rights of dominion and just war theory) that had been the exclusive province of theologians and canon lawyers during the thirteenth, fourteenth, and fifteenth centuries.[63] What's more, Mair's highly unusual amalgamation of theology, law, and philosophy had the effect of confusing two conceptions of "dominion" that had been understood to be separate in Scholastic natural law theory: the right of property on the one hand and the right to rule on the other. As Vitoria pointed out in "De indis," even *if* the American Indians were Aristotelian natural slaves who were destined by nature to be ruled by natural lords (such as the Spaniards), Aristotle certainly did not mean to say that such men thereby belong by nature to others and have no rights of ownership over their own bodies and possession (*dominium sui et rerum*). Such slavery is a civil and legal condition, to which no man can belong by nature. Nor did Aristotle mean that it is lawful to seize the goods and lands, and enslave and sell the persons, of those who are by nature less intelligent. What he meant to say was that such men have a natural deficiency, because of which they need others to govern and direct them. It is good that such men should be subordinate to others, like children to their parents until they reach adulthood, and like a wife to her husband. That this was Aristotle's true intention is apparent from his parallel statement that some men are "natural masters" by virtue of their superior intelligence. He certainly did not mean by this that such men had a legal right to arrogate power to themselves over others on the grounds of their superior intelligence, but merely that they are fitted by nature to be princes and guides. Hence, granting that these barbarians are as foolish and slow-witted as people say they are, it is still wrong to use this as ground to deny their true dominion (*dominium*); nor can they be counted among the slaves.[64]

Vitoria is referring here to the distinction that Aristotle had drawn in the *Politics* between two types of "slaves" (*doulos*)—natural slaves and those who are only slaves "by law."[65] Whereas, according to Aristotle, the former originates in the natural "fact" that all men are born unequal, legal slavery originates not in nature but in war or as a punishment for crime. Vitoria insisted on an absolute distinction between the two concepts because, in his understanding of Aristotle, a legal slave has no rights of dominion in either sense, whereas a natural slave is ruled but not owned, thus retaining his or her right to property (*dominium rerum*).

Although Mair was explicitly talking about not property but rule when referring to Aristotle's concept in the passage quoted above, the language he employed to describe the American Indians—"a nation who lives like beasts" (*populus ille bestialiter vivit*) and "men like wild animals" (*homines ferini*) living in the margins of the known world—clearly invoked not only the tradition of the wild man derived from the classical geographic imagination, with its environmental determinisms,[66] but also the category *Ferae bestiae* in Roman private law. If the Indians are themselves "like wild beasts," as Mair claimed, they are not legitimate holders of property but subject to appropriation by the first natural lord who discovers and "occupies" them (*primus eos occupans*). Indeed, in the *Digest of Justinian*, it was precisely the example of "wild beasts" that was used to elucidate the rights of discovery. As Andrew Fitzmaurice has explained, "Roman law discussions of occupation had been concerned with private law and dominion over things of property.... The distinction between the occupation of property, in private law, and of sovereignty, in the *ius gentium* (later the law of nations), would be vital to questions of the justice of empire through to the twentieth century."[67] This is an important observation that sheds light on the origins of the New World exceptionalism that emerged during the sixteenth century in the *ius gentium* with regard to the American Indians, to whom the distinction between the two senses of dominion—private property and the right to rule—would no longer apply by the nineteenth century, under the so-called Doctrine of Discovery referred to by Judge Marshall in *Johnson v. M'Intosh*.[68]

However, it would be a serious misreading of Vitoria to attribute to him the confusion of these two senses of dominion, as Fitzmaurice seems to do;[69] rather, the confusion of the right to property and the right to rule in the context of the conquest of America had originated with Mair's commentary on the Lombard, which brought classical pagan ideas derived from Ptolemy (only rediscovered in the Latin West in the fifteenth century) and Aristotle to bear on theological questions of dominion. Vitoria clearly recognized this when, in Question 2 ("Unjust Titles"), Article 3, he focused precisely on the law *Ferae bestiae* in order to refute its applicability to the *land* of America. His argument made explicit what the Scottish *neoterici* had left implicit—only to nip it in the bud:

> This title by right of discovery (*in iure inventionis*) was the only title alleged in the beginning, and it was with this pretext alone that Columbus of Genoa first set sail. And it seems [to some] that this title is valid because ... all things which are unoccupied or deserted become the property of the occupier by natural law and the law of nations, according to the law *Ferae bestiae* (*Institutes* II.1.12). Hence it follows that the Spaniards, who were the first to discover and occupy these countries, must by right possess them, just as if they had discovered a hitherto uninhabited desert.[70]

But, Vitoria objects, "we need not argue long" to dispense with this line of reasoning, given that he has already established (in Question 1) that "the barbarians possessed true public and private dominion" at the time of the Spaniards' arrival. Though the Indians may be "barbarians," they are humans, not "*Ferae bestiae*." As such, they were the lawful owners of their lands, and the Spaniards' arrival in the New World was not an act of "discovery" in the sense of this law (*in iure inventionis*)—which, hence, "provides no support for possession of these lands, any more than it would if they had discovered us."[71]

That Vitoria did not confuse dominion in property with dominion in rule is evident even where he does grant (in Question 3, Article 4) that the law *Ferae bestiae* may give Spanish titles to *some* things in the New World. Thus, he argues that "if there are any things among the barbarians which are held in common both by their own people and by strangers, it is not lawful for the barbarians to prohibit the Spaniards from sharing and enjoying them."[72] Perhaps not by coincidence, the first example that comes to his mind is that of "travelers [who] are allowed to dig for gold in common land or in rivers or to fish for pearls in the sea or in rivers." In this case, "the barbarians may not prohibit Spaniards from doing so," because hidden things that have not yet been discovered by the Indians (such as gold or pearls) "will belong by the law of nations to the first taker, just like the little fishes of the sea."[73] This line of reasoning was, as Orlando Bentancor has convincingly argued, highly influential for laying "the metaphysical basis of [Spanish] imperial ideology," an ideology rationalizing not the colonial appropriation of land or people but the exploitation of the land's hidden natural resources—the secrets of the New World.[74] The evaluation of this imperial ideology must be placed, however, in the context of several other, competing ideologies, such as that of Mair. Unlike Mair, Vitoria argues here that the Spaniards have a just title to these things not because the Indians are themselves a species of *Ferae bestiae* but because they have not themselves yet discovered them and therefore have no more right to them than do the Spaniards. However, according to Vitoria, this law of *Ferae bestiae* does not give the Spaniards a just title to rule the Indians: indeed, he qualifies that the Spaniards are only allowed to dig for gold "on the same terms as the former [i.e., the Indians] namely without causing offence to the native inhabitants and citizens."[75] It was for this reason that the Spanish exploitation of mineral resources in America was built (at least in theory) not on slavery but on pre-Columbian structures of exploiting resources and labor, such as the Andean system of the *mita,* a system of mandatory public service implemented by the Inca Empire and adapted (and intensified) in the Spanish viceroyalty of Peru.[76]

The fact that Vitoria apparently felt it necessary to clarify Aristotle's "true intention" with regard to natural slavery is significant, for it suggests that he was keenly aware of the slippery slope that Mair's confusion of natural slavery with just war theory implied with regard to the rights of dominion: according to Mair's logic, the Spaniards could lawfully force the Indian "natural slaves" into subjection without the latters' consent or provocation; if the Indians resisted their subjection to Spanish rule (*dominium jurisdictionis*), the ensuing armed conflict would be a just war in which the Indians' status would legally be transformed from that of natural slaves to that of legal slaves, who are no longer entitled to their property (*dominium rerum*) but become themselves the legal property of the Spaniards.[77] Essentially, Mair's interpretation of Aristotelian natural slavery as a *causus belli* as well as of American "barbarians" as living like "beasts" and "wild animals" could have the effect of rendering the Indians, though born free by nature, into chattel slaves. As we will see, it was precisely this rhetorical alchemy on which Sepúlveda's apology of the Spanish conquest was founded. Indeed, Sepúlveda explicitly named Mair in his *Apologia* among the authors whose works, he felt, support his defense of the conquest. Las Casas, for his part, called Mair's notions a "scandal and impediment to the faith" from which Sepúlveda had "taken his poison."[78]

The idea that the enslavement of barbarians constitutes a just reason for war was so preposterous to the Thomists that Domingo de Soto did not even mention it in his *Reclectio de dominio* (1534), written some five years before Vitoria gave his famous lecture "De indis" at Salamanca.[79] There, De Soto offered a general theory of dominion in the context of which he considered the arguments for Spanish titles in the New World customarily cited by the apologists of the Conquest, most notably the papal bulls *Inter caetera* and Charles V's claim to universal empire as sovereign of the Holy Roman Empire and as descendant of the ancient Roman Empire.[80] Some fifteen years before presiding over the debate between Sepúlveda and Las Casas at Valladolid, Domingo de Soto already concluded that any Spanish claims to temporal dominion in the New World were illegitimate and that the American Indians were the only rightful lords over their lands. Thus, he points out that the Roman Empire has never been a universal empire—not in ancient times and especially not in modern time, considering all the new lands that have been discovered and never known about. Similarly, he considers the argument that Pope Alexander VI's bulls *Inter cetera* constitute a just title for Spanish dominion in America but objects that the pope has no authority to grant pagan dominions to Christian lords because the pope is the temporal representative of Christ, who never had temporal dominion over even as little as a single village. So, by what right do Spaniards maintain an overseas empire in America?, De Soto asked. "In truth," he answered, "I have no idea."

> In the Gospels, it says "Go, preach the Gospel to all creatures." Here we are given the right of preaching in every place of the land and, consequently, we are also given the right to defend ourselves from whoever would impede the preaching.... But, beyond that, to take their property or to subdue them to our empire, I don't see from where such a right would be derived. When the Lord sent his disciples to preach, he did not send them like lions but like sheep in

the middle of wolves, not only without arms but without a stick, without a bag, without bread, and without money.[81]

From Nominalist Metaphysics to Humanist Philology: John Mair's Epistemological Eclecticism

Before turning to Sepúlveda, it will be useful to consider briefly Mair's argument in the context of the intellectual milieu in which it originated. The shifting political contexts and alignments discussed above would seem to provide one such plausible context: thus, Mair had written the first redactions of his commentaries on Peter Lombard's *Sentences* in Paris in the 1510s, before the impact of Montesinos's and Las Casas's indictments of Spanish cruelties was felt in Europe and before the election of Charles as Holy Roman Emperor.[82] By contrast, Vitoria wrote his "De indis" twenty years later at Salamanca in the wake of Las Casas's political activism and the Habsburgs' attempts to put into place stronger protections for the Indians and to roll back the neofeudal privileges that Ferdinand had granted to the conquerors. However, another (and overall more plausible) answer can be found in the fundamental differences between Vitoria's and Mair's theological alignments with regard to metaphysics and epistemology, specifically Vitoria's retrenchment into Neo-Scholastic Thomism on the one hand and Mair's "modern" epistemological eclecticism on the other. Mair's eclecticism had three basic and interrelated features that coalesced in his writing: his attachment to the nominalist metaphysics that was the hallmark of the College of Montaigu at the University of Paris; the influence of the Italian humanist understanding of just war theory; and the Parisian humanists' "recovery" of Aristotle from the Scholastic tradition. Nominalist metaphysics—due to its separation of the natural from the supernatural realm—had long predisposed its medieval Scholastic followers toward theological reform movements; and in the late fifteenth and sixteenth centuries, its followers in the western European academies were particularly receptive to the influences of Italian and northern European humanism. Due to his epistemological eclecticism, Mair has been notoriously difficult to categorize but most often has been described by modern historians as a Renaissance Aristotelian, as a transitory figure who straddled the early sixteenth-century divide between Scholastic Aristotelianism and the new humanist understanding of Aristotle that resulted in a new wave of translations whose authors, such as Leonardo Bruni, self-consciously attempted to distinguish their work from the "barbaric" translations produced by the Scholastics.[83]

Mair's writings about the nature of dominion offer important insights into the transition from Scholastic nominalist metaphysics to Renaissance humanist epistemology. Thus, his discussion of the American Indians (cited above) came in the forty-fourth "distinction" of his commentary on book 2 of Peter Lombard's *Sentences,* where he discussed the legitimacy of Christian rule not only over pagans (such as the American Indians) but also over infidels, mainly the "Saracens" (Arab Muslims) and Ottoman Turks—hardly people who could be mistaken as living like beasts or wild animals.[84] This discussion of Christian rule over infidels and pagans was presented as a series of examples in a more general discussion about the Scholastic concept of synderesis, the notion that all men were, by the nature of their reason, inclined to seek their true creator and endowed with a natural knowledge (the counterpart of animal instinct) of God's natural law. Specifically, Mair engaged there in a dispute with the German nominalist theologian Gabriel Biel. Mair followed Biel in his rejection of the Thomist idea that synderesis was a principle innate to universal human reason. But whereas Biel considered synderesis to be equivalent with the potency of practical human intellect itself, for Mair, it was a conscious act of assent that is not inherent in human reason but dependent on the truth of Christian revelation, law, and ethics, given that human conscience is often erroneous and the human will weak. In other words, the Christian faith was the precondition not only for salvation but also for true temporal civility, as natural reason unassisted by Christian religion was bound to result in perversion.[85]

This context is noteworthy for it suggests that there was a connection between Mair's defense of the Spanish conquest of America based on Aristotle's concept of natural slavery and his nominalist understanding of dominion. Following Gerson, Mair understood temporal dominion to originate only in postlapsarian human and natural law; and, like Gerson, he denied any metaphysical sanction of temporal dominion by divine or supernatural law. Temporal dominion was upheld not by divine law but only by the divine will. Mair hereby drew on the tradition of the Parisian Conciliarists not only in their attack on the Thomist concept of synderesis but also in their rejection of any temporal dominion of the pope. Thus, in his commentary on the Fourth Sentence of Peter Lombard, Mair categorically asserted that "the pope does not have temporal dominion over kings."[86] Nevertheless, as God wants all men to be saved, the church (meaning the pope, the council of bishops, and priests) does have the right to appoint temporal rulers to subdue infidels by force of arms in order to facilitate conversion. Thus, he argues in his commentary on book 1 of Lombard's *Sentences* that infidels who do not permit proselytization—or who permit it but do not convert—are "impeding God's glory" and are therefore "useless for the republic" and "enemies of the faith" who can be made war upon.[87] In the presence of a Christian lord attempting to proselytize, any natural rights by which a pagan or infidel lord might legitimately rule are suspended. To Mair's mind, the interference of the divine will in human affairs represents a justified suspension of natural law, as its correspondence with divine law is uncertain and ulimately unknowable.

But by introducing Aristotle's argument about natural slavery, Mair denied that Amerindian rule was sanctioned not only by supernatural law but also by natural law. And, given his denial of a connection between the two, his argument was hereby derived not from theology but from philosophy. Though not quite yet a humanist, Mair was willing to experiment with method and attempted to synthesize the old Scholastic approach to theology with the new ideas of Italian humanism. Thus, Mair asked in the typical fashion of the sixteenth-century moderns: "Has not Amerigo Vespucci in these times discovered lands that were unknown to Ptolemy, Pliny, and other geographers up to this present age? Why cannot the same happen in other realms?"[88] Mair's experimentalism with modern ideas and methods is perhaps nowhere as evident as in his *Dialogus de materia theologo tractanda* (Dialogue on the subject matter that should be investigated by a theologian), which appeared as a sort of preface to the first (1510) and second (1519) redactions of his commentaries on book 1 of Lombard's *Sentences*.[89] While the main parts of the commentaries are written in the conventional fashion of textual expositions, in the *Dialogue* he experiments with a form adopted from the Italian humanist tradition. The subject of the *Dialogue* is not Lombard's text but the question of what the task of a theologian such as himself should be. Thus, the *Dialogue* introduces two historical characters—Gavin Douglass and David Cranston—who discuss the merits of Mair's theological writings, as follow in the main part of the commentary. Douglass, a Scottish luminary at the University of St Andrews who had translated Virgil's *Aeneid* into Scots, plays the part of the humanist in assessing Mair's work. Cranston, a priest of the Glasgow diocese and one-time student of Mair's at Montaigu, plays the part of the defender of Mair's Scholastic method of writing theology, though (like Mair himself) he was knowledgeable of the new humanist scholarship, citing Gian Francesco Poggio Bracchiolini and other Italian Renaissance humanists. One of the questions that is being discussed is the role that "philosophy" (meaning Aristotle) should play in Christian theology. On the one hand, we have the Scholastic commentary tradition that had, in countless late medieval expositions and distinctions, explained what Aristotle, the Gospels, and the Testament "meant to say" (in Vitoria's phrase) by synthesizing classical pagan ideas with Christian theology. On the other hand, we have the humanists, who would dispense with the commentaries and return to the Greek and Hebrew originals of Aristotle and the Bible in order to discover what they had *in fact* said. The latter position is put into the mouth of Douglass: "I cannot see how it benefits theology to go on and on about so many futile topics, such as relations, intension of form, whether one should posit points in a continuum, and so on, because these things do not serve as an approach to theology. Instead they obfuscate and darken."[90] Douglass's modern criticism of the Scholastic method had earlier been put into the form of a biting satire on Mair by the German Protestant humanist Philip Melanchthon: "I have seen John Major's Commentaries on Peter Lombard," he wrote; "he is now, I am told, the prince of the Paris divines. Good heavens! What a wagon-load of trifling! What pages he fills with disputes whether there can be any horsemanship without a horse, whether the sea was salty when God made it."[91] Later, Mair again became the target of humanist satire by none less than François Rabelais, when his character Pantagruel discovers in the Library of St. Victor's in Paris a book entitled "*The Art of making Pudding,* by John Major."[92] Yet, it was an evident humanist influence, championed at the University of Paris by such prominent scholars as the Llullian Jacques Lefèvre d'Étaples, that informed Mair's ideas about just war. In the writings of Lefèvre d'Étaples and Mair, the Aristotelian idea of natural slavery was absorbed into a long tradition of Christian just war theory that has roots in Ciceronian ethics but was developed during the early Middle Ages by St. Augustine and his student Paulus Orosius, as well as, during the Italian Renaissance, by Andrea Alciato, Alberico Gentili, and the first humanist pope, Aeneio Silvio Piccolomini (Pope Pius II).[93]

Finally, besides the influence of nominalist metaphysics and the humanist interpretation of just war, yet another context for understanding Mair's use of natural slavery in the justification of the Spanish conquest can be found in the historical hermeneutics and textual transmission of the concept of natural slavery itself. This is to say that the "Aristotle" whom Vitoria cited in his "De indis" was not the same "Aristotle" cited by the "moderns" such as Mair and (later) Sepúlveda.[94] Whereas Vitoria's interpretation of Aristotle followed closely along the lines of the medieval translations of the Aristotelian corpus and the tradition of the Thomist commentaries, Mair's and Sepúlveda's interpretations of Aristotle were informed not only by a more eclectic range of Scholastic commentary traditions but also by the new humanist philology. The effect of this humanist recovery of Aristotle was the un- (or dis-)covery of a classical pagan worldview that had been utterly alien to late medieval Europe. This philology had cut through some of the obscurities of the medieval Latin translations of the *Politics* and its Scholastic commentary traditions, which, in ever-subtler distinctions and subdistinctions, had gradually overlaid Aristotle's pagan ideas with Christian hermeneutics. Martha Nussbaum and Amélie Rorty have called this process of reconciling Aristotle's pagan notions with Aquinas's Christian ideas in Scholastic (and especially Thomist) textual scholarship an enterprise in Aristotelian theodicy—the attempt to "use Aristotle's excellence and authority to bolster and flesh out a picture of the world that would be an acceptable foundation for Christian life and discourse."[95] One of the aspects of this "Aristotelian theodicy" concerned the adaptation of Aristotle's discussion of natural slavery to the context of late medieval Europe. It was this tradition that informed Vitoria's discussion of natural slavery in "De indis."[96]

The Hermeneutics of Natural Slavery

In order to elucidate the differences between Vitoria's and Sepúlveda's (and Mair's) readings of Aristotle, it is, at this point, necessary to take a closer look at the concept of natural slavery and its history. It is rooted in Aristotle's pagan understanding of nature as an ontologically more or less continuous hierarchical system in which the less perfect is destined to be ruled by the more perfect. Aristotle had called this the "ruling principle, as in the case of a musical scale," a principle that pervaded all of nature.[97] Within this hierarchical scale, a natural slave is a man "who participates in reason so far as to apprehend it but not to possess it," as Aristotle explained in the *Politics*. In *De anima,* he further theorized that all living things participate in "soul," but that there are three levels of soul: vegetative, sensitive, and rational.[98] Whereas plants participate only in the "vegetative soul," animals participate in both the vegetative and the sensitive soul, and man participates in all three levels, including also the highest level of rational soul. In this hierarchical scale, natural slaves still belong to the human race—whom Aristotle conceived as a higher form of animal—but his or her "participation" in the rational soul is limited, in comparison with that of a "freeman" (or a natural lord). That is, the natural slave participates in the rational soul only by "apprehending" its existence, but not by "possessing it."[99] The natural slave is thus lower on the scale of nature than a freeman (who not only apprehends but also possesses reason) and higher on the scale than an animal, "for animals other than man are subservient not to reason, by apprehending it, but to feelings."[100] As such, natural slaves might be comparable to madmen and children, except that, unlike madness, natural slavery is not a disease but a natural condition of birth; and, unlike children, natural slaves do not outgrow their rational deficiency, even though their reason can be improved by contact with freemen.

Although the difference between natural slaves and freedmen need not always be physically manifest, in the *Politics* Aristotle further ventured that there are entire nations who are natural slaves, who are called "barbarians" and who are destined by nature to be ruled by the Greeks. These barbarians are people who do not speak Greek and, more generally, are "far distant non-Greek races."[101] The distinguishing feature that marks the Greeks for freedom as citizens rather than slaves vis-à-vis these distant races is their well-balanced, median "temper," which is compromised in the latter by influences of the natural environment outside the Mediterranean, such as excessive heat or cold:

> Let us now speak of what ought be the citizens' natural character. Now this one might almost discern by looking at the famous cities of Greece and by observing how the whole inhabited world is divided up among the nations. The nations inhabiting the cold places and those of Europe are full of spirit but somewhat deficient in intelligence and skill, so that they continue comparatively free, but lacking in political organization and capacity to rule their neighbors. The peoples of Asia on the other hand are intelligent and skillful in temperament, but lack spirit, so that they are in continuous subjection and slavery. But the Greek race participates in both characters, just as it occupies the middle position geographically, for it is both spirited and intelligent; hence it continues to be free and to have very good political institutions, and to be capable of ruling all mankind if it attains constitutional unity. The same diversity also exists among the Greek races compared with one another: some have a one-sided nature, others are happily blended in regard to both these capacities.[102]

As both the natural lord and the natural slave benefit from the arrangement of natural slavery, war is for Aristotle a just means by which to procure slaves. It is akin to hunting animals in order to domesticate them for service. Both natural slave and natural lord benefit hereby, as the natural lord can dispose of the natural slave's labor, and the latter, like a domesticated animal, benefits from the former's protection. Thus, "the art of war will by nature be in a manner an art of acquisition (for the art of hunting is part of it) that is properly employed both against wild animals and against such of mankind as though designed by nature for subjections refuse to submit to it, inasmuch as this warfare is by nature just."[103] If there is war between two groups of natural lords, it may still happen that the vanquished is enslaved by the victor. In this case, the vaquished becomes a slave in law only, and his or her status would be unnatural and the war that caused the enslavement may have been unjust, unless there were other just reasons. (This, of course, would be especially unnatural and unjust in the case of barbarians enslaving Greeks.)

As we will see momentarily, it was this famous passage of Aristotle's *Politics*, 1256b20–25 in the Bekker numbering—in which the hunt for natural slaves is defined as a just war according to the laws of nature and in which human beings are put into the same category with "wild animals"—with which the Thomists had most difficulties, as it violated the Christian ontological distinction between man and animal. But for Aristotle a slave is, by definition, not owner of his or her person or things, "for he is by nature a slave who is capable of belonging to another (and that is why he does so belong)."[104] In fact, Aristotle discussed slavery in the context of "the art of acquiring property [as] a part of household management," which is the most basic unit of human social life: "The investigation of everything [with regard to politics] should begin with its smallest parts . . . and the primary and smallest parts of the household are master and slave, husband and wife, father and children."[105] Unlike husband, wife, and children, however, a slave is not only a part of the natural hierarchy of rule; rather he or she is a living "tool"; a slave is "a live article of property."[106]

As both legal and natural slavery can be a consequence of war, it may happen in Aristotle's scheme that some who are born natural slaves are legally free, while others who are born naturally free are legally slaves. A slave in law only is physically indistinguishable from a freeman, but a natural slave is often marked so by nature. For example, in *De anima,* Aristotle argued that, overall, the sense of smell is less developed in man than in other animals, but man excels in touch. However, with regard to touch, "the human race divides into the naturally well endowed and the naturally unendowed based on this sense organ rather than any other: the tough-skinned are naturally lacking in thinking, while the soft-skinned are naturally well-endowed."[107] And in the *Politics,* he argued that "the intention of nature . . . is to make the bodies . . . [of] Freemen and of slaves very different—the latter strong for necessary service, the former erect and unserviceable for such occupations, but serviceable for a life of citizenship." However, Aristotle admits nature has not always worked out this difference perfectly, so that natural slaves are not always physically distinguishable from natural freemen. Sometimes, even "the opposite comes about—slaves have the bodies of freemen and freemen the souls only; since this is certainly clear, that if freemen were born as distinguished in body as are the statues of the gods, everyone would say that those who were inferior deserved to be these men's slaves." Ultimately, the criterion differentiating between a natural slave and a freeman inheres in the difference in their rational soul. And since the soul rules the body, it is just that those with a superior rational soul should rule those with an inferior one.[108]

One important consequence of this natural difference between the slave and the lord concerns the capacity for science, for science depends on "prudence" and the "deliberative" intellect, which is restricted to the rational soul. While the deliberative intellect is imperfectly present in women and children, it is entirely absent in the natural slave: "All possess the various parts of soul, but possess them in various ways; for the slave has not got the deliberative part at all, and the female has it, but without full authority, while the child has it but in underdeveloped form."[109] With regard to cognitive abilities necessary for different kinds of labor, the natural slave is above livestock or inanimate tools that aid the natural lord in his work. While some of Aristotle's contemporaries, such as Xenophon, had extolled the virtues of manual labor in freemen (especially that of the farmer), Aristotle sees it as the expression of a servile nature.[110] The same is true for Aristotle's conception of intellectual labor necessary in science, for true science is for him both experiential *and* speculative. In the *Metaphysics,* Aristotle argued that all knowledge begins with experience, but he distinguishes between those who know by experience only from those who know by both experience as well as "skill" and "expertise." It is only the latter who can apprehend the significance and causes of experienced phenomena. And it is only the latter who can "move" another by teaching:

> We think that knowledge and expertise belong rather to skill than to experience, and we assume that the skilled are wiser than the experienced, in that it is more in connection with knowledge that wisdom is associated with anything. And the reason for this is that the skilled know the cause, whereas the experienced do not. For the experienced know the "that" but not the "because," whereas the skilled have a grasp of the "because," the cause. That is why in each field designers are thought more prestigious and to have more knowledge than craftsmen and to be wiser, in that they know the causes for what is being done. The assumption is that it is not being practical that makes them wiser but their possession of an account and their grasp of the causes. And in general the ability to teach is a distinguishing mark between the knowledgeable and the ignorant man, and that is why we think that skill is rather a form of knowledge than experience. For the skilled can, whereas the merely experienced cannot, teach.[111]

When considering the legacy of Aristotle's concept of natural slavery in late medieval and early modern Europe, it is important to bear in mind that the *Politics* was unknown in the Latin West until the thirteenth century. Apparently it had never been translated into Arabic and entered the Latin West only with two translations from the Greek by the Flemish Dominican William of Moerbeke (1215–1286), one of the first students of Greek in medieval western Europe who had also translated several other Aristotelian works, including *De anima,* the *Ethics,* the *Rhetoric,* and the *Metaphysics.* Moerbeke produced two translations of the *Politics,* the *translatio imperfecta* in ca. 1260, which included only the first two books, and in 1265 the *tranlatio completa.*

Both had been produced "ad instantiam fratris Thomae" (at the instigation of Fray Thomas [Aquinas]).[112] However, the first Scholastic to use the *Politics* in reference to the topic of slavery was not Aquinas but his teacher and fellow Dominican Albertus Magnus. In his commentary on passage 1256b20–25 of the *Politics,* Albertus wrote: "Whoever are born to subjection and are naturally slaves (as was shown earlier), if they refuse to be subjected, ought according to nature to be subjected (for it is just according to nature that they be subjected). Consequently just war can be made on them, and this was the cause of the first war."[113] How did Albertus reconcile this interpretation with Christian doctrine? Before the impact of the *Politics,* all Christian commentators followed the Apostle Paul and St. Augustine in assuming that all men were *born* equally free by nature and that slavery was essentially unnatural. The existence of slavery in the postlapsarian world was understood by Latin Christian writers as a punishment for human sin, both for collective original sin and individual sins. The key medieval text was book 4 of Peter Lombard's *Sentences,* which dealt with the sacraments and discussed the problem of slavery in the context of marriage—whether free and enslaved persons could marry, whether two enslaved persons belonging to two different lords could marry without their masters' consent, and so on. Starting from this basic tension between the Christian idea of man's natural equality in freedom and the Aristotelian understanding of man's natural inequality, Albertus began to assimilate the Aristotelian notion of natural slavery by introducing "distinctions" in his commentaries on the Lombard's *Sentences.* What do we mean, he asked, by human "nature": Is it (1) that which is common to all human beings, or is it that which has a natural reason? If the latter, is it (2) a natural reason in itself or (3) only something that originates in nature? From this point of view, slavery would not be natural in the first two senses, but it would be in the third sense.[114] Thus, war can be made on a person who possesses natural reason but whose reason "originates in nature."

We will return shortly to the question of what Albertus may have had in mind by "reason that originates in nature." Here, it will suffice to note that Albertus's interpretation that war can justly be made on natural slaves remained a possible view throughout the Middle Ages. However, it was soon qualified by the subsequent commentaries on the *Politics* by his student Thomas Aquinas, who utterly rejected the idea that enslavement could constitute a just reason for war.[115] Although Aquinas generally confined his commentaries to an "exposition" of Aristotle's text—which is to say that his commentaries do not present his own opinions or critiques of Aristotle but only his paraphrases and occasional explanations—they do provide insight into his distinctive interpretations of Aristotle's ideas, whether it be in the way of emphasis, clarification, or simply omission.[116] For example, in his commentary on book 1 of the *Politics*, Aquinas amplified Aristotle's original distinction between two types of slavery—natural and legal: "We speak of slavery and slaves in two ways. One way regards natural suitability, as he [Aristotle] has said before. But there is also a kind of slave or servitude by human law. For law declares that war captives are slaves of the victors, and almost all people observe it, and so also we call it a common law of peoples."[117]

With regard to Aristotle's notion of the "ruling principle" of nature, Aquinas's commentary on book 1 of the *Politics* echoes Aristotle's musical metaphor ("scale") by writing that "we can understand it in one way regarding musical harmony, since harmonious sounds always have one that predominates, one by which we judge the whole harmony. We can also understand it about the harmony of elements in a mixed material substance, in which one of the elements always predominates."[118] Aquinas's metaphor of predominance in harmonies of sounds and elements slightly shifts the emphasis on hierarchical instrumentality in Aristotle's original—where the less perfect exists in nature only to serve for the benefit of the more perfect—to an emphasis on interdependency, reciprocity, and mutual benefit of the organic whole of society: for a sound is not naturally dominant by itself but only becomes so in its relationship to other sounds in the context of a harmony. By the same token, an element such as fire is not naturally predominant over another such as earth except within the particular mixtures that constitute nature's diverse substances. In other words, inequality is for Aquinas not natural but social.

Moreover, whereas Aristotle's slave was not in possession of his body or things, Aquinas treats the issue of natural slavery entirely in terms of rule. In Aquinas's commentaries, natural slavery arises organically for the social benefit of all, given that some are suitable to rule while other are suitable to be ruled. As such, it is analogous to other natural distinctions in the universal hierarchy of the more perfect ruling the less perfect, such as that between soul and body, man and women, adult and child, and so on.[119] Even where he does acknowledge that Aristotle's slave "belongs absolutely to the master," he clarifies that this relationship of belonging is not one of possession or property but of rule and being ruled: "For those who are by nature fit to belong to other, namely, insofar as they can be governed only by the reason of another and not by their own reasons, whereby human beings are master of themselves."[120] The rule that the master has over the slave is a "despotic" rule, as opposed to the "political kind by which the ruler of the political community rules over free persons." This "despotic rule" is again likened to the rule that soul has over the "bodily member such as hands and feet," which "immediately execute their functions at the soul's bidding and without any resistance."[121] Thus, whereas Aristotle's natural slave is the master's possession and serves for the best functioning of the latter's household, Aquinas's natural slave and natural lord are connected in a hierarchical relationship of rule and being ruled that is predicated on mutual dependency and benefit: for a soul does not "own" its body; it *rules* it.

This is different, of course, with regard to legal slavery: while natural slavery proceeds from a difference in birth, legal slavery results from war (or sale). In this case, the slave is not in possession of his person and things, which belong to the master. According to Aquinas, such a form of slavery is "just" only by the standards of "relative justice" of postlapsarian human law but not by the standards of the "absolute justice" of natural law, considering that by nature all men are born free (i.e., not the property of somebody else).[122] Thus, in the *Summa*, he writes:

> A thing is said to belong to the natural law in two ways. First, because nature inclines thereto: e.g. that one should not do harm to another. Secondly, because nature did not bring in the contrary: thus we might say that for man to be naked is of the natural law, because nature did not give him clothes, but art invented them. In this sense, "the possession of all things in common and universal freedom" are said to be of the natural law, because, to wit, the distinction of possessions and slavery were not brought in by nature, but devised by human reason for the benefit of human life. Accordingly the law of nature was not changed in this respect, except by addition.[123]

In effect, Aquinas's interpretation of Aristotle's concept was not "natural" slavery at all but a Christianized version of the concept in which all mankind was still one in being born in the image of God and supplied with the same rational soul at birth. Although Original Sin had "wounded" man's natural reason, it was still universally intact at birth, even among those people whom Aristotle had called "barbarians." It was only after birth that men diversified into "barbarian" and "civilized" as a result of culture, depending on whether his laws and institutions were assisted not only by the natural light of reason but also by the additional light of Christian revelation. True religion thus provided a universal remedy for all but had given an advantage to the Christians, as beneficiaries of revelation. By contrast, the pagan Aristotle recovered by the humanists had seen the differences between natural slaves and natural lords as proceeding from natural (i.e., environmental) conditions in a man's place of birth at birth.

In order to appreciate Aquinas's distinctive interpretations of Aristotelian natural slavery, it is important to bear in mind that he did not read Aristotle in the Greek original but in Moerbeke's Latin translation. Thus, Moerbeke had rendered the Greek word *doulos* as the Latin word *servus*.[124] In Aristotle's ancient Greece, the existence of slavery, whether legal or natural, was normative. By contrast, in Aquinas's feudal society a slave (*sclavus*) was usually a non-Christian captured in a just war, according to St. Augustine's theory. One of those groups of non-Christians taken in a just war during the Middle Ages was the Slavs, and it is from that context that the modern word "slave" originates. By contrast, a "servus" in Aquinas's feudal society was a tenant farmer. While such a person was not the *dominus* in the sense of having rule or jurisdictional control over the land on which he worked, he or she still had rights to the land in the feudal system of divided dominion during the Middle Ages. Most importantly, such a person was not somebody else's property but had dominion over of his or her person and possessions (*dominium sui et rerum*). In this context, Aristotle's concept of natural slavery simply had no application in the social reality of late medieval Europe. There were the so-called monstrous races in the medieval geographical imagination, but those beings were hardly ever seen except in travel literature and maps. By definition, they played no part in medieval social life. The entire Aristotelean notion that there should be entire nations that were less than perfect human beings doubtlessly struck Aquinas as preposterous, considering that, in the Judeo-Christian tradition, man was created in the image of God.

Thus, throughout the later Middle Ages, the reception of Aristotle's theory of natural slavery was strongly filtered through the Scholastic commentaries on the *Politics* and *De anima,* which mediated and modified some of the more blatantly pagan aspects of Aristotle's ideas. As we can see in the example of Moerbeke's translation of the Geek word *doulos* as *servus,* the process of Aristotelian theodicy began even before Aquinas's commentaries, with Moerbeke's translations, which are often fragmentary and frequently differ from the "modern" translations prepared based on the standards of humanist textual scholarship. For example, in the first of his two translations, Moerbeke rendered the passage 1256b20–25 (quoted above) in which Aristotle had called the war on natural slaves "by nature just" (comparing it to a hunt for wild animals) by translating "as if by nature this fundamental and primary war is just."[125] For such obfuscations, Moerbeke was much maligned as a "barbarous" Latinist with limited expertise in classical Greek grammatical structures by the humanists in Aristotelian textual scholarship and translation. Some of these perceived shortcomings may have been the result of the fragmented nature of the Greek original texts from which he worked. But while some of the inaccuracies of his translations appear indeed to have originated from misapprehensions of the Greek original, others probably resulted from his attempt to render Aristotle's ideas in a way that made sense to him in a medieval Christian context.[126]

The "modern" (i.e., humanist) tradition of textual scholarship on Aristotle's *Politics* began with the fifteenth-century translations of several of Aristotle's works by Leonardo Bruni (1370–1444), including the *Politics* (1437), which was printed posthumously in Strasbourg in 1469 to become the most popular translation of the *Politics* in Renaissance Europe, replacing Moerbeke's translation as the preferred version in learned circles.[127] It was probably Bruni's translation, rather than Moerbeke's, that was cited by Mair.[128] But besides Bruni's, the next most influential humanist translation of Aristotle's *Politics* during the sixteenth century was that prepared by the Spanish humanist Juan Ginés de Sepúlveda, published in Paris in 1548. Entitled *Aristotelis de Republica Libri VIII*, it continued Bruni's humanist (and especially Ciceronian) tradition in Aristotelean scholarship. Like Bruni, the humanist Sepúlveda knew Aristotle not only (or primarily) from the Scholastic commentary tradition but also from the Greek manuscript tradition.[129] In that tradition, he would have discovered the concept of natural slavery in terms of a more-or-less continuous hierarchy of nature, in which the "barbarians" (or natural slaves) inhabited a liminal space between animals and humans.

Arguably the controversy between Sepúlveda and Las Casas at Valladolid revolved not only around the question of whether or not Aristotle's concept of natural slavery pertained to the American Indians but also around the question of what precisely was meant by the concept of the natural slave, especially when it came to laws of war and rights of conquest.[130] The different understandings of the concept emerged in part from the different traditions of "Aristotle" still current in the early sixteenth century—one as it had come down from the Scholastic (especially Thomist) tradition and another one from the humanist "recovery" of the classical Greek texts, which cut through the Latin translations and commentaries to expose a thoroughly pagan view of the relationship between human and nonhuman nature that was utterly at odds with Thomist natural law metaphysics. This epistemological difference between the Scholastic and the humanist understanding of the natural slave came to the fore in Sepúlveda's eighth "objection" to De Soto's summary of the debate at Valladolid in the *Disputa*. There, Sepúlveda charged that De Soto and Las Casas had misconstrued his sense of the concept of the natural slave, or the "barbarian." Quoting from Aquinas's commentary on the *Politics*—"Sancto Thomas. 1. politicorum lectione prima"—he explained that by natural slaves, he meant those who "do not live according to natural reason and have bad customs that are publicly approved." As Aquinas had interpreted Aristotle, these bad customs come from a "lack of religion," and a "lack of proper law and punishment," which make men brutal.[131] In other words, Sepúlveda here invokes Aquinas's Christian exposition of Aristotle's theory of natural slavery as a consequence not of birth but of culture and religion.

Why did Sepúlveda feel the need to clarify his position? Was it because De Soto and Las Casas had indeed misconstrued his earlier interpretation of Aristotle's natural slave in the *Democrates alter*? A closer look at the relevant passages in that text suggests that they had not misconstrued his meaning and that his additional elaboration in the *Disputa* was an attempt to qualify some of the more controversial passages of his earlier interpretation. As we will see, Sepúlveda's interpretation of Aristotle's concept in the *Democrates alter* was based on his very keen humanist understanding of the original Greek texts. Moreover, as I will argue in this last section, Sepúlveda's interpretation of natural slavery and his application of the theory to the American Indians was also influenced by another late medieval tradition of Aristotelianism distinct from Thomism: it was the earlier tradition not of Thomas Aquinas but that of his teacher Albertus Magnus, who had argued that war could justly be waged on natural slaves who participate in natural reason but whose reason "originates in nature," not in God's image imprinted upon Adam's original creation. Behind Albertus's interpretation of natural slavery lurked yet another Aristotle—the Aristotle that Albertus knew from the Arabic tradition, which knew of such things as "spontaneous generations," homunculi, alchemical transmutation, and demonic counterfeits.

The Second Democritus and the American Homunculus: Sepúlveda's Humanist Aristotelianism

When considering Sepúlveda's *Democrates alter*, it is first of all necessary to recognize that the rhetorical genre and purpose of the text were fundamentally different from those of Vitoria's *relectio*. In the prologue, Sepúlveda explains that it is his purpose to determine "Whether the wars in which the Kings of Spain and our compatriots have subjected and are subjecting the barbarians to their dominion are just or unjust."[132] But, unlike Vitoria's "De indis," Sepúlveda's text is not a Scholastic exercise in dialectical disputation in which various positions on a topic are subjected to a rigorous test of experience, authority, and syllogistic reason on an epistemologically consistent basis; rather, it is a dialogue in the Italian humanist tradition, adapted to his attempt to persuade his reader that the Spanish conquest of America was a just war. As such, Sepúlveda's argument was essentially a *historical* one; and for the purpose of justification he drew eclectically from a wide array of theological, metaphysical, and philosophical traditions that are often inconsistent with one another, including Thomism, pre-Thomist Scholasticism, and post-Thomist nominalism, classical Aristotelianism, as well as the traditions of Augustinian hierocratic canon law, humanist pre-Socratic materialism, and Machiavellian political philosophy.[133]

Sepúlveda had written the *Democrates alter* in the highly politicized aftermath of the promulgation of the New Laws of 1542, which had translated into law a royalist political assault on the encomienda and, thus, on the neofeudal pretensions of the Spanish conquerors in the New World. This political assault was largely based on the charges by Las Casas and other Dominicans that the conquest had not been a just war. By contrast, Sepúlveda's argument that the conquest had been justified implied that the conquerors and their descendants were entitled to the rights and privileges that are due to a Christian knight (i.e., an encomienda). For Vitoria, the question of Amerindian rights of dominion (in which the problem of natural slavery was only one among several considerations) was a question of *objective rights* as grounded in moral theology and natural law as it related to positive, divine, and eternal law; in other words, it was a question of discovering metaphysical truth by subjecting a question to the regimen of syllogistic reason. By contrast, for the humanist Sepúlveda, the entire *disputa* was primarily a *political* issue and a question of *subjective rights*, which is to say a question of the rights of different groups relative to one other—specifically, the rights of the conquerors and their descendants vis-à-vis the rights of the Indians and vis-à-vis the rights of the Crown. The question of Native American dominion (in which the argument about natural slavery was the centerpiece) was therefore for Sepúlveda one of political philosophy, in which questions of natural law and metaphysics were primarily of rhetorical interest. What mattered was not truth but persuasion; and as such the specific legal and political implications of Sepúlveda's defense of the conquest as a just war in the *Democrates alter* were immediately apparent. Thus, an anonymously published tract (possibly inspired by Las Casas) stated that "the royal chronicler Ginés de Sepúlveda ... composed in an elegant style a small work entitled *De justis belli causis,* in which he, without mentioning them, forcefully impugned the New Laws."[134] Although this judgment may have to be taken with a grain of salt (if indeed it originated with Las Casas or his orbit), a closer look at Sepúlveda's argumentation clearly reveals the political (rather than the metaphysical or theological) nature of the *Democrates alter.*

The main body of the *Democrates alter* is presented in form of a Socratic dialogue between Sepúlveda himself as "Democritus" and "Leopoldo," a German skeptic with regard to the possibility of just wars in general and of the Spanish conquest of America in particular. Leopoldo is a younger man, somewhat naïve and provincial, who appears to be "infected by the Lutheran errors, [which are] the epidemic of his country."[135] Thus, in Sepúlveda's *Democrates alter*, we can observe an interesting inversion of Lorenzo Valla's strategy of engaging with pre-Socratic philosophy that Stephen Greenblatt has called "dialogic disavowal," as well as of the Vespuccian New World variation that I have called "cannibal ventriloquism";[136] whereas in Valla and Vespucci, an interlocutor of pre-Socratic (i.e., Epicurean) materialism appeared in opposition to (and was ostensibly vanquished by) an interlocutor of Christian morality, here the pre-Socratic Democritus *is* the voice of Catholic orthodoxy in defending the justness of Christian conquest against a religious heretic and skeptic. Sepúlveda had already rehearsed this formula in his earlier (1535) *Democrates, sive de convenientia disciplinae militaris cum christiana religione dialogus*, which had also featured the character of Leopoldo, whom Democritus had met at the Vatican and engaged in a dialogue that proved to the young German that the profession of the soldier is not fundamentally in conflict with Christian principles. Basing his arguments mainly on the authorities of Aristotle, Augustine, and Isidore, Sepúlveda elaborated there a general theory of just war but made no reference to Aristotle's notion of natural slavery or the specific legality of the conquest of America. Rather, it was a general philosophical and theological treatment on the Christian humanists' *vita activa*, which entailed the occasional necessity of war.[137]

In this context, Sepúlveda's choice of Democritus in both texts as a mouthpiece for his just-war theory is significant. Democritus is of course best known as a pre-Socratic atomist whose materialist theory of matter was rejected by Scholastic hylomorphism but would play an important role in the scientific revolution after being revived in seventeenth-century mechanical philosophy.[138] However, Democritus's materialist philosophy had a long tradition not only in scientific theories of the structure of matter but also in the history of international law. Oleg Bazaluk (based on the work of the Russian philosopher Alexander Lyubishchev), has posited two central lines of philosophical thought on the question of war and peace in Western culture—the line of Democritus and that of Plato. The Democritan line of political "structural realism" actually had its origins in Thucydides's *History of the Peloponnesian War* (written in the fifth century BC), where the pre-Socratic historian argued that the use of force is "the norm of the political behavior of the fittest."[139] For Thucydides, the real reason for the war between Athens and Sparta—regardless of the moral justifications on both sides—simply came down to the fact that Athens had grown in power and was perceived as an existential threat by the Lacedaemonians. As articulated by Thucydides and Democritus, this idea became the foundation of the later (Christian) humanist theory of preemptive war. Thus, whereas the Stoics developed Plato's notion of a transcendental "'unified world state' formed and existing according to universal reason,"[140] the Democritans (following Thucydides) developed a "materialist" understanding of political being. The materialist line of Thucydides and Democritus was overshadowed by the Platonic line in Christian political philosophy regulating the relations within the Christian Republic as a result of Augustine's conversion to Plotinus's Platonism with regard to the transcendental unity of good and evil. But the Democritan materialist line of political philosophy survived in the tradition of a "realist" and "neorealist" conception of international relations. One of the most important pagan interlocutors of this realist tradition was Cicero, who argued in his *On Duties* (44 BC) that "war is a necessity of the world" and that "the rights of war are to be held sacred. Where there are two ways of contending, one by discussion, the other by force, the former belonging properly to man, the latter to beasts, recourse must be had to the latter if there be no opportunity for employing the former. Wars, then, are to be waged in order to render it possible to live in peace without injury."[141] While Cicero's former way of contending (discussion) was elaborated into an Augustinian and later Thomist metaphysics of just war and law of nations regulating international relations within the medieval Christian republic according to Augustine's Platonic principles, the latter (force) became the foundation of the "realist" tradition regulating man's relationship with beasts. It was Cicero's latter strand, the Democritan materialist tradition, of thinking about war that was revived in 1513 by Machiavelli in *The Prince*. There, Machiavelli announced a radical break with the Augustinian tradition of the Middle Ages of understanding the world in a metaphysical relationship between the City of God and the City of Man by making the earthly city alone the focus of empirical analysis, including the question of war and peace. Machiavelli hereby "revived and developed the ancient views on war and peace in line with Thucydides" and concluded that "Christian morality is not the basis of policy and political relations," thus "freeing politics from theological dogmas" and proving that "war and peace are immanent states of bilateral relations."[142]

Bazaluk's summary of the materialist line of Democritus in Western thinking about war and peace is instructive for understanding Sepúlveda's choice of the pre-Socratic atomist as a mouthpiece for his justification of the conquest of America in *Democrates alter*. Democritus and Leopoldo have met again, this time in Valladolid, taking a walk on the Pisguera River. Leopoldo explains that, during a recent stay with some friends at the palace of Prince Philip, he had the good fortune to meet Hernando Cortés, by whom he was informed of the "great feats that he and the other captains of the Emperor Charles had performed in the western and southern regions that had been entirely unknown to the ancients of our parts." However, Leopoldo was also haunted by "doubts and concerns about whether the war that the Spaniards have waged against those innocent mortals was sufficiently in conformity with Christian justice and piety, and whether they [the Natives] were not done some wrong."[143] Democritus replies by chiding Leopoldo for having relapsed into his earlier skepticism: "Now you again fall into your ineptitude, Leopoldo, and I can see that we wasted much time in that discussion at the Vatican ... about the dignity of the military profession, since I could [apparently] not convince you that sometimes waging war is not opposed to the law of the gospels."[144] An apologetic and deferential Leopoldo assures Democritus how much he had learned from the earlier conversation at the Vatican about the virtues of the military profession but confesses that he has again "been seduced by the new errors of his German countrymen," as a result of which he now has new doubts about the possibilities of a just war. In particular, he is curious to learn more about the Spanish conquest of America, which is to say "those remote islands and that other continent, which has recently been discovered by the Spaniards in their maritime incursions and subjected to their dominion by the force of arms." Of course, Democritus is happy to oblige in relieving his young friend with his moral dilemmas. Thus ensues a (rather monologic) "dialogue" in which Leopoldo gets to ask questions of clarification and make objections that provide the prompts for Democritus's disquisitions.

Though at first not addressing the Spanish conquest of America in particular, Democritus expounds on just war theory in terms of natural law, as defined by Thomas Aquinas as man's "participation in eternal law through reason."[145] In order to be just, he explains, a war must first of all be conducted by a legitimate authority, meaning a state.[146] In terms of the just causes for war, Democritus invokes Aristotelian-Thomist metaphysics in order to argue that, first, it is just and natural to oppose force with force.[147] Second, a war is justified when it rights a wrong, such as something wrongfully taken. Third, a war can be just when it is waged for revenge and punishment for offenses, such as mortal sins or violations of natural law. Leopoldo objects, citing Deuteronomy, that only God has the right to punish violations of higher law, such as natural and divine law. As the law of nations exists somewhere in between civil law and natural law, its violation stands beyond man's jurisdiction. However, Democritus replies, sometimes God does not punish personally or directly; nor does he wait until Judgment Day; rather, he often enacts temporal punishment through his "ministers" who carry out his divine will. Of course, this last point—essentially an argument for a messianic interpretation of history—presented a major departure from Thomist natural law metaphysics and had been utterly rejected by Vitoria (but embraced by Cortés and the Franciscans, as we saw).

Despite Leopoldo's explicit interest in the conquest of America, Democritus only at this point turns to those "barbarians" of the new continent, who are "commonly called Indians." And it is at this point only that he introduces "yet other reasons for just war." Although they are not of "wide or frequent application," he explains, they are nonetheless "held to be thoroughly just and based in natural and divine law. One of these, the most applicable to those barbarians commonly called Indians, whose defense you seem to have taken up, is as follows: that those whose natural condition is such that they must obey others, if they refuse that lordship and there is no other recourse, may be subdued by arms; and that this war is just according to the opinion of the most eminent philosophers."[148] The following exchange is worth quoting in full:

> Leopoldo: "What strange doctrine have you here expounded, Democritus, very remote from anything that humans have opined before."
> Democritus: "Strange perhaps, but only to those whose entry into philosophy has stopped at the doorstep. And so I wonder how a man as erudite as you could hold as new an ancient doctrine [known] among the philosophers and in conformance with natural law."
> Leopoldo: Should somebody have been born so unfortunately as to be condemned by nature to live in slavery?[149]

Democritus explains that the "philosophers" have since antiquity used the word "servitude" for innate slowness in understanding. He then rehearses the Aristotelian hylomorphic principle, according to which the less perfect serve the more perfect, a principle that includes both animate and inanimate things, which are composed of matter and form. Just as in inanimate things, form dominates and rules while matter is subjected and serves, so in animate objects, the soul rules and the body serves "like a slave."[150] Among mankind, the same sort of hierarchy exists between men and women, adults and children, as well as natural lords and natural slaves (barbarians). By this principle of natural law, everyone benefits, even those natural slaves who are "subjected to the rule of nations and princes more human and virtuous" than they are.[151] As we have seen, this argument is more or less consistent with the Thomists' interpretation of Aristotle. Then, however, Democritus advances arguments that go well beyond those permitted by the Thomist commentary tradition—arguments that eclectically draw from Sepúlveda's own translation of Aristotle's *Politics,* from the commentaries of Albertus Magnus, as well as from the Augustinian hierocratic tradition and the nominalism of Gerson. While these arguments do not add up to a coherent metaphysical or philosophical system, they elaborate an effective *ideology* justifying the Spanish conquest of America.

First, Democritus quotes from his "friend Ginés's" translation of the passage 1256b20–25 in Aristotle's *Politics,* where the enslavement of barbarians is said to be a just cause for war, similar to the hunt for a wild animal. Thus, he argues, force may be applied "not only against the beasts but also against those men who were born to obey but refuse domination."[152] (As we saw, this is precisely the interpretation that Moerbeke's translation had obscured and Aquinas's commentary had resisted.) Whereas war between civilized nations therefore needs a justification by the law of nations, war against natural slaves who resist their enslavement is sanctioned by natural law. The two kinds of war, Democritus argues, are fundamentally "two very distinct cases."[153] When reminded by Leopoldo that Christian wars against the barbarians result in "great slaughters" of innocent people and should therefore be avoided at all costs, Democritus replies that, "to the contrary," only unjust wars result in the slaughter of innocent people; by contrast, in a war against barbarians, "those who are defeated and fall have received their just punishment" for refusing to accept the station that nature had intended for them.[154]

In arguing for the justness of the war on American Indians who resist their natural place in subjection to the Spaniards, Democritus draws not only on his humanist (Ciceronian) understanding of war as a natural way of dealing with barbarians and on Aristotle's concept of barbarity but also on Augustine's hierocratic theory of dominion, according to which no heretic, infidel, or pagan has a right to his lands and property. (As we have seen, this idea, too, was utterly rejected by Vitoria, De Soto, and most of the other Thomists, beginning with Aquinas). According to Democritus, this is so because Christians "have an obligation, by divine and natural law, to ensure that they [pagans, heretics, and infidels] desist from their crimes, especially those that sin and transgress against natural law and its author, who is God, especially when it comes to the worst sin of idolatry."[155] Therefore, according to Augustine, Democritus continues, it is "entirely proper for a just prince to establish a law against pagans and their sacrifices, and to sanction with capital punishment and the confiscation for their property, not only that of the perpetrators of those impious sacrifices but also that of the governors of the provinces who do not care to punish those crimes."[156] Finally, according to St. Augustine, the barbarians should be subjected not only so that they listen to the preachers but also so that their Christian doctrine can be reinforced with "threats and the infusion of terror."[157] When Leopoldo raises the common Thomist objection that St. Augustine was speaking only about heretics, not about pagans, "whose case is very different" (considering that their ignorance of Christ is invincible), Democritus replies (in Franciscan fashion) that, regardless of whether committed by heretics or pagans, idolatry is a diabolic crime against natural law and all those addicted to it must be cured from it: "Just as a physician must often cure the sick against his will (and even has to tie him up), cutting and burning in order to restore his health, so too, San Augustine opines, we must watch over those who are deceived in religion and gone astray from true and Christian piety and force them even against their will and despite their opposition to participate in the evangelical banquet if they refuse it . . . and to force them to return to the Catholic Faith [*ut ad fidem catholicam redeant compelli*]."[158]

As Democritus explains in hierocratic fashion, Pope Alexander VI's bulls *Inter cetera* had called the Indians to Christ's banquet and charged the Catholic Monarchs of Spain with the mission to submit them to their dominion. Thus, those regions "passed to the dominion of the Spanish occupants by the law of nations, not because they didn't belong to anyone but because those mortals who occupied them earlier were completely devoid of Christian rule and civilized communities."[159] Finally, according to the law of nations, which is contained in natural law, those who are vanquished in a just war—as is the enslavement of natural slaves and those who resist Christianization—"both their persons and their possessions become the rightful possession of the victor . . . which is the origin of civil slavery."[160] Here we can see Democritus's rhetorical alchemy come full circle and arrive at precisely the conclusion that Vitoria had anticipated and utterly rejected: the subjection of natural slaves to the rule of natural lords is justified by Aristotelian natural law; if the natural slaves resist, they lose not only their sovereignty but also possession of their persons, lands, and things. Thus are natural slaves transformed into legal slaves.

Sepúlveda's choice of Democritus as his mouthpiece and the latter's claim vis-à-vis the ignoramus Leopoldo about the genuine ancientness of what *appears to be* a newfangled theory—the Aristotelian notion of the enslavement of barbarians as a justification of war—identify him as one of Vitoria's *neoterici*, which is to say as a nominalist, humanist, and philologist.[161] Democritus hereby positions himself as an Aristotelian whose knowledge of "Aristotle" is different from and superior to that derived from the Thomists' Scholastic tradition, especially hylomorphic metaphysics, where such ideas as atomism and the violent subjection of barbarians against their will were rejected (with some caveats, as we have seen). It is in light of this positioning of himself as a "pre-Socratic" (or materialist) Aristotelian that his reference to the American Indians as "*humunculos*" is significant.[162] It is probably in large part due to this claim that *Democrates alter* was judged by the academic theologians such as Melchor Cano to be contrary to "sound" theology and that Las Casas called its errors "enormous," ultimately resulting in the failure of Sepúlveda's efforts to see the book published in Spain.[163]

In late medieval and the early modern Aristotelianism, a homunculus (literally "little man") was known as an artificial human created in the alchemical flask. As such, the homunculus was a variety of "phenomena" that were explained in premodern times as products of "spontaneous generations"—extant species that could not possibly have had their origins in God's original Creation but "freak" accidents of nature—including spiders, toads, giants, and wild men. The theory of spontaneous generation has its origins in some of Aristotle's genuine works, such as *The History of Animals, The Generation of Animals,* and *The Parts of Animals.* At the root of the concept of spontaneous generation is the ancient Greek (male) idea that the sperm is the truly generative element in sexual reproduction and that the menstrual blood in the woman's womb merely plays a passive role as a receptacle or incubator, in analogy to the "dung" in a planting container in which a seed "putrefies," then germinates, and grows. According to this theory, the female womb was replaceable, though it was originally believed that creatures generated in artificial environments from male sperm would not be as perfect as those germinating and growing in the female womb. As William Newman explains: "The concept of the marvelous power of male sperm, like the ability of specific types of matter to generate life spontaneously, opened up a vast field of speculation about the possibilities of artificial life.... What would happen, they wondered, if human sperm were put into a matrix other than that of human menstrual blood?"[164] The idea of a miniature human created by alchemy came to Europe with some of the translations of Aristotle from the Arabic tradition and also with the Jewish tradition of the Golem. In one of the Arabic texts, the *Book of the Cow,* the homunculus is produced for supplying the bodily tissue used in organo-therapy, a form of medicinal cannibalism. In the Latin West, the homunculus makes frequent appearances in alchemical texts either written by or attributed to such famous Scholastic men of science as Albertus Magnus and Arnald of Villanova. It is one of the superb ironies of history that among the most influential medieval alchemical texts explaining the creation of a homunculus and its organo-therapeutic applications in alchemy, the *De essentiis essentiarum* (fourteenth century), should have been attributed to "Thomas" (i.e., Aquinas). Yet, as Newman points out, a type of homunculus plays a role also in Thomas Aquinas's authentic writings, the *Summa,* where the Dominican explained the Immaculate Conception by arguing that a miniature but fully formed baby Jesus was placed by God into Mary's womb. In other words, Jesus Christ (like spiders, giants, and monsters) was not descended by *natural* generation from one of the original creations of God (in this case, the semen of Adam). But, unlike these monstrous species, whose origin was uncertain, Jesus was a homunculus created by God.[165]

As we saw in chapter 6, one of the controversies that ensued between the Thomists and the Franciscans was over the question of whether or not art (demonic or human) could equal such divine feats. Whereas Franciscans such as Bonaventure thought it possible, the Thomists did not. One of the sworn enemies of alchemy who nevertheless involved himself in the debate about the homunculus was the Spanish theologian Alonso Fernández de Madrigal (1410–1455), also known as "El Tostado," one of the chief theorists of witchcraft and the author of *De malefic mulieribus, que vulgariter dicuntur bruxas* (1440), whom Sepúlveda cites in his *Democrates alter*.[166] However, whereas Aquinas had thought art—either demonic or alchemical—simply to be vain in relation to nature, El Tostado was skeptical about the powers of alchemy but convinced of the Devil's ability in artificially counterfeiting substantial forms, such as "incubi and succubi" in imitation of baby Jesus. To the extent that men also engaged in the pursuit of producing artificial men, they must be driven by the Devil. Thus, in *Beati Alphonsi Thostati Episcopi Abulensis* (a tract that was printed posthumously in 1528), El Tostado relates Arnald of Villanova's attempt to create a homunculus in a flask, which is called the "mother" of the man conceived there. In El Tostado's text, the attempt ultimately remained unsuccessful and the possibility of its success uncertain, due to Arnald's decision to smash the artificial "mother" holding his creature. Nevertheless, El Tostado embarks on a consideration of the demonic forces at work in Arnald's experiments.[167] Similarly, El Tostado relates the story of how Thomas Aquinas destroyed the homunculus created by his teacher Albertus Magnus.[168] His story contributes to the legend of Albertus Magnus as a famous alchemist, after dozens of alchemical tracts, such as the *Libellus de alchemia,* had spuriously been ascribed to him.[169] Although it is not clear whether Albertus himself practiced alchemy, he was a firm believer in the idea of spontaneous generation, which could happen as a result of a chance accumulation of different materials in nature or as a result of human or demonic artifice. In his commentaries on Peter Lombard's *Sentences,* he gave several examples of such spontaneous generations that were not descended from any species originally created by God.[170] Most likely, it was a humanoid generation (wild men, giants, and homunculi) that he had in mind when arguing that war could justly be waged on natural slaves who participate in natural reason but whose reason "originates in nature," not in God's image imprinted upon Adams's original creation.

Just before Sepúlveda branded the American Indians as *"humunculos"* in his *Democrates alter,* the most recent theory of the homunculus had resurfaced in the 1530s. In the *De natura rerum* (ca. 1529–32), the Swiss alchemist Philippus Aureolus Theophrastus Bombastus von Hohenheim, aka Paracelsus, wrote:

> We must now by no means forget the generation of homunculi. For there is something to it, although it has been kept in great secrecy and kept hidden up to now, and there was not a little doubt and question among the old philosophers whether it even be possible to nature and art that a man can be born outside the female body and [without] a natural mother. I give this answer—that it is by no means opposed to the spagyric art and to nature, but that it is indeed possible. But how this should happen and proceed—its process is thus—that the sperm of a man be putrefied by itself in a cucurbit for forty days with the highest degree of putrefaction in a horse's womb, or at least so long that it comes to life and moves itself, and stirs, which is easily observed. After this time, it will look somewhat like a man, but transparent, without a body. If, after this, it be fed wisely with the arcanum of human blood and be nourished for up to forty weeks, and be kept in the even heat of the horse's womb, a living human child grows therefrom, with all its members like another child, which is born of a woman, but much smaller.[171]

According to Paracelsus, the alchemical creation of the homunculus was the human equivalent of spontaneous generations found in nature. These were substantial forms not originally created by God and regenerated by natural (sexual) reproduction but by the demonic art of counterfeit. If the Devil generated the creatures that threatened (Christian) humanity, the divine gift of alchemy enabled Christians to counteract the Devil. As mentioned above, in another work, Paracelsus counts the American Indians among those spontaneous generations, writing that they were not the descendants of Adam but "of another Adam" (*von einem anderen Adam*):

> And so I cannot resist making a small notice on those who have been found in the hidden islands [*verborgenen insulen*] and those who are still hidden. As to whether they derive from Adam, it may be found that Adam's descendants [Kinder] have not come to the hidden islands; but it may be considered that those people derive from another Adam; and then it would hardly be the case that they share our flesh and blood and are therefore our friends. And it must be pondered that if Adam had remained in Paradise, perhaps another Adam would have come who did not possess God's image, like those from the new islands.[172]

If these children "of another Adam" did not possess God's image and were not our friends, but the creatures of the Devil, alchemy offered Christians the means to fight them in the metallurgical production of iron, and possibly even of homunculi that can serve as suppliers of the human tissue in the "spagyric art."

If Sepúlveda took the idea of the American homunculus from Paracelsus, it would be one of the earliest references to the Swiss alchemists in Spain.[173] However, as we have seen, the possibility of Sepúlveda's alchemical reference does not depend on a familiarity with Paracelsus. Already in El Tostado's works, the homunculus became a demonic creature that Paracelsus and Sepúlveda would later locate in America. Whereas the Franciscans had insisted that the Indians were creatures of God and the descendants of Adam, who were the victims of the Devil's art of counterfeit, the idea of the demonic origins of the American Indians emerged from Sepúlveda's synthesis of the alchemical tradition reaching back to Albertus Magnus, which insisted on the possibility of the creation of life by alchemy, on the one hand; and, on the other, of the Counter-Reformation's disavowal of such art as demonic in origin.

Historians have debated the significance of the confrontation between Las Casas and Sepúlveda at Valladolid. History would seem to suggest that Sepúlveda's "modern" Aristotelianism ultimately prevailed over the Dominicans' *via antigua* in both early modern science—with the coalescence of the Democritan ancient (atheist) tradition of atomism and the medieval Christian messianic tradition alchemy in the mechanical philosophy of the Scientific Revolution—and in international law with the consolidation of a "doctrine of the discovery" in the age of European settler colonialism. Even though the Crown imposed the so-called New Laws, intended to offer new protections for the American Indians, the catastrophic social, cultural, and demographic situation resulting from the European conquest was not markedly ameliorated. Nevertheless, the Dominican historian Venancio Diego Carro, the most eminent modern biographer of Domingo de Soto, begged to differ. As he pointed out, hardly ever did an empire before or after the sixteenth century seriously question its rights of conquest. As a case in point, Carro invoked the fate of the American Indians within the English colonial system: if Sepúlveda had indeed prevailed, he argued, the Spanish colonial system would have been "similar to that put into place by England a century later." The ultimate defeat of Sepúlveda's position in colonial Latin America was, according to Carro, evident in the differences between "the two colonial systems that has been known to [modern] history." Thus, "the indigenous element has been preserved in Hispano-American societies forty times in proportion to that of Anglo-American ones."[174]

Carro's point is borne out by the differences we have observed between the writings of Sepúlveda and Vitoria on the topic of the conquest of America.

While the concept of natural slavery did not occupy a very prominent place in Vitoria's "De indis" overall, it was central to Sepúlveda's entire argument. More importantly, whereas Vitoria had considered the concept of natural slavery in the context of an entirely speculative deliberation of possible Spanish rights of dominion in America, Sepúlveda discussed the subject in the context of a justification of war—particularly the justification of the Spanish conquest as it had happened in history—hereby coming to conclusions that would have been utterly abhorrent to Vitoria but that had momentous epistemological and geopolitical consequences for the history of the modern paradigm of discovery in the age of European settler colonialism. The differences between their treatments of the issue of natural slavery ultimately manifest a more fundamental difference in their respective epistemologies: whereas Vitoria approached the notion as a question of moral theology in the Scholastic tradition of Thomas Aquinas, for Sepúlveda the question of natural slavery was an issue of political philosophy in the Italian humanist tradition of Machiavelli. While Vitoria's Scholastic approach to the law of nations would play an important role in the history of international law in the Old World, Sepúlveda's Christian humanism became one of the key aspects in Francis Bacon's New World paradigm of discovery in science and, ultimately, the nineteenth-century "doctrine of discovery" in international law.

9

The Blood of the Dragon
Alchemy and New World *Materia Medica*

In 1571, the *sevillano* physician, businessman, and natural historian Nicolás Monardes (ca. 1512–1588) released the "second part" of his work on New World *materia medica,* the first part of which had appeared six years earlier (in 1565, republished in 1569). In this new volume, Monardes continued the task of describing the "things that are brought out of our Western Indies"—the great variety of exotic medicinal resins, gums, oils, stones, nuts, beans, flowers, roots, and woods to be found in the New World.[1] Although Monardes had never himself traveled to the New World, his project was to become one of the most successful publishing ventures in the early modern literature of discovery, his books being translated into several western European vernaculars, as well as Latin, by the end of the sixteenth century.[2] Monardes was widely cited by the most celebrated men of science from the sixteenth to the eighteenth centuries, including not only the Flemish translator of his works into Latin, Carolius Clusius,[3] but also such prominent Englishmen as Robert Boyle, William Castell, Nicholas Culpepper, Edmund Gardiner, and John Gerard, as well as the famous Swedish botanist Carl Linnaeus, who named the wild bergamot *Monarda fistulosa* in Monardes's honor.[4]

Some of the New World *materia medica* that Monardes described, like sassafras, had already been familiar to Europeans from their previous contact with the eastern "Indies" (i.e., Africa and Asia); others, like tobacco, were still new and known primarily from Amerindian medical traditions. Of the former category was apparently a certain fruit that had been brought back to Seville by the bishop of Cartagena and that Monardes called "El Dragon" (the dragon). One of the woodcuts included in the 1571 edition depicts several views of the fruit, including one of its inside (see figs. 22 and 23). Upon opening the fruit, Monardes writes, he and the bishop had made the startling discovery of a miniature dragon. It was "a marvelous thing to behold" (*cosa maravillosa de ver*), he wrote, for it was made "with so much art that it appeared to be alive, with a long neck, the mouth open, and bristles standing up like thorns, a long tail, and standing on its feet, so that surely nobody who saw it could help but marvel to see this figure, made with so much art it seemed

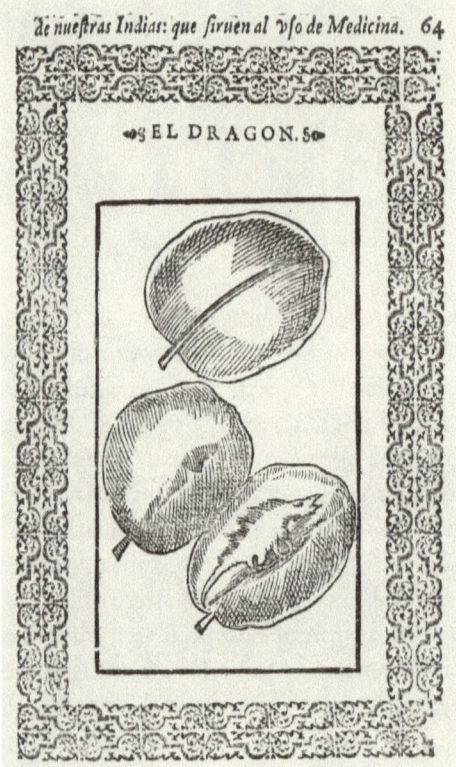

Figure 22. Nicolás Monardes, "El Dragon." (In Nicolás Monardes, *Primera y segunda y tercera partes de la historia medicinal* [1580]. Courtesy of the John Carter Brown Library at Brown University.)

that it was made of ivory and that no artisan, however accomplished, could have made it better."[5]

What should we make of Monardes's strange image and account? Some have suggested that the image of the dragon was (as a sort of biblical snake) intended to represent the "imprint of Satan," an instance of a European tendency to associate the unfamiliar aspects of New World nature with the demonic.[6] It is true that Monardes occasionally demonizes Native American uses of medicinal substances. Thus, even though he celebrated the medicinal virtues of tobacco, he claimed that its use in Native American culture was diabolical in origin, writing that "the Devil . . . showed them the virtues of this plant so that through it they might see those imaginings and phantasms that it represents before their eyes and through which they are deceived."[7] But while Monardes suspects that the Devil had indoctrinated the Indians in his preternatural knowledge of the secret properties of American plants, nowhere does he assert that nature is itself demonic in the New World, as did some

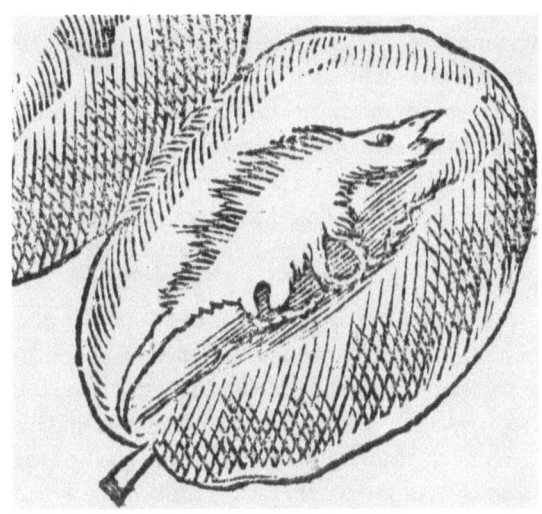

Figure 23. Nicolás Monardes, "El Dragon," detail. (In Nicolás Monardes, *Primera y segunda y tercera partes de la historia medicinal* [1580]. Courtesy of the John Carter Brown Library at Brown University.)

of his Franciscan contemporaries. We find a more likely context in which to read Monardes's dragon in the world of emblems in Renaissance natural history, which drew on a "complex web of associations" linking particular natural "things"—animals, plants, minerals, and metals—with history, mythology, etymology, and the entire cosmos.[8] In particular, I want to suggest that Monardes's "dragon" can be understood in the context of the iconographic language of alchemy that was an important feature of early modern European writings about American nature. We already encountered an example of this iconographic tradition in chapter 4, where I argued that in the context of Christopher Columbus's "ecstatic materialism," the elixir of the *lac virginis* is imagined as the special product of the tropical sun, distilled in a macrocosmic "crucible of the tropics"—analogous to the alchemical alembic that justified a curiosity about the natural secrets of the world in an apocalyptic rhetoric of Christian Reconquista and universal salvation. As we have seen, one tradition of empiricist "theoretical curiosity" about the natural secrets of the New World developed during the sixteenth century in the realm of missionary evangelical rhetoric and ethno-demonology, especially among the Franciscans and Jesuits. While few of the works in the missionary tradition had been published in the sixteenth century, the important forays into New World *materia medica* that had been made by Franciscans and their native collaborators, such as the *Libellus de medicinalibus indorum herbis,* was not lost on secular writers, especially among royal chroniclers and secretaries, such as Gonzalo Fernández de Oviedo y Valdés and Francisco Hernández, as well as among private physicians such as Monardes in Spain or Juan de Cárdenas in New Spain. Of course, their interest in New World *materia medica* was fundamentally different from that of the mendicant friars. Whereas the latter were interested in gathering information useful for the spiritual and physical healing of infidels and the extirpation of secret idolatries still persisting among the neophytes, the royal chroniclers and secretaries were primarily interested in America's natural secrets for their commercial and military value—an important aspect of "experimental" science since its first elaboration by Roger Bacon in the thirteenth century.

Yet, as we will see in this chapter, secular writers such as Monardes also justified their commercial interests in New World *materia medica* in the alchemical language of ecstatic materialism, hereby elaborating a modern (i.e., Christian humanist) critique of Scholastic Aristotelianism. When writing his natural history about exotic American plants during the second part of the sixteenth century, Monardes already had several rhetorical models on which he could draw. These models included, most prominently, the works of the royal chronicler Gonzalo Fernández de Oviedo y Valdés, one of the earliest Spanish writers to adapt the classical genre of Pliny's *Natural History* to an early modern Christian context. As we will see in this chapter, Monardes built on Oviedo's model of the "passionate" Christian natural historian, by presenting a curious mixture of scientific empiricism, Hermeticist mysticism, alchemical matter theory, and Christian messianism that played an important role in the subsequent European literature of overseas discovery and conquest, especially with regard to exotic *materia medica*. The rights of discovery over these exotic *materia medica* that reached Europe from the "Indies" in the early modern period are still being contested today in international legal disputes over Western companies' attempts to patent tropical foods and naturalia. In the sixteenth century, the language of alchemy offered an important rhetorical venue for the apprehension of American exotica by framing the interest in New World *materia medica,* both scientific and commercial, in strongly spiritual and even mystical terms.

In the first section of this chapter, I discuss Monardes's most important predecessor in the European discovery of New World *materia medica,* Gonzalo Fernández de Oviedo y Valdés, the "Pliny of the New World." The second section places Monardes's New World *materia medica* in the sixteenth-century context of intersecting traditions of humanist medicine and medieval alchemy. In that section, I also discuss the history of the emblem of the dragon in Renaissance alchemical iconography as well as natural history and painting. In the third section, I offer a reading of Monardes's tract "Diálogo del hierro" (Dialogue on iron), which was included beginning with the 1574 expanded edition of the *Historia medicinal* but that has, to date, received little critical attention.[9] I will argue that the inclusion of the "Diálogo del hierro" establishes alchemy as a key but little noted context in which to read Monardes's publications of his *Historia medicinal* and his project in New World natural history generally. In the final section, I will consider the legacy of Monardes's alchemification of New World *materia medica* in a discussion of another "hunter" of New World *materia medica,* Juan de Cárdenas, and his *Primera parte de los problemas y secretos maravillosos de las Indias* (1591).

Gonzalo Fernández de Oviedo y Valdés's "Passionate" Natural History of America

Gonzalo Fernández de Oviedo y Valdés was born in Madrid in 1478. His interest in the "Indies" had first been sparked in 1493, when, as a fourteen-year-old boy in the service of the Spanish *infante* Don Juan, he witnessed Christopher Columbus's triumphant entry into the city of Barcelona after his first transatlantic voyage. When writing many years later, Oviedo remembered being awed as Columbus presented the Catholic Monarchs with small quantities of gold as well as colorful arrays of exotic plants, animals, and even human beings never seen before in Europe. When, in 1497, crown prince Don Juan unexpectedly died, Oviedo, now in his early twenties, left for Italy, where he spent his intellectually formative years at the Renaissance courts of the Italian aristocracy in cities such as Genoa, Milan, and Mantua, becoming exposed to a humanist culture of classical learning. After having returned to Spain in 1502 and lived there in relative obscurity for several years, he first embarked for the New World in 1514, traveling as the official *veedor de las fundaciones de oro de la Tierra Firme* (inspector of gold mines on the mainland), in the expedition of Pedro Pedrarias Dávila. In 1523, he briefly returned to Spain in order to file official charges against the tyrannical government of Dávila. While at the royal court, Oviedo received a request from King Charles, recently elected Holy Roman Emperor, for a literary description of his overseas territories in the Indies. Oviedo had already begun such a work, but he had left the unfinished manuscript at his residence in Hispaniola. In order to oblige the king, he hastily composed a new book entitled *Oviedo de la natural hystoria de las Indias,* working largely from memory. Frequently referring the reader to the much larger and more detailed work he had already begun, he called the present work a mere *sumario* (summary), which is the title under which this work has also become known by historians. Published in 1526 in Toledo at Oviedo's private expense, the *Sumario* was the first book about the New World that offered not a narrative account of travel and conquest but a detailed and systematic description of the landscapes, flora, fauna, and human cultures of

Hispaniola and Tierra Firme, the mainland of what is today known as the Isthmus of Panama.[10]

In 1530, Oviedo was appointed by Charles as the official royal chronicler of the Indies, relieving him of his duties as inspector of mines. As a result, he was able to complete his longer work, but only parts of it would be published during his lifetime. In 1535, the first "part," containing the first nineteen "books," was published in Seville by the Cromberger printing house under the title *Historia general delas Indias*. It provided an account of the voyages of Columbus and a description of the Antilles, including also a chapter on shipwreck narratives (which would eventually become the fiftieth and final chapter of the complete manuscript).[11] "Book XX," the first book of the second part, was not published until the year of his death, in 1557. It treated Magellan's voyage to the Moluccas and the Southern Cone, Trinidad, Venezuela, and Colombia. The remaining books of the *Historia general* had to await publication until the nineteenth century, when the complete work of fifty books was edited for the first time, by José Amador de los Rios, for the Spanish Academy of History in 1851–55. It included all the materials that had remained in manuscript, which deal with the explorations and conquests of Panama, Central America, the Yucatán, Mexico, parts of North America, as well as Peru and Chile. Perhaps due to the incomplete availability of the *Historia general* in print, its dissemination remained somewhat limited during the early modern period. In 1556, Giovanni Battista Ramusio published a partial Italian translation as part of the third volume of his *Navigationi et viaggi* (1556), which included also a summary of the chapters on the discovery of the Marañon that Oviedo had sent in manuscript to Pietro Bembo in 1543 but that had been excluded from the Spanish edition. Also, a French translation of the printed materials available in Spanish was published by Michel de Vascosan twice (in 1555 and 1556).

Historians have speculated that one of the reasons why only a fraction of Oviedo's magnum opus was published during his lifetime—besides the prohibitive costs of publishing such a massive work—was the fierce opposition from the Dominican friar Bartolomé de las Casas, who regarded Oviedo's work as unhelpful to his political cause of defending the rights of the Indians.[12] It is true that Oviedo's portrayal of Native Americans and their cultures could be unflattering. For instance, in the *Sumario* he had occasionally attributed Indian knowledge and use of natural substances—such as the poison extracted from the raw yucca juice—to demonic revelations. Also, he had claimed that the Indians were exceptionally hardheaded in their resistance to peaceful conversion—a point of particular contention for Las Casas. Thus, Oviedo had written that the Indians' "skulls are four times thicker than those of the Christians. And so when one wages war with them and comes to hand to hand fighting, one must be very careful not to hit them on the head with the sword, because I have seen many swords broken in this fashion."[13] Overall, however, it must be acknowledged that Oviedo was also critical of the Spanish conduct in the Indies, which had led to a severe depopulation of the islands. For example, he wrote in the *Sumario:*

> There are very few Indians there [in Hispaniola] now, and not so many Christians as there should be, since many of those who once were on the island have gone to other islands or to Tierra Firme. Being men fond of adventure, those who go to the Indies for the most part are unmarried and therefore do not feel obligated to reside in any one place. Since new lands have been discovered and are being discovered every day, those men believe that they will swell their purses more quickly in new territory. Even though some may have been successful in this, most have been disillusioned, especially those who already have established homes and residences in Hispaniola.[14]

Unlike the *Historia general,* the shorter *Sumario,* enjoyed a broad dissemination throughout Europe. A complete Italian translation of the *Sumario* by the Venetian ambassador to Spain, Andrea Navigero, was first published in Venice in 1534 as part 2 of Ramusio's sequential *Summario de la generale historia de l'Indie Occidentali* and would be republished four more times in the next hundred years, three times as part of Ramusio's *Navigationi et viaggi.* As we will see in chapter 10, an English translation by Richard Eden was published twice during the sixteenth century and again (in extracts) during the seventeenth century, in Samuel Purchas's monumental *Purchas his Pilgrimes* (1625). A French translation (based on Navigero's Italian translation) by Jean Poleur was published in 1556. And it was even translated into Ottoman Turkish in the 1580s by Mehmet ibn Emir Hasan el Suudi, though this translation was not published in Istanbul until 1730, when it appeared together with Turkish translations from the New World histories written by Francisco López de Gómara and Agustín de Zárate.[15]

The great interest with which Oviedo's *Sumario* was greeted throughout Europe in the sixteenth century is not surprising, as it was the earliest natural history of the New World whose author could speak with the authority of an eyewitness when describing such exotic plants as the rubber tree, maize, tobacco, and cinnamon, as well as animals never seen before by Europeans, such as the armadillo or the anteater. Unlike the earlier accounts by explorers and conquerors such as Columbus or Vespucci, Oviedo did not organize his account chronologically as a narrative account, but as a topically and systematically arranged "scientific" catalogue of nature, hereby drawing in his descriptions on his classical training and taxonomic conventions that Italian Renaissance natural history had inherited from the Roman (and pagan) tradition of Pliny's *Historia naturalis,* which had divided up the natural world into general categories such as the elements, physical geography, man, animals, fishes, bird, insects, and the various types of plants, each category containing headers on the various subspecies. In the prologue to the *Sumario,* addressed to the emperor, Oviedo wrote:

> The wonders of nature are best preserved and kept in the memory of man by histories and books in which they are written by intelligent persons who have traveled over the world and who have observed at first hand the things they describe and who describe what they have observed and understood of such things. This was the opinion of Pliny.... A very accurate scholar, Pliny always cited his sources when he quoted a story which he had heard or read. He also included in this history many things which he had observed at first hand. In the manner of Pliny, then, in this short study I want to describe for your Majesty what I have seen in your Occidental Empire of the West Indies, Islands and Tierra Firme of the Ocean Sea.[16]

But despite paying homage to Pliny, Oviedo was also eager to distinguish himself from his classical pagan model, writing in his prologue to the *Historia general*:

> I have not culled them [these materials] from two hundred thousand volumes I might have read, as Pliny wrote ... where, it seems that he related what he had read.... I, however, compiled what I here write from two hundred thousand hardships, privations, and dangers in the more than twenty-two years that I have personally witnessed and experienced these things.... In one way my book will differ from Pliny's model: this will be to relate something of the conquest of these Indies, and ... justify the reason for their discovery.[17]

Unlike the classical pagan natural historian who may have described the local plants by direct observation but who relied on books regarding the exotic and remote ones, the Christian natural historian of the New World has no books on which to rely and so must suffer the hardships of travel and research in the hot, humid, and mosquito-infested parts of the world. And unlike that of his classical pagan model, Oviedo suggests, his inspiration for writing his natural history was not mere curiosity or the pleasure derived from nature but his Christian interest and duty in furthering the conquest of the Indies for the sake of spreading the faith and the expansion of the territories of the

Holy Roman Emperor. For Oviedo, it is the project of conquest that *justifies* scientific inquiry and discovery. Throughout his works, therefore, Oviedo underwrites the language of Aristotelian and Plinean *scientia* and the curiosity about the secrets of the Indies with the Christian language of passion, pilgrimage, and martyrdom.[18]

Indeed, there is in *Oviedo's Sumario* not only an "objective" rhetoric of science derived from the classical authority of books but also a self-conscious emphasis on the "subjective" or empirical qualities in its composition. While each individual chapter in the *Sumario* focuses on a particular "thing" (*cosa*)—a plant, animal, or ethnographic detail—this taxonomic organization, especially in the early part, is compromised by and synthesized with the imposition of a narrative time line that follows the trajectory of Oviedo's own travels. Thus, he begins with a chapter on the voyage—from the Casa de Contratación in Seville down the Guadalquivir River to San Lúcar de Barrameda, Seville's seaport, and out into the Atlantic on the first leg of the journey; the ten-day trip to the Canary Islands; the second leg, the twenty-five-day journey to Hispaniola; and finally the seven-day trip to Tierra Firme. From there, chapters proceed from general geographical observations, to descriptions of the cultural mores of the Natives—their foodways of making bread made from maize and yucca—and then finally to the myriad of plant and animal species. As several critics have noted, the subjectivism of this organization may have functioned as a sort of mnemonic device for Oviedo. Similar to Thomas Aquinas's technique of memorizing a long sermon by imagining its progress in analogy to a movement through the rooms of a building, Oviedo memorizes the particulars about the plants and animals by literarily reenacting his journey through space.[19]

In his descriptions of plants and animals, Oviedo adopted Pliny's basic model of natural history, including the Roman's "popular zoology." In his discussion of birds, for example, Oviedo categorizes them into those species which are "similar to those in Spain" and those that are different, singling out for special emphasis exotic birds such as the turkey, the pelican, and the hummingbird. Yet, if the Plinean tradition gave him a general taxonomic principle for organizing his materials, Oviedo soon realized the limits of its usefulness in approaching the nature of the New World. Recent critics such as Jeremy Paden and Andrés Prieto have investigated this "crisis in representation" in Oviedo's natural history, which is evident in the author's increasing realization of the relativity of Aristotelian descriptive categories once deemed to be universal. According to this Aristotelian system of classification, biological forms are categorized by way of mutually exclusive oppositions with regard to their natural habitat: "animals" live on land, "fish" in the sea, and "birds" in their air.

These very basic terms of this scientific taxonomy, however, break down in the description of such Caribbean animals such as flying fish or the iguana, based on the authority of the Christian scientific witness. In the "Indies," nature still appears to be in a primordial state of Chaos, a *prima materia,* in which the four elements of nature were not yet fully separate.[20] The idea of the primeval chaos that still reigns in the New World, though Aristotelian in its roots, signals Oviedo's critique of the Scholastic "Aristotle," a 'modern' (i.e., Christian humanist) critique that would become increasingly common in the historiography of the Americas in the course of the sixteenth century, culminating in José de Acosta's famous laughter at Aristotle's theory of climactic zones while standing in the snow in the equatorial Andes: "I will confess here that I laughed and jeered at Aristotle's meteorological theories and his philosophy, seeing that in the very place where, according to his rules, everything must be burning and on fire, I and all my companions were cold. For the truth is that no place in the world is there a calmer and more moderate region than that under the equator."[21] Like Acosta's a half century later, Oviedo's Christian critique of the pagan Aristotle, based on the authority of the Christian witness, proves that the Indies in Aristotle's torrid zone are fecund and temperate. It is by Christian passion and pilgrimage alone that God's providential design of the world is revealed. Oviedo's natural histories about the New World hereby provided an important model for later writers in synthesizing the Christian humanist critique of both Scholastic Aristotelianism and classical pagan naturalism with a messianic ideology of conquest and imperialist expansionism. As we will see in the next section, one of the most influential heirs of Oviedo's synthesis of classical *scientia* with Christian passion was the Sevillian physician Nicolás Monardes.

Nicolás Monardes: Commerce, Humanism, and Vernacular Medicine

Unlike Oviedo, Monardes had never traveled to the New World himself and therefore could not speak with the testimonial authority of the Christian martyr when writing his *Historia medicinal.* Also, whereas Oviedo had written his natural histories as an appointed royal chronicler of the Indies with the patronage of the emperor, Monardes was a businessman whose interests in New World *materia medica* was primarily private profit. The son of an Italian immigrant from Genoa, Monardes had received a humanist education at Cisneros's university at Alcalá de Henares, where he obtained, in 1530, a bachelor's degree in arts and philosophy as well as, in 1533, a bachelor's degree in medicine.[22] In 1547, he obtained a physician's degree from the Universidad de Santa María de Jesús de Sevilla. Doubtlessly, Monardes, like Acosta, came into contact with Llullism during his studies at Alcalá. Also, under the Cisnerean humanist curriculum at Alcalá, he had studied the classics—Hippocrates and Galen—and encountered (and greatly admired) Antonio de Nebrija's 1518 *Lexico artis medicamentae,* an edition that combined the classical *materia medica* of Dioscorides and Pliny. He began writing his own treatises on Spanish, Greek, and Arabic medicines as early as the 1530s;[23] but although in his early writings he was dismissive of the medicinal power of New World plants—comparing them unfavorably to the plants of Europe (and those of Spain in particular)—he apparently had a change of mind in the course of the following twenty years,[24] when he became increasingly interested in the natural secrets of the New World and their medicinal and economic potential. In 1565, he published the first results of his research on New World plants—the first two "books" of the *Historia medicinal de las cosas que se traen de nuestras Indias Occidentales,* a work that he would continue to revise and expand over the course of the following decade.[25] There, he described a plethora of New World *materia medica* and many of the Native healing practices involving the use of herbs and stones. He reported, for example, that the returning Spaniards were bringing from New Spain "two stones of great virtue" and describes in detail their use in Native healing rituals.

> The stone must be wet in cold water, and the sick man must take it in his right hand, and from time to time wet it in cold water. This is the way in which the Indians use them, for they hold it for certain that touching this stone unto a bleeding body part restrains the blood. They have great trust in this because they have witnessed the effects. We have also seen the great effects of this stone in staunching of blood. Those who suffer from the hemorrhoidal flow have cured themselves by moving this stone across the body in a circular motion and by wearing them continually upon their fingers.[26]

Significantly, unlike most of his earlier medical writings—such as the *De secanda vena in pleuriti* (1539), *De rosa et partibus ejus* (n.d.), and *De citris, avrantiis, ac limoniis* (n.d.), which manifested a rather conventional Galenism—all of Monardes's editions of the *Historia medicinal* about the New World were originally published not in Latin (the language of academic medicine) but in the vernacular Castilian. There are a number of reasons for this. For one, as José Pardo-Tomás and Marcy Norton have each pointed out, there were distinctly commercial aspects to Monardes's publications and his interest in New World *materia medica.*[27] Monardes was not only a physician but also a shrewd businessman who published his works not for a professional elite but for the general public, hoping to profit from the sale of New World *materia medica* in both sixteenth-century senses of the term—the actual medicinal "things" (*cosas*) imported from the New World (such as tobacco) and their "historia," meaning his treatment of them in writing and print. Thus, he had formed a mercantile enterprise that shipped slaves from Africa and manufactured goods from Spain to be sold in the port cities of the New World, while bringing back precious metals, spices, and other medicinal substances for sale in Spain. For this purpose, he had found a commercial partner on the other side of the Atlantic in Juan Núñez de Herrera, who sent him from Nombre de Dios cochineal as well as seeds and specimens of medicinal New World plants that he cultivated in his garden in Seville. However, due to some familial and commercial misfortunes involving the marriage of his daughter, he had to declare bankruptcy in 1567 and even seek refuge in a local Sevillian monastery to avoid being jailed by his creditors. When granting him permission to republish his work on New World *materia medica* in 1569, the Royal Council of the Indies noted that Monardes was still living in monastic asylum, and his final release from it was apparently granted mainly so that he could repay his creditors with the profits made from future editions of his medical writings.[28]

Monardes's books on New World *materia medica* were distinguished not only by their commercial but also by their philosophical character with regard to his practical approach to medicine. Despite his university degrees, Monardes was not an academic with a post at one of the universities but a practicing physician who combined his interest in the theory of medicine with its practice at patients' bedsides. This was remarkable in the sixteenth-century context, as the theory and practice of medicine were still generally considered to be separate realms.[29] As Gonzalo Aguirre Beltrán has observed, there were essentially two medical traditions in Europe: on the one hand, academic medicine that followed the classical theories of Hippocrates, Galen, Diocorides, and Avicena; and, on the other, what he calls "folk medicine" (*medicina-folk*), which flourished outside the official academies, in the streets. While the professors of the former despised the practitioners of the latter, the latter had a tendency toward empiricism and general irreverence with regard to the ecclesiastical and scholastic authorities.[30] During the sixteenth century, however, the separation between theory and practice was increasingly being challenged by humanist philosophers such as Juan Luis Vives (1492–1550) and Andreas Vesalius (1514–1564), who demanded that theoretical knowledge be based on an empirical footing. In order to reform knowledge, Vives recommended to scholars that they "should not be ashamed to enter into shops and factories, and to ask questions from craftsmen, and to get to know about the details of their work."[31] The calls by humanist philosophers for a reform of knowledge went hand in hand with the rise of what Pamela Smith has called the "artisanal epistemology" and the "vernacular philosophy" of a new brand of physicians such as Martín del Rio in Spain and Paracelsus in Switzerland.[32]

As already pointed out in the previous two chapters with regard to the medicinal use of mummy and the alchemical tradition of the homunculus, the Swiss physician Paracelsus (1493–1541) represents an important example of this "vibrant counterculture" to academic scholasticism in sixteenth-century natural philosophy. Particularly, his "chemical philosophy" was, as Walter Pagel has written, a *"scientia"* quite different from that which could be "learnt from books or by logical deduction." It was more akin to "empirical and experimental research, to testing, probing and 'knocking at the door' of nature," inspired by a deep distrust of the power of Scholastic rationalism. Despite Paracelsus's essentially premodern emphasis on correspondences between microcosm and macrocosm and his tendency to see similarities rather than differences in all natural phenomena, his occult philosophy contained "important proto-scientific ideas" by breaking out of text-bound knowledge and by participating in "those trends of skepticism and empiricism which were soon to contribute to the foundation of modern science." His *scientia* combined a highly eclectic and esoteric book learning with a popular and local folk knowledge passed down orally from generation to generation and the empirical knowledge gained from his everyday experience as a surgeon in the mines. However, precisely for his "artisan attitudes to life and medicine," Paracelsus was frequently shunned by the academics, despite his fame for producing effective remedies through his alchemical experiments which continued to secure him employment in the courts of local nobilities. While in the academic medical sciences of his day the active interference at the sick bed was seen as the task of the surgeon, who was considered to be merely a craftsman, this task was seen as beneath the dignity of the scholarly physician. Paracelsus's natural philosophy, by contrast, defied this institutionalized division between the physician and the surgeon, exemplifying what Richard Drayton has called "that peculiar Renaissance conjunction of the worlds of religion, philosophy, magic, and experimental science."[33] Despite being largely shunned by the academics at the universities, Paracelsus and his followers were increasingly gaining self-confidence and influence in the imperial cities and courts of Europe.[34]

These commercial, philosophical, alchemical, and "artisanal" contexts shed light also on many of Monardes's presentations of New World *materia medica* in his *Historia medicinal,* including the plant he called "El Dragon." Modern scholars have ventured several guesses about its identity in modern botanical nomenclature. While some have surmised that it was in fact the South American croton variety *Croton lechleri,* used by Native peoples for its wound-healing properties, others have speculated that it was the American cactus variety *Hylocereus,* producing the *pitaya* fruit, still today available in grocery stores under the popular name of "dragon fruit."[35] Whatever the modern identity of "El Dragon," Monardes's nomenclature and iconography of a miniature dragon (or lizard) suggest his attempt to identify and market this New World plant as a source of "Dragon's Blood." Thus, he writes that "we shall be certified that it [the juice of the fruit] is Dragon's Blood."[36] Dragon's Blood had traditionally been won from a variety of the Old World "dragon tree" (*Dracaena cinnabari*), native to southeastern Africa and India. Dragon's Blood (*sanguis draconis*) was believed to be an antidote with miraculous medicinal efficacy. Since Roman times, it also had been known to be a source of the bright-red mineral known as cinnabar, a mercury-sulfite compound used, in ground form, by painters, goldsmiths, instrument makers, book illustrators, and other artisans as a pigment to produce a deep red. In his *De materia medica,* Dioscorides had written that cinnabar "is brought from Libya. It is very expensive and so scarce that there is hardly enough for painters to variegate lines. It is also of a deep-color, wherefore some people thought that it is dragon's blood."[37] Since the late fourteenth century, it also had been harvested from a variety endemic to the Azores and Canary Islands (*Dracaena draco*), a specimen of which had been transplanted to Lisbon, where it was, in 1565, admired by the Flemish botanist Carolus Clusius, who later included a discussion of it in his *Rariorum aliquot stirpium per Hispanias observatarum historiae,* published in 1576.[38] By the time John Gerard published his monumental *Herbal and General History of Plants* in England in 1597, Monardes's American "El Dragon" had apparently become thoroughly identified with the Old World varieties of the Dracaena genus. In fact, Gerard claimed (wrongly) that some (patently referring to Monardes) held the opinion that the original dragon tree did not derive from Africa but "was first brought from Carthagena, in Noua orbe, by the bishop of the same prouince."[39] Although the identification of Monardes's "El Dragon" with the Old World dragon tree would be disproven by the end of the sixteenth century, his nomenclature stuck, and the extract of the American croton variety is still marketed today as "Dragon's Blood," known from Plinean and medieval natural history.

Much of the mystique surrounding Dragon's Blood derived from the rich web of associations that the substance had acquired in the course of centuries in natural history, art, and alchemy. At least since the thirteenth century, alchemists had produced an artificial substitute for cinnabar, known as vermilion, by heating mercury and sulfur together until they became a black paste which, when further heated and evaporated, condensed in the walls of the crucible as a bright-red cake.[40] This red substance—either from natural cinnabar or alchemical vermilion—was used in medieval manuscript illumination, especially to represent the blood of Christ, as it was the product of a "passion" that mercury and sulfur underwent in the crucible analogous to the passion undergone by Christ on the cross (the root of the word "crucible" is "cross"). Blood in general, and Dragon's Blood in particular (as an analogue to Christ's blood), was believed to have efficacious properties in medieval medicine. The dragon tree had therefore enjoyed a rich iconographic tradition, often appearing in Edenic landscapes as the tree of life, as in Michael Wohlgemut's *Liber chronicarum* (1493) or Hieronymous Bosch's famous *The Garden of Earthly Delights* (ca. 1510). It also appears in Martin Schongauer's and Albrecht Dürer's engravings of the story of the holy family's "flight into Egypt," recounted in the Gospel of Matthew, and, especially, in the apocryphal but widely known book of *Pseudo Matthew*, which tells the story of the so-called Dragon Wonder, in which baby Jesus tames wild dragons who subsequently praise and adore him, thus fulfilling the Old Testament prophecy of Psalms 148:7 ("Praise the Lord from the earth, ye dragons; ye dragons, and all ye deeps"). Frequently, the dragon tree is accompanied in this tradition by miniature dragons, or lizards (see figs. 24, and 25).[41]

In the Gospel of John (3:14–15), Jesus Christ is compared to a serpent.[42] As we saw in chapter 2, in medieval alchemy, this image is transformed into that of a winged serpent, which serves as the ubiquitous "sigil" (or seal) as an *ouroboros* (a dragon devouring its own tail) that emblematized the circulation of the elements during the alchemical opus. The dragon hereby symbolized the dark chthonic phase of the opus known as the Black Sun, in which the alchemist dissolves the base metal or matter into the original stuff of creation, the *prima materia*, in order to obtain the double seed of metals from which the Philosophers' Stone is "grown"—philosophical sulfur and philosophical quicksilver, the two "metals." These are compared to two dragons, one male and one female, which are united in a violent copulation to produce the mercurial water (also called "Dragon's Blood") and eventually transformed into the harmonious serpents entwined around the caduceus of Hermes.[43] In medieval Christian alchemy, mercury is often also associated with the lizard, as in a book of secrets attributed to Albertus Magnus. "Take a Lizard," the author wrote there, "and cut away the tail of it, and take that which cometh out, for it is like Quicksilver. After, take a wick and make it wet with oil, and put it in a new lamp and kindle it, and the house shall seem bright and white, or gilded with silver."[44]

Vermilion/cinnabar had been of interest to medieval alchemists such as Albertus because it was produced by the combination of what were believed to be the two principles of all metals, sulfur and mercury.[45] As we saw in chapter 2,

Figure 24. Martin Schongauer, *Flight into Egypt*. Woodcut. (Courtesy of the Harris Brisbane Dick Fund, 1929, the Metropolitan Museum of Art, New York.)

the idea that sulfur and mercury were the two basic components of all metals derived from the enormously influential medieval alchemical text *Summa perfectionis*, written by Pseudo-Geber (aka the Franciscan Paul of Taranto), which was one of the most foundational texts of medieval Western alchemy and corpuscular alchemical matter theory.[46] José María López Piñero, Mar Rey Bueno,

Figure 25. Martin Schongauer, *Flight into Egypt*. Woodcut, detail. (Courtesy of the Harris Brisbane Dick Fund, 1929, the Metropolitan Museum of Art, New York.)

María Luz López Terrada, and others have studied the extensive diffusion of alchemical texts by medieval Spanish authors, such as Arnald of Villanova, and sixteenth-century Italian and German authors, such as Girolamo Ruscelli and Paracelsus in sixteenth-century Spain, as well as the highly developed institutional infrastructure that alchemy had enjoyed there since the reign of Philip II.[47] The historical perspectives that these scholars have provided shed light on the rhetorical function that the language of alchemy plays in Monardes's natural history and in the early modern literature of the discovery of the New World more generally. The rich web of Christological, salvific, and messianic associations that the language of alchemy afforded justifies Monardes's curiosity about the occult qualities of tropical nature and underwrites his cultural appropriation and commodification of Amerindian (i.e., demonic) secret medical knowledge as a redemptive "conquest" of New World nature.[48]

The plausibility that Monardes's emblem of the dragon must be read in the context of alchemy and its medieval iconographic tradition finds further support if we consider the changing physical presentation of his work as it went through its various editions.[49] Thus, the 1571 edition—where "El Dragon" first appeared—was dedicated to King Philip II, a well-known aficionado and patron of both alchemy and exotic medicine, the latter of which he championed by sending scientific expeditions to the New World and the former by establishing alchemical laboratories at his monastic refuge of the Escorial.[50] Also, whereas the early (i.e., 1565 and 1569) editions had been published without illustrations (by the Sevillian publishing houses of Sebastian Trujillo and Hernando Díaz, respectively), beginning with the 1571 edition, the volumes also included a number of woodcuts that embellished Monardes's descriptions and had probably been prepared (or commissioned) by a new printer, Alonso Escribano, who published both the 1571 and the 1574 editions. The 1574 edition combined the already-published first (1565/1569) and second (1571) parts of New World *materia medica,* such as the Flower of Michoacán, the copal, and the guayacán wood (the latter believed to be a cure for the French pox). Also, it included a new, third part with discussions of spices and plants found in the New World, such as cinnamon, rhubarb, and coca, as well as two tracts (already included in the 1565 and 1569 editions) of two marvelous antidotes, the bezoar stone (a calcinated concretion found in the stomach or intestines of certain Andean quadrupeds, including the llama, the alpaca, the vicuna, and the guanaco)[51] and the *escorzonera,* an Iberian herb introduced into medicine by the Catalan physician Pere Carnicer. Most curiously, however, it featured two tracts that seem unusual in a volume ostensibly about New World *materia medica.* One of them, entitled "Libro que trata de la nieve," was a treatise on the medicinal uses of snow that had already been included in the 1571 edition. The other one was a new tract on alchemy and metallurgy entitled the "Diálogo del hierro y de sus grandezas." In the next section of this chapter, I would like to focus on the latter tract, in particular on the rhetorical purpose of its inclusion in Monardes's work about New World materia medica.

Monardes's "Dialogue on Iron"

The "Diálogo del hierro" appeared with a frontispiece that aptly sets the stage for the presentation of its content: an elderly, emaciated female figure, leaning on a spiny staff and devouring two snakes (see figs. 26 and 27). The image was the *impresa* (a signature device) of Escribano's publishing house, which specialized in the printing of Spanish Renaissance literature of discovery, science, marvels, and secrets, such as Agustin Zárate's *Historia del descubrimiento y conquista de las provincias del Peru* (1577), Bernadino de Escalante's *Discurso de la navegación que los portugueses hazen à los reinos y provincias del Oriente* (1577), and Jerónimo de Chaves's *Chronographía; ó, reportorio de los tiempos* (1572), as well as humanist linguistic treatises and dictionaries such as Christoval de las Casas's *Vocabulario de las dos lenguas, Toscana y Castellana* (1570).[52] The image of the woman devouring the snakes allegorized the common humanist topos of envy, following representations in Renaissance emblem books such as Andrea Alciato's *Los emblemas,* published in Lyon by Guillermo Rovilio in 1549.[53] Escribano's *impresa* makes for an appropriate fit with the content of Monardes's "Diálogo." On the one hand, the humanist conception of history as a degeneration from a superior classical age—in particular the four-age theory based on Hesiod—constitutes the utopian intellectual background of Monardes's didactic proposal about the virtues of iron in the context of his discussion of New World materia medica: the adoration of gold and silver common in present-day Europe, which had resulted in the rape of the New World and the wreck of the Spanish economy, serves as a vivid reminder of life in the Iron Age, when iron is abundant and cheap, whereas gold is scarce and precious.[54] However, America, where gold is abundant and iron scarce, still exists in the Golden Age and has a moral lesson to teach Europe. Thus, the true riches of the New World, Monardes suggests, consist not in the gold and silver it provides for the royal coffers but in its therapeutic resources—its medicinal plants, stones, metals, and minerals—the raw materials that would be transformed by the Spanish artisan. On the other hand, however, Monardes's text does not seem to corroborate the negative opinion held by many humanists of Arabic and medieval authorities on medicine. In fact, while the vast number of authorities cited in the "Diálogo" betrays a patent knowledge of metallurgy and alchemy on Monardes's part—so extensive that one modern historian speculated that he may have had "familiarity with the works of Paracelsus"—we find no references to the sixteenth-century Swiss physician or the Renaissance Italian and German Neoplatonists, such as Ficino, Pico della Mirandola, Agrippa, etc.[55] Instead, we find citations from an expansive, inclusive, and eclectic selection of Greek, Roman, Hellenistic, Arabic, Persian, Jewish, and medieval Christian authorities—Plato, Aristotle, Dioscorides, Galen, Hermes Trismegistus, Averoes, Avicenna, Al-Razi, (Pseudo-)Geber, Albertus Magnus, Ramón Llull, and Arnald of Villanova, and many others.[56]

The main body of the tract is written, as the title indicates, in the form of a Socratic dialogue, but Monardes's immediate inspiration seems to have been García d'Orta's *materia medica* about (East) India—the *Colóquios dos simples e drogas he cousas medicinais da Índia,* which had been published in 1563 at Goa in India. As does the character of "Orta" in García d'Orta's text, the "Doctor" in Monardes's "Diálogo" resembles the author himself, presented in the image of the humanist scholar who combines an interest in theory and book knowledge with the practice of medicine. In addition, Monardes uses the dialogue form to stage an intellectual exchange, not so much about colonial knowledge per se (as did García d'Orta) but about epistemology. Thus, while the doctor is on his way in the streets of Seville in order to see a patient, he meets one "Sr. Burgos," an apothecary, who is on his way to the Casa de Contratación (House of Trade) in order to view the gold, silver, and emeralds that have arrived with the latest fleet from the Indies. The doctor decides to accompany him, but, upon arrival at the Casa, they find the doors still locked and begin a conversation about metals. The doctor asks Burgos why he admires gold and silver—metals that are, in his opinion, much overrated. He announces that he will prove that iron is more excellent a metal than either gold or silver, because of both its medicinal properties and its usefulness to man in the making of tools. As though to dramatize Vives's call on scholars to "enter into shops and

Figure 26. Nicolás Monardes, frontispiece to "Diálogo del hierro" (1574). (Courtesy of the John Carter Brown Library at Brown University.)

Figure 27. Nicolás Monardes, frontispiece to "Diálogo del hierro," detail (1574). (Courtesy of the John Carter Brown Library at Brown University.)

factories, and to ask questions from craftsmen, and to get to know about the details of their work,"[57] the doctor therefore takes Burgos to the workshop of one Sr. Ortuño, a Basque miner and artisan who is an expert on iron mining and ironworking. At Ortuño's house, the three characters engage in a conversation in which each of the participants appears to personify one of the three branches in the Scholastic-Aristotelian division of knowledge between *episteme* (or *scientia*), *praxis,* and *techne.* Thus, the doctor personifies *episteme/scientia*—theoretical knowledge based on the logical syllogism and geometrical demonstration. Burgos, whose name invokes the historic Visigothic capital of Castile, seems to be associated with the civic and political realm, while his manifest interest in the treasure at the Casa also associate him with commercial life.[58] In short, he personifies *praxis* ("things done")—the Aristotelian term for human knowledge, including such branches as history, politics, ethics, and economics. Finally, the Basque artisan, Ortuño, seems intended to personify *techne* (things made).[59]

In the Scholastic order of knowledge, there was not only a strict separation between the three realms but also a clear epistemological, ethical, and social hierarchy—*scientia* being regarded as the noblest, most certain knowledge, practiced by the social elite, and *techne* being regarded as the lowliest and least stable knowledge, practiced by the lower ranks of society, who had to work with their hands.[60] In the "Diálogo," by contrast, Monardes underscores the equal "nobility" of artisanal work by giving his artisan character the name of "Ortuño"—an ancient Basque noble lineage whose name derives etymologically from the Latin roots fortuna (fortune) and hortus (garden), thus evoking the idea of empirical knowledge and the manipulation of nature by art and linking his Hermetic art to Monardes's own of botany or exotic horticulture.

Having underlined the equality of the three realms of knowledge, Monardes has his three characters engage in an egalitarian dialogue that is divided into two parts. In the first part, they discuss the genesis of iron and steel, the methods of their production, and their technological uses; in the second part, they treat the metals' elemental properties and uses in medicine. The doctor is hereby the expert on the physical, (al-)chemical, and medicinal aspects of iron and steel; Ortuño is the expert on their technological production and uses; and Burgos is the expert on their pharmaceutical uses. However, whereas Burgos's theoretical learning seems somewhat limited (he only cites the Al-Andalusians Albucasis and Averroes on the preparation of medicines, and is otherwise mostly responsible for raising questions), the doctor is the authority on the written record on iron and steel. Thus, he embarks on a learned disquisition on their origins and qualities. Iron and steel, he explains, are made "by means of alchemy and from them quintessence, as gold and silver are made: the alchemists say that the metal most suited to their designs and effects is iron."[61] Citing a formidable, if eclectic, array of alchemical authorities, the doctor argues not only that iron is created through the "same means and of the same matter as gold and silver" but also that it is "more excellent" than gold and silver because it is "more useful and necessary than all the other metals."[62] Although all metals were equally engendered in the earth from substances placed there by God at the Creation of the world, iron is singular in creation for its contrary qualities, being both hot and cold at the same time, thus having a perfect balance of properities. Citing Avicenna, the doctor explains that "iron has a complexion and temperament that participates in both qualities. Through its mercury, it is cold and because it has no moistness mixed with these qualities and is so dry, it is hard and strong. Through its sulfur, it is warm; it consumes, dries, opens, and is comfortative, it stimulates the appetite and does marvelous things because of its warmth that we will explain."[63] While he submits that some implements made of iron, such as the handgun, are surely inventions of the Devil, more generally, iron and steel, not gold and silver, are the keys to power and dominion in the form of weapons. Indeed, it was Europeans' possession not of gold, but of tools produced from iron, the doctor argues, that allowed them to discover and conquer the New World. Not only did the iron needle in the compass assist their transoceanic navigations, but it also awed the Indians into submission: "When they were first discovered, the Indians marveled at the Spaniards, who sewed with a needle, which seemed something miraculous, and they traded a great deal of gold for one needle."[64]

Significantly, Monardes dedicates the "Diálogo" to the second Duke of Alcalá de los Gazules, Fernando Enriquez de Ribera (1527–1594), who was not only one of the leading aristocrats of Andalusia but also the husband of Juana Cortés Ramírez de Arellano (?–1588), a daughter of the conqueror of Mexico, Hernando Cortés.[65] Monardes points out to the duke that iron has "great medicinal virtues" and also is an instrument by which the "brave have won great titles and renown."[66] The reference to titles and renown alludes to the role that the duke's own ancestors, the "Admirals of Castile," had played in the Reconquista after Fernando III had created the title following his conquest of Seville in 1248: "With powerful arms, gripping a lance, sword in hand, triumphing in battle, winning villages and towns, they won the name and immortal fame that they enjoy today."[67] Moreover, through his marriage to Juana, the duke had crossed his illustrious lineage with that of Cortés, who, through "immense travails," conquered the New World and there won not only "villages and towns" but also "kingdoms and empires."[68] Surely, the duke's own children will follow in the footsteps of these two great lines of ancestors and "emulate the feats and heroic deeds they did, taking for their instrument iron, which in such military endeavors will be a great and helpful tool."[69] Thus, from the very outset, Monardes emphasizes the technological applications of the scientific interest in metals and the salvific consequences of these practical applications by effecting the triumph of Christianity and Spanish civility over infidels in Spain and pagans in America.

Synthesizing empirical discovery with textual tradition, as well as the scientific interest in the material world, with Christian militancy and messianic salvation, the language of alchemy lent a strongly transcendent, spiritual, and magical character to the early modern "hunt" for exotic spices and drugs in early modern writings about the the discovery of the New World such as Monardes's *Historia medicinal*. Unlike gold or Dragon's Blood, however, which was associated with a rich cultural web of associations and analogies in a long tradition of Old World alchemy and natural history, the majority of New World exotic plants, such as tobacco, entered the early modern literature of discovery "naked," decontextualized from their meaning in Native American cultures—as a sort of "secret" knowledge that early modern Europeans came to associate with idolatry and diabolism. Thus, the sixteenth-century literature of the discovery and conquest of the New World represents the first step in early modern natural philosophy that Francois Jacob has described as a "scraping clean" of living bodies: things "shook off their crust of analogies, resemblances and signs," he writes, "to appear in all the nakedness of their true outer shape.... What was read or related no longer carried the weight of what was seen.... What counted was not so much the code used by God for creating nature as that sought by man for understanding it."[70]

It is at this juncture, then, that we can begin to see the significance of the European encounter with American nature to Stephen Gaukroger's question of why in the modern West the hermeneutic models of the natural sciences were able to establish cognitive hegemony—a hegemony that he deems to be "pathological" by comparative standards.[71] In medieval alchemy, the "hunt" for the secrets of nature between and beyond the categories of scientific reason had essentially been an esoteric tradition, limited in practice to private individuals, often operating in isolation and on the borders of religious orthodoxy. In the context of the European discovery and conquest of the New World, its rhetorical, hermeneutical, and epistemological models and methods became appropriated as instruments of the early modern and imperial state, such as the Spanish Casa de Contratación and Consejo de Indias (Council of the Indies). As historians of early modern Spanish science such as Antonio Barrera-Osorio, Maria Portuondo, Arndt Brendecke, and others have argued, if the decisive factor in the emergence of modern science was the interaction between artisans and scholars, through which scholars began to hold artisans and their methods in higher esteem than in the past, this process "took place within the European imperial and commercial expansion of the sixteenth and seventeenth centuries. Merchants, royal officials, artisans, natural historians, pilots, and cosmographers came together in institutions such as courts and academies, where their economic and political interests overlapped."[72] As we saw in chapter 6, New World missionaries such as José de Acosta also played a crucial role in legitimating empirical inquiry, giving rise to a new genre of ethno-demonology. But while missionaries such as Acosta still invoked the theme of the alchemical wedding in his *Historia natural y moral* in the context of the spiritual conquest, both Spanish colonial naturalists and Protestant imperialists were appropriating the motif for more temporal ends. In the last section of this chapter, I turn to one such Spanish colonial hunter of secrets—Juan de Cárdenas—while in the next chapter, I will turn to several Protestant alchemist writers about America, including Richard Eden, Walter Raleigh, and Thomas Harriot.

Juan de Cárdenas's Secrets and America's Watery Voids

Juan de Cárdenas (1563–ca. 1592) was born in Seville and emigrated to New Spain as a young man in 1577. After studying medicine at the University of Mexico, he dedicated his life to the study of New World nature and, in 1591, published his *Primera parte de los problemas y secretos marauillosos de las indias,* in which he described for his (mainly European) readers everything that was strange, new, and marvelous about the New World—the natural abundance of its flora and fauna, its excessive climates and earthquakes, its volcanoes, minerals, and metals, as well as its people and their physical constitutions and cultural habits. As he writes, "In the Indies, everything is portentous, everything is surprising, everything is different and on a larger scale than that of the Old World." And it was his aim to "find an explanation for so many phenomena and events, previously little known in the dogmatic scholarship of the ancient sages."[73]

For this purpose, the book is divided into three parts. In the first part (or "book"), Cárdenas focused on the land, as well flora and fauna. Like Monardes, he was especially interested in the marvelous medicinal properties of American plants, including tobacco, the cocoa bean, and the peyote mushroom.[74] Book 3 was devoted to a discussion of the people of New Spain—Indians, creoles, and Spaniards. He noted that creoles appeared to age more quickly than Spaniards; that the former are more prone to stomach problems than the latter; and that the former, while generally more prone to diseases while young, tend to be healthier in old age than are their Spanish counterparts. Still firmly informed by Aristotelian physics and Galenic medicine, Cárdenas explained the natural peculiarities of American plants, animals, and people in terms of the excessive humidity of the natural environment and the occult influences of the stars, which affected all aspects of nature, including also its people. The predominant physical complexion of the land in the Indies is hot and humid, resulting in the predominantly phlegmatic physiological and psychological complexion of its inhabitants. Although Cárdenas, being born in Spain, was not technically a creole, the book offered a defense of the character of New Spanish creoles, much maligned by Europeans for its alleged "degeneracy" induced by the occult influences of the humid natural environment and the stars in the New World. By contrast, Cárdenas offered a protoracialist explanation for human diversity, arguing that whereas the excessive phlegm in creole bodies was entirely contingent on the natural environment (and therefore "accidental" and reversible), in the Indians the phlegmatic constitution was "essential" to their nature. For this reason, his book has been called "the first modern treatise on racial psychology."[75]

In the second book, which is the focus of my interest here, Cárdenas dealt with the scientific "secrets" of New Spain's mineral resources and the technical "problems" of exploiting them, especially the extraordinary consumption of mercury that was required for silver mining. In order to remedy the problem, he recommended the use of salt, a new technique that had been developed in German mining in the wake of Paracelsian alchemy, in which salt was seen as one of the three most elemental substances in the composition of metal, besides mercury and sulfur.[76] Thus, he explains, the metallurgical process by which the ore is ground and mixed with salt and mercury until, after a few days, the mercury has thoroughly "embraced" the silver (*abraçarse la plata y el azogue*) and the miners can wash out the ore with water, leaving only the mixture or silver and mercury, which are then separated with the alchemical use of fire. In the mixture of silver and mercury, the salt is not itself involved in this "embrace" but merely acts as a provider of heat, as does the fire in the later process of separation, thus helping the "quicksilver [to] penetrate it [the ore] better, and embrace the silver."[77]

In trying to explain why in the amalgamation process mercury is lost in exact proportion with the silver extracted, he elaborates a distinctly corpuscular theory of matter, writing that "mercury is composed of very subtle and very penetrative parts, which are so thin that, at some point, fire or anything else causing heat makes them fly and converts them into smoke."[78] This penetration and subtlety can be empirically verified when mercury interacts with other substances, such as bones. Moreover, during the alchemical separation process, the vapor that is being generated condenses on the furnace wall as reconverted liquid mercury. This liquid mercury is the *same* mercury that was previously converted into gas, thus proving that the material particles survive the transformation of liquid into vaporous mercury and is not regenerated anew, as the Scholastic Aristotelian matter theory that was being taught at the universities would have it. In Scholastic Aristotelian matter theory, there was no need to inquire into the structure of matter, since it was presumed to be entirely homogeneous, continuous, solid, and infinitely divisible. Any inquiry into the microstructure would simply confirm what was already known about the elemental composition of all matter in terms of a particular mixture of the four elements and the qualities arising from the particularities of a given mixture. By contrast, alchemical matter theory presupposed a mixture of dissimilar smallest parts which behave in distinctive ways in any given mixture. In order to understand the qualities of a given substance, it was therefore important to understand the unique and individual qualities of its smallest parts and their unique interaction in a given compound.

Cárdenas's alchemical theory of matter as consisting of particles and pores also inspires his interest in the natural properties of New Spain's landscape, especially his fascination with the occult spaces of the subterranean caves that pervade New Spain and, like the stars, influence the qualities of the land, its flora and fauna, as well as its human civilizations. For Cárdenas, New Spain's subterranean world, flora and fauna, human culture, and the celestial world were all connected through occult correspondences that transcend the Aristotelian ontological division between the sublunar and superlunar regions and thus suggest a distinctly Llullified (i.e., Neoplatonic) alchemical understanding of the cosmos, in which every material thing and body is subject to the occult influences of the stars and planets. Each planet has hereby a special "dominion" over things in the sublunary realm:

> Although it is true that all the planets generally influence all things and bodies in the world, we have to understand that each one in particular has its own and most characteristic influence over those things with which it has most friendship [amistad] and afinity. Thus, the moon, to which pertains coldness and moistness, particularly dominates over water, the fish and silver, as well as over all cold and moist things, and so all these things noticeably change in their movements ascent, occasions, oppositions, and conjunctions. Mercury is the planet that is closest to the moon in the heavens, so its nature is such that it influences change and variety. It predominates over mercury, the chameleon, colorful stones, and all things that have a propensity to change.... The sun, as prince and lord of all the astral signs and planets has dominion over all precious and excellent things over every species. For example, among the animals, it has special dominion over man and the lion; among bird, over the eagle; among the bodily organs, the heat; and among the stones, the carbuncle; and among the spices, saffron.[79]

Through this web of occult influences in nature, each realm—the celestial, the sublunary, the terrestrial, and the subterranean—"penetrates" the other. "It is necessary to note," he writes, "that with the same chance that the sun and other planets of the heavens, penetrate with their celestial influence into the deepest abyss of the earth, there rise, from the humidity that is there contained, great volumes of humid vapors."[80] Just as the heat of the tropical sun influences sublunary nature, so does subterranean nature influence terrestrial nature. But whereas the former's dominant element is fire and its dominant quality heat, the latter's dominant element is water and its dominant quality moistness. The occult correspondences (*ocultos secretos*) between these different realms explain, for example, the exceptional humidity of the New World, which is more "porous" than the old and thus capable of absorbing more water. In fact, the continent of America is nothing but a number of islands that are highly concentrated but discrete parts (or particles) separated by voids filled with water that is easily penetrated. Thus, he writes:

> The humidity... takes its principle and origin from the part of the center and the abyss of this land; and so that we can better understand this, it will be necessary to note a strange property of the ground in the Indies, which is that in the inner part it is full, or better said, contaminated with terrible voids [*huecos*] and caverns [*cavernas*], which are the cause ... of the great and continuous earthquakes that happen in the Indies. As nature does not have a vacuum, these caverns are necessarily full of water.[81]

Because of the excessive tropical heat, the water contained in the subterranean pores evaporates and humidifies the air. The general principle of porousness affects all aspects of American nature—its plants, foods, medicine, and animal life as well as human bodies and cultures, making them less "solid" and substantial and more pervious to all sort of influences, including disease. American foods are less substantial because they consist mainly of holes, pores, and voids. American bodies are more susceptible to heat and cold because their "pores are open" and pervious to fluctuations in temperature from day to night, allowing subtle and small influences to "penetrate immediately through the said pores [*poros*] and thereby to effect sudden changes and do great damage."[82]

The language of embrace and penetration with regard to American matter in Cárdenas's *Secretos* has clear sexual overtones that echo the motif of the alchemical wedding that we already perceived (in chapter 6) in Acosta's *Historia natural y moral,* published the year before. Of course, whereas Acosta was primarily interested in the porousness of American souls in the act of religious conversion, Cárdenas, a Spanish American settler colonial, was interested in the porousness of American land. As we will see, the language of sexual penetration (*coniunctio*) in the motif of the alchemical wedding between Europe and America that was being articulated in the Spanish literature of the discovery and conquest of America would also have an afterlife in the literature of the English conquest of America. Thus, in his *Purchas his Pilgrimes,* Samuel Purchas applied the marriage allegory of an American bride taking an English husband.

> But looke upon Virginia; view her lovely looks (howsoever like a modest Virgin she is now vailed with wild Coverts and shadie Woods, expecting rather

ravishment then Mariage from her Native Savages) survey her Heavens, Elements, Situation; her divisions by armes of Bayes and Rivers into so goodly and well proportioned limmes and members; her Virgin portion nothing empaired, nay not yet improved, in Natures best Legacies; the neighbouring Regions and Seas so commodious and obsequious; her opportunities for offence and defence; and in all these you shall see, that she is worth the wooing and loves of the best Husband.[83]

In Purchas's version of the alchemy of conquest, a peculiar transformation of the marriage motif has occurred. Thus, whereas in Acosta's text, the bride personified the American Indians, and her dowry was American silver, in both Cárdenas and Purchas, the bride is the *land* of America, and her dowry is her natural fertility for which she has been "ravished" (rather than "married") by her Native American suitors, but which she is saving for her legitimate husband—the European miner or husbandman.[84] As we will see, this transformation of Acosta's alchemical wedding into a colonial ideology was the product of the alchemy of translation that resulted in the "White Legend" of the English discovery as a penetration of the virginal "maidenhead" of America.

Part IV

The Alchemy of the White Legend

10

Walter Raleigh's Legends
Black, Gold, and White

In the last paragraph of his *The Discoverie of the Large, Rich, and Bewtifvl Empyre of Guiana* (1596), Walter Raleigh reports that, during the time of the Spanish conquest of Peru, an ancient prophecy was found in one of the main temples at Cusco that foretold not only the fall of the old Inca capital to the Spaniards but also the Incas' eventual delivery from the Spanish colonial yoke and their restoration as legitimate lords of their empire. This restoration of the "Inga" would be brought about by men from "Inglatierra" and had, Raleigh averred, already begun with his own expedition up the Orinoco River in 1595 in search of "Manoa," a rich city rumored to be located in the remote interiors of the South American jungle. For, Raleigh explains, this "Inga" was none other than the legendary king of Manoa, also known as "El Dorado" for his alleged practice of an annual initiation rite during which he completely covered himself with gold dust and submerged in a lake. If this El Dorado had hitherto remained elusive, Raleigh appealed to his queen to "give order for the rest, and either defend it, and hold it as tributary, or conquer and keep it as empress of the same."[1]

Despite Raleigh's ardent appeal, however, Queen Elizabeth did not invest in his adventure to discover El Dorado; and Raleigh's own subsequent attempts, as well as those of his lieutenant, Lawrence Keymis, remained as unsuccessful as had been the previous Spanish endeavors. Worse, Raleigh's second expedition to Guiana in 1617 ended in the death of his son; in Keymis's suicide; and, ultimately, in his own execution in 1618 as a punishment for the illegal attack that Keymis had launched in Guiana against a Spanish garrison in defiance of King James's explicit order to honor the peace treaty with Spain. But for all these disasters, Raleigh's *Discoverie* was arguably a success in at least one respect—*not* as a historical chronicle of an actual English discovery and conquest but as a fiction that legitimated the *idea* of an English discovery of America, an America that had not yet been discovered by Spain but remained secret, saving itself for discovery by the English.[2] The legitimation of such an idea was no mean rhetorical feat in 1596, after more than a hundred years of Spanish discoveries and conquests in the Americas. In elaborating this idea,

Raleigh's narrative alchemy amalgamated ethnographic account and local lore with Spanish imperial historiography of the discovery and conquest as well as mythological, religious, and alchemical traditions derived from Classical antiquity, late medieval Aristotelianism, and early modern Neoplatonism. Thus, the story of the prophecy of the "Inga" who would be redeemed by a man from "Inglatierra" synthesized the classical story of Jason and the Argonauts and the late medieval millenarian tradition of the Last World emperor that had already inspired Columbus with the Andean apocalyptic tradition of *pachakuti*, the "turner of the world," with which Raleigh was patently familiar from his avid study of the Spanish chronicles of the conquest of Peru. Raleigh's *Discoverie* was hereby foundational in elaborating an English ideology of occupation as a *non*-conquest, resulting from the "discovery" of the secret void left in America by the Spanish conquest. It is an ideology that I want to call the "White Legend," in which the notion of an English "discovery" of a Golden America emerged in the discourse of the "Black Legend" of the Spanish conquest.

In this chapter, I investigate the role that alchemical ideas played in the history of this "White Legend" and its close dependence on the literature about the Spanish conquest. For this purpose, I focus on several of the earliest English texts about America during the sixteenth and early seventeenth centuries, written by promoters of English colonialism such as Richard Eden, John Dee, and Walter Raleigh. It is no coincidence, I will argue, that many of the early English writers about America not only were avid readers of Spanish accounts of the conquest of America but also had a strong interest in alchemy, for they saw the English penetration of a "secret" America in analogy to the alchemical inquiry into the structure of matter in terms of *minima naturalia* (corpuscles, atoms, etc.) and secret voids (or pores). However, whereas we will see in this chapter that the earliest English writers about America such as Eden and Raleigh imitated the model of the Spanish conquistadors in viewing America as a sort of macrocosmic crucible in the pursuit of gold, we will see in the next chapter that the English interest soon shifted from America's mineral wealth and pagan souls to its fecundity in "commodities," to be had through trade and the appropriation of land. If the early utopianism of the Protestant White Legend soon turned into a "cant of conquest" during the seventeenth century (as the historian Francis Jennings has argued),[3] the language of alchemy was at the root of an emerging English ethno-demonology that again heavily borrowed from Spanish historians of the conquest such as Acosta.

Richard Eden and the Alchemy of Translation

In his seminal 1970 study *Science in the British Colonies of America,* Raymond Stearns devoted his first chapter to what he called the "old science" in America—the sixteenth-century Spanish natural historians of the New World Gonzalo Fernández de Oviedo y Valdés, Nicolás Monardes, José de Acosta, and others—before turning to the actual topic of his book: science in the British colonies of America, which would presumably be the "new" (i.e., Baconian) science emerging during the seventeenth century.[4] The old/new binary in Stearns's organization of the history of science in the Americas was a common rhetorical feature among twentieth-century Anglophone and northern European historians of science. It undergirded narratives of the so-called Scientific Revolution that depended on a strict modern observance of modern national, cultural, and linguistic boundaries that obscured the significant intellectual debt that sixteenth- and seventeenth-century men of science in fact owed to the sixteenth-century tradition of natural history about the New World.[5] As a case in point, I want to begin here with the works of one of the most prolific English translators of the Spanish literature of the discovery and conquest of America, the noted alchemist Richard Eden.

Eden's interest in alchemy had apparently been inspired by his tutor at Queen's College, Thomas Smith, who had harbored a lifelong passion for distilling herbal remedies. In 1547, Eden was offered the position of distiller of waters in the royal household of Henry VIII, succeeding Thomas Seex at an annual salary of forty pounds. Eden was an avid student of the alchemical writings attributed to Roger Bacon, and the annotations of his copies of Bacon's texts betray a keen interest in the alchemical distillation of gold. After Henry's death, his successor, Edward VI, appointed someone else to the position, and Eden had to look around for gainful employment. He found a new patron in Richard Whalley, a Nottinghamshire gentleman and Receiver of the Court of Augmentations for Yorkshire, who employed Eden at his mansion so that he could devote himself to the search for the quintessence. During this time, Eden was also working on a translation of Vannoccio Biringuccio's enormously influential *De la pirotechnia,* which had been published at Venice in 1540 as the foundational work in alchemical metallurgy, foundry, mining, and explosives, offering detailed descriptions of furnaces, the processes of hardening antimony and of calcination, as well as the production of iron and steel.[6]

In 1552, Eden became secretary to Sir William Cecil and was charged to publicize the voyages to China and the Far East, in which Cecil was invested. Eden had good credentials for this appointment. After having translated Biringuccio's *De la pirotechnia,* he had begun to work on a translation of Sebastian Münster's monumental *Cosmographiae universalis,* written in Latin and published in Basel in 1550. Divided into two sections—one on east India and one on west India—Münster's work was one of the earliest and most comprehensive cosmographies to incorporate all the empirical knowledge gained with the new voyages of discovery. A scholar who had learned Hebrew and studied Jewish science,[7] Münster focused especially on the secret properties of the natural and mineral wealth of the newly discovered exotic places. Thus, the first section, which began with a summary of the Portuguese circumnavigation of Africa and the arrival at Calicut, details the virtues of "the diamond stone" and the secret uses to which it is put by Indian healers. The most precious among the stones, the diamond "not onely refuse[s] the forte of Iron but also resisteth the power of fyre, whose heate is so farre unable to melte it . . . and is also rather made purer thereby then anye wayes defiled or corrupted."[8] Its secret virtues counteract "poisons, and to frustrate the opperacion thereof, and being therefore greatly esteemed of kinges and Princes."[9] The second section (on the West Indies) provides an account of Columbus's first two voyages and of Magellan's circumnavigation; from there, it returns to Columbus's third voyage and the four voyages of Vespucci; it concludes with a theoretical discourse on "whether under the aequinoctial circle or burninge lyne (called Torrida zona) be habitable regions," in which he finds "no sufficiente causes why under that [equinoctial] line should be no habitable regions," citing diverse Greek, Roman, Alexandrian, and medieval textual authorities that appear to back up the empirical evidence derived from the recent explorations but which contradicted Aristotle.[10]

Eden published his translation of book 5 of Münster's text in 1553 under the title *A treatyse of the newe India, with other new founde lands and islandes, as well eastwarde as westware.* It provided accounts of India, China, and the Spice Islands, as well as the voyages of Columbus and Vespucci to the West Indies. Eden's last chapter, entitled "Whether under the Aequinoctial circle or burning lyne (called Torrida zona) be habitable regions," is not derived from Münster but from Aeneas Silvius Piccolomini (Pope Pius II, 1405–1464), whose *Cosmographia pii papae* had played a formative role in Christopher Columbus's geographic ideas by arguing that the habitable part of the globe extended beyond the Northern Hemisphere—in contradiction to Aristotle's theory of climactic zones.[11] In his prefatory address to John Dudley, the first Duke of Northumberland, Eden aligned Münster (and himself) with the tradition of the German Dominican friar, bishop, savant, and renowned man of science Albertus Magnus. As we saw in chapter 8, Albertus was a fabled alchemist whose occult knowledge was rumored not only to have made his garden bloom in the middle of winter but even to have constructed an artificial man, the homunculus, who was then allegedly destroyed by one of Albertus's most brilliant students, Thomas Aquinas, who warned his teacher against indulging in such "promethean ambitions."[12] Not only had Albertus already refuted Aristotle regarding the latter's claim of the uninhabitability of the equatorial regions of the earth, but his knowledge even exceeded that of St. Augustine, Eden explained, who fell into "erroure in the science of Astronomie in which he travayled but as a stranger."[13] Eden would most likely have been familiar with one of the numerous English translations of Albertus's writings on the magic properties of plants, such as *The Boke of Secretes of Albertus Magnus of the vertues of herbes, stones, and certaine beasts,* the fruit of his experiments with "herbes, stones, and certaine beasts" that have "great vertues" derived from "the influence of the planets . . . [as] every one of them taketh their vertue from the higher naturall powers."[14]

Like Columbus before him, Eden argued that the biblical Ophir and Tarshis, to which Solomon's navies sailed from Ezion-Gebir, lay in "the south parts of the world," and that these regions are most likely to produce precious metals, spices, and minerals: "For not only olde and new Histories, dayly experience, and the principles of Natural Philosophie doe agree, that the places moste apte to bring forth gold, spices, and precious stones, are the Southe and Southeast partes of the world, but also our Saviour Christ approveth the same declaring that the Quene of the Southe (meaning the Quene of Saba) came from the utmost partes of the worlde to hear the wisdom of Solomon."[15] Given Eden's apparent interest in the cosmology of precious metals, spices, and minerals, it is not surprising that the texts he chose to translate into English included not only works of alchemy and cosmography but also Spanish tracts on navigation. Thus, in 1561, he published *The Arte of Nauigation,* which was a translation of the *Breve compendio de la sphera y de la arte de navegar, con nuevos instrumentos y reglas, ejemplarizado con muy sutiles demostraciones* (Seville, 1551), written by the Spanish cosmographer Martín Cortés.[16]

In 1553, Mary I, a Catholic, ascended to the English throne and attempted to reverse the gains that the Protestant Reformation had made in England. The following year, she married Philip II of Spain, who promptly appointed Eden to a position in the treasury. In 1555, Eden published a second compilation of translations relating to the new geographic discoveries, entitled *The Decades of the New World*.[17] Clearly reflecting the new political reality in England, Eden's compilation included the first three decades of the *De orbo novo,* written by the Italian humanist and first official chronicler of the Indies, Peter Martyr; a Latin edition and English translation of Pope Alexander's bull *Inter cetera* (1493), which had divided the New World between Spain and Portugal; English translations of parts of Oviedo's *Natural hystoria,* and various other texts, such as Antonio Pigafetta's account of Magellan's cirumnavigation, a discourse by Francisco López de Gómara defending Spanish titles to the Americas as anchored in *Inter cetera;* accounts of South America by Amerigo Vespucci and Andrea Corsali; and accounts on Russia and Cathay. Also included was a part of his translation of Biringuccio's *Pyrotechnia,* in a chapter entitled "Of the generation of metalles and their mynes with the maner of fyndinge the same."[18]

Evidently, Eden saw a connection between the history of geographical discovery, navigation, cosmography, natural history, mining, and alchemy. Indeed, there were some striking similarities between the circumstances in which late medieval polymaths such as Roger Bacon delved into Hermetic-Arabic texts of alchemy and in which early modern English alchemists such as Eden translated Spanish texts about New World cosmography and navigation. Whereas Roger Bacon was incited by the rising tide of Islam and the imminent battles against the Antichrist in the Eschaton, Eden was preoccupied with England's geopolitical and economic crisis in the conflict with other European powers during the age of overseas expansionism. Thus, during the 1550s, England had been plagued by the economic repercussions of the war with France (1552–56), as specie had been leaving the country and created a chronic shortage of bullion. Efforts were stepped up to exploit the silver mines within England, but Dudley (the addressee of Eden's preface) had concocted a bolder scheme with Sebastian Cabot: they would sail an army in pinnaces up the Amazon River and wrest Peru from Spain, which was extracting enormous sums of silver during the 1540s from the newly discovered mines at Potosí. While the hare-brained scheme was prudently abandoned, both Dudley and Eden apparently conceived of the geographic secrets of the New World, which had been jealously guarded by Spanish cosmographers during the sixteenth century,[19] in analogy to the secrets of alchemy, jealously guarded by medieval adepts: both were branches of empirical and artisanal forms of knowledge whose trade secrets in the procurement of precious metals assumed enormous political importance in the context of imperial rivalry and warfare during the age of European expansionism. Eden hereby continued the tradition in what I have called the "ecstatic materialism" of Christopher Columbus, who, in times of exceptional political and spiritual crisis, found the "key" to the secrets of the world already contained in Scripture and medieval alchemical prophecy.[20]

The connections that Eden apparently saw between alchemy and the voyages of discovery shed light on his presentation of Oviedo's natural history. In his preface to the reader, Eden writes that, though Peter Martyr of Angleria is still unrivalled "in declarynge by philosophical discourses the secreate causes of naturall affectes bothe as touchynge the lande, the sea, the stares, and other straugne woorkes of nature . . . *Gonzalus Ferndinandus Ouiedus,* (whom the lerned *Cardanus* compareth to the ancient writers) is doubtless the chiefe" among those who can speak from eyewitness experience. However, Eden entirely reorganized Oviedo's natural history, getting rid of most of the subject headers, to the effect of enhancing its appearance as a coherent account and of almost entirely losing its taxonomic character as a catalogue of nature. Eden's reordering of materials betrays his primary interest in Oviedo's text. After Oviedo's introductory prologue to Charles V and the first chapter, which provides details about the voyage, Eden bypasses some eighty chapters that contain virtually all of Oviedo's naturalistic descriptions of the island of Hispaniola and Tierra Firme, their flora and fauna (including Oviedo's famous descriptions of New World animals and exotic fruits), as well as their Native populations and their cultural practices—in effect everything that had identified Oviedo's text as a natural history. Instead, Eden proceeds to the conclusion—in which Oviedo discusses the easy accessibility of the Caribbean from Europe—and then to chapter 82, which offers a discussion of the gold mines of Castilla de Oro, in Tierra Firme. Eden omits Oviedo's chapter 83 (on fish and fishing) and jumps to chapter 84 (on pearl fishing). Then, he returns to Oviedo's tenth chapter, entitled "Indians of Tierra Firme, Their Customs, Rites, and Ceremonies," but omits everything except for Oviedo's discussion of the *tequina*—the Indian warlords—and he retitles the chapter "Of the familiarity which certeyne of the Indians have with the deuyll, and howe they receaue answere of hym of thynges to come."[21] In sum, from Eden's reordering of Oviedo's natural history, it is evident that the English alchemist's newfound interest in cosmography lay primarily in American gold and silver.

In addition, Eden seemed interested in the philosophical and theoretical questions that Oviedo's natural history had raised about the New World and cosmography more generally. Thus, Eden picks up from an earlier part of Oviedo's chapter on the customs of the Indians, but he retitles it "Of the temperature of the regions under or neare to be burnt lyne cauled Torrida zona or the Equinoctiall: and of the dyvers seasons of the yeare." In this section Oviedo had presented his dispute with the ancients who had claimed that the torrid zone was uninhabitable. Eden inserts here a lengthy footnote in order to shed light on "the secreate woorke of nature" making it possible that the torrid zone should have temperate climates.[22] The reason for this, Eden explains, is the prevalence of water there, which has its "course toward the South as to the lowest part of the earth."[23] In other words, the Southern Hemisphere has more water because water has a tendency to flow "downward" into its proper, lower place (according to Aristotelian physics). As modern discoveries have revealed, the downward tendency of water is not just an accidental aspect of the natural order; rather, it is an *essential* part of a divine providential design that had been hidden from the ancients. Eden quotes from "De elementis"—specifically the *De subtilitate libri XXI* (1550)—by Girolamo Cardano, who had written that the ancients' belief that the world was mostly made up of land, with only little terrain being covered by the Ocean Sea, held true only for the Northern Hemisphere. The reason why God had made it this way was that "water by its couldnesse might temperate and not destroy the lyfe of beastes."[24] The hot South has therefore much water and the cold north has little. If it were any different, the torrid zone would indeed be uninhabitable, as Aristotle posited. The reason the pagan philosopher was wrong about the climate of the torrid zone was his ignorance of Christian Revelation and the gradual unveiling of God's providential design that only the experience of modern discoveries had brought.

One of the consequences of these revelations is the realization that the scientific knowledge derived from cosmological conjecture, as derived by way of reason, turns out to be erroneous. The defiance of West Indian climate to be reduced to European concepts of the seasons is a case in point. Whereas in Europe, July is hot because it is in summer and January is cold because it is in winter,

> in golden Castile or *Beragua,* it is contrary. For the sommer and tyme of greatest drowght and withowt rayne, is at Chrystman and a moneth before and a moneth after. And the tyme when it rayneth most, is about midsummer and a moneth before and a moneth after. And this season whiche they caule winter, is not for that it is any coulder then, then at any other tyme of the yeare, or hotter at Christmas then at other seasons, the tyme in these regions being ever after one maner, but for that that in this tyme which they caule winter, the soonne is hyd from theyr syghtes by reason of cloudes and rayne more then at other tymes. Yet forasmuch as for the moste parte of the yeare they lyue in a cleare, open, and temperate ayer, they sumwhat shrynke and feele a little coulde durynge the tyme of the said moist and cloudy ayer, althowth it bee not coulde in deede, or at the least such coulde as hath any sensible sharpenes.[25]

Thus, the experiential encounter with Caribbean climate turns (presumed) universal categories of realist metaphysics such as winter into the relative categories of nominalist metaphysics—"winter."

When Eden does finally return to Oviedo's botanical and zoological headings, he offers a rather condensed translation of Oviedo's descriptions of the animal world of the West Indies, discussing all of the plants as well as animals, fish, and birds summarily in one chapter each. Moreover, rather than translating Oviedo's sections devoted to Native American culture, Eden merely refers his reader to Peter Martyr's *Decades* (which preceded Oviedo's text in Eden's anthology). Eden closes with a few paragraphs from Oviedo dealing with "Bacalaos" (Isle of Cods) and assigns it its own chapter title: "Of the lande of Bacaoleos cauled Terra Baccalearum, situate on the North side of the firme lande."[26] Thus, Eden's reorganization of Oviedo's natural history clearly manifests the promotional character of his translations. They were written with a curious eye on the natural resources and especially the mineral riches of the New World, as well as their economic potential in order to entice English adventurers to invest in a lucrative overseas enterprise.

Yet, if Eden's English translations from Oviedo and Peter Martyr manifested a growing English interest in America, they also provided English readers with a first glimpse of America's Native peoples, as well as their cultures and religions. Overall, Eden's translations would have left his English readers with an ambivalent impression in this regard, especially with respect to Native American religions. On the one hand, Eden's translations conveyed Peter Martyr's utopian humanist impressions of Amerindian life in a state without property, a "golden world" that invokes Hesiod's idea of history as a degeneration from a primal Golden Age to a Silver and Bronze Age, and finally to the Iron present.[27] On the other hand, Eden's translations also conveyed Martyr's association of Caribbean and Mesoamerican sacred images and figures, called Zemes, with diabolism. Thus, translating from Peter Martyr, Eden writes:

> They make certeyne Images of gossampine cotton foulded or wrethed after theyr maner, and harde stopped within. These Images they make sytting, much lyke vnto the pictures of sprites [*sic*] and deuelles which owr paynters are accustomed to pain vppon waules. . . . These Images, th[e] inhabitants caule *Zemes:* wherof the leaste, made to the lykenes of younge devuels, they bind to theyr forheads when they goo to the warres ageynst their enemies. . . . For they thinke that these *Zemes* are the mediatours and messengers of the greate god, whom they acknowleage to be only one, eternall, withowte ende, omnipotent and inuisible.[28]

Eden also translated Martyr's account of an epic battle between two Indians, one of whom had embraced Christianity and another who still worships his "*Zemes,*" which are manifestations of "the deuyll to whose similitude theyr Images are made . . . who immediately appeared in his lykenes about the younge man that stoode in the defence of Sathans kyngedome."[29] But, as soon as the Christianized Native utters the Hail Mary, "there appeared a fayre virgin clothed in whyte, at whose presence the deuell vanguisshed immediately."

But despite such demonological passages in Peter Martyr's original text, in which the European conquest is framed as an epic battle between the forces of God and the forces of Satan, in the "Preface to the Reader," Eden offers an interpretation that mitigates the diabolism of his original. Rather, Eden follows the apologetic interpretations of Columbus and Las Casas of the Indians as spiritual blank slates awaiting inscription by the European Christian and civilizer. Thus, he writes, "These simple gentiles lyuinge only after the lawe of nature, may well bee likened to a smoothe and bare table vnpainted, or a white paper vnwritten, vpon the which yow may at the first paynte or wryte what yow lyste."[30] Yet, paradoxically, he also suggests that the Indians' spirituality was not a blank slate, or *prima materia,* but a "form" that had to be annihilated (rased) before it can be "painted" when writing that "as yow can not vppon tables alredy paynted, vnless yow rase or lot owt the fyrste forms."[31] This paradox suggests that Eden was familiar with both the hylomorphic and the alchemical hermeneutics of Amerindian spirituality and conversion that he had inherited from the Spanish tradition of ethnography about the Americas. But while Eden remains noncommittal in this regard, it is clear that his translations manifest a growing English interest in the Americas and that he envisioned the Spanish model of conquest and the extraction of America's mineral wealth as one to be emulated, rather than superseded, by the English. He hereby drew on the analogy that Spanish (or Latin) historians of the conquest saw between geographic discovery and alchemical inquiry, as well as between tropical nature and the alchemical crucible, which produce the redemptive gold or Philosophers' Stone that will bring about transformation and universal Christian empire.

John Dee and the Hermetic Empire

Not surprisingly, Eden's early works, published during the 1550s under the Catholic regime of Mary and Philip, were still distinctly pro-Spanish in their political orientation, as is evident in his reproduction of Pope Alexander's bulls *Inter cetera* with their apologia by López de Gómara. Unlike their French contemporaries, the earliest English writers about America did not usually challenge Spanish hegemony and rights of dominion in the New World as codified in the Alexandrine bulls. Although John Cabot had been the first early modern European to explore the North American coastline in 1497, his explorations had been undertaken under commission of Henry VII of England, who was still a Catholic and therefore bound to respect the Alexandrine bulls of donation.[32] His son and successor, Henry VIII, despite his defiance of the pope's authority with regard to the annulment of his marriage to Catherine of Aragon, was also reluctant to invest in the western enterprise, as was his son, Edward VI. English overseas exploration intensified during the reign of Elizabeth, who came to the throne after Mary's death in 1558. In the 1570s, Martin Frobisher and Michael Lok launched an expedition to the North Atlantic coastlines of America with the support of the Muscovy Company; but the Frobisher voyages were initially undertaken in search of a northwest passage to Asia rather than with the intent of gaining a colonial foothold in the Americas. Frobisher's crew also experimented with mining and settlement in the Arctic coasts of the Labrador Sea during the second and third voyage. However, the enterprise ended in financial disaster when Frobisher brought back from his third voyage (1578) 1,350 tons of what he thought was gold ore but turned out to be worthless iron pyrite, despite the fact that his expedition had included five trained assayers. Four years later, in 1583, Sir Humphrey Gilbert, who had been granted a royal patent for the exploration and colonization of North America, launched an expedition to found a colony in Newfoundland, but this enterprise also failed when Gilbert's flagship, the *Squirrel,* sank near the Azores in a storm, killing him and his crew. Thus, by the end of the first decade or so of Elizabeth's reign, English overseas activities had amounted mainly to privateering expeditions, culminating with Sir Francis Drake's spectacular raids in the Caribbean and the Spanish Main during the 1570s and 1580s.[33]

Nevertheless, during the 1570s Elizabethans did begin to devise more ambitious plans and rationales for challenging Spanish hegemony in the Atlantic and the Americas. The applied arts and sciences unlocking the secrets of nature were hereby regarded as vital for national survival in the new imperial rivalry with Spain. Among the most important theorists of the application of the arts and sciences for the purpose of empire during those years was the Elizabethan alchemist, astrologer, hermeticist, magician, necromancer, and mathematician John Dee (1527–1608). Dee had one of the largest libraries of Europe, with no fewer than ninety-two editions of works by Paracelsus, as well as other occultists such as Adam von Bodenstein, Alexander von Suchten, Gerhard Dorn, Leonhardt Thurneyesser zum Thurn, and Konrad Gesner.[34] In addition, Dee owned a large library of works written by (or attributed to) Ramón Llull, whom Dee had first studied while still a student at Cambridge and later during his stay in Leuven and in Prague at the court of the Holy Roman Emperor Rudolph II (1552–1612).[35] In his own works, Dee elaborated a comprehensive program for the application of the sciences in the national service of British imperialism. Whereas the medieval English polymath Roger Bacon had emphasized the practical applications of his "experimental science" in the Christian apocalyptic wars against infidels and the Antichrist, Dee, his early modern intellectual heir, insisted on the importance of the natural and applied sciences, including mathematics, for national survival in the imperial rivalry with Spain.

In 1564, Dee published his *Monas hieroglyphica*, where he employed arguments from Llull's combinatory logic, pseudo-Llullian alchemy, as well as kabbala, and mathematics to offer a theory of the Creation from a monistic unity of point, line, and circle. In 1570, Dee wrote a preface to the first English translation of Euclid's *Elements*, undertaken by the lord mayor of London, Sir Henry Billingsley, based on a Greek (rather than a Latin) original. In addition, in 1577, Dee published his *General and Rare Memorials Pertayning to the Perfecte Arte of Navigation,* in which he implored his queen to build a Royal Navy that would be able to stand up to Spanish maritime power, to protect English commercial and geopolitical interests in the Atlantic, and "to set furth Ships, for a Northwest Discouery."[36] Also, Dee offered there a mythological history of English discoveries going back to King Arthur and Prince Madoc. Thus, he presented a map of America on the back of which he outlined Elizabeth's "Title Royall to . . . foreyn Regions," especially in "Atlantis" (or America), by the right of discoveries made by "Lord Madoc, Sonne to Owen Gzynedd Prynce of Northwales." This Prince Madoc, Dee argued, founded a "Colonie and inhabited Terra Florida, or thereabouts," and Arthur, who allegedly "not only Conquered Iseland, Groenland, and all the Northern Iles compassing unto Russia, But even . . . the North Pole."[37] Finally, in "Of Famous and Rich Discoveries" (1577), "A brief Remembraunce of Sondrye foreyne Regions, discovered, inhabited, and partlie Conquered by the Subjects of this Brytish Monarchie" (1578), and especially in *The Limits of the British Empire* (*Brytanici Imperii Limites,* 1593), Dee elaborated a rationale of a comprehensive British claim to North America. Sidestepping the provisions of the Alexandrine bulls *Inter cetera* still accepted by Eden, Dee argued that, based on natural law, Roman law and the law of nations (*ius gentium*), "mere discovery" was no legal basis for titles of dominion without actual occupation.[38] Thus, he reasoned that, even though North America may have been included in the papal donation of 1493, the Spaniards had forfeited their titles there, due to their failure to occupy and settle. It was an imperial program that rested on the dual purpose of geographic discovery and historical recovery, a program that he called "this Brytish discovery and recovery enterprise."[39]

Although Queen Elizabeth and her advisers were initially reluctant to challenge Spanish naval power openly and therefore slow to implement Dee's proposals,[40] by the last decade of the sixteenth century, Dee's works had laid the ideological foundations for British imperial expansionism in the Americas. Dee's promotion of English overseas exploration and expansion abroad promised a political and spiritual renewal at home. It was a renewal in the sense of a reform or recovery of science and empire that was for him epitomized in the figure of Queen Elizabeth, who, according to Tudor mythology, was the heir to an Arthurian "British empire" (Imperium Brytanicum), whose divine destiny was to serve as the bulwark against the Catholic Hispano-Papal attempts at universal dominion.[41]

Walter Raleigh's Alchemical Wedding

The central figure in the attempt to translate Dee's dual reform of British science and empire into a coherent colonial enterprise in America during the Elizabethan period was the gentleman, soldier, courtier, and poet from Devon Walter Raleigh (1552–1618). Before becoming invested in the American colonial project, Raleigh had participated in the Elizabethan military campaigns in Ireland and was rewarded for his services with land confiscated from the native Irish. Due to the military valor he had demonstrated in Ireland, Raleigh's favors rose rapidly at Elizabeth's court, and he was knighted in 1585. The year before, on March 25, 1584, he had been granted a patent for the exploration and colonization of North America, after Gilbert's death in 1583 had left the earlier patant vacant. Thus, Raleigh was authorized by the queen to "discover search and fynde out and viewe such remote heathen and barbarous landes Contries and territories not actually possessed of any Christian Prynce" and "to haue holde occupy and enioye to him his heyres and assignes for ever."[42] Raleigh launched two attempts—one in 1585 and one in 1587—to found such a colony on Roanoke Island on the Outer Banks of what is today North Carolina, a land that he called "Virginia" in honor of the "Virgin Queen" Elizabeth. While both colonial ventures failed within a few years without having produced any of the anticipated riches from gold or trade with the Indians, they did result in some of the earliest and most seminal firsthand accounts originally written in English about North America (as we will see in the next chapter). With the immediate hopes for an English colony in North America dashed, Raleigh's standing at court further deteriorated sharply in 1591, when he secretly married one of the courtly ladies-in-waiting, Elizabeth Throckmorton, without obtaining the queen's permission—a transgression for which he was even briefly imprisoned in the Tower of London. In this moment of desperation, Raleigh turned his attention to South America, where the Spaniards had been extracting large sums of gold and silver and where a still undiscovered golden kingdom was rumored to exist in the remote interiors, known in the Spanish sources as the kingdom of El Dorado (the Golden One).[43]

In 1594, Raleigh sent, at his own expense, a reconnaissance mission to South America under the leadership of his lieutenant Jacob Whiddon. In February of the following year Raleigh set out on his own expedition to find the fabled city. During a stay-over on Trinidad, he sacked a Spanish garrison and captured the governor, Antonio de Berrío, who had also searched unsuccessfully for El Dorado during the 1580s. After interrogating Berrío, Raleigh proceeded to the South American mainland and slowly made his way up the Orinoco River to its junction with one of its tributaries, the Caroní River, near the Native village of Morequito. There, Raleigh attempted to forge an anti-Spanish alliance with the local Indians. Their leader, Topiawari, told Raleigh about a great city called Macureguarai farther to the west, which the Elizabethan took to be the legendary city of El Dorado he had heard and read about. The beginning summer rains, however, were making an already difficult navigation on the Orinoco utterly impossible, and so Raleigh promised Topiawari that he would return with more Englishmen the following year to make good on his promise of a military alliance in the struggle against the Spanish and to discover Macureguarai. In June, Raleigh returned to England and the following year (1596) published his account of his expedition, entitled *The Discoverie of the Large, Rich, and Bewtiful Empyre of Guiana,* in which he attempted to mobilize material support for a second expedition that would result in the English conquest of Guiana and the discovery of El Dorado. When such support did not materialize, Raleigh had to content himself with sending only two small vessels back to Guiana later in 1596 under his lieutenant Lawrence Keymis, who found Raleigh's previous point of entry into the Orinoco now blocked by Spanish fortifications and instead explored several other possible passages to the interior. Keymis reported on what he had learned during his voyage of reconnaissance in his *A Relation of the Second Voyage to Guiana,* which was published in London the same year.[44] However, due in part to the crisis of the Anglo-Spanish wars of the 1590s and in part to Raleigh's own political troubles, which culminated with his renewed imprisonment by James I in 1603, it would take more than twenty years until Raleigh and Keymis were able to embark on their final (and disastrous) attempt to conquer Guiana in 1617.

By the time they embarked on their first voyage to Guiana in 1595, both Raleigh and Keymis had a considerable reputation as alchemists. Although Raleigh's reputation rests primarily on the documented experiments that he conducted during imprisonment starting in 1603, his interest in alchemy had begun as early as the 1580s and was probably inspired by his association with John Dee's Hermetic circle. In 1596, the same year in which the *Discoverie* was published, a work on alchemy appeared that was dedicated to Raleigh and entitled *A hundred and fouretene experiments and cures of the famous physitian Philippus Aureolus Theophrastus Paracelsus.* Written by the distiller John Hester some ten years earlier, it claimed to be an English translation of the works of Paracelsus, who, though still controversial, was becoming increasingly influential among English occultists such as Dee and Robert Fludd.[45] Raleigh's library contained multiple works on alchemical medicine, Hermeticism, and the occult sciences, including Pietro Bairo's *Secreti medicinali* (1585) and Josephe du Chesne's *De ortu metallorum* (1576).[46] That Raleigh was well-versed in the Hermetic corpus is evident also from his massive *History of the World*. There, he embarked on a defense of the theory of astrological correspondence between microcosm and macrocosm. Citing "Mirandula," "Albertus," "Dionysius," "Apuleius the Platonist," and "Mercurius Trismegistus," he argued:

> It cannot be doubted, but the stars are instruments of far greater use, than to give an obscure light, and for men to gaze on after sunset; it being manifest, that the diversity of seasons, the winters, and summers, more hot and cold, are not so uncertained by the sun and moon alone, who always keep one and the same course, but that the stars have also their working therein. And if we cannot deny, but that God hath given virtues to springs and fountains, to cold earth, to plants and stones, minerals, and to the excremental parts of the basest living creatures, why should we rob the beautiful stars of their working powers?[47]

Similarly, Keymis was known as the "the great Alchemist of London."[48] He had been trained at Oxford before joining, in 1589, the scientific team at Raleigh's estate, which included also the mathematician Thomas Harriot. Keymis was probably chosen by Raleigh as his lieutenant on the Guiana voyages primarily for his expertise in metallurgy and mineralogy, but he was also one of Raleigh's most trusted associates, serving as his personal secretary.[49]

Given their background in alchemy, it is not surprising that both Raleigh and Keymis were intensely interested in the legend of El Dorado and his fabulously rich city, which was rumored to rival Mexico and Cusco in its imperial splendor. The sixteenth-century literary corpus about the European search for El Dorado is replete with classical mythological and medieval alchemical motifs. Among the mythological traditions that patently inspired the El Dorado legend are Ovid's account of the Golden Age in his *Metamorphoses,* the story of the biblical Ophir and golden mines of King Solomon that had already inspired Columbus, as well as the tales of giants familiar from medieval travel literature and romances of chivalry. But there was arguably no classical story that better captured the ambitions and hopes of the sixteenth-century conquerors seeking El Dorado than the epic tradition of Apollonius's *Argonautica,* which had been appropriated in the imperial ideology of the Spanish Habsburgs under Charles V and Philip II.[50] Indeed, the idea of a remote country of gold located on the shores of a lake in the El Dorado legend is distinctly reminiscent of the city of Colchis in the *Argonautica,* home of the Golden Fleece that Jason and his Argonauts succeeded in capturing after having fought fierce Amazons and drugged the dragon guarding the Fleece in a sacred grove with the aid of King Aeëtes's enchantress daughter, Medea. During the later Middle Ages and the early modern period, Jason's quest for the Golden Fleece became a common motif also in alchemical iconography to symbolize the *opus alchemicum.* Just as Jason had to undergo a perilous journey in order to obtain the Golden Fleece, so did the alchemist have to subject himself to arduous travails in order to obtain the Philosophers' Stone.[51] Thus, in his *History of the World,* Raleigh wrote, in a chapter devoted to the Argonauts, "Some there are, that by this journey of Jason understand the mystery of the philosopher's stone, called the golden fleece; to which also other superfine chymists draw the twelve labours of Hercules." However, as Raleigh notes, the Golden Fleece could also signify the secret alchemical text itself, written in "a book of parchment, which is of sheep's skin, and therefore called golden, because it was taught therein how other metals might be transmuted."[52] Having evolved into an alchemical allegory by the sixteenth century, the *Argonautica* would provide a seminal rhetorical model for narrativizing a modern scientific curiosity even still in twentieth-century ethnography.[53]

The *Argonautica* functions as an important literary subtext and frame of reference also in Raleigh's *Discoverie.*[54] For example, with regard to the mythological figures of the Amazons familiar from Apollonius's epic, Raleigh writes that he was "desirous to understand the truth of those warlike women, because of some it is believed, of others not." His personal journey in the remote region of the world believed to be populated by the Amazons affords him the opportunity of ascertaining their existence through empirical verification by local witnesses. Thus, he relates being told by a native "cacique" (lord) about a "nations of these women" who live

> on the south side of the river in the provinces of *Topago,* and their chiefest strengths and retracts are in the islands situate on the south side of the entrance, some 60 leagues within the mouth of the said river. The memories of the like women are very ancient as well in *Africa* as in *Asia.* In *Africa* those that had *Medusa* for queen; others in *Scythia,* near the rivers of *Tanais* and *Thermodon.* We find, also, that *Lampedo* and *Marthesia* were queens of the *Amazons.* In many histories they are verified to have been, and in divers ages and provinces; but they which are not far from *Guiana* do accompany with men but once in a year, and for

the time of one month, which I gather by their relation, to be in April; and that time all kings of the borders assemble, and queens of the *Amazons;* and after the queens have chosen, the rest cast lots for their valentines. This one month they feast, dance, and drink of their wines in abundance; and the moon being done they all depart to their own provinces. They are said to be very cruel and bloodthirsty, especially to such as offer to invade their territories. These *Amazons* have likewise great store of these plates of gold, which they recover by exchange chiefly for a kind of green stones, which the Spaniards call *piedras hijadas,* and we use for spleen-stones; and for the disease of the stone we also esteem them. Of these I saw divers in *Guiana;* and commonly every king or cacique hath one, which their wives for the most part wear, and they esteem them as great jewels.[55]

If Raleigh's exotic tropics produce extraordinary amounts of gold and efficacious medicines, they also produce, in alchemical and hermetic fashion, exceptionally fierce guards of these secret treasures against those unworthy of discovery.[56] Aside from the Amazons, Raleigh also reports the existence of many monstrous beasts in Guiana, including one that he calls by the Spanish name of *lagarto* (lizard), probably referring to the Amazonian caiman. It is of enormous size, abundant in number, and has a voracious appetite also for human flesh. Thus, Raleigh reports, "I had a negro, a very proper young fellow, who leaping out of the galley to swim in the mouth of this river, was in all our sights taken and devoured with one of those *lagartos.*"[57] This passage evokes images of ferocious dragons familiar not only from medieval novels of chivalry but also, as we have seen in chapter 9, from alchemical literature, where the dragon symbolized the dual-natured Mercurius, who both beckons the magus and wards off the uninitiated in the discovery of the secrets of nature (see fig. 28).

The text's chivalric and alchemical motifs invoked by Raleigh's account of mythical creatures familiar from the *Argonautica* are further enhanced by his practice of (re-)naming geographical markers in Guiana. Thus, he reports having named a river that (he claims) had no name "the River of the Red Cross, ourselves being the first Christians that ever came therein."[58] Most obviously, this designation invokes Saint George, the patron saint of England, whose emblem is the Red Cross. More specifically, however, it also recalls the Red Cross Knight, the chivalric knight errant in Edmund Spenser's *Faerie Queene* (1590), the Elizabethan epic that was published with a prefatory letter addressed to Raleigh and that offered an updated poetic version of Dee's pseudohistorical Arthurian British Empire. As has been noted, Spenser's use of the chivalric motif of the Red Cross Knight has distinctly alchemical resonances, possibly with early Rosicrucian flavor.[59] In light of these connotations of the motifs

Figure 28. Dragon being slain. Emblema XXV. "Draco non moritur, nisi cum fratre & sorore sua interficiatur, qui sunt Sol & Luna" ("The Dragon does not dye unlesse he be slain by a Brother and a Sister, which are Sol and Luna"). (In Michael Maier, *Atalanta fugiens* [1618]. Source: *Secretioris naturæ secretorum scrutinium chymicum, per oculis et et intellectui accuratè accommodata, firguri cupro appositissimè incisa, ingeniosissima emblemata, hisque confines, & ad rem egregiè facientes sententias, doctissimaque item epigrammata, illustratus.* Francofurti: Impensis Georgii Heinrici Oehrlingii...: 1687. Courtesy of the Library of Congress.)

of the dragon, the Amazons, and the Red Cross Knight, it seems plausible to conclude that Raleigh attempted to present himself in his *Discoverie* as a sort of alchemical Red Cross Knight errant, a British Jason on an alchemical quest for the "Golden King."

But Raleigh's *Discoverie* sheds light on the alchemical background of the El Dorado legend in the literature of the European discovery and conquest of America more broadly. Indeed, in early modern alchemical literature, the "Golden King" symbolizes the raw matter for the Philosophers' Stone, the Stone itself, or the Sol (sun), the male principle in the *coniunctio*. As we saw in chapter 6, European historians such as the Jesuit José de Acosta frequently presented the (spiritual) conquest of America in the metaphoric terms of the alchemical wedding. Raleigh was clearly influenced by this tradition, possibly even by Acosta's text (which had been published in 1590, though Raleigh does not explicitly cite it). Thus, in his own narrative, Raleigh builds on this sexual imagery of the alchemical *coniunctio*. However, he claims that, whereas Peru had been ravaged by the Spanish conquerors, Guiana is still saving herself for her legitimate English husband: "*Guiana* is a country that hath yet her maidenhead, never sacked, turned, nor wrought; the face of the earth hath not been torn, nor the virtue and salt of the soil spent by manurance. The graves have not been opened for gold, the mines not broken with sledges, nor their images pulled down out of their temples. It hath never been entered by any army of strength, and never conquered or possessed by any Christian prince."[60] In Raleigh's *Discoverie,* the idea of Guiana's "virginal" promise for English mineral extraction is driven home in an account of how he and his men chased three Spaniards in canoes to a riverbank. Although the Spaniards were able to get away on land, they left behind their two canoes, in which was hidden "an Indian basket ... which was the refiners basket, for I found in it quicksiluer, saltpeter, and divers things for the triall of mettals, and also the dust of such ore as he had refined, but in those *Canoas* which escaped there was a good quantify of ore and gold."[61] Passages such as this one underline the urgency of Raleigh's proposal that if the English do not intervene immediately in America, Guiana's "maidenhead" will also soon be lost to the Spaniards.

The idea of Guiana's virginal promise is further emphasized by the alchemical imagery that also pervades Raleigh's descriptions of Guiana's natural landscape. Virtually beginning on the first page of the *Discoverie,* Raleigh's Guianan landscape is littered with "signes" of something "secret" beneath the surface that he already knows to be there, of something "hidden" that beckons to be discovered. In Guiana, he writes, "all the rocks, mountains, all stones in the plaines, in woodes, and by the rivers sides are in effect thorow shining, and appear marveylous rich, which ... Are trew signes of rich mineralles, but are no other then *El madre del oro* (as the Spanyards terme them) which is the mother of golde, or as it is saide by others the scum of gold."[62] The "mother" or "scum" of gold is a sign that "the mine was farther in the ground,"[63] as gold (like medicinal plants) was known to "grow" in the tropics more rapidly than anywhere else in the world. A notably curious and recurrent image in Raleigh's descriptions of Guiana's natural landscape is hereby the church tower in reference to waterfalls:

> In this branch called *Cararoopana* were also many goodly islands, some of six miles long, some of ten, and some of twenty. When it grew towards sunset, we entered a branch of a river that fell into *Orenoque,* called *Winicapora;* where I was

informed of the mountain of crystal, to which in truth for the length of the way, and the evil season of the year, I was not able to march, nor abide any longer upon the journey. We saw it afar off; and it appeared like a white church-tower of an exceeding height. There falleth over it a mighty river which toucheth no part of the side of the mountain, but rusheth over the top of it, and falleth to the ground with so terrible a noise and clamour, as if a thousand great bells were knocked one against another. I think there is not in the world so strange an overfall, nor so wonderful to behold.[64]

Earlier, he had reported seeing "some ten or twelve overfalls in sight, every one as high over the other as a church tower."[65] The image of the tower more generally, and that of the church tower particularly, has a long tradition in alchemical literature as a symbol for the *athanor* or philosophical "furnace." This metaphoric connection was familiar not only to well-known English mystics such as Edward Kelly, close associate of John Dee in his alchemical work, but also to skeptics and satirists such as Ben Jonson.[66] In Raleigh's account, alchemical imagery functions to invoke a metaphoric analogy between the New World journey in quest for El Dorado and the alchemist's opus, which aims not only to transform base metal into gold but also to attain the Philosophers' Stone, bringing about transformation, spiritual renewal, and insight into the occult relations between microcosm and macrocosm.

Walter Raleigh as *Pachakuti*: The Narrative Alchemy of the White Legend

The emergence of the El Dorado myth in the sixteenth century may thus in part be understood in terms of a European alchemical fantasy, in which the age-old quest for the "Golden King" familiar from alchemical iconography was imposed upon the New World in the age of geographic discovery. In offering such an interpretation, Charles Nicholl relied primarily on the Jungian analysis of alchemy as a psychic phenomenon, as the struggle toward inner "wholeness" and the "projection" of an "image thrown out from the mind" and over the "emptiness of terra incognita."[67] Similarly, recent New Historicist literary critics have seen Raleigh's *Discoverie* primarily as a colonialist fantasy, as an example of "writing that conquers."[68] However, it would be a mistake to see the El Dorado legend *solely* in terms of a projection of European colonial fantasies. Thus, modern anthropologists have established that the El Dorado legend has a basis not only in classical European mythology as well as medieval chivalric and alchemical ideas but also in Native South American oral traditions about a probably actual cultural practice among the Muisca (or

Chibcha), an Indian nation living in the highlands of Bogotá, in which on an appointed day each year the tribal chief was stripped naked by his attendants and smeared from head to foot with a sticky layer of balsam gum and then powdered with gold that was puffed through tubes of cane until the cacique appeared like a living statue of gold.[69]

The earliest recorded version of the story of a rich kingdom or empire lying beyond South America's jungle and the coastal mountains seems to originate with Diego de Ordás's expedition to the Orinoco River in 1529 and was based on bits of gold and information that Ordás obtained from local Indians.[70] Having participated in the conquest of Mexico under Cortés, Ordás had hoped that this kingdom, which he referred to as "the Land of Meta," would equal that of Tenochtitlán in size and splendor. After the Spanish discovery and invasion of the Inca Empire in 1532–33 and occupation, in 1534, of the northern Inca city of Quito by Sebastián de Benalcázar, one of Pizarro's lieutenants, Spanish soldiers began to gather more details from indigenous informants about this fabulously rich city.[71] It was in these native accounts that the legendary figure known as "El Dorado" first emerged, subsequently inspiring numerous expeditions into the South American jungle, including the 1541 expedition led by Gonzalo Pizarro and Francisco de Orellana to "La Canela" (the land of cinnamon), which resulted in the discovery of the Amazon; the 1559 expedition by Pedro de Ursúa, which ended in disaster following the rebellion of Lope de Aguirre; and various expeditions undertaken by the agents of the German banking dynasty of the Welser, most notably the Swabian soldier Nikolaus Federmann.[72]

Far from being merely a European projection, the legend of El Dorado is thus an example of what Serge Gruzinksi has called a "mestizo mechanism," a *colonial* tradition that had precontact origins in both Amerindian and European cultures and that became hybridized in the intercultural exchanges between European and Native American historical and geographic traditions during the Spanish conquest.[73] Raleigh's adaptation of the El Dorado legend in his *Discoverie* provides an excellent example of the rhetorical interplay between alchemical imagery, ideas, and motifs on the one hand and ethnological curiosity and empirical knowledge on the other. As Neil Whitehead has observed, Raleigh's narrative is both an "enchanted text," indebted to European religious and mythological traditions, *and* an "ethnological text" based on empirical information. But while Whitehead (an anthropologist) was primarily interested in disentangling the "enchanted" from the "ethnological" elements in an attempt to make Raleigh's text acceptable as a documentary source for modern ethnohistorical scholarship, my interest here lies in how the interplay between the enchanted and ethnological elements is enabled rhetorically by the narrative alchemy of Raleigh's text.[74] As I want to argue, the language of alchemy pervading Raleigh's account functions as a portal that opens upon ethnological secrets of Amerindian culture by justifying an empiricist curiosity about "pagan" and "barbarous" words, ideas, and practices. Conversely, it is Raleigh's ethos as an ethnographic eyewitness that enables the epistemological authority of the *Discoverie* in a late sixteenth-century, early modern context. Thus, in Raleigh's *Discoverie*, the discourses of alchemy and ethnography are inseparable, feeding upon and enabling one another, hereby legitimating a modern idea of discovery as a *venatio* (hunt) for the secrets of nature.

As we have seen, this interplay between mythological and religious (especially Christological) imagery and motifs on the one hand and empirical observations and technical application on the other had been a characteristic feature of the alchemical tradition since the thirteenth century. Just as the medieval alchemists had inquired into the hidden structure of matter, so did the early modern explorers, missionaries, and ethnographers inquire into the secrets of a "new world." The rhetorical platform for detailed naturalist and ethnographic empirical descriptions, the language of alchemy in the *Discoverie* mediates between courtly and commercial interests, as well as between religious and scientific and concerns. Thus, at the outset of the *Discoverie*, Raleigh proposes two distinct motivations for the English colonization of Guiana: fealty and plunder. In fact, he wrote two separate prefatory addresses to his narrative, a courtly "Epistle Dedicatorie" addressed to Charles Howard, Knight of the Garter, and Privy Councillor Robert Cecil as well as a preface addressed to the common "reader." As Shannon Miller has noted, the two prefatory letters narrate "completely different version of Guiana, highlighting the conflicting conditions through which this project was pursued."[75] Thus, in the former, he compares his journey to a "painefull pilgrimage";[76] relates the Indians' desire for Queen Elizabeth's imperial "protection" against Spanish abuses and cruelties;[77] and the potential for national "glory" in the South American venture;[78] in the latter, by contrast, he appeals to the ambitions of the noncourtly reader by portraying Guiana as a geographic crucible in which gold grows naturally and simply needs to be gathered once the hardships of sea and land travel are overcome. Thus, he relates that, in Guiana there are entire mountains of a certain "white stone" wherein "gold is engendered and that will fetch 12000 or 13000 pounds a tunne" in London.[79] Yet, Raleigh takes pains to emphasize that his endeavor was ultimately not *solely* directed at attaining private profit: "I could have returned a good quantity of gold readie cast," he wrote, "if I had not shot at another marke, than present profit."[80] This "other marke" was local knowledge, particularly the "secrets" that the Indians had so far concealed from the Spaniards. Here and throughout Raleigh's text, the Hermetic language amalgamates the material with the spiritual, the empirical with the mythological, the mercantile with the mystical, the bourgeois with the courtly, as well as European with local indigenous knowledge.

It is in the context of this rhetorical interdependency of alchemical imagery and empirical observation that Raleigh's use of "hyper-ethnographic" language in the *Discoverie* can be understood. Thus, his account is replete with Amerindian geographic terminology and naturalistic nomenclature, which are rendered in italic font in the first print edition of 1596 in order to emphasize their exotic newness and strangeness. Raleigh's proto-ethnographic curiosity was directed not only toward the Indians' knowledge of the geographical location of El Dorado but also to their scientific knowledge of the properties of local animals and plants, including their art of preparing a very deadly poison with which they equip their arrows in warfare, and its antidotes. "There was nothing whereof I was more curious," he writes, "than to finde out the true remedies of these poisoned arrows, for besides the mortalitie of the wound they make, the partie shot indureth the most insufferable torment in the world, and abideth a most uglie and lamentable death, somtimes dying starke mad, somtimes their bowels breaking out of their bellies, and are presently discolored, as blacke as pitch, and so unsavory, as no man can endure to cure, or to attend them."[81] This medicine, commonly called *curare* by the Spaniards, was a mixture prepared from the Strychnos root and bark and the subject of many fables among the European colonists. While it is unclear whether this Native secret was actually disclosed to Raleigh, he makes great rhetorical use of it by emphasizing that, unlike the Spaniards, who failed in their attempt of attaining this knowledge through violent extortions, he was able to penetrate this secret, which was so occult that, even among the Indians, only the initiates were privy to this knowledge. "But every one of these Indians know it not," he writes, "no not one among thousands, but their southsaiers and priests, who do conceale it, and onely teach it but from the father to the sonne." Yet, he continues, "I was more beholden to the Guianians, than any other," and "they told me the best way of healing as well therof, as of all other poisons."[82] Among these remedies were many plants, minerals, and stones with magical properties, including one that the Natives call *takua* and that played an important role in Native healing ceremonies and cosmology.

Raleigh's claim that the Indians have been hiding secret information about El Dorado and the medicinal properties of plants from the Spaniards but are willing to divulge their secrets to the English "discoverers" is suggestive of how, in the *Discoverie,* the legend of El Dorado is connected rhetorically with another legend—the so-called Black Legend of the allegedly inordinate cruelty of the Spanish conquest. In the *Discoverie,* this Black Legend is personified by the governor of Trinidad, Antonio de Berrío. Thus, Raleigh reports that "every night there came some [of the Indians] with most lamentable complaints of his cruelty: how he had divided the island and given to every soldier a part; that he made the ancient cacique, which were lords of the country, to be their slaves; that he kept them in chains, and dropped their naked bodies with burning bacon, and such other torments, which I found afterwards to be true."[83] It is Berrío's cruelty that caused the Indians to withhold their secret knowledge about the location of El Dorado and explains why his discovery of El Dorado was doomed to failure. By contrast, Raleigh's Indians are most eager to become the subjects and collaborators of the English, who are the enemies of the Spaniards under their powerful Virgin Queen. Thus, he relates how "I made them understand that I was the servant of a queen who was the great cacique of the north, and a virgin, and had more *caciqui* under her than there were trees in that island; that she was an enemy to the *Castellani* in respect of their tyranny and oppression, and that she delivered all such nations about her, as were by them oppressed; and having freed all the coast of the northern world from their servitude, had sent me to free them also, and withal to defend the country of *Guiana* from their invasion and conquest."[84]

While the Black Legend ultimately originated, as we have seen, with earnest critiques of the Spanish conquest by Dominicans such as Bartolomé de las Casas, it was greatly embellished during the second half of the sixteenth century especially by northern European historians who wished to find a pretext for justifying Protestant encroachments into America. In 1583, Las Casas's *Brevíssima relación* had been translated into English and became a cornerstone of English colonialist ideology in countless promotional tracts and travel histories written by such Elizabethan imperialists as Dee and Richard Hakluyt.[85] Similarly, Raleigh argues that the cruelty, tyranny, and ultimately illegitimacy of Spanish rule caused the Indians to save their secrets for the discovery by their English friends, who were thus called upon to "defend" Guiana and "hold it as tributary, or conquer and keep it as empress of the same."[86] This fiction is further enhanced in Raleigh's text by his mimicry and ventriloquism of Native speech and ideas about the English. Thus, he writes that "I shewed them her Majesty's picture, which they so admired and honoured, as it had been easy to have brought them idolatrous thereof. The like and a more large discourse I made to the rest of the nations, both in my passing to *Guiana* and to those of the borders, so as in that part of the world her Majesty is very famous and admirable; whom they now call *Ezrabeta cassipuna aquerewana,* which is as much as 'Elizabeth, the Great Princess, or Greatest

Commander.'"[87] Thus, Raleigh emphasizes natural affinities between Guiana and England, between the Virgin Land and the Virgin Queen. Whereas the Spanish conquest represents in his text a rape of America, the English "discoverie" of Guiana is likened to a gentle "Platonic embrace."[88]

Raleigh's original contribution to the printed record about both the El Dorado legend and the Black Legend hereby lies in an ingenious connection he makes between the English "Discoverie" of Guiana and the Spanish conquest of Peru. It is at this point that I return to Raleigh's report of an Inca prophecy with which I began this chapter—the prophecy that "Inglatierra" will deliver the "Inga" from his cruel Spanish oppressor. In elaborating the idea that El Dorado is none other than the descendant of the Incas and that the Inca's redemption by an English *sanifex* had been foretold in an ancient prophecy found at Cusco, Raleigh's narrative alchemy in the *Discoverie* cunningly amalgamates ethnographic information obtained from the Spanish chronicles of the conquest of Peru and from the personal testimonies of various Spanish interlocutors.

Raleigh was an avid reader of the Spanish chronicles of the discovery and conquest. Despite his fierce anti-Catholic and anti-Spanish sentiments, he was enchanted with the Spanish dream of universal conquest. Indeed, for him, the exploitation of American gold was more than a dream; it was a necessity of *realpolitik* that would ensure English survival in the imperial rivalry with Spain for geopolitical hegemony. Thus, he writes, "We find that by the abundant treasure of that country the Spanish king vexes all the princes of *Europe,* and is become, in a few years, from a poor king of *Castile,* the greatest monarch of this part of the world, and likely every day to increase if other princes forslow the good occasions offered, and suffer him to add this empire to the rest, which by far exceedeth all the rest. If his gold now endanger us, he will then be unresistible."[89] Despite his polemical indictments of Spanish cruelties, Raleigh, like Eden, considered the Spanish conquest as a model to be emulated rather than to be superseded. "I shall willingly spend my life" in the conquest of Guiana, he writes, "And if any else shall be enabled thereunto, and conquer the same, I assure him thus much; he shall perform more than ever was done in *Mexico* by *Cortes,* or in *Peru* by *Pizarro,* whereof the one conquered the empire of *Mutezuma,* the other of *Guascar* and *Atabalipa.*"[90] For Guiana, being the land of the descendants of the Incas and being "directly east from *Peru,*"

> hath more abundance of gold than any part of *Peru,* and as many or more great cities than ever *Peru* had when it flourished most. It is governed by the same laws, and the emperor and people observe the same religion, and the same form and

policies in government as were used in *Peru,* not differing in any part. And I have been assured by such of the Spaniards as have seen *Manoa,* the imperial city of *Guiana,* which the Spaniards call *El Dorado,* that for the greatness, for the riches, and for the excellent seat, it far exceedeth any of the world, at least of so much of the world as is known to the Spanish nation.[91]

Guiana would be England's Peru, only better. The historical relationship that Raleigh constructs in the *Discoverie* between Guiana and Peru was not, however, only one of parallelism but also one of genealogy; for him, El Dorado *was* the descendant and heir of the Inca.

With regard to the Spanish conquest of Peru, Raleigh was informed by the Spanish historiography that had already appeared in print. He cites, for example (in Spanish with his own English translation), an extended passage from Francisco López de Gómara's *Historia general,* in which the Spanish historian described "the court and magnificence of *Guaynacapa* [Huayna Khapaq]."[92] Raleigh had also read Pedro Cieza de León's *Crónica del Peru,* which had been published in Seville in 1553 and which provided a detailed account of the Spanish conquest of Peru.[93] But besides drawing from the published sources written by Spanish authors, much of Raleigh's knowledge about South America generally, and the legend of El Dorado especially, was based on unpublished "secret" or local sources, some of which were spurious. Raleigh's statements on the subject suggest that one of his sources on the El Dorado legend was Berrío and the oral tradition that had inspired the Spanish seekers of El Dorado. Berrío also seems to have been one of the sources of Raleigh's conflation of the Inca and El Dorado. Thus, he writes, "Such of the Spaniards as afterwards endeavoured the conquest thereof, whereof there have been many, as shall be declared hereafter, thought that this *Inga,* of whom this emperor now living is descended, took his way by the river of *Amazons,* by that branch which is called *Papamene.*"[94] Berrío, while in Raleigh's captivity, had related how a certain Juan Martínez, a soldier who had been abandoned in a boat during one of these expeditions as punishment for his negligence in the explosion of a powder store, had been captured by Native Americans and brought to a golden city that the Indians called "Manoa," which allegedly stood on a lake up the Orinoco River and had been founded by El Dorado, the Golden King. Martínez (according to Raleigh) had related how every year El Dorado "carouseth with his captains, tributaries, and governors" as they are "stripped naked and their bodies anointed all over with a kind of white *Balsamum* (by them called *Curcai*).... When they are anointed all over, certain servants of the emperor, having prepared gold made into fine powder, blow it thorough hollow canes upon their naked bodies, until they be all shining from the foot to the head."[95]

But even before his capture and interrogation of Berrío, Raleigh had probably first heard of the story of El Dorado from Pedro Sarmiento de Gamboa, an official of the Spanish Crown who had been charged with the fortification of Spain's South American main and who had fallen captive to some of Raleigh's privateers in 1586 in the Strait of Magellan en route to Spain.[96] This is suggested by Raleigh's comment that "Many yeares since" he had knowledge, "by relation, of that mighty, rich, and beawtifull Empire of Guiana, and of that great and Golden City, which the Spanyards call El Dorado, and the naturals Manoa, which Citie was conquered, reedified, and inlarged by a younger sonne of Guainacapa [Huayna Khapaq] Emperor of Peru."[97] If Sarmiento de Gamboa was indeed Raleigh's earliest source for the connection between El Dorado and the last of the Incas while in English captivity in 1586, the Spaniard had patently pulled his leg. As the official chronicler of Peru (who had been commissioned by Viceroy Francisco de Toledo to write the *History of the Incas*) would have known, the city that was "reedified, and inlarged by a younger sonne of Guainacapa [Huayna Khapaq] Emperor of Peru" was called not Manoa but Vilcabamba, in the Amazonian foothills of the Andes, and had been conquered at last in 1572, after having resisted the Spaniards for some forty years. The last male descendant of the Incas, Tupac Amaru, had been executed by Toledo on the main square of Cusco the same year—more than a decade before Sarmiento's interview with Raleigh. In fact, one of the main reasons why Sarmiento de Gamboa had been commissioned by Toledo to write a history of the Incas was precisely to justify the viceroy's controversial decision to have the last Inca publicly executed. Thus, in his *Historia de los Incas* (which was completed in 1572 but not published until the twentieth century), Sarmiento de Gamboa had provided a detailed ethnographic account of Inca religious beliefs and practices in which the Incas were portrayed in an extremely unflattering light as devil worshippers, polygamists, and sodomites.

The last Inca, Tupac Amaru (1545–1572), was the son of Manco Inca (1516–1544), referred to by Raleigh as "a younger sonne of Guainacapa [Huayna Khapaq, 1464–1527] Emperor of Peru," who had at first been implemented as a puppet ruler by the Spaniards after their murder of his older half-brother, the Inca Atahualpa (ca. 1502–1533), but who had then risen up against them and laid siege to Cusco, only barely failing to retake it in 1536. After the failure of the siege, Manco Inca had withdrawn to Vilcabamba, where he reconstituted a neo-Inca state. After his assassination by some Spanish guests, Manco Inca's resistance was carried on by his sons, first Titu Cusi Yupanki (1529–1571) and then Tupac Amaru, who engaged in guerrilla warfare and occasional raids on Spanish merchants and "pacified" Indians until the final invasion.[98] Thus, when Sarmiento de Gamboa was in Raleigh's captivity and divulged historical and geographical information about Peru and South America, the last Inca had been dead for some twenty years, and the Spanish chronicler would surely have known it. Still, it is not inconceivable that Raleigh's conflation of the history of the Incas with the legend of El Dorado originated with Sarmiento de Gamboa during his captivity in England. As we know from other sources, Sarmiento de Gamboa frequently offered up entertaining tall tales that were probably meant to sow confusion among the English aspirants to empire in America. For example, in his *History of the World,* Raleigh relates that his captive responded to his demand for information about geographic information with a "pretty jest": "When I asked him, being then my prisoner, some question about an island in those straits, which methought might have done neither benefit or displeasure to his enterprise, he told me merrily, that it was to be called the Painter's Wife's Island saying, that whilst the fellow drew that map, his wife sitting by desired him to put in one country for her; that she, in imagination, might have an island of her own."[99]

Whatever the origin of Raleigh's narrative amalgamation of the history of the Incas with the legend of El Dorado, it seems likely that Sarmiento de Gamboa's oral testimony was the main source of Raleigh's story about a prophecy found during the Spanish conquest of Cusco foretelling the restoration of the "Inga" from Spanish oppression by a man from "Inglatierra." For, this prophecy is faintly reminiscent of an Inca apocalyptic tradition known as *pachakuti.* Thus, in his *Historia de los Incas,* Sarmiento de Gamboa had related the story of the defeat of the powerful Chancas by the Inca Yupanki (ca. 1438–1471). The Chancas had invaded the Inca homeland around Cusco and driven Viracocha Inca (Yupanki's father) and his designated successor, Urco Huaranca, to flee the capital. During the epic battle outside Cusco, the Inca Yupanki demonstrated great bravery and was miraculously assisted by mysterious warriors descending from the mountains, who were said to have been "sent by Viracocha, the creator, as succor for the Inca."[100] After the Inca Yupanki's victory over the Chancas, the Incas honored him for his triumph "with many epithets, especially calling him Pachacuti, which means 'overturner of the earth,' alluding to the lands and farms which they looked upon as lost by the coming of the Chancas. For he had made them free and safe again. From that time he was called Pachacuti Inca Yupanqui."[101] Moreover, Pachacuti Yupanki was made Inca and greatly expanded the empire all through South America, thoroughly reorganizing all facets of the Inca world in the process. It is because of his role as a transformer, both in war and in peace, that he received the title "Pachakuti."

Walter Raleigh's Legends   397

Under Spanish rule, the Inca Pachakuti Yupanki came to occupy a central role in Andean apocalyptic resistance movements as early as the sixteenth century. The Andean concept of *pachakuti* derives from the Quechua words *pacha* (meaning world, time, and space, or state of being) and *kuti* (meaning change, turn, or something that comes back on itself). The concept of *kuti*

Figure 29. "Taclla," Andean digging stick and symbol of *pachakuti*. (In Felipe Guaman Poma de Ayala, *Nueva corónica y buen gobierno* [1615]. Courtesy of the Royal Library, Denmark.)

is symbolized in Andean iconographic traditions by the digging stick, *taclla*, with its curved hook, with which the soil is plowed (see fig. 29). Sarmiento de Gamboa was thus literally correct when he defined a *pachakuti* as an "overturner of the earth." However, in an extended sense, the concept of *pachakuti* pertained also to "cycles of time and space and cataclysmic events" in Andean cosmogony, revolving around "oscillations of time/space in which periodic catastrophes define moments of transition separating epochs."[102] The legacy of the Inca Pachakuti Yupanki as an overturner of epochs has lived on in Andean chiliastic traditions from the time of the Spanish conquest to the present in the apocalyptic expectation that another Pachakuti will emerge who will shake off the colonial European yoke, just as the Inca Yupanki had shaken off the Chanca yoke. While in modern times, this concept lives on in the leftwing indigenist political movement originating in Bolivia called Pachakuti, in the post-conquest viceregal period, the prophetic tradition of *pachakuti* often revolved around the apocalyptic conflict between the Spanish king, *Españarrí*, and the Inca king, *Incarrí*. Although the present age is dominated by the *Españarrí*, another *pachakuti* will usher forth the victorious return of the *Incarrí*. Such a *pachakuti* appeared to have arrived during the late 1560s, when an indigenous prophetic movement called *taki unquy* (dancing sickness) arose in the Andes during which charismatic leaders called upon Andeans to resist the viceregal state and Spanish missionaries and to return to the old worship of *huacas* (sacred stones and places). Spanish officials were extremely concerned and convinced (probably correctly) that this prophetic movement had emanated from the neo-Inca state at Vilcabamba and therefore renewed their attempts to bring it under Spanish control, successfully invading it in 1572.[103] Still, the (post)colonial tradition of *pachakuti* has lived on as a millenarian prophecy of a return of the Inca bringing about an end to Spanish (or European) rule in the Andes throughout the Spanish viceregal period and (later) during the modern national period.

Raleigh's sixteenth-century contribution to this mestizo mechanism was to insert a role for himself and "Inglatierra" as an ally of "*Incarrí*" in the colonial Andean prophetic resistance movement of *pachakuti*. In devising the narrative ploy of bringing an indigenous prophetic tradition into connection with the European arrival in America, Raleigh was possibly also inspired by Hernando Cortés's "Second Letter to Charles V," which had been translated into multiple languages and printed throughout Europe. There, Cortés first told the tale that would later develop into the Mexican national myth of Quetzalcoatl, according to which the Mesoamerican deity had departed for the east in mythic times after being disobeyed by his people but prophesied his triumphant return to resume his legitimate rule over Anahuac, the high plateau of Mexico.

Although Cortés, in his letter, does not yet name this deity, he planted the seed of the legend by inventing a speech that Montezuma allegedly gave upon first facing the Spaniards on one of the causeways leading into Tenochtitlán. According to this speech, the Aztecs believed the Spaniards to be the emissaries of the returning god, who is called a "chieftain" there and who would resume his rightful place as lord of Anahuac, hereby replacing the ruling Aztec elite, who are but illegitimate newcomers. "For a long time we have known from the writings of our ancestors," Cortés has Moctezuma say,

> that neither I, nor any of those who dwell in this land, are natives of it, but foreigners who came from very distant parts; and likewise we know that a chieftain, of whom they were all vassals, brought our people to this region. And he returned to his native land and after many years came again, by which time all those who had remained were married to native women and had built villages and raised children. And when he wished to lead them away again they would not go nor even admit him as their chief; and so he departed. And we have always held that those who descended from him would come and conquer this land and take us as their vassals. So because of the place from which you claim to come, namely, from where the sun rises, and the things you tell us of the great lord or king who sent you here, we believe and are certain that he is our natural lord, especially as you say he has known of us for some time. So be assured that we shall obey you and hold you as our lord in place of that great sovereign of whom you speak; and in this there shall be no offense or betrayal whatsoever.[104]

It is unclear whether or not there was such a pre-Hispanic prophetic tradition foretelling the return of Quetzalcoatl. What is clear is that the speech ascribed to Montezuma is an act of colonial ventriloquism by Cortés. Similarly, Raleigh's account of an Inca prophecy foretelling the arrival of the English is clearly a colonial mestizo mechanism that is reminiscent of the late medieval alchemical tradition of the Last World emperor, which fuses in his text with the Andean tradition of *pachakuti,* familiar from the writings of missionary and imperial ethnographers. The product of this alchemical-ethnographical mestizo mechanism was an idea of an English "discoverie" that would have a long legacy in the history of British imperialism in America. Thus, while Raleigh's historical endeavors of discovering El Dorado and his secret city of Manoa remained fruitless, the narrative alchemy of his *Discoverie* laid one of the most foundational ideological building blocks in an emergent British imperialist ideology, the fiction that the English arrival in America fulfilled ancient Indian prophecies that foretold the liberation from the Spanish regime of terror and oppression. The alchemy of the White Legend—of an English idea of a "discovery" of America—hereby hinged on the notion that the Spanish conquest had not resulted in "actual occupation," that it had not converted America into a Spanish dominion that was *solid* but had instead left *voids* (or pores) that could still be penetrated by an English "husband" in ever new alchemical weddings in the New World.

11

Things of Darkness
Alchemy, Ethno-demonology, and the Protestant Cant of Conquest

Ten years before his South American venture, Raleigh had attempted to establish the first English colony in America on Roanoke Island on the Outer Banks of what today is North Carolina but what was called by Raleigh "Virginia," in honor of the "Virgin Queen" Elizabeth. Raleigh did not personally lead the colonizing expedition, but he put the fleet in charge of the soldier, mariner, and explorer Sir Richard Grenville and the colony under the command of Ralph Lane as governor. Also, he appointed the mathematician and natural philosopher Thomas Harriot, the Czech mineralogist Joachim Gans (Joachim Gaunse), as well as the painter John White to study the natural environment as well as flora, fauna, and Amerindian cultures. The colony failed after a year, due to its inability to sustain itself. Raleigh launched a second attempt in 1587, this time under the leadership of the painter John White, but this colony fared even worse than the first one. After a desperate White had embarked for England in order to secure supplies, he returned in 1590 only to find the colony abandoned, with no sign of the colonists save for the cryptic word "croatoan" carved into a wooden post. This second English venture came to be known as the "lost colony" of Roanoke, and speculations ran high (then as now) as to its fate. While these first colonial ventures at Roanoke of the 1580s ultimately failed, they produced some of the earliest records of the English colonial encounter with America. Thus, John White produced a series of watercolors that depicted aspects of Algonquian life and culture, as well as local flora and fauna, while Harriot made systematic scientific observations and took detailed notes, which he later compiled and published in 1588 under the title *Briefe and true report of the new found land of Virginia*.

Of common birth and obscure background, Thomas Harriot (1560–1621) had studied at Oxford, where he had met the mathematician and astronomer Thomas Allen, renowned as the Roger Bacon of his day; and the geographer and tireless promoter of British expansionism Richard Hakluyt. Through Hakluyt, the brilliant young Harriot came to the attention of Raleigh and, upon obtaining his master of arts degree in 1583, entered into the courtier's personal service. At his patron's residence at Durham House, Harriot taught mathematics, natural philosophy, and navigation. Like Dee before him, Harriot was interested in mathematics primarily because of his conviction of the central role that the arts and sciences would play in British imperial development. Also like Dee, he believed that a hidden symbolic logic undergirded all of creation that could be unlocked by human reason. Like Ramón Llull some three hundred years earlier, Harriot had therefore created a mathematical logic based on what he believed to be fundamental universal principles governing nature. Using algebraic symbols that were possibly inspired by Llull's Art, Jewish kabbala, or both, he attempted to create a phonetic alphabet that would express all languages and by which, he hoped, he would also be able to decipher the languages of the New World.[1] In 1584, Raleigh introduced Harriot to two Algonquian men, Manteo and Wanchese, who taught him some of their language (Roanok Algonquian) and assisted him as informants in the elaboration of his phonetic system before he embarked for America in 1585.[2]

Harriot's *Report* is divided into three parts. In the first part, he offered detailed descriptions of what he called Virginia's "merchantable commodities"—the natural resources furnished by the land that could be exploited and traded, such as copper, sugar, and furs; in the second part, he offered descriptions of the "commodities" that were being used as food by the Native population and that could also serve for the sustenance of an English colonial population, such as peas, beans, and corn. His descriptions were supplemented by commentaries informed by his research in Spanish New World herbals, such as Monardes's *Historia medicinal*, which had been translated into English in 1577 by John Frampton. For example, in the entry on sassafras, he wrote that it was so "called by the inhabitantes Winauk, a kinde of wood of most pleasand and sweete smel; and of most rare vertues in phisick for the cure of many diseases. It is found by experience to bee farre better and of more vses then the wood which is called *Guaiacum,* or *Lignum vitæ.* For the description, the manner of vsing and the manifold vertues thereof, I referre you to the booke of *Monardus,* translated and entituled in English, *The ioyfull newes from the West Indies.*"[3]

Following Monardes, Harriot presented his naturalistic descriptions and commentaries in form of a catalogue. In part 3, he also offered a prose account of the English colonists' interactions with the Native population subtitled "Of the nature and manners of the people," in which he portrayed the Algonquians as being generally docile and submissive. In their conquest of Virginia, the English would also be assisted by the European diseases that mysteriously cut down the Indians, weakening their military power to the effect that they "in respect of troubling our inhabiting and planting, are not to be feared; but that they shall haue cause both to feare and loue vs, that shall inhabite with them."⁴ Thus, Harriot reports the local medical healers' belief that the diseases resulted from "invisible bullets" dispatched by the English upon the Indians, who

> could not tel whether to think vs gods or men, and the rather because that all the space of their sicknesse, there was no man of ours knowne to die, or that was specially sicke: they noted also that we had no women amongst vs, neither that we did care for any of theirs. Some therefore were of opinion that wee were not borne of women, and therefore not mortall, but that wee were men of an old generation many yeeres past then risen againe to immortalitie. Some woulde likewise seeme to prophesie that there were more of our generation yet to come, to kill theirs and take their places, as some thought the purpose was by that which was already done. Those that were immediatly to come after vs they imagined to be in the aire, yet inuisible & without bodies, & that they by our intreaty & for the loue of vs did make the people to die in that sort as they did by shooting inuisible bullets into them. To confirme this opinion their phisitions to excuse their ignorance in curing the disease, would not be ashamed to say, but earnestly make the simple people beleue, that the strings of blood that they sucked out of the sicke bodies, were the strings wherewithal the inuisible bullets were tied and cast.⁵

Some of Harriot's claims about alleged Native American interpretations of the European arrival have a familiar ring, echoing as they do Columbus's notion that the Indians perceived the Europeans as being gods or demigods and Hernando Cortés's claim of the existence of Native prophecies of the European conquest. Interesting additions to this discursive "armature of conquest" here are Harriot's claims of an alleged Algonquian belief that the Englishmen were "not borne of women" and the belief that European diseases acted like "invisible bullets."⁶ Literary critics and historians have offered various interpretations of this curious and now iconic passage. In a seminal New Historicist reading, Stephen Greenblatt has argued that it manifests Harriot's attempt to discredit Native understanding of the world as a form of pagan superstition in order to construct a colonial difference by contrasting its apparent naivete with the scientifically superior understanding of disease by Europeans.⁷ By contrast, Kelly Wisecup has offered an ethnohistoricist reading arguing that Harriot's report may reflect a more or less accurate ethnographic account of Native medical beliefs, corroborated by other ethno-historical primary sources and scholarship.⁸ Earlier, Joyce Chaplin had suggested that the key to understanding this passage lies in Harriot's own intellectual and scientific milieu in late sixteenth-century Elizabethan England. Specifically,

Chaplin argues, this passage attributes to the Indians an atomistic theory of matter to which Harriot himself subscribed, a theory that combined medieval alchemical corpuscular matter theory with the pre-Socratic atomism of Democritus, Epicurus, and Lucretius that was considered to be atheistic, heretical, and therefore dangerous in late sixteenth-century Elizabethan England.[9] Similarly, Amir Alexander has suggested the influence of atomistic thinking on Harriot's account of exploration by showing how his representation of the English colonists' entry into American territories invokes a penetration of a "void" between smallest parts.[10] Alexander cites a letter from Harriot's correspondence with Johannes Kepler about the physics of refraction, in which Harriot elaborated an explanation derived from corpuscular (what Harriot called "atomic") matter theory. Thus, whereas Kepler had followed a Scholastic theory of matter as continuous by positing that the degree of refraction depended on the density (and therefore the weight) of a given medium, Harriot theorized that the phenomenon of refraction was in fact a species of *reflection*, as the light beams entering the medium collided with individual atoms and were reflected at different angles (see figs. 30 and 31). In explaining his theory of refraction in his correspondence with Kepler, Harriot fashioned himself in the distinct persona of the alchemical adept who would open a "door" into the secrets of nature: "I have now led you to the doors of the house of Nature, where her secrets lie hidden. If the doors are too narrow for you to enter, then mathematically abstract and contract yourself to an atom and then you will easily enter. Later, when you leave, tell me what marvels you have seen."[11] While Alexander entirely neglects the religious context in which Harriot offered his atomistic matter theory, Robert Goulding has noted that Harriot's language here invokes the *Corpus hermeticum,* especially Treatise XI (which also inspired the fellow atomist, Giordano Bruno), in which the spiritual alchemist celebrated his ability to penetrate into the most remote and secrets realms of nature. Harriot's posture as an alchemist, Goulding argues, "was not merely an expedient role"; rather, his research into refraction was profoundly connected with his alchemical interests. In fact, for Harriot, his optical researches "really *were* a species of alchemical experimentation, to which it was natural enough to apply the modes of alchemical concealment and allegory."[12]

In this chapter, I want to continue this line of inquiry into the relationship between atomistic and alchemical theories of matter on the one hand and Harriot's ethnographic account of Algonquian religious and medical beliefs on the other. Indeed, Chaplin's reading of Harriot's account of "invisible bullets" as a colonial ventriloquism about pre-Socratic atomism supports my larger argument here about a long tradition of European natural philosophers, starting with the Vespuccian during the early sixteenth century, who

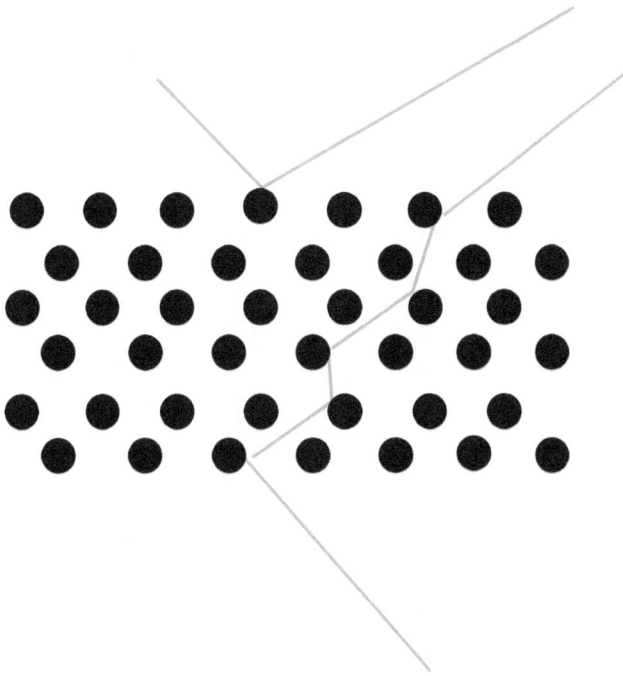

Figure 30. Passage of refracted light through a solid medium, according to Harriot's atomistic theory of matter. (Based on illustration from *Thomas Harriot and His World*, ed. Robert Fox [Burlington, VT: Ashgate, 2012].)

used the New World as a heterotopic foil for experimenting with morally and religiously problematic scientific ideas—especially pre-Socratic atomism, which reentered Europe (as we have seen in chapter 7) in form of a cannibal metaphysics in sixteenth-century accounts about Brazil. Similarly, in Harriot's account about America, which promised to open a new "door of the house of Nature" for Englishmen, atomistic theory of matter is justified by being presented in a narrative of conquest. This "alchemical" interpretation of Harriot's invisible bullets provides an apt context also for his claim of the Indians' alleged belief that the Englishmen were "not borne of women, and therefore not mortall, but that wee were men of an old generation many yeeres past then risen againe to immortalitie." As we have seen in chapter 8, while the idea of creatures not born of women is part of the long alchemical tradition about nature's "spontaneous generations" such as the homunculus—the "little man'" created by human or demonic artifice—the notion that man can achieve immortality, or at least near immortality, through art had been an integral part of alchemy virtually from its inception. The following section traces the history

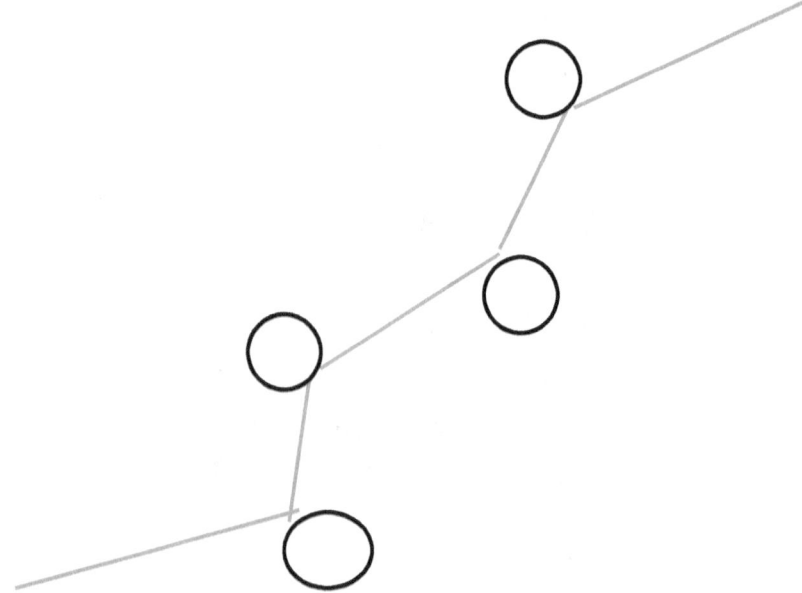

Figure 31. Diagram of refraction as reflection. (Based on British Library Add. MS 6789, f. 336. © The British Library Board.)

of English ethno-demonology from the earliest versions of Harriot's account to the later reeditions by the Flemish engraver Theodor de Bry. The remaining sections follow the ethno-demonological tradition in English colonial literature through the end of the seventeenth century.

Thomas Harriot, Theodor de Bry, and the Translation of Ethno-demonology

In the third part of the *Report,* Harriot described Algonquian dress, housing, warfare, and religion. "Some religion they haue alreadie," he wrote, "which although it be farre from the truth, yet beyng as it is, there is hope it may bee the easier and sooner reformed."[13] By using the word "reformed," Harriot suggested that Native religion might provide the elemental foundation for the Indians' conversion to the Protestant religion. For Harriot, Algonquians were hereby not essentially different from Europeans before the advent of the Protestant (or Anglican) Reformation, when local saints were widely worshiped alongside God, except that the "Virginians" use different words. "They beleeue that there are many Gods which they call *Mantóac,*" he wrote, "but of different sortes and degrees; one onely chiefe and great God, which hath bene from all eternitie. Who as they affirme when hee purposed to make the worlde, made first other goddes of a principall order to bee as meanes and instruments to bee vsed in the creation and gouernment to follow; and after the Sunne, Moone, and Starres, as pettie goddes and the instruments of the other order more principall."[14] If the Virginians' traditional belief in one "chiefe" god would presumably expedite their conversion to Christianity by the English, so would their belief in the "immortalitie of the soule" facilitate the translation of Christian concepts, such as heaven and hell. Thus, according to Harriot, the Indians hold that "after this life as soone as the soule is departed from the bodie according to the workes it hath done, it is eyther carried to heauē the habitacle of gods, there to enioy perpetuall blisse and happiness, or els to a great pitte or hole, which they thinke to bee in the furthest partes of their part of the worlde towarde the sunne set, there to burne continually: the place they call *Popogusso.*"[15] He explains that some of the apparent errors and uncertainties in Native accounts of the creation of the world by referring to their lack of "letters nor other such meanes as we to keepe recordes of the particularities of times past, but onelie tradition from father to sonne," hereby echoing monist Hermeticist explanations that all pagan religions contain faint memories of the true God, memories that have suffered somewhat in the New World due to a lack of writing, just as it had in Catholic Europe due to the church's corruption of the Latin canon. However, what is most important for Harriot is the positive social effects of religion more generally. "What subtilty soeuer be in the *Wiroances* and Priestes," he wrote, "this opinion worketh so much in manie of the common and simple sort of people that it maketh them haue great respect to their Gouernours, and also great care what they do, to auoid torment after death, and to enjoy blisse; although nothwithstanding there is punishment ordained for malefactours, as stealers, whoremoongers, and other sortes of wicked doers; some punished with death, some with forfeitures, some with beating, according to the greatnes of the factes."[16] If Harriot appears to offer a Machiavellian understanding of religion, his ethnographic descriptions emphasize the similarities with Christianity.

Harriot's emphasis on the Virginians' docility and the similarities between Native American and Christian religions can in part be understood in terms of his promotional intent of persuading adventurers to invest and potential colonists to enlist in the colonial enterprise. Thus, in his prologue, addressed to the "Adventurers, Favorers, and Wellwillers of the enterprise for the inhabiting and planting in Virginia," Harriot explained that his account was partially written to counteract the fallout of previous "reports with some slanderous and shamefull speeches bruited abroad by many that returned from thence."

These reports have "not done a little wrong to many that otherwise would have also favored and adventured in the action, to the honour and benefit of our nation."[17] Indeed, the colony had been afflicted by problems from the beginning, including an acute shortage of supplies that partially resulted from the mismanagement of relations with its Indian neighbors by Grenville and his men, who sacked and burned an entire village because one of the villagers had allegedly stolen a silver cup. In his report, Harriot therefore attempted to emphasize the natural abundance of Virginia and the docility of the Indians, as well as the ease with which they would be conquered and converted.

But while in Harriot's text, the similarities between the Christian and Algonquian religion suggest the easy convertibility of the Natives, these similarities would soon take on some darker connotations. In 1590, the Flemish Calvinist goldsmith, engraver, and book publisher from Liège working in Frankfurt Theodor de Bry republished Harriot's 1588 account as the launch title of his "Voyages" series, a lavishly illustrated collection of travel accounts about a century of European explorations, travels, and conquests in the overseas world that would become one of the most spectacularly successful publishing ventures of the early modern period. When the last volume was released by the De Bry publishing house in 1634, the series had grown to a total of twenty-five volumes, the first thirteen of which dealt with the Americas (commonly called the "Great Voyages"), while the remaining twelve (the "Small Voyages") treated European travel to Africa and Asia.[18] In part 8 of the Great Voyages, which was published in 1599, De Bry had reprinted Raleigh's *Discoverie*, along with narratives about several English expeditions by Francis Drake and Thomas Cavendish. In some respects, the De Bry Voyages were similar to the other great travel collections of the sixteenth century, such as the Italian Giovanni Battista Ramusio's *Navigationi et viaggi* (1550–1559) or the Englishman Richard Hakluyt's *Divers Voyages Touching the Discoverie of America* (1582) and *The Principal Navigations, Voiages, Traffiques and Discoueries of the English Nation* (1589–1600). More so than any sixteenth-century travel collectors before them, however, the De Brys made maximal use of the possibilities of early modern print technology, including some six hundred lavish copperplate engravings that indelibly coined European ideas about the peoples inhabiting the overseas world in centuries to come. Also more so than any travel collectors before them, the De Brys targeted an international and pan-European mass audience, releasing the first volume of the Great Voyages in Latin, German, French, and English and each of the subsequent volumes in Latin and German, to the effect that most Protestant Europeans had their first visual and textual encounter with the New World through the De Bry collection.[19]

The history of Harriot's account about Virginia as the launch title of choice for De Bry's "America" series began sometime in late 1584 or early 1585, when Theodor de Bry relocated to London, after the city of his previous residency, Antwerp, had come under Spanish siege. Apparently, de Bry had already had a reputation as an artist by the time he arrived in London in 1584 or 1585, for he quickly became associated with prominent figures at the Elizabethan court, including Raleigh, Richard Hakluyt, the heirs of Philip Sidney, and Anthony Ashley, the clerk of the Privy Council. Thus, in 1587, he was commissioned to engrave twelve plates illustrating the *Procession of the Knights of the Garter*, and a set of thirty-four plates illustrating the *Procession at the Obsequies of Sir Philip Sidney*. Also, when, in 1588, Ashley published his translation of Lucas Waghenaer's famous textbook *The mariners mirror*, he commissioned Theodor de Bry to create the copper plate for the frontispiece. After returning to the Continent, de Bry set up a new print shop at Frankfurt and, in 1590, republished Harriot's 1588 *Report* in four languages—English, Latin, German, and French—along with copperplate engravings that were based on John White's watercolor paintings about Virginia, copies of which de Bry had obtained from Hakluyt. This edition was the product not of the De Brys alone but of a collaboration between the De Bry publishing house at Frankfurt and several Englishmen including Harriot, who provided the captions for de Bry's engravings,[20] and Hakluyt, who translated Harriot's account and captions into Latin and who had persuaded de Bry to use Harriot's text as the launch title of the America series, which had already then been conceived as a multivolume work.[21] The new section of engravings following Harriot's text also included a brief introduction by de Bry and some additional engravings, also based on watercolors by White, of the "ancient Picts" who inhabited the British Isles in ancient times and who were supposed to illustrate the alleged cultural similarities between modern Virginians and ancient Britons.

Art historians and literary critics have noted several differences between White's and de Bry's images. For example, whereas the former's watercolors and captions generally defamiliarize and decontextualize Native religious practices, emphasizing ethnic difference and exotic strangeness, the latter's engravings recontextualize and refamiliarize ethnic elements by Europeanizing facial features in the stylistic convention of European mannerist visual art and by including landscape settings.[22] Of particular interest for my purposes here is the representation of Algonquian religion in the De Bry volume, which stands in marked contrast in this regard to both Harriot's earlier English publication (without images) of 1588 and John White's watercolors. For example, John White's watercolor painting of an Algonquian shaman was entitled *The Flyer* (see fig. 32). By contrast, the engraving based on this watercolor prepared for

Figure 32. John White, *The Flyer*. (© Trustees of the British Museum.)

the De Bry edition by Gijsbert van Veen, one of the artists working in de Bry's shop, was recaptioned in the Latin edition as *Prestigiator;* in the English edition as *The Coniuerer;* and in the German edition as *Der Schwarzkünstler oder Zauberer,* meaning "one adept in the black arts or a magician" (see figs. 33 and 34). In addition, the commentary on this engraving in the English edition reads: "They haue comonlye coniurers or iuglers which vse strange gestures, and often cótrarie to nature in their enchantments: For they be verye familiar with deuils, of whome they enquier what their enemys doe, or other suche thinges."[23]

The differences between White's watercolors and de Bry's engravings with regard to the representation of Native American shamanism can be understood in terms of what Sabine MacCormack has called the "battle over idols"

Figure 33. Theodor de Bry, *The Coniuerer* (In *America,* pt. 1 [Frankfurt, 1590]. Courtesy of the John Carter Brown Library at Brown University.)

that raged in Renaissance Europe. As she points out, during the era in which Europeans first encountered Native American religions, there was an active interest also in Europe in the power of images and idols, as well as in the agency of spirits and demons, especially in the wake of Ficino's Renaissance Neoplatonism and Hermeticism: "Seekers after occult knowledge, among them Ficino himself, speculated as to whether and how demons who possessed power of healing and divination might come to reside in statues or talismans and to bring their powers to bear on human lives."[24] Ficino derived these ideas from the Corpus Hermeticum, which he had translated, as well as from the alchemical Arabic tradition in such as the *Picatrix*. However, as MacCormack shows for the Spanish American archive, whereas in Europe, demons, statues,

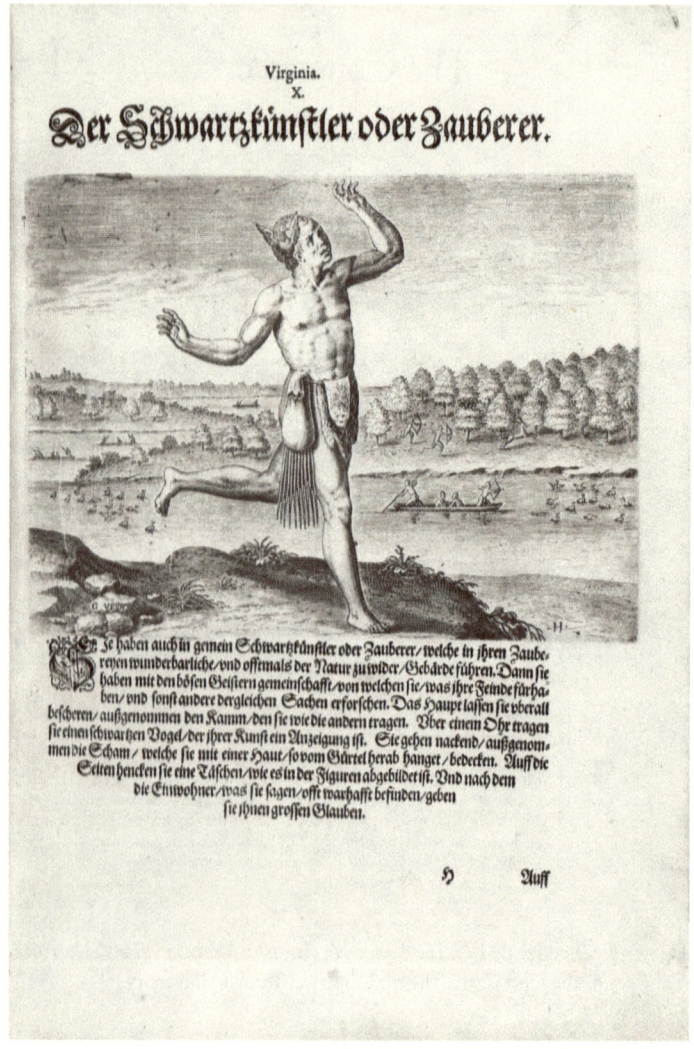

Figure 34. Theodor de Bry, *Der Schwarzkünstler oder Zauberer* (In America, pt. 1 [Frankfurt, 1590]. Courtesy of the Kraus Collection of Sir Francis Drake, Library of Congress)

images, and talismans figured, for the most part, "in the preoccupations of the learned," in the Americas, Europeans perceived the "idolatry" of Native American religions as "dirty" and "diabolic."

This emerging pattern of interpreting classical and Native American pagan "idolatry" would also become prevalent in the Protestant context and sheds light on the differences between White's watercolors and the representation in the De Bry volume. As we have seen in the last chapter, Walter Raleigh, in his *Discoverie*, still seemed to apply a Neoplatonic or Hermetic hermeneutics of idolatry when writing that it would have been "easy to have brought them [the Guianaians] idolatrous" of the image of Queen Elizabeth. Similarly, the title of White's portrait of the Algonquin shaman, *The Flyer*, would have reminded the reader of the Greek god Hermes (or the Roman Mercury), of European classical paganism generally, and especially of the Renaissance Hermetic tradition that had been brought to Elizabethan England by Giordano Bruno during his visit to London from 1583 to 1585 and that was associated with the members of the Hermetic circle that had gathered around John Dee, Edward Kelly, Sir Walter Raleigh, and even Harriot himself.[25] That White may have had the "white magic" of just such a learned, philosophical, or classical Hermes in mind when he portrayed the Algonquin shaman in his watercolor is suggested by the similarity that his *Flyer* bears, in posture and expression, to the Hermes in Botticelli's *Primavera*, which depicts a "magical" Renaissance garden with many medicinal herbs and references to alchemical motifs (figs. 35 and 36).[26]

By contrast, the new captions in the various editions of the De Bry volume strip the Native shaman of White's association of Native shamanism with the

Figure 35. Sandro Botticelli, *Primavera*, with Hermes (*left*). (Courtesy of the Uffizi Gallery and Wikimedia.org.)

"philosophical" Hermeticist or Christian alchemist in the Ficinian tradition of the Italian Renaissance. Instead, they associate Algonquian shamanism with the black magic of "dirty" and diabolic idolatry.[27] The association of Native American shamanism with diabolism and witchcraft is underscored by the iconography of de Bry's engravings depicting Algonquin religious rituals. Thus, in an engraving entitled "Their manner of prainge with Rattles abowt te fyer," de Bry organizes the image around a column of bellowing smoke that is reminiscent, as Michael Gaudio has shown, of an iconographic tradition representing the Witches Sabbath, such Hans Baldung's woodcut of that title.[28] The apparent similarities between Algonquin and Christian religious rites—which in Harriot's original 1588 text had still signified the Neoplatonic notion of pagans' faint memory of their true maker—imply in this new context of De Bry's publication diabolic counterfeit and perversions. The subtle variety in connotation of these captions in the different language editions of the De Bry volume are hereby instructive. For example, the "prestigiator" in the Latin edition refers to someone who causes a "praestigium," which, according to Isidore of Seville's *Etymolgia*, was the "'binding' of the pupil of the eye."[29] In other words, it involved visual deceptions primarily by the use of natural magic. As Stuart Clark observes, a prestige "might involve anything from high-class subtlety to low-class duping, provided the twin elements of artifice and imposture were present, but it was invariably a visual matter."[30] Modern English translations of *prestigiator* might thus include magician, trickster (one who practices deceit), juggler, impostor, cheat, or deceiver. Whereas the Latin *prestigiator* could imply white or black

Figure 36. Sandro Botticelli, *Primavera*, detail: Hermes. (Courtesy of the Uffizi Gallery and Wikimedia.org.)

magic, as well as learned or vulgar magic, the English "conjuror" has more limited connotations, invoking the European contexts of folk jugglers, witch doctors, and perhaps even diabolic "Catholic" superstitions, hereby foreshadowing an increasingly radical Protestant hermeneutics in which preternatural phenomena such as "flying" (or levitation) must no longer be associated with saints but only with witches.[31]

Perhaps most unequivocal in this context is the German translation as "Schwarzkünstler oder Zauberer." Three years earlier, in 1587, De Bry's rival printer in Frankfurt, Johann Spies, had published the *Historia von D. Johann Fausten,* one of the first in a series of narratives that would grow, in the 1590s (and subsequent centuries), into the Faust legend—the famous story about the scholar and physician who signs a contract with the Devil, selling his soul in exchange for magic powers in this world. The subtitle of Spies's publication was "*dem weitbeschreyten Zauberer und Schwarzkünstler / wie er sich gegen dem Teuffel auff eine benandte Zeit verschrieben*" (the notorious magician and adept in the black arts / how he enlisted himself with the devil for a named time) (see fig. 37). Spies's *Historia* was republished the following year, in 1588—two years before De Bry's publication of Harriot's account. In 1593, a sequel to Spies's *Historia* was published anonymously about Faust's *famulus,* Christoff Wagner, who, like his teacher, makes a pact with the Devil but only gets five years of preternatural power in exchange for his soul. Also, unlike his teacher, Wagner is a globe-trotter, traveling to the "newly discovered world" (*neuu erfundene Welt*) of America.[32] On his passage, he encounters various exotic animals such as the "flying fish," which had been depicted in one of John White's watercolors and described in numerous natural histories of the New World.[33] After the conventional ethnographic descriptions of stereotypically Amerindian customs—the use of tobacco, of poisoned arrows, and of going about naked—Wagner witnesses their religious practices, which clearly echo de Bry's depictions in his edition of Harriot's texts: "About their religion, it is like this. They pray to many and various gods, some are painted, some carved out of chalk or wood, or from gold and silver, strangely shaped, some have birds and other hideous animals, in the way we paint the devil, with craws' feet and long tails. . . . The devil deceives them often and in various form, and promises their priests something. . . . So, he confuses the poor people, this deceptive, lying charlatan."[34] As Keith Thomas has shown, the 1590s and the early decades of the seventeenth century saw an increasing level of anxiety about black magic and witchcraft in England and on the Continent. This shift in attitude toward magic provides the context also for the changing representations of Native American religions and cultures in the early years of English

Figure 37. *Historia von D. Johann Fausten* (Frankfurt: Johann Spies, 1587). (Courtesy of Goethe-Museum, Düsseldorf, CC BY-NC-SA.)

overseas exploration. Indeed, this shift in Europe may in part have been a response to the colonial encounter with non-Western forms of paganism in the Americas.

Another context for this new interpretation of paganism as idolatry can be found in the history of alchemy, the practice of which exploded in early modern European courts in the wake of the occult philosophy of Ficino and Agrippa, as well as the Paracelsian movement. As we have seen in chapter 6 with regard to the early Franciscan and Jesuit interpretations of Native American spirituality, the history of alchemy had long been connected with the history of demonology in Europe. By attributing significant agency to human art in effecting natural change, alchemists also had to make concessions to the power of demonic art. In early modern Protestant Europe, too, this alchemical nexus resulted in the interpretation of Native spirituality in terms of Satanism. Thus, Harriot's fledgling and ambivalent references to the Devil in the captions he provided for the 1590 De Bry edition of his *Report* may be seen mainly as a rhetorical gesture that participated in an increasingly negative interpretation of "idolatry" in the wake of Europe's colonial encounters with Native American religions, which gave rise to an unprecedented obsession with witchcraft and a general conviction of the Devil's unlimited power in the world.[35]

Indeed, in this changing religious climate during the 1590s, Harriot found himself repeatedly accused of being an atheist and even a sorcerer, as did some of his associates such as Raleigh and Dee, as well as Henry Percy, the Earl of Northumberland (known as the "Wizard Earl").[36] Thus, Christopher Marlowe was reported to have said "that it was an easy matter for Moyses being brought up in all the arte of the Egiptians to abuse the Jewes being a rude & grosse people," and "that Moyses was but a jugler, & that one Heriote [Harriot] being Sir W. Raleighs man can do more than he."[37] In order to extricate himself from the imputation of being a "jugler" himself, Harriot denounces the Algonquin "enchantments" and "idolatries," which impelled him to "make declaration of the contents of the Bible; that therein was set foorth the true and onelie God, and his mightie woorkes."[38] Like Shakespeare's Prospero in *The Tempest*, who casts his slave Caliban in a diabolic dye by invoking his mother, the alleged "witch" Sycorax, in order to absolve his own, "white" magic, both Harriot and de Bry, in the 1590 volume of the Great Voyages, conjure up images of pagan witchcraft while fashioning themselves as Hermetic Christian magi.[39] Thus, de Bry, in an enigmatic passage in the preamble to his engravings, makes the following cryptic threat to potential plagiarizers and pirates of his book: that "secret marks lye hiddin in my pictures, which wil breede Confusion unless they bee well observed" for the case that "any seeke to Contrefact thes my bookx, (for in this days many are so malicious that they seeke to gayne by other men labours) thow wouldest give noe credit unto suche counterfeited Drawghte."[40] When trying to make sense of this cryptic threat, it is helpful to keep in mind that the De Bry family was intimately connected with a pervasive culture of Hermeticism and the production of alchemical emblems and symbols. As we will see in the next chapter, Theodor de Bry's elder son and successor, Theodor Johann, not only continued his father's work on the Voyages but was also known for his printing of books of Hermetic alphabetology, alchemical symbolism and emblem books; and he had engraved the illustrations and published the alchemical works of Robert Fludd and the Rosicrucian Michael Maier, two influential seventeenth-century writers eager to disassociate the "Christian" Hermeticism of the Italian Neoplatonists such as Ficino from the vulgar magic of Europe's cunningmen and witch doctors.[41]

In the context of this generic interference between alchemy, demonology, and ethnography in late sixteenth-century Germany, subsequent volumes in the De Bry collections became less and less ambiguous in their representation of Amerindian spirituality. Volume 2, published in Latin and German in 1591, featured translations of René Goulaine de Laudonnière's account of Jean Ribault's French Huguenot colony in Florida, originally published in 1586 under the title *L'histoire notable de la Floride, contenant les trois voyages faits en icelles par des capitaines et pilotes français,* as well as engravings based on (now mostly lost) watercolors by the artist Jacques le Moyne. Although Laudonnière focused on the Native Floridians' idolatrous worship of sun and moon, while de Bry's engravings depicted them worshipping a column decorated with the French royal coat of arms and garlands (fig. 38), overall his volume refrained from associating Amerindian religions with diabolism. This changed, however, with parts 3 (1593) and 4 (1594), about Brazil and New Spain respectively. The frontispiece to part 3, which included De Bry's edition of the narratives of

Figure 38. Theodor de Bry, "Wie die Wilden in Florida die Seul vom Obersten in seiner ersten Schiffahrt aussgerichtet verehrt haben" (How the savages of Florida worshiped the column erected by the general during his first voyage). (In *America,* pt. 2 [Frankfurt, 1591]). Courtesy of the John Carter Brown Library at Brown University.

Hans Staden and Jean de Léry about their experiences among the Tupinamba of Brazil, displays several Tupis gorging themselves on human limbs (fig. 39).

In the dedication to the Duke of Palatine Ferdinand IV, de Bry reflected on the remarkable diversity of the peoples, cultures, and religions of the New World: "It is important when reading these three descriptions of mine, of Virginia, Florida, and Brazil, to take note of the great diversity (*Ungleichheit*) among these nations with regard to clothes, weaponry and armory, customs of life." This is not surprising, he continued, as "these lands are not small but each one extends over several hundred German miles."[42] Apart from their various styles of dress and hair, these nations also differ greatly in religion. In Virginia, for example, the Natives believe in a god that created everything, "but they have no knowledge of him, with the exception that they believe in life after death." In Florida, the Indians "have a different god, the sun and the moon. But these of which we are dealing with here [the Brazilians] believe in nothing else except in a great fruit that resembles the egg of an ostrich. This, they hold to be their god, as they are persuaded by their priests. Such is the great blindness of these poor people."[43] In other words, the Indians of Virginia, Florida, and Brazil provided a spectrum of demonically inspired paganism. Also, in his edition of Léry's narrative, De Bry included a prefatory poem that offers an allegorical reading of the Tupis' "wildness" and that links the Tupis' savagery in America to Catholic cruelty in Europe, making it clear that he understands the significance of New World ethnographies such as Léry's to be a commentary on human nature more general:

> I only want to tell you that in our country, where art and science is abundant, there can be found people much more terrible and monstrous so that you can better believe what I write here. Even though they may have a horrific way of life, cooking, roasting and eating their enemies, they have more peace than France right now. Take me there [to Brazil], learned Lery, before it gets any worse in France. You hear of monstrous people and hear of adventures in the New World, of people who live naked in the outdoors. This is the guilt of old Adam, who so pathetically scorned the image of God, through his sin and crime. That even though they are born in a good country and are without crime, they will remain wild like a beast without being subjected to [Christian] instruction.[44]

The degeneration of humans who live without the light of Christian revelation chronicled by De Bry's ethnographies comes to a nadir with part 4 of the America series, which presents translations (Latin and German in separate editions) of the first book of Girolamo Benzoni's *Historia del Mondo Nuovo*. The narrative provides a panoramic overview of the Spanish history

Figure 39. Theodor de Bry, frontispiece, *America,* pt. 3 (Frankfurt, 1593). (Courtesy of the John Carter Brown Library at Brown University.)

of the discovery and conquest, beginning with Columbus's voyages and culminating with the conquests of Mexico and Peru. The frontispiece of De Bry's edition of Benzoni presents a winged and wholly demonic Aztec god Huitzilopochtli, with claws of a large cat and a giant toothed mouth in his chest, demanding blood sacrifices (fig. 40).

If the sequence of frontispieces in De Bry's *America* series tells the story of

Figure 40. Theodor de Bry, frontispiece, *America,* pt. 4. Frankfurt, 1594. (Courtesy of the John Carter Brown Library at Brown University.)

an increasing obsession with witchcraft and idolatry in Continental Europe, in England, too, the interest in diabolism intensified, especially among the elite in church and state, with the succession of the Stuart dynasty, as well as the radicalization of the conflict between sectarians and an increasingly calcified orthodox Laudian church. Perhaps the most famous manifestation of this new interest in demonology on the part of the political elite is the publication of

King James's *Daemonologie* five years before his ascension to the throne of England in 1603. James's primary target was not malefic witchcraft but magic. He therefore attempted to delineate the lawful sciences (such as astronomy) from unlawful magic (such as divinatory astrology), as well as the art of conjuring spirits. As God is all-powerful, there is nothing that the Devil could do without God's permission. Instances of witchcraft were therefore to be interpreted as evidence of God's displeasure, which resulted in the withdrawal of his protection, thus allowing for malefic witchcraft. Witchcraft could therefore only be remedied by fasting and prayer rather than, as in the Catholic context, through rituals of exorcism. It is for this reason that Protestant demonologists such as James deemed magic a crime worse than witchcraft itself, as the witch was an instrument of God's wrath, whereas the conjurer had "knowledge" but still attempted to resist or "trick" his way out of God's providence through his magic, which made his crime an offense against the Holy Spirit. The "first cause" in witchcraft is God, he wrote, "and the Devill as his instrument and second cause shootes at in all these actiones of the Deuil, (as Gods hang-man)."[45] To be sure, James's treatise, written in a Socratic dialogue between two allegorical figures, Philomates and Epistemon, is primarily an attempt to persuade his readers of these theological implications of conjuring from the point of view of the Reformation. Nevertheless, what had previously been primarily a *moral* question—an opposition between white magic and black magic (or malifice)—became in his text, as in many others in seventeenth-century Protestant England, primarily a question of "conscience," as Stuart Clark has put it,[46] when any sort of conjuring was increasingly seen as a crime against the sovereignty of God, church, and state.

Ethno-demonology and Colonial British American Exceptionalism

It was in the context of this new intellectual climate that one of the greatest Counter-Reformation demonologies about the New World saw its first complete translation into English—José de Acosta's *Historia natural y moral,* translated in 1604 by Edward Grimstone.[47] The first Englishman who explicitly picked up on Acosta's contention that Native American religions were diabolic in origin was the biblical scholar and millenarian Joseph Mede, who, in the 1620s, argued in his "A Coniecture Concerning Gog and Magogs in the Revelations," that "the people of America are Colonies of the nation of Magog." Thus, Satan's army "shall come from those nations, which live in the Hemisphere opposite to us, whom the Best and most Great God in his secret judgment, for the most part shall not cherish with the light of his Gospel."[48]

Whereas the Old World (what he calls the "universal Hemisphere" of old), is the "onely ... partaker of the promised instauration, [and] shall become the camp of the Saints, and the seat of this [God's] blessed kingdome ... whatsoever nations are without this (in the places where the Ancients placed the seat of Hel) shall be reserved to the last triumph of Christ, to be destroyed by fire from heavn, by his just (though to us unknown) judgment." In other words, the New World will be redeemed from the Devil only with the coming of the apocalypse itself.[49]

Nevertheless, if Grimstone's translation of Acosta and Mede's millenarian speculations had set the stage for the interpretation of Native religions as diabolism by English writers, the ethnographic literature about British America during the first decades of the seventeenth century still reflected little of it. Even in Puritan New England, apologists for the English invasion of Native lands made little rhetorical recourse to the Devil at first. Some of the prominent New English clergymen, such as John Cotton, made typological use of the book of Exodus, in which the English Puritans became a type of New Israelites destined to drive out the Indians, a new type of Canaanites. The New Englanders hereby saw themselves as a people "set aside" from the worldly reign of the Antichrist in Catholic (and Anglican) Europe, and America was their "refuge."[50] For the English, land, rather than labor or souls, was the commodity they sought in the New World, despite some notable exception, such as the Puritan missionary John Eliot, who belatedly discovered the Puritans' apostolic mission during the 1640s.[51] Showing little interest in Native Americans as either an object of conversion or as a source of labor, the English colonists interpreted their removal into the New World through a typological exegesis of the book of Exodus, where the Devil did not play a prominent role. Thus, in "God's Promise to His Plantations" (1630), Cotton had admitted of "three ways" in which the Indian Canaanites may be deprived of their land: (1) "cast out" by "lawful war"; (2) "mak[ing] room ... by way of purchase" or simply "courtesy"; and (3) by acting as a "void."[52] The stunning devastation that European diseases had wrought among the Indians upon first contact with Europeans was interpreted by the Puritan observer, not as a sign of God's displeasure with the way Europeans had conducted themselves in the New World (as did Bartolomé de las Casas) but as a confirmation that the Indians were indeed a type of Canaanites who were making room for God's people. Thus, John Winthrop, the first governor of the Puritan Massachusetts Bay Colony, plausibly argued that "if God were not pleased with our inheriting these parts, why did he drive out the natives before us?"[53] This interpretation of events, and of the meaning of the Indian, not only proved the typological progress of sacred history but also conveniently provided the "answers" to certain "objections" voiced by enemies of the Puritan and Separatist colonial enterprises concerning the "warrant to enter upon that land which hath been so long possessed by others."[54]

One such critic was the Separatist ethnographer Roger Williams, who argued that the English king had no right to grant Indian lands to Englishmen, as the Indians were the legitimate owners of these lands. He had therefore purchased the land for his colony of Rhode Island from the Indians (even though he later still sought a royal patent for the purchased land). Williams became one of colonial British America's earliest ethnographers and linguists with the publication of *Key into the Language of America* (1643), the first sustained English study of an Amerindian language. It was a sort of language guide offering lists of words and phrases for various intercultural activities and communications (trade, proselytization, etc.) in the Narragansett dialect of the Algonquin language. Not unlike Ficino's "Key of the Thrice-Greatest Hermes," Williams's book offered a "key" that would unlock, he hoped, the "rarities concerning the Natives themselves not yet discovered." His key may "open a Box," he proposed, "where lies a bunch of the keyes" that will unlock "the secrets of those Countries." The Hermetic language of keys and secrets is unmistakable here. As in Raleigh's *Discoverie,* so also in William's *Key,* the language of Hermeticism affords the license for proto-ethnographic inquiry, hereby facilitating the importation of numerous Algonquin words into the English language—words such as squash, papoose, powwow, and squaw.[55]

Moreover, like Harriot, Williams adopted in the *Key* a Neoplatonic view on the origins of Algonquin culture and religion. "They have no *clothes, books,* nor *letters,* and conceive their *fathers* never had," he wrote, "and therefore they are easily persuaded that the *god* that made *English* men is a greater *god:* because He hath so richly endowed the *English* above *themselves:* But when they hear that about sixteen hundred years ago, *England* and the *Inhabitants* thereof were like unto *themselves,* and since have received from *God clothes, books,* &c. they are greatly affected with a secret hope concerning *themselves.*"[56] Even though without letters, the Indians still retained a faint memory of the son of God, whom they call "Wetucks." Thus, they "have many strange relations of one *Wetucks,* a man that wrought great *miracles* amongst them, and *walking upon the waters,* &c. with some kind of broken resemblance to the *son of God."* He even suggested that, based on certain linguistic affinities between Algonquin and Greek, the Indians may be descendants of the Greeks, while he also acknowledged the theory, increasingly popular during the 1640s, after the publication of Thomas Thorowgood's *Jews in America,* that the Indians may be descended from the Ten Lost Tribes of Israel, a theory that harked back to Spanish theorists during the sixteenth century.[57]

Throughout British America, however, writers did increasingly resort to a demonological interpretation of Native religions and cultures in the aftermath of armed conflict that inevitably erupted as a result of the English grab for Native land. In the literature about the first permanent English colony in America, Jamestown in Virginia, this moment arrived with the Powhatan confederacy's attack on the fledgling colony in 1622. Writing in 1625, and apparently remembering Acosta and Mede, the Anglican minister Samuel Purchas, Richard Hakluyt's successor as collector and historian of English overseas exploration and colonization, composed a short treatise entitled "Virginia's Verger," which offered an extended theoretical disquisition on what he called the "Law of Nature and Nations" and which was one of the most elaborate articulations yet in English of the justification of the English conquest. The English claim to the land had been established, he argued, by the rights of "first discovery, first actuall possession, prescription, gift, cession, and livery of seisin, sale for price natural Inheritance of the English their naturally borne, and the unnaturall outcries of many unnaturally murthered."[58] In order to preempt conceivable objections that the acts of violence committed by the Indians had been in legitimate self-defense, Purchas alleged their natural savagery and the diabolic origins of their religion:[59] "Considering so good a Country, so bad people, having little of Humanitie but shape, ignorant of Civilitie, of Arts, or Religion; more brutish then the beasts they hunt, more wild and unmanly then that unmanned wild Countrey, which they range rather then inhabite; captivated also to Satans tyranny in foolish pieties, mad impieties, wicked idlenesse, busie and bloudy wickednesse: hence have wee fit objects of zeale and pitie, to deliver from the power of darknesse."[60] Similarly, John Smith, in his *General History of Virginia* (1624), published two years after the massacre, portrayed the Powhattans' religion as satanic spectacles on which he claimed to report with the authority of an eyewitness captive. In his *General History* he reproduces de Bry's image from Harriot's account of "their idol Kiwasa," as well as de Bry/Harriot's designation of a Native shaman as a conjurer (fig. 41). In Smith's account the conjuror (as well as the priest) appear as minions to an idol with clearly demonic characteristics. Thus, Smith reports that, during his captivity among the Powhattans, "they entertained him with most strange and fearefull Coniurations";[61] and he concludes that the Powhattans' religion is essentially diabolic and entirely born of fear:

> All things that are able to doe them hurt beyond their prevention, [he writes] they adore with their kinde of divine worship; as the fire, water, lightning, thunder, our Ordnance, peeces, horses, &c. But their chiefe God they worship is the Devill. Him they call Okee, and serue him more of feare then loue. They say they

Fig. 41. John Smith, from *A map of Virginia vvith a description of the countrey, the commodities, people, government and religion* (Oxford: printed by Joseph Barnes, 1612). (Courtesy of the John Carter Brown Library at Brown University.)

haue conference with him, and fashion themselues as neare to his shape as they can imagine. In their Temples they haue his image euill favoured carved, and then painted and adorned with chaines of copper, and beads, and covered with a skin, in such manner as the deformitie may well suit with such a God.[62]

This Okee, Smith continues, demands yearly sacrifices of fifteen children, which "they held to be so necessary, that if they should omit it, their Okee or Devill, and all their other ... Gods, would let them haue no Deere, Turkies, Corne, nor fish, and yet besides, he would make a great slaughter amongst them." Although he also reports that the Indians held the English God as more powerful than theirs, given that he supplied them with weapons superior than theirs, they appear to be beyond salvation by human endeavors. "In this lamentable ignorance doe these poore soules sacrifice themselues to the Devill," he concludes, "not knowing their Creator; and we had not language sufficient, so plainly to expresse it as make them vnderstand it; which God grant they may."[63] This interpretation is a long way from Harriot's earlier portrayal of the "Virginians'" religion, as their alleged diabolism puts them beyond the possibility of salvation. For Smith, as for the majority of Protestant ethnographers in the seventeenth century, it is not man's business to extirpate or exorcise witchcraft. Thus, Smith, enduring the afflictions of Powhattan's satanic malefice, commends himself to God, who, miraculously, sends him a young Indian maiden, Powhatan's daughter Pocahontas, and Smith and Jamestown are restored to God's good protection.

In New England, a similar transformation in the perception of Native religions took hold in the second part of the seventeenth century, especially after King Philip's War. However, unlike the representations of Native religions of late sixteenth- and early seventeenth-century Spanish accounts of conquest, the Puritan accounts of King Philip's War, such as William Hubbard's *A Narrative of the Troubles with the Indians,* Increase Mather's *A Relation of the Troubles with the Indians,* or Mary Rowlandson's *The Sovereignty and Goodness of God,* conceive of Native diabolism not as something to be extirpated but to be suffered. It is interpreted entirely within the Protestant understanding of witchcraft as a matter of conscience, couched in the rhetoric of the jeremiad, in which Native Americans and their diabolic god prevail only while God's protection of his "new Jerusalem" in New England is temporarily lifted as the colony's collective punishment for some of its internal backsliders and degenerates. In Mary Rowlandson's *The Sovereignty and Goodness of God* (1682), for example, the interior "wilderness" of the colonial soul was projected upon an exterior "Indian wilderness"—upon irredeemable "black creatures in the night," as Rowlandson wrote, "which made the place [of her captivity] a lively resemblance of hell."[64]

Similarly, in *Wonders of the Invisible World,* his account of the Salem witch trials, Cotton Mather, the most prolific New England writer of the seventeenth century, synthesized Mede's notion of the hemisphere's satanic past with the providentialist understanding of witchcraft as a case of conscience. One of the reasons, he argues, why New England had been afflicted so severely by witchcraft in Salem and Andover in 1692 was the circumstance that New England was located in America, which, before the arrival of the Europeans, was "the *Devils* Territories."[65] "When the Silver-Trumpets of the Lord Jesus were so sound in the other *Hemisphere* of our World," he wrote in his *Seasonable Discourses,* "the Devil got a forlorn Crue over hither into America, in hopes that the Gospel never would come at them here."[66] One of the weapons that the Devil employed in his retaliation against the New England Christian vanguard was his art of mimesis, or imitation of the Christian church and rituals, such as an organization "after the manner of Congregational Churches," the celebration of a baptism and a supper, as well as "Officers among them, abominably Resembling those of our Lord." "Tis very Remarkable to see," he wrote, "what an Impious & Imputent *Imitation* of Divine Things, is Apishly affected by the Devil, in several of those matters, whereof the Confessions of our Witches . . . have informed us."[67] Mather echoed here José de Acosta's demonology a hundred years earlier, citing his *Historia natural y moral de las Indias* (1590) in Grimstone's 1604 translation in one of the editions of *Wonders* printed by Benjamin Harris in 1693, which added to the previous editions of this work also a number of natural and preternatural "curiosities" concerning the phenomenon of witchcraft, which Mather recorded in the empiricist spirit becoming of a member of the Royal Society of London.[68] "The Indians which came from far to settle about Mexico," Mather wrote, "were in their Progress to that Settlement, under a Conduct of the Devil, very strangely Emulating what the Blessed God gave to Israel in the Wilderness." Citing Acosta, Mather continues to relate the story of the Aztecs' migration to Mexico under the command of "the Devil" god Huitzilopochtli.[69]

For Mather, the witches of Salem perpetuated a long tradition of diabolism already begun by the Aztecs in Mexico. However, if the American Hemisphere, north as south, is thus more dangerously exposed than its Old World counterpart to the machinations of the raging Devil deprived of his last hideout, so well disguised by the Atlantic Ocean for millennia, it is only because of the sins of New Englanders that he was able to inflict any harm. Thus, Mather writes:

> The first Planters of these Colonies were a *Chosen Generation* of men, who were first so *Pure*, as to disrelish many things which they thought wanted *Reformation* else where; and yet withal so *Peaceable*, that they Embraced a Voluntary Exile in a Squalid, horrid, *American* Desert, rather than to Live in Contentions with their Brethren. . . . But alas, the Children, and Servants of those Old planters, must needs afford many, *Degenerate Plants*, and there is now Risen up a Number of people, otherwise Inclined than our *Joshua's* and the *Elders that outlived them*. . . . Hence tis, that the Happiness of *New-England*, has been, *but for a Time*, as it was foretold, and not for a *Long Time*, as ha's been desir'd for us. A Variety of Calamity ha's long follow'd this Plantation; and we have all the Reason imaginable to ascribe it unto the Rebuke of Heaven upon us for our manifold *Apostasies;* we make no Right use of our Disasters, if we do not, *Remember whence we are fallen, and Repent, and Do the first works*. But yet our Afflictions may come under a further Consideration with us: there is a further cause of our Afflictions, whose *Due* must be *Given* him.[70]

Mather's *Wonders of the Invisible World,* his tract on the "discovery" of witchcraft in New England, thus illustrates the historical connections between New World exceptionalism, heterotopianism, and ethno-demonology in a hermeneutics of discovery predicated on the esoteric construction of the occult that emerged from late medieval alchemy and translated into a state of exception in early modern science and international law. In a colonial context, both Spanish and English writers increasingly came to associate Native American religions not only with paganism but with Satanism in the course of their respective colonial encounters. By keeping a dual focus on Amerindian diabolism and savagery, colonial ethno-demonologists could provide rhetorically powerful arguments for Reformation and Counter-Reformation conceptions of human nature and natural reason, which, in turn, would provide (proto-)Hobbesean arguments rationalizing absolute monarchy and the early modern totalitarian state.[71] Unlike in Spanish America, however, in British America conquest was predicated on the legal notion of *terra nullius* and the fiction that America was a "virgin land" or "wilderness" that could be lawfully settled by Englishmen, not, as in the Spanish conquest, on the model of the Reconquista—the subjugation and conversion of infidels, new American vassals whose labor could be exploited. This fundamental difference had profound consequences for the encounter between Europeans and Native Americans, for the colonial societies that developed in each realm, and also for the role that "diabolism" played there. Thus, whereas Englishmen did, at times, see themselves victimized by the Devil and his New World minions, for Franciscans in New Spain such as Motolonía or Jerónimo de Mendieta, the Devil's victims who had to be redeemed were not European settlers but the Native neophytes, who had to be liberated from his clutches through extirpation and exorcism. In predominantly Protestant British America, by contrast, diabolism continued to be interpreted as a "matter of conscience," as something that had to be suffered and endured as a sign of God's righteous displeasure, and therefore is most typically subsumed in the rhetorical structure of the American jeremiad. When considered comparatively, the histories of both Spanish and British American perceptions of Native American religions suggest the important role that the colonial encounter itself played in the shaping of Western Christianity in the religious transformations of the early modern period.

12

Eating Bacon
Alchemy and Cannibal Science

> No, there are no longer cannibals in this region. We ate the last one yesterday.
> —Slavoj Žižek, *For They Know Not What They Do*

Below the image of the sixteenth-century galleon passing through the Pillars of Hercules in the iconic frontispiece of Francis Bacon's *Instauratio magna* (1620), we find an inscription from the book of Daniel (12:4): "Multi pertransibunt et augebitur scientia" (Many shall go to and fro and knowledge shall be increased) (see fig. 42). Book 12 of Daniel contains a prophecy of the End Times, when "there shall be a time of trouble" and when the dead, "buried in the dust of the earth, shall awake" to face judgment. In the *New Organon* (1620), Bacon explains that the prophecy of Daniel on the last times of the world "signifies enigmatically that it is in the fates, that is, in providence, that the circumnavigation of the world (which after so many long voyages now seems quite complete or on the way to completion) and the increase of the sciences should come to pass in the same age."[1] According to Bacon, this age had been inaugurated by Christopher Columbus's "wonderful voyage across the Atlantic Sea," which gave proof "that new lands and continents, beyond those previously known, could be found" and which have been "the causes and beginnings of great things."[2] The discovery of America had made manifest what Bacon's Columbus already knew to be true: the existence of new worlds beyond the Pillars of Hercules. Columbus's discovery was thus both an act of revelation that fulfilled Daniel's prophecy and an announcement of a new world of science yet to come, which would leave behind the old book-bound world of knowledge circumscribed by the ancients' Circle of Knowledge. This new, reformed, or purified science would repudiate what Bacon called "received philosophy"—the world of Aristotelian Scholasticism, including alchemy and magic. It would be a "science" in the sense of the study not of books (the works of men) but of the works of nature by way of observation and experimentation. As Bacon wrote in *Of the Interpretation of Nature* (1603), it is as if "the opening of the world by navigation and commerce and the further discovery of knowledge should meet in

Figure 42. Francis Bacon, frontispiece, *The Great Instauration* (1620), detail. (Courtesy of the Library of Congress.)

one time or age," which is the "autumn of the world": "Let it be believed, and appeal thereof made to *Time,* (with renunciation nevertheless to all the vain and abusing promises of Alchemists and Magicians, and such like light, idle, ignorant, credulous, and fantastical wits and sects,) that the new-found world of land [i.e., America] was not greater addition to the ancient continent than there remaineth at this day a world of inventions and sciences unknown, having respect to those that are known."[3] The only difference between the New World of America and the New World of science, Bacon notes, was that "the ancient regions of knowledge will seem as barbarous compared with the new, as the new regions of people seem barbarous compared to many of the old."[4]

Francis Bacon was an English natural philosopher of note as well as a statesman, a common law jurist, and, above all, a great allegorist. Indeed, much of the postmortem success of his program in the reform of natural philosophy arguably owes to his talents as a rhetorician. But it is often one of his limping allegories that is most revealing about the nature of modern scientific discovery. Thus, in the example above, the imperfection that he notes in his own allegory—the New World of America that Columbus discovered was like his new world of science in every respect *except* its barbarity—alerts us to the degree to which the legitimacy of the modern idea of discovery turned on the age-old European notion of barbarism. As we have seen in chapters 7 and 8, it is a concept that had reentered sixteenth-century Europe in the guise of the cannibal in the encounter with America. While it is perhaps a commonplace to assert that Bacon conceived of scientific discovery as an act of conquest— the "conquest of nature"—in the late sixteenth and early seventeenth centuries, "conquest" had a concrete context that is important to bear in mind when investigating the origins of Bacon's notion of scientific discovery. As I will argue in this chapter, the conceptual language Bacon employs in elaborating his idea of scientific discovery was intimately related not only to the spatial logic of early modern transoceanic expansionism but also to the sixteenth-century debate about natural law and the rights to "dominion" as it had emerged from the legal debate about the sixteenth-century conquest of America.

As we have seen in chapter 4, Columbus had also invoked the prophetic book of Daniel in order to lend apocalyptic significance to his transatlantic voyages. But unlike Bacon's Columbus, the historical Columbus had not, of course, intended to prove by experiment the existence of new lands and continents. While new *(is-)lands* were to be expected on the way to Asia, new *continents* (or "parts") were the last thing that either Columbus or his backers, the Catholic Monarchs, had bargained for. Insofar as the idea of a "New World" emerged at all in Columbus's later writings, it did so only as a fulfillment of ancient biblical prophecies and (as I have argued) as late medieval alchemical ideas about the apocalyptic recovery of the Earthly Paradise. Indeed, despite the increasing amount of information brought back during the early sixteenth century from the Americas to Europe by mariners, soldiers, travelers, and imperial administrators, the Renaissance episteme fusing Aristotelian with Judeo-Christian knowledge traditions proved to be remarkably flexible and resilient in accommodating the new discoveries of the fifteenth and sixteenth centuries. Still in 1512, the Nuremberg humanist Johann Cochlaeus declared, in his publication of yet another unaltered edition of Pomponius Mela's first-century *Cosmographia,* that "Whether it is true or fabricated," the discovery of America "matters not at all or very little to the knowledge of Cosmography and History." Cochlaeus could make this declaration because the pagan Roman cosmographer Mela had already posited the existence of a southern part of the world, which he had called "Antichthones," after the people who inhabit the "Antipodes," a Southern Hemisphere represented in some classical and medieval world maps. The news about the recent discovery of new lands merely proved to Cochlaeus that there really was nothing new under the sun.[5]

During the early sixteenth century, cosmography as practiced in the academies still belonged to that enterprise of textual scrutiny to which humanism was as committed as had been Scholasticism.[6] Sixty years after Columbus's landfall, in 1552, the Spanish Renaissance historian Francisco López de Gómara famously announced that "the greatest thing after the creation of the world, excepting the incarnation and death of him who created it, was the discovery of the Indies." But for López de Gómara, the "discovery of the Indies" meant the *recovery* of something already known, for the "Indies" were for him nothing but Plato's Atlantis ("Atlantide"). While there had been a protracted debate about the question of whether "Plato's story was a fable or a true history," there can now be "no debate nor doubt," he explained, for "the discovery and conquest of the Indies plainly affirm that which Plato wrote about those lands"; and he points to the Nahuatl word for water (*atl*) to prove that Plato had been very well informed when naming the Indies "Atlantis." For López de Gómara, the discovery of America did not challenge authority and tradition; rather, it *affirmed* them. For him, the significance of America lay not in the fact that Columbus had discovered a new continent—which was not a "fact" at all—but in the fact that the Indies had been conquered, thus opening the door to the conversion of millions of pagan souls and the extension of Spain's imperial dominion.[7]

When, seventy years after López de Gómara's assertion that the Indies were Plato's Atlantis, Francis Bacon wrote his *New Atlantis* as a blueprint for England's own scientific future, he was describing a utopian society that had, unlike the Old Atlantis, remained entirely unknown to the Ancients, its discovery by the Moderns signaling a radical break from tradition. If Baconianism is often taken as a stand-in for the beginnings of scientific modernity—looking forward rather than backward—it is arguably due to the lasting persuasive power of one of its most prominent *rhetorical* features—its claim of a radical discontinuity between premodern and early modern scientific thought. Indeed, as Charles Whitney has argued, the very word "instauration" in the Baconian language of natural philosophy strategically exploits an ambiguity in invoking the notion of a revolutionary break from the past on the one hand while, on the other, drawing on a long Judeo-Christian chiliastic tradition of "reform related to Biblical prophecy."[8] It is this Judeo-Christian tradition—not a break from it—that underwrites the rhetorical power of Bacon's modern hermeneutics of discovery.

This chapter explores the role that the nexus of alchemy and conquest plays in Francis Bacon's elaboration of a modern paradigm of discovery. Focusing on *New Atlantis*, I argue that the institutional infrastructure imagined by Bacon for his project in scientific reform is modeled on the Spanish imperial knowledge production, and his idea of scientific inquiry as a "conquest of nature" profoundly informed by the language of the conquest of America, especially regarding the questions it had raised about the rights of dominion. Moreover, Bacon's elaboration of a modern paradigm of discovery, both in his science fiction and in his philosophical works, is rooted in the language of alchemy transposed onto an American heterotopia that not only justified a modern curiosity but also rationalized its own cannibalistic relationship with scientific tradition. Thus, Bacon's "Great Instauration" aims at a restoration of the atomist science of the pre-Socratics that is inspired by his dialogues not only with Montaigne but also with his heterotopic Other in "Of Cannibals" when devouring and digesting (even while suppressing) the textual tradition of the alchemists and that of the Spanish conquerors of America. In Bacon's natural philosophy, the language of alchemy not only sublimates pagan materialism (especially New World cannibalism) but also purifies the violence of the Spanish conquest of America in the epistemic violence of the "conquest of nature."

New Atlantis: An Empire of Knowledge

Bacon wrote *New Atlantis* only late in his life, probably in 1623, after his political career as lord chancellor had ended in his impeachment for taking bribes and after having failed in his lifelong pursuit to persuade his monarchs to create state institutions that would implement the programs in scientific reform for which he had been advocating for some twenty years in his theoretical writings on natural philosophy. Left unfinished upon his death in 1626 and first published in Latin in 1627, *New Atlantis* represents Bacon's last effort to convince the Stuart Monarchy of the sociopolitical benefits of his program in scientific reform—this time in the form not of a treatise in natural philosophy but of a piece of fiction in the tradition of Thomas More's *Utopia*.

New Atlantis is the story of a Spanish ship crew that had set out from Peru but was blown off course and landed on an island called Bensalem, which is home to an advanced civilization composed of citizens with an apparently quite unimpeachable moral character. The Bensalemite form of government is that of an authoritarian scientocracy whose administrative and intellectual center is Solomon's House, a hub of state-sponsored corporate empirical research in which scientists live in detachment from the larger society and conduct experiments producing knowledge that is tightly controlled and managed by the state through censorship and publication for the purpose of harnessing it for the maximal benefit of the social order in the commonwealth. As the Spaniards are informed by their host, the governor of "Strangers' House," the purpose of Solomon's House is to attain "the knowledge of Causes, and secret motions of things; and the enlarging of the bounds of Human Empire, to the effecting of all things possible."[9] Thus, the Spaniards are confronted in Bensalem with a model of empire more highly evolved than their own—not a political empire built on military conquest for the purpose of enlarging the bounds of one nation at the expense of another but a "human empire" extending its bounds into nonhuman nature for the good of humanity at large.

Bensalem's empire thrives on a mercantilist economy not of "gold, silver, or jewels; nor for silks; nor for spices; nor any other commodity of matter; but only for God's first creature, which was *Light*," which is to say knowledge.[10] Yet, in terms of its social organization, Solomon's House is a hierarchical corporation that operates as a colonial economy of knowledge production that I have elsewhere described as a form of "epistemic mercantilism"—a territorially and socially stratified division of intellectual labor that Bacon had first theorized twenty years earlier, in his *The Advancement of Learning* (1605).[11] We may think of the place of Solomon's House within this epistemic economy in terms of Bruno Latour's notion of a "center of calculation" governing modern scientific networks of knowledge production.[12] Thus, Bensalem employs a company of "merchants of light" who sail into foreign countries and "bring us the books, and abstracts, and patterns of experiments of all other parts." Another company, called the "Depredators," collect the experiments to be found in books. The "Mystery-men" collect the experiments of the mechanical arts and liberal sciences. Those who conduct "new experiments" are called the "Pioneers or Miners;" those who draw the experiments of the miners into "titles and tables" are called the "Compilers;" those who devise practical uses of these experiments are the "Dowry-men or Benefactors;" those who analyze the results of the experiments and plan new ones based on those results are the "Lamps;" those who execute and report on them are the "Inoculators;" finally, those who build the theoretical axioms based on this human machinery of knowledge are the "Interpreters of Nature."[13]

Although the Bensalemites had once engaged in free and open trade, 1,900 years ago a king named Solamona forbade any general navigation to parts of the world that were not under his rule. Instead, he commanded that every twelve years two ships should be dispatched containing a "mission of three of the Fellows or Brethren of Solomon's House," whose purpose it was "only to give us knowledge of the affairs and state of those countries to which they were designed, and especially of the sciences, arts, manufactures, and inventions of all the world."[14] When departing Bensalem for their periodic voyages, the Merchants of Light would take with them not Bensalemite knowledge that could be traded for foreign knowledge but a "store of victuals, and good quantity of treasure to remain with the brethren, for the buying of such things and rewarding of such persons as they should think fit." In other words, like the conquerors of America, the Merchants of Light trade not foreign knowledge for local knowledge but foreign knowledge for local trinkets. "We know well most parts of the habitable world," the host tells the Spaniards, "and are ourselves unknown."[15] In order to prevent local knowledge from leaving the island, the Bensalemites rarely admit strangers, and those who are admitted (such as the Spanish narrator and his crew) are kept under strict surveillance in "Strangers' House." Also, their government imposes upon its own travelers strict "laws of secrecy," and the Merchants of Light travel under the stealth of a false national identity. Thus, in its scientific relations to other nations, Bensalem is entirely parasitic and even cannibalistic; it is an epistemic black hole. In its internal relationship between Solomon's House and Bensalemite society at large, it resembles a dictatorship that tightly controls the knowledge it produces.[16] Thus, the Spaniards' self-appointed guide, a Jewish man named Joabin enjoying Bensalem's religious tolerance, explains, "We have consultations which of the inventions and experiences which we have discovered shall be published, and which not; and take all an oath of secrecy for the concealing of those which we think fit to keep secret; though some of those we do reveal sometime to the State, and some not."[17] Despite the protestation that the mission of Solomon's House is the enlargement of human knowledge at large, the beneficiaries of the Bensalemite epistemic economy are only Bensalemites, and especially the scientocratic ruling class.[18]

Bacon's *New Atlantis* thus dramatized in fictional form how his program in the reform of knowledge would benefit Britain's monarchical state and fledgling overseas empire.[19] Twenty-five years prior to his writing *New Atlantis*, in 1594, Bacon had delivered an address as chancellor of Gray's Inn, one of the four academies and guild houses of professional common law jurists, on the occasion of an exceptionally lavish Elizabethan Christmas masque. We find there an early iteration of some of the proposals for scientific reform that he later put into fictional form in *New Atlantis*. They all revolve around the role that the monarchical state should play in the advancement of learning, including "the collecting of a most perfect and general Library wherein whatsoever the Wit of Man had heretofore committed to Books of worth, be they ancient or modern, printed or Manuscript, European or of the other Parts, of one or other Language." Also, a "spacious, wonderful Garden, wherein whatsoever Plant, the Sun of Divers Climates, out of the Earth of divers Moulds, either wild, or by the Culture of Man, brought forth." This garden would also contain stables and cages to house rare beasts and birds, as well as lakes, one fresh and one saltwater, with a variety of fish. Finally, a "goodly huge Cabinet" displaying the ingenious products of the human mechanical arts, as well as a "Still-house so furnished with Mills, Instruments, Furnaces and Vessels, as may be a Palace fit for a Philosopher's Stone." Only when "your Excellency shall have added depth to Knowledge to the fineness of Spirits and greatness of your Power," he declared, addressing the queen, "shall you lay a Trismegistus."[20] In other words, only when the monarch gives a state-sponsored institutional application to science and the mechanical arts will she become another Hermes Trismegistus, a philosopher king.

While Bacon apparently intended his utopian island as a model and blueprint for England's own scientific future, historians have speculated about his sources of inspiration. Frank Manuel and Fritzie Manuel, for example, argued that it can be traced to Sir Humphrey Gilbert's proposals for Queen Elizabeth's Academy, designed to train a civil service elite; and Anthony Wallace has noted the similarities between Bacon's Solomon's House and the Royal Office of Ordnance's navy yards.[21] But another source of inspiration is suggested by the similarities, already noted in the introduction of this book, between the frontispiece of Bacon's *Great Instauration* and García de Céspedes's *Regimiento de navegación,* a treatise that was produced for the Spanish Casa de Contratación (House of Trade), the clearinghouse in Seville instituted for the gathering of all information about the New World. In his *Principal Navigations* (1598), Richard Hakluyt described the creation of the Spanish House of Trade in Seville like this:

> [The] late Emperour Charles the fifth, considering the rawness of his Seamen, and the manifolde shipwracks which they systeyened in passing and repassing betweene Spaine and the West Indies, with an high reach and great foresight, established not onely a Pilote Major, for the examination of such as sought to take charge of ships in that voyage, but also founded a notable Lecture of the Art of Navigation, which is read to this day in the Contractation house at Sivil. The readers of which Lecture have not only carefully taught and instructed the Spanish Mariners by word of mouth, but also have published sundry exact and worthy treatises concerning Marine causes, for the direction and incouragement of posteritie. The learned works of three of which readers, namely of Alonso de Chavez, of Hieronymo de Chavez, and of Roderigo Zamorano came long ago very happily to my hands, together with the straight and severe examining of all such Masters as desire to take charge of the West Indies.[22]

Although not all of Hakluyt's information is accurate—the House of Trade was already established by Ferdinand, not by Charles—this passage shows that Englishmen like Hakluyt and Bacon interested in promoting overseas

English expansionism were keenly aware of the formidable infrastructure that undergirded Spanish imperial knowledge production. In fact, the House of Trade was only one among a number of Spanish state-sponsored institutions of imperial knowledge production as imagined by Bacon. Others included the Council of the Indies and the royal court of Philip II itself, especially the treasure house of art and learning he had built outside Madrid at his monastic refuge of the Escorial, which included alchemical laboratories, botanical gardens, as well as research libraries and archives.[23]

All of these institutions had operated during the greater part of the sixteenth century under strict directives of secrecy that condemned much of the knowledge that the early modern Spanish men of science produced to the vaults of the archive rather than adding them to the rapidly expanding early modern world of print. The reasons why Spanish officials in the sixteenth century strove to keep secret the new technical knowledge that was being produced by these institutions were primarily of a geopolitical and military-strategic nature. Thus, any new findings about the exact locations of newly discovered overseas territories would have to be reconciled with Spanish territorial claims as founded on the Treaty of Tordesillas (1494), which divided the world into a Spanish and a Portuguese half along a geometrical coordinate along a meridian 370 leagues west of the Cape Verde Islands in the Atlantic Ocean and a corresponding antimeridian in the Pacific, as later stipulated in the Treaty of Zaragoza (1529). But more importantly, the court of Philip II was convinced that particular geographic intelligence (about ports, straits, resources, and routes) was of vital strategic value in the defense of Spanish possession against the encroachments by Spain's jealous European neighbors, and his court therefore implemented policies of strict secrecy intended to keep sensitive information out of foreign reach.[24]

To be sure, the court of Philip II was not alone on the continent in championing the experimental sciences and technical arts. As pointed out in chapter 1, another influential patron was the court of Rudolf II, king of Bohemia and Holy Roman Emperor, whose court in Prague had been visited and admired by the two Elizabethan alchemists Edward Kelly and John Dee. But it was Spain's example that, to Bacon, demonstrated most fully the connection between imperial knowledge and monarchical power—a connection of which he was such an astute student. Although he was highly critical of Catholicism, he openly admired Spanish military might as well as institutions of imperial administration and its scientific knowledge production. In his essay "Of the True Greatness of Kingdoms and Estates," he conceded that in modern Christian Europe, only the Spaniards could be compared to the ancient Romans and Macedonians. Although he sensed that Spanish power was waning (and tried to understand the reasons for this), and even pushed for war with Spain in 1624, he admired Spanish imperial administration. "I have marveled sometimes at Spain," he wrote, "how they clasp and contain so large dominions with so few natural Spaniards; but sure the whole compass of Spain is a very great body of a tree; far above Rome and Sparta at first."[25] In part, this success owed to the Spanish practice of incorporating soldiers from all nations in its armies. But, as Bacon understood, even more important to Spanish success was the vast corporate information network that Spanish imperial administrators had built up in producing useful information about its overseas empire, and he repeatedly urged James I to emulate it. In *Of the Interpretation of Nature,* for instance, Bacon wrote that an implementation of his proposals for collaborative, corporate, and state-sponsored production of knowledge "leadeth us to an administration of knowledge in some such order and policy as the king of Spain in regard of his great dominions useth in state; who though he hath particular councils of State or last resort, that receiveth the advertisements and certificates from all the rest."[26]

But while the institutional infrastructure of Solomon's House in *New Atlantis* is patently modeled on Spanish institutions of imperial knowledge production, Bensalem is not a representation of imperial Spain. Rather, Bacon told the story from the point of view of Spanish mariners precisely so that they can be convinced of the superiority of Bensalem to their own empire, which was, for Bacon, still an empire built on the conquest of men by the force of arms. Indeed, for him, imperial Spain resembled more closely the ancient (rather than the "New") Atlantis, which was destroyed by divine intervention as a punishment for its imperial ambitions of conquering territories and enslaving their people. The "New Atlantis," by contrast, would be known for its conquest not of subjects but of objects. Bacon's project of scientific discovery as the "conquest of nature" for the benefit of humanity at large was thus engaged in what might be called a "purification" of conquest, a purification that borrowed its militant and salvific rhetoric from the Spanish conquest of America in order to *reform* it. As a reformed conquest, the Baconian project in natural philosophy held out the promise of a restoration of man's dominion over God's creation, lost as a consequence of the Fall. But in order to explore the genealogy of Bacon's notion of discovery as a "reformed conquest," it will be necessary to take a closer look at the epistemological and philosophical foundations of Baconian empiricism, specifically with regard to its roots in Renaissance humanism, medieval alchemy, and natural law.

The Finger of God: Heterotopia and Prisca Philosophia

If the infrastructure of Spanish imperial knowledge production provides a concrete historical context for the conception of Solomon's House, one of the most obvious literary models for *New Atlantis* more generally was Thomas More's *Utopia,* first published, also in Latin, some hundred years earlier, in 1516.[27] Indeed, Bacon himself invoked More's *Utopia* as a literary subtext against which to read his own tract. But whereas More's Utopians had the notorious custom of inspecting their spouses naked before agreeing to marry them, the Bensalemites practice a chaster version of the Utopians' mating rites. As one of the Bensalemites explains to the Spanish visitors:

> I have read in a book of one of your men, of a feigned commonwealth, where the married couple are permitted, before they contract, to see one another naked. This they [the Bensalemites] dislike; for they think it a scorn to give a refusal after so familiar knowledge; but because of many hidden defects in men and women's bodies, they have a more civil way; for they have near every town a couple of pools (which they call Adam and Eve's pools), where it is permitted to one of the friends of the man, and another of the friends of the woman, to see them severally bathe naked.[28]

This allusion (as well as the obvious parallels in plot) suggests that Bacon wished his *New Atlantis* to be read in intertextual dialogue with More's *Utopia,* calling the reader's attention to the *differences* between More's prototype and Bacon's revision. Thus, we first note that, whereas Utopia was literally "nowhere"—a place of purely philosophical speculation that never existed and would never exist in the real world—the Bensalem of *New Atlantis* projected a social and scientific vision for a reformed but potentially real English future. With regard to the literary representation of reality, we might say that whereas More's text is *fantastic*—the real and the imaginary strictly divided by an ocean so that they never shall meet—Bacon's is *realistic* in the sense that Bensalem is an extrapolation of and blueprint for his ideas for real-world scientific and social reform. Perhaps one of the earliest modern science fictions, it hereby represents not two worlds (as *Utopia* had done) but only one—one that has already been attained by Bensalem and that will eventually also be attained by England, which merely lags behind in a historical teleology that is universalist and apocalyptic.[29]

As I have suggested in the introduction, Michel Foucault's notion of heterotopia as a transcultural "other space" illuminates the history of the early modern idea of discovery in New World exceptionalism in both science and international law. It also illuminates Bacon's second major revision of *Utopia* in *New Atlantis:* the Bensalemites are not pagans but Christians; however, unlike the Catholic Spaniards from whose point of view the story is told, they practice a form of revealed religion that was older and "purer" than the Christianity practiced in Catholic Europe, meaning it had remained unadulterated by pagan and Muslim Aristotelianism and even (presumably) medieval (i.e., Augustinian) Neoplatonism. Thus, the reader learns early in the narrative that "about twenty years after the ascension of our Saviour" the people of Renfusa (a city on the eastern coast of the island) received Christianity in a revelation of the "finger" of God: It was in the shape of a "great pillar of light" in the night sky, "not sharp, but in form of a column, or cylinder, rising from the sea, a great way up toward heaven; and on the top of it was seen a large cross of light." Awestruck by such a revelation, one of the wise men from Solomon's House "fell down upon his face; and then raised himself upon his knees" to utter the following prayer:

> Lord God of heaven and earth; thou hast vouchsafed of thy grace, to those of our order to know thy works of creation, and true secrets of them; and to discern, as far as appertaineth to the generations of men, between divine miracles, works of nature, works of art and impostures, and illusions of all sorts. I do here acknowledge and testify before this people that the thing we now see before our eyes is thy finger, and a true miracle. And forasmuch as we learn in our books that thou never workest miracles, but to a divine and excellent end (for the laws of nature are thine own laws, and thou exceedest them not but upon great cause), we most humbly beseech thee to prosper this great sign, and to give us the interpretation and use of it in mercy; which thou dost in some part secretly promise, by sending it unto us.[30]

After the wise man had concluded his prayer, the boat resumed its approach, but at once the pillar disappeared, leaving only a "small ark or chest of cedar, dry and not wet at all with water, though it swam." The ark opened, and inside the Bensalemites found a "book and a letter" both written on parchment. The book contained the Old and New Testaments, including John's Apocalypse and even books of the New Testament that "were not at that time written." The letter was from St. Bartholomew and addressed the Bensalemites in the following manner: "I, Bartholomew, a servant of the Highest, and apostle of Jesus Christ, was warned by an angel that appeared to me in a vision of glory, that I should commit this ark to the floods of the sea. Therefore I do testify and declare unto that people where God shall ordain this ark to come to land, that in the same day is come unto them salvation and peace, and good-will from the Father, and from the Lord Jesus."³¹ In Bacon's reformed history of science, Christianity had thus arrived in Bensalem purely by divine revelation, in an apocalyptic and mystical moment without the involvement of any human agency of modern historical memory. But, unlike the arrival of Christianity in America, its arrival in Bensalem did not destroy but rather perfected pre-Christian culture on the island; it represented the typological fulfillment of Bensalem's originary pre-Christian ("Solomonic") and pre-Socratic wisdom.

Although Bensalem is emphatically not (Spanish) America, Bacon's fiction betrays a surprisingly intimate knowledge of colonial Latin American history in religious *mestizaje*. St. Bartholomew was, like St. Thomas, known as the apostle who had evangelized (East) India. Most likely, Bacon's source for the legend of St. Bartholomew as the apostle of the *New* (West) India, or America, was the *Comentarios reales del los Incas* (1609/1617) by the Peruvian mestizo Garcilaso de la Vega, el Inca, whom Bacon cites in his *An Advertisement Touching an Holy War* (1622) and whom he had apparently read in the Spanish original. Thus, Garcilaso had explained that a confraternity of Peruvian mestizos had claimed St. Bartholomew as their patron for having brought Christianity to Peru long before the Spanish conquerors.³² Indeed, the notion of a pre-Hispanic evangelization of the "the Indies" by St. Bartholomew or St. Thomas had (as we have seen in chapter 5) medieval roots and a wide circulation in colonial Latin America during the early modern period among both indigenous and creole historians. According to one tradition cited by the Native Andean chronicler Felipe Guaman Poma de Ayala (roughly a contemporary of the Inca Garcilaso and Bacon), a large cross that was found by Spanish conquerors in the vicinity of Lake Titicaca (the so-called Cross of Carabuco) had been left by St. Bartholomew (see fig. 43). According to another tradition from Mesoamerica, St. Thomas was the same historical figure as Quetzalcoatl (the Plumed Serpent), the Toltec king-deity later adopted by the Mexica ("Aztecs") and finally during colonial times in the myth of the prophecy that foretold his return in the arrival of the European conquerors.³³ Like the Hermetic tradition in the Old World from late antiquity to the seventeenth century, the traditions of St. Thomas and St. Bartholomew in the New World were forms of religious *mestizaje* that fused Christian and non-Christian forms of knowledge. Whereas the Old World tradition of Hermes Trismegistus had combined the wisdom of the Judeo-Christian Moses with that of the Greek Hermes and the Egyptian Thoth (as we have seen in chapter 1), the New World traditions of St. Thomas and St. Bartholomew fused Christian and indigenous forms of religious messianism.³⁴

Figure 43. *Apóstol S[an] Bart-olomé*, depicting the arrival of St. Bartholomew in pre-Columbian Peru. (In Felipe Guaman Poma de Ayala, *Nueva corónica y buen gobierno* [1615]. Courtesy of the Royal Library, Denmark.)

The Alchemy of Digestion: Bacon's Epistemic Cannibalism

At first glance, it would appear that Bacon's Bensalemites are not, like the Vespuccian's or Montaigne's Epicureans, savage cannibals; nor are they, like More's Utopians, philosophers. Rather, they are alchemists and experimentalists. Alchemical experiments are conducted in underground laboratories located in caves called "the lower region." The purpose of these alchemical experiments is the "imitation of natural mines and the producing also of new artificial metals, by compositions and materials which we use and lay there for many years. We use them also sometimes (which may seem strange) for curing of some diseases, and for prolongation of life, in some hermits that choose to live there, well accommodated of all things necessary, and indeed live very long; by whom also we learn many things."³⁵ Besides alchemical laboratories, the Bensalemites have

> dispensatories, or shops of medicines. Wherein you may easily think, if we have such variety of plants and living creatures more than you have in Europe, (for we know what you have,) the simples, drugs, and ingredients of medicines, must likewise be in so much the greater variety. We have them likewise of divers ages, and long fermentations. And for their preparations, we have not only all manner of exquisite distillations and separations, and especially by gentle heats and percolations through divers strainers, yea and substances; but also exact forms of composition, whereby they incorporate almost, as they were natural simples.³⁶

But while the Bensalemites are clearly not Montaigne's savage cannibals, one might wonder about the exact nature and purpose of their alchemical experiments, which include "coagulations, indurations, refrigerations, and conservations of bodies."³⁷ Were the Bensalemites experimenting with medicinal cannibalism? Although there are no direct references to mummy or blood medicine in *New Atlantis,* such an inference would not be far-fetched for the seventeenth-century reader. As we have seen in chapter 7, the medicinal use of human bodily matter had a long tradition in alchemy generally and was an especially prominent feature of Paracelsian spagyrics, or medicinal alchemy, which included the use of human blood and "mummy"—the flesh of deceased persons. Paracelsian alchemy had fused the medieval (i.e., pseudo-Aristotelian) alchemy originating in the works of Pseudo-Geber and Roger Bacon with the Pseudo-Llullian Neoplatonic "occult philosophy" of Ficino and Agrippa, positing correspondences between the microcosm (man) and the macrocosm of the celestial and supracelestial universe. Although Paracelsus had remained a Catholic, he found particularly loyal followers among Protestants, including German Rosicrucians such as Michael Maier; English Paracelsians such as Robert Fludd and Nicholas Culpepper; as well as New English Puritans such as Michael Wigglesworth, John Allin, George Starkey, John Wintrop II, and Edward Taylor.³⁸ Karen Gordon-Grube has suggested that, among Protestants, the alchemical practice of medicinal cannibalism may in part have "fulfilled a substitute function to that of the transubstantiated flesh and blood in the Sacrament."³⁹ Indeed, while we now know that Paracelsus had a considerable influence also in early modern Catholic Spain,⁴⁰ we will presently see that there was a close affinity between alchemy, cannibalism, the Protestant Reformation, and the rise of the "New Sciences" in seventeenth-century England.

While the influence of Paracelsianism on many of the seventeenth-century Englishmen connected with the New Science seems now indisputable, Bacon's own relationship to Paracelsus and alchemy more generally is ambiguous. In his philosophical works, Bacon frequently disavowed what he called the "sect of the chemists," especially the sixteenth-century occult philosophers who engaged in the "making of Paracelsus's pygmies, or any such prodigious follies."[41] Bacon's attacks on "the chemists" have sometimes been taken at face value—as evidence of the need to distinguish between "scientific" and "occult" mentalities during the early modern period.[42] However, they must be seen in the context of his ostensible disavowal of nearly *all* scientific traditions, not just that of alchemy. Thus, he offends the acolytes of Aristotle (that "cheap dupe of words"), Plato (whose philosophy was but "scraps of borrowed information polished and strung together"), Galen ("Plague of the human race!"), Ramus ("that pestilent book-worm"), and Agrippa ("a trivial buffoon").[43] Reading Bacon's insults of these philosophers as evidence of their insignificance in the formation of his scientific program would mean falling into the rhetorical trap of his oracular pronouncements that his "new science" would deliver maxims that are not indebted to the works of men but exclusively derived from the "things themselves" in the experimental unlocking of the secrets of nature.

For all of Bacon's disavowals of alchemy, several historians of science have demonstrated the profound intellectual debts that Bacon's natural philosophy owed to the Hermetic art, especially Paracelsianism.[44] William Newman, for example, has shown that Bacon's position on the status of natural and artificial objects is "practically identical" to the one promoted by alchemists and their supporters from the thirteenth century onward and that "it would not be an exaggeration to say that the art of chymistry was for Bacon the model upon which he built his concept of experiment pushing nature to the limit so that it would reveal its deepest secrets."[45] Indeed, in his posthumously published *Sylva sylvarum* (1627), Bacon revealed the alchemical sources of his thinking about matter when writing that "of all powers in nature heat is the chief."[46] As he goes on to explain:

> The power of heat is best perceived in distillations which are performed in close vessels and receptacles. But yet there is a higher degree; for howsoever distillations do keep the body in cells and cloisters, without going abroad, yet they give space unto bodies to turn into vapour, to return into liquor, and to separate one part from another. So as nature doth expatiate, although it hath not full liberty; whereby the true and ultimate operations of heat are not attained. But if bodies may be altered by heat, and yet so such reciprocation or rarefaction and of

condensation and of separation admitted, then it is like that this Proteus of matter, being held by the sleeves, will turn and change into many metamorphoses.[47]

When Bacon goes on to describe the furnace that produces the heat causing the "strange transmutation of bodies" as a "womb and matrices of living creatures," his description is reminiscent of the alchemists' "philosophical egg," believed to be capable of producing the homunculus (an artificial man).[48] Beyond the metaphors of his scientific experimentalism, Bacon is indebted to the alchemists also in the reconciliation of his belief in the persistence of matter with religion. The idea of a corpuscular structure of matter, while contradicting Aristotle, is in no way in contradiction with Christian doctrine, he explained, for just as it required an act of God to create something out of nothing, so will it require an act of God to make nothing out of something: "There is nothing more certain in nature than that it is impossible for any body to be utterly annihilated; but that as it was the work of the omnipotency of God to make somewhat of nothing, so it requireth the like omnipotency to turn somewhat into nothing. And therefore it is well said by an obscure writer of the sect of the chemists, that there is no such way to effect the strange transmutations of bodies, as to endeavor and urge by all means the reducing of them to nothing."[49]

Moreover, Bacon shared with the alchemists the belief in chrysopoeia, the alchemical making of gold, writing that "the work itself [of chrysopoeia] I judge to be possible . . . for we conceive indeed that a perfect good concoction or digestion or maturation of some metals will produce gold."[50] Finally, Bacon also subscribed to the alchemical belief in the medicinal efficacy of mummy, explaining that "any part taken from a living creature newly slain, may be of greater force than if it were taken from the like creature dying of itself, because it is fuller of spirit."[51] For example, fresh mummy "hath great force in stanching of blood; which, as it may be ascribed to the mixture of balms that are glutinous; so it may also partake of a secret propriety, in that the blood draweth man's flesh. And it is approved that the moss which groweth upon the skull of a dead man unburied, will stanch blood potently: and so do the dregs, or powder of blood, severed from the water, and dried."[52] Although this moss growing on corpses' heads—known as *usnea*–was hard to come by in England, Bacon thought that the "slain bodies, laid on heaps unburied" in Ireland would provide a good supply in the future.[53]

But beyond the technical descriptions of the medicinal use of mummy, cannibalism was also central as an idea in Bacon's elaboration of his ethos as a natural philosopher in his relationship with scientific tradition. As Stephen Gaukroger has observed, Bacon frequently attributes his ideas to the ancients but "rarely discusses his immediate sources." This is especially the case with regard to the alchemists, upon whom he frequently heaps contempt.[54] Arguably, however, Bacon's strident attacks on the alchemists were part of a rhetorical strategy that he had inherited from the alchemists, especially the Paracelsians, whose writings had cultivated an artisanal and anti-academic ethos as well as a characteristically impolite and irreverent style in their handling of tradition. This irreverent ethos had been cultivated by nonacademic physician-authors who operated outside the medical academies and who used their writings for social and economic advancement by carefully crafting their individual professional brands. This rhetorical aspect of the trade was amplified once alchemy had moved out of the medieval convents and into the early modern courts, where alchemists had to compete for patronage, especially given the Janus-faced ambiguity that had beset the figure of the alchemist in the Latin West since the thirteenth century—prophet and magus on the one hand and impostor (*Betrüger*) on the other.[55] Interestingly, in his savage attacks on the alchemists, Bacon often singled out Paracelsus, the so-called father of early modern alchemy, whose notoriety rested as much on his innovative use of mummy and the surgical applications of salt as it did on his polemical and abrasive style as an author.[56] Just as Paracelsus had heaped contempt on Galen and his early modern followers, so did Bacon heap contempt on Paracelsus, calling him the "adopted son of the family of asses" who must have been "blinded I suppose by his distillations."[57]

Bacon's disparagement of Paracelsus is characteristic of his oedipal relationship with the alchemists more generally.[58] On the one hand, Bacon was clearly familiar with both Paracelsus's original works such as *De generatione rerum naturalium*, as well as the works by prominent sixteenth-century followers of Paracelsus, such as the *Idea medicinae philosophicae* (1571) by the Danish physician Peter Severinus (Peder Soerensen).[59] He borrowed from these works much of his technical vocabulary, including terms such as distillation, digestion, assimilation, nourishment, generation, putrefaction, irritation, and fixation. But, on the other hand, if little alchemical gold had actually been produced by the alchemists, he argued, it was because their "practice [is] full of error and imposture and in the theory, full of unsound imaginations."[60] While Bacon subscribed to the belief in the theoretical possibility of alchemical transmutation and chrysopoeia, he objected to all mysticism and Christological iconography that characterized many alchemical texts of the Middle Ages, especially the analogy between the Eucharist and the alchemical opus. Bacon especially rejected the Neoplatonic notion of cosmic correspondences and analogies between the microcosm and the macrocosm, which overemphasized (in his view) the agency of the magus in imposing or projecting himself upon, rather than observing, nature. "All these are but dreams," he wrote; "and so are many other grounds of alchemy. And to help the matter, the alchemists call in likewise many vanities out of astrology, natural magic, superstitious interpretations of Scriptures, auricular traditions, feigned testimonies of ancient authors, and the like."[61] They had mixed "the divine with the natural, the profane with the sacred, heresies with mythology, you have corrupted, O you sacrilegious impostor, both human and religious truth."[62] In the *Novum organum*, Bacon attacks the Scholastics more generally for "mix[ing] the prickly and contentious philosophy of Aristotle more thoroughly into the body of religion." They "have not been afraid to deduce and confirm the truth of the Christian religion from the principles and authority of the philosophers. With much pomp and ceremony they celebrate the marriage of faith and sense as a legitimate union, and charm men's minds with a pleasing variety of things, but at the same time mix things human with things divine."[63] In essence, Bacon aimed to secularize Paracelsus's occult philosophy. He was among the earliest proponents of the "New Science" who caricatured "the alchemists" as being primarily a tribe of medieval occultists, even while absorbing their basic ideas, including their theories of matter and their understanding of the relationship between art and nature.[64]

Chastizing the Aristotelian-Arabic alchemists, Bacon's *Great Instauration* announced a restoration of the "true" alchemy of the ancients, of a pre-Socratic (i.e., Greek) "chymistry" that was unadulterated by Aristotle, the Arabs, and the Latin Scholastics. Bacon had studied the pre-Socratics from 1603 to 1612, especially the atomism of Democritus. But the problem he faced was that pre-Socratic science was largely lost to the moderns. Therefore, the pre-Socratics' ancient wisdom had to be retrieved from scientific tradition, much of which had been corrupted by the Aristotelians. "Has not time, like a river, brought down to us the light and inflated, and sunk the solid and weighty," Bacon asked; "What of those ancient inquiries after truth, Heraclitus, Democritus, Pythagoras, Anaxagoras, Empedocles, and others, known by the writings of others, not by their own?"[65] The project of his *Great Instauration* was to restore the "solid and weighty" science of the pre-Socratics that had been corrupted by the "received philosophy" of Aristotelianism.[66] And the key to such a reformation of pre-Socratic knowledge lay, for Bacon, in humanist philology, as Gerard Passannante has shown.[67] Indeed, Bacon's humanist understanding of such a philological restoration was, like his understanding of matter, thoroughly materialist and atomistic. Thus, Bacon attempted to retrieve the eternal particles of pre-Socratic wisdom from the textual "matter" of tradition—from "the scattered fragments of the pre-Socratic philosophers he collected and assembled, in the shadow of movable type, and most of all in his dialogue with Montaigne, and the ancient Epicurean poet [Lucretius]."[68]

But if Bacon's conception of ideas was atomistic, his philological method and his notion of tradition were thoroughly alchemical in principle. I say "alchemical" because Bacon believed that scientific tradition, like material substances, was subject to the natural processes of corruption in the sublunar world but still contained a mixture of the quintessence that could be distilled and harnessed through art. Thus, he attempted to retrieve pre-Socratic science not only from the texts of the Epicureans but also from those of the Aristotelians, especially the alchemists. In effect, Bacon's philology was a form of textual alchemy; and he borrowed the methodological language not only from the materialist philosophy of Lucretius but also (and, I would argue, primarily) from the alchemists, particularly from the Paracelsians. Like that of the Paracelsians, Bacon's understanding of physics was an ambivalent mixture of mechanistic and vitalistic conceptions of nature. This included the Hermetic doctrine of the transmutation of substances based on the notion that they share a common "spirit" that is homogeneous except for varying levels of impurity. Bacon judged it as "one of the greatest *magnalia naturae,* to turn water or watery juice into oil or oily juice: greater in nature, than to turn silver or quicksilver into gold."[69] This transformation is achieved by an alchemical process called "digestion":

> The intention of version of water into a more oily substance is by digestion; for oil is almost nothing else but water digested; and this digestion is principally by heat; which heat must be either outward or inward: again, it may be by provocation or excitation; which is caused by the mingling of bodies already oily or digested; for they will somewhat communicate their nature with the rest. Digestion is also strongly effected by direct assimilation of bodies crude into bodies digested; as in plants and living creatures, whose nourishment is far more crude than their bodies: but this digestion is by a great compass, as hath been said. As for the most full handling of these two principles, whereof this is but a taste, (the inquiry of which is one of the profoundest inquiries of nature), we leave it to the title of version of bodies; and likewise to the title of the first congregations of matter; which, like a general assembly of estates, doth give law to all bodies.[70]

Bacon had borrowed the concept of digestion from Paracelsian spagyrics, in which the stomach is an alchemist. According to Paracelsus, for the stomach, "the matter is the same as for a spagyric who renders all things subtle and separates them, purifies in many ways, now this, then that way, for as long as it takes to find what he desires."[71] For Paracelsus, there "is no food that does not contain within it poison.... Therefore, the stomach is such that it must separate things afterward and make them excrement and expel them."[72] Human digestive organs, including the stomach, the liver, and kidneys are thus "all three fires, which separate these three from the others."[73] The only difference is that the digestive fires operate at lower temperatures than do the alchemical fires. It is this principle of digestion, Bacon believed, that is the secret of true alchemical transmutation of base metals into gold: "We will direct a trial touching the maturing of metals, and thereby turning some of them into gold: for we conceive indeed that a perfect good concoction or digestion or maturation of some metals will produce."[74] He relates the story of a certain "Dutchman, that had wrought himself into the belief of a great person by undertaking that he could make gold, whose discourse was, that gold might be made; but that the alchemists over-fired the work: for (he said) the making of gold did require a very temperate heat, as being in nature a subterrany work, where little heat cometh; but yet more to the making of gold than of any other metal; and therefore that he would do it with a great lamp that should carry a temperate and equal heat, and that it was the work of many months."[75]

The Paracelsian idea of digestion was a key concept also in Bacon's project in philological alchemy by which he attempted to restore the pre-Socratic wisdom of the ancients. It is in this context that the watery simile "time, like a river" in the passage quoted above is significant. Not unlike "digested" water, pre-Socratic science can be digested from the Scholastic texts through philology. In other words, Bacon borrowed his philological method not only from Montaigne but also from Montaigne's heterotopic other in "Of Cannibals." Like Montaigne's Tupinamba, Bacon digested from the enemy's body the substance of the ancestors in a process of epistemic cannibalism. For Bacon, this enemy was, of course, Aristotle and his tribe—the enemies of the science of nature. Indeed, Bacon explicitly resorts to the imagery of cannibalism precisely when explaining the relationship between tradition and innovation in science. For example, in the *Advancement of Learning*, he wrote that "it seemeth the children of time to take after the nature and malice of the father. For as he devoureth his children, so one of them seeketh to devour and suppress the other; while antiquity envieth there shold be new additions, and novelty cannot be content to add but it must deface."[76] His allegory refers to Hesiod's *Theogony*, particularly the story of Kronos (also identified with Saturn), who castrated his father Uranus and later devoured his own children in order to avoid being himself overcome by them, as had been foretold in a prophecy. It is for his cannibalistic, all-devouring characteristics that Kronos was known as the god of time in the *Orphic Theogonies*. Among the victims of all-devouring

Kronos were, for Bacon, many of the pre-Socratic writings, which were themselves lost to the modern world but could be digested from its scattered "substances" in tradition—the references in Aristotle, Cicero, Plutarch, Lucretius, and the Scholastic alchemists.

Yet, it is again the slight limp in Bacon's allegory of a "river of time" that betrays something barbaric about the modern hermeneutics of discovery. First, in Bacon's allegory of tradition, it was not the oedipal murder of the father but the murder of his children by a cannibalistic father that constitutes the act of transgenerational cannibalism. Bacon's own cannibal philology is thus not a project in intellectual history but an act of epistemic revenge against scientific tradition. Second, as he was surely aware, "digested" oil would rise to the surface, being more "light and windy" than water. Ultimately, Bacon's was a cannibal philology whose logic was committed not to the reconstruction but to the *de*struction of tradition. For ultimately, it was a philology that would lead to a past (as well as to a future) when philosophers no longer studied texts—the works of men—but the works of nature, in a pure "Science of Nature" consisting of direct observation and experiment. Like the *ouroboros*, Bacon's alchemical philology devoured itself.

The (Mytho-)Alchemy of Bacon's Christian Epicureanism

Devouring and disavowing the tradition of the medieval alchemists, Bacon invokes, in *New Atlantis*, the ancient authority of neither the pagan philosopher Aristotle nor the Alexandrian magus Hermes Trismegistus but King Solomon of the Old Testament, whom Bacon viewed as a proto-Christian scientist.[77] For example, in *Of the Interpretation of Nature*, he writes that "Salomon the king, as out of a branch of his wisdom extraordinarily petitioned and granted from God, is said to have written a natural history of all that is green from the cedar to the moss ... and also of all that liveth and moveth ... the same Salomon the king affirmeth directly that the glory of God *is to conceal a thing, but the glory of a king is to find it out,* as if according to the innocent play of children the divine Majesty took delight to hide his works, to the end to have them found out."[78] Evoking St. Augustine's notion of *iusta curiositas,* Bacon writes that those are in error who "think that the inquisition of nature is in any part interdicted or forbidden. For it was not that pure and uncorrupted natural knowledge whereby Adam gave names to the creatures according to their property, which gave occasion to the fall.... Whereas of the sciences which regard nature, the divine philosopher [in Proverbs 25:2] declares that 'it is the glory of God to conceal a thing, but it is the glory of the King to find a thing out.'"[79] There was for Bacon a difference between "true magic"—the ancient study of nature—and false magic—the modern study of texts. "A little natural philosophy inclineth the mind to atheism," he wrote, "but a further proceeding bringeth the mind back to religion."[80] While magic had been disparaged by the Roman Church, he proposed in *In the Advancement of Learning* (1605) a restoration of the original honor and esteem in which it was held among the ancients:

> But I must here stipulate that magic, which has long been used in a bad sense, be again restored to its ancient and honourable meaning. For among the Persians magic was taken for a sublime wisdom, and the knowledge of the universal consents of things; and so the three kings who came from the east to worship Christ were called by the name of Magi. I however, understand it as the science which applies the knowledge of hidden forms to the production of wonderful operations; and by uniting (as they say) actives with passives displays the wonderful works of nature.[81]

A few years later, in *The Wisdom of the Ancients* (1609), Bacon attempted to elaborate a synthesis of pre-Socratic wisdom (as retrievable from the "digestion" of Ovid, Hesiod, and Lucretius) with Christian doctrine. Thus, each chapter offers an allegorical interpretation of a figure from Greek mythology as a prototype of Christian moral principles or artisanal technical terms familiar from the mechanical arts. Thus, Daedalus is "the Mechanic"; Proteus, "Matter"; and so on. In "Cupid; or the Atom," Bacon explains that the fable of the pagan god of love "relates to the cradle and infancy of nature and pierces deep. This Love I understand to be the appetite or instinct of primal matter; or to speak more plainly, *the natural motion of the atom;* which is indeed the original and unique force that constitutes and fashions all things out of matter. Now this is entirely without parent; that is, without cause. For the cause is as it were parent of the effect; and of this virtue there can be no cause in nature (God always excepted): there being nothing before."[82] Cupid is forever a child, Bacon explains, for unlike "things compounded," which are "affected by age," he is like "the primary seeds of things, or atoms," which "are minute and remain in perpetual infancy." Cupid is naked because, unlike compounds (which are "masked and clothed"), atoms are the "primary particles of things." And he is blind, because he "has very little providence; but directs his course, like a blind man groping, by whatever he finds nearest." This makes the "supreme divine Providence all the more to be admired," Bacon adds in the fashion of the Christian Epicurean, as "that which contrives out of subject peculiarly empty and destitute of providence, and as it were blind, to educe by a fatal and necessary law all the order and beauty of the universe."[83]

The Bensalemites' alchemical caves in *New Atlantis*—"in the lower region"—are particularly reminiscent of Bacon's essay on Proteus in *The Wisdom of the Ancients*. As Newman has pointed out, the figure of Proteus as an allegory of matter was in wide use in alchemical literature during the sixteenth and seventeenth centuries, in texts such as Willem Mennens's *Aureus vellus* (1604) and Blaise de Vigenère's *De igne et sale* (1608).[84] Bacon builds on this tradition when explaining that the Greek god, who was a "prophet" whose "dwelling was under an immense cave," was a personification of "the secrets of nature and the conditions of matter."[85] Like Proteus, matter is eternal (indestructible) and "has its habitation under the vault of heaven, as under a cave." The only way to enlist Proteus's help, is "first to secure his hands with handcuffs, and then to bind him with chains. Whereupon he on his part, in order to get free, would turn himself into all manner of strange shapes—fire, water, wild beasts, &c., till at last he returned again to his original shape." The chaining of Proteus, Bacon explains, is an allegory of the discovery of the secrets of nature:

> If any skillful Servant of Nature shall bring force to bear on matter, and shall *vex it and drive it to extremities as if with the purpose of reducing it to nothing*, then will matter (since annihilation or true destruction is not possible except by the omnipotence of God) finding itself in these straits, turn and transform itself into strange shapes, passing from one change to another til it has gone through the whole circle and finished the period; when, if the force be continued, it returns at last to itself. And this constraint and binding will be more easily and expeditiously effected, if matter be laid hold on and secured by the hands; that is, by its extremities.[86]

While the classical poets had provided the allegories and philosophies of nature, Bacon's Bensalemites, "skillful Servant[s] of Nature," put these allegories into practice by forcing nature to give up its subterranean secrets. By "vexing" and "driving" nature to its extremities, however, they act neither as pagan philosophers nor as humanist philologists but as New World alchemical experimentalists who extort nature's secrets by subjecting her to a "passion" by the use of the gehennical fire.

If Bacon's debt to alchemical ideas is particularly evident in his discussions of the relationship between art and nature, it is also this relationship that is at the heart of his critique of the alchemists. Thus, in *The Wisdom of the Ancients*, he included an essay entitled "Atalanta: or Profit," based on a fable in Ovid's *Metamorphoses*: The beautiful virgin huntress Atalanta lived a solitary life in the woods, after she had been warned against marriage by Apollo. When she receives suitors, she challenges them to race. The suitor who can beat her will win her in marriage as a prize, but invariably she pierces every suitor during the race with her spear. Enter Hippomenes, who tricks her during the race by dropping three golden apples given to him by Aphrodite from the garden of the Hesperides. A distracted Atalanta stops to pick up the apples and therefore loses the race. When Atalanta and Hippomenes become lovers they copulate in a temple dedicated to Aphrodite, who punishes them for the defilement by transforming them into two lions (lions were in antiquity believed to mate not with each other but with panthers, who then beget leopards).

Bacon sees in this fable an allegory of the "contest of Art with Nature."[87] But his interpretation is strangely unconvincing and out of character with the gendered language he usually employs in his natural philosophy. Whereas he usually renders nature as female,[88] here he interprets Atalanta as art and Hippomenes as nature. The somewhat contrived lesson he draws from this allegory is that, while art is usually swifter than nature in transforming matter—the artificial baking of clay into bricks versus the natural turning of clay into stone, for example—art is often hampered and loses out against nature by human greed after "profit and commodity." Hence, he concludes, it "is no wonder if Art cannot outstrip Nature, and . . . remains subject to Nature, as the wife is subject to her husband."[89] The awkwardness of Bacon's readings of this fable is especially striking in light of the fact that the fable of Atalanta had long been one of the favorite allegories in alchemical literature, particularly the sixteenth-century variety known as "mythoalchemy," written by alchemists who had come under the sway of humanism and who attempted to interpret the ancient Greek and Roman myths as allegories of the alchemical opus.[90] In this tradition Atalanta is conventionally interpreted as the fugitive and elusive mercurial water and Hippomenes as the fiery elemental sulfur, who "fixes" mercury by the coagulating power of salt (the golden apples). Atalanta's and Hippomenes's copulation in Aphrodite's temple represents there an allegory of the alchemical wedding and their transformation into lions, the Green Lion (philosophical mercury) and the Red Lion (philosophical sulfur), the earliest stage of the alchemical opus (see fig. 44). Perhaps the best-known example of this mythoalchemy is Michael Maier's alchemical emblem book *Atalanta fugiens,* which was published in 1618 with lavish copperplate engravings produced by Matthäus Merian in the printing house of his father-in-law, Johann Theodor de Bry (1561–1623), the son of Theodor de Bry. After his father's death in 1598, Johann Theodor had taken over the De Bry business and published (together with his brother Johannes Israel) most of the remaining volumes of the Great Voyages series. Also, he had begun to specialize in the publication of alchemical literature and emblem books, including the works

Figure 44. The Green and Red Lion. (From Michael Maier, *Atalanta fugiens* [1618]. Source: *Secretioris naturæ secretorum scrutinium chymicum, per oculis et et intellectui accuratè accommodata, firguri cupro appositissimè incisa, ingeniosissima emblemata, hisque confines, & ad rem egregiè facientes sententias, doctissimaque item epigrammata, illustratus* [Francofurti: Impensis Georgii Heinrici Oehrlingii . . . : 1687]. Courtesy of the Library of Congress.)

of Maier as well as of the English Paracelsian Robert Fludd. Where Theodor de Bry's distinctive engraving of Amerindian smoke had invited a demonological interpretation of Native American religion and culture (as we have seen in the previous chapter), Merian adopted this technique for Maier's *Atalanta fugiens* in his engraving of the alchemical-hermetic emblem of "windy smoke" (*windigten Rauch*), which "carried in its belly" the mercurial vapor necessary for the process of sublimation in Christian alchemy (see figs. 45 and 46).[91]

Although Maier's *Atalanta fugiens* was not published until eight years after Bacon's *Wisdom of the Ancients,* it is likely that the two natural philosophers had met, as Maier had spent five years (1611–16) in London at the royal court working as a physician for various courtiers and publishing, in 1613 and 1614, his *Arcana arcanissima* (The most secret of secrets), a work that he had written before his arrival in England, during his stay at the court of Rudolf II in

Figure 45. "Portavit eum ventus in ventre suo" (The wind carried him in his belly). Emblema I. (In Michael Maier, *Atalanta fugiens* [1618]. Source: *Secretioris naturæ secretorum scrutinium chymicum, per oculis et et intellectui accuratè accommodata, firguri cupro appositissimè incisa, ingeniosissima emblemata, hisque confines, & ad rem egregiè facientes sententias, doctissimaque item epigrammata, illustratus* [Francofurti: Impensis Georgii Heinrici Oehrlingii . . . : 1687]. Courtesy of the Library of Congress.)

Prague, as is evident in an early manuscript that survives today at the university library of Leipzig under the title *De theosophia Aegyptiorum*. These works offered an interpretation of Egyptian and Greek myths as representations of universal alchemical processes as well as a genealogy of the Adamic (i.e., proto-Christian) genealogy of alchemy. There, Maier argued that the art of alchemy was a *Prisca Philosophia* first revealed to Adam, passed down to the Jewish patriarchs, who passed them on to the Egyptians, who passed them on to the Greek pre-Socratics via Pythagoras, who had traveled to Egypt. In 1616, Maier published another work, the *Symbola aureae mensae,* which added the argument that Hermes Trismegistus, the most ancient of spiritual alchemists,

Figure 46. Theodor de Bry, "Their matter of prainge vvith Rattels abowt te fyer." (From *America,* pt. 1 Frankfurt, 1590. Courtesy of the John Carter Brown Library at Brown University.)

had derived his knowledge from Abraham, to whom it had been passed down by Seth, the son of Adam.[92]

Thus, despite these Protestant and humanist attempts to purge alchemy of its Catholic iconography and Aristotelian filiopiety, and despite Bacon's insistence on a separation of the realms of science and religion, it would be a mistake to see his reform of science in merely secular terms, as it remains profoundly indebted to the alchemical tradition in its prophetic apocalypticism and millenarian redemptive teleology. While the methods of science and religion are distinct, Bacon argued, both serve the same end. "*All knowledge is to be limited by religion,*" he wrote in *Of the Interpretation of Nature*, "*and to be referred to use and action.*"[93] For Bacon, science and religion are separate from but complementary to one another; for true science, like true religion, "leadeth to the greater exaltation of the glory of God." In fact, failing to study nature would do injury to the majesty of God, "as if we should judge of the store of some excellent jeweler by that only which is set out to the street in his shop." Like the alchemists, Bacon believed that science would ultimately undo the consequences of the Fall and lead to a partial "restitution and reinvesting ... of man to the sovereignty and power ... which he had in his first state of creation."[94]

From the Secrets of Nature to the Secrets of State: Discovery, Torture, and the Law

If Bacon attempted to rid alchemy of its Christological iconography and mysticism, he also aimed to harness its practical applications and potentials for the benefit of the monarchical state. We have already seen how, in *New Atlantis*, he offered a model of science that was based on Spanish imperial knowledge production and that transformed the medieval alchemist's solitary pursuits into a corporate program of state-sponsored research. Bacon believed that, whereas the mechanical arts had steadily progressed throughout history from their primitive beginnings, philosophy and science (*scientia*) had degenerated from their original heights in classical antiquity: "In the former many wits and industries contributed in one: In the latter many men's wits spent to deprave the wit of one."[95] In other words, where the technical arts succeeded due to their corporate and collaborative nature, the liberal arts and sciences have failed due to their individualistic character. Alchemy, as a technical art, was a curious mix in this regard: it was artisanal but also solitary, enveloped in Hermetic language and esoteric spirituality, especially in the context of sixteenth-century Neoplatonic occult philosophy. Whereas Bacon's "alchemists" were like Homer's heroes, who employed their art for their own glorification, the Baconian natural philosopher would be like Virgil's pious Aeneas, whose higher purpose was the glory of his *patria*.[96] In the model of science proposed by Bacon, the discoveries of the secrets of nature that alchemy produces would become the secrets of the state, the domain of secretaries such as himself. Thus, while Bacon aimed to purify the "experimental science" first theorized by his medieval namesake Roger Bacon of its Christological and Eucharistic iconography, he hybridized it not only with classical mythology but also with the languages of politics and the law.

According to Bacon, observation can lead to the revelation of nature's secrets under three conditions: by observing the regular operations of nature; by observing its "errors" (such as deformed creatures); and by forcing nature into man's "bonds." In chapter 2, I have discussed the role that the analogy between the "torture" of metal through fire and the passion of Christ played in the medieval notion of alchemical transmutation in texts such as Ullmann's *Buch der Heiligen Dreieinigkeit.* Bacon utterly rejected such analogies; yet his discoverer, like the alchemist, must "hound nature," as he wrote in *The Advancement of Learning,* and force her to reveal her secrets by subjecting her to the violence of human artifice. For, "like as a man's disposition is never well known or proved til he be crossed, nor Proteus ever changed shapes till he was straitened and held fast; so nature exhibits herself more clearly under the *trials and vexations of art* than when left to herself."[97] As he explained in *Description of the Intellectual Globe:*

> Natural history therefore treats either of the *liberty* of nature or her *errors* or her *bonds.* And if any one dislike that arts should be called the bonds of nature, thinking they should rather be counted as her deliverers and champions, because in some cases they enable her to fulfill her own intention by reducing obstacles to order; for my part I do not care about these refinements and elegancies of speech; all I mean is, that nature, like Proteus, is forced by art to do that which without art would not be done; call it what you will,—force and bonds, or help and perfection.[98]

Bacon's description of the process of scientific discovery here is reminiscent not only of the alchemical torture of metals but also, as Carolyn Merchant has observed, of the early modern legal practice of torturing suspected criminals, especially in the context of witch hunts.[99] Indeed, Bacon had himself invoked the connection between the trying and vexing of nature and the use of instruments of torture in the inquisition of witchcraft, which works with preternatural causes: "A useful light may be gained," he wrote in *The Advancement of Learning,* "not only for a true judgment of the offenses of persons charged with such practices, but likewise for the further disclosing of the secrets of nature. Neither ought a man to make scruple of entering and penetrating into these holes and corners, when the inquisition of truth is his whole object—as your majesty has shown in your own example" (referring to James I's tract *Daemonology*, 1597).[100] Both Baconian "forensic" science and inquisitorial torture are rooted in a hermeneutics of secrecy that presumed that the truth is hidden from us but can be made manifest through the violent operations of art. Not coincidentally, inquisitorial torture had emerged on the Continent at roughly the same time as alchemy—during the thirteenth century—hereby replacing the early medieval legal practice of the ordeal.[101] By the sixteenth century, torture was a common forensic procedure the results of which were widely deemed admissible evidence in Continental European legal proceedings. We know that Bacon was himself involved in the practice, as he is listed as a commissioner on five torture warrants issued during both Elizabeth's and James's reigns.[102] Also, he publicly supported the use of torture in cases of crimes against the state, especially treason, though only for purpose of "discovery, and not for evidence," as he explained in one of his letters.[103] Thus, torture can lead to new evidence and facts in cases of treason, conspiracy, and other crimes against the state, but it cannot constitute sufficient ground for conviction in a court of law.

It is not surprising that Bacon's natural philosophy should be inflected by the language of the law. After all, Bacon's father had been Lord Keeper of the Seal and head of the Chancery. Bacon himself was a trained common law jurist who lived at Gray's Inn, one of the law guilds established especially to train jurists in common law, as both Oxford and Cambridge were ecclesiastic institutions that traditionally specialized in canon law. Later, under James I, he became lord chancellor. As Harvey Wheeler has shown in a series of erudite studies, Bacon's idea of scientific discovery was profoundly inspired by his innovations in interpreting the precedents embedded in common law rulings, which (like the law of nature) had never been codified. Thus, in his *Maximes of the Common Law* and the *Elements of the Common Law* (published together posthumously in 1630), Bacon proceeded by analyzing the case reports in search for a higher law (or metalaw) hiding behind them. In other words, he was searching for the "grammar" hiding behind a recorded tradition of cases. Then, applying a "reversed Platonism" to this metalaw, he created an empirical phenomenological substance that he called "*schematismus*," which led to the creation of a sort of "logic engine" that was then, in the *Novum organum*, applied to the laws of nature. Thus, Bacon's new case method, Wheeler argued, provided "the basis for the law-finding method he applied to science" and was the model of the inductive method of scientific discovery that he laid out in his *New Organon*.[104]

But while the English common-law tradition may have informed Bacon's idea of the laws of nature as a grammar that is invisible on the surface of observable phenomena, it would not have legitimated his notion of torture as a metaphor and method of scientific discovery by experiment. Indeed, his own stance on torture as a legal practice was highly anomalous in the English common law tradition. The practice of torture was confined to only a few decades during the late sixteenth and early seventeenth centuries in England, and even then it was used only sporadically.[105] Bacon was hereby among a small minority of English jurists—perhaps even "the only English lawyer"—who asserted the permissibility of a practice that most English jurists of the day, including Sir Edward Coke, held to be "directly against the common laws of England."[106] The emergence of this temporary "aberration" in English juridical practice, lasting from roughly the 1560s to the 1620s, has usually been explained as the result of a political state of exception in early modern England, mainly the aftermath of the Recusant crisis after the papal bull *Regnans in excelsis* had absolved Elizabethan Catholics from loyalty to their queen. Torture was occasionally used in this context not to extort confessions of guilt but for the purpose of gathering more information and discovering more covert activities that could be used in the trial.[107]

Bacon's rhetorical recourse to the language of torture in his natural philosophy seems at odds, then, with the fact that English jurists generally prided themselves on the absence of torture from the English common law system, which they often contrasted favorably in this regard to what they regarded as the "Catholic" practices on the Continent, especially as associated with the Spanish Inquisition. Bacon himself, though supporting torture under certain circumstances, generally rejected the practice as inconsistent with English piety and civility. In "Observations on a Libel," he wrote that in England, "we do not much emulate the greatness and glory of the Spaniards; who having not only excluded the purity of religion, but also fortified against it, by their device of the inquisition, which is a bulwark against the entrance of the truth of God."[108] But, as Bacon knew, the "entrance of the truth," or knowledge, was ultimately a question of power that could be rationalized in the face of an existential threat to the state, as was Spanish military power. From this point of view, the pervasiveness of the language of torture in Bacon's natural philosophy appears to be a purified form of inquisition in the law, the torture not of subjects but of objects. As such, it represents the early modern continuation of the state of exception that had legitimated alchemy in a Scholastic context, where, as I have suggested in chapter 2, medieval alchemists legitimated the appropriation of the foreign art ("Egyptian gold") in the face of moral or theological reservations through apocalyptic rhetoric.

Indeed, the corporate nature of the scientific enterprise in *New Atlantis* renders Solomon's House reminiscent not only of the Spanish House of Trade, the Spanish Council of the Indies, and the Escorial but also of the

Spanish Inquisition. As Irene Silverblatt has argued, the Spanish Inquisition was the first modern legal institution of state-sponsored production and control of knowledge created by Ferdinand and Isabella in the context of their unification of the kingdoms or Aragon and Castille, the expulsion of the Jews, the completion of the Reconquista, and the incipient conquest of America, where it had established two Holy Offices by the 1570s.[109] If, in *New Atlantis*, Bacon confronts the Spanish travelers with a Jewish guide enjoying an empire that practices religious tolerance, benevolent totalitarianism, and internal social peace built on scientific principles of government, Solomon's House, Bensalem's department of scientific discovery, operates on the principles derived from a *supersession* (rather than a rejection) of the "Spanish" model of imperial knowledge production. Bensalem represents a more highly evolved empire that had purified not only its practices of inquest but also, as we will see in the last section of this chapter, its practices of conquest.

The Purification of Conquest

Bacon was highly critical not only of the Spanish Inquisition but also of the Spanish conquest of America. Conquerors are like the "great Rovers and Witches," he said in his masque performance in the *Gesta Grayorum* in 1594, "whose Power is in Destruction, and not in Preservation." In this regard, conquerors are the antithesis of Bacon's natural philosophers. Yet, there is a fundamental similarity between the conqueror and the natural philosopher for Bacon. For the occupation of the natural philosopher was the "Conquest of the Works of Nature; making his Proportion, that you bend the Excellency of your Spirit to the searching out, inventing and discovering of all whatsoever is hid in secret in the World."[110] As the Hermes-like speaker in "The Masculine Birth of Time" put it, the purpose of science was "to stretch the deplorably narrow limits of man's dominion over the universe to their promised bounds." This extension of man's "dominion" over the universe will deliver "Nature with all her children to bind her to your service and make her your slave."[111]

The legacy of Bacon's notorious formulations for the course of Western culture has been amply discussed in modern scholarship. While some have blamed Bacon's notion of the conquest of nature for all the environmental degradations that modern Western culture has inflicted on the planet since the seventeenth century, others have defended Baconian science from such charges, pointing out that the Baconian idea of discovery also entailed the notion that nature must be served and obeyed. Thus, in the *New Organon*, Bacon wrote that man, who is the "servant" of nature, "does not have empire over nature except by obeying her."[112] Only by observing, serving, and obeying nature, he wrote in *The Natural and Experimental History of the Foundation of Philosophy*, will man regain his prelapsarian "dominion over creatures."[113]

In part, this apparently paradoxical idea—domination through obedience—seems again to derive, as Paolo Rossi has shown, from medieval alchemy and early modern occult philosophy. Specifically, the idea appears in Agrippa's *De incertitudine et vanitate scientiarum atque artium declamatio invectiva* (*Declamation Attacking the Uncertainty and Vanity of the Sciences and the Arts*, 1527), where he wrote that "Natural magic is that which having contemplated the virtues of all natural and celestial things and carefully studied their order proceeds to make known the hidden and secret powers of nature.... For this reason, magicians are like careful explorers of nature only directing what nature has formerly prepared.... Therefore those who believe the operations of magic to be above or against nature are mistaken because they are only derived from nature and in harmony with it."[114] Thus, if Bacon conceived of scientific discovery as the conquest of nature, it is a conquest in the sense not of an imposition of one's will or reason but of an act of artifice, trickery, and cunning, the harnessing not of one's own power but the power of nature after closely observing and understanding the hidden laws of its operations through art. It is an idea that was probably inspired, as William Eamon has suggested, by Bacon's study of classical mythology, particularly by the allegory of Pan's "hunt" (*venatio*) and the Greek concept of *mêtis* (cunning).[115] Thus, in a chapter on the Greek god of nature in *Wisdom of the Ancients*, Bacon wrote that "every natural action, every motion and process of nature, is nothing else than a hunt. For the sciences and arts hunt after their works, human counsels hunt after their ends, and all things in nature hunt either after their food, which is like hunting for prey, or after their pleasures, which is like hunting for recreation."[116] Pan's knowledge is based on "sagacious experience and the universal knowledge of nature, which will often by a kind of accident, and as it were while engaged in hunting, stumble upon such discoveries."[117] From the knowledge gained by accident or experiment, he then proceeds by analogy and conjecture, extrapolating from known results to unknown situations. As Bacon wrote in *Of the Interpretation of Nature*, "the discovery of new works and active directions not known before, is the only trial to be accepted of; and yet not that neither, in case where one particular giveth light to another; but where particulars induce an axiom or observation, which axiom found out discovereth and designeth new particulars."[118] Baconian inductivism was thus an attempt, Eamon argues, to "translate *mêtis*—whether it be the artisan's cunning or the natural magician's intuition—into a method."[119]

But, as Eamon also notes, there had been more recent examples of conquest by cunning. For, an entirely new field of "secrets" emerged with Europe's overseas expansionism in the New World.[120] Indeed, the sixteenth-century Spanish conquest of the New World provides a concrete and immediate context for understanding not only Bacon's idea of the role of cunning in scientific discovery but also the connection he saw between discovery and dominion, or property. Bacon conceived of his inductivist program in natural philosophy not only as a reformed alchemy but also as reformed conquest, a conquest that was conceptually inspired and ethically legitimated by the Spanish conquest of the New World but that was "reformed" in the sense that it was a conquest not of subjects but of objects. While some men seek to extend their own power over their own native country, Bacon explained in the *New Organon,* others seek to extend their country's power by establishing dominion over other territories. Although the latter is more laudable than the former, it ultimately still stems from covetousness. The noblest ambition, therefore, Bacon argues, is that which seeks to extend the "power and empire [*dominium*] of the human race itself over the universe of things. . . . [A]nd the empire of man over things lies solely in the arts and sciences. For one does not have empire over nature except by obeying her."[121] The purpose of the arts and sciences was for Bacon the restoration of man's prelapsarian state of dominion (*dominium naturale*), which had partially been lost due to Adam's Fall.

The figurative language that Bacon employs here in theorizing the scientific discovery of the secrets of nature—territorial conquest and the extension of man's "dominion"—no longer derives from the language of alchemy nor from that of natural philosophy but rather from that of politics and the Judeo-Christian religion. In a general sense, the idea has its roots in the book of Genesis in the Old Testament. There, God is said to have sovereignty over the universe and, likewise, man over the living creatures on the earth. Thus, Genesis 1:26 in the King James version (1611) reads: "And God said, Let us make man in our image, after our likeness: and let them have dominion over the fish of the sea, and over the fowl of the air, and over the cattle, and over all the earth, and over every creeping thing that creepeth upon the earth." Similarly, Genesis 1:28 reads: "And God blessed them, and God said unto them, Be fruitful, and multiply, and replenish the earth, and subdue it: and have dominion over the fish of the sea, and over the fowl of the air, and over every living thing that moveth upon the earth." In the Latin biblical commentary tradition, there had been a protracted debate about whether and how the Fall affected Man's dominion over nature, but the existence of wild animals in postlapsarian times was usually interpreted to signify that man had at least partially lost his former God-given dominion, as the animals were said to have lived in peaceful subjection to man in prelapsarian times.[122]

As William Leiss has observed, the word "dominion" in Genesis 1:26 conveys a picture of God as the "absolute ruler of the universe who has delegated subordinate authority to man for the management of affairs of earth."[123] More specifically than that, as we have seen in chapter 8, the word *dominium*—at its root a legal concept, derived from Roman law—meant the right to property, which grants the owner the right to treat his property exactly as he wishes, as he is the "master" (*dominus*). This right is the *ius utendi et abutendi re sua* (the right to make use of and consume what is yours). Thus, to think of discovery as an act of extending one's dominion over nature is to think of discovery as an act of taking territorial possession, or of making the thing discovered your legal property. It is instructive to note here, however, that when comparing Genesis 1:26 in the King James Version to that in the earlier Geneva Bible (1557–60), we get slightly divergent connotations regarding man's relationship to nature. Thus, Genesis 1:26 reads in the Geneva Bible: "Let vs make man in our image according to our likenes, and let them rule ouer the fish of the sea, and ouer the foule of the heauen, and ouer the beastes, and ouer all the earth." Instead of the King James Version's phrase "have dominion," the Geneva Bible simply has "rule." Also, in the Latin Vulgate, Genesis 1:26 reads as follows: "et ait faciamus hominem ad imaginem et similitudinem nostram et praesit piscibus maris et volatilibus caeli et bestiis universaeque terrae omnique reptili quod movetur in terra." The connotation of "praesit piscibus maris" is not exactly the same as having "dominion" over the fishes of the sea, as the verb *praesse* simply means "being before something," "presiding or ruling over," "taking the lead" over something, or "commanding" something. It does not necessarily connote ownership. The absence of the noun "dominium" in the Vulgate version of Genesis 1:26 and 1:28 strongly suggests that the idea in the King James Version of man's rule as a territorial, undivided *ownership* is of early modern (British) origins.[124]

In chapter 8, I have explored the late Scholastic and early modern debate about the concept of *dominium* and the "rights of dominion"—from John Wycliffe and Richard Fitzralph to John Mair and School of Salamanca, particularly Francisco de Vitoria and Domingo de Soto. I have investigated the connections between Vitoria's and De Soto's opposition to violent conquest in America on the one hand and a Franciscan nominalism that had provided the metaphysical context for the rise of scientific Baconianism on the other. Likewise, I have argued for a connection between the school's notion of "peaceful conquest" and De Soto's epistemology of "regressus" in the Thomist notion of synderesis. It is significant that Bacon was patently very well informed about history of the idea of "dominion" in early modern political philosophy and metaphysics, as it had emerged in the Spanish debate about the conquest of America. In his *An Advertisement Touching on Holy War,* published in 1622, Bacon presents a fictional disputation reminiscent of Sepúlveda's *Democrates alter,* between four characters, Martius, Pollio, Zebedaeus, and Eupolis, about the question of whether or not Christians have the right of conquest by the mere virtue of being Christians. "There cannot be a better ground laid to declare this," Zebedaeus argues (clearly drawing from the King James Version), "than to look into the original donation of government. Observe it well, especially the inducement, or preface. Saith God: *Let us make man after our own image, and let him have dominion over the fishes of the sea, and the fowls of the air, and the beasts of the land, etc.*" As Zebedaeus goes on explaining, "De Victoria [*sic*], and with him some others, infer excellently, and extract a most true and divine aphorism, *Non fundatur dominium, nisi in imagine Dei*" (There is no foundation for dominion but in the image of God).[125] It is clear from this reference that the debate between the opposing traditions of Fitzralph/Wycliffe on the one hand and Vitoria/De Soto on the other provides the theoretical cornerstones of Zebedaeus's disquisition. The colonial record of eyewitnesses constitutes the evidentiary basis for Zebedaeus's arguments that Native Americans had lost their natural rights to dominion based on their violations of natural law—violations such as cannibalism, idolatry, sodomy, and human sacrifice.

Bacon's own stance on the justification of "holy war," based on considerations of natural law, ultimately remains ambiguous, for his tract was left unfinished, ending abruptly after Zebedaeus's lengthy disquisition and leaving some modern historians with the impression that Bacon agreed with his character Zebedaeus's defense of the European conquest.[126] However that may be, I would argue that Bacon's apparent interest in this debate was primarily for the implications it held for the question of the legitimacy not of the conquest of men (subjects) but of the conquest of nature (objects)—a conquest that drew its territorial logic and theological justification from the Spanish conquest of America, which had turned (as we have seen) the Augustinian theological interdiction against "vain curiosity" (*vana curiositas*) about the occult into a theologically justified curiosity (*iusta curiositas*) with apocalyptic ends. Bacon's was a more radical attack on the Realist-Thomist notion of natural law as a basis for moral and natural philosophy more generally that had grown out of the Franciscan nominalist tradition holding that human conceptions of the laws of nature derived from reason are not a reliable guide to understanding the universe as it *really* was, whose ultimate principles are known only to God but forever hidden from us and open-ended in their number. His natural philosophy was aimed not at a demonstration of moral and universal truths but at advancing human power. While his idea of scientific discovery as an extension of man's "dominion" into the realm of nature was clearly inflected by the Roman legal notion of a *terra/res nullius,* it derived its legitimacy from the medieval nominalist tradition that held that truth was not the dominion of universal reason but the process of Christian empirical discovery and revelation. Bacon's reform of the sixteenth-century ideology of conquest simply replaced the Christian/pagan binary in holy war for the binary of man/nature or subject/object in science.

Barbarians, and especially cannibals, fall, in this binary, on the side of natural objects, as a species of *ferae bestiae,* for they lack the fundamentally defining trait of civility—the technical arts, especially the arts of transforming metals—that are the instruments of discovery. Thus, Bacon argues that it is only the technical arts that distinguish the civilized people of Europe from American "barbarians": "Again (if you please), let anyone reflect how great is the difference between the life of men in any of the most civilised provinces of Europe and in the most savage and barbarous region of New India; and he will judge that they differ so much that deservedly it may be said that 'man is a God to man,' not only for help and benefit, but also in the contrast between their conditions. And this is due not to soil, climate or bodily qualities, but to Arts."[127] Only "civilised" people in possession of the (mechanical) arts are capable of making discoveries that will lead to progress, most notably printing, gunpowder, and the magnet. For "these three things have changed the face and condition of things all over the globe: the first in literature; the second in the art of war; the third in navigation; and innumerable changes have followed; so that no empire or sect or star seems to have exercised a greater power and influence on human affairs than those mechanical things."[128]

The prominence of the concept of "dominion" in Bacon's hermeneutics of discovery highlights the connection between sixteenth-century European expansionism and the hegemony that the logic of Baconian science would attain in the context of a burgeoning British colonial project in the New World. Thus, whereas in the sixteenth century, the word was used in English mainly to refer to dominions inherited by kings (i.e., the dominion of France), its first usage in terms of territorial conquest appears to have been in 1606 in the *First Charter of Virginia,* which refers to "The said several Colonies and Plantations, . . . they being of any Realms, or Dominions under our Obedience." Three years later, Bacon would coauthor and sign the *Second Charter* of Virginia, which repeats the phrase and uses the word "dominion" in terms of British overseas possessions nine times. Five years later, the translators of the King James Version adopted the word in their rendering of the relationship between man and nature as ordained by the Word of God. And a decade or so later, Francis Bacon extended the legal logic of the acquisition of new territorial dominions through conquest into the realm of natural philosophy in order to articulate a hermeneutics of discovery in terms of a penetration of natural secrets in order to extend man's dominion over nature.[129]

Indeed, the analogy between political and epistemic conquest pervades Bacon's writings, as had the analogy between the Body of Christ and the Philosophers' Stone in the alchemical tradition. For example, in "Certain Considerations touching the Plantation in Ireland" (1606), he wrote:

> Although it be a great fortune for a king to deliver or recover his kingdom from long continued calamities: yet in the judgment of those that have distinguished of the degrees of sovereign honour, to be a founder of estates or kingdoms, excelleth all the rest. For, as in arts and sciences, to be the first inventor is more than to illustrate or amplify: and as in the works of God, the creation is greater than the preservation: and as in the works of nature, the birth and nativity is more than the continuance: so in kingdoms, the first foundation or plantation is of more noble dignity and merit than all that followeth. Of which foundations there being but two kinds; the first, that maketh one of more; and the second, that maketh one of none: the latter resembling the creation of the world, which was *de nihilo ad quid;* and the former, the edification of the Church, which was *de multiplici ad simplex, vel ad unum:* it hath pleased the divine providence, in singular favour to your majesty, to put both these kinds of foundations or regenerations into your hand: the one, in the union of the island of Britain [i.e., of England and Scotland]; the other, in the plantation of great and noble parts of the island of Ireland.[130]

The *recovery* of dominions in politics is like the Scholastic Thomist scientific method of producing knowledge: by illustration and amplification of things already known. By contrast, the creation of *new* plantations is like first invention, or the discovery of something new. Whereas the recovery of dominions is achieved by "natural" means (procreation and succession), the creation of plantations is achieved by artificial means (conquest). But whereas most political conquests—such as the Spanish conquest of the New World—"have been founded in the effusion of blood," the English conquest of nature will be a reformed or purified conquest, built *"in solo puro, et in area pura,* that shall need no sacrifices expietory for blood; and therefore, no doubt, under an higher and more assured blessing."[131] While the violence of conquest thus survives in Bacon's language of scientific discovery, it is a violence directed not against (European) subjects but against nature.

If, as I have argued, Bacon's conception of discovery as territorial appropriation was based on the idea of a reform of the Spanish conquest of America, there is a certain irony in the fact that it was predicated on a misunderstanding of the de jure (if not de facto) identity of the Indies within the constitutional structure of the Spanish Empire and the framework laid out by the Alexandrine bulls of *Inter cetera*. For the bulls did not confer territorial ownership but only Spain's monopoly of *access* to the Indies; and Spanish imperial law conferred ownership only over America's natural resources first "discovered" by Spaniards and only Spanish "rule" over its lands and people, who were, at least in theory, free subjects of the Crown (a *república de los indios*) and the owners of their dominions. It was a fine, technical, and legalistic distinction, to be sure, with little practical significance, which would have easily been lost on the seventeenth-century observer in England, where a concept of land as alienable property had developed earlier than on the Continent.[132] Nevertheless, the analogy between the Spanish dominion over the Americas and man's dominion over nature was further elaborated in English biblical commentaries throughout the seventeenth century. As the English jurist Matthew Hale declared in his *The Primitive Origination of Mankind* (1677):

> In relation . . . this inferior World of Brutes and Vegetables, the End of Man's Creation was, that he should be the Vice-Roy of the great God of Heaven and Earth in this inferior World. . . . [T]his was one End of the Creation of Man, namely, To be the Vicegerent of Almighty God, in the subordinate Regiment especially of the Animal and Vegetable Provinces. The Earth, and Vegetables, and Animals stand in need of such a Superior Nature to keep them in a competent order: an ordinary Observation lets us see how soon those Regions uninhabited by Mankind become rude Forests and Wildernesses, how destitute they are of those mansuete Animals, being exposed without a protector to be the prey of savage Beasts.[133]

Similarly, John Donne, in his sermons, explains that in Genesis, "God creates man, whom he constitutes His Viceroy in the World" and then "extends man's term in his viceregency to the end of the world."[134] Finally, in 1651, the alchemist Noah Biggs would define the "New" (Baconian) sciences as the "investigation into the America of nature."[135]

Thus, if alchemy had provided much of the salvific language for Bacon's legitimation of an atomistic materialism and a modern sense of scientific curiosity about the secrets of nature, the sixteenth-century literature about the conquest of America had provided the conceptual model for his notion of naturalist inquiry and discovery as a "conquest"—as an extension of man's "dominion" into the realm of nature and, thus, as an act of spatial and territorial appropriation. As I have argued, Bacon's reform of natural philosophy can be understood in terms of a "purification" or "reformation" not only of the alchemical tradition but also of the idea of conquest—as a conquest not of subjects but of objects. Despite his critique of Spanish political expansionism, his natural philosophy remained profoundly indebted to the sixteenth-century Neo-Scholastic debate about the "rights of discovery" and the "rights of dominion," as well as to the spatial logic of transoceanic expansionism. Although his proposals for scientific reform for the conquest of nature largely fell on deaf ears during his own time in the early seventeenth century, many of them would later be embraced by the Royal Society of London during the second part of the seventeenth century, in the aftermath of Great Britain's own first experiences with imperial expansionism in America.

CODA

Alexander von Humboldt, Alchemist of the Tropics

In his old age, Melchíades, in the late Gabriel García Márquez's *Cien años de soledad,* withdraws into the seclusion of one of the bedrooms in the Buendía home, spending "hours on end scribbling his enigmatic literature on the parchments that he had brought with him" and talking to himself in inscrutable monologues.[1] The only thing that could be made out was an "insistent hammering on the word *equinox, equinox, equinox,* and the name of Alexander von Humboldt."[2] Although this is the only time that the famous Prussian naturalist is mentioned by name, he seems to have a dark presence in the novel through his association with the ancient (and ageless) Melchíades.[3] For, as the reader learns on the last page of the novel, it was Melchíades—Mephistophelan alchemist, chronicler, and prophet of scientific progress—who had condemned Macondo to a hundred years of solitude and its apocalyptic end in his enigmatic manuscript, which, written in the ancient Indo-European language of Sanskrit, is finally translated by the last of the Buendías family in the moment of his own demise.[4] Thus, "the city of mirrors (or mirages) would be wiped out by the wind and exiled from the memory of men ... because races condemned to a hundred years of solitude did not have a second opportunity on earth."[5]

If, in his Nobel Prize address, "The Solitude of Latin America," García Márquez later reiterated this dramatic ending with a twist—calling for a "utopia of life" in Latin American writing, "where the races condemned to one hundred years of solitude will have, at last and forever, a second opportunity on earth"—he underscores his novel's metafictional critique of a Melchíadean dystopia of death that had entrapped Latin Americans within a "city of mirrors" for a hundred years. Moreover, García Márquez suggests that Melchíades's text was but one version of a much grander European master script about America, a script at least as old in the European literature of discovery as Antonio Pigafetta's account of Magellan's first circumnavigation during the sixteenth century. In that narrative, Pigafetta had related how, during their stay-over in Patagonia, Magellan's men encountered a giant cannibal who, when confronted with a mirror given to him by the Europeans, "lost his senses to the terror of his own image."[6] In presenting "a strictly accurate account that nonetheless resembles a venture into fantasy," García Márquez suggested, Pigafetta's narrative "already contained the seeds of our present-day novels." *Cien años de soledad* can thus be read as a metafictional reflection on Latin America's heterotopian experience with scientific modernity, which has continuously forced Latin Americans to look at themselves through the eyes of European technologies of representation.[7] The novel's "magical realism"—which has often been hailed by modern literary critics as an autochthonous literary expression of a distinctly Latin American "magical" ontology—turns out to be a parodic literary device punning on a European discourse of discovery that has been inventing (Latin) America since the fifteenth century.[8]

In this book, I have attempted to imagine a cultural history of Melchíades's enigmatic manuscript by exploring how the idea that America was discovered by Europeans in the fifteenth century became a "paradigm" in modern Western science; I have investigated the theological roots of this modern paradigm in the synthesis between science and religion in late medieval alchemy; I have emphasized the epistemic violence of this synthesis and explored its early modern legacies in the literature of discovery, from the writings of Christopher Columbus to those of Francis Bacon; and I have argued that the conquest of America underwrote this alchemical synthesis with early modern state power, giving rise to the modern European subject in the discovery of American objects (or "things"). The language of alchemy in *Cien años de soledad* has been amply studied in literary criticism and does not need further elucidation here.[9] Apparently in possession of the miraculous Philosophers' Stone, Melchíades has "achieved immortality" in his continuous reinventions of Latin America as an object of scientific inquiry.[10] I return to García Márquez's novel in this coda in order to offer some concluding remarks about its apparent critique of the so-called Second Discoverer of (Latin) America, Alexander von Humboldt (1769–1859). By associating Humboldt with Melchíades—"*equinox, equinox, equinox*"—García Márquez seems to attribute special significance to the nineteenth-century savant and his voluminous scientific travel writings about the American tropics in the long literary history of Macondo, the dystopian linguistic city of mirrors.

Whereas Humboldt was largely forgotten in the United States until recently, his fame as a scientist during the nineteenth century was substantial, as is attested to by his wide-ranging influence on such nineteenth-century naturalists as Charles Darwin, who wrote that all of the preconceived ideas he held about the tropics "were taken from the vivid descriptions in the *Personal Narrative* of Humboldt."[11] In Latin America, especially, Humboldt's legacy has been continuous and formidable. Simón Bolívar even allegedly once declared that Humboldt was "the *real* discoverer of South America ... for captivating the world with his depictions of the region's aesthetic and scientific wonders."[12] Since the second half of the twentieth century, however, the assessment of Humboldt's legacy has been more ambivalent. On the one hand, a number of postcolonial critics have seen his "godlike, omniscient stance over both the planet and the reader" as the expression of a European imperial gaze, implicated especially in the nineteenth-century neocolonial exploitation of Latin America and its resources by Europe and (later) the United States.[13] On the other hand, several scholars have recently objected that Humboldt was not an agent of any European imperial power while traveling through and writing about Latin America. In fact, Humboldt, following Kant, had overtly condemned Europe's global imperialism. His *Vue des Cordillères et monuments des peuples indigènes de l'Amérique* (1810) was one of the first European treatises of the New World to give due credit to the cultural achievements of America's pre-Columbian civilizations;[14] and he vehemently condemned slavery in both his *Political Essay on the Island of Cuba* and his *Personal Narrative*.[15] Admittedly, he equivocated about the rise of Anglo-American power in the Western Hemisphere, especially with regard to the US annexation of Mexican territory; nonetheless, he abhorred the development of a virulently racist ideology of Manifest Destiny in the United States that underwrote not only Andrew Jackson's policy of Indian Removal and slavery but also the Mexican-American War.[16] Contemporary critics have even suggested that the Humboldtian understanding and desire to represent the "whole of nature" anticipated much of the contemporary environmentalist and ecocritical thinking that has exposed the (neo)colonial historical roots of the modern Anthropocene.[17]

García Márquez's novel challenges us to ask not what Humboldt had to say about African slavery, European empire, neocolonialism in Latin America, or the rise of US power, but what role his writings about the Americas played in the long history of a modern Western *paradigm of discovery* that not only transformed our conception of the world from Oikoumene to Cosmos—from a bound to a boundless world—but that also rationalized indigenous peoples' dispossession of that world around the globe by Europeans beginning in the fifteenth century.[18] In other words, García Márquez invites us to ask what role Humboldt's writings about America played in the history of the legitimation of a particular idea of discovery underwriting both the modern empirical sciences and the so-called Doctrine of Discovery as it emerged in nineteenth-century international law and could be invoked by Justice John Marshal in the 1823 Supreme Court case *Johnson v. M'Intosh*. On the one hand, it is a history that links the Humboldtian desire to discover the secrets of America's volcanoes, caves, isothermal patterns, and magnetic fields to the tradition of Francis Bacon's *Great Instauration* and to the rise of nuclear physics roughly fifty years after Humboldt's death; on the other hand, it is a history that links Christopher Columbus's acts of taking possession of Caribbean islands in the late fifteenth century with the early twenty-first-century opposition of four former British colonies to the United Nation's Declaration on the Rights of Indigenous Peoples.

Humboldt and his companion, the French botanist Aimé Bonpland (1773–1858), had arrived in the Americas on a ship aptly named the *Pizarro* during the final years of the Spanish Empire, in 1799, not long before Spain's own invasion by Napoleon's forces in 1808. Having served the Prussian state as an inspector of mines in the 1790s, the polymath from Berlin had witnessed, at the Second Congress of Rastatt in 1797, the beginning of the end of another empire that once included Spain—the thousand-year-old Holy Roman Empire, whose territories were now being carved up by France, Prussia, and Austria. Before embarking from Spain for America, Humboldt explained the purpose of his journey in a letter to a friend in Berlin by invoking Bacon:

> I will collect flora and fauna; I will investigate the heat, elasticity, and magnetic and electrical charge of the atmosphere, and chemically analyze it; I will determine latitudes and longitudes, and measure mountains. But all this is not the aim of my voyage. My sole true object is to investigate the confluence and interweaving of all physical forces, and the influence of dead nature on the animate animal and plant creation. To this end, I have had to instruct myself in every empirical discipline. Thence the complaints of those who have no idea what I'm doing, that I'm pursuing too many things at once. We have botanists, we have mineralogists, but no physicists, as [Bacon] called for in the *Sylva Sylvarum*.[19]

Humboldt's description of his empirical eclecticism as "chemical" analysis and his reference to Bacon are significant for the light it sheds on the epistemological roots of his scientific project. As Michael Dettelbach has explained, Humboldt's conception of science can be understood in the context of eighteenth-century Prussian cameralism, the "systematic science of administration that emerged and was codified in the curricula of eighteenth-century German universities and academies."[20] Known in German as *Staatswissenschaft*, it was a natural science placed in the service of the state that had its roots in the seventeenth century, particularly in the reforms of natural philosophy proposed by Bacon in England and in the work of alchemists such as

Johann Becher, patronized by courts in the Holy Roman Empire, as well as in the Spanish imperial administration in the Americas.[21]

Just as Bacon's New Science had been inspired by alchemical experimentalism, so was Humboldt's project inspired by what he called the "vital chemistry" of such French chemists as Antoine Lavoisier, Pierre Simon Laplace, and Claude Berthollet, whose forays into calorimetry and eudiometry by way of elaborate scientific instruments such as the eudiometer, barometer, thermometer, and electrometer he had studied as a student of mining at the University of Freiburg and that he had himself applied in his program to reform the mining industry while serving the Prussian state as an inspector of mines in Ansbach-Bayreuth, Franconia. Indeed, like Bacon's, Humboldt's experimentalism in the discovery of the secrets of the cosmos had originated on the microcosmic scale, as is evident in one of his earliest scientific writings, a work on organic chemistry entitled *Versuche über die gereitzte Muskel- und Nervenfaser* (Experiments on stimulated muscle and nerve fibers). "For several years now," he wrote there, "I have been engaged in the comparison of the phenomena of organic matter with the laws of inanimate nature. In the course of this work, I conducted successful experiments that led to the discovery of the chemical process of life. A severed animate organ, with irritable and sensible fibers, can be stimulated in the course of a few seconds from a state of profound numbness to the highest level of sensitivity toward external stimuli, and vice versa be reduced to a state of numbness."[22]

In the course of his experiments, Humboldt discovered that the stimulation (*Reizung*) of organic matter does not depend, as previously believed, merely on the amount of oxygen but also (and mainly) on mercury and hydrogen, or rather on "a combination of effects and the antagonism between multiple substances."[23] It was in the course of these experiments in organic chemistry, which he performed in various cities throughout Germany and Austria, that Humboldt cultivated his characteristic habit of traveling with his entourage of scientific instruments; and it was this cameralist background in mining, metallurgy, and organic chemistry that would also inspire his scientific approach to questions of cosmology, an approach that he called "terrestrial physics" and meant to put to the test experimentally during his American travels. Thus, on July 16, 1799, he and Bonpland disembarked at Cumaná, Venezuela, with hundreds of boxes containing scientific instruments and tools, poised to commence their epic five-year journey crisscrossing Spanish America—through the Orinoco delta to Caracas; through the Caribbean to Colombia, Ecuador, and Peru; and finally to New Spain (Mexico).[24]

Perhaps the most well-known contribution that Humboldt's project in "physical geography" made to modern science lay in his invention of the isobar and the isotherm—lines on the map connecting points of equal atmospheric pressure or median surface temperature (see fig. 47). It was this method of making manifest what remains hidden from the bare eye, the occult principles of physical geography, that came to represent Humboldtian science per se—the depiction of nature as a unified and interconnected whole, a "microcosm on one page."[25] For example, in his 3′ × 2′ *Naturgemälde* (painting of nature) of the Chimborazo, he presented the famous Ecuadorian volcano in cross-sections that showed plants distributed according to their altitudes. To the left and right of the mountain he placed columns that provided related details and correlated information about temperature, gravity, humidity to elevation, information that that he had gathered with his instruments during his own climb of the volcano (see fig. 48). But perhaps more consequential than Humboldt's theories about physical geography was his elaboration of a new transnational ethos of scientific authorship in the purification of nature and the separation of scientific subjects from objects. Unlike such Enlightenment travelers and men of science as Charles Marie de La Condamine, Jorge Juan,

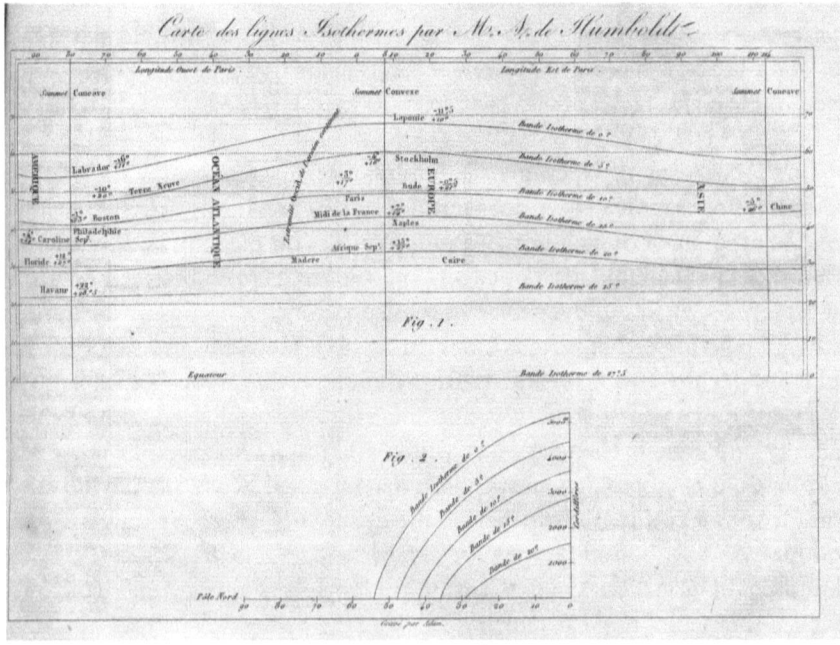

Figure 47. Alexander von Humboldt, *Carte de lignes isothermes*, showing mean temperature around the world as dependent on latitude, longitude, and altitude. (Source: MM. Gay-Lussac et Arago, *Annales de chimie et de physique*, vol. 5, bk. 1 [Paris: Chez Crochard, Libraire, rue de Sorbonne, 1817].)

Figure 48. Alexander von Humboldt's *Naturgemelde* of the Chimbarrazo. (Source: A. de Humboldt, *Essai sur la géographie des plantes* [Paris: Levrault, Schoell et Compagnie, Libraires, XIII, 1805].)

and Antonio de Ulloa before him, Humboldt traveled the Americas not in the service of a state but as a private individual in the service of extending what he called the "empire" of human knowledge over nature for a cosmopolitan republic of science that would be independent of political empires and nationalist politics. Thus, in his *Cosmos* (1845), he wrote that "the knowledge of the laws of nature, whether we can trace them in the alternate ebb and flow of the ocean, in the measured path of comets, or in the mutual attractions of multiple stars, alike increase our sense of the rest (*Ruhe*) of nature, while the chimera so long cherished by the human mind in its early and intuitive contemplations, the belief in a 'discord of the elements,' seems gradually to vanish in proportion as science extends her empire."

Humboldt's chemical notion of *Reizung*—a German noun that can mean stimulation in general but also irritation and excitement—sheds light on his fascination with the American tropics. There, he believed, the secrets of nature are revealed to the philosophical traveler equipped with scientific instruments more readily than in any other region on earth, due to the extraordinary power of the sun. To Humboldt, as for Columbus before him, the tropics were the cosmological analogue of the alchemical crucible in the discovery of the secrets of nature. "If [tropical] America does not occupy an important place in the history of mankind," he wrote in his *Personal Narrative*, "it does offer a wide field for the naturalist. Nowhere else does nature so vividly suggest general ideas on the cause of events, and their mutual interrelationships."[26] And in his later *Cosmos* he wrote that the "regions of the torrid zone not only give rise to the most powerful impressions by their organic richness and their abundant fertility, but they likewise afford the inestimable advantage of revealing to man, by the uniformity of the variations of the atmosphere and the development of vital forces and by the contrasts of climate and vegetation exhibited at different elevations, the invariability of the laws that regulate the course of heavenly bodies, reflected as it were in terrestrial phenomena."[27] For Humboldt, tropical America was exceptional not because the universal laws of nature did not apply there but because the occult laws of nature were manifest and measurable there to exceptional degrees. The tropics were for him *pure* nature, as yet unconquered by human culture. "Nowhere does nature impart on us more the feeling of her power more," he wrote, "than in the tropics: under the 'Indian Heaven,' as the climate of the Torrid Zone was known in the early Middle Ages."[28] After his arrival at Cumaná and during his first foray into the South American jungle, Humboldt marvels at the "great seal" of tropical nature but finds himself confused by its entangled profusion. Overawed, he does not know

> what shocks him more: whether the *restful silence of the solitude,* or the beauty of the diverse, contrasting objects, or that fullness and freshness of plant life in the Tropics. It could be said that the earth, overloaded with plants, does not have sufficient space to develop. Everywhere tree trunks are hidden behind a thick green carpet. If you carefully transplanted all the orchids, all the epiphytes that grow on one single American fig tree (Ficus gigantea) you would manage to cover an enormous amount of ground. The same lianas that trail along the ground climb up to the tree-tops, swinging from one tree to another 100 feet up in the air. As these parasitical plants form a real tangle, a botanist often confuses flowers, fruit and leaves belonging to different species.[29]

The observation of tropical nature is akin to the experience of a volcanic eruption, when solid and cold earth turns into glowing liquid: it shakes and overthrows human conceptions and categories, preparing the mind for new ideas. Tropical nature and volcanic eruptions are the macrocosmic crucibles of modern geographic discovery, where substantial forms are reduced to their *prima materia:*

From our infancy, the idea of certain contrasts becomes fixed in our minds: water appears to us an element that moves; earth, a motionless and inert mass. These impressions are the result of daily experience; they are connected with everything that is transmitted to us by the senses. When the shock of an earthquake is felt, when the earth which we had deemed so stable is shaken on its old foundations, one instant suffices to destroy long-fixed illusions. It is like awakening from a dream; but a painful awakening. We feel that we have been deceived by the apparent stability of nature; we become observant of the least noise; we mistrust for the first time the soil we have so long trod with confidence. But if the shocks be repeated, if they become frequent during several successive days, the uncertainty quickly disappears.[30]

The trope of the tropical entanglement of South American nature that confuses European categories of knowledge is a pervasive theme in all of Humboldt's travel narratives. As we have seen, the history of this trope reaches back to the earliest European accounts of America in the sixteenth century and still inspired García Márquez's defamiliarization of Bacon's emblem of purification in the image of the Spanish galleon with which I began this book.[31] Indeed, it was probably Humboldt's *Personal Narrative* that inspired García Márquez's memorable literary image. There the Prussian naturalist writes: "On the 1st of July we came across the wreck of a sunken ship. We could distinguish its mast covered in floating seaweed. In a zone where the sea is perpetually calm the boat could not have sunk. Perhaps its remains came from the northerly stormy area and were dragged there by the extraordinary whirling of the Atlantic Ocean in the Southern hemisphere."[32] But tropical nature threatens to entangle not only European technologies but also most basic cultural categories, such as that of human food. Thus, Humboldt marvels at the culinary habits of the Otomac people in eating earth without becoming ill (a trope that may have partially inspired the character of Rebeca in García Márquez's novel). It is a custom, he explains, that is found in "hot regions among inert people, who live in the most glorious and fertile part of the world."[33] He witnessed the practice in the small village of La Concepción de Uruana:

> They [the Otomacs] distinguish one type of earth from another by taste, for not all muds are equally agreeable to them. They knead this soil into balls of four to six inches in diameter and burn its exterior with a smalls fire until it becomes reddish. While eating, the balls are moistened again. These Indians are mainly wild men who shun the cultivation of plants.... One Indian consumes ... between three and five quarters of a pound [of earth] daily. According to the Otomacs'

own testimony, this earth is their main food during the rainy season.... Indeed, they crave the mud so much that, even when they have enough fish to eat, they have it daily as a snack after the meal.[34]

Whereas in temperate zones, this pathological craving is very rare and limited to children and pregnant women, in "tropical countries of all continents, earth eating is endemic."[35] In all tropical countries, men have this "marvelous, almost irresistible craving to eat earth, not the so-called alkaline kind to neutralize the acids, but rather the fat kind with a strong smell."[36]

The entanglement of human culture by nature has the effect of the solitude of tropical existence and a permanent state of cultural arrested development. Thus, Humboldt claims that the "pastoral life, this beneficent middle stage that binds nomadic hordes of hunters to the soil and prepares them for agriculture, remained unfamiliar to America's indigenous population, which is the reason for the emptiness of South' America's prairie."[37] Whereas in temperate Europe, historical change proceeded at a revolutionary pace even while he was traveling through South America, in tropical America history appears static. Even

> very populous provinces appear almost deserted; because man, to find nourishment, cultivates but a small number of acres. These circumstances modify the physical appearance of the country and the character of its inhabitants, giving to both a peculiar physiognomy; the wild and uncultivated stamp which belongs to nature, ere its primitive type has been altered by art. Without neighbors, almost unconnected with the rest of mankind, each family of settlers forms a separate tribe. This insulated state arrests or retards the progress of civilization, which advances only in proportion as society becomes numerous, and its connections more intimate and multiplied. But, on the other hand, it is solitude that develops and strengthens in man the sentiment of liberty and independence; and gives birth to that noble pride of character which has at all times distinguished the Castilian race.[38]

One consequence of tropical man's solitude is the inability to preserve historical memory. Thus, in several passages that may well have inspired the outrageous episode of the insomnia plague in *Cien años de soledad,* Humbodt writes that in the tropics, "the settler vainly tries to name the mountains, rivers and valleys with names that recall his motherland; these names soon lose their charm, and mean nothing to later generations. Under the influence of an exotic nature new habits are born for new needs, national memories are slowly effaced, and those remembered, like ghosts of our imaginations, are not attached to any time or place."³⁹ This absence of memory seems to afflict the people not only of tropical America but of the New World more generally, including even "these new people in the United States of America" as well as "the Spanish and Portuguese possessions." However, the location of the United States in a temperate zone affords it certain advantages in Humboldt's terrestrial physics: "When we reflect on the great political upheavals in the New World, we note that Spanish Americans are in a far less fortunate position than the inhabitants of the United States, who were more prepared for independence by constitutional liberty. Internal feuds are inevitable in regions where civilization has not yet taken root and where, thanks to the climate, forests soon cover all cleared land if agriculture is abandoned."⁴⁰ While the "wild aspect" of nature has been destroyed in temperate climates by the cultivation of grain (*graminées*), man in the tropics has "less extended his empire [*a moins éxtendu son empire*]" and "may be said to appear, not as an absolute master, who changes at will the surface of the soil, but as a transient guest, who quietly enjoys the gifts of nature [*bienfaits de la nature*]."⁴¹

Thus, unlike the Enlightenment philosophes before him, who had subscribed to a New World exceptionalism that apprehended the biological and cultural differences of the entire Western Hemisphere in terms of a "degeneration" of the biological and cultural forms of the Old World,⁴² Humboldt reshapes this economy of difference in ways that illuminate his hermeneutics of discovery: First, he emphasizes latitude (as well as elevation) over longitude in explaining the climatological and environmental characteristics, the "character of the landscape," that explain the forms of human culture; in effect, he replaces a New World exceptionalism with a tropical exceptionalism the history of which originates in the late medieval cosmology of the famed alchemist Albertus Magnus and that still inspired Christopher Columbus in reaching the East by sailing not only West but also South.⁴³ Instead of emphasizing the difference between America (the "New World") and Europe, Africa, and Asia (the "Old World"), Humboldt emphasizes the difference between the tropical and the temperate zones:

> When a traveler recently arrived from Europe steps into the South American jungle for the first time he sees nature in a completely unexpected guise. The objects that surround him only faintly bring to mind those descriptions by famous writers of the banks of the Mississippi, of Florida and of other temperate regions of the New World. With each step he feels not at the frontiers of the torrid zone but in its midst; not on one of the West Indian Islands but in a vast continent where everything is gigantic; mountains, rivers and the masses of plants. If he is able to feel the beauty of landscape, he will find it hard to analyze his many impressions.⁴⁴

Second, Humboldt apprehends cultural difference not in terms of a degeneration but in terms of progress (or its retardation), hereby betraying the influence of the Romantic idea that man's original state of nature was the savage, not the pastoral state. Unlike Rousseau, however, he does not see this savage state as being noble in the least. Contemplating the custom among some tribes living along the Orinoco of killing their children when they are born with deformities or as twins, he writes that "Such is the candor and simplicity of manners, such the boasted happiness of man in the *state of nature* [*état de nature*]! He kills his son, to escape the ridicule of having twins, or to avoid journeying more slowly; in fact to avoid a little inconvenience."[45]

While the tropical climate affords the European natural philosopher superior opportunities for scientific discovery, it is averse to the development of an indigenous scientific culture. Scientific progress is therefore restricted to man living in the temperate zone. In other words, while the tropics produce the objects of scientific discovery, the temperate zone produces its subjects:

> Notwithstanding the obstacles opposed in northern latitudes to the discovery of the laws of nature, owing to the excessive complication of phenomena, and the perpetual local variations and the distribution of organic forms, it is to the inhabitants of a small section of the temperate zone that the rest of mankind owe the earliest revelation of an intimate and rational acquaintance with the forces governing the physical world. Moreover, it is from the same zone (which is apparently more favorable to the progress of reason, the softening of manners, and the security of public liberty) that the germs of civilization have been carried to the regions of the tropics, as much by the migratory movement of races as by the establishment of colonies, differing widely in their institutions from those of the Phoenicians or Greeks.[46]

Thus, the tropics reveal the secrets of nature to temperate man but not to tropical man, as Humboldtian discovery requires the aid of human art and instrumentation the development of which are retarded by the tropical entanglement of nature and culture.

In elaborating this Eurocentric cosmology of scientific subjectivity, Humboldt brings to a culmination a long tradition of travel writers and natural historians who legitimated a modern paradigm of discovery in the idea that America was a "New World" that had been discovered by Europeans. Whereas Humboldt's representation of native tropical curiosity as a quiet enjoyment of the gifts of nature is distinctly reminiscent of Epicureanism (i.e., paganism), his idea of Western discovery as an extension of man's empire over nature betrays his profound debt to Bacon's Christian humanism and the alchemical construction of the occult. But whereas Columbus and Bacon had legitimated this modern idea of discovery as a providential fulfillment of ancient apocalyptic prophecies of the impending millennium (Scripturally, a time of rest and "the refreshment of the saints"),[47] Humboldt's scientific rediscovery of tropical America ends not in an eschatological apocalypse but in a revelation of another kind—the transcendental aesthetic experience of the *Ruhe* (restfulness) of nature, which gives reprieve from the buzzing changes and turmoil of (European) history. It is this transcendent aesthetic experience of *Ruhe* (following *Reizung*) that legitimates the curiosity about the occult in the secular age. Thus, like the Vespuccian travel writer three hundred years earlier, Humboldt confesses that he is reminded of Dante's *Purgatory*, according to which prelapsarian man was still able to see the Southern Cross before being deprived of its aspect as a result of his expulsion from Paradise:

> At a period when I studied the heavens, not with the intention of devoting myself to astronomy, but only to acquire a knowledge of the stars, I was disturbed by a feeling unknown to those who are devoted to sedentary life. It was painful to me to renounce the hope of beholding the beautiful constellations near the south pole. Impatient to rove in the equinoctial regions, I could not raise my eyes to the starry firmament without thinking of the Southern Cross, and recalling the sublime passage of Dante, which the most celebrated commentators have applied to that constellation—
>
> > Io mi volsi a man' destra e posi mente
> > All' altro polo, e vidi quattro stele
> > Non viste mai fuorch' alla prima gente.
> >
> > Goder parea lo ciel di lor fiammelle;
> > O settentrional vedovo sito
> > Poiche privato sei di mirar quelle![48]
> > (*Purgatory* 1:22–27)
>
> (The pleasure we felt on discovering the Southern Cross was warmly shared by those of the crew who had visited the colonies. In the solitude of the seas we hail a star as a friend, from whom we have long been separated.)[49]

Whereas Dante's poem had allegorized the Augustinian pessimism about the possibility of worldly redemption as well as the notion of the providential sacredness of the occult and the sinfulness of a "vain curiosity" that seeks to penetrate it, the early modern discovery and conquest of America had restored the Southern Cross to (northern) humanity and transformed the curiosity about the occult into a "just curiosity" (*iusta curiositas*)—a curiosity justified in the name of the progress of the Christian faith and Redemption history.[50] If the Portuguese and the Spaniards on the *Pizarro* are particularly susceptible to the experience of the sublime elicited by the contemplation of the Southern Cross, it is "due to a religious sentiment [that] attaches them to a constellation, the form of which recalls the sign of the faith planted by their ancestors in the deserts of the New World."[51] Similarly, in his *Ansichten der Natur,* Humboldt recalls Columbus's third voyage, particularly his entry into the *boca del drago* (the Dragon's Mouth, aka the Orinoco delta), which had impressed upon the Italian explorer the notion that he found himself in the presence not of islands but of an enormous continent: India. All of this, Humboldt writes, led Columbus to believe that he "had approached the Garden of Eden, the holy site of the first generation of men. The Orinoco River appeared to him as one of the four rivers that, according to the honorable fable of the Ancient world, flowed from Paradise to quench and divine the earth newly adorned with plants."[52] This poetic passage, Humboldt continues, "has a special psychological interest. It teaches anew that the creative imagination of the poet is expressed in the discoverer, just as in any greatness of the human character."[53] For Humboldt, scientific discovery is essentially an *aesthetic* experience.

Although Humboldt rejects the religious "fanaticism and superstition" that had motivated his Iberian predecessors in New World travel during the sixteenth century,[54] his own curiosity also had to be legitimated and distinguished from vain Epicurean pleasure in nature characterizing tropical curiosity. Thus, by the time he writes his *Personal Narrative,* his journey represents no longer the mere fulfillment of the dreams of his youth. "What attracted me about the Torrid Zone," he writes, "was no longer the promise of a wandering life full of adventures, but a desire to see with my own eyes a grand, wild nature rich in every conceivable natural product, and the prospect of collecting facts that contribute to the progress of science."[55] Whereas Humboldt's early modern Iberian predecessors had employed the salvific rhetoric of conquest, political empire, and apocalypse in order to justify their forays into a New World that had been "hidden" by God (or the Devil) from Christendom until the providentially appointed time, Humboldt's hermeneutics of discovery is legitimated by a modern, "purified" conquest. He is himself the modern personification of what he called the "scientific conqueror" (*wissenschaftliche[r] Eroberer*) rediscovering tropical America for the secular age.[56] It is a conquest not in the sense of the expansion of the Christian faith or of the political dominions of empires centered in Europe but in the sense of an extension of "the empire of science" by mobile, liberal, and cosmopolitan subjects such as himself at the end of which stands not the Second Coming but a "time of rest" of a different sort—the transcendent experience of *Ruhe* in the contemplation of the sublime "whole" of nature.

Thus, although Humboldt did not condone European geopolitical imperialist ambitions, his scientific writings about the American tropics played an important role in the history of a Western hermeneutics of discovery by relegitimating the idea that America was discovered by Europeans in the fifteenth century and that the American tropics continued to produce objects of scientific discovery for the scientific conqueror even in a secular and liberal age—in the "second discovery" of tropical America by temperate man, equipped with natural philosophy and scientific instrumentation. While his modern hermeneutics of scientific discovery disavows its affiliation with the nineteenth-century geopolitical Doctrine of Discovery, it shares with it a logic and a history of conquest that produced scientific objects in the New World and political subjects in the Old. If, as late as 1955, the famous French anthropologist Claude Lévi-Strauss could write, in his *Tristes tropiques,* that nature in the tropics "displayed a higher degree or presence and permanence" than in the temperate zone, it is largely thanks to the scientific writings of Alexander von Humboldt, the alchemist of the tropics, who rearticulated the modern hermeneutics of discovery in nineteenth-century terms of scientific progress, the aesthetic sublime, and the Global South.[57] If the first (early modern) conquest had legitimated this purification in the language of Christian alchemical apocalypticsim, Humboldt's crucial intervention in the history of the idea that America was discovered lay in the secularization of its millenarian telos in the language of the aesthetic sublime: the Romantic concept of *Ruhe*. In Bruno Latour's terms, we might thus say that Humboldt's voluminous travel writings about South America constitute a central moment in the construction of the "Modern Constitution,"[58] which casts the European naturalist at the "center of calculation" from where he separates nature from culture as well as American objects from European subjects. South America hereby emerges from his travel writings as a sort of "crucible of the tropics"—a geographical analogue to Robert Boyle's air pump—where the secrets of nature are revealed to the (northern European) "philosophical traveler" equipped with instrumentation but never to the South American Native him- or herself. In a permanent state of arrested development (or "solitude"), Humboldt's tropical America becomes the foil against which the modern Western narrative of scientific progress continues to unfold in a colonial history scientific modernity that I have called the alchemy of conquest.

Notes

Introduction

1. Gabriel García Márquez, *Cien años de soledad,* Edición Conmemorativa (Madrid: Real Academia Española, 2007), 7; English translations from Gabriel García Márquez, *One Hundred Years of Solitude,* trans. Gregory Rabasa (New York: Avon, 1971), 6.
2. Ibid.
3. Ibid., 422.
4. See Juan Pimentel, "The Iberian Vision: Science and Empire in the Framework of a Universal Monarchy, 1500–1800," *Osiris,* 2d ser., vol. 15 (2000): 17–30; Jorge Cañizares-Esguerra, *Nature, Empire, and Nation: Explorations of the History of Science in the Iberian World* (Stanford: Stanford University Press, 2006), 16–19; and Victor Navarro Brotóns and William Eamon, eds., *Más allá de la leyenda negra: España y la revolución científica/Beyond the Black Legend: Spain and the Scientific Revolution* (València: Universitat de València, Inst. de Historia de la Ciencia y Documentación López Piñero, 2007), 27–40.
5. Noah Biggs, *Mataeotechnia medicinae praxeos: The Vanity of the Craft of Physick* (London: Giles Calvert, 1651), 57; my emphasis. On Bigges, see Allen G. Debus, *The Chemical Philosophy: Paracelsian Science and Medicine in the Sixteenth Century* (New York: Science History Publications, 1977), 499–512.
6. On the emblematic relationship between geographic and intellectual discovery in modern Western scientific culture, see Denis Cosgrove, *Apollo's Eye: A Cartographic Genealogy of the Earth in the Western Imagination* (Baltimore: Johns Hopkins University Press, 2001), esp. 139–75. On the notion of a paradigm, see Giorgio Agamben, "What Is a Paradigm?," in *The Signature of All Things* (New York: Zone, 2009), 18–19.
7. Thomas S. Kuhn, *The Structure of Scientific Revolutions,* 2nd ed. (1962; Chicago: University of Chicago Press, 1970), 35–42. It is this absolutist claim to truth in modern science that David Noble has called "religion of technology" (see Noble, *The Religion of Technology: The Divinity of Man and the Spirit of Invention* [New York: Knopf, 1997]; and Stephen Gaukroger, *The Emergence of a Scientific Culture: Science and the Shaping of Modernity, 1210–1685* [Oxford: Clarendon, 2006]).
8. Roland Greene, *Five Words: Critical Semantics in the Age of Shakespeare and Cervantes* (Chicago: University of Chicago Press, 2013), 15–40.
9. See Russell Stannard, *The End of Discovery* (Oxford: Oxford University Press, 2010), 209–22.
10. *Johnson v. M'Intosh,* 21 U.S. 543, 5 L.Ed. 681, 8 Wheat. 543 (1823), 573–74 (my emphases). On the significance of Marshall's ruling for the evolution of the doctrine

of the "rights of discovery" in the United States, see Steven Newcomb, *Pagans in the Promised Land: Decoding the Doctrine of Christian Discovery* (Golden, CO: Fulcrum, 2008); James Muldoon, "John Marshall and the Rights of the Indians," in *Latin America and the Atlantic World/El mundo atlántico y América Latina (1500–1850)*, ed. Renate Pieper and Peer Schmidt, 67–82 (Cologne: Böhlau, 2005); Robert Miller, "The Legal Adoption of Discovery in the United States," in *Discovering Indigenous Lands: The Doctrine of Discovery in the English Colonies*, by Miller, Jacinta Ruru, Larissa Behrent, and Tracey Lindberg, 26–65 (Oxford: Oxford University Press, 2010), esp. 53–61; and Lindsay Robertson, *Conquest by Law: How the Discovery of America Dispossessed Indigenous Peoples of Their Lands* (Oxford: Oxford University Press, 2005).

11. Bruno Latour, *We Have Never Been Modern,* trans. Catherine Porter (Cambridge: Harvard University Press, 1993), 10–15.

12. For critiques of the British American historical tradition that has sought to avoid thinking about the English occupation as a "conquest," see Jorge Cañizares-Esguerra, *Puritan Conquistadors: Iberianizing the Atlantic, 1550–1700* (Stanford: Stanford University Press, 2006); Francis Jennings, *The Invasion of American: Indians, Colonialism, and the Cant of Conquest* (Chapel Hill: University of North Carolina Press, 1975); and Andrew Fitzmaurice, *Sovereignty, Property and Empire, 1500–2000* (Cambridge: Cambridge University Press, 2014), 8.

13. See Ralph Bauer, "Colonial Discourse and Early American Literary History: Ercilla, the Inca Garcilaso, and Joel Barlow's Conception of a New World Epic," *Early American Literature* 30, no. 3 (1995): 203–32.

14. Daniel J. Boorstin, *The Discoverers* (New York: Vintage, 1985), 8, xv–xvi.

15. David Stannard, *American Holocaust: Columbus and the Conquest of the New World* (New York: Oxford University Press, 1992); Kirkpatrick Sale, *The Conquest of Paradise: Christopher Columbus and the Columbian Legacy* (New York: Knopf, 1990); Jennings, *Invasion*.

16. For accounts of the ecological consequences of the Columbian exchange, see Alfred Crosby, *The Columbian Exchange: Biological and Cultural Consequences of 1492* (Westport, CT: Greenwood, 1972); and Alfred Crosby, *Ecological Imperialism: The Biological Expansion of Europe, 900–1900* (Cambridge: Cambridge University Press, 1986). Crosby did not, of course, use the term "Anthropocene," but for a definition, see P. L Gibbard and M. J. C. Walker, "The Term 'Anthropocene' in the Context of Formal Geological Classification," *Geological Society, London, Special Publications* 395, no. 1 (2014): 29–37. On the proposition that the Columbian encounter, with its catastrophic demographic and significant ecological consequences for the Americas, marks the beginning of the Anthropocene, see S. L. Lewis and M. A. Maslin, "Defining the Anthropocene," *Nature* 519 (2015): 171–80. For a critique of this view, see Jan Zalasiewicz et al., "Colonization of the Americas, 'Little Ice Age' Climate, and Bomb-Produced Carbon: Their Role in Defining the Anthropocene," *Anthropocene Review* 2, no. 2 (August 2015): 117–27.

17. Annette Kolodny, for example, has explored the cultural history of the idea that America was discovered not in 1492 by Christopher Columbus but by Leif Eiriksson and other Norsemen in the eleventh century. It is an idea, she shows, that has been fraught in the United States with racial anxieties and imperialist ambitions from colonial times to the twentieth century (see Kolodny, *In Search of First Contact: The Vikings of Vinland, the Peoples of the Dawnland, and the Anglo-American Anxiety of Discovery* [Durham, NC: Duke University Press, 2012]). For other accounts of "prediscovery," see Ivan Van Sertima, *They Came before Columbus: The African Presence in Ancient America* (New York: Random House, 2003); Rowan Gavin Paton Menzies, *1421: The Year China Discovered the World* (New York: Bantam, 2004); and Jack Forbes, *The American Discovery of Europe* (Urbana: University of Illinois Press, 2007).
18. Hans Selye, *From Dream to Discovery* (New York: McGraw-Hill, 1964), 88.
19. For the best account of Native American stories of origin with a hemispheric scope, see Gordon Brotherston, *Book of the Fourth World: Reading the Native Americas through Their Literature* (Cambridge: Cambridge University Press, 1992).
20. Augustine Brannigan, *The Social Basis of Scientific Discoveries* (Cambridge: Cambridge University Press, 1981), 121–23.
21. James Dougal Fleming, introduction to *The Invention of Discovery: Humanism, Science, and Hermeneutics,* ed. Fleming (Aldershot, UK: Ashgate, 2011), 7, 8; see also Fleming's monograph *Milton's Secrecy* (Aldershot, UK: Ashgate, 2009), 1–4.
22. Edmundo O'Gorman, "Do the Americas Have a Common History?," in *Do the Americas Have a Common History? A Critique of the Bolton Theory,* ed. Lewis Hanke, 103–11 (New York: Knopf, 1964).
23. Edmundo O'Gorman, *La idea del descubrimiento de América: Historia de esa interpretación y crítica de sus fundamentos* (Mexico City: Centro de Estudios Filosóficos, 1951); Edmundo O'Gorman, *The Invention of America* (1958; Westport, CT: Greenwood, 1972). The Spanish translation of Heidegger's *Sein und Zeit* (1927) had been published by José Gaos in 1951 in Mexico. On the encounter between Latin American intellectuals with German phenomenology, see Enrique Dussel, "Philosophy in Latin America in the Twentieth Century: Problems and Currents," in *Latin American Philosophy: Currents, Issues, Debates,* ed. Eduardo Mendieta, 11–53 (Bloomington: Indiana University Press, 2003), esp. 16–19.
24. O'Gorman, *Invention*, 129.
25. Ibid., 41.
26. Amerigo Vespucci, *Letters from a New World: Amerigo Vespucci's Discovery of America,* ed and introd. Luciano Formisano, trans. David Jacobson (New York: Marilio, 1992), 49. For a critique of O'Gorman's failure to engage with the historicity of the idea of discovery, see Marcel Bataillon, "The Idea of the Discovery of America among the Spaniards of the Sixteenth Century," in *Spain in the Fifteenth Century, 1369–1516: Essays and Extracts by Historians of Spain,* ed. J. R. Highfield, trans. F. López Morilla, 426–64 (London: Macmillan, 1972); see also Wilcomb Washburn, "The Meaning of 'Discovery' in the Fifteenth and Sixteenth

Centuries," *American Historical Review* 68, no. 1 (1962): 1–21; and Silvio Zavala, "Excursión por el Diccionario de la Academia de la Lengua, con motivo del V centenario del descubrimiento de América," *Nueva Revista de Filología Hispánica* 35, no. 1 (1987): 265–81. For O'Gorman's response to Bataillon, see Marcel Bataillon and Edmundo O'Gorman, *Dos conceptiones de la tarea histórica: Con motivo de la idea del descubrimiento de América* (Mexico City: Imprenta Universitaria, 1955). For other critiques of O'Gorman's thesis, see Iris Zavala, ed., *Discursos sobre la invención de América* (Amsterdam: Rodopi, 1992); and Luis N. Rivera, *A Violent Evangelism: The Political and Religious Conquest of the Americas* (Louisville, KY: Westminster/John Knox, 1992), 3–7.

27. In the history and philosophy of science, there is an extensive literature on the problem of discovery. Some of the milestones of this literature include Karl Popper, *The Logic of Scientific Discovery* (1935; London: Routledge, 2002); Norwood Russel Hanson, *Patterns of Discovery* (Cambridge: Cambridge University Press, 1958); David Gooding, R. J. Pinch, and Simon Schaffer, *The Uses of Experiment Studies in the Natural Sciences* (Cambridge: Cambridge University Press, 1989); and Ahron Kantorovich, *Scientific Discovery: Logic and Tinkering* (Buffalo: State University of New York Press, 1993). For a useful overview of this literature, see Ahron Kantorovich, "Scientific Discovery: A Philosophical Survey," *Philosophia* 23, no. 1–4 (1994): 3–23.

28. An exception here is David Abulafia's *The Discovery of Mankind: Atlantic Encounters in the Age of Columbus* (New Haven: Yale University Press, 2008), in which the author assumes an oddly parochial posture toward "literary," "post-modernist," and "post-colonialist" scholarship (xvi).

29. For only a few landmark examples, see Stephen Greenblatt, ed., *New World Encounters* (Berkeley: University of California Press, 1993); José Rabasa, *Inventing America: Spanish Historiography and the Formation of Eurocentrism* (Norman: University of Oklahoma Press, 1993); Jerry M. Williams and Robert E. Lewis, eds., *Early Images of the Americas: Transfer and Invention* (Tucson: University of Arizona Press, 1993); Djelal Kadir, *Columbus and the Ends of the Earth: Europe's Prophetic Rhetoric as Conquering Ideology* (Berkeley: University of California Press, 1992); and Michael Householder, *Inventing Americans in the Age of Discovery: Narratives of Encounter* (Farnham, UK: Ashgate, 2011).

30. On postcolonial critiques of the ontological erasure of indigenous knowledge, see Walter Mignolo, *The Darker Side of the Renaissance: Literacy, Territoriality, and Colonization* (Ann Arbor: University of Michigan Press, 1995); 75; Mignolo, *Local Histories/Global Designs: Coloniality, Subaltern Knowledges, and Border Thinking* (Princeton: Princeton University Press, 2000); Elizabeth Hill Boone and Walter Mignolo, eds., *Writing without Words: Alternative Literacies in Mesoamerica and the Andes* (Durham, NC: Duke University Press, 1994); and Enrique Dussel, *The Invention of the Americas: Eclipse of the Other and the Myth of Modernity* (New York: Continuum, 1995).

31. Chris Tiffin and Alan Lawson, introduction to *De-scribing Empire: Postcolonialism and Textuality,* ed. Tiffin and Lawson (London: Routledge, 1994), 3. Tiffin and Lawson were discussing English narratives about the "discovery" of Chomolungma, commonly known as Mt. Everest. On the notion of a transcultural hermeneutics, see Helen Watson-Verran and David Turnbull, "Science and Other Indigenous Knowledge Systems," in *Handbook of Science and Technology Studies,* ed. Sheila Jasanoff, Gerald E. Marble, James C. Peterson, and Trevor Pinch, 115–39 (Thousand Oaks, CA.: 1995); and David Turnbull, *Masons, Tricksters and Cartographers: Comparative Studies in the Sociology of Scientific and Indigenous Knowledge* (London: Routledge, 2000).
32. Only a few examples of this vast social history of early modern science can be mentioned here. On the role of "invisible technicians" in the Scientific Revolution, see Stephen Shapin, *A Social History of Truth: Civility and Science in Seventeenth-Century England* (Chicago: University of Chicago Press, 1994); on artisans, see Pamela Smith, *The Body of the Artisan: Art and Experience in the Scientific Revolution* (Chicago: University of Chicago Press, 2004); on merchants, see Pamela Smith and Paula Findlen, eds., *Merchants and Marvels: Commerce, Science, and Art in Early Modern Europe* (New York: Routledge, 2002).
33. Although no study of the colonial history of the idea of scientific discovery exists to my knowledge, the literature on the connections between empire and science has recently proliferated. For only a few recent examples, see Londa L. Schiebinger and Claudia Swan, eds., *Plants and Empire: Science, Commerce, and Politics in the Early Modern World* (Philadelphia: University of Pennsylvania Press, 2005); James Delbourgo and Nicholas Dew, eds., *Science and Empire in the Atlantic World* (London: Routledge, 2008); Neil Safier, *Measuring the World: Enlightenment Science and South America* (Chicago: University of Chicago Press, 2008); Harold Cook, *Matters of Exchange: Commerce, Medicine, and Science in the Dutch Golden Age* (New Haven, CT: Yale University Press, 2007); Cañizares-Esguerra, *Nature;* Nicolás Wey-Gómez, *The Tropics of Empire: Why Columbus Sailed South to the Indies* (Cambridge: MIT Press, 2008); Antonio Barrera-Osorio, *Experiencing Nature: The Spanish American Empire and the Early Scientific Revolution* (Austin: University of Texas Press, 2006); Daniela Bleichmar et al., eds., *Science in the Spanish and Portuguese Empires* (Stanford: Stanford University Press, 2009); Bleichmar, *Visible Empire: Botanical Expeditions and Visual Culture in the Hispanic Enlightenment* (Chicago: University of Chicago Press, 2012); Bleichmar, *Visual Voyages: Images of Latin American Nature from Columbus to Darwin* (New Haven: Yale University Press, 2017); Maria Portuondo, *Secret Science: Spanish Cosmography and the New World* (Chicago: University of Chicago Press, 2009); Antonio Sánchez Martínez, *La espada, la cruz y el padrón: Soberanía, fe y representación cartográfica en el mundo ibérico bajo la Monarquía Hispánica, 1503–1598* (Madrid: CSIC, 2013); and Arndt Brendecke, *Empirical Empire: Spanish Colonial Rule and the Politics of Knowledge* (Berlin: De Gruyter, 2016).

34. For a discussion of the colonial history of scientific and technological modernity in India during the eighteenth century, see Rajani Sudan, *The Alchemy of Empire: Abject Materials and the Technologies of Colonialism* (New York: Fordham University Press, 2016).
35. On the question of the uncertain or "blunted" impact of the New World on the Old, see also J. H. Elliott, *The Old World and the New, 1492–1650* (Cambridge: Cambridge University Press, 1970); Fredi Chiappelli et al., eds., *First Images of America: The Impact of the New World on the Old*, 2 vols. (Berkeley: University of California Press, 1976); Anthony Pagden, *European Encounters with the New World: From Renaissance to Romanticism* (New Haven: Yale University Press, 1993); and Felipe Fernández-Armesto, *1492: The Year the World Began* (New York: Harper Collins, 2014).
36. Stephen Greenblatt, *Marvelous Possessions: The Wonder of the New World* (Chicago: University of Chicago Press, 1991), 2, 72–73, 17–20, 7. For other accounts operating under this hermeneutic, see Beatriz Pastor Bodmer, *The Armature of Conquest: Spanish Accounts of the Discovery of America, 1492–1589* (Stanford: Stanford University Press, 1992), which presents the literary history of the European discovery as a dialectic between "mythification" and "demythification."
37. On the notion of a "second" (or multiple states of) encounter and discovery, see Susanne Burghartz, "Alt, neu oder jung? Zur Einheit der Neuen Welt," in *Die Wahrnehmung des Neuen in der Antike und Renaissance*, ed. Achatz von Müller and Jürgen von Ungern-Sternberg (Munich: Saur, 2004), 188; and Michael Giesecke, *Von den Mythen der Buchkultur zu den Visionen der Informationsgesellschaft* (Frankfurt: Suhrkamp, 2002).
38. Anthony Grafton, *New Worlds, Ancient Texts: The Power of Tradition and the Shock of Discovery* (Cambridge: Harvard University Press, 1995), 51, 54, 41; see also Grafton's *Defenders of the Text: The Traditions of Scholarship in an Age of Science 1450–1800* (Cambridge: Harvard University Press, 1991). Similarly, David Freedberg has pointed out that "science" (*scientia*) for early moderns compassed "a much larger field than it does now. It ranged from what we call the humanities to fundamental physical phenomena and to mathematics," as well as the occult sciences (9). While Grafton's argument runs counter to the Foucaultian idea of a seismic epistemic shift, Freedberg emphasizes how natural historical discourse about the New World put considerable pressure on the old world of science derived from texts (see Freedberg, *The Eye of the Lynx: Galileo, His Friends, and the Beginnings of Modern Natural History* [Chicago: University of Chicago Press, 2013]).
39. On the notion of discovery as a "hunt" for the secrets of nature, see chapters 1 and 12 of this book. On alchemy in early modern Spain, particularly at the court of Philip II, see chapter 9.
40. On the emergence of the modern idea of the secretary, see Jacques Derrida and Maurizio Ferraris, *A Taste for the Secret*, trans. Giacomo Donis, ed. Donis and David Webb (Cambridge, UK: Polity, 2001). On the history of secrecy in Western culture, especially in the technical arts, from antiquity to the early modern period,

see Pamela Long, *Openness, Secrecy, Authorship: Technical Arts and the Culture of Knowledge from Antiquity to the Renaissance* (Baltimore: Johns Hopkins University Press, 2001); and Daniel Jütte, *The Age of Secrecy: Jews, Christians, and the Economy of Secrets, 1400–1800,* trans. Jeremiah Riemer (New Haven: Yale University Press, 2015).

41. Jill Kraye, Charles B. Schmitt, and W. F. Ryan, *Pseudo-Aristotle in the Middle Ages: The Theology and Other Texts* (London: Warburg Institute, University of London, 1986); Anthony Grafton, *Forgers and Critics: Creativity and Duplicity in Western Scholarship* (London: Collins and Brown, 1990); William Newman, introduction to *The Summa Perfectionis of Pseudo-Geber: A Critical Edition, Translation, and Study* (Leiden: Brill, 1997).

42. Christopher Columbus, cited in Karl Marx, *Das Kapital: Kritik der politischen Ökonomie,* 3 vols. (Berlin: Dietz, 1983), 1:145. On Marx and alchemy, see David Holt, "Jung and Marx: Alchemy, Christianity, and the World against Nature," in *The Psychology of Carl Jung: Essays in Application and Deconstruction,* by Holt (Lewiston, NY: Mellen, 1992).

43. On the significance of gold in the Spanish conquest and imperial economy, see Elvira Vilches, *New World Gold: Cultural Anxiety and Monetary Disorder in Early Modern Spain* (Chicago: University of Chicago Press, 2010).

44. Marx, *Das Kapital,* 1:145–46. Some modern English translations have "gold" here instead of "money." However, the German original cited here has "Geld" (money), not "Gold" (gold).

45. Aristotle, *Nicomachean Ethics* 5.5 (Kitchener, Ontario: Batoche, 1999), 80.

46. Aristotle, *Metaphysics,* quoted in Richard Seaford, *Money and the Early Greek Mind: Homer, Philosophy, Tragedy* (Cambridge: Cambridge University Press, 2004), 217.

47. Seaford, *Money,* 218, 220, 221.

48. Ibid., 225.

49. Ibid., 94.

50. Marx, *Das Kapital,* 1:145.

51. There, Arnald is called a "necromancer" who was "impotent since childhood because of a scorpion bite" (García Márquez, *One Hundred Years of Solitude,* 377). I have not been able to establish the basis for this idea.

52. (Pseudo-)Arnaldus, "Rosarius philosophorum," in Jean-Jacques Manget, *Bibliotheca chemica curiosa, seu rerum ad alchemiam pertinentium thesaurus instructissimus,* 2 vols. (Geneva: Chouet, G. de Tournes, Cramer, Perachon, Ritter & S. de Tournes, 1702), 1:665. See also Titus Burckhardt, *Alchemy: Science of the Cosmos and the Soul,* trans. William Stoddart (Longmead: Element, 1986), 92–96.

53. See Lyndy Abraham, *A Dictionary of Alchemical Imagery* (Cambridge: Cambridge University Press, 1998), 138.

54. See William Newmann, *Atoms and Alchemy: Chymistry and the Experimental Origins of the Scientific Revolution* (Chicago: University of Chicago Press, 2006), 35–44; Newman, *Gehennical Fire: The Lives of George Starkey. An American Alchemist in the Scientific Revolution* (Chicago: University of Chicago Press, 1994);

Lawrence Principe, *The Secrets of Alchemy* (Chicago: University of Chicago Press, 2013); W. Newman and L. Principe, *Alchemy Tried in the Fire: Starkey: Boyle, and the Fate of Helmontian Chymistry* (Chicago: University of Chicago Press, 2002); and Gideon Manning, *Matter and Form in Early Modern Science and Philosophy* (Leiden: Brill, 2012).

55. Marx, *Das Kapital,* 1:146–47.
56. Ibid., 147.
57. Pamela Smith, *The Business of Alchemy. Science and Culture in the Holy Roman Empire* (Princeton: Princeton University Press, 1994), 5–6.
58. Karen Pinkus, *Alchemical Mercury: A Theory of Ambivalence* (Stanford: Stanford University Press, 2010), 8–10; and Michael Nerlich, *The Ideology of Adventure,* 2 vols. (Minneapolis: University of Minnesota Press, 1995), 1:29, 43, 60, 71.
59. Augustine, *The Confessions,* ed. Albert Cook Outler (Louisville, KY: Westminster Press, 1955), 233.
60. On the significance of alchemy in the history of modern science, see Bruce Moran, *Distilling Knowledge: Alchemy, Chemistry, and the Scientific Revolution* (Cambridge: Harvard University Press, 2005); William Eamon, *Science and the Secrets of Nature: Books of Secrets in Medieval and Early Modern Culture* (Princeton: Princeton University Press, 1994); William Newman and Anthony Grafton, eds., *Secrets of Nature: Astrology and Alchemy in Early Modern Europe* (Cambridge: MIT Press, 2001); William Newman, "From Alchemy to 'Chymistry,'" in Lorraine Daston and Katheirne Park, *The Cambridge History of Science,* vol. 3: *Early Modern Science* (Cambridge: Cambridge University Press, 2006), 497; Newman, *Atoms and Alchemy;* Newman, *Gehennical Fire;* Lawrence Principe, *The Secrets of Alchemy* (Chicago: University of Chicago Press, 2013); W. Newman and L. Principe, *Alchemy Tried in the Fire;* Smith, *The Business of Alchemy;* Pamela Smith, *The Body of the Artisan: Art and Experience in the Scientific Revolution* (Chicago: University of Chicago Press, 2004); Chiara Crisciani, *From the Laboratory to the Library: Alchemy According to Guglielmo Fabri* (Cambridge: MIT Press, 1999); and Tara Nummedal, *Alchemy and Authority in the Holy Roman Empire* (Chicago: University of Chicago Press, 2007).
61. Giorgio Agamben, *State of Exception,* trans. Kevin Attell (Chicago: University of Chicago Press, 2005), 41, 25.
62. Schmitt, *The "Nomos" of the Earth in the International law of the "Jus Publicum Europaeum,"* trans. and annotated G. L. Ulmen (New York: Telos, 2003), 131.
63. Carl Schmitt, *The "Nomos,"* 86. It must be pointed out here that, despite Schmitt's many interesting insights, he has also rightly been critiqued for some of his Eurocentric ideas (to say nothing of his affiliations with Nazism) (see Peter Sloterdijk, "The Signs of the Explorers: On Cartography and Imperial Name Magic," in *In the World Interior of Capital* [Cambridge, UK: Polity, 2013], EBL digital edition, n.p.; and Stephen Legg, ed. *Spatiality, Sovereignty, and Carl Schmitt: Geographies of the Nomos* [London: Routledge, 2011]).

64. Schmitt, *The "Nomos,"* 92.
65. Ibid.
66. On the role that the idea of the "void" played in seventeenth-century matter theory, see Antonio Clericuzio, *Elements, Principles, and Corpuscles: A Study of Atomism and Chemistry in the Seventeenth Century* (Dordrecht: Kluwer, 2000).
67. Hugo Grotius, *The Free Sea*, trans. Richard Hakluyt, ed. David Armitage (Indianapolis: Liberty Fund, 2014), 13–14. On Grotius, see Richard Tuck, *The Rights of War and Peace: Political Thought and the International Order from Grotius to Kant* (Oxford: Oxford University Press, 1999), 78–108.
68. Fritz Bleiber, *Die Entdeckung im Völkerrecht: Eine Studie zum Problem der Okkupation* (Greifswald: Universitätsverlag Ratsbuchhandlung L. Bamberg, 1933), 21. On the concept of "occupation," see Fitzmaurice, *Sovereignty*, 33–58.
69. Luis Weckmann-Muñoz, *Las bulas alejandrinas de 1493 y la teoría política del papado medieval: Estudio de la supremacia papal sobre islas, 1091–1493* (Mexico City: Universidad Nacional Autónoma de México, 1949), 27–33; see also Manuel Giménez Fernández, *Nuevas consideraciones sobre la historia, sentido, y valor de las bulas Alejandrinas de 1493 referentes a las Indias* (Seville: Consejo Superior de Investigaciones Científicas Escuela de Estudios Hispano-Americanos de la Universidad de Sevilla, 1944); Pedro de Leturia, "Las grandes bulas misionales de Alejandro VI, 1493," *Biblioteca Hispana Missionum* (Barcelona, 1930), 211–51; Miguel Batllori, *Del descubrimiento a la independencia: Estudios sobre Iberoámerica y Filipinas* (Caracas: Universidad Católica Andrés Bello, 1979); James Muldoon, *Popes, Lawyers, and Infidels: The Church and the Non-Christian World, 1250–1550* (Philadelphia: University of Pennsylvania Press, 1979); and Muldoon, *Empire and Order: The Concept of Empire, 800–1800* (Houndmills, Basingstoke, Hampshire: Macmillan, 1999).
70. See Katherine Walsh, *Richard FitzRalph in Oxford, Avignon, and Armagh: A Fourteenth-Century Scholar and Primate* (Oxford: Clarendon, 1981); and Stephen Lahey, *Metaphysics and Politics in the Thought of John Wyclif* (Cambridge: Cambridge University Press, 2003), esp. 68–107; see also Lahey, *John Wyclif* (Oxford: Oxford Univeristy Prss, 2009), esp. 199–221; Gordon Leff, *Bradwardine and the Pelagians* (Cambridge: Cambridge University Press, 1957); Leff, "The Place of Metaphysics in Wycliff's Theology," in *From Ockham to Wyclif*, ed. A. Hudson and M. Wilks, *SCH* Subsida 5 (Oxford: Published for the Ecclesiastical History Society by B. Blackwell, 1987), 217–31. On Fitzralph, see Leff, *Richard Fitzralph, Commentator of the Sentences: A Study in Theological Orthodoxy* (Manchester, UK: Manchester University Press, 1963).
71. See Silvio Zavala, introduction to *"De las islas del mar Océano," por Juan López de Palacios Rubios y "Del dominio de los Reyes de España sobre los indios," por Fray Matias de Paz* (Mexico City: Fondo de Cultura Económica, 1954), ix–cxxx; see also Zavala, *New Viewpoints on the Spanish Colonization of America* (Philadelphia: University of Pennsylvania Press, 1943), 6–7; Zavala, *Las instituciones jurídicas en la conquista de América* (Madrid: Centro de Estudios Históricos, 1953);

and Patricia Seed, *Ceremonies of Possession in Europe's Conquest of the New World, 1492–1640* (Cambridge: Cambridge University Press, 1995).

72. See Muldoon, *Popes,* 6, 47; and David Traboulay, *Columbus and Las Casas: The Conquest and Christianization of America, 1492–1566* (Lanham, MD: University Press of America, 1994), 85–91.

73. See Francis Oakley, *The Conciliarist Tradition: Constitutionalism in the Catholic Church, 1300–1870* (Oxford: Oxford University Press, 2003), 60–110; Heiko Oberman, *The Harvest of Medieval Theology: Gabriel Biel and Late Medieval Nominalism,* rev. ed. (Grand Rapids, MI: Eerdmans, 1967); Oberman, "Via Antigua and Via Moderna: Late Medieval Prolegomena to Early Reformation Thought," *Journal of the History of Ideas* 48 (1987): 23–40; Oberman, *The Two Reformations: The Journey from the Last Days to the New World* (New Haven: Yale University Press, 2003), 21–43. On nominalism and the conquest of America, see also Pedro Leturia in "Maior y Vitoria ante la conquista de América," *Conferencia Anual de la Asociación Francisco de Vitoria* III (1930–31): 43–83; Venancio Diego Carro, in *La teología y los teólogos-juristas españoles ante la conquista de América* (Salamanca: Apartado, 1951), 287–92; and Anthony Pagden, *The Fall of Natural Man: The American Indian and the Origins of Comparative Ethnology* (Cambridge: Cambridge University Press, 1982), 27–56, esp. 39.

74. See Ernst Kantorowicz, introduction to *Las bulas alejandrinas de 1493 y la teoría política del Papado medieval: Estudio de la supremacía papal sobre islas, 1091–1493,* by Luis Weckmann-Muñoz (Mexico City: DF UNAM, 1949), 8. Incidentally, Kantorowiczs's (and Weckmann-Muñoz's) point sheds a comic light on Buendía's dismay at and obsession with the hybrid or "peninsular" ontology of Macondo ("La idea de un Macondo peninsular," in García Márquez, *Cien años,* 7). On the relationship between insularity and colonialism, see Antonio Benítez Rojo, *La isla que se repite: El Caribe y la perspectiva postmoderna,* rev. ed. (San Juan, Puerto Rico: Editorial Plaza Mayor, 2010).

75. See John Boyd Thacher, *Christopher Columbus: His Life, His Works,* 3 vols. (New York: G. P. Putnam's Sons, 1903), 2:86n1.

76. Although Peter Martyr's *De orbe novo* would not be published until 1511, it was written as a series of private letters the earliest of which dates from 1493.

77. Miguel Batllori, "The Papal Division of the World and Its Consequences," in *First Images of America: The Impact of the New World on the Old,* ed. Fredi Chiappelli et al., 2 vols. (Berkeley: University of California Press, 1976), 1:217. Indeed, as Batllori notes, from the point of view of the Catholic Monarchs, the significance of Alexander's *Inter cetera* bulls seems to have mainly been in their creation of a break of the long fifteenth-century tradition of similar bulls by which the Popes Martin V (*Sieut carissimus,* 1418), Eugene IV (*Cum dudm,* 1433), Nicholas V (*Romanus pontifex,* 1455), Calixtus III (*Inter cetera,* 1456), and Sixtus IV (*Aeterni regis,* 1481) had granted the Portuguese monarchs titles to the lands and islands that their sailors had "discovered" during their exploration of the African coast line. Portugal's claims to all lands to the south of Cape Bojador in Africa had been recognized by

the Catholic Monarchs themselves in the Treaty of Alcáçobas, which was based on Calixtus's bull *Inter cetera* and reaffimred by Sixtus's *Aeterni Regis*. The Treaty of Tordesillas appeared to have successfully resolved the dispute between Spain and Portugal by revising the terms of Alcáçobas and of *Inter cetera* to mutual satisfaction, at least for the moment. See also Wey-Gómez, *The Tropics of Empire*, 105–6, 308–13.

78. Francisco de Vitoria, "On the American Indians," in *Political Writings*, ed. and trans. Anthony Pagden and Jeremy Lawrance (Cambridge: Cambridge University Press, 1991), 264–65; my emphasis. On Vitoria, see chapter 8 of this book; on his legacy, see Benton and Strauman, "Acquiring," 20–29; Anthony Pagden, *Lords of All the World: Ideologies of Empire in Spain, Britain and France c. 1500–c. 1800* (New Haven: Yale University Press, 1995), 46–61; and Robert Williams, *The American Indian in Western Legal Thought: The Discourses of Conquest* (New York: Oxford University Press, 1990), 96–97. On the School of Salamanca, see Bernice Hamilton, *Political Thought in Sixteenth-Century Spain: A Study of the Political Ideas of Vitoria, De Soto, Suárez, and Molina* (Oxford: Clarendon, 1963); and J. A. Fernández-Santamaria, *The State, War, and Peace: Spanish Political Thought in the Renaissance, 1516–1559* (Cambridge: Cambridge University Press, 1977). On the history and literary history of this early modern debate, see Zavala, *Las instituciones jurídicas;* Rolena Adorno, *The Polemics of Possession in Spanish American Narrative* (New Haven: Yale University Press, 2007), 101–24; and Pagden, *The Fall of Natural Man*, 27–56.

79. George Edward Ellis, *The Indians of Eastern Massachusetts* (Boston: Massachusetts Historical Society, 1885), 248; Peter Oliver, *The Puritan Commonwealth* (Boston: Little, Brown, 1856), 102. On the debate about the rights of "occupation" from the sixteenth century onward, see Fitzmaurice, *Sovereignty;* see also Ken MacMillan, *Sovereignty and Possession in the English New World: The Legal Foundations of Empire, 1576–1640* (Cambridge: Cambridge University Press, 2006). For a discussion of the history of the use of "vacuum domicilium," see Paul Corcoran, "John Locke on the Possession of Land: Native Title vs. the 'Principle' of *Vacuum domicilium*," Proceedings, Australasian Political Studies Association Annual Conference 2007, refereed paper, Social and Political Theory Stream, Australasian Political Studies Association and Monash University, September, 24–26, 2007, http://arts.monash.edu.au/psi/news-and-events/apsa/refereed-papers/political-theory/corcoran.pdf.

80. "The Bull Inter Caetera," in *European Treaties Bearing on the History of the United States and Its Dependencies to 1648*, ed. Francis Gardiner Davenport (Washington, DC: Carnegie Institution of Washington, 1917), 58, 73.

81. See Leturia, "Las grandes bulas," 224.

82. Ibid., 250.

83. Ibid., 118.

84. On the massive resettlement undertaking in the Viceroyalty of Peru in the 1570s under viceroy Francisco de Toledo, see Jeremy Ravi Mumford, *Vertical Empire:*

The General Resettlement of Indians in the Colonial Andes (Durham, NC: Duke University Press, 2012). On the comparison between the early American reductions and the modern concentration camp, see David Stannard, "Uniqueness as Denial: The Politics of Genocide Scholarship," in *Is the Holocaust Unique? Perspectives on Comparative Genocide,* ed. Alan Rosenbaum (Boulder, CO: Westview, 2009), 311; Stannard, *American Holocaust;* and Mark Sutton, *An Introduction to Native North America* (Boston: Pearson, 2012), 44. On the debate about "genocide" in early America, see George E. Tinker, *Missionary Conquest: The Gospel and Native American Cultural Genocide* (Minneapolis: Fortress, 1993). Tinker uses the phrase "cultural genocide" to distinguish the early American missionary projects from those of outright "military extermination," which are nevertheless "no less devastating to a people" (5). See also Clark University, "Ned Blackhawk: Colonial Genocides in Native North America—Varying Methods and Approaches" (2016), Clark University Event Archive, 232; http://commons.clarku.edu/videoarchive/232; and Ned Blackhawk, *Violence over the Land: Indians and Empires in the Early American West* (Cambridge: Harvard University Press, 2006). For the Latin American context, see Alfonso García Isaza, "Nueva leyenda negra," *Boletín de historia y antiquidades* 776 (February-March 1992); Antonio Cacua Prada, "Religión y lengua, fundamentos de la unidad Iberoamericana," in *Actas il congreso de academias iberoamericanistas de la historia, 1992,* ed. Juan Pérez de Tudela (Madrid: Taravilla, 1994), 135–50; and Rivera, *A Violent Evangelism,* 52.

85. Nicholas Goodrick-Clarke, *Black Sun: Aryan Cults, Esoteric Nazism, and the Politics of Identity* (New York: New York University Press, 2002), 145.
86. Schmitt, *The "Nomos,"* 93–94. On Hobbes, see Tuck, *The Rights of War and Peace,* 109–39. Thomas Hobbes stated that even hard bodies are composed of parts which are in continuous and rapid motion: "Durissima corpora illa sunt in quibus partium motus et velocissimus est, et intra spatia brevissima" (*Problemata Physica,* 1662, in T. Hobbes, *Opera philosophica,* 5 vols. [London, 1839–45], 4:333–41); see also Clericuzio, *Elements,* 95 (on Hobbes).
87. On the influence of the pre-Socratic "atomist" tradition of Thucydides and Democritus on Hobbes's political philosophy, see Alexander Lyubishchev, *Lines of Democritus and Plato in the History of Culture* (St. Petersburg: Altheia, 2000); see also Oleg Bazaluk, *The Theory of War and Peace: The Geophilosophy of Europe* (Plaats: Uitgever, 2017), 15–16, 124–30; and Richard E. Flathman, *Thomas Hobbes: Skepticism, Individuality, and Chastened Politics* (Lanham, MD: Rowman and Littlefield, 2002).
88. Michel Foucault, "Of Other Spaces: Utopias and Heterotopias," *Diacritics* (Spring 1986): 23–27. See also Micol Seigel, Lessie Jo Frazier, and David Sartorius, "The Spatial Politcs of Radical Change, an Introduction," *Transnational American Studies* 4, no. 2 (2012), online.
89. Foucault, "Of Other Spaces," 24.
90. For example, as Jeremy Ravi Mumford points out, the "grid" of modern urban landscapes originated not in Europe but in America, when millions of Indians in

the Andes were resettled in artificially created towns (*reducciones*) and their ancestral villages destroyed (see Ravi Mumford, *Vertical Empire,* 41–52).
91. See Seigel, Frazier, and Sartorius, "The Spatial Politics."
92. For the medieval background on this debate, see Richard Tuck, *Natural Rights Theories: Their Origin and Development* (New York: Cambridge University Press, 1979); Harold Johnson, ed., *The Medieval Tradition of Natural Law* (Kalamazoo, MI: Medieval Institute Publications, 1987); and Brian Tierney, *The Idea of Natural Rights* (Atlanta: Scholars, 1997). On its (early) modern legacy, see Quentin Skinner, *The Foundations of Modern Political Thought,* 2 vols. (Cambridge: Cambridge University Press, 1978), 2:135–73; and Marco Sgarbi, ed., *Francisco Suárez and His Legacy: The Impact of Suarezian Metaphysics and Epistemology on Modern Philosophy* (Milan: Vita e Pensiero–Largo A. Gemelli, 2010).
93. On the role that the Franciscan poverty controversy played in late medieval debate about dominion, see Annabel Brett, *Liberty, Right, and Nature: Individual Rights in Later Scholastic Thought* (Cambridge: Cambridge University Press, 1997); on the legacies of this debate in Franciscan America, see Julia McClure, *The Franciscan Invention of the New World* (Cham: Springer International, 2016), esp. 23–48.
94. Latour, *We Have Never Been Modern,* 10–15.
95. Ibid., 71, 37.
96. Ibid., 97, 30–31.
97. On Hobbes's significance for the development of the law of nations, see David Armitage, "Hobbes and the Foundations of Modern International Thought," in *Rethinking the Foundations of Modern Political Thought,* ed. Annabel Brett, James Tully, and Holly Hamilton Bleakley (Cambridge: Cambridge University Press, 2006), 219–35.
98. Ibid., 38, 99. On the colonial nexus of this constitution, especially in terms of peripheries and "centers of calculation" as well as "immobile mobiles," see also Latour, *Science in Action: How to Follow Scientists and Engineers through Society* (Cambridge: Harvard University Press, 1987), 215–57.
99. Sandra Harding critiques Latour for his failure to engage with both feminist and postcolonial studies in *Science from Below: Feminisms, Postcolonialities, and Modernities* (Durham, NC: Duke University Press, 2008), 36, 42–43. In fact, in *Science in Action,* Latour did discuss European colonialism in an eighteenth-century context, especially with regard to "centers of calculation" and "immobile mobiles" (215–57), but he does not address the sixteenth-century Spanish conquest of America.
100. According to the *Oxford English Dictionary Online,* the verb "to entangle" means "to intertwist (threads, branches, or the like) complicatedly or confusedly together; to intertwist the threads or parts of (a thing) in this way." On the trope of entanglement in recent historiography, see Ralph Bauer and Marcy Norton, introduction to "Entangled Trajectories: Indigenous and European Histories," special issue, *Colonial Latin American Review* 26, no. 1 (March 2017): 1–17.

101. Richard Eden, *The Decades of the newe worlde or west India* (London: William Powell, 1555), 160r.
102. Ibid., 157r.
103. Ibid., 16r.
104. The emphasis on Protestantism (and Puritanism in particular) in the history of modern science has a long tradition that has its roots in Max Weber's seminal *The Protestant Ethic and the Spirit of Capitalism,* first published in 1905. Inspired by Weber's work, the Anglo-American sociologist of science Robert K. Merton argued for a strong connection between the simultaneous rise of Puritanism and of scientific empiricism in seventeenth-century England in his *Science, Technology and Society in Seventeenth Century England* (1970 [1938]) and later in his *The Sociology of Science* (1977). On the impact and legacy of the so-called Merton Thesis, see R. Hooykass, *Religion and the Rise of Modern Science* (Grand Rapids, MI: Eerdmans, 1972); see also the special issue of *Science in Context* devoted to the Merton Thesis (3, no. 1 [1989]). The connection between the Protestant Reformation and the Scientific Revolution has recently been reinforced by Peter Harrison's seminal *The Bible, Protestantism, and the Rise of Natural Science* (Cambridge: Cambridge University Press, 1998), in which he argued that the "major catalyst in the emergence of science" was the "Protestant approach to the interpretation of texts" (8), specifically Protestantism's assault on the allegorical interpretation of texts and nature, which facilitated "a new conception of the order of nature" (4) as understood by modern science. While Harrison is certainly correct that the rise of modern science must be seen in connection with the history of textual (especially biblical) hermeneutics, he fails to consider not only the important role that the allegorical interpretation of nature played in legitimating naturalist inquiry during the Middle Ages but also that the skepticism toward allegory did not arise with (and was not confined to) the Protestant Reformation, which was but a (admittedly very successful) iteration of a long tradition of Christian reform (see Gordon Leff, *The Dissolution of the Medieval Outlook: An Essay on the Intellectual and Spiritual Change in the 14th Century* [New York: New York University Press, 1976]).
105. Navarro Brotóns and Eamon, introduction to *Más allá de la leyenda negra,* 27–40. See also Cañizares-Esguerra, *Puritan Conquistadors;* and Cañizares-Esguerra, *Nature.*
106. For an example of how the notion of an epochal break informed the historiography on early American science, see Raymond Phineas Stearns, *Science in the British Colonies of America* (Urbana: University of Illinois Press, 1970), who distinguishes between an "Old" (i.e., Spanish) and a "New" (i.e., "British") scientific tradition in the Americas. Other seminal works on early American science, such as Silvio Bedini's *Thinkers and Tinkers: Early American Men of Science* (New York: Scribner's, 1975), do not deal with Spanish contributions to modern science at all. More recent important studies, such as Joyce Chaplin's *Subject Matter: Technology, the Body, and Science on the Anglo-American Frontier, 1500–1676* (Cambridge:

Harvard University Press, 2001), acknowledge the importance of sixteenth-century Spanish science in the Americas but do not give it an extensive treatment.
107. Juan Rodríguez Freyle, *El Carnero*, prologue, notes, and chronology by Dario Achury Valenzuela (Caracas: Biblioteca Ayacucho, n.d. [1979]), 38, 50, 56, 37.
108. Dario Achury Valenzuela, prologue to Juan Rodríguez Freyle, *El carnero*, prologue, notes, and chronology by Valenzuela (Caracas: Biblioteca Ayacucho, n.d. [1979]), LVII.
109. Roberto González Echevarría, *Myth and Archive: A Theory of Latin American Narrative* (Cambridge: Cambridge University Press, 1990), 90.
110. Rodríguez Freyle, *El carnero*, 71–72.
111. Ibid., 74.
112. See Claudio Sánchez-Albornoz, *España y el Islam* (Buenos Aires: Editorial Sudamericana, 1943), esp. 181–99; James Phelan, *The Millennial Kingdom of the Franciscans in the New World* (Berkeley: University of California Press, 1970), 18–19; Georges Baudot, "Los precursores Franciscanos de Sahagún del siglo XIII al siglo XVI en Asia y América," *Estudios de Cultura Náhuatl* 32 (2001): 159–73; Luis Weckmann-Muñoz, *The Medieval Heritage of Mexico* (New York: Fordham University Press, 1992); Bataillon, *Erasmo;* José Antonio Maravall, "La utopia político-religiosa de los Franciscanos en Nueva España," *Estudios Americanos* 2 (1949): 199–227; Osvaldo Pardo, *The Origins of Mexican Catholicism: Nahua Rituals and Christian Sacraments in Sixteenth-Century Mexico* (Ann Arbor: University of Michigan Press, 2007); and Jaime Marroquín Arredondo, *Diálogos con Quetzalcóatl: Humanismo, etnografía y ciencia (1492–1577)* (Madrid: Iberoamericana Vervuert, 2014).
113. James Holstun, *A Rational Millennium: Puritan Utopias of Seventeenth-Century England and America* (New York: Oxford University Press, 1987).
114. David Hill Scott, "From Boston to the Baltic: New England, Encyclopedics, and the Hartlib Circle" (PhD diss., University of Notre Dame, 2003); Sarah Rivett, *The Science of the Soul in Colonial New England* (Chapel Hill and Colonial Williamsburg: University of North Carolina Press for the Omohundro Institute of Early American History and Culture, 2011). On the Renaissance background of missionary linguistics, see also Robert Young, *Comenius and the Indians of New England* (London: School of Slavonic and East European Studies in the University of London, Kings College, 1929); and Allison Bigelow, "Imperial Translations: New World Missionary Linguistics, Indigenous Interpreters, and Universal Languages in the Early Modern Era," in *American Literature and the New Puritan Studies*, ed. Bryce Traister, 93–110 (New York: Cambridge University Press, 2017); on the Hartlib Circle, see also Mark Greenglass, Michael Leslie, and Timothy Raylot, *Samuel Hartlib and Universal Reformation: Studies in Intellectual Communication* (Cambridge: Cambridge University Press, 1994); and Richard Yeo, *Notebooks, English Virtuosi, and Early Modern Science* (Chicago: University of Chicago Press, 2014).
115. Hill Scott, *From Boston to the Baltic*, 38.

116. Howard Hotson, *Paradise Postponed: Johann Heinrich Alsted and the Birth of Calvinist Millenarianism* (Dordrecht: Kluwer Academic, 2000), 79–80.
117. J. T. Young, *Faith, Alchemy and Natural Philosophy: Johann Moriaen, Reformed Intelligencer, and the Hartlib Circle* (Aldershot, UK: Ashgate, 1998); see also Newman, *Gehennical Fire,* 54–84.
118. Walter Woodward, *Prospero's America: John Winthrop, Jr., Alchemy, and the Creation of New England Culture, 1606–1676* (Chapel Hill and Williamsburg, VA: University of North Carolina Press for the Omohundro Institute of Early American History and Culture, 2009), esp. 93–137.

1. The Hermeneutics of Secrecy

1. See the *OED* entry for the word "to discover"; see also Sebastián Covarrubias's *Tesoro de la lengua castellana* (1611), which has the following entry on *descubrir*: "manifestar lo que estava cubierto. . . . Vale hallar cosas nuevas, o tierras antes no conocidas, como el descubrimiento de las Indias. Descubrir tierra, es inquirir lo que puedo aver en un negocio, como hazen en la Guerra los Adalides, que van delante a enterarse de lo que ay: dichos en la sagrada Escritura Exploradores, que yvan delante del pueblo de Dios a descubrir la tierra." For a discussion of the various early modern meanings of the word "to discover" in Spanish and Portuguese, see Francisco Machado, *História da expansão Portuguesa no mundo,* ed. António Baião (Lisbon, 1937), 55; Samuel Eliot Morison, *Portuguese Voyages to America in the Fifteenth Century* (1940; New York: Octagon, 1965), 5–10; Armando Cortesao, *"Descobrimento" e descobrimentos* (Coimbra: Junta de Investigações do Ultramar, 1972), 3–6; and Silvio Zavala, "Excursión por el Diccionario de la Academia de la Lengua, con motivo del V Centenario del Descubrimiento de América," *Nueva Revista de Filología Hispánica* 35, no. 1 (1987): 265–81.
2. Roger French and Andrew Cunningham, *Before Science: The Invention of the Friars' Natural Philosophy* (Aldershot, UK: Scholar Press, 1996), 19.
3. Aristotle, *Metaphysics,* trans. and introd. Hugh Lawson-Tancred (London: Penguin, 1998), 4.
4. See Edward Grant, *The Foundation of Modern Science in the Middle Ages: Their Religious, Institutional, and Intellectual Contexts* (Cambridge: Cambridge University Press, 1996); and Stephen Gaukroger, *The Emergence of a Scientific Culture: Science and the Shaping of Modernity, 1210–1685* (Oxford: Clarendon, 2006).
5. On the various Aristotelian traditions of discovery, see also R. J. Hankinson, "Science," *The Cambridge Companion to Aristotle,* ed. Jonathan Barnes (Cambridge: Cambridge University Press, 1995), 140–67; Jonathan Barnes, "Aristotle's Theory of Demonstration," in *Articles on Aristotle,* ed. Barnes, Malcolm Schonfield, and Ricard Sorabji, vol. 1: *Science* (London: Duckworth, 1975), 65–87; and Chumaru Koyama, ed., *Nature in Medieval Thought: Some Approaches East and West* (Leiden: Brill, 2000).

6. See French and Cunningham, *Before Science*, 19–24.
7. See Giacinta Spinosa, "*Translatio Studiorum* through Philosophical Terminology," in *Translatio Studiorum: Ancient, Medieval, and Modern Bearers of Intellectual History*, ed. Marco Sgarbi (Leiden: Brill, 2012), 80; and Tullio Gregory, *La "reductio Artium" da Cassiodoro a S. Bonaventura* (Citta De Castello: Società Poligrafica Editoriale, 1964). On the Franciscan intellectual tradition, see Ilia Delio, O.S.F, "The Franciscan Intellectual Tradition: Contemporary Concerns," in *Franciscan Intellectual Tradition: Tracing Its Origins*, ed. Kenan B. Osborne et al., 1–19 (St. Bonaventure, NY: Franciscan Institute, St. Bonaventure University, 2003).
8. Thomas Aquinas, *Summa theologiae* (New York: Cosimo Classics, 2007), 1334.
9. Ibid., 1295.
10. On the history of metaphysical nominalism, see Heiko Oberman, *The Harvest of Medieval Theology: Gabriel Biel and Late Medieval Nominalism.* (Cambridge: Harvard University Press, 1963); Vicente Muñoz Delgado, *La lógica nominalista en la Universidad de Salamanca (1510–1530)* (Madrid: Publicaciones del Monasterio de Poyo, 1964); Gordon Leff, *The Dissolution of the Medieval Outlook: An Essay on Intellectual and Spiritual Change in the Fourteenth Century* (New York: New York University Press, 1976); and David Lindberg and Ronald Numbers, eds., *When Science and Christianity Meet* (Chicago: University of Chicago Press, 2002).
11. See Heiko Oberman, *The Two Reformations: The Journey from the Last Days to the New World*, ed. Donald Weinstein (New Haven: Yale University Press, 2003), 6–8. On Duns Scotus and Ockham, see Leff, *Dissolution;* on the late medieval intersections between religion, science, and metaphysics more generally, see Lindberg and Numbers, *When Science and Christianity Meet*. On Gerson and d'Ailly, see Francis Oakley, *The Political Throught of Pierre d'Ailly: The Voluntarist Tradition* (New Haven: Yale University Press, 1964).
12. David Herlihy, *The Black Death and the Transformation of the West* (Cambridge: Harvard University Press, 1997), 72.
13. Oberman, *The Two Reformations*, 8.
14. See Oberman, *The Harvest of Medieval Theology*.
15. Oberman's division of late medieval thought into metaphysical realism and nominalism has been criticized recently by scholars who have pointed out that many late medieval theologians straddled this division or that their position in the *Wegestreit* often depended on the subject matter on which they wrote (see Maarten Hoenen, "Via Antiqua and Via Moderna in the Fifteenth Century: Doctrinal, Institutional, and Church Political Factors in the *Wegestreit*," in *The Medieval Heritage in Early Modern Metaphysics and Modal Theory, 1400–1700*, ed. Russell L. Friedman and Lauge O. Nielsen [Dordrecht: Kluwer, 2003], 9–36). Nevertheless, Oberman's schema remains conceptually useful for my purposes here. On nominalism at Salamanca, see Muñoz Delgado, *La lógica nominalista*.
16. See note 38 in the introduction to this book.

17. Charles Schmitt, *Aristotle and the Renaissance* (Cambridge: Harvard University Press, 1983); Christoph Lüthy, Cees Leijenhorst, and Johannes M. M. H. Thijssen, "The Tradition of Aristotelian Natural Philosophy: Two Theses and Seventeen Answers," in *The Dynamics of Aristotelian Natural Philosophy from Antiquity to the Seventeenth Century,* ed. Leijenhorst, Lüthy, and Thijssen, 1–29 (Leiden: Brill, 2002).
18. The classic study of Domingo de Soto's "regressus theory" and its influence on Galileo is Pierre Duhem, *Études sur Léonard de Vinci* (Paris: Hermann, 1913), but for more recent treatments, see William Wallace, *Domingo de Soto and the Early Galileo* (Aldershot, UK: Ashgate, 2005), esp. 113–29; and Wallace, *Galileo's Logic of Discovery and Proof: The Background, Content, and Use of His Appropriated Treatises on Aristotle's "Posterior Analytics"* (Dordrecht: Kluwer Academic, 1992). On the Neo-Aristotelian School of Padua, see John Randall, *The School of Padua and the Emergence of Modern Science* (Padua: Editrice Antenore, 1961); and Heikki Mikkeli, *An Aristotelian Response to Humanism: Jacopo Zabarella on the Nature of Arts and Sciences* (Helsinki: SHS, 1992). On Galileo, see Freedberg, *The Eye of the Lynx.*
19. Gaukroger, *Emergence,* 163; also 161–65. On Polydore Vergil's notion of discovery, see Brian Copenhaver, "The Historiography of Discovery in the Renaissance: The Sources and Composition of Polydore Vergil's *De inventoribus rerum, I–III,*" *Journal of the Warburg and Courtauld Institutes* 41 (1978): 192–214. On Ramus, see Walter Ong, *Ramus, Method, and the Decay of Dialogue: From the Art of Discourse to the Art of Reason* (1983; Chicago: University of Chicago Press, 2005).
20. Stephen Shapin and Simon Shaffer, *Leviathan and the Air-Pump: Hobbes, Boyle, and the Experimental Life: Including a Translation of Thomas Hobbes, Dialogus physicus de natura aeris by Simon Schaffer* (Princeton: Princeton University Press, 1985). On the early modern history of the notion of discovery, see also Nicholas Jardine, "Epistemology of the Sciences," in *The Cambridge History of Renaissance Philosophy,* ed. Charles Schmitt, Quentin Skinner, Eckhard Kessler, and Jill Kraye, 685–711 (Cambridge: Cambridge University Press, 1988); and Neal W. Gilbert, *Renaissance Concepts of Method* (New York: Columbia University Press, 1960). On Bacon's idea of discovery in particular, see Lisa Jardine, *Francis Bacon: Discovery and the Art of Discourse* (Cambridge: Cambridge University Press, 1974), esp. 76–132.
21. See Ahron Kantorovich, *Scientific Discovery: Logic and Tinkering* (Buffalo: State University of New York Press, 1993), 4.
22. On the humanist notion of discovery as a "hermeneutics of recognition," see Hans Georg Gadamer, *Truth and Method* (1960; York: Continuum, 2004), esp. 113. Gadamer built on the Heidegger's critique in *Sein und Zeit* (1927; Frankfurt: Vittorio Klostermann, 1976). On the history of the modern distinction between truth and fiction, see Luiz Costa Lima, *The Control of the Imaginary: Reason and Imagination in Modern Times* (Minneapolis: University of Minnesota Press, 1989).
23. See the introduction of this book.

24. Aristotle, *Metaphysics*, 59.
25. Stephen Greenblatt, *Marvelous Possessions: The Wonder of the New World* (Chicago: University of Chicago Press, 1991). Greenblatt maintains that this acquisitiveness derives from the concept of discovery in natural law, according to which an uninhabited territory (*terra nullius*) and a thing without an owner (*res nullius*) "become the possession of the first to discover them" (60). But as pointed out in the introduction of this book, the Roman law concept of *terra nullius* was not generally applied to the Americas until the eighteenth century.
26. Peter Sloterdijk, "The Signs of the Explorers: On Cartography and Imperial Name Magic," in *In the World Interior of Capital* (Cambridge, UK: Polity, 2013), EBL digital edition.
27. Ibid. For Martin Heidegger, the modern age first manifested itself in the conquest of the world as picture. "Whenever we have a world picture," Heidegger wrote, "an essential decision occurs concerning beings as a whole. The beings of beings is sought and found in the representedness of beings.... The world picture does not change from an earlier medieval to a modern one; rather, that the world becomes picture at all is what distinguishes the essence of modernity.... To be 'new' belongs to a world that has become picture" (Martin Heidegger, "The Age of World Picture," in *The Question Concerning Technology and Other Essays*, by Heidegger, trans. William Lovitt [New York: Harper and Row, 1977], 115–54).
28. Thus, as Lorraine Daston and Katherine Park have explained, in the High Middle Ages, "wonder existed apart from curiosity," whereas in the early modern period, "wonder and curiosity interlocked" (see Lorraine Daston and Katherine Park, *Wonders and the Order of Nature, 1150–1750* [New York: Zone, 1998], 15).
29. See Pamela Long, *Openness, Secrecy, Authorship: Technical Arts and the Culture of Knowledge from Antiquity to the Renaissance* (Baltimore: Johns Hopkins University Press, 2001).
30. See Daniel Jütte, *The Age of Secrecy: Jews, Christians, and the Economy of Secrets, 1400–1800*, trans. Jeremiah Riemer (New Haven: Yale University Press, 2015), 8.
31. Girolamo Cardano, *De secretis*, in *Opera omnia*, ed. C. Spon (Lyon: Huguetan and Ravaud, 1663; repr., Stuttgart: Friedrich Frommann, 1966), 2:537–38.
32. James Dougal Fleming, introduction to *The Invention of Discovery: Humanism, Science, and Hermeneutics*, ed. Fleming (Aldershot, UK: Ashgate, 2011), 1–4.
33. Ibid. On the history of early modern secrecy, see Heidrun Kugeler, "'Ehrenhafte Spione': Geheimnis, Verstellung und Offenheit in der Diplomatie des 17. Jahrhunderts," in *Die Kunst der Aufrichtigkeit im 17. Jahrhundert*, ed. Claudia Benthien and Stefffen Martus (Tübingen: Niemeyer, 2006); William Eamon, *Science and the Secrets of Nature: Books of Secrets in Medieval and Early Modern Culture* (Princeton: Princeton University Press, 1994), 54; and Keith Hutchinson, "What Happened to Occult Qualities in the Scientific Revolution?" *Isis* 73 (1982): 233–53.
34. *Aeneid*, 6.13–16: "Aeneas, In duty bound, went inland to the heights / where overshadowing Apollo dwells / And nearby, in a place apart—a dark enormous

cave—the Sibyl feared by men" (Virgil, *The Aeneid,* trans. Robert Fitzgerald [New York: Vintage, 1990], 159).
35. Sloterdijk, "The Signs of the Explorers."
36. Hildegard Elizabeth Keller, "Absonderungen: Mystische Texte als literarische Inszenierung von Geheimniss," in *Deutsche Mystik im abendländischen Zusammenhang: Neu erschlossene Texte, neue methodische Ansätze, neue theoretische Konzepte,* ed. Walter Haug and Wolfram Schneider-Lastin, 195–22 (Tübingen: Max Niemeyer, 2000), 197. See also Hans-Martin Gauger, "Geheimnis und Neugier—in der Sprache," *Geheimnis und Neugierde,* 13–28, 20; and Hans Kippenberg and Guy Stroumsa, eds, *Secrecy and Concealment: Studies in the History of Mediterranean and Near Eastern Religions* (Leiden: Brill, 1995).
37. Georg Simmel, "Das Geheimnis," in *Aufsätze und Abhandlungen, 1909–1918,* ed. Rüdiger Kramme and Angela Rammstedt (Frankfurt: Suhrkamp, 2001), 2:317.
38. Michel Serres, *Hermes: Literature, Science, Philosophy,* ed. Josué Harari and David F. Bell (Baltimore: Johns Hopkins University Press, 1982), xxxiii. See also Jacques Derrida and Maurizio Ferraris, *A Taste for the Secret,* trans. Giacomo Donis, ed. Donis and David Webb (Cambridge, UK: Polity, 2001).
39. Aleida Assmann and Jan Assmann, introduction to *Schleier und Schwelle,* ed. Assmann and Assmann, 3 vols., vol. 3: *Geheimnis und Neugierde* (Munich: Wilhelm Fink, 1997), 7–11.
40. Michel de Certeau, *The Mystic Fable. Volume One: The Sixteenth and Seventeenth Centuries,* trans. Michael B. Smith (Chicago: University of Chicago Press, 1992), 97, 99.
41. Ibid.
42. Isidore of Seville, *The Etymologies of Isidore of Seville,* ed. Stephen Barney, W. J. Lewis, J. A. Beach, and Oliver Berghof, with the collaboration of Muriel Hall (Cambridge: Cambridge University Press, 2006), 401.
43. Assmann and Assmann, introduction to *Schleier und Schwelle,* 7–11.
44. On "cunning intelligence" in the Western tradition, see Marcel Detienne and Jean-Pierre Vernant, *Cunning Intelligence in Greek Culture and Society* (Sussex: Harvester, 1978). The *OED* describes the meaning of the Latin word *conquærĕre* as "to seek for, search for, procure, whence the later sense 'to procure by effort, gain, win, conquer,'" with *con-* expressing "completion" and *quærĕre* to "seek." Its governing metaphor is not one of a "frontier" of knowledge expanding into empty or new space but that of redrawing boundaries, of "gathering together" and "procuring" not objects but subjects, of incorporating knowledge that has been "locally discreet" (or "secret").
45. Eamon, *Science,* 266–300.
46. Ibid., 39, 270, 272–73, 416n24. On the courtly context of early modern alchemy in particular, see also Smith, *The Business of Alchemy.*
47. Eamon, *Science,* 416n24.
48. Hernando Cortés, "Second Letter to Charles V," in *Letters from Mexico,* trans. and ed. Anthony Pagden (New Haven: Yale University Press, 1971), 77.

49. Chris Tiffin and Alan Lawson, introduction to *De-scribing Empire: Post-Colonialism and Textuality,* ed. Tiffin and Lawson (London: Routledge, 1994), 3.
50. See chapter 6 of this book; and Jaime Marroquín Arredondo and Ralph Bauer, introduction to *Translating Nature: Transcultural Histories of Science in the Early Modern Atlantic World,* ed. Marroquín Arredondo and Bauer (Philadelphia: University of Pennsylvania Press, 2019).
51. Kellie Robertson, "Medieval Materialism: A Manifesto," *Exemplaria* 22, no. 2 (Summer 2010): 103. See also Robertson's *Nature Speaks: Medieval Literatura and Aristotelian Philosophy* (Philadelphia: University of Pennsylvania Press, 2017), esp. 1–38.
52. Hans Blumenberg, *The Legitimacy of the Modern Age,* trans. Robert M. Wallace (Cambridge: MIT Press, 1999), 240, 282.
53. Augustine, *The Confessions,* ed. Albert Cook Outler (Louisville, KY: Westminster, 1955), 233.
54. Blumenberg, *The Legtimacy,* 249.
55. Dante Alghieri, *Inferno,* trans. Allen Mandelbaum (New York: Bantam, 1982), 12–13 (canto I:10, 22–27). For more recent accounts of curiosity, see Susan Scott Parrish, *American Curiosity: Cultures of Natural History in the Colonial British American World* (Chapel Hill and Colonial Williamsburg: University of North Carolina Press for the Omohundro Institute of Early American History and Culture, 2006); and Barbara Benedict, *Curiosity: A Cultural History of Early Modern Inquiry* (Chicago: University of Chicago Press, 2001).
56. For Löwith's account of the connection between Christian apocalyptic eschatology and scientific "progress," see Karl Löwith, *Meaning in History* (Chicago: University of Chicago Press, 1949), esp. 188–90.
57. Heiko Oberman, "*Contra vanam curiositatem*": *Ein Kapitel der Theologie zwischen Seelenwinkel und Weltall* (Zürich: Theologischer Verlag, 1974), 17–18. See also David Lindberg, "The Medieval Church Encounters the Classical Tradition: Saint Augustine, Roger Bacon, and the Handmaiden Metaphor," in *When Science and Christianity Meet,* ed. Lindberg and Numbers, 7–32; Eamon, *Science,* 58–66; Edward Peters, "The Desire to Know the Secrets of the World," *Journal of the History of Ideas* 62, no. 4 (October 2001): 593–610. For other accounts of the early modern notion of curiosity, see Neil Kenny, *The Uses of Curiosity in Early Modern France and Germany* (Oxford: Oxford University Press, 2004); Toby Huff, *Intellectual Curiosity and the Scientific Revolution: A Global Perspective* (Cambridge: Cambridge University Press, 2011); and Gaukroger, *Emergence,* 16, also 17–19.
58. St. Augustine, *De doctrina Christiana,* ed. and trans. R. P. H. Green (Oxford: Clarendon, 1995), 17.
59. Gaukroger, *Emergence,* 161, 163, 165; see also Christopher Kaiser, *Toward a Theology of Scientific Endeavour: The Descent of Science* (Aldershot, UK: Ashgate, 2007).
60. See chapter 2 for bibliographical references to this historiography.

61. William Newman, introduction to the *The Summa Perfections of Pseudo-Geber*, ed. Newman (Leiden: Brill, 1991), 1–108.
62. Lactantius, *Divine Institutes*, trans., introd., and annotated Anthony Bowen and Peter Garnsey (Liverpool: Liverpool University Press, 2003), 69.
63. Ibid., 152.
64. Ibid., 232.
65. Ibid., 232–33.
66. Ibid., 275.
67. Ibid., 69.
68. The classic study of premodern Hermticism is A. J. Festugière, *Hermétisme et mystique païenne* (Paris: Aubier Montaigne, 1967); see also Claudio Moreschini, *Hermes Christianus: The Intermingling of Hermetic Piety and Christian Thought* (Turnhout, Belgium: Brepols, 2011); Roelof van den Broek and Wouter J. Hanegraaff, eds., *Gnosis and Hermeticism from Antiquity to Modern Times* (Albany: State University of New York Press, 1998); and Jan Assmann, *Moses the Egyptian: The Memory of Egypt in Western Monotheism* (Cambridge: Harvard University Press, 1997), 1–22.
69. St. Augustine of Hippo, *The City of God*, trans. Marcus Dods; introd. Thomas Merton (New York: Modern Library, 1950), 270.
70. Ibid., 271.
71. Ibid., 273.
72. Ibid.
73. Moreschini, *Hermes Christianus*, esp. 33–47.
74. Lactantius, *Divine Institutes*, 96.
75. St. Augustine, *The City of God*, 174.
76. On the often subterranean life of the Lucretian tradition of Epicurean atomism from Virgil through the Middle Ages, see Gerard Passannante, *The Lucretian Renaissance: Philology and the Afterlife of Tradition* (Chicago: University of Chicago Press, 2011), esp. chap. 1.
77. Nicolaus Cusanus, *De docta ignorantia*, ed. H. G. Senger (Hamburg: Felix Meiner, 1993), 96–97.
78. On the textual history of the *Corpus Hermeticum*, see *Hermetica: The Greek "Corpus Hermeticum" and the Latin Asclepius in a New English Translation with Notes and Introduction by Brian Copenhaver* (Cambridge: Cambridge University Press, 1992), xiii–lxii; and Maurizio Campanelli, introduction to *Mercurii Trismegisti*, Campanelli (Turin: Aragno, 2011) xxiii–ccl.
79. Marsilio Ficino, *Platonic Theology*, trans. Michael J. B. Allen, ed. James Hankins with William Bowen, 6 vols. (Cambridge: Harvard University Press, 2005), 5:321; see also James G. Snyder, "Marsilio Ficino's Critique of the Lucretian Alternative," *Journal of the History of Ideas* 72, no. 2 (2011): 165–81. On the "return" of Lucretius to Renaissance Europe more generally, see Allison Brown, *The Return of Lucretius to Renaissance Florence* (Cambridge: Harvard University Press, 2010); Stephen

Greenblatt, *The Swerve: How the World Became Modern* (New York: Norton, 2011); and Passannante, *The Lucretian Renaissance*.
80. Marsilio Ficino, "Argumentum," in *Mercurii Trismegisti Pimander, sive, De potestate et sapientia Dei* (1471), ed. Maurizio Campanelli (Turin: Aragno, 2011), 3–6, 4, 6.
81. Ficino, "Mercuri Trismegisti *Clavis,* ad Tatium," *Mercurii Trismegisti*, 59–71.
82. Ficino, *Platonic Theology*, 1:79.
83. Ibid., 6:83.
84. On Alexander's interest in Hermeticism, kabbala, and alchemy, see chapter 5.
85. See Paolo Rossi, *"Clavis universalis," Arti mnemoiche e logica combinatorial da Lullo a Leibnitz* (Milan: Ricciardi, 1960), 41; Frances Yates, *Llull and Bruno: Collected Essays* (London: Routledge and Kegan Paul, 1982), 67; and Mark Johnston, "The Reception of the Llullian Art, 1450–1530," *Sixteenth-Century Journal* 12, no. 1 (Spring 1981): 31–48. On occult philosophy in the Counter-Reformation, see Paula Findlen, ed, *Athanasius Kircher: The Last Man Who Knew Everything* (London: Routledge, 2004); and Juan Pimentel, "Juan E. Nieremberg, American Wonders, Preterimperial Natural History," in *Science in the Spanish and Portuguese Empires,* ed. Daniela Bleichma et al., 93–114 (Stanford: Stanford University Press, 2009).
86. Moreschini, *Hermes Christianus*, 162–70.
87. See Antony Grafton and Joanna Weinberg, *"I Have Always Loved the Holy Tongue": Isaac Casaubon, the Jews, and a Forgotten Chapter in Renaissance Scholarship* (Cambridge: Harvard University Press, 2011), 30–42.
88. Elias Ashmole, *The way to bliss. In three books: Made publick* (London: Printed by John Grismond for Nath. Brook, at the Angel in Corn-hill, 1658), 9. On Ashmole, see Bruce Janacek, *Alchemical Belief: Occultism in the Religious Culture of Early Modern England* (University Park: Pennsylvania University Press, 2011), 128–59. On the history of Ficinco's translation during the sixteenth and seventeenth centuries, see Frances Yates, *Giordano Bruno and the Hermetic Tradition* (Chicago: University of Chicago Press, 1974), 20–43. On the Hermetic tradition from early modern to modern times, see Assman, *Moses the Egyptian*. On Cotton Mather, see Jan Stievermann, *Prophecy, Piety, and the Problem of Historicity: Interpreting the Hebrew Scriptures in Cotton Mather's "Biblia Americana"* (Tübingen: Mohr Siebeck, 2016). On John Winthrop Jr., see Walter Woodward, *Prospero's America: John Winthrop, Jr., Alchemy, and the Creation of New England Culture, 1606–1676* (Chapel Hill and Williamsburg, VA: University of North Carolina Press for the Omohundro Institute of Early American History and Culture, 2009).
89. Nicholas Goodrick-Clarke, *The Western Esoteric Tradition: A Historical Introduction* (Oxford: Oxford University Press, 2008), 13. On the history of Western Hermeticism and esotericism, see also Antoine Faivre, *The Eternal Hermes: From Greek Good to Alchemical Magus,* trans. Joscelyn Godwin (Grand Rapids, MI: Phanes, 1995); Kocku von Stuckrad, *Locations of Knowledge in Medieval and Early*

Modern Europe: Esoteric Discourse and Western Identities (Leiden: Brill, 2010). R. van den Broek, *Gnosis and Hermeticism from Antiquity to Modern Times* (Binghamton: State University of New York Press, 1998); Olav Hammer and Kocku von Stuckrad, *Polemical Encounters: Esoteric Discourse and Its Others* (Leiden: Brill, 2007); and Arthur Versluis, *The Esoteric Origins of the American Renaissance* (Oxford: Oxford University Press, 2001). On the role of "productive" knowing from antiquity to the early modern period, see Antonio Perez-Ramos, *Francis Bacon's Idea of Science*.

90. Robert Bonfil, *Rabbis and Jewish Communities in Renaissance Italy* (Oxford: Published for the Littman Library by Oxford University Press, 1990), 285, 292.
91. See Yates, *Giordano Bruno;* Frances Yates, *The Rosicrucian Enlightenment* (London: Routledge, 1972); Wayne Schumaker, *The Occult Sciences in the Renaissance* (Berkeley: University of California Press, 1972); D. P. Walker, *Spiritual and Demonic Magic from Ficino to Campanella* (London: Warburg Institute, 1958); and Anthony Grafton and Moshe Idel, *Der Magus: Seine Ursprünge und seine Geschichte in verschiedenen Kulturen* (Berlin: Akademie, 2001).
92. For critiques of the Yates Thesis, see Brian Vickers, introduction to *Occult and Scientific Mentalities in the Renaissance,* ed. Vickers (Cambridge: Cambridge University Press, 1984); Herbert Butterfield, *The Origins of Modern Science: 1300–1800* (New York: Free Press, 1965); and Charles Schmitt, "Reappraisals in Renaissance Science," *History of Science* 16 (1978): 200–214.
93. John Henry, *The Scientific Revolution and the Origins of Modern Science,* 2nd ed. (New York: Palgrave, 2002), 65; see also Newman, *Atoms and Alchemy,* 129–70.
94. See Thomas S. Kuhn, *The Structure of Scientific Revolutions,* 2nd ed. (1962; Chicago: University of Chicago Press, 1970), 35–42.
95. Gerhard Dorn, *Comentaria in Archidoxorum Libros X. D. Doctoris Theophrasti Paracelsi* (Frankfurt, 1584), 452.
96. Henry Cornelius Agrippa of Nettesheim, *Three Books of Occult Philosophy,* trans. James Freake, ed. Donald Tyson (Woodbury, MN: Llewellyn, 1992), 46, 70.
97. See Daston and Park, *Wonders,* 215–54; Scott Parrish, *American Curiosity;* and Benedict, *Curiosity*.
98. Agrippa, *Three Books of Occult Philosophy,* 70.
99. Paracelsus, "*Caput de morbis somnii,*" in *Theophrast von Hohenheim genannt Paracelsus: Sämtliche Werke,* ed. Karl Sudhoff, Wilhelm Matthiessen, and K. Goldammer, 9:359–62 (Munich: R. Oldenbourg, 1923), 9:361.
100. William Newman, "From Alchemy to 'Chymistry,'" in *The Cambridge History of Science,* vol. 3: *Early Modern Science,* ed. Katharine Park and Lorraine Daston, 497–512 (Cambridge: Cambridge University Press, 2006), 497.
101. On the historical connections between early modern absolutist monarchies and modern nation-states, see Perry Anderson, *Lineages of the Absolutist State* (London: Humanities Press, 1974).
102. See José María López Piñero, "Paracelsus and His Work in 16th and 17th Century Spain," *Clio Medica* 8 (1973): 119–31. On alchemy in early modern Spain,

particularly at the court of Philip II, see Mar Rey Bueno, *Los señores del fuego: Destiladores y espagiricos en la corte de los Austrias* (Madrid: Corona Borealis, 2002); "La Mayson pour Distiller des Eaües at El Escorial: Alchemy and Medicine at the Court of Philip II, 1556–1598," *Medical History Supplement* 29 (2009): 26–39; "El informe Valles: Los desdibujados límites del arte de boticarios a finales del siglo XVI (1589–1594)," *Asclepio* 56, no. 2 (2004): 243–68; "Juntas de herbolarios y tertulias espagíricas: El círculo cortesano de Diego de Cortavila (1597–1657)," *Dynamis* 24 (2004): 243–67; "Los paracelsistas españoles: Medicina química en la España moderna," in *Más allá de la leyenda negra: España y la revolución científica / Beyond the Black Legend: Spain and the Scientific Revolution,* ed. Victor Navarro Brotóns and William Eamon (Valencia: Instituto de Historia de la Ciencia y Documentación López Piñero, 2007), 41–56; see also Javier Puerto Sarmiento, "La panacea áurea: Alquimia y destilación en la corte de Felipe II (1527–1598)," *Dynamis* 17 (1997): 107–40; Javier Puerto Sarmiento, M. E. Alegre Pérez, Mar Rey Bueno, and Miguel López Pérez, eds., *Los hijos de Hermes: Alquimia y espagiria en la terapéutica española moderna* (Madrid: Ediciones Corona Borealis, 2001); Javier Ruiz, "Los alquimistas de Felipe II," *Historia* 16 (1977) 12:49–55; Mar Rey Bueno and María Esther Alegre Pérez, "Los destiladores de su majestad: Destilación, espagiria y paracelsismo en la corte de Felipe II," *Dynamis* (2001): 323–50; Miguel López Pérez, *Asclepio renovado: Alquimia y medicina en la España Moderna (1500–1700)* (Madrid: Ediciones Corona Borealis, 2003); "Ciencia y pensamiento hermético en la Edad Moderna española," in *Más allá,* ed. Victor Navarro Brotóns and William Eamon, 57–72; David Goodman, *Power and Penury: Government, Technology, and Science in Philip II's Spain* (Cambridge: Cambridge University Press, 1988); María Luz López Terrada, "Medical Pluralism in the Iberian Kingdoms: The Control of Extra-Academic Practitioners in Valencia," *Medical History Supplement* 29 (2009): 7–25; and José Rodriguez-Guerrero, "La primera gran red comercial de un medicamento *chymico:* Vittorio Algarotti y su quintaesencia del oro medicinal," *Azogue* 6 (2008–9): 12–67. On the special role of the Jesuits in alchemy, see Camenietzki Ziller, "Jesuits and Alchemy in the Early Seventeenth Century: Father Johannes Roberti and the Weapon-Salve Controversy," *Ambix* 48, pt. 2 (July 2001): 83–101; and Martha Baldwin, "Alchemy and the Society of Jesus in the Seventeenth Century: Strange Bedfellows?" *Ambix* 40, pt. 2 (July 1993): 41–64.

103. See Allen G. Debus, *The English Paracelsians* (New York: Franklin Watts, 1966); Debus, *The Chemical Philosophy: Paracelsian Science and Medicine in the Sixteenth and Seventeenth Centuries,* 2 vols. (New York: Science History Publications, 1977); Walter Pagel, *Paracelsus: An Introduction to Philosophical Medicine in the Era of the Renaissance* (New York: Karger, 1984); and Tara Nummedal, *Alchemy and Authority in the Holy Roman Empire* (Chicago: University of Chicago Press, 2007); on Dee, see Jennifer Rampling, "John Dee and the Alchemists: Practising and Promoting English Alchemy in the Holy Roman Empire," *Studies in History and Philosophy of Science* 43 (2012): 498–508.

104. See Michael Dettelbach, "Describing the Nation: Local and Universal in Humboldt's Administrative Practice and in Late Eighteenth-Century Cameralism," in *Alexander von Humboldt and the Americas,* ed. Vera Kutzinski, Ottmar Ette, and Laura Dassow Walls (Berlin: Walter Frey, 2012), 183–208.
105. See Agostino Paravicini Bagliani, *The Pope's Body* (Chicago: University of Chicago Press, 2000).

2. Egyptian Gold

1. Mircea Eliade, *The Forge and the Crucible* (New York: Harper, 1962), 99–100, 75.
2. Ibid.
3. Carl Jung, "Paracelsus as Spiritual Phenomenon," in *Alchemical Studies,* trans. R. R. C. Hull, vol. 13 of *The Collected Works,* ed. Sir Herbert Read (Princeton: Princeton University Press, 1967), 140, 137.
4. Ibid., 179.
5. Ibid., 159–60.
6. Jung, "The Spirit Mercurius," in *Alchemical Studies,* 193. See also vol. 12, *Psychology and Alchemy* (Princeton: Princeton University Press, 1953).
7. Jung, "The Spirit Mercurius," 368. On the religious and spiritual aspects of alchemy, see also "Paracelsus."
8. Jung, "The Spirit Mercurius," 368. On the Eucharist and alchemy, see also Katherine Eggert, *Disknowledge: Literature, Alchemy, and the End of Humanism in Renaissance England* (Philadelphia: University of Pennsylvania Press, 2015), 66; Urszula Szulakowska, "The Apocalyptic Eucharist and Religious Dissidence in Stefan Michelspacher's *Cabala:* Spiegel der Kunst und Nature, in Alchymia (1616)," *Aries* 3, no. 2 (2003): 211; and Karen Gordon–Grube, "Evidence of Medicinal Cannibalism in Puritan New England: 'Mummy' and Related Remedies in Edward Taylor's 'Dispensatory,'" *Early American Literature* 28, no. 3 (1993): 185.
9. Carl Jung, "The Spirit Mercurius," 191–250.
10. See Sabine Doran, *The Culture of Yellow: Or the Visual Politics of Late Modernity* (New York: Bloomsbury, 2013).
11. Ibid., 8.
12. See Lyndy Abraham, *A Dictionary of Alchemical Imagery* (Cambridge: Cambridge University Press, 1998).
13. See William Newman and Lawrence Principe, "Some Problems with the Historiography of Alchemy," in *Secrets of Nature: Astrology and Alchemy in Early Modern Europe,* ed. Anthony Grafton and Newman (Cambridge: MIT Press, 2001), 385–432. For a critique of Jung's universalism from the point of view of literary criticism, see Karen Pinkus, *Alchemical Mercury: A Theory of Ambivalence* (Stanford: Stanford University Press, 2010), 8–10.
14. Jung, "Paracelsus," 189.
15. Ibid., 127–28, 115.

16. Leah DeVun, *Prophecy, Alchemy, and the End of Time: John of Rupescissa in the Late Middle Ages* (New York: Columbia University Press, 2009), 102. On the important role that religion played in the history of alchemy more generally, see "Alchemy and Religion in Christian Europe," ed. Tara Nummedal, special issue, *Ambix* 60, no. 4 (2013); on the close connection between alchemy and especially Franciscan spirituality during the later Middle Ages, see Zachary Matus, *Franciscans and the Elixir of Life: Religion and Science in the Later Middle Ages* (Philadelphia: University of Pennsylvania Press, 2017); and Agostino Paravicini-Bagliani, "Ruggero Bacone e l'alchimia della lunga vita," in *Alchimia e medicina nel medioevo*, ed. Chiara Crisciani and Paravicini-Bagliani (Tavarnuzze: SISMEL Edizioni del Galluzzo, 2003). On the connection between alchemy and spirituality beyond the Franciscan milieu, see Hereward Tilton, *The Quest for the Phoenix: Spiritual Alchemy and Rosicrucianism in the Work of Count Michael Maier (1569–1622)* (Berlin: Walter de Gruyter, 2003); Charles Webster, *From Paracelsus to Newton: Magic and the Making of Modern Science* (Cambridge: Cambridge University Press, 1982); and Webster, *Paracelsus: Medicine, Magic, and Mission at the End of Time* (New Haven: Yale University Press, 2008).
17. St. Augustine, *De doctrina Christiana,* ed. and trans. R. P. H. Green (Oxford: Clarendon, 1889), 124.
18. French and Cunningham, *Before Science,* 18–19. See also David Lindberg, *The Beginnings of Western Science: The European Scientific Tradition in Philosophical, Religious, and Institutional Context, Prehistory to A.D. 1450* (1992; Chicago: University of Chicago Press, 2007).
19. Roger Bacon, *The Opus Majus of Roger Bacon,* trans. Robert Belle Burke, 2 vols. (Philadelphia: University of Pennsylvania Press, 1928), 2:644. On this figure of speech in Bacon, see also David Lindberg, "Science as Handmaiden: Roger Bacon and the Patristic Tradition," *Isis* 78 (1987): 518–36; and Lindberg, "The Medieval Church Encounters the Classical Tradition: Saint Augustine, Roger Bacon, and the Handmaiden Metaphor," in *When Science and Christianity Meet,* ed. Lindberg and Ronald Numbers (Chicago: University of Chicago Press, 2003), 7–32.
20. Jesús Montoya Martínez and Ana Domínguez Rodríguez, eds., *El Scriptorum alfonsi: De los libros de astrología a las "Cantigas de Santa Maria"* (Madrid: Editorial Complutense, 1999); Emmanuelle Poulle, "The Alfonsine Tables and Alfonso X of Castille," *Journal for the History of Astronomy* 19 (1988): 99–105; K. Sudhoff, "Daniels von Morley, *Liber de naturas inferiorum et superiorum* nach der Handschrift Cod. Arundel 377 des Britischen Museums zum Abdruck gebracht," *Archiv für die Geschichte der Naturwissenschaften und der Technik* 8 (1917) 1–40, reprinted in Gregor Maurach, "Daniel von Morley Philosophia," *Mittellateinisches Jahrbuch* 14 (1979): 204–55; French and Cunningham, *Before Science,* 81–82; see also Thomas Glick, Steven Levesy, and Faith Wallis, eds., *Medieval Science, Technology, and Medicine* (New York: Routledge, 2005), 424; and William Newman, *Promethean Ambitions: Alchemy and the Quest to Perfect Nature* (Chicago: University of Chicago Press, 2004), 43.

21. See William Newman and L. Principe, *Alchemy Tried in the Fire: Starkey: Boyle, and the Fate of Helmontian Chymistry* (Chicago: University of Chicago Press, 2002); Lawrence Principe, *The Secrets of Alchemy* (Chicago: University of Chicago Press, 2013); William Newman and Anthony Grafton, eds., *Secrets of Nature: Astrology and Alchemy in Early Modern Europe* (Cambridge: MIT Press, 2001); Newman, "From Alchemy to 'Chymistry,'" in *The Cambridge History of Science,* vol 3: *Early Modern Science,* ed. Katharine Park and Lorraine Daston, 497–512 (Cambridge: Cambridge University Press, 2006), 497; Pamela Smith, *The Business of Alchemy: Science and Culture in the Holy Roman Empire* (Princeton: Princeton University Press, 1994); Pamela Smith, *The Body of the Artisan: Art and Experience in the Scientific Revolution* (Chicago: University of Chicago Press, 2004); Chiara Crisciani, *From the Laboratory to the Library: Alchemy According to Guglielmo Fabri* (Cambridge: MIT Press, 1999); and Bruce Moran, *Distilling Knowledge: Alchemy, Chemistry, and the Scientific Revolution* (Cambridge: Harvard University Press, 2005).
22. On the differences between Thomist and alchemical matter theory, see William R. Newman, *Atoms and Alchemy: Chymistry and the Experimental Origins of the Scientific Revolution* (Chicago: University of Chicago Press, 2006), 1–44.
23. Ibid., 36.
24. Ibid., 25.
25. On the pre-Socratics, see G. S. Kirk, J. E. Raven, and M. Schofield, *The Presocratic Philosophers: A Critical History with a Selection of Texts* (Cambridge: Cambridge University Press, 1983), 402–33. On the "New World" return of Lucretius to Europe, see chapter 7 of this book. On alchemical matter theory, see Newman, *Atoms and Alchemy;* Newman, *Gehennical Fire,* 92–114; Newman, "Corpuscular Alchemy and the Tradition of Aristotle's Meteorology, with Special Reference to Daniel Sennert," *International Studies in the Philosophy of Science* 15, no. 2 (2001): 145–53; and Antonio Clericuzio, *Elements, Principles, and Corpuscles: A Study of Atomism and Chemistry in the Seventeenth Century* (Dordrecht: Kluwer Academic, 2000).
26. Newman, *Atoms and Alchemy,* 17.
27. The text of John XXII's decretal *Spondent quas non exhibent* is reproduced and translated with a discussion in Robert Halleux, *Les textes alchimiques* (Turnhout, Belgium: Brepols, 1979), 124–26.
28. On the concept of "creative duplicity," see Anthony Grafton, *Forgers and Critics: Creativity and Duplicity in Western Scholarship* (London: Collins and Brown, 1990); on this tradition in alchemy, see Jill Kraye, Charles B. Schmitt, and W. F. Ryan, *Pseudo-Aristotle in the Middle Ages: The Theology and Other Texts* (London: Warburg Institute, University of London, 1986); and William Newman, introduction to *The Summa Perfectionis of Pseudo-Geber: A Critical Edition, Translation, and Study* (Leiden: Brill, 1997).
29. See William Eamon, *Science and the Secrets of Nature: Books of Secrets in Medieval and Early Modern Culture* (Princeton: Princeton University Press, 1994), 38–45.

30. DeVun, *Prophecy*, 6.
31. Arthur Williamson, *Apocalypse Then: Prophecy and the Making of the Modern World* (Westport, CT: Praeger, 2008), 16.
32. Ibid. On Joachimite millenarianism and its impact, see Marjorie Reeves, *The Influence of Prophecy in the Later Middle Ages: A Study of Joachimism* (Oxford: Clarendon, 1969); Reeves, *Joachim of Fiore and the Prophetic Future: A Medieval Study in Historical Thinking* (London: S.P.C.K., 1976); and Bernard McGinn, *The Calabrian Abbot: Joachim of Fiore in the History of Western Thought* (New York: Macmillan, 1985).
33. Joachim qtd. in Williamson, *Apocalypse*, 19.
34. Williamson, *Apocalypse*, 19. On the evolution of medieval anti-Semitism, see Jeremy Cohen, *The Friars and the Jews: The Evolution of Medieval Anti-Judaism* (Ithaca, NY: Cornell University Press, 1982). On Aquinas's complicated attitudes toward the Jews, see Steven Boguslawski, O.P., *Thomas Aquinas on the Jews: Insights into His Commentary on Romans 9–11* (New York: Paulist Press, 2008). On the history of late medieval Christian apocalyptic thought more generally, see Bernard McGinn, *Apocalyptic Spirituality* (New York: Paulist Press, 1979); and McGinn and Richard Emmerson, eds., *The Apocalypse in the Middle Ages* (Ithaca, NY: Cornell University Press, 1992).
35. See Wilfrid Theisen, O.S.B., "The Attraction of Alchemy for Monks and Friars in the 13th–14th Centuries," *American Benedictine Review* 46, no. 3 (1995): 239–53; Bert Roest, *A History of Franciscan Education, ca. 1210–1517* (Leiden: Brill, 2000), 144–45; and Tara Nummedal, *Alchemy and Authority in the Holy Roman Empire* (Chicago: University of Chicago Press, 2007), 150; on John of Rupescissa, see DeVun, *Prophecy*; on Paul of Tarento, see Newman, *Atoms and Alchemy*, 23–44; on Paul of Tarento and Elia da Cartona, see H. M. Briggs, "De duobus fratribus minoribus medii aevi alchemistis fr. Paolo de Tarento et. Fr. Elia," *Archivum Francisanum Historicum* 20 (1927): 305–13. On alchemy among the Jesuits, see Martha Baldwin, "Alchemy and the Society of Jesus in the Seventeenth Century: Strange Bedfellows?," *Ambix* 40, no. 2 (July 1993): 41–64; Carlos Ziller Camenietzki, "Jesuits and Alchemy in the Early Seventeenth Century: Father Johannes Roberti and the Weapon-Salve Controversy," *Ambix* 48, no. 2 (July 2001): 83–101; Zachary Matus, *Franciscans and the Elixir of Life*; and Agostino Paravicini-Bagliani, "Ruggero Bacone e l'alchimia della lunga vita."
36. On Albertus Magnus and Aquinas, see Newman, *Promethean Ambitions*, 44–52.
37. On the connection between the European encounter with the New World and the history of the idea of polygenesis in general, see also David N. Livingstone, *Adam's Ancestors: Race, Religion, and the Politics of Human Origins* (Baltimore: Johns Hopkins University Press, 2008).
38. Lynn Thorndike, *A History of Magic and Experimental Science* (New York: Columbia University Press, 1923), 3:347.
39. Ibid.
40. See Matus, *Franciscans*.

41. Father Ullmann, *Das "Buch der Heiligen Dreifaltigkeit" in seiner zweiten, alchemistischen Fassung (Kadolzburg, 1433)*, ed. and introd. Uwe Junker (Cologne: Arbeiten der Forschungsstelle des Instituts für Geschichte der Medizin der Universität zu Köln, 1986), 201–8.
42. Ibid., 207.
43. Edmund Brehm, "Roger Bacon's Place in the History of Alchemy," *Ambix* 23 (1976): 53–57, 54.
44. See Abraham, *Dictionary*, 135–36, 202–3.
45. Ullmann, *Buch*, 243.
46. See Uwe Junker, introduction to Ullmann, *Buch*, 1–48.
47. Roger Bacon, *The Opus Majus of Roger Bacon*, trans. Robert Belle Burke, 2 vols. (Philadelphia: University of Pennsylvania Press, 1928), 2:583.
48. Lynn Thorndike, "Roger Bacon and Experimental Method in the Middle Ages," *Philosophical Review* 23, no. 3 (May 1914): 271.
49. See David Lindberg, introduction to *Roger Bacon's "Philosophy of Nature": A Critical Edition, with English Translation, Introduction, and Notes of "De multiplicatione specierum" and "De speculis comburentibus"* (Oxford: Clarendon, 1983), xv–lxxxi; Lindberg, introduction to *Roger Bacon and the Origins of "Perspectiva" in the Middle Ages* (Oxford: Clarendon, 1996), xvii–cxi; Lindberg, *The Beginnings of Western Science*, 228–39; Lindberg, "Science as Handmaiden;" Lindberg, "The Medieval Church Encounters"; see also Noble, *Religion of Technology*, 26–28; Steward C. Easton, *Roger Bacon and His Search for a Universal Science* (New York: Russel and Russel, 1971); Thorndike, *History*, 2:863–65; DeVun, *Prophecy*, 80–89, 134–36; and French and Cunningham, *Before Science*, 237–43.
50. Agostino Paravicini Bagliani, *The Pope's Body* (Chicago: University of Chicago Press, 2000), 201–11.
51. Newman, "An Overview of Roger Bacon's Alchemy," in *Roger Bacon and the Sciences*, ed. Jeremiah Hacket (Leiden: Brill, 1997), 328; see also William R. Newman, "The Philosopher's Egg: Theory and Practice in the Alchemy of Roger Bacon," *Micrologus* 3 (1995): 76–77. On the notion of Bacon as an "armchair alchemist," see Dorothea Waley Singer, "Alchemical Writings Attributed to Roger Bacon," *Speculum* 7 (1932): 80–86.
52. Bacon, *Opus Maius*, 2:583–84.
53. Ibid., 2:587.
54. Ibid., 2:631–32.
55. On the medieval history of this text, see Steven Williams, *The Secret of Secrets: The Scholarly Career of a Pseudo-Aristotelian Text in the Latin Middle Ages* (Ann Arbor: University of Michigan Press, 2003). On the importance of the *Secretum secretorum* to Bacon, see Eamon, *Science*, 50–52.
56. See Brehm, "Roger Bacon's Place," 54.
57. Roger Bacon, *Opus tertium*, in *Opera quaedam hactenus inedita Fr. Rogeri Bacon*, ed. J. S. Brewer (London: Longman, Green, Longman, and Roberts, 1859), 39–40. See also Newman, "An Overview," 318.

58. Bacon, *Opus maius*, 2:626–27.
59. Ibid., 2:645–46.
60. On Bacon's apocalypticism, see Amanda Power, *Roger Bacon and the Defense of Christendom* (Cambridge: Cambridge University Press, 2012); on alchemy, see esp. 118–20; see Alexsey Klemeshov, "The Conversion and Destruction of the Infidels in the Works of Roger Bacon," in *Religion and Power in Europe: Conflict and Convergence,* ed. Joaquim Carvalho (Pisa: Edizioni Plus, Pisa University Press, 2007), 15–28; Zachary Matus, "Reconsidering Roger Bacon's Apocalypticism in Light of His Alchemical and Scientific Thought," *Harvard Theological Review* 105, no. 2 (2012): 189–222; and Matus, *Franciscans and the Elixir,* esp. 76–85.
61. Bacon, *Opus maius*, 2:633.
62. Ibid., 2:634.
63. Ibid.
64. Ibid., 2:625.
65. See Newman, "An Overview," 332–35.
66. Bacon, *Opus maius*, 2:620; see also Paravicini-Bagliani, *The Pope's Body,* 204–11.
67. See Paravicini-Bagliani, *The Pope's Body,* 207.
68. Bacon, *Opus maius*, 2:620.
69. Ibid.
70. Ibid., 2:620–21.
71. Ibid., 2:621.
72. Roger Bacon, *Frater Rogerus Bacon in libro sex scientiarum,* in Fratris Rogeri Bacon, *De retardatione accidentium senectutis cum aliis opusculis de rebus medicinalibus,* ed. A. G. Little and E. Withington (Oxford: Clarendon, 1928), 183.
73. See Newman, "An Overview," 326. On Bacon's alchemical theory, see also Newman, "The Philosopher's Egg"; Holmyard, *Alchemy,* 119–25, 148–52; DeVun, *Prophecy,* 80–89; Michela Pereira, *L'oro dei filosofi: Saggio sulle idee di un alchmista del trecento* (Spoleto: Centro Italiano di studi sull'alto medioevo, 1992), 43–83; Faye Marie Getz, "Roger Bacon and Medicine: The Paradox of the Forbidden Fruit and the Secrets of Long Life," in *Health, Disease, and Healing in Medieval Culture,* ed. Sheila Campbell, Bert S. Hall, and David N. Klausner (New York: St. Martin's, 1992), 141–51; and Brehm, "Roger Bacon's Place."
74. See Brehm, "Roger Bacon's Place," 54; and F. Sherwood Taylor, *The Alchemists: Founders of Modern Chemistry* (London: Heinemann, 1958), 115.
75. Newman, "The Philosopher's Egg."
76. Bacon, *In libro sex scientianum in 3°gradu sapiencie,* in *De retardatione accidentium senectutis; cum aliis opusculis de rebus medicinalibus,* 181–86 (Oxonii, 1928), 183. Translation in Newman, "The Philosophers' Egg," 78.
77. Thorndike, "Roger Bacon," 283.
78. On Arnald's medical writings, see Thorndike, *History,* 2:841–61; Marcelino Menéndez Pelayo, *Arnaldo de Vilanova, médico catalán del siglo XIII: Ensayo histórico sequido de tres opúsculos inéditos de Arnaldo, y de una colección de documentos relativos á su persona* (n.p.: Nabu Public Domain Reprints, 2011); Michael McVaugh,

"Arnald of Vilanova and Bradwardine's Law," *Isis* 58 (1967); McVaugh, ed., *Arnaldi de Villanova Opera Medica Omnia,* 2: *Aphorismi de gradibus* (Granada: Seminarium Historiae Medicae Granatensis, 1975), 76–82; McVaugh, *Medicine before the Plague: Practitioners and Their Patients in the Crown of Aragon, 1285–1345* (Cambridge: Cambridge University Press, 1993); and McVaugh, "Chemical Medicine in the Medical Writings of Arnau de Vilanova," *Arxíu de textos Catalans antics* 23/24 (2005): 256–64; see also Joseph Ziegler, *Medicine and Religion, c. 1300: The Case of Arnau de Vilanova* (Oxford: Clarendon, 1998). On Arnald's service to rulers and popes, see Robert Lerner, "The Pope and the Doctor," *Yale Review* 78 (1988–89): 62–79; and Paravicini-Bagliani, *The Pope's Body,* 225–26, 343–44.

79. On Arnald's prophetic writings, see Heinrich Finke, *Aus den Tagen Bonifaz VIII* (Münster: Druck und Verlag der Aschendorffschen Buchhandlung, 1902), 191–226; Paul Diepgen, *Arnald von Villanova als Politiker und Laientheologe* (Berlin: Abhandlungen zur mittleren und neueren Geschichte, 1909); Marcelino Menéndez Pelayo, *Historia de los Heterodoxos Españoles,* 2nd ed. (Madrid, 1918), 179–225; Jose M. Pou y Marti, *Visionarios, beguinos, y fratricelos* in *Archivo Ibero-Americano* 6 (1919): 143–221; Raoul Manselli, "Un compagno di strada: Arnaldo da Vilanova," in *Spirituali e beghini in Provenza, Instituto Storico Italiano per il Medio Evo* (Rome: Nella sede dell'Istituto, 1959); and Manselli, *La Religiosità D'arnaldo da Villanova* (Rome: Istituto Storico Italiano per il Medio Evo, 1951); Ernst Benz, *Ecclesia Spiritualis: Kirchenidee und Geschichtstheologie der Franziskanischen Reformation* (Stuttgart: W. Kohlhammer, 1964), 368–86; Harold Lee, "Scrutamini Scripturas: Joachimist Themes and Figurae in the Early Religious Writing of Arnald of Vilanova," *Journal of the Warburg and Coutauld Institutes* 37 (1974): 33–56; and Robert Lerner, "Ecstatic Dissent," *Speculum* 67, no. 1 (January 1992): 33–57.

80. As Juanita Daly has noted, in modern scholarship there exist "two Arnalds: Arnald the physician and Arnald the prophet" (Daly, "Arnald of Vilanova: Physician and Prophet," *Essays in Medieval Studies* 4 [1997]: 29–41). For examples of more comprehensive views of this dual aspect of Arnald's works, see Michael McVaugh, "Moments of Inflection: The Careers of Arnau de Vilanova," in *Religion and Medicine in the Middle Ages,* ed. Peter Biller and Joseph Ziegler (York: York Medieval Press, 2001); and Ziegler, *Medicine;* and DeVun, *Prophecy*. Important bibliographic information on Arnald can be found in René Verrier, *Etudes sur Arnaud de Villeneuve 1240–1311,* 2 vols. (Leiden: Brill, 1947).

81. See Ziegler, *Medicine,* 81.

82. Ibid.

83. On the alchemical works attributed to Arnald, see Thorndike, *History,* 3:52–84; Antoine Calvet. "Étude d'un texte alchimique Latin du xive siècle: Le 'Rosarius Philosophorum' attribué au médecin Arnaud de Villeneuve (ob. 1311)," *Early Science and Medicine* 11, no. 2 (2006): 162–206; A. Calvet, *La version d'oc du rosarius philosophorum attribué à Arnaud de Villeneuve (introduction, Étude de Langue, Édition, Traduction)* (Paris, 1995); Antoine Calvet, *Le de secretis*

naturae du Pseudo-Arnaud de Villeneuve (Paris: Société d'Étude de l'Histoire de l'Alchimie, 1999) (1997–99), 155–206; A. Calvet, "Alchimie et Joachimisme dans les alchimica pseudo-arnaldiens," in *Alchimie et philosophie à la Renaissance: Actes du Colloque International de Tours (4–7 Décembre 1991)*, ed. Jean-Claude Margolin and Sylvain Matton, 93–107 (Paris: Vrin, 1993); A. Calvet and Giralt Sebastià, *Les oeuvres alchimiques attribuées à Arnaud de Villeneuve: Grand Œuvre, médecine et prophétie au Moyen-Âge* (Paris: S.É.H.A., 2011); A. Calvet and Sylvain Matton, "Quelques versions de la 'Flos Florum' du Pseudo-Arnaud de Villeneuve," *Chrysopœia* 6 (1997–99): 207–71; DeVun, *Prophecy, Alchemy*, 89–95; and Matus, *Franciscans*, 123–24.

84. See Ziegler, *Medicine*, 40.
85. See Antoine Calvet, "Le tractatus parabolicus du Pseudo-Arnaud de Villeneuve," *Chrysopœia* 5 (1992–96): 145–71.
86. Pseudo-Arnald, *Tractatus parabolicus*, ed. and trans. Antoine Calvet, in *Chrysopœia* 5 (1992–96): 160. On Arnald's alchemical works, see also Lawrence Principe, *The Secrets of Alchemy* (Chicago: University of Chicago Press, 2013), 64–69.
87. Antoine Calvet, *Le rosier alchimique de Montpellier: Lo rosari, XIVe siècle* (Paris: Presses de l'Université de Paris-Sorbonne, 1997), xvii.
88. (Pseudo-)Arnald of Villanova, "Rosarius philosophorum," in Jean-Jacques Manget, *Bibliotheca chemica curiosa, seu rerum ad alchemiam pertinentium thesaurus instructissimus*, 2 vols. (Geneva: Chouet, G. de Tournes, Cramer, Perachon, Ritter & S. de Tournes, 1702), 1:664.
89. Ibid.
90. Ibid.
91. Ibid., 1:665.
92. Ibid.
93. Ibid., 1:667.
94. Ibid.
95. Ibid., 1:676.
96. On Rupescissa's prophetic writings, see Thorndike, *History*, 3:347–69; DeVun, *Prophecy*; Josep Perarnau i Espelt, "La traducció catalana resumida del *Vademecum in tribulatione* (Ve ab mi en tribulació) de fra Joan de Rocatalhada," *Arxiu de textos Catalans antics* 12 (1993): 43–140; Robert Lerner, "John, the Astonishing," *Oliviana* (online journal), placed online March 31, 2009; URL: http://oliviana.revues.org/335; Robert E. Lerner and Christine Morerod-Fattebert, *Johannes de Rupescissa, Liber secretorum eventuum: Édition critique, traduction et introduction historique* (Fribourg: Éditions Universitaires, 1994); Robert E. Lerner, "Popular Justice: Rupescissa in Hussite Bohemia," in *Eschatologie und Hussitismus*. ed. Alexander Patschovsky et al. (Prague: Historisches Institut, 1996), 39–52; Josep Perarnau i Espelt, "La traducció catalana medieval del *Liber futurorum eventuum* de Joan de Rocatalhada: Edició i estudi," *Arxiu de Textos Catalans antics* 17 (1998): 7–219; Elizabeth Casteen, "John of Rupescissa's Letter *Reverendissime pater* (1350) in the Aftermath of the Black Death," *Franciscana* 6 (2004): 139–84;

Barbara Ferrari, "La prima traduzione francese del *Vade mecum in tribulatione* di Giovanni di Rupescissa (Parigi, BNF f. fr. 24254)," *Studi mediolatini e volgari* 50 (2004): 59–76; Barbara Ferrari, "Le *Vade mecum in tribulatione* de Jean de Roquetaillade en Moyen Français (ms. BAV, Reg. lat. 1728)," in *Pour acquerir honneur et pris: Mélanges de Moyen Français offerts à Giuseppe Di Stefano*, ed. M. Colombo & C. Galderisi (Montreal: Ceres, 2004), 225–36; André Vauchez et al., *Jean de Roquetaillade, Liber ostensor quod adesse festinant tempora* (Rome: École française de Rome, 2005), XIII–1041; Sylvain Piron, "L'ecclésiologie franciscaine de Jean de Roquetaillade," *Franciscan Studies* 65 (2007): 281–94.

97. On John of Rupescissa's alchemical writings, especially the *De quinta essentia*, see Thorndike, *History of Magic*, 4:355–69; DeVun, *Prophecy*; Matus, *Franciscans and the Elixir*, 121–38; Principe, *The Secrets of Alchemy*, 64–69; and Marguerite Halversen, "*The Consideration of Quintessence:* An edition of a Middle English translation of John of Rupescissa's *Liber de consideratione de quintae essentiae omnium rerum* with introduction, notes, and commentary" (PhD diss., Michigan State University, 1998).

98. See Thorndike, *History of Magic*, 4:355–69; DeVun, *Prophecy*; Matus, *Franciscans and the Elixir*, 121–38; and Principe, *The Secrets of Alchemy* (Chicago: University of Chicago Press, 2013), 64–69.

99. John of Rupescissa, "Liber lucis," in Manger, *Biblioteca chemica*, 2:84. On the Christian militancy of the Franciscan alchemists, see also Principe, *The Secrets of Alchemy*, 64–69.

3. The Alchemy of Conversion

1. Ramon Llull, *A Contemporary Life*, ed. and trans. by Anthony Bonner (Barcelona: Barcino Tamesis, 2010), 35.
2. Ibid., 41.
3. See Harvey J. Hames, *The Art of Conversion: Christianity and Kabbalah in the Thirteenth Century* (Leiden: Brill, 2000), 8–10.
4. See Harvey J. Hames, ed., *Jews, Muslims, and Christians in and around the Crown of Aragon: Essays in Honour of Professor Elena Lourie* (Leiden: Brill, 2004).
5. St. Augustine, *The City of God* (New York: Modern Library, 1950), 658–59. See also Jonathan Boyarin, *The Unconverted Self: Jews, Indians, and the Identity of Christian Europe* (Chicago: University of Chicago Press, 2009), 7; Charles Tilly, *Coercion, Capital and European States, 990–1992* (Cambridge: Basil Blackwell, 1992); Kenneth Stowe, *Alienated Minority: The Jews of Medieval Latin Europe* (Cambridge: Harvard University Press, 1992); Robert Bartlett, *The Making of Europe: Conquest, Colonization, and Cultural Change, 950–1350* (Princeton: Princeton University Press, 1993); and David Nirenberg, *Communities of Violence: Persecution of Minorities in the Middle Ages* (Princeton: Princeton University Press, 1996).
6. Richard Konetzke, "Points of Departure for the History of Missions in Hispanic America," *Americas* 14, no. 4 (1958): 517; Mark D. Meyerson, *The Muslims*

of Valencia in the Age of Fernando and Isabel: Between Coexistence and Crusade (Berkeley: University of California Press, 1991).

7. See Karen Melvin, *Building Colonial Cities of God: Mendicant Orders and Urban Culture in New Spain* (Nashville: Vanderbilt University Press, 2012), 8, 97–99.

8. For examples of medieval Franciscan travel accounts about China, see Friar Giovanni DiPlano Carpini, *The Story of the Mongols Whom We Call the Tartars,* trans. and introd. Erik Hildinger (Boston: Branden, 2014); and William Rubruck, *The Journey of William of Rubruck to the Eastern Parts of the World,* trans. William Woodville Rockhill (n.p.: Alex Struik, 2012). On the medieval hagiographic and martyrologic tradition as a precursor to Franciscan missionary narratives in the Americas, see José Sánchez Herrero, "Precedentes franciscanos del descubrimiento de América," in *Actas del I Congreso Internacional sobre los Franciscanos en el Nuevo Mundo,* 15–76 (Madrid: Editorial Deimos, 1986); Georges Baudot, "Los precursores Franciscanos de Sahagún del siglo XIII al siglo XVI en Asia y América," *Estudios de Cultura Náhuatl* 32 (2001): 159–73; and James Phelan, *The Millennial Kingdom of the Franciscans in the New World* (Berkeley: University of California Press, 1970), 18–19; Claudio Sánchez-Albornoz, *España y el Islam* (Buenos Aires: Editorial Sudamericana, 1943), esp. 181–99. On Montecorvino, see *Epistolae fr. Iohannis de Monte Corvino,* III, in *Sinica Franciscana I: Itinera et relationes fratrum Minorum saeculi XIII et XIV,* ed. Anastasius Van den Wyngaert (Ad Claras Aquas-Quaracchi, 1919), 352. On the question of missionary successes, see J. D. Ryan, "Conversion vs. Baptism? European Missionaries in Asia in the Thirteenth and Fourteenth Centuries," in *Varieties of Religious Conversion,* ed. James Muldoon (Gainesville: University Press of Florida, 1997), 146–67; and Bert Roest, "Early Mendicant Mission in the New World: Discourses, Experiments, Realities," *Franciscan Studies* 71, no. 1 (2013): 197–217.

9. See David Burr, *The Spiritual Franciscans: From Protest to Persecution in the Century after Saint Francis* (University Park: Pennsylvania State University Press, 2001), 43–66. See also chapters 5 and 6 of this book.

10. See Steven McMichael and Susan Myers, eds., *The Friars and the Jews in the Middle Ages and Renaissance* (Leiden: Brill, 2004).

11. Robin Vose, *Dominicans, Muslims, and Jews in the Medieval Crown of Aragon* (Cambridge: Cambridge University Press, 2009), 54. On conversion in medieval Europe, see Kenneth Mills and Anthony Grafton, eds., *Conversion in Late Antiquity and the Early Middle Ages: Seeing and Believing* (Rochester: University of Rochester Press, 2003); and Michael Sievernich, *Die Christliche Mission: Geschichte und Gegenwart* (Darmstadt: Wissenschaftlich Buchgesellschaft, 2009), 39–82. On the Dominican translation of their traditional mission into the America, see Pedro Fernández Rodríguez, O.P., *Los Dominicos en la primera evangelización de México* (Salamanca: Editorial San Estéban, 1994).

12. See Brian Davies, *Thomas Aquinas's Summa Contra Gentiles: A Guide and Commentary* (New York: Oxford University Press, 2016), 8–10.

13. Hames, *The Art of Conversion,* 1–30.

14. See R. D. F. Pring-Mill, *El microcosmos Lullià* (Palma de Mallorca: Editorial Moll, 1961), 1–32; also Mark Johnston, *The Evangelical Rhetoric of Ramon Llull: Lay Learning and Piety in the Christian West around 1300* (New York: Oxford University Press, 1996), 3–11; Marcelino Menéndez y Pelayo, *Historia de los heterodoxos españoles* (Madrid: F. Maroto é hijos, 1880): 464–525; and Jean Henri Probst, *Caractère et origine des idées du bienheureux Raymond Lulle* (Toulouse: Hachette Livre, 1912).
15. See Hames, *The Art of Conversion*, 9.
16. On the notion of Llull's Art as a "frontier philosophy," see Joaquín Carreras y Artau and Tomas Carreras y Artau, *Historia de la filosofía española: Filosofía cristiana de los siglos XIII al XV*, 2 vols. (Madrid: Real academia de ciencias exactas, fisicas y naturales, 1939), 1:635; Johnston, *The Evangelical Rhetoric;* Nicholas Goodrick-Clarke, "Ramon Llull's New World Order: Esoteric Evangelism and Frontline Philosophy," *Aries* 9, no. 2 (2009): 175–94; and Pere Villalba I Varneda, *Ramon Llull: Escriptor i filòsof de la diferència* (Bellaterra: Universitat Autònoma de Barcelona, 2015).
17. See Amy Remensnyder, *La Conquistadora: The Virgin Mary at War and Peace in the Old and the New Worlds* (New York: Oxford University Press, 2014), 166–70.
18. J. N. Hillgarth, *Ramon Lull and Lullism in Fourteenth-Century France*. Oxford-Warburg Studies (Oxford: Clarendon, 1971), 30.
19. See Frances Yates, "Ramon Lull and John Scotus Erigena," *Journal of the Warburg and Courtauld Institutes* 23, no. 1–2 (1960): 1–44.
20. For a comprehensive catalogue and description of Llull's works, see Lull, *Selected Works,* ed. Bonner, 2:1256–304.
21. Llull, *A Contemporary Life,* 51.
22. Ibid., 53.
23. See Johnston, *The Evangelical Rhetoric,* 8; also George Terhune Peck, *The Fool of God, Jacopone da Todi* (Tuscaloosa: University of Alabama Press, 1980).
24. See Lola Badia, Joan Santanach, and Albert Soler, *Ramon Llull as a Vernacular Writer: Communicating a New Kind of Knowledge* (Woodbridge, Suffolk, UK: Boydell and Brewer, 2016).
25. Ramon Lull, *Book of Knighthood and Chivalry,* trans. William Caxton and modernized by Brian R. Price (n.p.: Brian Price, 2001), 1.
26. Ibid., 22.
27. Ibid.
28. Ibid., 25.
29. Ramón Llull, *Blanquerna,* trans. E. Allison Peers (London: Jarrolds, 1926), 68.
30. Ibid., 317. See also Roberto González-Casanovas, *The Apostolic Hero and Community in Ramon Llull's "Blanquerna": A Literary Study of a Medieval Utopia* (New York: P. Lang, 1995).
31. Llull, *Blanquerna,* 162.
32. Ibid., 162–63.

33. Ibid., 166.
34. Ramon Llull, *The Book of the Lover and the Beloved,* trans. Mark Johnston (Bristol: Centre for Mediterranean Studies, University of Bristol, 1995), 139n215.
35. Ibid., 5.
36. Sebastián Trias Mercant, "La ideología Lulliana de Miramar," *Esutios Lulianos* 22, no. 64–66 (1978): 12.
37. Ramón Llull, "The Book of the Gentile and the Three Wise Men," in *Selected Works,* by Llull, ed. Bonner, 1:91–304. See also L. Badia, *Teoria I pràctica de la literature en Ramón Llull* (Barcelona: Quadems Crema, 1992), 19–29; Hames, *Art of Conversion,* 155–82; and Cohen, *The Friars and the Jews,* 205–14.
38. See note 8 above.
39. See Albert Soler i Llopart, "El *Liber super Psalmum Quicumque* de Ramon Llull i l'opció pels Tàrtars," *Studia Lulliana* 32 (1992): 3–19.
40. Llull, "Felix: or the Book of Wonders," in *Selected Works,* ed. Bonner, 2:982.
41. Llull, *Blanquerna,* 330–31.
42. Benjamin Liu, "The Mongol in the Text," in *Under the Influence: Questioning the Comparative in Medieval Castile,* ed. Cynthia Robinson and Leyla Rouhi (Leiden: Brill, 2005), 297.
43. Llull, *Blanquerna,* 400–401.
44. See Martin Gardner, *Logic Machines and Diagrams* (New York: McGraw-Hill, 1958), 1–27; Paolo Rossi, *"Clavis universalis," Arti mnemoiche e logica combinatorial da Lullo a Leibnitz* (Milan: Ricciardi, 1960); and Erhard-Wolfram Platzeck, "Gottfried Wilhem Leibniz y Raimundo Llull," *Estudios Lulianos* 16 (1972): 129–93.
45. See Miguel Cruz Hernández, *El pensamiento de Ramon Llull* (Madrid: Castalia, 1977); and Mark Johnston, *The Spiritual Logic of Ramon Llull* (Oxford: Clarendon, 1987), 15–27. On Llull's significance for the history of modern computational systems, see Bonner, *The Art and Logic of Ramon Lull: A User's Guide* (Leiden: Brill, 2007), 295.
46. In Llull, *Selected Works,* ed. Bonner, 1:425.
47. See Bonner, *The Art and Logic of Ramon Lull;* see also Johnston, *The Evangelical Rhetoric,* 12–33; Hames, *The Art of Conversion;* Annemarie Mayer, "Charting the Attributes of God: The Common Ground of Three Religions According to Ramon Llull (1232–1316)," *International Journal for the Study of the Christian Church* 9, no. 2 (2009): 95–117; Frances Yates, "The Art of Ramon Lull: An Approach to It through Lull's Theory of the Elements," *Journal of the Warburg and Courtault Institutes* 17 (1954): 115–73; and Charles Lohr, "Metaphysics," in *The Cambridge History of Renaissance Philosophy,* ed. Charles Schmitt, Quentin Skinner, and Eckhard Kessler, 537–638 (Cambridge: Cambridge University Press, 1988).
48. Mary Franklin-Brown, *Reading the World: Encyclopedic Writing in the Scholastic Age* (Chicago: University of Chicago Press, 2012), 35; on Llull, see 129–81. On Llull's tree, see also Paolo Rossi, "The Legacy of Ramon Llull," *Medieval and*

Renaissance Studies (Warburg Institute) 5 (1961): 182–213; and Fernando Domínguez Reboiras, Pere Villalba Verneda, and Peter Walter, eds., *Arbor scientiae: Der Baum des Wissens von Ramon Llull* (Turnhout, Belgium: Brepols, 2002).
49. Higuera Rubio, "Saint Louis and Llull's 'Plan,'" 178. On St. Francis, see Bert Roest, "Early Mendicant Mission," 197.
50. On Llull and John Scotus Erigena, see Yates, "Ramon Lull," 1–44. On Llull and Bonaventure, see Johnston, *The Evangelical Rhetoric*, 17–20; on Bonaventure's concept of *reductio artium ad theologiam,* see Saint Bonaventure, *Breviloquium: De reduction atrium ad theologiam: Collationes in Hexaemeron,* in *Opera omnia,* 5 vols. (Quaracchi: Collegium S. Bonventure, 1891); Jay Hammond, "Contemplation and the Formation of the *vir spiritualis* in Bonaventure's *Collationes in Hexaemeron,*" in *Franciscans at Prayer,* ed. Timothy Johnson (Leiden: Brill, 2007), 123–66; and Guy Allard, "La technique de la 'reductio,' chez Bonaventure," in *S. Bonaventure, 1274–1974,* ed. Jacques Guy Bougerol et al., 2 vols. (Grottaferrata, Italy: Collegio S. Bonaventure, 1973).
51. Llull, "The Principles of Medicine," in *Selected Works,* ed. Bonner, 2:1199. See also R. D. F. Pring-Mill, *The Analogical Structure of the Lullian Art* (Oxford, UK: Cassirer, 1972); Anthony Bonner, "Lull's Thought," in *Selected Works,* by Llull, 1:66–67; and Yates, "Art." On the metaphorical dimension of Llull's medicine, see Joseph Ziegler, *Medicine and Religion, c. 1300: The Case of Arnau de Vilanova* (Oxford: Clarendon, 1998), 54–59; and E. Gisbert, "Metaforice loquendo: De l'analogia a la metàfora en els Començaments de medicina de Ramon Llull," *Studia Lulliana* 44, no. 100 (2004): 17–52; Johnston, *Evangelical,* 101–2.
52. Llull, "Principles of Medicine," 1128–29.
53. Ibid., 1129.
54. Ibid.
55. Ibid., 1128.
56. Qtd. in Yates, "Art," 114.
57. Ziegler, *Medicine,* 59.
58. Qtd. ibid., 180.
59. Ramon Llull, *Doctrina pueril,* ed. Gret Schib (Barcelona: Editorial Barcino, 1972), 194. It is not clear when Llull wrote this text, but see S. Garciás Palou, "Que año escribió Ramon Lull la 'Doctrina Pueril'?," *Estudios Lulianos* 12 (1968): 33–45; and E. Blanco Gómez, "La fecha de composición de la 'Doctrina Pueril,'" *Estudios Lulianos* 29 (1989): 147–54. The text, originally written in Catalan, circulated widely in multiple languages already during medieval times and has been reedited in modern times (see *La versione occitanica della "Doctrina pueril" di Ramon Llull,* ed. Maria Carla Marinoni [Milan: LED, 1997]; Maria Carla Marinoni, "Per il testo della 'Doctrina Pueril' provenzale," in *Filologia romanza e cultura medievale: Studi in onore di Elio Melli,* ed. Andrea Fassò et al. [Alessandria: Edizioni Dell'Orso, 1998], 509–23; *Doctrine d'enfant,* ed. A. Llinarès [Paris, 1969]).
60. Llull, *Doctrina pueril,* 194–95.

61. See, for example, David Abulafia, *The Discovery of Mankind: Atlantic Encounters in the Age of Columbus* (New Haven: Yale University Press, 2008), 23; see also Baéz-Rubí, "Die 'Rhetorica Christiana' (Perugia 1579) des Fray Diego de Valadés als Ausdruck franziskanischer Missionstheologie," *Zeitschrift für Missionswissenschaft und Religionswissenschaft* 92, no. 3 (2008): 335; and Edgar Allison Peers, *Ramon Llull: A Biography* (London: Society for Promoting Christian Knowledge, 1929), 97. For a critical discussion of this issue, see Gabriel Ensenyat, "Pacifism and Crusade in Ramon Llull," *Quaderns de la Mediterrània* 9 (2008): 137–44.
62. On Llull and Jewish expulsion, see Jeremy Cohen, *The Friars and the Jews: The Evolution of Medieval Anti-Judaism* (Ithaca, NY: Cornell University Press, 1982), 199–225.
63. On the dual *ordinatio* of *bellandi* and *convertendi*, see José Higuera Rubio, "Saint Louis and Llull's 'Plan' for the Crusade in the Western Mediterranean," in *Life and Religion in the Middle Ages,* ed. Flocel Sabaté (Newcastle, UK: Cambridge Scholars Publishing, 2015), 163–83; and Bert Roest, "Medieval Franciscan Mission: History and Concept," in *Strategies of Medieval Communal Identity: Judaism, Christianity and Islam,* ed. Wout J. van Bekkum and Paul M. Cobb (Paris: Peeters, 2004), 137–61. On violence in Franciscan missionology in the New World, see Julia McClure, *The Franciscan Invention of the New World* (Cham, Switzerland: Springer International, 2016), esp. chap. 5, "Franciscan Landscapes of Identity and Violence: The Franciscan Invention of Coloniality" (117–58); and Andrew L. Toth, *Missionary Practices and Spanish Steel: The Evolution of Apostolic Mission in the Context of New Spain Conquests* (Bloomington: Universe Com, 2012).
64. Llull, "Felix: or the Book of Wonders," in *Selected Works,* ed. Bonner, 2:660.
65. Ibid., 777. On Llull's disapproval of alchemy, see A. Llinarès, "L'idée de nature et la condemnation de l'alchimie d'après le 'Livre des merveilles' de Raymond Llulle," *La filosofia della natura nel medioevo: Atti del III Congreso Internazionale di Filosofía Medioevale* (Milan: Società Editrice Vita E Pensiero, 1966), 536–41n.
66. Pseudo-Llull, *Il testamentum alchemico attribuito a Raimundo Lullo,* ed. Michela Pereira and Barbara Spaggiari (Florence: Sismel, 1999), 512–14. On the textual problems and variations, see the introduction to that volume; and Dorothea Waley Singer, "The Alchemical Testament Attributed to Raymund Lull," *Archeion* 9, no. 1 (1928): 43–52.
67. See Pereira and Spaggiari, introduction to Pseudo-Llull, *Il testamentum,* cxxxviii–clxiv.
68. Pseudo-Llull, *Il testamentum,* 396, 130.
69. See Michela Pereira, "Ramon Llull and the Alchemical Tradition," *Catalonia* 43 (1995): 40–43. On the *Testamentum* in particular and the pseudo-Llullian alchemical tradition in general, see Pereira, *The Alchemical Corpus Attributed to Raymond Llull* (London: Warburg Institute, 1989); see also Pereira, "Lullian Alchemy: Aspects and Problems of the Corpus of Alchemical Works Attributed to Ramon Llull (XIV–XVII Centuries)," *Catalan Review* 4, no. 1–2 (1990): 41–54;

Pereira, "La leggenda di Llullo alchmista," *Estudios Lulianos* 27 (1987): 145–63; Pereira, "Il santo alchimista: Intrecci leggendari attorno a Raimondo Lullo," *Micrologus: Natura, scienze e società medievali* 21 (2013): 471–516; Carreras y Artau and Carreras y Artau, *Historia de la filosofía española*, 2:45–58; Lynn Thorndike, *A History of Magic and Experimental Science* (New York: Columbia University Press, 1923–41), 1:862–73, 4:3–64; Leah DeVun, *Prophecy, Alchemy, and the End of Time: John of Rupescissa in the Late Middle Ages* (New York: Columbia University Press, 2009), 95–99; Miguel Pérez-Lopez, "Algunos rasgos sobre la relación entre lulismo y pseudolulismo en la Edad Moderna," *Biblid* 22 (2002): 327–50; and Lawrence Principe, *The Secrets of Alchemy* (Chicago: University of Chicago Press, 2013), 71–73. The last great defender of the idea of Llull as an alchemist was the eighteenth-century German Llulist Ivo Salzinger, who collected, edited, and published Llull's works, including the seventy-seven alchemical works attributed to Llull (see the *Raymundi Llulli opera omnia*, ed. Ivo Salzinger [Mainz, 1721–42]). The first critical assessment of the legend was Gabriel Naudé's *Apologie pour toutes les grands personnages* (1625); see Pereira, *Alchemical*, 59. While there were a few other scholars who doubted the authenticity of Llull's alchemical works, including Benito Jerónimo Feijóo y Montenegro in the eighteenth century, the first modern study debunking the myth of Llull the alchemist was José Ramón de Luanco's *Ramon Lull (Raimundo Lulio) considerado como alquimista* (Barcelona: Establecimiento tipográfico de Jaime Jepús Roviralta, 1870).

70. Pereira, *Alchemical corpus*, 6; see also Pereira, "Introduzione storica," in *Testamentum*, vii–lxii. However, Pereira and Spaggiari, in their bilingual edition cited here, divide the work into three parts, omitting the last.

71. Thorndike, *History*, 4:40.

72. Llull, *Testamentum*, 12.

73. Ibid., 14–16.

74. Ibid., 306.

75. On Bacon's and Arnald's alchemical theories, see chapter 2 of this book.

76. *Ars operativa*, in Jean de Roquetaillade, et al., *Ioannis de Rupescissa, qui vixit ante CCCXX annos, De consideratione quintae essentiae rerum omnium, opus sanè Egregium. Accessere Arnaldi De Villanoua Epistola de sanguine humano distillato. Raymundi Lullii Ars Operatiua, & alia quaedam. Michaelis Sauanarolae Libellus optimus de aqua vitae, nunc valde correctior quàm ante annos LXX editus. Omnia ad selectissimam materiam medicam, & morborum curationem, vitaeque conseruationem mirabiliter facientia* (Basel: per Conradum Waldkirch, 1597), 151. See also M. Pereira, "*Medicina* in the Alchemical Writings Attributed to R. Lull (14th–17th Centuries)," *Alchemy and Chemistry in the 16th and 17th Centuries*, ed. Piyo Rattansi and Antonio Clericuzio (Dordrecht: Kluwer Academic, 1994), 1–16.

77. In Jean-Jacques Manget, *Bibliotheca chemica curiosa, seu rerum ad alchemiam pertinentium thesaurus instructissimus*, 2 vols. (Geneva: Chouet, G. de Tournes, Cramer, Perachon, Ritter & S. de Tournes, 1702), 1:908. On the *Codicillus*, see Thorndike, *History* 4:32; M. Pereira, "Un innesto sull' *Arbor scientiae*: L'alchima

nella tradizione lulliana," *Studia Lulliana* 36, no. 92 (1996): 79–97; and Bruce Moran, *Distilling Knowledge: Alchemy, Chemistry, and the Scientific Revolution* (Cambridge: Harvard University Press, 2005), 20.
78. In Manget, *Biblioteca chemica curiosa*, 1:884.
79. Ibid., 1:880–81, 888.
80. On Paracelsus's notion of "Elias the Artist," see William Newman, *Gehennical Fire: The Lives of George Starkey, an American Alchemist in the Scientific Revolution* (Cambridge: Harvard University Press, 1994), 3.
81. Ramon Llull, *Sacri Doctoris Raymundi Lulii de secretis nature siue de quinta essentia libellus* (Augsburg, 1518), n.p. On the *Liber*, see also M. Pereira, "'Vegetare seu transmutare': The Vegetable Soul and Pseudo-Lullian Alchemy," in *Arbor scientiae*, ed. Fernando Domínguez Reboiras, Pere Villalba Varneda, and Peter Walter, 93–119; see also Pereira, "Filosofia naturale lulliana e alchimia: Con l'inedito epilogo del 'Liber de secretis naturae seu de quinta essentia,'" *Revista di storia della filosofia* 4 (1986): 747–80.
82. This epilogue is omitted from the printed edition of the *Liber* cited here but has been edited and published by Pereira in "Filosofia naturale lulliana e alchimia: Con l'inedito epilogo del 'Liber de secretis naturae seu de quinta essentia,'" *Rivista de storia della filosofia* 4 (1986): 747–80.
83. See Pereira, *Alchemical*, 11–17.
84. Pereira, "Vegetare," 94.
85. Ettore Ausonio, *Trattato sopra l'arte dell' alchimia* (Biblioteca Ambrosiana, Milan, MS IMILAQ1k185/00: Varia Miscellanea, Inter Quae). See also Pereira, "La leggenda" and *The Alchemical Corpus*, 46–47, 93–94.

4. The Secrets of the World

1. "Relación del Cuarto Viaje," in *Cristóbal Colón: Textos y documentos completos*, ed. Consuelo Varela and Juan Gil, 485–503 (1982; Madrid: Alianza Editorial, 2003), 492; my translation. For the textual history and historical context of this letter, also known as the "lettera rarissima," see Antonio Rumeu de Armas, *Libro Copiardor de Cristóbal Colón: Correspondencia inédita con los Reyes Católocos sobre los viajes a América, Estudio histórico-crítico y edición*, 2 vols. (Madrid: Testimonio Compañía Editorial, 1989), 1:375–430.
2. Samuel Eliot Morison, *Admiral of the Ocean Sea* (Boston: Little, Brown, 1942), 6. The notion of Columbus's "madness" originated already during the nineteenth century, for example, in H. Harrisse's *Notes on Columbus* (New York: privately printed 1866), 156. M. Fernández de Ybarra speculated that Columbus's religious vision was the result of a "psychical perturbation" induced by a combination of blood poison, grief and disappointment, hardship, unhygienic surroundings, and the want of proper treatment (see "The Medical History of Christopher Columbus," *Journal of the American Medical Association* 12, no. 18 [May 5, 1894]: 651, 652). For more recent speculations on Columbus's delirium, madness, or senility, see

Antonello Gerbi, *Nature in the New World: From Christopher Columbus to Gonzalo Fernández de Oviedo,* trans. J. Moyle (Pittsburgh: University of Pittsburgh Press, 1986), 26–27; Gianni Gronzotto, *Cristoforo Colombo* (Milan: Arnoldo Mondadori, 1984), 292; and Felipe Fernández-Armesto, *Columbus* (New York: Oxford University Press, 1991). For "revisionist" accounts asserting the materialist rationalism of Columbus, see Edmundo O'Gorman, *The Invention of America* (Westport, CT: Greenwood, 1972); Stephen Greenblatt, *Marvelous Possessions: The Wonder of the New World* (Chicago: University of Chicago Press, 1991); David Stannard, *American Holocaust: Columbus and the Conquest of the New World* (New York: Oxford University Press, 1992); Kirkpatrick Sale, *The Conquest of Paradise: Christopher Columbus and the Columbian Legacy* (New York: Knopf, 1990). For interpretations of the prophetic and millenarian themes as rhetorical strategies, see Ramón Iglesia, *El Hombre Colón* (Mexico City: Colegio de México, 1944); Djelal Kadir, *Columbus and the Ends of the Earth: Europe's Prophetic Rhetoric as Conquering Ideology* (Berkeley: University of California Press, 1992); and Elise Bartosik-Vélez, "The Three Rhetorical Strategies of Christopher Columbus," *Colonial Latin American Review* 11, no. 1 (2002): 33–46.

3. As Margarita Zamora has shown in her meticulous study of Columbus's writings, the religious motivations of Columbus's project were introduced into his official correspondence with the court not by the Catholic Monarchs (whose interest in Columbus's project appears to have been of a strictly commercial nature) but by Columbus himself (see Margarita Zamora, *Reading Columbus* [Berkeley: University of California Press, 1993], 21–38 and 95–151). See also Pauline Moffitt Watts, "Prophecy and Discovery: On the Spiritual Origins of the Enterprise of the Indies," *American Historical Review* 90, no. 1–2 (1985): 73–102, 83. On Columbus's marginalia, see also Moffitt Watts, "Science, Religion, and Columbus's Enterprise of the Indies," *OAH Magazine of History* 5, no. 4 (Spring 1991): 14–17; and "Apocalypse Then: Christopher Columbus's Conception of History and Prophecy," in *Medievalia et Humanistica: Studies in Medieval and Renaissance Culture,* n.s., no. 19: "Renaissance and Discovery," ed. Paul Maurice Clogan (Lanham, MD: Rowman and Littlefield, 1993), 1–10. On the importance of millenarianism, prophecy, and the spiritual aspects of Columbus's project more generally, see Marcel Bataillon, "Evangélisme et millénarisme au Nouveau Monde," *Courants religieux et humanism a la fin de xve et au début de xvie siècle* (Paris: Presses Universitaires de France, 1959), 25–36; James Phelan, *The Millennial Kingdom of the Franciscans in the New World* (Berkeley: University of California Press, 1970), 17–28; Adriano Prosperi, "America e apocalisse: Note sulla 'conquista spirituale,'" *Critica Storica* 13 (1976): 1–61; Prosperi, "New Heaven and New Earth: Prophecy and Propaganda at the Time of the Discovery and Conquest of the Americas," in *Prophetic Rome in the High Renaissance Period,* ed. Marjorie Reeves (London: Clarendon, 1992), 279–304; Alain Milhou, *Colón y su mentalidad mesiánica en el ambiente franciscanista español* (Valladolid: Casa-Museo de Colón Seminario americanista de la Universidad de Valladolid, 1983); Leonard Sweet, "Christopher

Columbus and the Millennial Vision of the New World," *Catholic Historical Review* 72, no. 3 (July 1986): 369–82; Delno West, "Wallowing in a Theological Stupor or a Steadfast Consuming Faith: Scholarly Encounters with Columbus's *Libro de Profecías,*" in *Columbus and His World: Proceedings, First San Salvador Conference,* ed. Donald T. Gerace (Fort Lauderdale: College Center of the Finger Lakes, 1987), 45–56; West, "Christopher Columbus, Lost Biblical Sites, and the Last Crusade," *Catholic Historical Review* 78 (1992): 519–41; Valerie Flint, *The Imaginative Landscape of Christopher Columbus* (Princeton: Princeton University Press, 1992), 54–70; Flint, "Christopher Columbus and the Friars," in *Intellectual Life in the Middle Ages,* ed. Lesley Janette Smith (New York: Continuum, 2002), 295–310; James Romm, "Biblical History and the Americas: The Legend of Solomon's Ophir, 1492–1591," in *The Jews and the Expansion of Europe to the West, 1400–1800,* ed. Paolo Bernadini and Norman Fiering, 27–46 (New York: Berghahn, 2001), 29; Carol Delaney, *Columbus and the Quest for Jerusalem* (New York: Free Press, 2011); and Pablo Pérez García, "Dos usos y dos sentidos de la propaganda política en la España tardomedieval: El profetismo hispánico encubertista trastámara y el profetismo épico imperial carolino," *Res publica* 18 (2007): 179–223.
4. While the intellectual debate about the concept of "tradition" was long dominated by the sociological approach laid out by Edward Shils in *Tradition* (Chicago: University of Chicago Press, 1981) as well as by Eric Hobsbawm and Terence Ranger in their coedited volume *The Invention of Tradition* (Cambridge: Cambridge University Press, 1983), more recent approaches have critiqued their social constructivism. See, for example, *Questions of Tradition: Exploring the Concept of Tradition across the Disciplines,* ed. Mark Salber Phillips and Gordon Schochet (Toronto: Toronto University Prss, 204). For an anthropological critique of the paradigm, see Marshall Sahlins, "Two or Three Things I Know about Culture," *Journal of the Royal Anthropological Institute,* n.s., vol. 5, no. 3 (1999): 299–421; and Néstor García Canclini, *Hybrid Cultures: Strategies for Entering and Leaving Modernity,* trans. Christopher L. Chappari and Silvia L. López (Minneapolis: University of Minnesota Press, 1995). For an approach from the humanities, I am especially indebted to Stephen Prickett, *Modernity and the Reinvention of Tradition: Backing into the Future* (Cambridge: Cambridge University Press, 2009); and *Words and the Word: Language, Poetics, and Biblical Interpretation* (Cambridge: Cambridge University Press, 1986); and Stephen Prickett, *Narrative, Religion and Science: Fundamentalism Versus Irony, 1700–1999* (Cambridge: Cambridge University Press, 2004).
5. Colón, *Textos,* 498.
6. Robert Lerner, "Ecstatic Dissent," *Speculum* 67, no. 1 (January 1992): 54. As Lerner points out (54n78), the exception in this tradition of "spiritual intelligence," was ironically Joachim himself, who held the laity subordinate to the clergy.
7. For claims for the Joachimite roots of Columbus's spirituality, see Marjorie Reeves, *The Influence of Prophecy in the Later Middle Ages: A Study in Joachimism*

(Oxford: Clarendon, 1969), 360; Roberto Rusconi, introduction to *The "Book of Prophecies" edited by Christopher Columbus*, ed. Rusconi, trans. Blair Sullivan, vol. 3 of Repertorium Columbianum (Berkeley: University of California Press, 1997), 33; see also Prosperi, "America"; and "New Heaven"; Delaney, *Columbus*, 285.

8. Colón, *Textos*, 89.
9. On Columbus's plan for writing a poem about his voyages, see Delno West and August Kling, introduction to *The Libro de las profecías of Christopher Columbus*, ed. West and Kling (Gainesville: University of Florida Press, 1991), 5; and West, "Medieval Ideas of Apocalyptic Mission and the Early Franciscans in Mexico," *Americas* 45, no. 3 (January 1989): 304.
10. Rusconi, introduction to *The "Book of Prophecies,"* 8–11. On the history of Columbus's interest in biblical prophecy, see Hector Avalos, "Columbus as Biblical Exegete: A Study of the *Libro de las profecías*," in *Religion in the Age of Exploration: The Case of Spain and New Spain*, ed. Bryan F. Le Beau and Menachem Mor (Omaha, NE, Creighton University Press, 1996), 59–80.
11. "Christ Bearer" is the interpretation that Bartolomé de las Casas gave this signature, writing that "Llamose por nombre Cristóbal, conviene a saber *Christum Ferens*, que quiere decir traedor o llevador de Cristo, y así se firma él algunas veces" (*Las Casas on Columbus: Background and The Second and Fourth Voyages*, ed. Nigel Griffin, vol. 7 of Repertorium Columbianum [Turnhout, Belgium: Brepols, 1999], 25, 29, 116, 154); see also *Las Casas on Columbus: The Third Voyage*, ed. Jesús Carillo, trans. Michael Hammer and Blair Sullivan, vol. 11 of Repertorium Colombianum (Turnhout, Belgium: Brepols, 2001), 134. However, as Consuelo Varela has pointed out, Columbus's signature reads not "Christum Ferens" but "Christo Ferens"; i.e., Christ is not the direct but the indirect object, which would have to be more accurately rendered as the "bearer for Christ" (see introduction to *Textos*, 83).
12. Juan Pérez de Tudela dated the earliest document bearing this distinctive signature at 1501 (see *Las armadas de Indias y los origins de la política de colonización [1492–1505]* [Madrid: CSIC, 1956], 216). However, more recent textual scholarship suggests that the first time Columbus used this signature was much earlier, specifically in his letter to Rodrigo de Escobedo, written on January 4, 1493, from Hispaniola (see *Textos*, 219). For interpretations of its meaning, see Morison, *Admiral*, 356–57; and Milhou, *Colón*, 65.
13. *The Vulgate*, Luke 24:25–26, http://vulgate.org/nt/gospel/luke_24.htm.
14. *The "Book of Prophecies,"* ed. Rusconi, 296–97. Further references to this edition will appear abbreviated as *BP*. See also Las Casas, *Las Casas on Columbus . . . Second and Fourth voyages*, 25. On Columbus's realist metaphysics, see Kadir, *Columbus*, 11.
15. *The Vulgate*, Revelation 1:9–10, http://vulgate.org/nt/epistle/revelation_1.htm.
16. *BP*, 346–47.
17. Ibid., 147.

18. *The Vulgate,* Revelation 20:4, http://vulgate.org/nt/epistle/revelation_20.htm.
19. On the multiple early modern meanings of the word "discovery," see chapter 1 of this book.
20. *The Book of Privileges Issued to Christopher Columbus by King Ferdinand and Queen Isabel,* ed. and trans. Helen Nader, vol. 2 of Repertorium Columbianum (Berkeley: University of California Press, 1996), 63–66, 63.
21. On the idea of Columbus's secret foreknowledge of the existence of the American continent, see Juan Manzano Manzano, *Colón y su secreto: El predescubrimiento* (Madrid: Ediciones de Cultura Hispánica, 1989). For a critique of this idea, see Antonio Rumeu de Armas, *Nueva luz sobre las Capitulaciones de Santa Fe de 1492* (Madrid: Consejo Superior De Investigaciones Científicas, 1985); Stuart Schwartz, *The Iberian Mediterranean and Atlantic Traditions in the Formation of Columbus as a Colonizer* (Minneapolis: University of Minnesota, the Associates of the James Ford Bell Library, 1986); and William D. Phillips Jr. and Carla Rahn Phillips, *The Worlds of Christopher Columbus* (Cambridge: Cambridge University Press, 1992), 133–35.
22. Zamora, *Reading Columbus,* 27
23. Colón, *Textos,* 95–96.
24. *BP,* 144–47; my emphasis.
25. Ibid., 63, 136–55, 162–63.
26. Ibid., 64–65.
27. Ibid., 66–67.
28. In John Boyd Thacher, *Christopher Columbus: His Life, His Works,* vol. 3 (New York: G. P. Putnam's Sons, 1903), 2:423–38, 424, 431.
29. *BP,* 74–75.
30. Ibid., 179.
31. Ibid., 185.
32. *Las Casas on Columbus: The Third Voyage,* 137–38, 297.
33. Colón, *Textos,* 497–98.
34. *BP,* 322–23.
35. James Romm, "Biblical History and the Americas," 29. On Columbus's alleged Jewish ancestry, see Salvador de Madariaga, *Christopher Columbus* (London: Hollis and Cater, 1949), 54–65; Juan Gil, "Colón y la Casa Santa," *Historiografía y Bibliografía Americanistas* 21 (1977): 125–35; and Jonathan Sarna, "The Mythical Jewish Columbus and the History of America's Jews," in *Religion in the Age of Exploration: The Case of Spain and New Spain,* ed. Bryan F. Le Beau and Menachem Mor (Omaha, NE, Creighton University Press, 1996), 81–116.
36. Columbus's copy of the Bible has not been found, and it is not known with certainty which edition of the Vulgate was the basis for the Scriptural excerpts in the *Book of Prophecies.* In the introduction to their edition of the *Book of Prophecies* (1991), Delno West and August Kling assume that it was an early printed edition of the Sixto-Clementine "Vulgate *textus receptus,*" and they note that, if their assumption is correct, many of the transcriptions were faulty (*The Libro de las*

profecías, 81–83, 86). Héctor Ignacio Avalos ("The Biblical Sources of Columbus's 'Libro de las Profecías,'" *Traditio* 49 [1994]: 331–35), however, has pointed out that the earliest edition of this Sixto-Clementine *textus receptus* only dates back to 1592 and therefore did not exist when the *Book of Prophecies* was being compiled. He showed that the Scriptural excerpts of the *Book of Prophecies* correspond rather faithfully to two editions of the *Biblia sacra cum glosa ordinaria et interlineari* that contain the scriptural commentary of Nicholas of Lyra, *Biblia sacra . . . cum postillis Nicolai de Lyra* published in 1492 and 1498 and particularly to the latter (333). Nicholas of Lyra's commentary on Ophir excerpted in the *Book of Prophecies* can be found in Nicholas de Lyra, *Postilla super totam bibliam* (Frankfurt: Minerva, 1971), n.p., 3 Kings, chap. 9.

37. On the idea of late Scholastic "ancient texts" as a living tradition, see Anthony Grafton's *New Worlds, Ancient Texts: The Power of Tradition and the Shock of Discovery* (Cambridge: Harvard University Press, 1995), which considers especially the fifteenth-century dissemination of Ptolemy (13–27). On the colonialist dimensions of the rise of humanism in the sixteenth century, see Walter Mignolo, *The Darker Side of the Renaissance* (Ann Arbor: University of Michigan Press, 1994), 125–69.

38. *BP,* 164–65.

39. Robert Lerner, "The Refreshment of the Saints: The Time after Antichrist as a Station for Earthly Progress in Medieval Thought," *Traditio* 32 (1976): 143–44. See also his *The Power of Prophecy: The Cedar of Lebanon Vision from the Mongol Onslaught to the Dawn of the Enlightenment* (Berkeley: University of California Press, 1983); and Brett Edward Whalen, *Dominion of God: Christendom and Apocalypse in the Middle Ages* (Cambridge: Harvard University Press, 2009). On the connection between the Christian millenarian tradition and the history of the Western idea of progress, see David Noble, *The Religion of Technology: The Divinity of Man and the Spirit of Invention* (New York: Knopf, 1997), 21–42.

40. St. Augustine of Hippo, *The City of God,* trans. Marcus Dods and introd. Thomas Merton (New York: Modern Library, 1950), 718–19.

41. Ibid. See also Richard Landes, "Lest the Millennium Be Fulfilled: Apocalyptic Expectations and the Pattern of Western Chronography, 100–800 CE," in *The Use and Abuse of Eschatology in the Middles Ages,* ed. Werner Verbke, Daniel Verhelst, and Andrien Welkenhuysen (Louvain: Leuven University Press, 1988), 137–211; Noble, *Religion,* 22–23; Norman Cohn, *The Pursuit of the Millennium: Revolutionary Millenarians and Mystical Anarchists of the Middle Ages* (Oxford: Oxford University Press, 1961), 27–29.

42. Ernst Sackur, *Sibyllinische Texte und Forschungen: Pseudomethodius, Adso und die Tiburtinsche Sibylle* (Halle: Max Niemeyer, 1898), 1–96; Agostino Pertusi, *Fine di Bisanzio e fine del mondo: Significato e ruolo storico delle profezie sulla caduta di costantinopoli in oriente e in occidente* (Rome: Nella Sede Dell Istituto Palazzo Borromini, 1988); Benjamin Garstad, introduction to *Apocalypse of Pseudo-Methodius. An Alexandrian World Chronicle,* ed. and trans. Benjamin Garstad (Cambridge:

Harvard University Press, 2012), vii–xxxix; José Guadalajara Medina, *Las profecías del Anticristo en la edad media* (Madrid: Gredos, 19960), 133–71; G. J. Reinink, introduction to *Die Syrische Apokalypse des Pseudo-Methodius* (Louvain, Belgium: Corpus Scriptorum Christianorum Orientalium, 1993), vii–xl.

43. *BP,* 76–77.
44. Joachim of Fiore, *Expositio in Apocalypsim* (Frankfurt: Minerva, 1964), 127; see also Ernst Benz, *Evolution and Christian Hope* (Garden City, NY: Doubleday, 1975). The literature on the Joachimite millenarian tradition is extensive, but for some landmark studies see Marjorie Reeves, *The Influence of Prophecy in the Later Middle Ages: A Study in Joachimism* (Oxford: Oxford University Press, 1969); Reeves, *Joachim of Fiore and the Prophetic Future: A Medieval Study in Historical Thinking* (1976; London: Sutton, 1999); Bernard McGinn, *The Calabrian Abbot: Joachim of Fiore in the History of Western Thought* (New York: Macmillan, 1985); Richard K. Emerson and Bernard McGinn, eds., *The Apocalypse in the Middle Ages* (Ithaca, NY: Cornell University Press, 1992); Delno West, ed., *Joachim of Fiore in Christian Thought: Essays on the Influence of the Calabrian Prophet,* 2 vols. (New York: Burt Franklin, 1975); Gian Luca Potestà, ed., *Il profetismo gioachimita tra Quattrocento e Cinquecento, Atti del III Congresso Internazionale di Studi Gioachimiti S. Giovanni in Fiore, 17–21 settembre 1989* (Genoa: Marietti, 1991); and Julia Eva Wannenmacher, *Hermeneutik der Heilsgeschichte: "De Septem Sigilis" und die sieben Siegel im Werk Joachims von Fiore* (Leiden: Brill, 2005).
45. Noble, *The Religion of Technology,* 22.
46. On Columbus's naming practices, see also Leonardo Olschki, "The Columbian Nomenclature of the Lesser Antilles," *Geographical Review* 33, no. 3 (1943): 397–414.
47. Colón, *Textos,* 126, 134.
48. Juan Gil, introduction to *Textos,* 15–79, 27; Evelina Gužauskytė, *Christopher Columbus's Naming in the Diarios of the Four Voyages (1492–1504): A Discourse of Negotiation* (Toronto: University of Toronto Press, 2014). On the alchemical motifs in Columbus's place-names, see esp. 82–102.
49. *BP,* 67.
50. See Klaus Wagner, *Judicia Astrologica Colombiniana: Bibliographisches Verzeichnis einer Sammlung von Praktiken des 15. und 16. Jahrhunderts der Biblioteca Colombina Sevillla* (Frankfurt: Buchhändler-Vereinigung, 1975); on Columbus's interest in astrology, see also Nicolás Wey Gómez, *The Tropics of Empire: Why Columbus Sailed South* (Cambridge: MIT Press, 2008), 242–69.
51. Hernando Colón, *The History of the Life and Deeds of the Admiral Don Christopher Columbus: Attributed to His Son Fernando Colón,* ed. Illaria Caraci Luzzana, trans. Geoffrey Symox and Blair Sullivan, vol. 13 of Repertorium Columbianum (Turnhout, Belgium: Brepols, 2004), 222.
52. Ibid.
53. For Las Casas's version, see *Las Casas on Columbus, . . . the Second and Fourth Voyages,* 230. Thacher, *Christopher Columbus,* 2:631; Morison, *Admiral,* 653–54, 655.

For more critical accounts of these colonial encounters involving Western science and technology, see Stephen Greenblatt's seminal essay "Invisible Bullets; Renaissance Authority and Its Subversion," *Glyph* 8 (1981): 40–61; see also Joyce Chaplin's critique of Greenblatt's reading in *Subject Matter: Technology, the Body, and Science on the Anglo-American Frontier, 1500–1676* (Cambridge: Harvard University Press, 2001).

54. Colón, *Textos,* 113.
55. Ibid., 488.
56. *BP,* 292–93.
57. Morison, *Admiral,* 655.
58. *BP,* 290–91.
59. Colón, *Textos,* 490.
60. See Gil, introduction to *Textos,* 27–28.
61. Laura Ackerman Smoller, *History, Prophecy, and the Stars: The Christian Astrology of Pierre d'Ailly* (Princeton: Princeton University Press, 1994), 24. On Neoplatonic astrology, see Cirilo Flórez Miguel, Pablo García Castillo, and Roberto Albares Albares, *La ciencia del cielo: Astrología y filosofía natural en la universidad de Salamanca, 1450–1550* (Salamanca: Caja de Ahorros y Monte de Piedad de Salamanca, 1989); and Anthony Grafton and William Newman, introduction to *Secrets of Nature: Astrology and Alchemy in Early Modern Europe* (Cambridge: MIT Press, 2001), 1–38. On the technical applications of astronomy for early modern navigation, see José Luis Comellas, *El cielo de Colón: Técnicas Navales y Astronómicas en el Viaje del Descubrimiento* (Madrid: Tabapress, 1991).
62. Plato, *The Essential Plato,* trans. Benjamin Jowett with M. J. Knight, introd. Alain de Botton (New York: Quality Paperback Book Club, 1999), 803.
63. *BP,* 71, 169.
64. On the dissemination of Neoplatonic astrology through the Arabs into Spain and beyond, see Alejandro García Avilés, "Alfonso X y a tradición de la magia astral," in *El Scriptorum alfonsi: De los libros de astrología a las "Cantigas de Santa Maria,"* ed. Jesús Montoya Martínez and Ana Domínguez Rodríguez (Madrid: Editorial Complutense, 1999), 83–104; Flórez Miguel, García Castillo, and Albares Albares, *La ciencia del cielo,* 19; Manuel Sánchez Mariana, Ana Domínguez, Julio Samsó, and Manuel Rico y Sinobas, eds., *Libros del saber de astronomía del rey D. Alfonso X* (Barcelona: Ebrisa, 1999); Mercè Comes, Honorino Mielgo, and Julio Samsó, *Ochava espera y astrofísica: Textos y estudios sobre las fuentes Árabes de la astronomía de Alfonso X* (Barcelona: Universidad de Barcelona, Instituto "Millás Vallicrosa" de Historia de la Ciencia Árabe, 1990).
65. Raymond Klibanski, Erwin Panofsky, and Fritz Saxl, *Saturn und Melancholy: Studies in the History of Natural Philosophy, Religion, and Art* (London: Nelson, 1964), 44.
66. Ibid., 50, 54, 190.
67. *BP,* 70–73.

68. See Moffit Watts, "Prophecy," 82; on Columbus's notions about the "torrid zone" or the tropics, see Wey Gómez, *Tropics,* 380–81. On d'Ailly's astrology and apocalypticism, see Ackerman Smoller, *History,* esp. 85–101; also Lynn Thorndike, *A History of Magic and Experimental Science:* vols. 3 and 4, *Fourteenth and Fifteenth Centuries* (New York: Columbia University Press, 1934), 4:101–13; on d'Ailly's nominalism or voluntarism, see Francis Oakley, *The Political Throught of Pierre d'Ailly: The Voluntarist Tradition* (New Haven: Yale University Press, 1964).
69. *BP,* 170–75. On Pseudo-Methodius's influence on d'Ailly, see Ackerman Smoller, *History,* 106–7; on d'Ailly as Columbus's source on Pseudo-Methodius, see Moffits Watts, "Prophecy."
70. *BP,* 71–77, 23.
71. Ibid., 70–71.
72. Ibid. On the Toledo School of Translators, see Montoya Martínez and Domínguez Rodríguez, *El Scriptorum alfonsi.* Emmanuelle Poulle has argued that the Latin "Alfonsine tables," which would have been the ones consulted by d'Ailly, actually originated in Paris during the early fourteenth century and differed from the tables from the Castillian version produced by Alfonso's School (see Poulle, "The Alfonsine Tables and Alfonso X of Castille," *Journal for the History of Astronomy* 19 [1988]: 99–105). On Albumassar's influence on d'Ailly (and, by extension, Columbus), see Ackermann Smoller, *History,* 10–12, 65–71, 144n34; and Moffit Watts, "Prophecy," esp. 86–92. On the role of the Tartars in Columbus's eschatology, see Milhou, *Colón,* 145–68.
73. Roger Bacon, *The Opus Majus of Roger Bacon,* trans. Robert Belle Burke, 2 vols. (Philadelphia: University of Pennsylvania Press, 1928), 1:116. On Bacon's influence on Columbus's cosmological ideas, see Alexander von Humboldt, *Examen critique de l'histoire de la géographie du nouveau continent, et des progrès de l'astronomie nautique aux quinzième et seizième siècles* (Paris: Gide, 1836), 1:110; Moffit Watts, "Prophecy," 79; and Wey Gómez, *Tropics,* 380–81.
74. On Albumasar's role in Christian prophecy, see Alejandro García Avilés, "Alfonso X, Albumasar y la profecía del nacimiento de Cristo," *Imafronte* 8–9 (1992–93): 189–200. On d'Ailly's appropriation of Alubmasar's conjunction theory (via Bacon), see Ackerman Smoller, *History,* 61–84.
75. Pierre d'Ailly, *Ymago mundi y otros opúsculos,* ed. Antonio Ramírez de Verger (Madrid: Alianza Editorial, 1992), 333, postil 545. See also Moffit Watts, "Prophecy," 82.
76. *BP,* 164–65.
77. Ibid., 166–67.
78. Columbus in d'Ailly, 345, postil 821.
79. Moffit Watts, "Prophecy," 82; Wey-Gómez, *Tropics,* 380; and Milhou, *Colón.*
80. Bacon, *Opus majus,* 1:116.
81. Ibid., 1:129.
82. Ibid., 2:164–66.

83. *BP*, 74–75.
84. Ibid.
85. Ibid., 70–71.
86. Colón, *Textos*, 498.
87. Pierre d'Ailly, *Tractatus de ymagine mundi, Eppilogus mape mundi, Tractatus de legibus et sectis* (Lovanii: Johannes de Westfalia, ca. 1477–1483), fol. 118, recto; see also Rusconi, introduction to *The "Book of Prophecies,"* 32.
88. *BP*, 170–71.
89. Ibid., 316–17.
90. Rusconi, introduction to *The "Book of Prophecies,"* 31.
91. The first among modern scholars to make the connection between Columbus's pseudo-Joachimite prophecy about a Spanish restorer of the Holy Sepulchre and Arnald of Villanova was James Phelan (*Millennial*, 136n27), though he could not substantiate it at the time. Meanwhile, the Catalan Franciscan scholar José Pou y Martí (*Visionarios, beguinos, y fraticelos catalanes [siglos XIII–XV]* [1930; Madrid: Ed. Colegio "Cardenal Cisneros," 1991], 54–55) had edited and published Arnald's prophecy, though he did not mention Columbus there. Then, Alain Milhou, citing Pou y Martí, substantiated Phelan's supposition (*Colón*, 374–79). While scholars have since occasionally returned to this connection in order to account for Columbus's religious messianism, scholarship has yet to consider the admiral's scientific mentality in light of it, particularly of Arnald's alchemical ideas (see Flint, *Spiritual*, 186; Moffit Watts, "Prophecy," 90; Pérez García, "Dos usos," 198; and Rusconi, introduction to *The "Book of Prophecies,"* 31–32).
92. Arnald of Villanova, "Der tractatus de tempore adventus Antichristi. 1297," in Finke, *Aus den Tagen Bonifaz VIII*, CXXIX–CLIX, es. CXXXI–CXXXII. See also Paul Diepgen, *Arnald von Villanova als Politiker und Laientheologe* (Berlin: Abhandlungen zur mittleren und neuren Geschichte, 1909), 15–171; and Robert Lerner, "Ecstatic Dissent," *Speculum*, 67, no. 1 (January 1992): 33–57, 42–57.
93. Arnald of Villanova, "De misterio cymbalorum ecclesie," in J. Perarnau i Espelt, "El text primitiu del *De mysterio cymbalorum ecclesiae* D'Arnau de Vilanova," in *Arxiu de Textos Catalans Antics*, VII/VIII (1988–89), 102.
94. Ibid.
95. Ibid., 103. On this tract, see also Isabel Alfonso Antón, Julio Escalona, Georges Martin, Séminaire D'études Médiévales Hispaniques de l'Ecole Normale Supérieure Lettres et Sciences Humaines, Séminaire Interdisciplinaire de Recherches sur L'Espagne Médiévale, Casa de Velázquez, and Instituto de Historia (Spain), *Lucha Política: Condena y Legitimación en la España Medieval*. Annexes des Cahiers de Linguistique et de Civilisation Hispaniques Médiévales, vol. 16 (Lyon: ENS Editions, 2004), 71–73.
96. See Alain Milhou, "La chauve-souris, le nouveau David et le roi caché (trois images de l'empereur des derniers temps dans le monde ibérique: XIIIe–XVIIes.)," *Mélanges de la Casa de Velázquez* 18, no. 1 (1982): 61–78; and Matthias Kaup and

Robert Lerner, "Gentile of Foligno Interprets the Prophecy 'Woe to the World' with an edition and English translation," *Traditio* 56 (2001): 149–211.

97. Pico de la Mirandola in his *De rerum praenotione,* cap. V, lib. IX. See also Jaume Mensa I Valls, *Arnau de Vilanova* (Madrid: Ediciones del Orto), 47.

98. See Delno West, "The Abbott and the Admiral: Influences in the Life and Writings of Christopher Columbus," in *Il profetismo gioachimita tra Quattrocento e Cinquercento (Atti del III Congresso Internazionale di Studi Giochimiti),* a cura di Gian Luca Potestà (Genoa: Marietti, 1991), 461–73, 468, 473–74; and A. Atiya, *The Crusade in the Later Middle Ages,* 2nd ed. (New York: Kraus Reprint, 1965), 467; on the Colombo and Guistiniani family, see Paolo Emilio Taviani, *Christopher Columbus: The Grand Design* (London: Orbis, 1985), 275.

99. See Cinthia María Hamlin, "La traducción en la España pre-humanista y sus causas político-ideológicas: El caso de la Divina Comedia y los Reyes Católicos," *Revista De Literatura Medieval* 24 (2012): 86; see also Milhou, *Colón,* 381; Adolfo Bonilla y San Martin, *Libros de caballerías* (Madrid: N.B.A.E., 1907), 6:160; and Guadalajara Medina, *Las profecías del Anticristo en la Edad Media* (Madrid: Gredos, 1996), 206.

100. Arnaldus de Villanova, "De conservanda iuventute et retardanda senectute," in *3 Tractate: 1) De Arte Cognoscendi Venena (1473): 2) De Vinis (1505); 3) De Conservatione Iuventntutis [sic] (1511),* ed. Anton F. W Sommer (Vienna: Im Selbstverlag, 2012), n.p. On Chanca's commentary, see Martín Fernández de Navarrete, *Colección de los viajes y descubrimientos que hicieron por mar los Españoles desde fines del siglo XV* (Madrid: en la Imprenta Nacional, 1848), 1:69; Gerbi, *Nature,* 23n2.

101. Las Casas, *Las Casas on Columbus: The Third Voyage,* 39. Carillo and Symox were not able to identify Las Casas's reference, but it almost certainly refers to Arnald of Villanova.

102. See Jeanne Bignami-Odier, *Etudes sur Jean de Roquetaillade (Johannes de Rupescissa)* (Paris: Vrin, 1952), 130–39, 242; and Milhou, *Colón,* 379.

103. Andrés Bernáldez, *Historia de los Reyes Católicos Don Fernando y Doña Isabel* (Seville: Impr. Que Fué De J.M. Geofrin, 1879), 678.

104. Juan Manzano y Manzano, *Fray Antonio Marchena: Principal depositario del gran secreto colombino* (Seville: [s.n.], 1984); José Coll, *Colón y la Rábida: Con un studio acerca del los Franciscanso en el Nuevo Mundo* (Madrid: Librería Católica de Gregorio del Amo, 1891); Antonio Rumeu de Armas, *La Rábida y el descubrimiento de América: Colón, Marchena, y Fray Juan Pérez* (Austin: Instituto de Cultura Hispánica, 1968); Ángel Ortega, *La Rábida: Historia documental crítica,* 4 vols. (Seville: Impr. y Editorial de San Antonio, 1925).

105. Hernando Colón, *History,* 55.

106. Antonio Rumeu de Armas, "El cosmógrafo Fray Antonio de Marchena, amigo y confidente de Colón," *Anuario de estudios americanos* 24 (1967): 793–829; Rumeu de Armas, *La Rábida y el descubrimiento de América;* Fernández de Navarrete, *Colección* 1:69.

107. Hernando Colón, *History*, 58.
108. *Las Casas on Columbus*, 63.
109. Ibid.
110. Ortega, *La Rábida*, 1:19; Lino Gómez Canedo, *Evangelización y conquista: Experiencia Franciscana en Hispanoamérica* (Mexico City: Edición Porrúa, 1977), 1–2; Rumeu de Armas, *La Rábida*, 45; see also Lucas Wadding, *Annales Minorum seu trium Ordinum a Francisco institutorum*, 3rd ed. (Quaracchi Prope Florentiam: Ad Claras Aquas, 1933), 13:147; Antanasio López, "El franciscanismo en España (1455–1471)," *Archivo Ibero-Americano* 12 (1943): 555–56. The sixteenth-century Franciscan chronicler Jerónimo de Mendieta, in his *Historia eclesiástica indiana*, conflated the two Franciscans into one person, whom he called "Juan Pérez de Marchena" (see Fray Gerónimo de Mendieta, *Historia eclesiástica indiana*, ed. Joaquín García Icazbalceta [Mexico City: Antigua Libreria, Portal de Agustinos, 1870] 15).
111. José Luis de Pando Villarroya, *Colón y el Oro* (Madrid: Pando Ediciones, 1985), 9–43. See also Elvira Vilches, "Columbus's Gift: Representations of Grace and Wealth and the Enterprise of the Indies," *MLN* 119, no. 2 (2004): 201–25; Elvira Vilches, *New World Gold: Cultural Anxiety and Monetary Disorder in Early Modern Spain* (Chicago: University of Chicago Press, 2010), 59, 78; and William D. Phillips and Carla Rahn Phillips, *The Worlds of Christopher Columbus* (Cambridge: Cambridge University Press, 1992), 219.
112. Colón, *Textos*, 375.
113. Ibid., 377.
114. Ibid., 380.
115. See *Book of the knowledge of all the kingdoms, lands, and lordships that are in the world, and the arms and devices of each land and lordship, or of the kings and lords who possess them, written by a Spanish Franciscan in the middle of the XIV century*, trans. and ed. Sir Clements Markham (London: Hakluyt Society, 1912), 36.
116. Qtd. in Thorndike, *History*, 4:361.
117. Ibid.
118. Ibid., 4:366.
119. See here esp. Wey Gómez, *Tropics*, 242–69.
120. Colón, *Textos*, 497.
121. Las Casas, *Las Casas on Columbus, the Third Voyage*, 38.
122. Ibid., 40.
123. Ibid.
124. Colón, *Textos*, 110–11.
125. Ibid., 120.
126. On this topic, see Gerbi, *Nature;* see also Wey Gómez, *Tropics;* and Pamela Smith, *Merchants and Marvels: Commerce, Science, and Art in Early Modern Europe* (London: Routledge, 2001).
127. Colón, *Textos*, 93.
128. See Sebastian Münster, *A treatyse of the New India*, trans. Richard Eden (London, 1553), n.p.

129. Michael Nerlich, *The Ideology of Adventure*, 2 vols. (Minneapolis: University of Minnesota Press, 1995), 1:29, 43, 60, 71.
130. Antoine Faivre, *The Eternal Hermes: From Greek Good to Alchemical Magus*, trans. Joscelyn Godwin (Grand Rapids, MI: Phanes, 1995).
131. *BP*, 291.

5. The Llullian Renaissance and European Expansionism

1. The legend about Llull's martyrdom in North Africa goes back to at least the middle of the fifteenth century, when his final tomb was constructed in Palma de Majorca (see Erhard Wolfram Platzeck, *Raimund Lull: Sein Leben, seine Werke, die Grundlagen seines Denkens [Prinzipienlehre]*, 2 vols. [Düsseldorf: L. Schwann, 1962], 1:39–41). It first appeared in print in the sixteenth century, in two biographies of Llull, namely the "Officium gloriosissimi et beatissime martyris magistri raymundi lulli," included in Jacobus Janer's *Ars methaphisicalis naturalis ordinis cuiuslibet rei intelligibilis arboris nature reuerendi doctoris... Jacobi Juanuarij monachi Terraconensis diocesis* (1506), 633; and Nicolás de Pax's *Illuminati Doctoris et Martyris Raymundi Llulli: Opusculum de anima rationali: Et vita eiusdem Doctoris* (Alcalá: Arnau Guillem Brocar, 1519). The story of the delivery of Llull's body by the two Genoese merchants named Stephanus Colon and Ludovici Pastorga first appears in Luke Wadding's seventeenth-century annals of the Franciscan order, *Annales Minorum seu trium Ordinum a Francisco institutorum*, 3rd ed. (Quaracchi Prope Florentiam: Ad Claras Aquas, 1931), 6:231. But the legend of a Llullian tradition about the existence of another continent in the west seems to date back only to the eighteenth century (see below). The story about Llull's prophecy of its discovery seems to originate in the nineteenth century and was still uncritically repeated in the twentieth, especially in Franciscan, Majorcan, and missionary scholarship (see, for example, Mossén Salvador Bové, "Lo Beat Ramon Llull y l'descubriment de les Ameriques," *Revista Luliana* 1 [1901]: 105–14; Joan Aviñyó, *El terciari francescá Ramón Llull: Doctor arcantélic y martre de Crist, sa vida y la historia contemporanea* [Igualada: N. Poncell, 1912], 229–37; Nesta De Robeck, *Among the Franciscan Tertiaries* [London: J. M. Dent and Sons, 1930], 165; and Francis Borgia Steck, "Christopher Columbus and the Franciscans," *Americas* 3, no. 3 [January 1947]: 320). For the first critical assessment of this story, see Edgar Allison Peers, *Ramon Llull: A Biography* (London: Society for Promoting Christian Knowledge, 1929), 372n2. By most recent scholarly accounts, Llull died a natural death after his safe return from Africa (see Anthony Bonner, ed., *Selected Works of Ramon Llull (1232–1316)*, 2 vols. [Princeton: Princeton University Press, 1985], 1:50n192; and *Doctor Illuminatus: A Ramon Llull Reader* [Princeton: Princeton University Press, 1993], 44n138; see also J. N. Hillgarth, *Ramon Llull and Llullism in Fourteenth-Century France* [Oxford: Clarendon, 1971], 134n369). For a summary of the debate, see Miguel Batllori, *Humanismo y renacimiento: Estudios Hispano-Europeos* (Barcelona: Círculo de Lectores, 1996); and Batllori, "Un

problema hagiogràfic entorn de Ramon Llull: El martiri," *Orientacions i recerques segles XII–XX* (Montserrat: Curial Edicions Catalanes, 1983), 141–56, esp. 148–49.

2. Raimundo Pascual, *Descubrimiento de la aguja náutica, de la situación de la América, del arte de navegar, y de un nuevo método para el adelantamiento en las artes y ciencias* (Madrid: en la imprenta de Manuel González, 1789), 54. The tract *Quaestiones* from which Pascual quotes (50) actually dates from 1290 or 1291. There, Llull employs the methods of the *Ars demonstrativa* and *Ars inventiva* in order to supply 206 questions about God, the afterlife, the angels, as well as the sublunary elemental world. In Question 155, Llull also asked why the Atlantic Ocean, which he called the "English Sea" (Mare Angliae), has high and low tides (*fluat* and *refluat*)—a phenomenon hardly measurable in the Mediterranean. As an answer, he posited that another landmass must lie opposite the known one, on the western side of the Ocean Sea, because "Land and sea are a spherical body and, because the sphere of water is situated in the concavity above the spherical earth, a great sea naturally seeks to submerge the land" (*Beati Raymundi Lulli Doctoris Illuminati et Martyris Operum* [Mainz: Ex Officina Typographica Mayerianak, Johannes Georg Häffner, 1724], 4:151). Llull made a similar argument in his *Félix: or the Book of Wonders,* where he wrote: "The ocean is salty because it rises and falls. Its upward movement is caused by fire and the sun heating it and drawing upward its hot and dry vapors; and since water is by nature heavy, the cold and moist vapors move downward. And since water is round, it moves circularly and lengthwise, according to the obliquity of its roundness, which makes for the movement of waves toward land and for the movement of the English sea [i.e., the Atlantic]; for this obliquity inclines one way some of the time and another way the rest of the time" (in Llull, *Selected Works,* ed. Bonner, 2:751). In essence, Llull's logic in positing the existence of a landmass on the western end of the Atlantic rests on an Aristotelian cosmology, according to which there needs to be a landmass beyond the Ocean Sea that acts as a "counterweight" to the known lands to keep the entire world, which is spherical and composed of both land and water, in balance. However, nowhere did Llull say that such a landmass was a "continent" or was hitherto unknown and therefore new. For an early critique of Pascual's thesis, see Fernando Weyler Laviña, *Raimundo Lulio, juzgado por sí mismo* (Palma de Mallorca: Imprenta de Pedro José Gelabert, 1866), 339–41. On Llull's geography, see Miguel Massutí Alzamora, "La teoría lulliana de les marees," *LNT* 7 (1934): 304–15; and "Una teoría medieval sobre la marea," *Las Ciencias (Anales de la Asociación Española para el Progreso de las Ciencias)* 8 (Madrid, 1943): 259–67; Josep Maria Millas I Vallicrosa, "El 'Tractatus novus de Astronomía' de Ramon Llull," *Estudios Lulianos* 6 (1962): 257–73; and Miguel Batllori, "Les idées géographiques de Ramon Llul (R. Lulle) et leur diffusion en Italie aux XVIe et XVe siècles," *Studi Colombiani* 3 (1951): 49–55, translated into Spanish in Batllori, *Del descubrimiento a la independencia: Estudios sobre Iberoamérica y Filipinas* (Caracas: Universidad Católica Andres Bello, 1979), 3–12.

3. Pascual, *Descubrimiento*, 50–65.
4. On the idea of Columbus's secret foreknowledge of the existence of the American continent, see Juan Manzano Manzano, *Colón y su secreto: El predescubrimiento* (Madrid: Ediciones de Cultura Hispánica, 1989), which represents a modern proponent of this theory.
5. Pascual, *Descubrimiento*, 58, 61.
6. Ibid., 64.
7. For later assessments of the significance of Llull's tract for the discovery of America, see Emilia Pardo Bazán, *Los Franciscanos y Colón* (Madrid: Establecemiento Tipográfico 'Sucesores de Rivadeneyra,' 1892), who went so far as to assert that "it was Llull who really discovered America," whereas Columbus, benefiting from the Llullian tradition, was the one who merely "found" it (21); see also Ángel Ortega, *La Rábida: Historia documental crítica*, 4 vols. (Seville: Impr. y Editorial de San Antonio, 1925), 2:65–66; and Leandro Tormo Sanz, "De Llull a Serra: Contribución de las Baleares al descubrimiento y cristianización de las indias," *Missionalia hispánica* 41, no. 120 (1984): 323–40.
8. Ramon Llull, *A Contemporary Life*, ed. and trans. by Anthony Bonner (Barcelona: Barcino Tamesis, 2010), 49.
9. Both Pardo Bazán, *Los Franciscanos y Colón* (24–25), and Ángel Ortega, *La Rábida* (2:65–73), suggest that Columbus may have come across Llull's *Questiones* at La Rábida through Pérez and Marchena, though Bazán points out the contradiction between the notion of Columbus's foreknowledge of another continent and his stated aim of reaching Asia, whereas Ortega points out that the theories about the size of the globe, the extent of the Atlantic, and the flux and reflux of its waters were not particular to Llull but part of a Franciscan tradition of learning reaching back to John Duns Scotus (72–73).
10. See Carmen Álvarez Márquez, *El itinerario de adquisiciones de libros de mano de Hernando Colón* (Seville: Universidad de Sevilla, Secretariado de Publicaciones, 2004), 86; and Tomás Marín Martínez, José Manuel Ruiz Asencio, and Klaus Wagner, *Catálogo concordado de la biblioteca de Hernando Colón* (Seville: Fundación Mapfre América, Cabildo de la Catedral de Sevilla, 1993).
11. Bonner, "Llull's Influence," in *Selected Writings*, by Llull, ed. Bonner, 71–72. On Llull and Cusa, see Charles Lohr, "Metaphysics," in *The Cambridge History of Renaissance Philosophy*, ed. Charles Schmitt, Quentin Skinner, and Eckhard Kessler (Cambridge: Cambridge University Press, 1988), 537–638, esp. 545–67; and Ermenegildo Bidese et al., *Ramon Llull und Nikolaus von Kues: Eine Begegnung im Zeichen der Toleranz: Akten des Internationalen Kongresses zu Ramon Llull und Nikolaus von Kues (Brixen und Bozen, 25.–27. November 2004) = Raimondo Lullo E Niccolo Cusano: Un incontro nel segno della tolleranza; Atti del Congresso Internazionale su Raimondo Lullo e Niccolo Cusano (Bressanone e Bolzano, 25–27 Novembre 2004)* (Turnhout, Belgium: Brepols, 2005).
12. See Juan de Herrera, *Sobre la figura cúbica*, ed. Manuel Arrate Peña (Santander: Universidad de Cantabria-Ayuntamiento de Camargo, 1998).

13. On Llull's influence on Protestant pansophic movements, see Howard Hotson, *Paradise Postponed: Johann Heinrich Alsted and the Birth of Calvinist Millenarianism* (Dordrecht: Kluwer Academic, 2000), esp. 75–84; and Kieran Egan, "Comenius at the Aera," *Journal of Curriculum and Supervision* 8, no. 1 (Fall 1992): 56–61. On Becher, see Pamela Smith, *The Business of Alchemy: Science and Culture in the Holy Roman Empire* (Princeton: Princeton University Press, 1994), 97. On Starkey, see William Newman, *Gehennical Fire: The Lives of George Starkey. An American Alchemist in the Scientific Revolution* (Chicago: University of Chicago Press, 1994), 98–103. On Donne, see Roberta Albrecht, *The Virgin Mary as Alchemical and Lullian Reference in Donne* (Selinsgrove, PA: Susquehanna University Press, 2005). On Newton, see Michael White, *Isaac Newton: The Last Sorcerer* (Reading, MA: Addison-Wesley, 1997), 119.
14. Frances Yates, *Llull and Bruno: Collected Essays* (London: Routledge and Kegan Paul, 1982), 67. On the late medieval and early modern history of Llullism, see Hillgarth, *Ramon Llull,* 135–317; Joan Avinyó, *Història del lulisme* (Barcelona: Libreria tipografía católica, 1925); Joaquín Carreras y Artau and Tomas Carreras y Artau, *Historia de la filosofía española: Filosofía cristiana de los siglos XIII al XV,* 2 vols. (Madrid: Real academia de ciencias exactas, físicas y naturales, 1939), 2:177–278; Paolo Rossi, *Clavis Universalis: Arti mnemoniche e logica combinatoria da Lullo a Leibniz* (Milan: R. Ricciardi, 1960); Mark Johnston, "The Reception of the Lullian Art, 1450–1530," *Sixteenth-Century Journal* 12, no. 1 (Spring 1981): 31–48; Miguel Batllori, *Ramón Llull i el Lul·Lisme* (Valencia: Tres i Quatre, 1993); and Pere Villalba I Varneda, *Ramon Llull: Escriptor i filòsof de la diferència* (Bellaterra: Universitat Autònoma de Barcelona, 2015), 463–558.
15. Rossi, *Clavis Universalis,* 41. On Llull's mnemo-technology, see Frances Yates, "The Art of Ramon Lull: An Approach to It through Lull's Theory of the Elements," *Journal of the Warburg and Courtault Institutes* 17 (1954): 115–73; and Paolo Rossi, *Logic and the Art of Memory: The Quest for a Universal Language,* ed. Stephen Clucas (Chicago: University of Chicago Press, 2000). On the "Llullian renaissance" (my term), see Joseph Victor, "The Revival of Lullism at Paris," *Renaissance Quarterly* 28, no. 4 (1975): 504–34; and Victor, *Charles de Bovelles, 1479–1553: An Intellectual Biography* (Geneva: Droz, 1978).
16. "The Bull Inter Caetera," in Frances Gardiner Davenport, *European Treaties Bearing on the History of the United States and Its Dependencies to 1648,* ed. Gardiner Davenport (Washington, DC: Carnegie Institution of Washington, 1917), 59. On this change, see Manuel Giménez Fernández, *Nuevas consideraciones sobre la historia, sentido, y valor de las bulas Alejandrinas de 1493 referentes a las Indias* (Seville: Consejo Superior de Investigaciones Científicas Escuela de Estudios Hispano-Americanos de la Universidad de Sevilla, 1944); and Giménez Fernández, *La política religiosa de Fernando V en Indias* (Madrid, 1943), 1–58. On the papal bulls, see A. García Gallo, "Las bulas de Alejandro VI y el ordenamiento jurídico de la expansión portuguesa y castellana en Africa e Indias," *Anuario de Historia*

del Derecho español 27–28 (1957–58): 461–829; Luis Weckmann-Muñoz, *Las bulas alejandrinas de 1493 y la teoría política del papado medieval: Estudio de la supremacia papal sobre islas, 1091–1493* (Mexico City: Universidad Nacional Autónoma de México, 1949).

17. Richard Konetzke, ed., *Colección de documentos para la historia de la formación social de Hispanoamérica, 1493–1810,* 3 vols. (Madrid: Consejo Superior de Investigaciones Científicas, 1953), 1:1.
18. *Recopilación de las leyes de los reinos de las Indias* (Madrid: Boix, 1841), 1:1.
19. Weckmann-Muñoz, *Las bulas,* 27–33; see also Luis Weckmann-Muñoz, *Constantino El Grande y Cristóbal Colón: Estudio de la Supremacía Papal Sobre Islas (1091–1493),* 2nd ed. (Mexico City: Fondo de Cultura Económica, 1992); Hector Avalos, "Pope Alexander VI, Slavery and Voluntary Subjection: 'Ineffabilis et Summi Patris' in Context," *Journal of Ecclesiastical History* 65, no. 4 (2014): 738–60; Pedro de Leturia, "Las grandes bulas misionales de Alejandro VI, 1493," *Biblioteca Hispana Missionum* (Barcelona, 1930), 211–51; Giménez Fernández, *Nuevas;* Batllori, *Del descubrimiento;* James Muldoon, *Popes, Lawyers, and Infidels: The Church and the Non-Christian World, 1250–1550* (Philadelphia: University of Pennsylvania Press, 1979); and Muldoon, *Empire and Order: The Concept of Empire, 800–1800* (Houndmills, Basingstoke, Hampshire: Macmillan, 1999).
20. Although the Spanish missionaries used the word *reducir* interchangeably with *convertir,* the usage in this sense remained particular to missionary discourse. Thus, it does not appear in that sense in Sebastián Covarrubias's *Tesoro de la lengua castellana,* which defines *reduzir* as *convencerse* and *buelto a major orden* (Madrid: por Luis Sánchez, impressor del Rey N. S. 1611), R5. The *Diccionario de la lengua española,* published by the Real Academia Española, notes several modern definitions, including "volver algo al lugar donde antes estaba o al estado que tenia" (i.e., in the classical Latin sense); "mudar algo en otra cosa equivalente"; "cambiar moneda"; "sujetar a la obediencia a quienes se habían separado de ella"; "persuader o atraer a alguien con razones y argumentos"; "En culinaria, hervir un líquido para que se concentre"; "Fil[osofía] convertir en perfecta la figura imperfecta de un silogismo"; "med[icina] restablecer en su situación natural los huesos dislocados o rotos, o bien los tejidos protruidos en la hernias"; and "Quím[ica] eliminar el oxígeno de un compuesto" (http://dle.rae.es/?id=Va98hEO). On the use of the word in missionary discourse in America, see Jeremy Ravi Mumford, *Vertical Empire: The General Resettlement of Indians in the Colonial Andes* (Durham, NC: Duke University Press, 2012), 48; and William Hanks, *Converting Words: Maya in the Age of the Cross* (Berkeley: University of California Press, 2010), 4.
21. See Nicolau Eimeric, *Directorivm Inqvisitorvm R.P.F. Nicolai Eymerici, Ord. Præd. S. Theol. Mag. Inquisitoris hæreticæ prauitatis in Regnis Regis Aragonum, Denvo Ex Collatione Plvrivm, exemplarium emendatum, et accessione multarum literarum, Apostolicarum, officio Sanctæ Inquisitionis deseruientium, locupletatum, Cvm Scholiis Sev Annotationibvs eruditissimis D. Francisci Pegnæ Hispani, S. Theologiæ*

et Iuris Vtriusque Doctoris. Accessit rerum et verborum multiplex et copiosissimus Index. Cum Priulegio, et Superiorum approbatione, ed. Francisco Peña (Rome: In Aedibvs Pop. Rom., 1578).

22. See Platzeck, *Raimund Lull,* 1:103–4.
23. Leen Spruit, "Censorship and Canon: A Note on Some Medieval Works and Authors," in *How the West Was Won: Essays on the Literary Imagination, the Canon, and the Christian Middle Ages for Burcht Pranger,* ed. Willemien Otten et al. (Leiden: Brill, 2010), 177–94; on Llull's use of the vernacular as a source of controversy, see Lola Badia et al., *Ramon Llull as a Vernacular Writer: Communicating a New Kind of Knowledge* (Rochester, NY: Boydell and Brewer, 2016), 34.
24. Spruit, "Censorship," 185.
25. For a discussion of this, see Batllori, *Humanismo,* 30–32.
26. Alberto María Carreño, "The Books of Don Fray Juan de Zumárraga," *Americas* 5, no. 3 (January 1949): 311–30; W. Michael Mathes, "Humanism in Sixteenth- and Seventeenth-Century Libraries of New Spain," *Catholic Historical Review* 82, no. 3 (1996): 412–35.
27. Linda Báez-Rubí, *Die Rezeption der Lehre des Ramon Llull in der "Rhetorica Christiana" [Perugia, 1579] des Franziskaners Fray Diego de Valadés* (Frankfurt: Peter Lang, 2004); Báez-Rubí, *Mnemosine novohispánica: Retórica e imágenes en el siglo XVI* (Mexico City: Universidad Nacional Autónoma de México, 2005).
28. Batllori, *Humanismo,* 16–38.
29. Qtd. in D. Francisco de Bofarull y Sans, *El Testamento de Ramon Lull y la Escuela Luliana en Barcelona, memoria leida en La Real Academia De Buenas Letras* (Barcelona: Establecimiento Tipográfico de Jaime Jesús, 1896), 441. On the Escuela Luliana, see also Josep Maria Madurell Marimon, "La Escuela de Ramón Llull, de Barcelona. Sus alumnos, lectures y protectores," *Estudios Lulianos* 9 (1965): 93–103.
30. See Álvaro Santamaría, *La promoción universitaria en Mallorca: Época de Fernando el Católico (1479–1516)* (Palma de Mallorca: Servei de Publicacions de la Universitat de Palma de Mallorca, 1983), 118–21; Batllori, *Ramón Llull,* 373–83; Álvaro Fernández de Córdova Miralles, "El pontificado de Alejandro VI (1492–1503)," *Revista Borja. Revista de l'IIEB, 2: Actes del II Simposi Internacional sobre els Borja* (2009): 231; and J. Custurer, *Disertaciones históricas del Beato Raymundo Lullio Doctor iluminado, y mártir: Con un apendix de su vida* (Palma de Mallorca, 1700), 347.
31. See John Monfasani, *Fernando of Cordova: A Biographical and Intellectual Profile* (Philadelphia: American Philosophical Society, 1992), 51–53; see also Lorenzo Pérez Martínez, "El Maestro Pedro Daguí y el lulismo mallorquín de fines de siglo XV," *Estudios Lulianos* 4 (1960): 291–306.
32. Monfasani, *Fernando of Cordova,* 52.
33. *Clementissime Deus cum tua gratia & auxilio incipit liber qui uocatur Ianua Artis Magistri Raymundi Lull* (Impressum Rom[a]e: Eucharius Silber, 1485).

Notes to Pages 192–194   545

34. Pedro Daguí, *Formalitates breves in artem Raimundi Lulli* (Seville: Paulus de Colonia, Johannes Pegnitzer, Magnus Herbst and Thomas Glockner, 1491); Pedro Daguí, *Tractatus de differentia* (Seville: Stanislao Polono, 1500).
35. *Barcelona: Biblioteca de la Universitat (II)* (Barcelona: Institut d'Estudis Catalans, 2002), 245.
36. On Alexander's interest in Llullism, see Álvaro Fernández de Córdova Miralles, "El pontificado de Alejandro VI (1492–1503)," *Revista Borja. Revista de l'IIEB, 2: Actes del II Simposi Internacional sobre els Borja* (2009): 231; and Batllori, *Humanismo*, 30.
37. Batllori, *Humanismo*, 30.
38. See Miguel Batllori, *La familia de Los Borjas* (Madrid: Real Academia de la Historia, 1999), 149–244.
39. See A. J. Festugière, *Hermétisme et mystique païenne* (Paris: Aubier Montaigne, 1967); Claudio Moreschini, *Hermes Christianus: The Intermingling of Hermetic Piety and Christian Thought* (Turnhout, Belgium: Brepols, 2011); Roelof van den Broek and Wouter J. Hanegraaff, eds., *Gnosis and Hermeticism from Antiquity to Modern Times* (Albany: State University of New York Press, 1998); and Jan Assmann, *Moses the Egyptian: The Memory of Egypt in Western Monotheism* (Cambridge: Cambridge University Press, 1997), 1–22.
40. On Alexander's interest in Hermeticism and kabbala, see Karl Giehlow, "Die Hieroglyphenkunde des Humanismus in der Allegorie der Renaissance, besonders der Ehrenpforte Kaisers Maximilian I," in *Jahrbuch der Kunsthistorischen Sammlungen des Allerhöchsten Kaiserhauses*, ed. Karl Grafen Lanckoronski, 1–232 (Vienna: F. Tempsky, 1915), 41–47; Fritz Saxl, "The Appartamento Borgia," in *Lectures*, 2 vols. (London: Warburg Institute, 1957), 1:174–88; and Frances Yates, *Giordano Bruno*, 113–16.
41. On Llull and the bellicose cult of the Virgin Mary, see Amy Remensnyder, *La Conquistadora: The Virgin Mary at War and Peace in the Old and the New Worlds* (New York: Oxford University Press, 2014), 15–17, 109–10; on the Virgin Mary as a "mother of conversion," see 175–208. See also chapter 3 of this book.
42. Samuel Purchas, *Purchase, His Pilgrimes,* part 1 In fiue books (London: Printed by William Stansby for Henrie Fetherstone, and Are to Be Sold at His Shop in Pauls Church-Yard at the Signe of the Rose, 1625), 23.
43. These five bulls include: (1) The original bull of donation, *Inter cetera* I (dated May 3); (2) *Piis filelium* (dated June 25, establishing Spain's apostolic mission); (3) *Inter cetera* II (dated May 4 but written at the end of June); (4) *Eximic devotionis* (dated May 3 but not written until early July); and (5) *Dudum siquidem* (dated and written September 25). Although the series is collectively known as "the bulls *Inter cetera*" (or also "the Columbian bulls"), only two them began with the phrase "inter cetera" (after the customary salutations). For a comparison of the two versions, see H. Vander Linden, "Alexander VI and the Demarcation of the Maritime and Colonial Domains of Spain and Portugal, 1493–1494," *American Historical Review* 22, no. 1 (1916): 8–10, 17. The attribution of the idea of a

line of demarcation to Columbus, rather than to Pope Alexander, was first made by Alexander von Humboldt and has been accepted as almost certainly correct since the twentieth century (see Alexander von Humboldt, *Examen critique de l'histoire de la géographie du nouveau continente* [Paris: Gide, 1814–34], 251).

44. *Cristóbal Colón: Textos y documentos completos,* ed. Consuelo Varela and Juan Gil (1982; Madrid: Alianza Editorial, 2003), 375. See also chapter 4 of this book; and Giménez Fernández, *Nuevas consideraciones,* 28.

45. See Giménez Fernández, *Nuevas consideraciones,* 76.

46. See Worldcat.org (http://www.worldcat.org/identities/lccn-n2001130381/).

47. *Storia degli scavi di Roma: E notizie intorno le collezioni Romane di Antichità,* vol. 1 (Rome: Ermanno Loescher, 1902), 204; Mario Emilio Cosenza, *Biographical and Bibliographical Dictionary of the Italian Humanists and the World of Classical Scholarship in Italy, 1300–1800* (Boston: G. K. Hall, 1962), 2854.

48. According to legend, the pope was treated with blood by a Jewish physician by the name of Giacomo de San Genesio. The evidence for this is unreliable, however, and the story may be the product of anti-Semitism. On this legend, see Jacalyn Duffin, *History of Medicine: A Scandalously Short Introduction* (Toronto: University of Toronto Press, 1999), 171–72; see also Richard Sugg, *Mummies, Cannibals, and Vampires: The History of Corpse Medicine from the Renaissance to the the Victorians* (London: Routledge, 2016), 24–25.

49. "usque ad Indos," Pope Calixtus III, "Inter cetera," in *European Treaties,* ed. Davenport, 29. See also Giménez Fernández, *Nuevas consideraciones,* 79.

50. I have not been able to find the word *reducere* used in the sense of *convertere* in any Latin dictionaries. Charles de Fresne's *Glossarium mediae et infimae Latinitatis,* vol. 6 (Graz: Akademischer Druck und Verlagsanstalt, 1883–87) lists the general sense of "return" [something or somebody], to "lead back" or "take back" (i.e., an exile back to her country, a strayed wife back to her marriage, an actor back to the stage). Also, he lists the alchemical sense as found in Arnald of Villanova's *Rosarius* (discussed in the introduction and in chapter 2 of this book), as well as the sense of "to withdraw," as in "hominibus fugiendo se Reduxit at Tyrum." The etymological note for the English word "to reduce" in the *OED* also notes the early modern sense of "to conquer" or "subdue": "*redūcere* to lead or bring back, to withdraw, to retire, to draw back, to revive, to bring back (earlier) in time, to restore, to recall, to represent, to bring (to a state), to bring down (in degree or quality), in post-classical Latin also to subdue (10th cent.), (in logic) to bring a syllogism (or proposition) into a different but equivalent form (*a*1250 in a British source), to set (a broken bone), to bring down, diminish to a smaller number, amount, quantity, extent, etc. (1363 in Chauliac), to restore a metal to the unchanged or metallic state (1537 in Paracelsus) < *re-* RE- *prefix* + *dūcere* to lead, bring (see DUCT *n.*)."

51. "The Bull Romanus Pontifex," in *European Treaties,* ed. Gardiner Davenport, 14.

52. Cardinal Henry Edward Manning (Archbishop of Westminster, England), *The Vatican Decrees in Their Bearing on Civil Allegiance* (New York: Catholic Publication Society, 1875), 172–73.
53. Catholic Church, Pope (1305–14: Clement V), *Regestum Clementis Papae V: ex Vaticanis archetypis sanctissimi Domini nostri Leonis Xiii Pontificis Maximi iussu et munificentia* (Ex Typographia Vaticana, 1885), 40, col. 2.
54. *Liber de civitate mundi,* in *Raimundi Lulli opera latina,* ed. Fridericus Stegmüller, 5 vols. (Palma de Mallorca, 1959), 2:200–221. See also Johannes Stöhr, "Missionsvorstellung in Llulls Spätschriften," *Estudios Lulianos* 22 (1978): 140; and Pedro Ramis, *Lectura del "Liber de civitate mundi" de Ramón Llull* (Barcelona: PPU, 1992).
55. Ramon Llull, *Disputatio Petri clerici et Raymundi phantastici,* in *Raimundi Lulli opera latina,* ed. F. Stegmüller, 5 vols., (Turnhout, Belgium: Brepols, 1975) 4:28.
56. Reproduced in E. Longpré, "Deux opuscules inedits du B. Raymond Lulle," *La France Franciscaine* 18 (1935): 153. See also Josep Perarnau i Espelt, "Un text català de Ramon Llull desconegut: La 'Petitició de Ramon al Papa Celestí V per a la conversió dels infidels," *Arxiu de Textos Catalans Antics* 1 (1982): 9–46; and Pamela May Beattie, "Evangelization, Reform and Eschatology, Mission and Crusade in the Thought of Ramon Llull" (PhD. diss., University of Toronto, 1995), 71–115.
57. "usque ad Indos," Pope Calixtus III, "Inter cetera," in *European Treaties,* ed. Gardiner Davenport, 29.
58. Thomas Aquinas, *Summa theologiae* (New York: Cosimo Classics, 2007), 1247; see also chapter 8 of this book.
59. *European Treaties,* ed. Gardiner Davenport, 15.
60. See Friedrich Zarncke, *Der Priester Johannes* (Leipzig: S. Hirzel, 1876), 837–43; 945–46; see also Keagan Brewer, trans. and ed., *Prester John: The Legend and Its Sources* (Burlington, VT: Ashgate, 2015); and L. N. Gumilev, *Searches for an Imaginary Kingdom: The Legend of the Kingdom of Prester John,* trans. R. E. F. Smith (New York: Cambridge University Press, 1987).
61. See Brewer, introduction to *Prester John,* 8.
62. Lynn Thorndike, *A History of Magic and Experimental Science* (New York: Columbia University Press, 1923), 2:244. The story about Alexander III's "reply" is now also believed to be spurious (see Brewer, introduction to *Prester John,* 13).
63. Friar Giovanni DiPlano Carpini, *The Story of the Mongols Whom We Call the Tartars,* trans. and introd. Erik Hildinger (Boston: Branden, 2014), 55; see also William Rubruck, *The Journey of William of Rubruck to the Eastern Parts of the World, 1253–55,* trans. William Woodville Rockhill (Farnham: Ashgate, 2011).
64. Roger Bacon, *The Opus Majus of Roger Bacon,* trans. Robert Belle Burke, 2 vols. (Philadelphia: University of Pennsylvania Press, 1928), 2:384.
65. *The Travels of Marco Polo,* bk. 1, chap. 59, https://en.wikisource.org/wiki/The_Travels_of_Marco_Polo/Book_1/Chapter_59. On the medieval idea of an alliance between Christians and Mongols against Islam, see Toby Lester's popular

The Fourth Part of the World: An Astonishing Epic of Global Discovery, Imperial Ambition, and the Birth of America (New York: Free Press, 2009).

66. In the fourteenth century, some writers also located the Kingdom of Prester John in Africa. For example, the anonymous Franciscan author of the *Libro del conoscimiento* wrote that Prester John was "the Patriarch of Nubia and Etiopia," whose capital is the city of Malsa (see *Book of the knowledge of all the kingdoms, lands, and lordships that are in the world, and the arms and devices of each land and lordship, or of the kings and lords who possess them, written by a Spanish Franciscan in the middle of the XIV century,* trans. and ed. Sir Clements Markham [London: Hakluyt Society, 1912], 36).

67. See Jacques Lafaye, *Quetzalcóatl and Guadalupe: The Formation of Mexican National Consciousness,* trans. Benjamin Keen (Chicago: University of Chicago Press, 1987).

68. On Conill, Rodrigo Borgia, and the Llullian circle at Valencia, see Miguel Batllori, *La familia de los Borjas,* 150–51. On the history of early modern Spanish Llullism, see Carreras y Artau and Carreras y Artau, *Historia,* 2:177–278; see also Marcelino Menéndez y Pelayo, *Historia de los heterodoxos españoles* (Madrid: F. Maroto é hijos, 1880), 513–39; and Avinyó, *Història del lulisme.* On the history of Llulism beyond Spain, see Hillgarth, *Ramon Llull.*

69. Jacobus Janer, *Ars methaphisicalis naturalis ordinis cuiuslibet rei intelligibilis arboris nature* (Valencia: Leonhart Hutz, 1506), 633.

70. Johannes Matthaeus Ferrarius de Gradibus, Moses Maimonides, and Raimundus Lullus, *Consiliorum . . . secundum viam Avicenne ordinatorum utile repertorium: Additis antiquissimi medici Rabbi Moysi De regimine vite quinque tractatibus ad Sultanum inscriptis* (Venice: Georgium Arrivabenum, 1514); see also Thorndike, *History,* 5:535–36.

71. Joseph Pérez, *Cisneros, el cardenal de España* (Madrid: Santillana Ediciones Generales, 2014), 146.

72. On Llull's influence on Cardinal Cisneros, see also Marcel Bataillon, *Erasmo y España: Estudios sobre la historia espiritual del siglo XVI* (1937; Mexico City: Fondo de Cultura Económica, 1966), 52–57; Joaquín Carreras y Artau and Tomas Carreras y Artau, *Historia de la filosofía española: Filosofía cristiana de los siglos XIII al XV,* 2 vols. (Real academia de ciencias exactas, físicas y naturales, 1939), 2:251–53; Alberto Jiménez, *Selección y reforma: Ensayo sobre la Universidad renacentista española* (Mexico City: El Colegio de México, 1944); Miriam Therese Olabarrieta, *The Influence of Ramon Llull on the Style of the Early Spanish Mystics and Santa Teresa* (Washington, DC: Catholic University of America Press, 1963), 14–15; and José López Rueda, *Helenistas españoles del siglo XVI* (Madrid: Instituto Antonio de Nebrija, 1973). On Cisneros and his reform programs more generally, see José García Oro, *La reforma de los religiosos Españoles en tiempo de los reyes Católicos* (Valladolid: Instituto "Isabel la Católica" de Historia eclesiastica, 1969), 111–13, 195–96; García Oro, *El cardenal Cisneros: Vida y empresas* (Madrid: BAC, 1992); and García Oro, *La Universidad de Alcalá en la*

etapa fundacional (1458–1578) (Santiago de Compostela: Independencia Editorial, 1992).

73. See *Divi Raymundi Lulli Doctoris Illuminatissimi Ars inventiva veritatis: Tabula generalis: Comentum in easdem ipsius Raymundi* (Valencia: Diego de Gumiel, 1515); and *Libellus illuminati Raymundi de amico et amato* (Alcalá: Arnau Guillem Brocar, 1517). The former text was edited by Cisneros's associates Alfonso de Proaza and Nicolás de Pax, the latter having been appointed by Cisneros as the first chair of Llullian studies at Alcalá. On Cisneros's involvement in these editions, see Noel Blanco Mourelle, *Lullus complutensis* (Research blog, http://laic.columbia.edu/blog/lullus-complutensis/). On Cisnero's collection of Llullian books, see *Cuentas de los gastos efectuados por cuenta del Cardenal Cisneros para adquirir e imprimir libros para el Colegio de San Ildefonso, entre los años 1497–1509* (Madrid: Biblioteca Nacional de España, MSS/20056/47); see also "Index omnium librorum bibliotece collegii santi illefonsy oppidi complutensis" (Madrid: Archivo Histórico Nacional, Universidades L. 1090ff. 33r–54v); and Ramón de Alós y de Dou, *Los catálogos lulianos: Contribución al studio de la obra de Ramón Lull* (Barcelona: Imprenta de Francisco J. Altés y Alabart, 1918), 55–66. On the Universtiy of Alacalá more generally, see Stafford Poole, *Juan de Ovando: Governing the Spanish Empire in the Reign of Philip II* (Norman: Universtiy of Oklahoma Press, 2004), 56–63.

74. Nicolás de Pax, *Illuminati Doctoris et Martyris Raymundi Lulli: Opusculum de anima rationali: Et vita eiusdem Doctoris* (Alcalá: Arnau Guillem Brocar, 1519).

75. Ibid. On Pax and Cisneros, see Carreras y Artau and Carreras y Artau, *Historia*, 2:253; and Pérez, *Cisneros*, 232–33.

76. See Pérez, *Cisneros*, 250.

77. *Divi Raymundi Lulli Doctoris Illuminatissimi Ars inventiva veritatis: Tabula generalis: Comentum in easdem ipsius Raymundi* (Valencia: Diego de Gumiel, 1515).

78. On Proaza, see D. W. McPheeters, *El humanista español Alonso de Proaza* (Madrid: Castalia, 1961).

79. On Llullism in fifteenth-century Italy, see Miguel Batllori, *Il Lullismo in Italia: Tentativo di sintesi* (Rome: Antonianum, 2004).

80. See Báez Rubí, *Rezeption,* 83; Victor, *Charles de Bovelles,* 57; Augustin Renauder, *Préréforme et humanisme à Paris pendant les premières guerres d'Italie (1494–1517)* (Paris: D'Argences, 1953); and Buy Bedouelle, *Lefèvre d'Etaples et l'intelligence des ecritures* (Geneva: Librairie Drosz, 1976).

81. See Pérez, *Cisneros,* 146–47, 249.

82. Qtd. in Victor, "Revival;" see also Báez Rubí, *Rezeption,* 84; and Bataillon, *Erasmo,* 64–65.

83. On Llull's influence on Zumárraga, see Báez Rubí, "La herencia del Ars Lulliana contemplativa en el orbe cultural de la evangelización franciscana: Fray Juan de Zumárraga y la via de los beneficios en tierras de la Nueva España," *Antonianum; Periodicum trimester* 80, no. 3 (2005). On Zumárraga's millenarian utopianism, see Silvio Zavala, Guillermo Tovar de Teresa, and Miguel León Portilla, *La*

Utopía Mexicana del siglo XVI: Lo bello, lo verdadero, y lo bueno (Mexico City: Grupo Azabache, 1992).

84. Richard Tuck, *The Rights of War and Peace: Political Thought and the International Order from Grotius to Kant* (Oxford: Oxford University Press, 1999), 16–50. On the militant humanism of Sepúlveda, see chapter 8 of this book.

85. On Lavinheta, see Carreras Artau and Carreras Artau, *Historia* 2:209–16; Hillgarth, *Ramon Llull,* 288–93; Erhard-Wolfram Platzeck, introduction to *Explanatio compendiosaque applicatio Artis Raymundi Lulli,* by Bernard de Lavinheta, ed. Platzeck (Hildesheim: Gerstenberg, 1977), 11; and Báez Rubí, *Rezeption,* 89–97.

86. Pedro Daguí, *Janua artis Lulli. Introductorium admodum breue et succinctum ad omnes scientias quod Ianua artis illuminati doctoris magistri Raymundi Lulli runcupatur . . . (compositum a Petro Degui, correctum per Bernardum De Lavinheta)* (1516).

87. Bernard de Lavinheta, *Explanatio compendiosaque applicatio Artis Raymundi Lulli,* ed. Erhard-Wolfram Platzeck (Hildesheim: Gerstenberg, 1977), 13 (original fol. Xxi).

88. Ibid.

89. Ibid., 348.

90. Platzeck, introduction to *Explanatio compendiosaque applicatio Artis Raymundi Lulli,* by Bernard de Lavinheta, 13; see also Hillgarth, *Ramon Llull,* 292; Thorndike, *History,* 4:22; Carreras Artau and Carreras Artau, *Historia* 2:212; and Michela Pereira, "Bernardo Lavinheta e la diffusione del Lullismo a Parigi nei primi anni del '500,'" *Interpres* 5 (1983/84): 242–65.

91. Lavinheta, *Explanatio,* 348–49 (original fol. 174–75).

92. On Llull's legacy in the history of Spanish religious mysticism, see Olabarrieta, *The Influence*. On his influence on English Renaissance thought, see Yates, *Llull and Bruno;* Rossi, *Logic;* and Bonner, "Llull's Influence," 75–89.

93. *In rhetoricam Isagoge,* in Raimundus Lullus, *Opera,* reprint of the Strasbourg 1651 edition with an introduction by Anthony Bonner, 2 vols. (Stuttgart: Frommann-Holzboog, 1996), 1:178–223, 179. On Rufo, see also Rossi, *Logic,* 38–39; Gerardo Ramírez Vidal, "Fray Diego Valadés y el tratado seudoluliano *In rhetoricam isagoge,*" *Nova tellus* 30, no. 1 (2012): 167–97; Marcelino Menéndez y Pelayo, *Historia de las ideas estéticas en España,* 2nd ed. (Buenos Aires: Editorial Glem, 1943), 164–79; and Carreras y Artau, *Historia,* 2:214–16.

94. *In rhetoricam Isagoge,* 179.

95. Báez Rubí, *Rezeption,* 107.

96. See Rossi, *Logic,* 276. On Pico's debt to Llull, see Carreras y Artau and Carreras y Artau, *Historia,* 2:198–201. On Pico's kabbalism, see Yates, *Giordano Bruno,* 84–116; Menéndez y Pelayo, *Historia de los heterodoxos españoles,* 464, 525; François Secret, *La kabbala Cristiana del Renacimiento* (Madrid: Taurus, 1979); and Joseph Leon Blau, *The Cristian Interpretation of the Cabala in the Renaissance* (Port Washington, NY: Kennikat, 1965). Some scholars have also argued that Llull's Art was itself influenced by Jewish kabbala (see J. M. Millas Vallicrosa, "Algunas

relaciones entre la doctrina Juliana y la Cabala," *Sefarad* 18 [1958]: 241–53; Josep Maria Millàs i Vallicrosa, *The Doctrine of the "Lullian Dignities" and the Sefiroth* [Jerusalem: Historical Society of Israel, 1960]; and Blau, *The Christian Interpretation*, 117–18).

97. On the early modern fusion between the previously separate traditions of alchemy and astrology, see William Newman and Anthony Grafton, eds., *Secrets of Nature: Astrology and Alchemy in Early Modern Europe* (Cambridge: MIT Press, 2001).

98. Ramón Llull, *De conversione subjiecti et praedicati et Medii*, in *Raimvndi Lvlli Opera Latina*, ed. Helmut Riedlinger (Turnhout, Belgium: Brepols, 1978), 251–76.

99. Antonio Rumeu de Armas, *El obispado de Telde* (Madrid: Patronato de la "Casa De Colón" Biblioteca Atlántica, 1960), 44.

100. Ibid., 43–50; see also Johannes Vincke, "Die Evangelisation der Kanarischen Inseln im 14. Jahrhundert im Geiste Raimund Lulls," *Estudios Lullianos* 4 (1960): 307–17; Leonardo Francalanci, "Humanism and Llullism in Fifteenth-Century Majorca: New Information on the Case of Arnau Descós," in *Humanism and Christian Letters in Early Modern Iberia (1480–1630)*, ed. Barry Taylor and Alejandro Coroleu (Newcastle, UK: Cambridge Scholars Publishing, 2010), 93–104; A. Oliver, "Conquista y evangelización de las Canarias," in *Historia de la Iglesia en España* (Madrid: Biblioteca de Autores Cristianos, 1982), 408; J. Zunzunegui, "Los orígenes de las misiones en las Islas Canarias," *Revista Española de Teologia* 1 (1941): 361–408; Enrique Manuel Pareja Fernández, *El manuscrito luliano Torcaz I. del Seminario de Canarias* (La Laguna: Universidad de la Laguna, 1949); Elías Serra Rafols, "La missió de Ramón Llull i els missioners mallorquins del segle XIV," *Studia monografica et recentiones* XI (1954): 169–75; Tormo, "De Llull a Serra," 330–32; Felipe Fernández-Armesto, *Before Columbus: Exploration and Colonisation from the Mediterranean to the Atlantic, 1229–1492* (Philadelphia: University of Pennsylvania Press, 1987), 229; Eyda M. Merediz, *Refracted Images: The Canary Islands through a New World Lens: Transatlantic Readings* (Tempe, AZ: Center for Medieval and Renaissance Studies, 2004), 13; Julia McClure, *The Franciscan Invention of the New World* (Cham, Switzerland: Springer International, 2016), 85–91.

101. *Bula piis fidelium (25–VI–1493)*, in Giménez Fernández, *Nuevas consideraciones*, 195–204.

102. On the Llullism of the missionaries on Columbus's second voyage, see José M. Rodríguez Tejerina, "El lulismo en el descubrimiento de América," *Estudios Lulianos* 19, no. 55–57 (1975): 172–83; Odette D'Allerit, "Ramon Llull y la tradición del eremitismo apostólico," *Estudios Lulianos* 6 (1962): 105–15; Pere Villalba i Varneda, *Ramon Llull: Escriptor i filòsof de la diferència: Palma de Mallorca, 1232–1316* (Bellaterra: Universitat Autònoma De Barcelona, 2015), 504–5. On Llullism in early American missionary history more generally, see also Tormo Sanz, "De Llull a Serra." On Boyl, see Carlos Dobal, *El primer apostol del Nuevo Mundo* (Santiago, Dominican Republic: Pontificia Universidad Católica Madre y Maestra, 1991); and Fidel Fita, *Fray Bernal Buyl ó el primer apóstol del Nuevo Mundo: Colección*

de Documentos Raros é Inéditos, Relativos á Este Varon Ilustre (Madrid: Impr. De la Viuda é Hija de Fuentenebro, 1884). On Boyl's Llullism, see Anselm Albareda, "Lullisme a Montserrat al segle XVè: L'ermtà Bernat Boil," *Estudios Lulianos* 9 (1965): 5–22; and Pérez Martínez, "El Maestro Pedro Daguí." There has been a long-standing controversy between the Franciscans and the Benedictines about the historical identity and character of Boyl. While the former claim that he was a Franciscan (Minim) friar, the latter claim that he was a Benedictine; yet others claim that there were actually two contemporaries—Boil the Franciscan and Boyl the Benedictine. According to the latter theory, the Franciscan was the one appointed by the papal bull, but Ferdinand, taking advantage of the similarities in names, sent the latter on Columbus's second voyage (see José Gabriel Navarro, *Los Franciscanos en la conquista y colonización de América* [Madrid: Ediciones Cultural Hispánica, 1955], 17; and McClure, *The Franciscan Invention*, 97).

103. For the letters that passed between Boyl and Descós, see Fidel Fita Colomé, ed., "Escritos de Fray Bernad Boyl," *Boletín de la Real Academia de la Historia* 19 (1891): 344–47. On Descós, see Leonardo Francalanci, "Humanism and Lullism in Fifteenth-Century Majorca: New Information on the Case of Arnau Descós," in *Humanism and Christian Letters in Early Modern Iberia (1480–1630)*, ed. Barry Taylor and Alejandro Coroleu (Newcastle: Cambridge Scholars, 2010), 93–103. For the letters that passed between Boyl and Cisneros, see McClure, *The Franciscan Invention*, 95, 113.

104. Mendieta was intent on absolving Columbus from Boyl's indictments of his abuses and enslavement of the Indians, writing that Boyl "spent two years on the island, most of them quarrelling with the Admiral instead of looking after the Indians" (see Fray Gerónimo de Mendieta, *Historia eclesiastica indiana,* ed. Joaquín García Icazbalceta [Mexico City: Antigua Libreria, Portal de Agustinos, 1870], 33).

105. Honorius Philoponus, *Nova typis transacta navigatio: Novi Orbis Indiæ Occidentalis admodum reverendissimorum PP. . . . Dn. Buellii Cataloni abbatis montis Serrati, & in vniversam Americam, sive Novum Orbem sacræ sedis Apostolicæ Romanæ à latere legati, vicarij, ac patriarchæ: Sociorumq[ue] monarchorum ex Ordine S.P.N. Benedicti ad suprà dicti Novi Mundi barbaras gentes Christi S. Evangelium prædicandi gratia delegatorum sacerdotum dimissi per S.D.D. Papam Alexandrum VI. Anno Christi. 1492. Nunc primum e varijs scriptoribus in vnum collecta, & figuris ornata* (Linz, 1621).

106. See Marriano Errasti, *Los primeros franciscanos en América, isla Española, 1343–1520* (Santo Domingo: Custodia Franciscana del Caribe, 2003); and McClure, *The Franciscan Invention*, 97.

107. See Ramón Pané, *An Account of the Antiquities of the Indians: Chronicles of the New World Encounter,* ed. José Juan Arrom (Durham, NC: Duke University Press, 1999), 3. Although the original manuscript is lost, Columbus's son Hernando included a transcription of the text in his biography of his father. Because of the unfavorable political climate toward the Columbus family in Spain during the early decades of the sixteenth century, Hernando was unable to publish his

biography, written in Spanish; but an Italian translation was published after Hernando's death by Alfonso de Ulloa in 1571. The original manuscript of the biography is now also lost. Ulloa's translation is riddled with Italian transliterations and other problems, but both Pietro Martire d'Anghiera and Bartolomé de las Casas, who were apparently in possession of a copy of Pané's manuscript or had at least seen a copy, used it in their own accounts of Columbus's expeditions.

108. Some historians of religion in America have therefore seen Pané as a distant intellectual heir of Llull (see, for example, Tormo Sanz, "De Llull a Serra," 323–40). However, Tormo Sanz does not provide any concrete evidence of Pané's distinctly Llullian orientation, and we know next to nothing about Pané's life and education, except that he was, like Llull, a native speaker of Catalan and grew up in the vicinity of Barcelona, where he witnessed Columbus's triumphant entry after returning from his first voyage. Given that Barcelona was one of the centers of the Llullist revival during the last decades of the fifteenth century, it is possible that he was partially inspired by Llull's example of missionary hermitage.

109. See I. Vázquez Janeiro, "Un lector de Raimundo Lulio y de Arnaldo de Vilanova entre los evangelizadores de la América Colombina?," *Humanismo, Reforma y Teología* 4 (1979): 1–36. It should be noted here that Vázquez Janeiro's identification of the Robles who was in possession of these Llullian and Arnaldian texts with the Robles who arrived in Hispaniola in 1500 was somewhat speculative. Previously, the former Robles had been identified as a Benedictine by J. Perarnau, though, as Vázquez Janeiro pointed out, such an identification is questionable for chronological reasons (see J. Perarnau, "Dos tratados 'espirituales' de Arnau de Vilanova en traducción castellana medieval: 'Dyalogus de elementis catholice fidei' y 'De helemosyna et sacrificio,'" *Anthologica Annua*, 22–23 [1975-16 (1978)]: 477–630).

110. Qtd. in Vázquez Janeiro, "Un lector," 28. See also Pedro Borges, "Primeras expediciones misioneras a América," *Archivo Ibero-Americano* 27 (1967): 123–33.

111. Reproduced in Ortega, *La Rábida*, 2:303–9.

112. See José Torrubia, *Crónica de la provincia franciscana de santa cruz,* ed. Odilo Gómez Parente (Caracas: Academia Nacional de la Historia, 1972); see also Antonine S. Tibesar, "The Franciscan Province of the Holy Cross of Española, 1505–1559," *Americas* 13, no. 4 (April 1957): 377–89; and Livarius Onger, "The Earliest Record on the Franciscan Missions in America," *Catholic Historical Review* 6, no. 1 (April 1920): 59–65. Tibesar and, before him, Onger heavily draw on an account written in 1501 in Nuremberg by the Franciscan chronicler Nicholas Glassberger, a correspondent of Maillard. See also José Gabriel Navarro, *Los franciscanos en la conquista y colonización de América* (Madrid: Ediciones Cultura Hispánica, 1955), 23; and McClure, *The Franciscan Invention,* 98.

113. Hernán Cortés, *Letters from Mexico,* ed. Anthony Pagden (New Haven: Yale University Press, 2001), 332–33.

114. Ibid., 334.

115. See Francisco Morales, "The Native Encounter with Christianity: Franciscans and Nahuas in Sixteenth-Century Mexico," *Americas* 65, no. 2 (2008): 137–59;

Morales, "Franciscanos y mundo religioso en el México virreinal: Algunas consideraciones generales," in *Franciscanos y mundo religioso en México,* ed. Morales et al. (Mexico City: Universidad Nacional Autónoma de México, 1993), 9–30; Morales, *Ethnic and Social Background of the Franciscan Friars in Seventeenth-Century Mexico* (Washington, DC: Academy of American Franciscan History, 1973); Elsa Cecila Frost, *La historia de dios en las Indias: Visión franciscana del Nuevo Mundo* (Mexico City: Tiempo de Memoria Editores, 2002); Bert Roest, "Early Mendicant Mission in the New World: Discourses, Experiments, Realities," *Franciscan Studies* 71 no. 1 (2013): 197–217; Roest, "From *Reconquista* to Mission in the Early Modern World," in *A Companion to Observant Reform in the Late Middle Ages and Beyond,* ed. James Mixson and Bert Roest (Leiden: Brill, 2015), 346; see also Vicente Beltrán de Heredia, *Historia de la reforma de la provincial de España (1450–1550)* (Rome: Institutum Historicum Ff. Praedicatorum, Romae Ad S. Sabinae. Dissertationes Historicae, Fasc. Xi. Romae: Ad S. Sabinae, 1939); García Oro, *La reforma,* 91–125; and García Oro, *Prehistoria y primeros capítulos de la evangelización de América* (Caracas: Ediciones Trípode, 1988); Mónica Ruiz Bañuls, "El franciscanismo en el contexto evangelizador novohispano: raíces del mensaje missional," *Semata, Ciencias Sociais e Humanidades* 26 (2014): 491–507; and Hervé Pujol, "La christianisation de la Nouvelle-Espagne ou le rêve d'une église indienne: Les agents de l'évangélisation," *Cahiers d'études du religieux. Recherches interdisciplinaires* 10 (2012).

116. Karen Melvin, *Building Colonial Cities of God: Mendicant Orders and Urban Culture in New Spain* (Nashville: Vanderbilt University Press, 2012), 8, 97–99; on mendicant reformism, see García Oro, *La reforma,* 91–125.
117. Bernal Díaz del Castillo, *The True History of the Conquest of New Spain,* ed. David Carrasco (Albuquerque: University of New Mexico Press, 2008), 355.
118. On the notion of a "spiritual conquest," see chapter 6.

6. Physicians of the Soul

1. Robert Ricard, *The Spiritual Conquest of America: An Essay of the Apostolate and the Evangelizing Methods of he Mendicant Orders in New Spain, 1523–1572,* trans. Lesley Byrd Simpson (Berkeley: University of California Press, 1966). Since the original publication of this seminal work in 1933, historians have long challenged Ricard's notion of a "spiritual conquest." Some have emphasized the active and continual Nahua resistance to the Spanish attempt at evangelization, speaking instead of "spiritual conflict" and "warfare" (see Jorge Klor de Alva, "Spiritual Conflict and Accommodation in New Spain: Toward a Typology of Aztec Responses to Christianity," in *The Inca and Aztec States, 1400–1800: Anthropology and History,* ed. George Collier, Renato Rosaldo, and John Wirth [New York: Academic, 1982], 345–66; and David Tavárez, *The Invisible War: Indigenous Devotions, Discipline, and Dissent in Colonial Mexico* [Stanford, CA: Stanford University Press, 2011]). Others have pointed out not only the many compromises and negotiations that

the mendicants had to make in their missionary efforts but also the active role that indigenous actors and their diverse responses played in the making not of one but many Christianities in the early Americas (see Louise Burkhart, *The Slippery Earth: Nahua-Christian Moral Dialogue in Sixteenth-Century Mexico* [Tucson: University of Arizona Press, 1989]; Ana de Zaballa Beascoechea, *Transculturación y misión en Nueva España: Estudio histórico-doctrinal del libro de los "Coloquios" de Barnadino de Sahagún* [Barañáin-Pamplona: Ediciones Universidad de Navarra, 1990]; Serge Gruzinski, *The Mestizo Mind: The Intellectual Dynamics of Colonization and Globalization* [New York: Routledge, 2002]; Stephanie Wood, *Transcending Conquest: Nahua Views of Spanish Colonial Mexico* [Norman: University of Oklahoma Press, 2003]; Osvaldo Pardo, *The Origins of Mexican Catholicism: Nahua Rituals and Christian Sacraments in Sixteenth-Century Mexico* [Ann Arbor: University of Michigan Press, 2007]; and David Tavárez, ed., *Words & Worlds Turned Around: Indigenous Christianities in Colonial Latin America* [Boulder: University Press of Colorado, 2017]).

2. Ricard, *Spiritual Conquest*, 102; and Ricard, "Morisques et Indiens: Notes sur quelques procédés d'évangélisation," *Journal de la société des Américanistes* 18 (1926): 350–57.
3. Although Pope Clement V—partially in response to Llull's persistent urging—issued a decree at the Council of Vienne (1312), that called for the establishmenet of chairs in Greek, Hebrew, Arabic, and Aramaic at the papal curia and in Paris, Oxford, Rome, and Salamanca, the plan languished until the sixteenth century (see Bert Roest, *A History of Franciscan Education, ca. 1210–1517* [Leiden: Brill, 2000], 152).
4. See Ricard, "Morisques et Indiens," 350–57.
5. Josep-Maria Riera Sans, though acknowledging several similarities between Llull's and Molina's texts observed by Ricard, ultimately concluded that a direct dependency is altogether unlikely (see his "Fray Alonso de Molina y Ramon Llull: A propósito de una hipótesis de Robert Ricard," *10 Simposio Internacional de Teología de la Universidad de Navarra* [1990], 2:1021–32).
6. The primary focus has hereby been on the *Rhetorica Christiana* (1579), written by the American-born Franciscan missionary Fray Diego de Valadés (see Pauline Moffitt Watts, "Hieroglyphs of Conversion: Alien Discourses in Diego Valadés's *Rhetorica Christiana*," *Memoriae Domenicane* 22 [1991]: 405–33; and Moffitt Watts, "Talking to Spiritual Others: Ramon Llull, Nicholas of Cusa, Diego Valadés," in *Travellers, Intellectuals, and the World beyond Medieval Europe*, ed. James Muldoon [Farnham, Surrey: Ashgate, 2010], 129–44; see also Mauricio Beuchot, "Retórica y lulismo en Diego de Valadés," *Studia Lulliana* 32 [1992]: 153–61; Linda Báez-Rubí, *Die Rezeption der Lehre des Ramon Llull in der "Rhetorica Christiana" [Perugia, 1579] des Franziskaners Fray Diego de Valadés* [Frankfurt: Peter Lang, 2004]; Báez-Rubí, *Mnemosine novohispánica: Retórica e imágenes en el siglo XVI* [Mexico City: Universidad Nacional Autónoma de México, 2005]; Báez-Rubí, "Die 'Rhetorica Christiana' [Perugia 1579]

des Fray Diego de Valadés als Ausdruck franziskanischer Missionstheologie," *Zeitschrift für Missionswissenschaft und Religionswissenschaft* 92, no. 3 [2008]: 330–49; César Chaparro Gómez, "Enciclopedia y retórica: De Raimundo Lulio a Diego Valadés," *Fortunatae* 19 [2008]: 9–25; and D. Alcala Mendizabal, "La Influencia Lulista en Fray Diego Valadés: Y su análisis desde la Hermenéutica Analógica," *Utopia y Praxis Latinoamericana* 21, no. 72 [2016]: 95–102). Báez Rubí has also investigated the influences of Llullian natural theology on Fray Toribio de Benavente and Fray Juan de Zumárraga in "La herencia del Ars Lulliana contemplativa en el orbe cultural de la evangelización franciscana: Fray Juan de Zumárraga y la via de los beneficios en tierras de la Nueva España," *Antonianum; periodicum trimester* 80, no. 3 (2005) and "De harmonia mundi: ¿un reino de Saturno novohispano?," *Anales del Instituto de Investigaciones Estéticas* 73 (1998): 41–67. Rodolfo Fernández has explored the influence of Llullian encyclopedic rhetoric in the *Relación de Michoacán* written by the Franciscan missionary Fray Jerónimo de Alcalá in his *Retórica y antropología del mundo Tarasco: Textos sobre la relación de Michoacán* (Mexico City: Instituto Nacional de Antropología e Historia, 2011), 137–66; see also his "Ramón Llull y los rétores del mundo novohispano Valadés y Alcalá," in *Transformaciones socioculturales en México en el contexto de la conquista y colonización: Nuevas perspectivas de investigación: [reunión en amatitán]*, ed. Barbara Potthast-Jutkeit et al., 107–27 (Mexico City: Instituto Nacional de Antropología e Historia, 2009). D. Urvoy has argued (without giving specific evidence) that Sahagún's project (as well as that of the Jesuit working in China Matteo Ricchi) represented the historical realization the program envisioned by Llull (see "L'apport de Fr. B. de Sahagún a la solution du problem lullien de la comprehension d'autrui," *Estudios Lulianos* 52–54 [1974]: 5–24). For an overview of Llullism in New Spain, see Francisco José Díaz-Marcilla, "Tierras de penumbra: Las vicisitudes del lulismo novohispano (1519–1750)," *Revista de Hispanismo Filosófico* 21 (2016): 13–33; and Rafael Ramis Barceló, "La Inquisición de México y la calificación del *Árbol de la ciencia* de Ramon Llull (1665–1669)," *Estudios de Historia Novohispana* 48 (2013):189–214. On the impact of Llullian memory technology on early modern Spanish culture generally, see Fernando Rodríguez de la Fior, *Emblemas: Lecturas de la imagen simbólica* (Madrid: Alianza Forma, 1995).

7. On the notion of a "missionary science," see Andrés Prieto, *Missionary Scientists: Jesuit Science in Spanish South America, 1570–1810* (Nashville: Vanderbilt University Press, 2011).

8. Barbara Rosenwein and Lester Little, "Social Meaning in the Monastic and Mendicant Spirituality," *Past and Present* 63, no. 1 (1974): 24; and Jonathan Boyarin, *The Unconverted Self: Jews, Indians, and the Identity of Christian Europe* (Chicago: University of Chicago Press, 2009). On the growth of religious intolerance, especially anti-Judaism and anti-Islamic crusading, in this late medieval socioeconomic context, see Jeremy Cohen, *The Friars and the Jews: The Evolution of Medieval Anti-Judaism* (Ithaca, NY: Cornell University Press, 1982), 15–16; and Robert

Bartlett, *The Making of Europe: Conquest, Colonization, and Cultural Change, 950–1350* (Princeton: Princeton University Press, 1993).

9. Calvin Kendall, introduction to *Conversion to Christianity from Late Antiquity to the Modern Age: Considering the Process in Europe, Asia, and the Americas*, ed. Kendall, Oliver Nicholson, William Phillips, and Marguerite Ragnow (Minneapolis: Center for Early Modern History, 2009), 3. On the history of conversion before the thirteenth century, see Kenneth Mills and Anthony Grafton, eds., *Conversion in Late Antiquity and the Early Middle Ages* (Rochester: Univeristy of Rochester Press, 2003). On conversion during the Middle Ages more generally, see James Muldoon, ed. *Varieties of Religious Conversion in the Middle Ages* (Gainesville: University Press of Florida, 1997).

10. Kendall, introduction to *Conversion to Christianity*, 1; see also William James, *The Varieties of Religious Experience: A Study of Human Nature*, ed. Matthew Bradley (Oxford: Oxford University Press, 2012), 210.

11. Mark Johnston, introduction to *The Book of the Lover and the Beloved* by Ramon Llull, trans. Johnston (Bristol: Centre for Mediterranean Studies, University of Bristol, 1995), xvii.

12. See Caroline Walker Bynum, *Resurrection of the Body in Western Christianity, 200–1336* (New York: Columbus University Press, 1995), 215; and R. I. Moore, *The Formation of a Persecuting Society: Power and Deviance in Western Europe, 950–1250* (Oxford: Basil Blackwell, 1987).

13. *La disputa de Tortosa*, ed. Antonio Pacios López, 2 vols. (Madrid: Consejo Superior de Investigaciones Científicas, 1957), 2:21. See also David Boruchoff, "Sahagún and the Theology of Missionary Life," in *Sahagún at 500: Essays on the Quincentenary of the Birth of Fr. Bernadino de Sahagún*, ed. John Frederick Schwaller (Berkeley: Academy of American Franciscan History, 2003), 59–102, 86–87.

14. Boyarin, *The Unconverted Self*, 12.

15. Karl Morrison, *Understanding Conversion* (Charlottesville: University Press of Virginia, 1992), ix–xxii, xiii.

16. See William Newman and Lawrence Principe, *Alchemy Tried in the Fire: Starkey, Boyle, and the Fate of Helmontian Chymistry* (Chicago: University of Chicago Press, 2002). On the belief in the power of art in the context of alchemy, see William Newman, *Promethean Ambitions: Alchemy and the Quest to Perfect Nature* (Chicago: University of Chicago Press, 2004). On the phrase "alchemy of words," see chapter 5 and below in this chapter.

17. See Charles Schmitt, *Aristotle and the Renaissance* (Cambridge: Harvard University Press, 1983); Christoph Lüthy, Cees Leijenhorst, and Johannes M. M. H. Thijssen, "The Tradition of Aristotelian Natural Philosophy: Two Theses and Seventeen Answers," in *The Dynamics of Aristotelian Natural Philosophy from Antiquity to the Seventeenth Century*, ed. Leijenhorst, Lüthy, and Thijssen (Leiden: Brill, 2002), 1–29; see also chapter 1 of this book.

18. Orlando Bentancor, *The Matter of Empire: Metaphysics and Mining in Colonial Peru* (Pittsburgh: Pittsburgh University Press, 2017), 3.

19. Ibid., 27.
20. Ibid., 10.
21. This applies especially to Llullian legal thought, which derives from the canon law tradition (see Rafael Ramis Barcelo, "El pensamiento jurídico de Santo Tomás y de Ramon Llull en el contexto político e institucional del siglo XIII," *Angelicum* 90, no. 2 [2013]: 189–216; Ramis Bercelo, "La recepción de las ideas jurídicas de Ramon Llull en los siglos XV y XVI," *Revista de Estudios Históricos-Jurídicos* 34 [2012]: 431–56; Ramis Barcelo, "La fundamendación y la estructura del derecho en el *Ars brevis*," *Scintilla* 10, no. 1 [2013]: 79–97; and Ramis Barcelo, "Raimundus Lullus on Canon Law," *Zeitschrift der Savigny-Stiftung für Rechtsgeschichte: Kanonistische Abteilung* 102, no. 1 [2016]: 445–70). For the important role that the traditions of Duns Scotus and William of Ockham still played in sixteenth-century Franciscan natural theology in New Spain, see Verónica Murillo Gallegos, *La ley natural en el pensamiento Franciscano: Su presencia en Nueva España* (Zacatecas, Mexico: Policromía, 2016), 9–26; and Julia McClure, *The Franciscan Invention of the New World* (Cham, Switzerland: Springer International, 2016), 7.
22. Fray Bernadino de Sahagún, *Historia general de las cosas de la Nueva España,* ed. Ángel María Garibay, 4 vols. (Mexico City: Editorial Porrúa, 1956), 1:27. Although *Historia general* is the title by which modern editors and authors have most commonly referred to Sahagún's text, Jesús Bustamente García has shown that this is based on an error originating with Carlos María de Bustamente's 1829–30 edition of Sahagún's work. Bustamente García shows that Sahagún intended his history to be entitled "Historia universal" (see Jesús Bustamente García, *Fray Bernadino de Sahagún: Una revisión crítica de los manuscritos y de su proceso de composición* [Mexico City, DF: Universidad Nacional Autónoma de México, 1990], 249).
23. Sahagún, *Historia general,* 1:27.
24. See Roest, *A History of Franciscan Education,* 150.
25. St. Augustine, *De doctrina Christiana,* ed. and trans. R. P. H. Green (Oxford: Clarendon, 1995), 24.
26. On the history of the analogy in a late medieval context (particularly that of Parisian nominalism), see Thomas Tentler, *Sin and Confession on the Eve of the Reformation* (Princeton: Princeton University Press, 1977), 100–102.
27. Joseph Ziegler, *Medicine and Religion, c. 1300: The Case of Arnau de Vilanova* (Oxford: Clarendon, 1998), 182, 9, 102.
28. See also E. Gisbert, "Metaforice loquendo: De l'analogia a la metàfora en els Començaments de medicina de Ramon Llull," *Studia Lulliana* 54, no. 100 (2004): 17–52; and Mark Johnston, *The Evangelical Rhetoric of Ramon Llull: Lay Learning and Piety in the Christian West around 1300* (New York: Oxford University Press, 1996), 101–2.
29. Andrés de Olmos, *Tratado de hechicerías y sortilegios,* ed. Georges Baudot (Mexico City: Universidad Nacional Autónoma de México, 1990), 24.
30. Ricard, *The Spiritual Conquest,* 285.

31. See Luis N. Rivera, *A Violent Evangelism: The Political and Religious Conquest of the Americas* (Louisville, KY: Westminster/John Knox, 1992), 52.
32. Thomas Aquinas, *Summa theologiae* (New York: Cosimo Classics, 2007), 1334.
33. See Rivera, *A Violent Evangelism*. On the significance of the distinction between Franciscan nominalist and Thomist realist metaphysics in missionology, see Fernando Cervantes, *The Devil in the New World: The Impact of Diabolism in New Spain* (New Haven: Yale University Press, 1994), 21–39. On Dominican theology of conversion more generally, see Vinencio Carro, in *La teología y los teólogos-juristas españoles ante la conquista de América* (Salamanca: Apartado, 1951); and Pedro Fernández Rodríguez, *Los Dominicos en la primera evangelización de México* (Salamanca: Editorial San Estéban, 1994).
34. See Paula Findlen, ed., *Athanasius Kircher: The Last Man Who Knew Everything* (London: Routledge, 2004); Daniel Stolzenberg, *Egyptian Oedipus: Athanasius Kircher and the Secrets of Antiquity* (Chicago: University of Chicago Press, 2013); Juan Pimentel, "Juan E. Nieremberg, American Wonders, Preterimperial Natural History," in *Science in the Spanish and Portuguese Empires,* ed. Daniela Bleichmar et al. (Stanford: Stanford University Press, 2009), 93–114; Daniel Stolzenberg, *Egyptian Oedipus: Athanasius Kircher and the Secrets of Antiquity* (Chicago: University of Chicago Press, 2013); Brian Curran, *The Egyptian Renaissance: The Afterlife of Ancient Egypt in Early Modern Italy* (Chicago: University of Chicago Press, 2007).
35. Joseph-François Lafitau, *Customs of the American Indians Compared with the Customs of Primitive Times* (Toronto: Champlain Society, 1974), 31. On Lafitau's "comparative ethnology," see Anthony Pagden, *The Fall of Natural Man: The American Indian and the Origins of Comparative Ethnology* (Cambridge: Cambridge University Press, 1982), 198–209.
36. Ricard, *The Spiritual Conquest,* 284.
37. Edwin Edward Sylvest Jr., *Motifs of Franciscan Mission Theory in Sixteenth-Century New Spain Province of the Holy Gospel* (Washington, DC: Academy of American Franciscan History, 1975), 101–2; see also Stafford Poole, "Some Observations on Mission Methods and Native Reactions in Sixteenth-Century New Spain," *Americas* 50, no. 3 (1994): 337–49; and Pedro Borges, *Métodos misionales en la Cristianización de América, siglo XVI* (Madrid: Consejo Superior de Investigaciones Científicas, Departamento de Misionología Española, 1960).
38. See Arthur Anderson, introduction to *Bernadino de Sahagun's* Psalmodia Christiana (Christian Psalmody), trans. Arthur J. O. Anderson (Salt Lake City: University of Utah Press, 1993), xv–xxxv; Miguel León Portilla, *Bernardino de Sahagun, First Anthropologist* (Norman: University of Oklahoma Press, 2002), 139; F. Vicente Castro and José-Luis Rodríguez Molinero, *Bernardino de Sahagún: Primer antropólogo en Nueva España (siglo XVI)* (Salamanca: Ediciones Universidad De Salamanca, 1986); and Louise Burkhart, "On the Margins of Legitimacy: Sahagún's *Psalmodia* and the Latin Liturgy," in *Sahagún at 500: Essays on*

the *Quincentenary of the Birth of Fr. Bernadino de Sahagún,* ed. John Frederick Schwaller (Berkeley: Academy of American Franciscan History, 2003), 103–16.

39. On *mestizaje,* see Gruzinski, *The Mestizo Mind* and his forthcoming *The Time Machine;* Pardo, *Origins;* Jacques Lafaye, *Quetzalcóatl and Guadalupe: The Formation of Mexican National Consciousness,* trans. Benjamin Keen (Chicago: University of Chicago Press, 1987); and Viviana Díaz Balsera, *The Pyramid under the Cross: Franciscan Discourses of Evangelization and the Nahua Christian Subject in Sixteenth-Century Mexico* (Tucson: University of Arizona Press, 2005). On the architecture that grew out of the cultural *mestizaje,* see Samuel Edgerton, *Theaters of Conversion: Religious Architecture and Indian Artisans in Colonial Mexico,* with photographs by Jorge Pérez de Lara (Albuquerque: University of New Mexico Press, 2001).
40. See Georges Baudot, *Utopia and History in Mexico: The First Chroniclers of Mexican Civilization* (1979; Boulder: University Press of Colorado, 1995), 76–80.
41. The New Spanish Franciscans' alleged indebtedness to Joachimite eschatology has been the subject of a protracted historiographic debate. Besides Baudot, the most important proponent of Franciscan apocalyptic urgency was James Phelan in his *The Millennial Kingdom of the Franciscans in the New World* (Berkeley: University of California Press, 1970); other proponents include Luis Weckmann-Muñoz, "Las esperanzas milenaristas de los franciscanos de la Nueva España," *Historia Mexicana* 32 (1982): 89–105; and José Rabasa, *Inventing America: Spanish Historiography and the Formation of Eurocentrism* (Norman: University of Oklahoma Press, 1993), 151–64. Skeptical assessments include José Antonio Maravall, "La utopia politico-religiosa de los Franciscanos en Nueva España," *Estudios Americanos* 2 (1949): 199–227; Marcel Bataillon, "Evangélisme et millénarisme au Nouveau Monde," *Courants religieux et humanism a la fin de xve et au début de xvie siècle* (Paris: Presses Universitaires de France, 1959), 25–36; and Delno West, "Medieval Ideas of Apocalyptic Mission and the Early Franciscans in Mexico," *Americas* 45 (1989): 293–313.
42. Baudot, *Utopia,* 75; see also Díaz Balsera, *The Pyramid,* 165.
43. The relationship between the so-called missionary ethnography of the sixteenth century and modern anthropology has been the subject of much debate. For a good overview of this debate, see Victoria Ríos Castaño, *Translation as Conquest: Sahagún and "Universal History of the Things of New Spain"* (Madrid: Iberoamericana, 2014), 1–36.
44. There were, however, exceptions. For example, although Fray Andrés de Olmos often employed "brutal means" in his campaigns to extirpate idolatry and polygamy, he apparently came to have doubts about the usefulness of force and violence, exclaiming "let there be no conquest" (see Baudot, *Utopia,* 137, 148).
45. Toribio de Motolinía [Benavente], "Carta de fray Toribio de Motolinía al Emperador Carlos V, Enero 2 de 1555," in *Historia de los Indios de la Nueva España,* ed. Edmundo O'Gorman (Mexico City: Editorial Porrúa, 1979), 211. On the use of force in conversion, see also Rivera, *A Violent Evangelism,* 217–34.
46. Toribio de Motolinía [Benavente], "Carta."

47. See Cervantes, *The Devil*, 21–39. Cervantes posits a preponderance of the nominalist point of view only after the Council of Trent. However, as we have seen, the Franciscan preoccupation with the active power of evil was already evident during the Middle Ages, especially among Franciscan alchemists. Also, as John Monfasani has pointed out, until the fifteenth and sixteenth centuries, Ockham's most prominent followers appear to have been secular theologians at the University of Paris such as Gabriel Biel and John Mair (see John Monfasani, "Aristotelians, Platonists, and the Missing Ockhamists: Philosophical Liberty in Pre-Reformation Italy," *Renaissance Quartely* 46, no. 2 [1993]: 247–76). In Spain, this changed in the sixteenth century with the rise of influential Spanish Franciscan humanists such as Jiménez de Cisneros.
48. Cervantes, *The Devil*, 21–22.
49. Mark Evan Davis, "'The Evangelical Prophecies over Jerusalem Have Been Fulfilled': Joachim of Fiore, the Jews, Fray Diego de Landa and the Maya," *Journal of Medieval Iberian Studies* 5, no. 1 (2013): 86–103.
50. On Zumárraga, see Joaquín García Icazbalceta, *Don Fray Juan de Zumárraga: Primer obispo y arzobispo de México* (Mexico City: Antigua Librería de Andrade y Morales, 1881). On the trial of Don Carlos, see Tavárez, *The Invisible War*, 26. As Julia McClure has pointed out, the Franciscans' tendencies toward violence was directed not only at their neophytes but also (and often primarily) at themselves in a "ritualized and salvific violence" that expressed itself in elaborate procedures of penitence disciplining their bodies and their minds (McClure, *The Franciscan Invention*, 124).
51. Olmos, *Tratado*, 27–29. On Olmos's pioneering efforts in ethnography, see Baudot, *Utopia*, 121–334.
52. Gerónimo de Mendieta, *Historia eclesiastica indiana*, ed. Joaquín García Icazbalceta (Mexico City: Antigua Libreria, Portal de Agustinos, 1870), 75.
53. Baudot, *Utopia*, 131.
54. Elsa Cecilia Frost, *La historia de Dios en las Indias: Visión franciscana del Nuevo Mundo* (Mexico City: Tusquets Editores, 2002), 183. On the concept of extirpation in the Andes, see also Pierre Duviols, *La destrucción de las religiones andinas durante la conquista y la colonia* (Mexico City: Universidad Nacional Autónoma de México, 1977); Nicolas Griffiths, *The Cross and the Serpent: Repression and Resurgence in Colonial Peru* (Norman: University of Oklahoma Press, 1996); Kenneth Mills, *Idolatry and Its Enemies: Colonial Andean Religion and Extirpation, 1640–1750* (Princeton: Princeton University Press, 1997); and Sabine MacCormack, "Gods, Demons, and Idols in the Andes," *Journal of the History of Ideas* 67, no. 4 (October 2006): 623–48.
55. See Fabián Alejandro Campagne, "Witches, Idolaters, and Franciscans: An American Translation of European Radical Demonology (Logroño, 1529–Hueytlalpan, 1553)," *History of Religions* 44, no. 1 (2004): 1–35; Cervantes, *The Devil*, 25; and Baudot, *Utopia*, 121–245.

56. See Baudot, *Utopia,* 191.
57. McClure, *The Franciscan Invention,* esp. chapter 5, "Franciscan Landscapes of Identity and Violence" (117–58). Although McClure does not address questions of metaphysics and the connection to alchemy, she provides an excellent discussion of the Franciscans' peculiar relationship to violence. On Franciscan violence, see also Jorge Klor de Alva, "Colonizing Souls: The Failure of the Indian Inquisition and the Rise of the Penitential Discipline," in *Cultural Encounters: The Impact of the Inquisition in Spain and in the New World,* ed. Mary Elizabeth Perry et al. (Berkeley: University of California Press, 1991), 3–22; on the notion of conversion in terms of warfare, see Tavárez, *The Invisible War.*
58. Newman, *Promethean Ambitions,* 43–53.
59. Ibid., 52; see also Newman, *Atoms and Alchemy: Chymistry and the Experimental Origins of the Scientific Revolution* (Chicago: University of Chicago Press, 2006), 17.
60. Newman and Principe, *Alchemy Tried in the Fire,* 78.
61. See Newman, *Promethean Ambitions,* 51–76.
62. Burkhart, *The Slippery Earth,* 9. As Burkhart shows, the attempt to turn dialogue into monologue was often successfully resisted by the Mexica participants. See also Thomas S. Bremer, "Reading the Sahagún Dialogues," in *Sahagún at 500: Essays on the Quincentenary of the Birth of Fr. Bernardino De Sahagún,* ed. John Frederick Schwaller (Berkeley, CA: Academy of American Franciscan History, 2003), 13.
63. Ramón Sugranyes de Franch has argued that Las Casas may also have been influenced by certain aspects of the Llullian art, whose emphasis on dialogue and rational argumentation accorded with Llull's project for peaceful conversion (see Ramón Sugranyes de Franch, "¿Bartolomé de las Casas, discípulo de Raimundo Lulio?," in *De Raimundo Lulio Al Vaticano Ii: Articulos Escogidos* [Lausanne: Sociedad Suiza De Estudios Hispánicos, 1991], 107–21, and 111–12). As I have pointed out, however, Llull and the Llullists considered peaceful dialogue only as one method among other, more coercive methods, including war—something that Las Casas categorically rejected.
64. For an English translation of the Nahuatl text of the *Colloquios,* see Jorge Klor de Alva, "The Aztec-Spanish Dialogues of 1524," *Alcheringa* 4 (1980): 52–193; for a modern Spanish edition, see Bernardino de Sahagún, *Coloquios y doctrina Cristiana: Con que los doce frailes de San Francisco, Enviados por el Papa Adriano Vi y por el Emperador Carlos V, convirtieron a los indios de la Nueva España: En lengua Mexicano y Española. Los diálogos de 1524,* ed. Miguel León Portilla (Mexico City: Universidad Nacional Autónoma de México, Fundación De Investigaciones Sociales, 1986). For some seminal discussions of this text, see Klor de Alva, "La historicidad de los *Coloquios* de Sahagún," *Estudios de Cultura Náhuatl* 15 (1982): 147–84; Christian Duverger, *La conversión de los indios de Nueva España con el texto de los "Coloquios de los Doce" de Bernadino de Sahagún (1564),* trans. María Dolores de la Peña (Mexico City: Fondo de Cultura Económica, 1993); Burkhart,

The Slippery Earth; Ana de Zaballa Beascoechea, *Transculturación y mision en Nueva España: Estudio histórico-doctrinal del libro de los "Coloquios" de Bernadino de Sahagún* (Barañáin-Pamplona: Ediciones Universiddad de Navarra, 1990); and Díaz Balsera, *The Pyramid,* 15–52.
65. Sahagún, *Coloquios,* 81.
66. Díaz Balsera, *The Pyramid,* 24–25.
67. Klor de Alva, "The Aztec-Spanish Dialogues," 72.
68. Ibid., 87.
69. Díaz Balsera, *The Pyramid,* 179; and Burkhart, 170–83.
70. Mendieta, *Historia eclesiástica,* 281.
71. Ibid., 5.
72. See Díaz Balsera, *The Pyramid,* 22.
73. Mendieta, *Historia eclesiastica,* 75.
74. Ibid.
75. On the considerable continuities between pre- and post-Conquest Nahua religions, see James Lockhard, *The Nahuas after the Conquest: A Social and Cultural History of the Indians of Central Mexico, Sixteenth through Eighteenth Centuries* (Stanford: Stanford University Press, 1992); Poole, "Some Observations"; on the violent reaction to the discovery of these continuities, see Klor de Alva, "Colonizing Souls"; and Tavárez, *The Invisible War.*
76. The classic works on Franciscan New World utopianism include Justino Fernández and Edmundo O'Gorman, *Santo Tomas More y "La Utopia de Tomas Moro en la Nueva España"* (Mexico City: Alcancia, 1937); Phelan, *The Millennial Kingdom of the Franciscans;* Patricia Nettel Díaz, *La utopia franciscana en la Nueva España* (Mexico City: UNAM, 1989); Silvio Zavala, Guillermo Tovar de Teresa, Miguel León Portilla, *La Utopía Mexicana del siglo XVI: lo bello, lo verdadero, y lo bueno* (Mexico City: Grupo Azabache, 1992); Baudot, *Utopia;* Stelio Cro, *Realidad y utopía en el descubrimiento y conquista de la América Hispana, 1492–1682* (Madrid: Fundación Universitaria Espanola, 1983); and Cro, *The American Foundations of the Hispanic Utopia* (Tallahassee, FL: DeSoto, 1994).
77. Peter Martyr D'Anghera, *De orbe novo,* trans., introd., and annotated Francis Augustus MacNutt, 2 vols. (New York: Putnam's Sons, 1912), 1:103. As we saw in chapter 7, this claim originated with the *Mundus novus* attributed to the Florentine explorer Amerigo Vespucci.
78. Fray Toribio de Benavente [Motolinía], *Historia de los Indios de la Nueva España: Escrita a mediados del siglo XVI.* ed. Daniel Sánchez García (Barcelona: Herederos De J. Gili, 1914), 168. The English translation is taken from Elizabeth Andros Foster in *Motolinia's History of the Indians of New Span,* trans. Elizabeth Andros Foster (Berkeley, CA: Cortes Society, 1950), 193.
79. Motolinía, *Historia,* 73 (English, 98).
80. "A estas dos maneras de tiranía infernal se reducen e ser resuelven o subalternan como a géneros todas las otras diversas y varias de asolar aquellas gentes, que son infinitas" (Bartolomé de las Casas, *Brevísima relación de la destruición de las*

Indias, ed. Martínez-Torrejón José Miguel [Madrid: Real Academia Española, 2013], 4).
81. Motolinía, *Historia,* 12 (English, 38).
82. Ibid.
83. Motolinía, *Historia,* 182 (English, 207).
84. Hernando Cortés, "Second Letter to Charles V," in *Letters from Mexico,* trans. and ed. Anthony Pagden (New Haven: Yale University Press, 1971), 62.
85. Mendieta, *Historia eclesiastica indiana,* 15.
86. On the comparison with Anglo-American exodus narratives, see David Boruchoff, "New Spain, New England, and the New Jerusalem: The 'Translation' of Empire, Faith, and Learning (Translatio Imperii, Fidei Ac Scientiae) in the Colonial Missionary Project," *Early American Literature,* vol. 43, no. 1 (2008): 5–34.
87. Mendieta, *Historia,* 175.
88. Ibid.
89. Ibid., 174–75.
90. On Mendieta's apocalypticism, see especially Phelan, *The Millenial Kingdom;* and Baudot, *Utopia.*
91. Mendieta, *Historia,* 463, 538. On the role of the Virgin Mary in late medieval and early modern Christian militancy, see Amy Remensnyder, *La conquistadora: The Virgin Mary at War and Peace in the Old and the New Worlds* (New York: Oxford University Press, 2014).
92. As pointed out in chapter 4, Mendieta conflated the two Franciscan friars Juan Pérez and Antonio de Marchena into one person, whom he called "Juan Pérez de Marchena."
93. Mendieta, *Historia,* 15.
94. On Franciscan militancy, see Bert Roest, "From *Reconquista* to Mission in the Early Modern World," in *A Companion to Observant Reform in the Late Middle Ages and Beyond,* ed. James Mixson and Bert Roest (Leiden: Brill, 2015), 331–62.
95. Mendieta, *Historia,* 18.
96. Ibid., 17.
97. Ibid., 18–19. English translation is from Fray Gerónimo de Mendiea, *Historia eclesiásitca Indiana: A Franciscan's View of the Spanish Conquest of Mexico,* trans. Felix Jay (Lewiston, NY: Edwin Mellen, 1997), 24.
98. Ibid.
99. Ibid.
100. Ibid.
101. "Instrucción y obediencia del Ministerio General Francisco de los Angeles Quiñonez a Martín de Valencia, custodio de los doce franciscanos enviados para plantar el evangelio en Tenochtitlan," reproduced in Juan Meseguer Fernández, "Contenido misionológico de la obediencia e instrucción de Fray Francisco de los Ángeles a los doce Apostoles de México," *Americas* 11, no. 3 (1955): 491.
102. See note 21 in chapter 5 of this book.
103. Valadés, *Rhetorica,* "Prefatio ad Lectorem," n.p.

104. Focher, *Itinerario del misionero en América,* ed. and trans. Antonio Eguíluz (Madrid: Librería General V. Suárez, 1960), 371–75.
105. Ibid., 371.
106. Ibid., 372.
107. Ibid. 374.
108. I thank Allison Bigelow for the reference about "mineros," which was Ovando's terms for some of his fifteen villas.
109. Reproduced in Lino Gómez Canedo, *Evangelización y conquista: Experiencia Franciscana en Hispanoamérica* (Mexico City: Edición Porrúa, 1977), 217–20. On Mexía and the *experiencia,* see ibid., 102–7. José Torrubia, *Crónica de la provincia franciscana de santa cruz,* ed. Odilo Gómez Parente (Caracas: Academia Nacional de la Historia, 1972); see also Antonine S. Tibesar, "The Franciscan Province of the Holy Cross of Española, 1505–1559," *Americas* 13, no. 4 (April 1957): 377–89; and Livarius Onger, "The Earliest Record on the Franciscan Missions in America," *Catholic Historical Review* 6, no. 1 (April 1920): 59–65. See also José Gabriel Navarro, *Los franciscanos en la conquista y colonización de América* (Madrid: Ediciones Cultura Hispanica, 1955), 23; and McClure, *The Franciscan Invention,* 98.
110. On Quiroga, see Ross Dealy, *The Politics of an Erasmian Lawyer, Vasco de Quiroga* (Malibu: Undena Publications, 1976); Francisco Martín Hernández, *Don Vasco de Quiroga, Protector de los Indios* (Salamanca: Publicaciones Universidad Pontificia de Salamanca, 1993); Felipe Tena Ramírez, *Vasco de Quiroga y sus Pueblos de Santa Fe en los siglos XVIII y XIX* (Mexico City: Editorial Porrúa, 1990); and Silvio Zavala, *Sir Thomas More in New Spain: A Utopian Adventure of the Renaissance* (Mexico City: Colegio Nacional de México, 1955); Zavala, "The American Utopia of the Sixteenth Century," *Huntington Library Quarterly* 4 (1947): 337–47; Zavala, "En torno de tratado *De Debellanis Indis de Vasco de Quiroga,*" *Historia mexicana* 18 (1969): 623–26; Zavala, *Ideario de Vasco de Quiroga* (Mexico City: El Colegio de México, 1941); and Zavala, *Por la Senda Hispana de la libertad* (Madrid: Editorial MAPFRE, 1992).
111. On the notion of *reducción* as a space of ethnic concentration, isolation, and catechization, see Johann Specker, *Die Missionsmethode in Spanisch-Amerika im 16. Jahrhundert* (Schöneck-Beckenried: Administration der Neuen Zeitschrift für Missionswissenschaft, 1953), 22–23; Sylvest, *Motifs,* 23, 122; Fidel Chauvet, "Métodos misionales empleados en México en la primera evangelización," *Signo* 32 (1976): 19–27; and Chauvet, "Las Misiones Franciscanas," 28–48, in *Historia general de la Iglesia en América Latina* (Salamanca: Ediciones Sígueme, 1984); Pedro Borges Morán, *Misión y civilización en América* (Madrid: Alhambra, 1987), 104–37; Lluís Duch, *La Memòria dels sants: El projecte dels franciscans de Mèxic* (Barcelona: Publicacions del'Abada de Montserrat, 1992), 234–37; Erick Langer and Robert H. Jackson, introduction to *The New Latin American Mission History,* ed. Langer and Jackson (Lincoln: University of Nebraska Press, 1995), vii–xviii, vii; and Abdon Yaranga Valderrama, "Las 'reducciones,' uno de los instrumentos del etnocidio," *Revista Complutense de Historia de América* 21 (1995): 241–62.

112. In Joaquín García Icazbalceta, *Don Fray Juan de Zumárraga: Primer Obispo y Arzobispo de México* (Mexico City: Andrade y Morales, 1881), Appendix of Documents, 166.
113. In *Recopilación de leyes reynos de las Indias,* vol. 2 (1681; repr., Madrid: Ediciones Cultura Hispánica, 1973), 198 (bk. 6 titulo 3, ley 1). See also Tom Cummins, "Forms of Andean Colonial Towns, Free Will, and Marriage," in *The Archaeology of Colonialism,* ed. Claire Lyons and John Papadopoulos (Los Angeles: Getty Research Institute, 2002), 199–240, whose English translation I use here (201).
114. Cummins, "Forms of Andean Colonial Towns," 201–2.
115. Ibid., 202. On Nebrija, see also Walter Mignolo, *The Darker Side of the Renaissance: Literacy, Territoriality, and Colonization* (Ann Arbor: University of Michigan Press, 1995), 29–31.
116. Cummins, "Forms of Andean Colonial Towns," 203.
117. As already mentioned, the first Native language instruction books in Spanish America were Andrés de Olmos's *Arte para aprender la lengua mexicana* (1547) and his *Vocabulario en lengua mexicana* (1547). These were followed, in New Spain, by Alonso de Molina's *Vocabulario en lengua castellana y mexicana* (1555) and Alonso de Rangel's *Arte de la lengua mexicana,* Maturino Gilberti *Arte de la lengua de Michoacán* (1558) and *Vocabulario en lengua de Michoacán* and *Diccionario tarasco-español* (1559), as well as Pedro de Palacio, *Arte de la lengua otomí.* Important linguistic works produced by Dominicans include Domingo de Santamaría's *Arte de la lengua mixteca,* Pedro de Feria's *Vocabulario de la lengua,* and Francisco de Cepeda's *Arte de la lengua zoque.*
118. See Ricard, *Spiritual,* 39–60; Edward Gray and Norman Fiering, eds., *The Language Encounter in the Americas, 1492–1800: A Collection of Essays* (New York: Berghahn, 2000); see also Pardo, *Origins;* and Jaime Marroquín Arredondo's *Diálogos con Quetzalcóatl: Humanismo, etnografía y ciencia (1492–1577)* (Madrid: Iberoamericana Vervuert, 2014).
119. See Báez-Rubí, *Die Rezeption;* Báez-Rubí, *Mnemosine novohispánica:* Báez-Rubí, "Die 'Rhetorica Christiana.'"
120. Ziegler, *Medicine,* 53–59; see also E. Gisbert, "Metaforice loquendo: De l'analogia a la metàfora en els Començaments de medicina de Ramon Llull," *Studia Lulliana* 44, no. 100 (2004): 17–52; Johnston, *Evangelical,* 101–2.
121. Ziegler, *Medicine,* 53.
122. Ibid., 191, 102, 185.
123. See Lyndy Abraham, *A Dictionary of Alchemical Imagery* (Cambridge: Cambridge University Press, 1998), 186.
124. Pseudo-Llull, "Testamentum alchemicum," in Jean-Jacques Manget, *Bibliotheca chemica curiosa, seu rerum ad alchemiam pertinentium thesaurus instructissimus,* 2 vols. (Geneva: Chouet, G. de Tournes, Cramer, Perachon, Ritter & S. de Tournes, 1702), 1:763; see also Michaela Periera, "*Medicina* in the Alchemical Writings Attributed to Raimond Lull (14th–17th Centuries)," in *Alchemy and Chemistry,* ed. Rattansi and Clericuzio, 11.

125. Bernardo de Lavinheta, *Explanatio compendiosaque applicatio Artis Raymundi Lulli*, ed. Erhard-Wolfram Platzeck (Hildesheim: Gerstenberg, 1977), 434.
126. See Dane T. Daniel, "Medieval Alchemy and Paracelsus' Theology: Pseudo-Lull's *Testamentum* and Paracelsus's *Astronomia Magna*," *Nova Acta Paracelsica*, 22/23 (2008–9): 121–35.
127. See Roest, *A History of Franciscan Education*, 272–324. On the importance of preaching among Franciscans, see Timothy Johnson, *Franciscans and Preaching: Every Miracle from the Beginning of the World Came about through Words* (Leiden: Brill, 2012). On medieval rhetoric and preaching more generally, see James J. Murphey, *Rhetoric in the Middle Ages: A History of Rhetorical Theory from St. Augustine to the Renaissance* (Berkeley: University of California Press, 1974); and James Murphey, ed., *Medieval Eloquence: Studies in the Theory and Practice of Medieval Rhetoric* (Berkeley: University of California Press, 1978). On preaching in early modern England, see Debra Shuger, *Sacred Rhetoric: The Christian Grand Style in the English Renaissance* (Princeton: Princeton University Press, 1988).
128. On Granada, see Manuel López Muñoz, *Fray Luis de Granada y la Retórica* (Almería: Universidad de Almería, Servicio de Publicaciones, 2000). On his legacy in the New World, see Don Paul Abbott, *Rhetoric in the New World: Rhetorical Theory and Practice in Colonial Spanish America* (Columbia: University of South Carolina Press, 1996), 15.
129. See Gwendolyn Barnes-Karol, "Religious Oratory in a Culture of Control," in *Culture and Control in Counter-Reformation Spain*, ed. Anne Cruz and Elizabeth Perry (Minneapolis: University of Minnesota Press, 1992), 53.
130. Anne Cruz and Elizabeth Perry, introduction to *Culture and Control in Counter-Reformation Spain*, xv–xvi.
131. On the importance of Cisneros's reforms to the education of the American missionaries and their need to adapt to local circumstances in the Americas, see Pardo, *Origins*, 2–3.
132. See Fidel Chauvet, "Fray Jacobo de Testera, misionero y civilizador del siglo XVI," *Estudios de Historia Novohispana* 3 (1970): 7–33.
133. See Pedro de Gante, *Doctrina Christiana en Lengua Mexicana. Per signum crucis. Icamachiotl cruz yhuicpain toya chua Xitech momaquixtili Totecuiyoc diose. Ica inmotocatzin. Tetatzin yhuan Tepilizin yhuan Spiritus Sancti. Amen Jesús* [1547], ed. Ernesto de la Torre Villar (Mexico City: Centro De Estudios Históricos Fray Bernardino de Sahagún, 1981); and *Catecismo de la doctrina cristiana con jeroglíficos, para la enseñanza de los indios de México*, in *El catecismo en pictogramas de Fr. Pedro de Gante*, ed. Justino Cortés Castellanos (Madrid: Fundación Universitaria Española, 1987).
134. On Pedro de Gante and his use of music and visual rhetoric in the missionary effort, see Ezequiel A. Chávez, *Fray Pedro de Gante* (Mexico City: Editorial Jus, 1962); Justino Cortés Castellanos, *El catecismo en pictogramas de Fray Pedro de Gante* (Madrid: Fundación Universitaria Española, 1987); Mariner Ezra Padwa,

Peter of Ghent and the Introduction of European Music in the New World (Santa Fe, NM: Hapax, 1993).

135. Diego de Valadés, *Rhetórica Christiana,* introd. Estéban J. Palomera, adv. Alfonso Castro Pallares, pre. and trans. Tarsicio Herrera Zapién (Mexico City: UNAM, 1989), 9. See also Patricia Nettel, "Cosmovisión y cultura material Franciscana en los pueblos de indios de Nueva España según Fray Diego de Valadés (una perspectiva etnográfica)," in *Franciscanos y mundo religioso en México,* ed. Francisco Morales, et al. (Mexico City: UNAM, 1993), 39–53.
136. Valadés, *Rhetorica Christiana* (Preface to Pope Gregory XIII, n.p. [21]).
137. See Báez-Rubí, *Die Rezeption;* Báez-Rubí, *Mnemosine novohispánica;* and Báez-Rubí, "Die 'Rhetorica Christiana.'" On Llull's scheme, see also chapter 3 of this book.
138. Valadés, *Rhetorica Christiana,* pars segunda, cap. VII, 57.
139. Ibid., cap, XVII, 72.
140. Báez-Rubí, "Die 'Rhetorica Christiana,'" 336.
141. Linda Báez-Rubí, "De harmonia mundi: ¿Un reino de Saturno novohispano?," *Anales del Instituto de Investigaciones Estéticas* 73 (1998):41–67.
142. Walden Browne, *Sahagún and the Transition to Modernity* (Norman: University of Oklahoma Press, 2000), 133–34.
143. From autopsía: "seeing with one's own eyes, eye-witnessing; personal observation or inspection." On the "autopic imagination," see Anthony Pagden, *European Encounters with the New World* (New Haven: Yale University Press, 1993), 51–88.
144. Stuart Clark, *Vanities of the Eye,* 9; see also J. M. Hernández-Mansilla, "Autopsía, embalsamamiento y signos de santidad en el cuerpo de Ignacio de Loyola," *Ilu* 21 (2016): 79–91.
145. See Baudot, *Utopia,* 110–15.
146. Sahagún, *Historia general,* 3:161.
147. Baudot, *Utopia,* 107.
148. See Luis Nicolau D'Olwer, *Fray Bernadino de Sahagún (1499–1590)* (Mexico City: Instituto Panamericano de Geografía e Historia, 1952), 29–41; Ricard, *The Spiritual Conquest,* 35–42; Manuel Casado Arboniés and Pedro Manuel Alonso Marñón, "Alcalá de Henares y América: un nexo universitario," in *Estudios sobre América: Siglos XVI–XX,* ed. Antonio Gutiérrez and María Luisa Laviana (Seville: AEA, 2005), 255–89; Pardo, *Origins;* Francis Borgia Steck, *El primer colegio de América, Santa Cruz de Tlaltelolco* (Mexico City: Centro de estudios Franciscanos, 1944); José Maria Kobayashi, *La educación como conquista* (Mexico City: El Colegio de México, 1974).
149. See Ricard, *The Spiritual Conquest,* 219–38; and Baudot, *Utopia,* 99–103.
150. On Sahagún's date of matriculation at Salamanca, see Arthur Anderson, "Sahagún's Career and Character," in *Florentine Codex. Introductions and Indices,* preface by Miguel León Portilla (Santa Fe, NM: School of American Research and the University of Utah, 1982), 31; and León Portilla, *Bernadino de Sahagún,* 36.

151. See León Portilla, *Bernardino de Sahagun*, 116–23.
152. See Emily Walcott Emmart, introduction to *The Badianus Manuscript (Codex Barberini 2141, Vatican Library). An Aztec Herbal of 1552*, ed. and trans. Emily Walcott Emmart (Baltimore: Johns Hopkins University Press, 1940), 3–82; also Donald Robertson, *Mexican Manuscript Painting of the Early Colonial Period: The Metropolitan Schools* (1959; Norman: University of Oklahoma Press, 1994), 156–58.
153. See Marcy Norton, "The Quetzal and *The Ornithology of Francis Willughby*: Microhistory, Mesoamerican Knowledge and Early Modern Natural History," in *Translating Nature: Transcultural Histories of Early Modern Science*, ed. Jaime Marroquín and Ralph Bauer (Philadelphia: University of Pensylvania Press, 2019); Daniela Bleichmar, *Visual Voyages: Images of Latin American Nature from Columbus to Darwin* (New Haven: Yale University Press, 2017), 28–42; Simon Varley et al., eds., *Searching for the Secrets of Nature: The Life and Works of Dr. Francisco Hernández* (Stanford: Stanford University Press, 2000), 127–34; and David Freedberg, *The Eye of the Lynx: Galileo, His Friends, and the Beginnings of Modern Natural History* (Chicago: University of Chicago Press, 2002), 198–350.
154. Sahagún, *Historia general*, 1:27.
155. Ibid.
156. Bernadino de Sahagún, "Arte Adivinatoria," in Joaquín García Icazblaceta, *Bibliografía mexicana del siglo XVI*, ed. Agustín Millares Carlo, 2nd rev. ed. (Mexico City: Fondo de Cultura Económica, 1981), 383.
157. Sahagún, *Historia general*, 1:28.
158. Bustamente García, *Fray Bernadino*, 376. One prominent example of scholarship celebrating Sahagún as a forerunner of modern anthropology is León Portilla, *Bernadino de Sahagún*.
159. Sahagún, *Historia general*, 1:105
160. For a summary of the debate about the authorship of the *Nican Mopohua*, see David Brading, *Mexican Phoenix: Our Lady of Guadalupe: Image and Tradition across Five Centuries* (Cambridge: Cambridge University Press, 2001), 117–18.
161. See León Portilla, *Bernadino de Sahagún*, 144; Robertson, *Mexican Manuscript Painting*, 46–48, 167–78; Wigberto Jiménez Moreno, "Fray Bernadino de Sahagún y su obra," introduction to his edition (with Spanish translations by Elizabeth Gott) of *Historia general de las cosas de la Nueva España*, 5 vols. (Mexico City: Pedro Robredo, 1938), 1:1–9; Alfonso Toro, "Importancia etnográfica y linquistica de las obras del padre Fray Bernardino de Sahagún," *Anales del Museo Nacional e Arqueología, Historia y Etnografía*, ser. 4 vol. 2 (1930): 1–18; and Ríos Castaño, *Translation as Conquest*.
162. Sahagún, *Historia general*, 1:105.
163. Ibid., 1:106.
164. See Victoria Ríos Castaño, "From the 'Memoriales con escolios' to the Florentine Codex: Sahagún and His Nahua Assistants' Co-Authorship of the Spanish Translation," *Journal of Iberian and Latin American Research* 20, no. 2 (2014): 214–28.

165. See Toro, "La importancia etnográfica;" also Robertson, *Mexican Manuscript Painting,* 167–70; and Donald Robertson "The Sixteenth Century Mexican Encyclopedia of Fray Bernardino De Sahagún," *Cahiers d'histoire mondiale: Journal of World History* 9, no. 1 (1965): 617–26; León Portilla, *Bernadino de Sahagún,* 138–40.
166. See Jiménez Moreno, "Fray Bernadino de Sahagún"; and Wigberto Jiménez Moreno, *Primeros memoriales de fray Bernadino de Sahagún* (Mexico City: Instituto Nacional de Antropología e Historia, 1974).
167. See the bilingual English/Nahuatl edition prepared by Arthur Anderson and Charles Dibble, *Florentine Codex: Introductions and Indices,* preface by Miguel León Portilla (Santa Fe, NM: School of American Research and the University of Utah, 1982), which is based on the manuscript at the Laurentian library. See also Jiménez Moreno, *Primeros memoriales;* and León Portilla, *Bernadino de Sahagun,* 139.
168. See Ángel María Garibay, *Historia de la literature náhuatl,* 2 vols. (1954; Mexico City: Editorial Porrúa, 1971), 2:71; and Ríos Castaño, *Translation as Conquest,* 111–50.
169. See Bustamente García, *La obra etnográfica y lingüistica de fray Bernadino de Sahagun* (Madrid: Universidad Complutense, 1989), 706–17; also Bustamente García, *Fray Bernadino,* 355–64.
170. Donald Robertson, "The Sixteenth-Century Mexican Encyclopedia," 622–26; see also Robertson, *Mexican Manuscript Painting,* 169–72.
171. Robertson, *Mexican Manuscript Painting,* 172; see also his more recent "The Sixteenth-Century," which concludes that the form of the *Historia* is essentially medieval and backward-looking (626).
172. Browne, *Sahagún,* 127–32.
173. On the unprecedented popularity of Llull's *Arbor scientiae* among humanist encyclopedists, see Franklin-Brown, *Reading the World,* 167–69; see also Joseph Victor, "The Revival of Lullism at Paris," *Renaissance Quarterly* 28, no. 4 (1975): 504–34; and Mark Johnston, "The Reception of the Llullian Art, 1450–1530," *Sixteenth-Century Journal* 12, no. 1 (Spring 1981): 31–48.
174. Franklin-Brown, *Reading the World,* 179.
175. On Sahagún and Velasco, see Poole, *Juan de Ovando,* 142–45.
176. Sahagún, *Historia general,* 1:30. On the providentialism of Sahagun's history, see Boruchoff, "Sahagún and the Theology of Missionary Life."
177. Sahagún, *Historia general,* 4:17.
178. Ibid., 4:8.
179. Ibid., 4:18.
180. Ibid., 1:30.
181. Ibid., 1:31.
182. Ibid.
183. Ibid.
184. See León Portilla, *Bernadino de Sahagún,* 199–211.

185. Jeremy Ravi Mumford, *Vertical Empire: The General Resettlement of Indians in the Colonial Andes* (Durham, NC: Duke University Press, 2012), 1, 10. On the comparison between the missionary reductions in colonial Latin America and the modern concentration camp, as well as on the notion of the European conquest of Latin America as a "genocide" or "ethnocide," see pp. 497–89n84 of this book; see also Centre National de la Recherche Scientifique (France), Groupe de Recherches sur L'Amérique Latine, Universite de Toulouse-le Mirail, and Centre Interdisciplinaire D'études Latino-americaines, *Indianite, Ethnocide, Indigenisme en Amerique Latine* (Paris: Editions du CNRS, 1982). For colonial British America, see Francis Jennings, *The Invasion of American: Indians, Colonialism, and the Cant of Conquest* (Chapel Hill: University of North Carolina Press, 1975). For the nineteenth century, see Ned Blackhawk, *Violence over the Land: Indians and Empires in the Early American West* (Cambridge, Mass.: Harvard University Press, 2006). On the connection between genocide/ethnocide and spatial relocation projects more generally, see Andrea Fischer-Tahir and Sophie Wagenhofer, *Disciplinary Spaces: Spatial Control, Forced Assimilation and Narratives of Progress since the 19th Century*. Sozial- und Kulturgeographie, volume 14 (Bielefeld: Transcript-Verlag, 2017). On the notions of genocide and ethnocide more broadly, see Samantha Power, *A Problem from Hell: America and the Age of Genocide* (New York: Basic Books, 2002); Adam Jones, *Genocide: A Comprehensive Introduction*, 2nd ed. (London: Routledge, 2011); and Jacques Sémelin, *Purify and Destroy: The Political Uses of Massacre and Genocide*, the Ceri Series in Comparative Politics and International Studies (New York: Columbia University Press, 2007).
186. Ravi Mumford, *Vertical Empire*, 3.
187. On Acosta's life, see David Brading, *The First America: The Spanish Monarchy, Creole Patriots, and the Liberal State, 1492–1867* (Cambridge: Cambridge University Press, 1991), 184–86; Claudio Burgaleta, *José De Acosta, S.J., 1540–1600: His Life and Thought* (Chicago: Jesuit Way, 1999); and Bentancor, *Matter of Empire*, 151–53.
188. On the eclecticism of Jesuit education, see Prieto, *Missionary Scientists*, 1–12; on Acosta in particular, see 143–68.
189. On this difference, see Rolena Adorno, *The Polemics of Possession in Spanish American Narrative* (New Haven: Yale University Press, 2007), 194–98.
190. See Prieto, *Missionary Scientists*, 145.
191. José de Acosta, *Peregrinación de Bartolomé Lorenzo, Hermano de la Compañía* (Madrid: Confrontado por Juan Bautista Muñoz, 1586).
192. José de Acosta, *De natura Novi Orbis libri dvo: Et De promvlgatione Evangelij, apvd barbaros, sive De procvranda Indorvm salvte libri sex.* (Salmanticæ: Apud Guillelmum Foquel., M.D.LXXXIX [1589]).
193. José de Acosta, *Historia natural y moral delas Indias* (Impresso en Seuilla: en casa de Iuan de Leon, 1590).
194. See Antonio Barrera-Osorio, *Experiencing Nature: The Spanish American Empire and the Early Scientific Revolution* (Austin: University of Texas Press, 2006),

114–20; Prieto, *Missionary Scientists*, 143–68; and Jorge Cañizares-Esguerra, *Nature, Empire, and Nation: Explorations of the History of Science in the Iberian World* (Stanford: Stanford University Press, 2006), 24–26.

195. On Acosta's attempt to engage with the Augustinian notion of *vana curiositas*, see Prieto, *Missionary Scientists*, 149–56. On Acosta's diabolism, see also Cervantes, *The Devil*, 25–33; and Jorge Cañizares-Esguerra, *Puritan Conquistadors: Iberianizing the Atlantic, 1550–1700* (Stanford: Stanford University Press, 2006). Cañizares-Esguerra writes there that Acosta's history is "actually a treatise on demonology" (120); however, in *Nature, Empire, and Nation*, Cañizares-Esguerra argues that Acosta was "not willing to cede the realm of the natural and the marvellous in the New World to the devil" and "sought to steer early modern European perceptions of nature in the New World away from the realm of the preternatural and thus the demonic" (26). As I argue here, the two impulses—empiricist and demonological—are not in contradiction but enable one another in the missionaries' discourse of medical autopsy.

196. As scholars have pointed out, Acosta's understanding of writing systems, based often on second-hand information is not reliable. This is especially true for his information on Asia, much of which he obtained from the Jesuit Alonso Sánchez, whom he had met in New Spain. On Acosta's comparative ethnology, see Anthony Pagden, *The Fall of Natural Man: The American Indian and the Origins of Comparative Ethnology* (Cambridge: Cambridge University Press, 1982), 146–97; and Ivonne Del Valle, "From José de Acosta to the Enlightenment: Barbarians, Climate Change, and (Colonial) Technology as the End of History," *Eighteenth Century: Theory and Interpretation* 54, no. 4 (2013): 435–59.

197. Bentancor, *Matter*, 151–216.

198. José de Acosta, *Historia natural y moral de las Indias*, 2 vols. (Madrid: R. Anglés, 1894), 2:288. English translations are from José de Acosta, *Natural and Moral History of the Indies*, trans. Frances López-Morillas, ed. Jane E. Mangan, introd. and commentary by Walter Mignolo (Durham: Duke University Press, 2002), 162.

199. Acosta, *Natural History*, 1:316–17 (English, 178).

200. Ibid., 1:291 (English, 164).

201. See Bernard McGinn, *The Growth of Mysticism: From Gregory the Great to the Twelfth Century* (London: SCM, 1994).

202. Acosta, *Natural History*, 1:342–43 (English, 191–92).

203. Bentancor, *Matter*, 151.

204. Ibid., 211.

205. *The Vulgate*, Psalms 11.7, http://vulgate.org/ot/psalms_11.htm.

206. On the alchemical origins of this technique in mining, see Tara Nummedal, *Alchemy and Authority in the Holy Roman Empire* (Chicago: University of Chicago Press, 2007), 33–39, 85–95; and Pamela Long, *Openness, Secrecy, Authorship: Technical Arts and the Culture of Knowledge from Antiquity to the Renaissance* (Baltimore: Johns Hopkins University Press, 2001), 175–209.

207. See Thorndike, *History* 3:137; Newman, *Promethean*, 188.

208. Richard Bonney, *The European Dynastic States, 1494–1660* (Oxford: Oxford University Press, 1991), 422; Nummedal, *Alchemy*, 79; Arthur Whitaker, *The Huancavelica Mercury Mine: A Contribution to the History of the Bourbon Renaissance in the Spanish Empire* (Cambridge: Harvard University Press, 1941); Guillermo Lohmann Villena, *Las minas de Huancavelica en los siglos XVI y XVII* (Seville: Escuela de Estudios Hispano-Americanos, 1949); Peter Bakewell, *Miners of the Red Mountain: Indian Labor in Potosí, 1545–1650*, 1st ed. (Albuquerque: University of New Mexico Press, 1984); see also Bakewell, *Mines of Silver and Gold in the Americas* (Brookfield, VT: Variorum, 1997). As Allison Bigelow has shown, some of the metallurgical practices of amalgamation that were imported from Europe to America during the second part of the sixteenth century may actually have originated with pre-Columbian Native American practices in the Andes, which were observed by Europeans such as Álvaro Alonso Barba, taken to Europe and developed there, and then reimported as official "science" back to the viceregal Americas (see Allison Bigelow, "Transatlantic Quechuañol: Reading Race Through Colonial Translations," *PMLA* 134, no. 2 (2019): 242–59; see also Bigelow's monograph *Cultural Touchstones: Mining, Refining, and the Languages of Empire in the Early Americas* [forthcoming from the University of North Carolina Press for the Omohundro Institute of Early American History and Culture]).
209. Acosta, *Natural and Moral History*, 1:339–42 (English 190–91; my italics).
210. See Newman, *Gehennical Fire*, 24.
211. On the differences between a "unitist" versus the "pluralist" understanding of the relationship between matter and form, as well as between alchemical (corpuscular) and Thomist (continuous) understanding of matter, see chapter 2 of this book.
212. Newman and Principe, *Alchemy*, 78; see also Newman, *Gehennical Fire*, 29. Bentancor is thus correct when arguing that Acosta sees the purification of "metals not as a transformation of their essence" (211). However, it is precisely the fact that the silver contained in ore is still there in the "pores" of the mercury after having become "incorporated" by it that suggests that Acosta's understanding of matter does not follow Thomist Aristotelian theory of matter as continuous and "fixed" but the alchemical corpuscular theory of *minima naturalia*.
213. Newman and Principe, *Alchemy*, 77–78.
214. Bentancor, *Matter*, 156.
215. See Abraham, *Dictionary*, 35–39.
216. Arnald of Villanova, "Rosarius philosophorum," in Manget, *Bibliotheca chemica curiosa*, 1:676.
217. Andrés Pérez de Ribas, *History of the Triumphs of Our Holy Faith amongst the Most Barbarous and Fierce Peoples of the New World*, ed. Daniel T. Reff (Tucson: University of Arizona Press, 1999), 491.
218. Ibid., 68.

7. Cannibal Heterotopias in the Sixteenth Century

1. Michel Serres, *Hermes: Literature, Science, Philosophy,* ed. Josué Harari and David F. Bell (Baltimore: Johns Hopkins University Press, 1982), 99.
2. See Alison Brown, *The Return of Lucretius to Renaissance Florence* (Cambridge: Harvard University Press, 2010); Stephen Greenblatt, *The Swerve: How the World Became Modern* (New York: Norton, 2011); Gerard Passannante, *The Lucretian Renaissance: Philology and the Afterlife of Tradition* (Chicago: University of Chicago Press, 2011); and Catherine Wilson, *Epicureanism at the Origins of Modernity* (Oxford: Clarendon, 2008). On the importance of Lucretius from the point of view of the history of science, see Monte Ransome Johnson and Catherine Wilson, "Lucretius and the History of Science," in *The Cambridge Companion to Lucretius,* ed. Stuart Gillespie and Philip R. Hardie, 131–48 (Cambridge: Cambridge University Press, 2007).
3. Lucretius, *On the Nature of Things,* trans., intod., and annotated Martin Ferguson Smith (1969; Indianapolis: Hackett, 2001), 68.
4. Ibid., 62.
5. Augustine, *The Confessions,* ed. Albert Cook Outler (Louisville, KY: Westminster, 1955), 233. Augustine explained there that curiosity was one of the Christian vices, one of the three forms of concupiscence, namely that of the "lust of the eyes" (*concupiscentia oculorum*).
6. See Greenblatt, *The Swerve,* 222.
7. See Stephen Gaukroger, *Francis Bacon and the Transformation of Early-Modern Philosophy* (Cambridge: Cambridge University Press, 2001).
8. For a discussion of the Foucauldian concept of "heterotopia," see the introduction of this book.
9. Francesca Lardicci et al., *A Synoptic Edition of the Log of Columbus's First Voyage* (Turnhout, Belgium: Brepols, 1999), Repertorium Columbianum, 6:116. On the history of the word, see Peter Hulme, *Colonial Encounters: Europe and the Native Caribbean, 1492–1797* (London: Methuen, 1986), 13–43.
10. Amerigo Vespucci, *Letters from a New World: Amerigo Vespucci's Discovery of America,* ed. and introd. Luciano Formisano, trans. David Jacobson (New York: Marilio, 1992), 49. The authenticity of the *Mundus novus* and the "Soderini" letter, published under Vespucci's name in multiple editions and languages during his lifetime, has long been disputed. Antonello Gerbi, for example, in his *Nature in the New World,* trans. Jeremy Moyle (Pittsburgh: University of Pittsburgh Press, 1985), treats the "authentic" writings of Vespucci—the three private letters addressed to Lorenzo di Pierfrancesco de' Medici—separately from those he attributes to a "Pseudo-Vespucci" (45–49). Gerbi doubts the authenticity of these published versions mainly based on a contrast he perceives between their sensationalist style and the very learned style of Vespucci's unpublished letters to Lorenzo. For a less charitable interpretation of Vespucci's learning, see Felipe Fernández Armesto's biography, *Amerigo: The Man Who Gave His Name to America*

(New York: Random House, 2007), in which he argues that there was only one Vespucci, who was essentially a self-promoting charlatan. For a sober and convincing rehabilitation not only of Vespucci but also of the authenticity of *Mundus movus* and the Soderini letter, see Robert Wallisch, *Der Mundus Novus des Amerigo Vespucci* (Vienna: Verlag der Oesterreichischen Akademie der Wissenschaften, 2002). However, as the identity of the author who wrote the tracts published under Vespucci's name is immaterial to my argument, I will simply refer to him as "the Vespuccian" in this book.

11. *Letters from a New World*, 49–50, 49, 48, 64.
12. Among the scholars who approach the phenomenon of cannibalism primarily as an aspect of colonialist discourse are William Arens (*The Man-Eating Myth: Anthropology and Anthropophagy* [New York: Oxford University Press, 1979]); Francis Barker, Peter Hulme, and Margaret Iversen (*Cannibalism and the Colonial World* [Cambridge: Cambridge University Press, 1998]); and Gananath Obeyesekere (*Cannibal Talk, The Man-Eating Myth and Human Sacrifice in the South Seas* [Berkeley: University of California Press, 2005]); and Cătălin Avramescu (*An Intellectual History of Cannibalism* [Princeton: Princeton University Press, 2009]). Among scholars who are interested in the ontology of cannibalism from an anthropological perspective are Laurence Goldman (*The Anthropology of Cannibalism* [Westport, CT: Bergin and Garvey, 1999]); Peggy Reeves Sanday (*Divine Hunger: Cannibalism as Cultural System* [Cambridge: Cambridge University Press, 1986]); Hans Askenasy (*Cannibalism: From Sacrifice to Survival* [Amherst: Promethus, 1994]); and Maggie Kilgour (*From Communion to Cannibalism: An Anatomy of Metaphors of Incorporation* [Princeton: Princeton University Press, 1990]).
13. Sigmund Freud, *Totem and Taboo* (1913; London: Routledge, 2001); see also Freud, *Moses and Monotheism*, trans. Katherine Jones (Letchworth: Hogarth, 1939).
14. Slavoj Žižek, *For They Know Not What They Do: Enjoyment as a Political Factor* (London: Verso, 1991), 233.
15. Caroline Walker Bynum, *Resurrection of the Body in Western Christianity, 200–1336* (New York: Columbia University Press, 1995), 15.
16. Richard Sugg, *Mummies, Cannibals, and Vampires: The History of Corpse Medicine from the Renaissance to the the Victorians* (London: Routledge, 2016), 24–25; see also Piero Camporesi, *Juice of Life: The Symbolic and Magic Significance of Blood* (New York: Continuum, 1995); and Jacalyn Duffin, *History of Medicine: A Scandalously Short Introduction* (Toronto: University of Toronto Press, 1999), 171–72.
17. Karl Dannenfeldt, "Egyptian Mumia: The Sixtenth-Century Experience and Debate," *Sixteenth Century Journal* 16, no. 2 (Summer 1985): 164.
18. Ibid., 166.
19. André Thevet, *Cosmographie de Levant* (Lyon: J. De Tournes et G. Gazeau, 1554), 152–56; *La cosmographie universelle*, 2 vols. (Paris: Huillier, 1575), 1:42–43; see also Dannenfeldt, "Egyptian Mumia," 168.

20. Dannenfeldt, "Egyptian Mumia," 170.
21. Paracelsus, *Bücher und Schriften,* ed. J. Huster, 6 vols. (Basel, 1589–99), 1:290–98, 302.
22. Ibid.; see also Dannenfeldt, "Egyptian Mumia," 173.
23. Qtd. Dannenfeldt, "Egyptian Mumia," 173.
24. Ibid., 173–74.
25. See Louise Christine Noble, *Medicinal Cannibalism in Early Modern English Literature and Culture* (New York: Palgrave Macmillan, 2011), 20; and Karen Gordon-Grube, "Evidence of Medicinal Cannibalism in Puritan New England: 'Mummy' and Related Remedies in Edward Taylor's 'Dispensatory,'" *Early American Literature* 28, no. 3 (1993): 185–221. On the English disciples of Paracelsus, see Allen Debus, *The English Paracelsians* (New York: F. Watts, 1966).
26. Francis Bacon, *Sylva sylvarum* (London: 1627), Cent. X, 980, 262; qtd. in Dannenfeldt, "Egyptian Mumia," 178.
27. Robert Boyle, *Works,* 6 vols. (London, 1772), 2:451, qtd. in Dannenfeldt, "Egyptian Mumia," 178.
28. Thomas Moffett, *Health's Improvement* (London: printed by Tho. Newcomb for Samuel Thomson, 1655), 139–40; see also Sugg, *Mummies,* 16.
29. Eduardo Viveiros de Castro, *Cannibal Metaphysics: For a Post-Structural Anthropology,* trans. and ed. Peter Skafish (Minneapolis: Univocal and the University of Minnesota Press, 2014); see also Viveiros de Castro, *From the Enemy's Point of View: Humanity and Divinity in an Amazonian Society,* trans. Catherine Howard (Chicago: University of Chicago Press, 1992); and James Maffie, *Aztec Philosophy: Understanding a World in Motion* (Boulder: University of Colorado Press, 2014).
30. Walker Bynum, *Resurrection,* 27–58, 31.
31. St. Augustine of Hippo, *The City of God,* trans. Marcus Dods, introd. Thomas Merton (New York: Modern Library, 1950), 843–44.
32. St. Augustine, *The City of God,* 844.
33. Vespucci, *Letters from a New World,* 49–50.
34. Ibid., 45.
35. On Traversari's *Life of Epicurus,* see Brown, *The Return of Lucretius,* 16.
36. Marsilio Ficino, *Platonic Theology,* trans. Michael J. B. Allen, ed. James Hankins with William Bowen (Cambridge: Harvard University Press, 2005), 5:321. See also James G. Snyder, "Marsilio Ficino's Critique of the Lucretian Alternative," *Journal of the History of Ideas* 72, no. 2 (2011): 165–81.
37. G. Savonarola, *Prediche sopra Amos e Zaccaria,* ed. P. Ghiglieri, 3 vols. (Rome: Belardetti, 1971), 1:80; see also Allison Brown, "Intellectual and Religious Currents in the Post-Savonarola Years," in *La figura de Jerónimo Savonarola O.P. y su infuencia en España y Europa,* ed. Donald Weinstein, Júlia Benavent, and Inés Rodriguez (Florence: Edizioni del Galluzzo per la Fondazione Ezio Franceschini, 2004), 35.
38. See Greenblatt, *The Swerve,* 119.
39. Vespucci, *Letters from a New World,* 45.

40. See Pauline Moffitt Watts, "Prophecy and Discovery: On the Spiritual Origins of the Enterprise of the Indies," *American Historical Review* 90, no. 1–2 (1985): 73–102.
41. Revelation 7:9 reads, "I saw a great multitude, which no man could number, of all nations and tribes and peoples and tongues, standing before the throne and in sight of the Lamb, clothed with white robes, and palms in their hands" (http://vulgate.org/nt/epistle/revelation_7.htm).
42. Vespucci, *Letters from a New World,* 57.
43. On curiosity, see chapter 1 of this book.
44. N. G. Wilson has pointed out that a possible source for *daios* in Raphael's name (Hythlo-daios) may be a quote from Epicurus in Plutarch's *Moralia,* where it has the connotation of "cunning" (see Wilson, "The Name Hythlodaeus," *Moreana* 29, no. 110 [1992]: 33).
45. Thomas More, *Utopia,* trans. and introd. Paul Turner (Harmondsworth, Middlesex, UK: Penguin, 1965), 83.
46. Ibid., 93.
47. Ibid., 96. On More's Epicureanism, see Edward Surtz, S.J., *The Praise of Pleasure: Philosophy, Education, Communism in More's "Utopia"* (Cambridge: Harvard University Press, 1957); George G. M. Logan, *The Meaning of More's "Utopia"* (Princeton, NJ: Princeton University Press, 1983), esp. 145–49, 154–56, 161–63, and 166–68; Dominic Baker-Smith *More's "Utopia"* (1991; repr., Toronto: Toronto University Press, 2000), 172–78; and A. D. Cousins, *Pleasure and Gender in the Writings of Thomas More: Pursuing the Common Weal* (Pittsburgh: Duquesne University Press, 2010); see also Gianni Paganini and Edoardo Tortarolo, eds., *Der Garten und die Moderne: Epikureische Moral und Politik vom Humanismus bis zur Aufklärung* (Stuttgart: Frommann-Holzboog, 2004). On More's ambivalent reception of Lucretian atomism, see Greenblatt, *The Swerve,* 219–41.
48. See Mikhail Bakhtin, *Rabelais and His World: Carnival and Grotesque* (Cambridge: MIT Press, 1968); and Bakhtin, *Problems of Dostoyevsky's Poetics: Polyphony and Unfinalizability* (Minneapolis: University of Minnesota Press, 1984).
49. Michel de Montaigne, *Montaigne's Annotated Copy of Lucretius: A Transcription and Study of the Manuscript, Notes, and Pen-Marks,* ed. M. A. Screech (Geneva: Librairie Droz, 1998), 251.
50. Michel de Montaigne, *Essays,* trans. and introd. J. M. Cohen (London: Penguin, 1993); for references to Epicurus, see, for example, 345, 347. For a discussion of Montaigne's intense engagement with Lucretius, see Passannante, *The Lucretian Renaissance,* 104–19; and Greenblatt, *The Swerve,* 243–49. For Montaigne's quotes from Lucretius, see *Essays,* 264, 275, 276.
51. Montaigne, *Essays,* 113.
52. Ibid., 110.
53. Ibid., 117.
54. Ibid., 105, 108.

55. André Thevet, *Les singularitez de la France Antarctique,* ed. Paul Gaffarel (Paris: Maisonneuve & Cie, 1878), 199.
56. Jean de Léry, *History of a Voyage to the Land of Brazil, Otherwise Called America,* trans. and introd. Janet Whatley (Berkeley: University of California Press, 1990), 128, 132–33.
57. On Montaigne's interest in cannibalism, see George Hoffmann, "The Anatomy of the Mass: Montaigne's 'Cannibals,'" *PMLA* 117, no. 2 (March 2002): 207–21; and Hoffmann, "The Investigation of Nature," in *The Cambridge Companion to Montaigne,* ed. Ullrich Langer, 163–82 (Cambridge: Cambridge University Press, 2005), 164. For a discussion of the role played by the New World in the *Essays,* see Tom Conley, "The *Essays* and the New World," in *The Cambridge Companion to Montaigne,* ed. Ullrich Langer (Cambridge: Cambridge University Press, 2005), 74–95. Conley aptly describes the *Essays* as a "keystone in the literature of discovery" (75).
58. Léry, *History,* 127.
59. Ibid., 125. On the *point d'honneur,* see Janet Whatley's note 8 in her edition of Léry, *History,* 245. On Thevet and Léry, see Sara Castro-Klarén, "What Does Cannibalism Speak?," in *Carnal Knowledge: Essays on the Flesh, Sex, and Sexuality in Hispanic Letters and Film,* ed. Pamela Barcarisse, 23–42 (Pittsburgh: Tres Rios, 1992); and Castro-Klarén, "Parallaxes: Cannibalism and Self-Embodiment; or, the Calvinist Reading of Tupi A-Theology," in *Thinking the Limits of the Body,* ed. Jeffrey Jerome Cohen and Gail Weiss, 101–28 (Albany: State University of New York Press, 2003).
60. Florestan Fernandes, *A função social da guerra na sociedade Tupinambá,* 2nd ed. (1952; São Paulo: Pioneira/Editôra de Universidade de São Paulo, 1970), 339; see also Fernandes, "La guerre et le sacrifice humain chez les Tupinamba," *Journal de la Société des Américanistes de Paris* 40 (1952): 139–220; Viveiros de Castro, *From the Enemy's Point of View,* 278, 283; Viveiros de Castro, *Cannibal Metaphysics,* 139–44; Alfred Métraux, *La civilisation matérielle des tribus Tupi-Guarani* (Paris: Geuthner, 1927); Métraux, *Religions et magies indiennes d'Amerique du Sud* (Paris: Gallimard, 1967), esp. 67–73; and Suzanne Lussagnet, *Le Brésil et les Brésiliens* (Paris: PUF, 1953), esp. 192–93. On pre-Columbian Mesoamerican metaphysics, see Maffie, *Aztec Philosophy.*
61. Viveiros de Castro, *From the Enemy's Point of View,* 286.
62. See also Viveiros de Castro's reading of the passage in Montaigne, quoted above (*From the Enemy's Point of View,* 285). All of this is not to suggest, of course, that the metaphysics that informed the Tupinamba cultural practice of cannibalism was in any way related or even similar to Epicurean materialism. As Viveiros de Castro and the other anthropologists cited above suggest, Tupinamba cannibalism was an integral part of an intricate shamanistic complex that involved many spiritual and supernatural dimensions, including the idea of an afterlife and a mythology populated by cannibalistic deities that cannot be considered here.
63. Montaigne, *Essays,* 357.

64. Michiel van Groesen, *The Representation of the Overseas World in the De Bry Collection of Voyages (1590–1634)* (Leiden: Brill, 2008), 103. The most influential reading of de Bry in terms of sectarianism is Bernadette Bucher's *La sauvage aux seins pendants* (Paris: Herman, 1977). Critical reappraisals of this position include Pol-Pierre Gossiaux, "Hiérarchie du monde sauvage et eschatologie protestante selon l'iconographie des Grands Voyages des de Bry," in *Protestantisme san frontièrs: La réforme dans la duché de Limbourg et dans la Prinicipauté de Liège,* ed. Philippe Denis and Richard Stauffer (Aubel: Gason, 1985), 99–169; Gloria Deák, *Discovering America's Southeast: A Sixteenth-Century View Based on the Mannerist Engravings of Theodor de Bry* (Birmingham, AL: Birmingham Public Library Press, 1992); Maike Christadler, "Die Sammlung zur Schau gestellt: Die Titelblatter der America-Serie," in *Inszinierte Welten: Die west- und ostindische Reisen der Vergleger de Bry, 1590–1630 / Staging New Worlds: De Bry's Illustrated Travel Reports,* ed. Susanne Burghartz, 47–93 (Basel: Schwabe, 2004); Anna Greve, *Die Konstruktion Amerikas: Bilderpolitik in den "Grands Voyages" aus der Werkstatt de Bry* (Cologne: Böhlau, 2004); Jörg Dünne, "Die Karte als imaginierter Ursprung: Zur frühneuzeitlichen Konkurrenz von textueller und kartographischer Raumkonstitution in den America-Reisen Theodor de Brys," in *Topographien der Literatur: Deutsche Literatur im transnationalen Kontext,* ed. Hartmut Böhme (Stuttgart: Metzler, 2005), 73–99; Michael Gaudio, *Engraving the Savage: The New World and Techniques of Civilization* (Minneapolis: University of Minnesota Press, 2008); Patricia Gravatt, "Rereading Theodor de Bry's Black Legend," in *Rereading the Black Legend: The Discourses of Religious and Racial Difference in the Renaissance Empires,* ed. Margarete Greer, Walter Mignolo, and Maureen Quilligan, 225–43 (Chicago: University of Chicago Press, 2008).
65. I would like to thank my colleague Andrea Frisch for pointing this out to me and for sharing the paper she delivered at the Sixteenth-Century Conference in New Orleans in October 2014.

8. Homunculus americanus

1. Juan Ginés de Sepúlveda, *Democrates Segundo, o de las Justas causas de la Guerra contra los indios,* ed. and trans. Angel Losada (Madrid: Consejo Superior de Investigaciones Científicas Instituto Francisco de Vitoria, 1951), 22.
2. On the circumstances of this publication, see *Aqui se contiene una disputa entre el ... Bartolome de las Casas ... y el doctor Gines Sepúlveda* (Seville: Casa de Sebastián Trujillo, 1552), i–xii; this pamphlet contains a summary of the circumstances that led up to the debate, as well as summaries by the president of the *junta* of judges, Domingo de Soto, along with responses by Sepúlveda and Las Casas. See also Teodoro Andres Marcos, *Los imperialismos de Juán Ginés de Sepúlveda en su "Democrates alter"* (Madrid: Instituto de Estudios Políticos, 1947), 29–32.
3. This was published as *Apologia Ioannis Genesii Sepuluedae pro libro de iustis belli causis* (Rome: Apud Valerium Doricum et Ludouicum, 1550).

4. *Aqui se contiene,* ii.v. This is from the introductory "argument" of the tract, whose author is not internally identified, but historians, such as Lewis Hanke, assume that it was written by Las Casas (see Hanke, *All Mankind Is One: A Study of the Disputation between Bartolomé de Las Casas and Juan Ginés de Sepúlveda in 1550 on the Intellectual and Religious Capacity of the American Indians* [DeKalb: Northern Illinois University Press, 1974], 63).
5. *Aqui se contiene,* ii.v: It is not clear what Spanish translations of both works are being referred to here. If they existed in manuscript, they have never been published. An edition containing the Latin facsimiles and Spanish translations of Sepúlveda's and Las Casas's apologias has been published by Angel Losada in *Apologia de Juan Ginés de Sepúlveda contra Fray Bartolomé de las Casas y de Fray Bartolomé de las Casas contra Juan Ginés de Sepúlveda,* trans., ed., and introd. Angel Losada (Madrid: Editora Nacional, 1975).
6. On the "Great Debate," see David Brading, *The First America: The Spanish Monarchy, Creole Patriots, and the Liberal State, 1492–1867* (Cambridge: Cambridge University Press, 1991), 59–80.
7. Anthony Pagden, introduction to *Political Writings,* by Francisco de Vitoria, ed. and trans. Pagden and Jeremy Lawrance (Cambridge: Cambridge University Press, 1991), xiii–xxix. On Vitoria and his legacy, see Lauren Benton and Benjamin Straumann, "Acquiring Empire by Law: From Roman Doctrine to Early Modern European Practice," *Law and History Review* 28 (2010): 20–29; Anthony Pagden, *Lords of All the World: Ideologies of Empire in Spain, Britain and France c. 1500–c. 1800* (New Haven: Yale University Press, 1995), 46–61; and Robert Williams, *The American Indian in Western Legal Thought: The Discourses of Conquest* (New York: Oxford University Press, 1990), 96–97. On the School of Salamanca, see Bernice Hamilton, *Political Thought in Sixteenth-Century Spain: A Study of the Political Ideas of Vitoria, De Soto, Suárez, and Molina* (Oxford: Clarendon, 1963); J. A. Fernández-Santamaria, *The State, War, and Peace: Spanish Political Thought in the Renaissance, 1516–1559* (Cambridge: Cambridge University Press, 1977); and Richard Tuck, *The Rights of War and Peace: Political Thought and the International Order from Grotius to Kant* (Oxford: Oxford University Press, 1999), 51–77. On the history and literary history of this early modern debate, see Silvio Zavala, *Las instituciones jurídicas en la conquista de América* (1935; Mexico City: Porrúa, 1971).
8. In this camp, we might place Venancio Diego Carro (*La teología y los teólogos-juristas españoles ante la conquista de América* [Salamanca: Apartado, 1951]); and Lewis Hanke (*All Mankind Is One* and *The Spanish Struggle for Justice in the Conquest of America,* ed. Hanke, James H. Sutton Jr., and Sylvia Leal Carvajal Collection [Boston: Little, Brown, 1965]).
9. Orlando Bentancor, *The Matter of Empire: Metaphysics and Mining in Colonial Peru* (Pittsburgh: Pittsburgh University Press, 2017), 3; see also Rolena Adorno, *The Polemics of Possession in Spanish American Narrative* (New Haven: Yale University Press, 2007), 101–24; and Anthony Pagden, *The Fall of Natural Man: The American Indian and the Origins of Comparative Ethnology* (Cambridge:

Cambridge University Press, 1982), 27–56. For a survey of these positions, see Joseph E. Capizzi, "The Children of God: Natural Slavery in the Thought of Aquinas and Vitoria," *Theological Studies* 63 (2002): 31–52.

10. On the complexity of Renaissance Aristotelianism, see Charles B Schmitt, *Aristotle and the Renaissance* (Cambridge: Published for Oberlin College by Harvard University Press, 1983); Charles Lohr, *Latin Aristotle Commentaries, II: Renaissance Authors* (Florence: Leo S. Olschki, 1988); and Günter Frank and Andreas Speer, eds., *Der Aristotelismus in der Frühen Neuzeit—Kontinuität oder Wiederaneignung* (Wiesbaden: Harrossowitz, 2007).

11. On the continuities and discontinuities between Scholastic Aristotelianism and the "New" sciences, see Edward Grant, *The Foundations of Modern Science in the Middle Ages: Their Religious, Institutional, and Intellectual Contexts* (Cambridge: Cambridge University Press, 1996); and Marco Sgarbi, *The Aristotelian Tradition and the Rise of British Empiricism: Logic and Epistemology in the British Isles (1570–1689)* (Dordrecht: Springer Netherlands, 2013).

12. See Hanke, *All Mankind Is One*; Hanke, Sutton Jr., and Sylvia Leal Carvajal Collection, *The Spanish Struggle for Justice in the Conquest of America*; also Adorno, *Polemics*, 101–24; Pagden, *Fall*, 27–56; and Anthony Pagden, *Spanish Imperialism and the Political Imagination: Studies in European and Spanish-American Social and Political Theory, 1513–1830* (New Haven: Yale University Press, 1990).

13. See Carro, *La teología*, 1–35.

14. Ibid., 46.

15. See Lesley Byrd Simpson, *The Encomienda in New Spain: The Beginning of Spanish Mexico*, rev. and enlarged ed. (Berkeley: University of California Press, 1966).

16. See Pagden, *Fall*, 27–56; Brading, *The First America*, 59–80; Caro, *La teología*, 33–48.

17. See Pagden, *Spanish Imperialism*, 13–14.

18. Las Casas qtd. in Juan López de Palacios Rubios, et al. *De las islas del mar océano*, ed. Silvio Zavala (Mexico City: Fondo de Cultura Económica, 1954), xviii, 108, 112.

19. Qtd. in Bartolomé de las Casas, *Historia de las indias*, in *Obras Competas*, ed. Miguel Angel Medina (Madrid: Alianza, 1994) vol. 5, pt. 3, 1915.

20. Pope Paul III, "Sublimus Dei," *Papal Encyclicals Online*, http://www.papalencyclicals.net/Paul03/p3subli.htm.

21. Francisco de Vitoria, "On the American Indians," in *Political Writings*, ed. and trans. Anthony Pagden and Jeremy Lawrence (Cambridge: Cambridge University Press, 1991), 233.

22. Important exceptions here include Pagden, *Fall*; Fernández-Santamaria, *The State*; and Hamilton, *Political Thought*, which consider the important roles played in the debate by John Mair and De Soto respectively.

23. Vitoria, "On the American Indians," 239.

24. Ibid., 250.

25. Ibid., 259–60.

26. Ibid., 264–65. This is basically the idea of "terra nullius," though Vitoria does not use this term here; rather he invokes "ferrae bestiae." On the significance of this choice, see Andrew Fitzmaurice, *Sovereignty, Property and Empire, 1500–2000* (Cambridge: Cambridge University Press, 2014), 56–60.
27. Vitoria, "On the American Indians," 277; my emphasis.
28. Ibid., 290.
29. For example, Rolena Adorno has seen the differences between the two as consisting mainly in the degree of certitude in which each applied Aristotle's concept of natural slavery to the American Indians. "Vitoria equivocates and qualifies," she writes, "Sepúlveda is certain" (*Polemics*, 109–13). Walter Mignolo also offers a harsh judgment of Vitoria as a colonialist (see "Cosmopolitanism and the De-Colonial Option," *Studies in Philosophy & Education* 29, no. 2 [March 2010]: 111–27).
30. Anthony Pagden and Jeremy Lawrance, introduction to Francisco de Vitoria, *Political Writings*, ed. Pagden and Lawrance (Cambridge: Cambridge University Press, 1991), xiii–xxix, vii. This edition also includes an excerpt from Vitoria's lecture on the evangelization of unbelievers (339–52), as well as an English translation of several of Vitoria's *relectiones*, including "De indis."
31. See Alexander Broadie, "John Mair on the Writing of Theology," in *A Companion to the Theology of John Mair*, ed. John Slotemaker and Jeffrey Witt, 25–40 (Leiden: Brill, 2015).
32. Vitoria, "On the American Indians," 276.
33. Ibid., 238.
34. Henry Raup Wagner and Helen Rand Parish, *The Life and Writings of Bartolomé de las Casas* (Albuquerque: University of New Mexico Press, 1967), 106; see also Adorno, *Polemics*, 112.
35. Letter of Charles V to the prior of the Dominican monastery San Esteban, November 10, 1539, qtd. in Adorno, *Polemics*, 113.
36. Vitoria, "On the American Indians," 235.
37. Ibid.
38. On the Scholastic notion of conscience, see Michael Baylor, *Action and Person: Conscience in Late Scholasticism and the Young Luther* (Leiden: Brill, 1977); and Douglas Langston, *Conscience and Other Virtues: From Bonaventure to MacIntyre*. (University Park: Pennsylvania State University Press, 2001).
39. Vitoria, "On the American Indians," 238.
40. On the literature of this intra-imperial contest for administrative control between the conquerors and the Crown, see chapter 2 of my *The Colonial Geography of Colonial American Literatures: Empire, Travel, Modernity* (Cambridge: Cambridge University Press, 2003).
41. See the discussion by Pagden and Lawrance, introduction to *Political Writings*, by Vitoria, xvi–xvii; and Quentin Skinner, *The Foundations of Modern Political Thought*, 2 vols. (Cambridge: Cambridge University Press, 1978), 2:135–73.
42. Wycliffe qtd. by Vitoria, "On the American Indians," 240.

43. See the introduction and chapter 5 of this book.
44. See Francis Oakley, *The Political Thought of Pierre d'Ailly: The Voluntarist Tradition* (New Haven: Yale University Press, 1964), 72–73; and Katherine Walsh, *Richard FitzRalph in Oxford, Avignon, and Armagh: A Fourteenth-Century Scholar and Primate* (Oxford: Clarendon, 1981).
45. Vitoria, "On the American Indians," 241.
46. Ibid., 243.
47. As Pagden and Lawrance explain (Vitoria, *Political Writings*, 126n20), the word *neoterici* originates with Cicero, who used it sarcastically to refer to certain "avant-garde" modes of thought. In the Renaissance, it was applied to mock the adherents of the *via moderna,* the "modern school of Dunces" (followers of Duns Scotus).
48. On the connections between the Ockhamian *via moderna* as developed by Biel in the fifteenth century and the Protestant Reformation, see Heiko Oberman, "Via Antigua and Via Moderna: Late Medieval Prolegomena to Early Reformation Thought," *Journal of the History of Ideas* 48 (1987): 23–40; Oberman, *The Two Reformations: The Journey from the Last Days to the New World* (New Haven: Yale University Press, 2003), 21–43; and Oberman, *The Harvest of Medieval Theology: Gabriel Biel and Late Medieval Nominalism,* rev. ed. (Grand Rapids: Eerdmans, 1967); see also Leif Grane, *Contra Gabrielem: Luthers Auseinandersetzung mit Gabriel Biel: Der Disputatio contra scholasticam theologiam 1517,* Acta Theologica Danica vol. 4 (Copenhagen: Gyldendal, 1962); Harvey Owen Brown, "Martin Luther: A Natural Law Theorist?" in *The Medieval Tradition of Natural Law,* ed. Harold Johnson (Kalamazoo, MI: Medieval Institute Publications, 1987), 13–26; and Mads Jensen, "By Convention or by Nature: Melanchton's Criticism of Late Medieval Ockhamist Political Thought in the *Commentarii in Aliquot Polticos Libros Aristotel,*" *History of Political Thought* 35, no. 1 (2014): 1–28.
49. This is admittedly but necessarily an overly schematic characterization of the issue. For a more detailed analysis of the complex politics of Wycliffe's hierocratic thought and nominalism, see Stephen Lahey, *Metaphysics and Politics in the Thought of John Wyclif* (Cambridge: Cambridge University Press, 2003), esp. 68–107; see also Lahey, *John Wyclif* (Oxford: Oxford Univeristy Press, 2009), esp. 199–221; Gordon Leff, *Bradwardine and the Pelagians* (Cambridge: Cambridge University Press, 1957); Leff, "The Place of Metaphysics in Wycliff's Theology," in *From Ockham to Wyclif,* ed. A. Hudson and M. Wilks, 217–31, SCH Subsida 5 (Oxford: published for the Ecclesiastical History Society by B. Blackwell, 1987). On Fitzralph, see Leff, *Richard Fitzralph, Commentator of the Sentences: A Study in Theological Orthodoxy* (Manchester, UK: Manchester University Press, 1963).
50. See Francis Oakley, *The Conciliarist Tradition: Constitutionalism in the Catholic Church, 1300–1870* (Oxford: Oxford University Press, 2003), 60–110.
51. D'Ailly qtd. in Oakley, *Political Thought,* 76.
52. Ibid., 77–92.
53. On the nominalism or voluntarism of Gerson and d'Ailly, see Oakley, *Political Thought;* on Biel, see Oberman, *Harvest.*

54. On Vitoria's years in Paris, see Ricardo Villoslada, *La Universidad de París durante los estudios de Francisco de Vitoria, O.P.* (Rome: Gregorian University, 1938).
55. Vitoria, *Political Writings,* 100–101.
56. Ibid., 342–44.
57. See ibid., 172n22.
58. See Heiko Oberman's provocative chapter "From Luther to Hitler" in *The Two Reformations* (81–96).
59. Vitoria, "On the American Indians," 290–91; my emphasis.
60. Pagden, *Fall,* 39; see also Marcos, *Los imperialismos.* As far as I am able to tell, the first historian to draw attention to the significance of Mair's commentary in this context was Pedro Leturia in "Maior y Vitoria ante la conquista de América," *Conferencia Anual de la Asociación Francisco de Vitoria* III (1930–31): 43–83. See also Carro, *La teología,* 287–92. On Mair at Paris, see Villoslada, *La Universidad,* 127–64; and Silvio Zavala, *Servidumbre natural y libertad cristiana según los tratadistas españoles de los siglos XVI y XVII* (1944; Buenos Aires: Editorial Porrúa, 1975).
61. Villoslada, *La Universidad de París,* 245–78.
62. John Mair, *In secundum librum sententiarum* (Paris, 1519), xlxxxvii, r.
63. Pagden, *Fall,* 39, 40–41.
64. Vitoria, "On the American Indians," 251.
65. Aristotle, *Politics,* trans. H. Rackham (Cambridge: Harvard University Press, 1959), 25.
66. See Surekha Davies, *Renaissance Ethnography and the Invention of the Human* (Cambridge: Cambridge University Press, 2016), 39–46. The theory that some groups of people are prone to natural servitude based on the geography of their birth was elaborated in Aristotle's *Nicomachean Ethics,* where he wrote that certain nations consist entire of "foolish people, those who are naturally lacking in reason and live by perception alone . . . like some of the far distant non-Greek races," which are "brutish" (*Nicomachean Ethics,* ed. and trans. Roger Crisp [Cambridge: Cambridge University Press, 2004], 128).
67. Fitzmaurice, *Sovereignty,* 45.
68. See the introduction of this book.
69. Fitzmaurice (*Sovereignty,* 45) writes here (somewhat confusingly): "Vitoria and Soto, by contrast, extended the sense in which it was possible to occupy to the question of supremacy, the Roman law equivalent of *dominium jurisdictionis.*"
70. Vitoria, "On the American Indians," 264–65.
71. Ibid., 265.
72. Ibid., 280.
73. Ibid. See here also Bentancor, *The Matter of Empire,* 45–46.
74. Vitoria, "On the American Indians," 280.
75. Ibid.
76. See Jeffrey Cole, *The Potosí Mita, 1573–1700: Compulsory Indian Labor in the Andes* (Stanford: Stanford University Press, 1984).

77. On this circular logic in the Spanish conquest, see Zavala, *Las instituciones jurídicas en la conquista de América* (Madrid: Centro de Estudios Históricos, 1953), 240.
78. *Apologia de Juan Ginés de Sepúlveda,* 69, 79. Las Casas's response can be found on pages 363–75. The point about the Indians' alleged "bestiality" is discussed on pages 373–75; the quotes are on pages 363 and 373. See also Angel Losada, "Bartolomé de las Casas y Juan Maior ante la colonización Española de América," *Cuadernos Hispanoamericanos* 286 (April 1974): 5–23.
79. On De Soto's political writings, see Venancio Diego Carro, *El Maestro Fr. Pedro de Soto, O.P. (Confesor de Carlos V) y las controversias político-teológicas en el siglo XVI* (Salamanca: Convento de San Esteban, 1931); Venancio Diego Carro and Vicente Beltrán De Heredia, *Domingo de Soto y su Doctrina Jurídica: Estudio teológico-jurídico e histórico,* 2nd ed. (Salamanca: Los Dominicos, 1944); Carro et al., *Domingo de Soto y el derecho de gentes* (Madrid: Bruno Del Amo, 1930); Jaime Brufau Prats, *El pnsamiento político de Domingo de Soto y su concepción del poder* (Salamanca: Universidad de Salamanca, 1960); Vicente Beltrán de Heredia, *Domingo de Soto: Estudio biográfico documentado* (Madrid: Ediciones Cultura Hispánica, 1961); Hamilton, *Political Thought;* Annabel S. Brett, *Liberty, Right, and Nature: Individual Rights in Later Scholastic Thought* (Cambridge: Cambridge University Press, 1999), 137–64; David Jiménez Castaño, "Domingo de Soto," in *La Escuela De Salamanca: Filosofía y humanismo ante el mundo moderno,* ed. Ángel Poncela González (Madrid: Verbum, 2015); and Jörg Alejandro Teilkamp, "Über den Zusammenhang von Freiheit und Sklaverei," in *Politische Metaphysik: Die Entstehung moderner Rechtskonzeptionen in der Spanischen Scholastik,* ed. Matthias Kaufman and Rober Schnept (Frankfurt: Peter Lang, 2007). On his scientific writings, see William Wallace, *Domingo de Soto and the Early Galileo: Essays on Intellectual History* (Aldershot, UK: Ashgate, 2004); see also Wallace, *Galileo's Logic of Discovery and Proof: The Background, Content, and Use of His Appropriated Treatises on Aristotle's "Posterior Analytics"* (Dordrecht: Kluwer Academic, 1992).
80. For a history of the idea of universal empire, see Pagden, *Lords.*
81. Domingo de Soto, *Relección "De dominio,"* ed., trans., and introd. Jaime Brufau Prats (Granada: Universidad de Granada, 1964), 162.
82. The passage quoted above appeared in his second redaction of the commentaries on book 2 of Lombard's *Sentences,* published in 1519, the year of Charles's coronation as emperor and three years after his accession to the throne of Spain. The first two redactions of the commentaries appeared in the 1510s; in the 1520s, he undertook a third redaction. In total, Mair published two redactions of book 1, three redactions of book 2, two redactions of book 3, and two redactions of book 4. The last one (of book 1) appeared in 1530 (see Severin Kitanow, John Slotemaker, and Jeffrey Witt, "John Major's [Mair's] Commentary on the *Sentences* of Peter Lombard: Scholastic Philosophy and Theology in the Early Sixteenth Century," in *Mediaeval Commentaries on the "Sentences" of Peter Lombard,* vol. 3, ed. Philipp Rosemann [Leiden: Brill, 2015], 373–75).

83. On Mair, see J. H. Burns, *The True Law of Kingship: Concepts of Monarchy in Early Modern Scotland* (Oxford: Clarendon, 1996), 39–92; Burns, "Politica regalis et opima: The Political Ideas of John Mair," *History of Political Thought* 2, no. 1 (January 1981): 31–61; John Thomas Slotemaker, ed., *A Companion to the Theology of John Mair* (Leiden: Brill, 2015); and Alexander Kaufman, "John Mair's Historiographic Humanism: Portraits of Outlaws, Robbers, and Rebels in his *Historia maioris Britanniae tam Angliae quam Scotiae* (*History of Greater Britain*)," *Enarration: Publications of the Medieval Association of the Midwest* 19 (2015): 104–18.
84. Mair, *In secundum,* xlxxxvii.
85. See Pekka Kärkkäinen, "Conscience and Synderesis in John Mair's Philosophical Theology," in *A Companion to the Theology of John Mair,* ed. John Slotemaker and Jeffrey Witt (Leiden: Brill, 2015), 175–93.
86. John Mair, *Joannis Majoris, . . . In quartum sententiarum quaestiones utilissimae suprema ipsius lucubratione enucleatae: Denuo tamen recognitae: & majoribus formulis impressae: Cum duplici tabella: Videlicet alphabetica materiarum decisarum in fronte: & quaestionum in calce* (Vaenundantur a sui impressore Jodoco Badii, 1519), ccxiiii.
87. John Mair, *In primum sententiarum* (Paris: Henri Estienne for Josse Bade, Jean Petit and Constantin Lelièvre, 1510), 121.
88. John Mair, *Joannis Majoris, . . . In quartum sententiarum,* fol. Ivb., trans. in Durkan, "John Major: After 400 Years," *Innes Review* 1 (1950): 135.
89. John Mair, *In primum sententiarum* (Paris: Henri Estienne for Josse Bade, Jean Petit and Constantin Lelièvre, 1510); and *In primum sententiarum* (Paris: Josse Bade, 1519). There was a third redaction of Mair's commentaries on book 1, which did not include the *Dialogue.* For a discussion of this, see Broadie, "John Mair," 25.
90. I cite A. Broadie's translation in his "John Mair's *Dialogus de materia theologo tractanda:* Introduction, Text, and Translation," in *Christian Humanism: Essays in Honor of Arjo Vanderjagt,* ed. A. A. MacDonald, Zweder R. W. M. von Martels, and Jan R. Veenstra, 419–30 (Leiden: Brill, 2009), 423.
91. Cited in Peter Hume Brown, *George Buchanan, Humanist and Reformer: A Biography* (Edinburgh: D. Douglas, 1890), 43.
92. Ibid., 43–44.
93. Tuck, *The Rights of War and Peace,* 19–50; on Mair, see 41.
94. See here also Scott Davis, "Humanist Ethics and Political Justice: Soto, Sepúlveda, and the 'Affair of the Indies,'" *Annual of the Society of Christian Ethics* (1999): 197.
95. Martha Nussbaum and Amélie Rorty, *Essays on Aristotle's "De anima"* (Oxford: Clarendon, 1992), 55.
96. To be clear, I am not interested in arguing here that the humanist reinterpretation of Aristotle was more historically "accurate'" than that of the Scholastics (though some might wish to argue this), but merely that it was different. Nor am I suggesting that Vitoria's understanding of Aristotle was less capacious than that of Mair or Sepúlveda. Clearly, Vitoria was aware not only of the various Scholastic commentary traditions on the *Politics* but also of the new humanist theology and its philological epistemology. His adherence to a

strictly Thomist hermeneutics must be seen as a conscious *rejection* of both the nominalist metaphysics and the humanist philology on Aristotle embraced, to varying degrees, by Mair and Sepúlveda (by the latter more so than the former). Arguably, Vitoria decided to tackle the issue of natural slavery at the end of his "De indis" precisely in order to reclaim Aristotle's natural slave from that portrayed by Mair in an attempt to reign in some of its more excessive implications—implications, as we will see, that would indeed play out in the subsequent history of the colonial Americas.

97. Aristotle, *Politics*, 21.
98. Aristotle, *De anima*, ed. Ronald Polansky (Cambridge: Cambridge University Press, 2007), 145–70.
99. Aristotle, *Politics*, 23.
100. Ibid.
101. Ibid., 7.
102. Ibid., 567.
103. Ibid., 37.
104. Ibid., 23.
105. Ibid., 15, 13.
106. Ibid., 16–17.
107. Aristotle, *De anima*, 2.ix, trans. and introd. Mark Shifman (Newburyport, MA: Focus, 2011), 67.
108. Aristotle, *Politics*, 23; *Nicomachean Ethics*, 128.
109. Aristotle, *Politics*, 63.
110. See Winston Ashley, *The Theory of Natural Slavery According to Aristotle and St. Thomas* (Notre Dame, IN: University of Notre Dame, 1941), 70.
111. Aristotle, *Metaphysics*, trans. and introd. Hugh Lawson-Tancred (London: Penguin, 1998), 5.
112. Martino Grabmann, *Guglielmo de Moerbeke, O.P. il traduttore delle opera di Aristotele* (Rome: Pontífica Università Gregoriana, 1946), 62; see also Eckart Schütrumpf, *The Earliest Translations of Aristotle's "Politics" and the Creation of Political Terminology* (Paderborn: Wilhelm Fink, 2014). On the dating of the two translations, see F. Bossier, "Méthode de traduction et problems de chronologie," in *Guillaume de Moerbeke: Recueil d'études à l'occasion du 700e aniversaire de sa mort (1286)*, ed. J. Brams and W. Vanhamel, 257–94 (Leuven: Leuven University Press, 1989), 288, 292.
113. Albertus Magnus, *Opera*, 5.2 (Lyon, 1561), 29 (I.i.6); qtd. in Tuck, *The Rights of War and Peace*, 66.
114. See Christoph Flügler, *Rezeption und Interpretation der Aristotelischen "Politica" im späten Mittelalter*, 2 vols. (Amsterdam: B. R. Grüner, 1992), 1:42–43; see also Tuck, *The Rights of War and Peace*, 67.
115. Tuck, *The Rights of War and Peace*, 67, 68–77.
116. See Winston Norman Ashley, "The Theory of Natural Slavery According to Aristotle and St. Thomas" (PhD diss., University of Notre Dame, 1941); and Harold J.,

Johnson. *The Medieval Tradition of Natural Law* (Kalamazoo: Medieval Institute Publications, Western Michigan University, 1987).
117. Saint Thomas Aquinas, *Commentary of Aristotle's "Politics,"* trans. and. ed. Richard Regan (Indianapolis: Hackett, 2007), 34.
118. Ibid., 28.
119. Ibid., 26.
120. Ibid., 30.
121. Ibid., 29.
122. Ibid., 35.
123. Thomas Aquinas, *Summa theologiae* (New York: Cosimo Classics, 2007), 1355.
124. Aristotle, *Politica: Libri I–II.ll: Translatio prior imperfecta interprete Guillelmo de Moerbeka,* ed. Petrus Michaud-Quantin (Bruges: Desclée de Brouwer, 1961).
125. "Propter quod et bellica natura possessiva aliqualiter erit; predativa enim pars ipsius, qua oportet uti et ad bestias et hominum quicumque nati sunt subici et non volunt, velut natura iustum hoc existens bellum primum" (ibid., 14). See also Tuck, *The Rights of War and Peace,* 66.
126. See Nicolai Rubinstein, "The History of the Word *Politicus* in Early-Modern Europe," in *The Languages of Political Theory in Early-Modern Europe,* ed. Anthony Pagden (Cambridge: Cambridge University Press, 1987), 41–56; and James Hankins, "Exclusivist Republicanism and the Non-Monarchical Republic," *Political Theory* 38, no. 4 (2010): 452–82.
127. On Bruni's translation, see Schmitt, *Aristotle,* 16–17, 67–71; Paul Botley, *Latin Translation in the Renaissance: The Theory and Practices of Leonardo Bruni, Giannazzo Manetti and Desiderius Erasmus* (Cambridge: Cambridge University Press, 2004), 58–59; and Thomas Izbicki, "Badgering for Books: Aeneas Sylvius Piccolomini and Leonardo Bruni's Translation of Aristotle's *Politics,*" in *Essays in Renaissance Thought and Letters: In Honor of John Monfasani,* ed. Alison Frazier and Patrick Nold (Leiden: Brill, 2015), 12–22. On Bruni's influence in Spain, see Anthony Pagden, "The Diffusion of Aristotle's Moral Philosophy in Spain, ca. 1400–ca. 1600," *Traditio* 31 (1975): 287–313.
128. Burns ("Politica regalis et opima," 59) assumes that Mair read Moerbeke's translation but notes that Mair's citations and references appear to be "mistaken," as they do not correspond with Moerbeke's text. Given the wide circulation of Bruni's translation in early modern Spain, it is likely that Vitoria also used Bruni. If so, it would provide an additional reason (in addition to his exposure to Mair) that he felt obliged to address the issue of natural slavery; on Bruni in early modern Spain, see Pagden, "The Diffusion of Aristotle's Moral Philosophy in Spain, ca. 1400–1660."
129. See A. Coroleu, "The Fortuna of Juan Ginés de Sepúlveda's Translations of Aristotle and of Alexander of Aphrodisias," *Journal-Warburg and Courtauld Institutes* 59 (1996): 325–31; and Schmitt, *Aristotle,* 70–85.
130. Daniel R. Brunstetter and Dana Zartner, "Just War against Barbarians: Revisiting the Valladolid Debates between Sepúlveda and Las Casas," *Political Studies* 59, no. 3 (2011): 733–52.

131. In De Soto, *Una disputa*.
132. Sepúlveda, *Democrates Segundo*, 1.
133. On Machiavelli and Sepúlveda, see Ángel Poncela González, "The Simulated Dispute between Machiavelli and Ginés de Sepúlveda about the Profession of Soldier and Its Relation to Moral," *Revista de la Sociedad Española de Italianistas* 9 (2013): 137–48.
134. Antonio Maria Fabié, *Vida y escritos de don fray Bartolomé de las Casas* (Madrid: Impr. De Miguel Ginesta, 1879), 2:540. See also Vicente Beltrán De Heredia, *Domingo de Soto: Estudio biográfico documentado* (Madrid: Ediciones Cultura Hispánica, 1961), 237.
135. Sepúlveda, *Democrates Segundo*, 2.
136. See chapter 7 of this book.
137. See Fernández-Santamaria, *The State*, 172–95.
138. See Lancelot Law Whyte, *Essay on Atomism: From Democritus to 1960* (Middletown, CT: Wesleyan University Press, 1961); Ernan McMullin, ed., *The Concept of Matter in Greek and Medieval Philosophy* (Notre Dame, IN: Notre Dame University Press, 1965); David Furley, *Two Studies in the Greek Atomists* (Princeton: Princeton University Press, 1967); Paul Cartledge, *Democritus* (London: Routledge, 1997); and C. C. W. Taylor, "The Atomists," in *The Cambridge Companion to Early Greek Philosophy*, ed. A. A. Long, 181–204 (Cambridge: Cambridge University Press, 1999).
139. See Oleg Bazaluk, "The Problem of War and Peace: A Historical and Philosophical Analysis," *Philosophy and Cosmology* 18 (2017): 89; Bazaluk, *The Theory of War and Peace: The Geophilosophy of Europe* (Newcastle: Cambridge Scholars, 2017), 5–34, esp. 11–13; and Alexander Lyubishchev, *Lines of Democritus and Plato in the History of Culture* (St. Petersburg: Altheia, 2000).
140. Bazaluk, "Problem," 95
141. Marcus Tullius, Cicero, *De officiis,* trans., introd., and annotated Andrew P. Peabody (Boston: Little, Brown, 1887), http://oll.libertyfund.org/titles/ciceroon-moral-duties-de-officiis; qtd. in Bazaluk, *Theory*, 90.
142. Bazaluk, *Theory*, 90.
143. Sepúlveda, *Democrates Segundo*, 7.
144. Ibid., 6.
145. Ibid., 11.
146. Ibid., 13.
147. Ibid., 16.
148. Ibid., 19.
149. Ibid., 19–20.
150. Ibid., 21.
151. Ibid., 22.
152. Ibid.
153. Ibid., 25.
154. Ibid., 27.

155. Ibid., 60
156. Ibid., 70.
157. Ibid., 73.
158. Ibid., 75.
159. Ibid., 83.
160. Ibid., 90.
161. On the connection between Renaissance atomism and philology, see Gerard Passannante, *The Lucretian Renaissance: Philology and the Afterlife of Tradition* (Chicago: University of Chicago Press, 2011).
162. On Sepúlveda's use of this idea, see Ben Kiernan, *Blood and Soil: A World History of Genocide and Extermination from Sparta to Darfur* (New Haven: Yale University Press, 2007); 97–100; Michael Palencia-Roth, "The Cannibal Law of 1503," in *Early Images of the Americas: Transfer and Invention,* ed. Jerry M. Williams and Robert Earl Lewis, 21–64 (Tucson: University of Arizona Press, 1993), 48; and Edmondo Lupieri, *In the Name of God: The Making of Global Christianity* (Grand Rapids, MI: Eerdmans, 2011), 45.
163. See Marcos, *Los imperialismos,* 39, 48, 50.
164. Newman, *Promethean Ambitions: Alchemy and the Quest to Perfect Nature* (Chicago: University of Chicago Press, 2004), 171.
165. See Newman, *Promethean Ambitions,* 164–208; and Mary Baine Campbell, "Artificial Men: Alchemy, Transubstantiation and the Homunculus," in "Between Experience and Experiment," special issue of *Republics of Letters* (Arcades Project, Stanford University), 1, no. 2 (2010): 3–15.
166. Sepúlveda, *Democrates alter,* 52.
167. Newman, *Promethean Ambitions,* 195.
168. Alonso Fernández de Madrigal, *Beati Alphonsi Thostati Episcopi Abulensis super explanatio litteralis amplissima nunc primum edita in apertum* (Venice, 1528), II, 15a.
169. *Libellus de alchimia, ascribed to Albertus Magnus,* trans. Virginia Heines (Berkeley: University of California Press, 1958).
170. See Newman, *Promethean Ambitions,* 66.
171. Theophrast von Hohenheim, gen. Paracelsus, *Sämtliche Werke,* ed. Karl Sudhoff (Munich: Druck und Verlag von R. Oldenbourg, 1929), 11:316–17. The Paracelsian authorship of this text is contested. On Paracelsus's homunculus, see Walter Pagel, *Paracelsus: An Introduction to Philosophical Medicine in the Era of the Renaissance,* 2nd rev. ed. (Basel: Karger, 1982), 117.
172. Paracelsus, *Sämtliche Werke,* ed. Sudhoff, 12:35. On Paracelsus's idea of the American Indians as a type of homunculi, see Allen Debus et al. *Reading the Book of Nature: The Other Side of the Scientific Revolution* (Kirksville, MO: Sixteenth Century Journal, 1998), 63; and Wilhelm Schmidt-Biggemann, *Philosophia Perennis: Historical Outlines of Western Spirituality in Ancient, Medieval and Early Modern Thought* (Dordrecht: Springer, 2004), 186.

173. See chapter 1, note 106. In the modern history of science, it was generally assumed that the works of Paracelsus were not known in Renaissance Spain. More recently, historians of Spanish science have recovered not only the profound influence of Paracelsus but the rich tradition of alchemy in early modern Spain. However, most of the documentation of a tradition of Spanish Paracelsianism provided by these historians derived from the second part of the sixteenth century (see José María López Piñero, "Paracelsus and His Work in 16th- and 17th-Century Spain," *Clio Medica* 8 [1973]: 119–31; López Piñero, *El "Dialogus" [1589] del paracelsista Llorenç Coçar y la cátedra de medicamentos químicos de Valencia [1591]* [Valencia: Cátedra e Instituto de Historia de la Medicina, 1977]; and Mar Rey Bueno, "Los paracelsistas españoles: medicina química en la España moderna," in *Más allá de la leyenda negra: España y la revolución científica / Beyond the Black Legend: Spain and the Scientific Revolution,* ed. Victor Navarro Brotóns and William Eamon [Valencia: Instituto De Historia De La Ciencia Y Documentación López Piñero], 41–55).
174. Carro and Beltrán de Heredia, *Domingo de Soto,* 65, 68, 64.

9. The Blood of the Dragon

1. The complete title of this "second part" was *Segunda parte del libro, de las cosas que se traen de nuestras Indias Occidentales, que siruen al vso de medicina: Do se trata del tabaco, y de la sassafras: y del carlo sancto [. . .] / Hecho por el doctor Monardes medico de Seuilla. ; va añedico [sic] vn libro de la nieue. Do veran los q[ue] beuen frio conella . . . fecho, por el mismo doctor Monardes.*
2. The Italian translation by Annibale Briganti appeared in Venice in 1576; the English translation by John Frampton appeared in London in 1577.
3. This translation was entitled *De simplicicibus medicamentis ex Occidentali India Delatis, quorum in Medicina usus est* (Antwerp, 1574).
4. For recent assessments of Monardes's significance for the history of science, see José María López Piñero and María Luz López Terrada, eds., *La influencia española en la introducción en Europa de las plantas americanas: 1493–1623* (Valencia: Instituto de Estudios Documentales e Históricos Sobre la Ciencia, Universitat de València, C.S.I.C, 1997); and José Pardo Tomás, *Oviedo, Monardes, Hernández: El tesoro natural de América: Colonialismo y ciencia en el siglo XVI* (Madrid: Nivola, 2002), 77–126; on Spanish natural history writing about the New World more generally, see María Luz López Terrada and José Pardo Tomás, *Las primeras noticias sobre plantas americanas en las relaciones de viajes y crónicas de Indias, 1493–1553* (Valencia: Instituto de Estudios Documentales e Históricos Sobre la Ciencia, Universitat de València, C.S.I.C, 1993); and Daniella Bleichmar, "Books, Bodies, and Fields: Sixteenth-Century Transatlantic Encounters with New World Materia Medica," in *Colonial Botany: Science, Commerce, and Politics in the Early Modern World,* ed. Londa Schiebinger and Claudia Swan, 83–99 (Philadelphia: University of Pennsylvania Press, 2005).

5. Nicolás Monardes, *Historia medicinal de las cosas que se traen de nuestras indias occidentales que sirven en medicina* (Seville: Padilla Libros, 1988), 79r. Unless noted otherwise, further citations refer to this edition, which is a facsimile reproduction of the 1574 edition. In the 1571 edition (where it appeared for the first time), this passage can be found on page 91r.
6. Jorge Cañizares-Esguerra, *Puritan Conquistadors: Iberianizing the Atlantic, 1550–1700* (Stanford: Stanford University Press, 2006), 130; Similarly, Marcia Stephenson has placed Monardes's natural history in the context of the missionary campaigns to extirpate Native idolatry—on a trajectory from inquiry to Inquisition—and suggested that New World *materia medica* often came to be associated with diabolism in European natural histories. Stevenson, however, distinguishes between Monardes's attitude toward New World *materia medica* per se and Native American medicinal and religious uses of them (see Marcia Stephenson, "From Marvelous Antidote to the Poison of Idolatry: The Transatlantic Role of Andean Bezoar Stones during the Late Sixteenth and Early Seventeenth Centuries," *Hispanic American Historical Review* 90, no. 1 [2009]: 3–39). On Monardes's treatment of the bezoar stone, see also Miguel de Asúa and Roger French, *A New World of Animals: Early Modern Europeans on the Creatures of Iberian America* (Aldershot, UK: Ashgate, 2005), 106–10.
7. Monardes, *Historia medicinal*, 48v–r.
8. William Ashworth, "Natural History and the Emblematic World View," in *The Scientific Revolution: The Essential Readings,* ed. Marcus Hellyer, 132–56 (Malden, MA: Blackwell, 2003), 135. On the continuities of the emblematic tradition in New World natural history, see Andrés Prieto, *Missionary Scientists: Jesuit Science in Spanish South America, 1570–1810* (Nashville, TN: Vanderbilt University Press, 2011) with regard to Counter-Reformation historians; and Christopher Iannini, *Fatal Revolutions: Natural History, West Indian Slavery, and the Routes of Early American Literature* (Chapel Hill and Colonial Williamsburg, VA: University of North Carolina Press for the Omohundro Institute of Early American History and Culture, 2012). On early modern natural history more generally, see Brian Ogilvie, *The Science of Describing: Natural History in Renaissance Europe* (Chicago: Chicago University Press, 2006); Harold John Cook, *Matters of Exchange: Commerce, Medicine, and Science in the Dutch Golden Age* (New Haven: Yale University Press, 2007); Nicholas Jardine, James Second, and Emma Spary, eds., *Cultures of Natural History* (Cambridge: Cambridge University Press, 1996); Paula Findlen, *Possessing Nature: Museums, Collecting, and Scientific Culture in Early Modern Italy* (Berkeley: University of California Press, 1996); and Lorraine Daston and Katherine Park, eds., *Wonders and the Order of Nature, 1150–1750* (New York: Zone, 1998).
9. For some brief discussions of Monardes's treatment of iron, see Javier Lasso de la Vega y Cortezo, *Biografía y estudio crítico de las obras del médico Nicolás Monardes* (Seville: Padilla Libros, 1988), 40–42; and Raymond Phineas Stearns, *Science in the British Colonies of America* (Urbana: University of Illinois Press, 1970), 32.

10. For an annotated bibliography of Oviedo's works, see Daymond Turner, *Gonzalo Fernández de Oviedo y Valdés: An Annotated Bibliography* (Chapel Hill: University of North Carolina Press, 1966); for a comprehensive study of Oviedo's works, see Antonello Gerbi, *Nature in the New World: From Christopher Columbus to Gonzalo Fernández de Oviedo* (Pittsburgh: University of Pittsburgh Press, 1985); and Kathleen Ann Myers, *Fernández de Oviedo's Chronicle of America* (Austin: University of Texas Press, 2007).
11. This "first part" was republished in Salamanca in 1547 together with an account of the conquest of Peru by Francisco de Xérez. This edition was entitled *Coronica delas Indias: La hystoria general de las Indias agora nueuamente impressa corregida y emendada. 1547: Y con la conquista del Peru* (Impreso en Salamanca: por Iuan de Iunta: Acabose a cinco dias del mes de julio año del nascimiento de nuestro señor Iesu Christo, de mil [y] quinientos [y] quarenta [y] siete años. [July 5, 1547]).
12. See Anthony Pagden, introduction to *Las Casas on Columbus: Background and the Second and Fourth Voyages,* by Bartolomé de las Casas, trans. Nigel Griffin, ed. and introd. Anthony Pagden, Reportorium Colombianum VII (Turnhout, Belgium: Brepols, 1999), 16–19.
13. Gonzalo Fernández de Oviedo y Valdés, *Ouiedo dela natural hystoria delas Indias* (Toledo: se imprimio a costas del autor Go[n]çalo Ferna[n]dez de Ouiedo al[ia]s e Valdes: Por industria de maestre Remo[n] de Petras: & se acabo en la cibdad de Toledo, a. xv. dias del mes de Hebrero. de M.D. xxvj. años [February 15, 1526]), fo. x; English translation in Gonzalo Fernández De Oviedo Y Valdés, *Natural History of the West Indies,* trans. Sterling A. Stoudemire (Chapel Hill: University of North Carolina Press, 1959), 43.
14. *Ouiedo,* fo. ii; *Natural History,* 9.
15. For a description and discussion of this work, see Thomas Goodrich Day, "Ottoman Americana: The Search for the Sources of the Sixteenth-Century Tarih-I Hind-I Garbi," *Bulletin of Research in the Humanities* 85 (Autumn 1982): 269–94; see also Goodrich Day, "Sixteenth-Century Ottoman Americana or Study of Tarih-I Hind-I Garbi" (PhD diss., Columbia University, 1968).
16. *Ouiedo,* "Proemio," fo. ii; *Natural History,* 3.
17. Gonzalo de Fernández de Oviedo y Valdés, *La historia general de las Indias* (Seville: enla empre[n]ta de Iuam Cromberger, 1535), 11.
18. The English word "martyr" derives, as Anthony Pagden notes, from a Greek word that means simply "witness." A martyr is a Christian hero who has "seen" but failed to persuade others of the unique authenticity of his or her vision, a pilgrim who has not returned; and Christianity is a "religion of observance" (Pagden, *European Encounters with the New World: From Renaissance to Romanticism* [New Haven: Yale University Press, 1993], 67).
19. For a discussion of the role that the medieval and Renaissance art of memory played in the composition of the *Sumario,* see Antonio Sánchez Jiménez, "Memoria y utilidad en el *Sumario de la natural historia de las Indias,*" *Colonial Latin American Review* 13, no. 2 (2004): 263–73; Andrés Prieto, "Classification,

Memory, and Subjectivity in Gonzalo Fernández de Oviedo's *Sumario de la natural historia* (1526)," *MLN* 124, no. 2 (March 2009): 329–49.

20. See Jeremy Paden, "The Iguana and the Barrel of Mud: Memory, Natural History, and Hermeneutics in Oviedo's *Sumario de la natural historia de las Indias*," *Colonial Latin American Review* 16 (2007): 203–26; on Renaissance natural history more generally, see Ogilvie, *The Science of Describing;* see also Henry Lowood, "The New World and the European Catalogue of Nature," in *American in European Consciousness 1493–1750*, ed. Karen Ordahl Kupperman (Chapel Hill and Williamsburg, VA: University of North Carolina Press for the Omohundro Institute of Early American History and Culture, 1995), 295–23.

21. José de Acosta, *Historia natural y moral de las Indias*, 2 vols. (Madrid: R. Anglés, 1894), 1:144; trans. Frances López-Morillas, ed. Jane E. Mangan, and introduction and commentary by Walter Mignolo, *Natural and Moral History of the Indies* by José de Acosta (Durham: Duke University Press, 2002), 89.

22. On Monardes's life, see Javier Lasso de la Vega y Cortezo, *Biografía y estudio crítico de las obras del médico Nicolás Monardes* (Seville: Padilla Libros, 1988); Francisco Guerra, *Nicolás Bautista Monardes su vida y su obra, ca. 1493–1588* (Mexico City: Compañia Fundidora de Fierro y Acero de Monterrey, 1961); C. R. Boxer, *Two Pioneers of Tropical Medicine: Garcia d'Orta and Nicolás Monardes* (London: Hispanic and Luso-Brazilian Councils, 1963); Francisco Rodríguez Marín, *La verdadera biografía del doctor Nicolás de Monardes* (1925; Seville: Padilla, 1988); and José Pardo Tomás, *Oviedo, Monardes, Hernández: El tesoro natural de América: Colonialismo y ciencia en el siglo XVI* (Madrid: Nivola, 2002), 77–126.

23. These include the *Diálogo llamado pharmacodilosis o declaración medicinal* (1536), the *De secanda vena in pleuriti* (1539), *De rosa et partibus ejus* (n.d.), and *De citris, avrantiis, ac limoniis* (n.d.). For a discussion of the question of authorship surrounding these tracts, see Rodríguez Marín, *La verdadera biografía*, 22–23.

24. Guerra (*Nicolás Bautista Monardes,* 87–88) explains Monardes's apparent change of heart toward exotic plants by the influence of the Portuguese natural historian of India, Garcia d'Orta; see also Boxer (*Two Pioneers,* 20–22), who disagrees with Guerra and explains Monardes's change as a result of his own experience as a collector and cultivator of New World plants in his garden in Seville. On Garcia d'Orta's influence on Monardes, see also Allison Bigelow, *Cultural Touchstones: Mining, Refining, and the Languages of Empire in the Early Americas* (forthcoming from the University of North Carolina Press for the Omohundro Institute of Early American History and Culture), chap. 4.

25. Nicolás Monardes, *Dos libros: El vno trata de todas las cosas q[ue] trae[n] de n[uest]ras Indias Occide[n]tales, que siruen al vso de medicina [. . .] El otro libro, trata de dos medicinas marauillosas q[ue] son co[n]tra todo veneno* (1565). This edition was reprinted in 1569 by the publishing house of Hernando Díaz.

26. Monardes, *Dos libros,* 19.

Notes to Pages 347–350   595

27. See Pardo-Tomás, *Oviedo*, 96–103; and Marcy Norton, *Sacred Gifts and Profane Pleasures: A History of Tobacco and Chocolate in the Atlantic World* (Ithaca, NY: Cornell University Press, 2008), 107–28.
28. See Pardo-Tomás, *Oviedo*, 101–3.
29. On the distinction between *theoria* and *practica* in early modern medicine, see Harold Cook, "Medicine," in *Early Modern Science,* ed. K. Daston and L. Park, vol. 3 of *The Cambridge History of Science* (Cambridge: Cambridge University Press, 2006); and Cook, *Matters of Exchange.* On Monardes's practices, see Pardo-Tomás, *Oviedo,* 86–91.
30. Gonzalo Aguirre Beltrán, *Medicina y magia: El proceso de aculturación en la estructura colonial* (Jalapa México: Universidad Veracruzana, 1992), 23–24.
31. Juan Luis Vives, *De tradendis disciplinis* (1531), trans. Foster Watson (Totowa, NJ: Rowman and Littlefield, 1971), 209. On Vives, see also Paolo Rossi, *Philosophy, Technology, and the Arts in the Early Modern Era,* trans. Salvator Attanasio (New York: Harper and Row, 1970); and Pamela Smith, *The Body of the Artisan: Art and Experience in the Scientific Revolution* (Chicago: University of Chicago Press, 2004), 66–67.
32. See Martín del Rio, *Investigations into Magic,* ed. and trans. P. G. Maxwell-Stuart (Manchester: Manchester University Press, 2000).
33. Charles Gunnoe, "Erastus and Paraceslsianism: Theological Moties in Thomas Erastus' Rejection of Paracelsian Natural Philosophy," in *Reading the Book of Nature: The Other Scientific Revolution,* ed. Allen G. Debus and Michael Walton, 45–66 (Kirksville, Mo.: Sixteenth Century Journal, 1998); Walter Pagel, *Paracelsus: An Introduction to Philosophical Medicine in the Era of the Renaissance* (Basel: Karger, 1982), 15, 24, 51; see also Richard Drayton, *Nature's Government* (New Haven: Yale University Press, 2000), 9.
34. On "artisanal epistemology," see Smith, *Body,* 59–93; on "vernacular philosophy," see Smith, "What Is a Secret? Secrets and Craft Knowledge in Early Modern Europe," in *Secrets and Knowledge in Medicine and Science, 1500–1800,* ed. Elaine Leong and Alisha Rankin (Aldershot, UK: Ashgate, 2011), 60. On Paracelsus's challenge to the division of labor between the theory and the practice of medicine, see Walter Pagel, *Paracelsus: An Introduction to Philosophical Medicine in the Era of the Renaissance* (Basel: Karger, 1982); Allen Debus, "Paracelsianism and the Diffusion of the Chemical Philosophy in Early Modern Europe," in *Paracelsus: The Man and His Reputation, His Ideas and Their Transformation,* ed. Ole Peter Grell (Leiden: Brill, 1998), 225–44; Debus, "Paracelsus and the Delayed Scientific Revolution in Spain: A Legacy of Philip II," in *Reading the Book of Nature,* ed. A. G. Debus and M. T. Walton, 139–52; Debus, *Chemistry and Medical Debate* (Canton, MA: Science History Publications, 2001); and Debus, "The Chemical Philosophy and the Scientific Revolution," in *The Scientific Revolution,* ed. Marcus Hellyer (London: Blackwell, 2003), 159–77.
35. See Cañizares-Esguerra, *Puritan Conquistadors,* 130; by contrast, the cataloguer of John Carter Brown's online image collection, Luna, believes that Monardes's "El

Dragon" was the *pitaya* cactus (https://jcb.lunaimaging.com/luna/servlet/detail/JCB~1~1~2178~3600006:El-dragon-?qvq=q:monardes&mi=2&trs=21).

36. "Y de aqui adelante, estaremos certificados, que sea sangre de Drago" (Monardes, *Historia medicinal,* 80v–r).

37. Dioscorides, *De Materia Medica: Being an Herbal with Many Other Medical Materials Written in Greek in the First Century of the Common Era: A New Indexed Version in Modern English by T. A. Osbaldeston and R. P. A. Wood* (Johannesburg, South Africa: Ibidis, 2000), 375.

38. Carolius Clusius, *Rariorum aliquot stirpium per Hispanias observatarum historiae* (Antwerp: Ex officina Christophori Plantini, 1576), 11–12.

39. John Gerard, *The Herbal or General Historie of Plantes* (London: John Norton, 1597), 1340.

40. On alchemically produced vermillion, see Pamela Smith, "What Is a Secret?," 60; and Smith, "Vermilion, Mercury, Blood, and Lizards: Matter and Meaning in Metalworking," in *Materials and Expertise in Early Modern Europe: Between Market and Laboratory,* ed. Ursula Klein and Emma Spary (Chicago: University of Chicago Press, 2010), 29–49.

41. On the iconography of the dragon tree, see Renée Gicklhorn, Walter Göpfert, Irmgard Müller, and Hans Schadewaldt, "Bemerkungen zur Geschichte und Ikonographie des Drachenbaumes," *Deutsche Apotheker Zeitung* 120, no. 27 (1980): 1260–66; on the cultural history of the Canary variety, see Jost Casper, *Die Geschichte des Kanarischen Drachenbaumes in Wissenschaft und Kunst: Vom Arbor Gadensis des Posidonius zur Dracaena draco* (Jena: Thüringische Botanische Gesellschaft, 2000). Peter Mason ("A Dragon Tree in the Garden of Eden," *Journal of the History of Collections* 18, no. 2 [2006]: 169–85) argues that the iconographic tradition of the dragon tree can be seen as a movement from "religious" to a "secular" or "scientific" understanding. The alchemical treatment of the dragon tree in Monardes, however, offers a concrete example of how the religious is not so easily disassociated from the "scientific" in the sixteenth and seventeenth centuries, but how the two realms were inextricably interlocked.

42. For an excellent discussion of the history of the symbol of the snake in Western culture, see James Charlesworth, *The Good and Evil Serpent: How a Universal Symbol Became Christianized* (New Haven: Yale University Press, 2010).

43. On dragon imagery in Western alchemy, see Lyndy Abraham, *A Dictionary of Alchemical Imagery* (Cambridge: Cambridge University Press, 1998), 59–60.

44. *The Book of Secrets of Albertus Magnus: Of the Virtues of Herbs, Stones, and Certain Beasts, Also a Book of the Marvels of the World,* ed. Michael R. Best and Frank H. Brightman (Oxford: Oxford University Press, 1999), 104. On the alchemical significance of the lizard, see also Smith, "Vermilion," 45–47.

45. Smith, "Vermilion" 39–40.

46. See chapter 2 of this book; see also William Newman, *Atoms and Alchemy: Chymistry and the Experimental Origins of the Scientific Revolution* (Chicago: University of Chicago Press, 2006), 26–27; and Newman, *The Summa Perfectionis of*

Pseudo-Geber: A Critical Edition, Translation and Study (Leiden: Brill, 1991). On Newton's alchemy, see Michael White, *Isaac Newton: The Last Sorcerer* (Reading, MA, Addison-Wesley, 1997); and Betty Jo Teeter Dobbs, *The Foundations of Newton's Alchemy: or, "The Hunt for the greene lyon"* (New York: Cambridge University Press, 1975). On Boyle's alchemy, see Lawrence M. Principe, *The Aspiring Adept: Robert Boyle and His Alchemical Quest* (Princeton: Princeton University Press, 1998); and Michael Hunter, "Robert Boyle and Secrecy," in *Secrets and Knowledge in Medicine and Science, 1500–1800,* ed. Elaine Leong and Alisha Rankin, 87–104 (Aldershot, UK: Ashgate 2011),

47. See chapter 1, note 102.
48. On the notion of a "conquest" of nature, see Raquel Álvarez Peláez, *La conquista de la naturaleza Americana* (Madrid: Consejo Superior de Investigaciones Científicas, 1993), esp. 293–338.
49. Pardo-Tomás notes that Monardes did not share the general antipathy against alchemy prevailing at the universities (*Oviedo,* 86).
50. On Philip's sponsorship of New World natural history and *materia medica,* see Simon Varey, Rafael Chabrán, and Dora Weiner, eds., *Searching for the Secrets of Nature: The Life and Works of Dr. Francisco Hernández* (Stanford: Stanford University Press, 2000).
51. As with the Old-World "dragon tree" and Monardes's New World "Dragon's Blood," relatively familiar names, such as "rhubarb" and "cinnamon," were applied to plants from the East and West Indies alike; the "rhubarb of the Indies" was Michoacán root, for example. For a discussion of Monardes's treatment of the bezoar stone, see Stephenson, "From Marvelous Antidote," 3–39.
52. On the role of the *impresa* or "device" during the sixteenth century, see Ashworth, "Natural History," 140–42. On Escribano's *impresa* in particular, see Francisco Escudero y Perosso, *Tipografías Hispalense: Anales bibliográficos de la ciudad de Sevilla desde el establecimiento de la imprenta hasta fines del siglo xviii* (Madrid: Impresores de la Real Casa, 1894), 28.
53. I thank Consolación Baranda, of the Instituto Universitario "Menéndez Pidal," Faculty of Philology at the Universidad Complutense at Madrid for alerting me to this allusion to Alciato.
54. On the debate of the effects that the influx of American gold had on the Spanish economy, see Elvira Vilches, *New World Gold: Cultural Anxiety and Monetary Disorder in Early Modern Spain* (Chicago: University of Chicago Press, 2010).
55. Raymond Phineas Stearns, *Science in the British Colonies of America* (Urbana: University of Illinois Press, 1970), 39. On the diffusion of Paracelsianism in sixteenth-century Spain, see José María López Piñero, *El "Dialogus" (1589) del paracelsista Llorenç Coçar y la cátedra de medicamentos químicos de Valencia (1591)* (Valencia: Cátedra e Instituto de Historia de la Medicina, 1977); López Piñero, "Paracelsus and His Work in 16th- and 17th-Century Spain," *Clio Medica* 8 (1973): 119–31; and Mar Rey Bueno, "Los paracelsistas españoles: Medicina química en la España moderna," in *Más allá de la leyenda negra: España y la revolución científica / Beyond*

the Black Legend: Spain and the Scientific Revolution, ed. Victor Navarro Brotóns and William Eamon (Valencia: Instituto de Historia de la Ciencia Y Documentación López Piñero), 41–55.
56. Monardes, *Historia medicinal,* 161r–171v.
57. Vives, *De tradendis disciplinis,* 209.
58. Burgos is derived from gothic baurgs, or walled villages.
59. On these Aristotelian categories and their Scholastic afterlife, see Pamela Long, *Openness, Secrecy, Authorship: Technical Arts and the Culture of Knowledge from Antiquity to the Renaissance* (Baltimore: Johns Hopkins University Press, 2001), 16–45.
60. See Cook, "Medicine."
61. Monardes, *Historia medicinal,* 167v.
62. Ibid., 163v.
63. Ibid., 172v.
64. Ibid., 166v–r.
65. On the duke's family history, see Joaquín González Moreno, *Don Fernando Enríquez De Ribera, Tercer Duque de Alcalá de los Gazules, 1583–1637: Estudio Biográfico* (Sevilla: Ayuntamiento De Sevilla, Delegación De Cultura, Sección De Publicaciones, 1969). On the history of the title of the Admiral of Castile, see Esteban Ortega Gato, "Los Enriquez, almirantes de Castilla," *Publicaciones de la Institución Tella Téllez de Meneses* 70 (1999): 23–65.
66. Monardes, *Historia medicinal,* 158v.
67. Ibid.
68. Ibid.
69. Ibid.
70. Francois Jacob, *The Logic of Life: A History of Heredity* (New York: Pantheon, 1971), 28.
71. Stephen Gaukroger, *The Emergence of a Scientific Culture: Science and the Shaping of Modernity, 1210–1685* (Oxford: Clarendon, 2006), 18.
72. Antonio Barrera-Osorio, *Experiencing Nature: The Spanish American Empire and the Early Scientific Revolution* (Austin: University of Texas Press, 2006), 8. See also Maria Portuondo, *Secret Science: Spanish Cosmography and the New World* (Chicago: University of Chicago Press, 2009); Antonio Sánchez Martínez, *La espada, la cruz y el padrón: Soberanía, fe y representación cartográfica en el mundo ibérico bajo la Monarquía Hispánica, 1503–1598* (Madrid: CSIC, 2013); Arndt Brendecke, *Empirical Empire: Spanish Colonial Rule and the Politics of Knowledge* (Berlin: De Gruyter, 2016).
73. Juan de Cárdenas, *Primera parte de los problemas y secretos marauillosos de las indias* (Mexico City: En casa de Pedro Ocharte, 1591), 3.
74. On Cárdenas, see Barrera-Osorio, *Experiencing Nature,* 75–79; and Norton, *Sacred Gifts,* 134–37.
75. Jorge Cañizares-Esguerra Jorge. *Nature, Empire, and Nation: Explorations of the History of Science in the Iberian World* (Stanford: Stanford University Press, 2006), 87.

76. On salt in Paracelsan alchemy and mining, see Tara Nummedal, *Alchemy and Authority in the Holy Roman Empire* (Chicago: University of Chicago Press, 2007), 23–25. On Cárdenas's metallurgy and its alchemical roots, see Barrera-Osorio, *Experiencing Nature*, 75–79.
77. Juan de Cárdenas, *Problemas y secretos maravillosos de las Indias* (Mexico City: Bibliófilos Mexicanos, 1965), 102.
78. Cárdenas, *Problemas y secretos,* 107.
79. Ibid., 99.
80. Ibid., 32.
81. Ibid., 29.
82. Ibid., 79.
83. Samuel Purchas, *Purchase, His Pilgrimes,* part 1 In fiue books (London: printed by William Stansby for Henrie Fetherstone, and Are to Be Sold at His Shop in Pauls Church-Yard at the Signe of the Rose, 1625), 2.
84. See Allison Bigelow, *Cultural Touchstones: Mining, Refining, and the Languages of Empire in the Early Americas* (Chapel Hill: University of North Carolina Press for the Omohundro Institute of Early American History and Culture, forthcoming).

10. Walter Raleigh's Legends

1. Walter Ralegh, *The Discoverie of the Large, Rich and Bewtiful Empyre of Guiana,* ed. Neil Whitehead (Norman: University of Oklahoma Press, 1997), 199.
2. In the introduction to his 1928 edition of Raleigh's *Discoverie,* V. T. Harlow wrote that, while Raleigh's fame cannot justly be based on his record as a "man of action," it is justified based on his accomplishments as a "man ideas . . . his prophetic imagination [which] called up a vision of England overseas which was translated by his successors into glorious reality." Harlow, introduction to *The Discoverie of Guiana by Sir Walter Raleigh* (London: Argonaut, 1928), xvi, xliii.
3. See Francis Jennings, *The Invasion of American: Indians, Colonialism, and the Cant of Conquest* (Chapel Hill: University of North Carolina Press, 1975).
4. Raymond Phineas Stearns, *Science in the British Colonies of America* (Urbana: University of Illinois Press, 1970), 32.
5. See David Freedberg, *The Eye of the Lynx: Galileo, His Friends, and the Beginnings of Modern Natural History* (Chicago: University of Chicago Press, 2013).
6. See David Gwyn, "Richard Eden: Cosmographer and Alchemist," *Sixteenth Century Journal* 15, no. 1 (1984): 12–34; C. J. Kitching, "Alchemy in the Reign of Edward VI: An Episode in the Career of Richard Whalley and Richard Eden," *Bulletin of the Institute of Historical Research* 44 (1971): 308–15. On Eden, see also Michael Householder, *Inventing Americans in the Age of Discovery: Narratives of Encounter* (Farnham, UK: Ashgate, 2011), 49–78; and Andrew Hadfield, *Literature, Travel, and Colonial Writing in the English Renaissance, 1545–1625* (Oxford, UK: Clarendon, 1998).

7. Anthony Grafton, *New Worlds, Ancient Texts: The Power of Tradition and the Shock of Discovery* (Cambridge: Harvard University Press, 1992), 103.
8. Richard Eden, *A treatyse of the New India, as it is known and found in these our days* (London: In Lombard Strete, by S. Mierdman for Edward Sutton, 1553), n.p.
9. Ibid.
10. Ibid.
11. On Aeneas Silvius's influence on Columbus, see Nicolás Wey Gómez, *The Tropics of Empire: Why Columbus Sailed South* (Cambridge: MIT Press, 2008); and chapter 4 of this book.
12. William Newman, *Promethean Ambitions: Alchemy and the Quest to Perfect Nature* (Chicago: University of Chicago Press, 2004), 44–52; on Albertus Magnus and Aquinas, see also chapter 8 of this book.
13. Richard Eden, "To the Reader," in *A treatyse of the New India*, n.p.
14. Albertus Magnus, *The Boke of Secretes of Albertus Magnus of the vertues of herbes, stones, and certayne beastes. Also, a boke of the same aucthor of the maruaylous thinges of the worlde: and of certaine effectes, caused of certayne beastes* (London: In Poules Chuchyarde [sic] by Wyllyam Seres, 1570), Biii.
15. Eden, *A treatyse*, A8.
16. Richard Eden, *The Arte of Nauigation: Conteyning a compendious description of the Sphere,* by Martín Cortés (London: Richard Iugge, 1561).
17. Richard Eden, *The decades of the newe worlde or west India, conteynyng the nauigations and conquestes of the Spanyardes, with the particular description of the moste ryche and large landes and ilandes lately founde in the west ocean perteynyng to the inheritaunce of the kinges of Spayne. . . . Wrytten in the Latine tounge by Peter Martyr of Angleria, and translated into Englysshe by Rycharde Eden* (London: Guilhelmi Powell [for Robert Toy], 1555).
18. Ibid., 326.
19. See Maria Portuondo, *Secret Science: Spanish Cosmography and the New World* (Chicago: University of Chicago Press, 2009).
20. See chapter 4 of this book.
21. Eden, *Decades,* 215.
22. Ibid., 184.
23. Ibid.
24. Ibid.
25. Ibid., 185.
26. Ibid., 214.
27. Ibid., 71, 78.
28. Ibid., 99.
29. Ibid., 125.
30. Ibid., 57.
31. Ibid.

32. On Cabot's voyages, see Evan T. Jones and Margaret M. Condon, *Cabot and Bristol's Age of Discovery: The Bristol Discovery Voyages 1480–1508* (Bristol: University of Bristol Press, 2016).
33. On Frobisher and his voyages, see Samuel Eliot Morison, *The European Discovery of America: The Northern Voyages, A.D. 500–1600* (New York: Oxford University Press, 1971), 497–500; David B. Quinn, "Frobisher in the Context of Early English Exploration," in *Meta Incognita: A Discourse of Discovery—Martin Frobisher's Arctic Expeditions, 1576–1578*, ed. Thomas Symons, 2 vols. (Hull: Canadian Museum of Civilization, 1999), 1:7–18; Joyce Chaplin's *Subject Matter: Technology, the Body, and Science on the Anglo-American Frontier, 1500–1676* (Cambridge: Harvard University Press, 2001), 43–59; and Alden T. Vaughn, *Transatlantic Encounters: American Indians in Britain, 1500–1776* (Cambridge: Cambridge University Press, 2006), 1–3.
34. Nicholas H. Clulee, "John Dee and the Paracelsians," in *Reading the Book of Nature: The Other Side of the Scientific Revolution,* ed. Allen G. Debus and Michael Walton, 111–32 (Kirksville, MO: Sixteenth Century Journal, 1998). 113. See also Peter French, *John Dee: The World of an Elizabethan Magus* (London: Routledge, 1972), 40–61; William Sherman, *John Dee: The Politics of Reading and Writing in the English Renaissance* (Amherst: University of Massachusetts Press, 1995), 29–52, as well as 40 and 165 on the connections between Raleigh, Gilbert, and Dee; and Deborah Harkness, *John Dee's Conversations with Angels: Cabala, Alchemy, and the End of Nature* (Cambridge: Cambridge University Press, 1999), 124.
35. See Frances Yates, *The Art of Memory* (London: Routledge, 1966), 262–63; and French, *John Dee*, 44–47.
36. John Dee, *General and Rare Memorials Pertayning to the Perfect Arte of Nauigation: Annexed to the Paradoxal Cumpas, in Playne: Now First Published: 24. Yeres, After the First Inuention Thereof* (London: By Iohn Daye, 1577), 2.
37. Ibid., A2. See also E. G. R. Taylor, *Tudor Geography, 1485–1583* (London: Methuen, 1930); on the history of the concept of occupation and English claims to dominion in the New World, see Andrew Fitzmaurice, *Sovereignty, Property and Empire, 1500–2000* (Cambridge: Cambridge University Press, 2014), 85–124.
38. John Dee et al., *John Dee: The Limits of the British Empire* (Westport, CT, Praeger, 2004), 53.
39. Ibid. See also French *John Dee*, 197; and Sherman, *John Dee*, 150–51.
40. For a discussion of the Elizabethan consideration of these legal issues, see Robert Miller, "The Legal Adoption of Discovery in the United States," in *Discovering Indigenous Lands: The Doctrine of Discovery in the English Colonies*, by Miller, Jacinta Ruru, Larissa Behrent, and Tracey Lindberg, 26–65 (Oxford: Oxford University Press, 2010), 15–19; and Anthony Pagden, *Lords of All the World: Ideologies of Empire in Spain, Britain and France c. 1500–c. 1800* (New Haven: Yale University Press, 1995), 90.

41. Taylor, *Tudor Geography*, 119–38; see also French, *John Dee* 180. On Dee's "Christian Cabbalism," see Frances Yates, *The Occult Philosophy in the Elizabethan Age* (London: Routledge, 1979), 76.
42. Qtd. in David B. Quinn, *The Roanoke Voyages, 1584–1590*, 2 vols. (London: Hakluyt Society, 1955), 1:82–89.
43. Joyce Lorimer, introduction to *Sir Walter Ralegh's "Discoverie of Guiana,"* ed. Lorimer (Aldershot, UK: Ashgate for the Hakluyt Society, 2006), xvii–xcvi, xx. On the background of Raleigh's composition and promotion of this text, see also Surekha Davies, *Renaissance Ethnography and the Invention of the Human* (Cambridge: Cambridge University Press, 2016), 183–216; and Anna Beer, *Sir Walter Raleigh and His Readers in the Seventeenth Century* (Basingstoke: Macmillan, 1997).
44. Lawrence Keymis, *A Relation of the Second Voyage to Guiana* (London: Thomas Dawson, 1596); see also Mary Fuller, "Ralegh's Fugitive Gold," in *New World Encounters*, ed. Stephen Greenblatt, 177–217 (Cambridge: Cambridge University Press, 1993).
45. For a discussion of Raleigh's reputation as an alchemist, see Charles Nicholl, *The Creature in the Map: A Journey to El Dorado* (New York: William Morrow, 1995), 278–87.
46. See Nicholl, *Creature*, 280.
47. Walter Raleigh, "The History of the World," in *The Works of Sir Walter Ralegh*, 8 vols. (New York: Burt Franklin, 1964), 2:3, 4, 27, 28. On Raleigh's use of these sources, see also Nicholas Popper, *Walter Ralegh's History of the World and the Historical Culture of the Late Renaissance* (Chicago: University of Chicago Press, 2012), 12–76, 91, and 96.
48. See Nicholl, *Creature*, 75, 279.
49. Ibid., 75–76.
50. In 1565, Philip II, who styled himself the "Chief and Sovereign" of the Golden Fleece, even had the Argo reconstructed as a royal war galley, which became the flagship in the victorious Catholic fleet at the sea battle at Lepanto against the Turks (see Mary Tanner, *The Last Descendant of Aeneas: The Hapsburgs and the Mythic Image of the Emperor* [New Haven: Yale University Press, 1993], 5–9, 150–51). On the relationship between the *Argonautica* and the El Dorado legend, see Demetrio Ramos Pérez, *El mito del Dorado: Su génesis y proceso* (Caracas: Academia Nacional De La Historia, 1987), 404; Gil Munilla, *Descubrimiento del Marañón* (Seville: n.p., 1954), 175; and Manuel Ferrandis Torres, *El mito del oro en la conquista de América* (Valladolid: Talleres tipográficos "Cuesta," 1933), 158–70.
51. See Lyndy Abraham, *A Dictionary of Alchemical Imagery* (Cambridge: Cambridge University Press, 1998), 88; on the history of this connection, see Antoine Faivre, *The Golden Fleece and Alchemy* (Albany: State University of New York Press, 1993).
52. Raleigh, *Works*, 4:413.

53. On the Argonautica and modern science, see Bronislaw Malinowski's introduction to this seminal anthropological work on the western Pacific, *Argonauts of the Western Pacific: An Account of Native Enterprise and Adventure in the Archipelagoes of Melanesian New Guinea* (London: Routledge, 1922).
54. See Nicholl, *Creature,* 309–13; and Ralph Bauer, "A New World of Secrets: Occult Philosophy and Local Knowledge in the Sixteenth-Century Atlantic World," in *Science and Empire in the Atlantic World,* ed. James Delbourgo and Nicholas Dew (London: Routledge, 2007), 99–126.
55. Raleigh, *Discoverie,* 145–46.
56. On monsters in Raleigh's *Discoverie,* see Davies, *Renaissance Ethnography,* 183–216.
57. Raleigh, *Discoverie,* 163. Whitehead, in his introduction to the edition of *Discoverie* cited here (1–116, 23), has pointed out that there is no record of a "negro" among Raleigh's crew. He therefore speculates that the entire episode was invented by Raleigh for rhetorical effect in order to enhance the "enchanted-ethnological" poetics of the text. By contrast, Joyce Lorimer, in the annotation to her edition, disputes Whitehead's interpretation (see *Sir Walter Ralegh's "Discoverie of Guiana,"* ed. Lorimer, 113).
58. Raleigh, *Discoverie,* 157.
59. See Yates, *The Occult Philosophy,* 170; and Nicholl, *Creature,* 309–13.
60. Raleigh, *Discoverie,* 196.
61. Ibid., 164.
62. Ibid., 125.
63. Ibid., 176.
64. Ibid., 188.
65. Ibid., 176.
66. Thus, Edward Kelly, in his *The Theatre of Terrestrial Astronomy,* refers to the gates of the "furnace" as open "towers" (see *Two excellent Treatises on the Philosophers Stone together with the Theater of Terristrial Astronomy* [London, 1676], 141). In Ben Jonson's *The Alchemist,* Subtle says to Ananias: "O are you come?" 'Twas time. Your threescore minutes / Were at the last thred, you see, and downe had gone / Furnus acediae, Turris circulatorius. . . . Had all been cinders (3.2.1–5). For a discussion of the symbol of the tower in alchemical literature, see Abraham, *Dictionary of Alchemical Imagery,* 203–4.
67. Nicholl, *Creature,* 319–20.
68. Louis Montrose, "The Work of Gender in the Discourse of Discovery," in *New World Encounters,* ed. Stephen Greenblatt, 177–217 (Berkeley: University of California Press, 1993), 182; see also Greenblatt, introduction to *New World Encounters;* Fuller, "Ralegh's Fugitive Gold," ibid., 226–27; Fuller, *Voyages in Print: English Travel to America, 1576–1624* (Cambridge: Cambridge University Press, 1995), esp. 55–84; William Hamlin, "Imagined Apotheosis: Drake, Harriot, and Ralegh in the Americas," *Journal of the History of Ideas* 57, no. 3 (1996): 405–28; and Greenblatt, *Sir Walter Raleigh: The Renaissance Man and His Roles* (New Haven: Yale University Press, 1973), 55–84.

69. See Whitehead, introduction to Walter Raleigh's *The Discoverie of the Large, Rich and Bewtiful Empyre of Guiana*, ed. Whitehead (Norman: University of Oklahoma Press, 1997),72–91.
70. See Ramos Pérez, *El mito del Dorado*, 28, 38; Enrique de Gandía, *Historia crítica de los mitos y leyendas de la conquista Americana* (Buenos Aires: Centro Difusor Del Libro, 1946), 125–26; and John Hemming, *The Search for El Dorado* (New York: Dutton, 1978).
71. For a summary of these indigenous accounts, see Ramos Pérez, *El mito del Dorado*, 293–304.
72. Both of these expeditions resulted in the production of written accounts, Gaspar de Carvajal's *Descubrimiento del Río de las Amazonas* and Francisco Vázquez's *Relación de Omagua y Dorado* respectively. An interesting sixteenth-century account of the Welsers' search for El Dorado is Nicolas Federmann's "Indianische Historia," in *N. Federmanns und H. Stades Reisen in Südamerica, 1529 bis 1555* (1558; Stuttgart: Bibliothek des Litterarischen Vereins in Stuttgart, Bd. 47, 1859).
73. Serge Gruzinksi, *The Mestizo Mind: The Intellectual Dynamics of Colonization and Globalization* (New York: Routledge, 2002), 27, 31, 43, 50–51.
74. Thus, Whitehead wrote not one but two separate introductions to his edition of the *Discoverie* in two parts, one devoted to the "enchanted text" and one to the "ethnological" text (see Whitehead, introduction to Walter Ralegh's *The Discoverie of the Large, Rich and Bewtiful Empyre of Guiana*, ed. Whitehead, 1–91).
75. Shannon Miller, *Invested with Meaning: The Raleigh Circle in the New World* (Philadelphia: University of Pennsylvania Press, 1998), 154.
76. Raleigh, *Discoverie*, 121.
77. Ibid., 122.
78. Ibid.
79. Ibid., 126.
80. Ibid., 165.
81. Ibid., 170–71.
82. Ibid., 171.
83. Ibid., 28.
84. Ibid., 134.
85. See Charles Gibson, ed., *The Black Legend: Anti-Spanish Attitudes in the Old World and the New* (New York: Knopf, 1971); and Margaret Rich Greer, Walter Mignolo, and Maureen Quilligan, eds., *Rereading the Black Legend: The Discourses of Religious and Racial Difference in the Renaissance Empires* (Chicago: University of Chicago Press, 2007).
86. Raleigh, *Discoverie*, 219.
87. Ibid., 134.
88. Nicholl, *Creature*, 289.
89. Raleigh, *Discoverie*, 138.
90. Ibid., 136.
91. Ibid.

92. Ibid., 137.
93. For a discussion of the Spanish sources of Ralegh's *Discoverie*, see Pablo Ojer, *La formación del oriente venezolano* (Caracas: Universidad Católica "Andrés Bello," Facultad de Humanidades y Educación, Instituto de Investigaciones Históricas, 1966), 496–97.
94. Raleigh, *Discoverie*, 138.
95. Ibid., 140.
96. See Lorimer, introduction to *Sir Walter Ralegh's "Discoverie of Guiana,"* ed. Lorimer, xli; and Hemming, *Search*, 165.
97. Ralegh, *Discoverie*, 121–22. The earliest Spanish written account bringing the history of the Incas in connection with the legend of El Dorado appears to have been written by the Spanish soldier de Pedro Maraver de Silva, though this account was not published, and it is therefore unlikely that Raleigh would have been aware of it (see Pedro Maraver de Silva, "Relación del viaje de Pedro Maraver de Silva: El Dorado" [1576] [Archivo General de Indias, PATRONATO, 26, R. 28]; and Hemming, *Search*, 43–45).
98. For a historical overview of these events, see Ralph Bauer, introduction to *An Inca Account of the Conquest of Peru, by Titu Cusi Yupanki* (Boulder: University Press of Colorado, 2006), 1–56.
99. Ralegh, *Works*, 4:684.
100. Pedro Sarmiento de Gamboa, *Historia de los Incas* (Madrid: Miraguano, 2001), 88; English, Pedro Sarmiento de Gamboa, *History of the Incas,* trans. Clemens Markham (1907; Mineola, NY: Dover, 1999), 92.
101. Sarmiento de Gamboa, *Historia.,* 89; English, Sarmiento de Gamboa, *History,* 92.
102. Paul Richard Steele and Catherine Allen, *Handbook of Inca Mythology* (Santa Barbara, CA: ABC Clio, 2004), 226–27.
103. See ibid.; Sabine MacCormack, *Religion in the Andes: Vision and Imagination in Early Colonial Peru* (Princeton: Princeton University Press, 1991), 284; MacCormack, "Pachacuti: Miracles, Punishments, and Last Judgment: Visionary Past and Prophetic Future in Early Colonial Peru," *American Historical Review* 93, no. 4 (1988): 960–1106; and Bauer, introduction to *An Inca Account of the Conquest of Peru, by Titu Cusi Yupanki.*
104. Hernando Cortés, "Second Letter to Charles V," in *Letters from Mexico,* trans. and ed. Anthony Pagden (New Haven: Yale University Press, 1971), 85–86.

11. Things of Darkness

1. See Ethel Seaton, "Thomas Harriot's Secret Script," *Ambix* 4 (October 1956): 111–14; John W. Shirley, *Thomas Harriot: A Biography* (Oxford, UK: Clarendon, 1983), 109–12; and Daniel J. Cohen, *Equations from God: Pure Mathematics and Victorian Faith* (Baltimore: Johns Hopkins University Press, 2008), 26.
2. On Harriot's early biography, see Shirley, *Thomas Harriot*, 38–112; John W. Shirley, introduction to *Thomas Harriot; Renaissance Scientist,* ed. Shirley (Oxford,

UK: Clarendon, 1974); and Robert Fox, introduction to *Thomas Harriot and His World: Mathematics, Exploration, and Natural Philosophy in Early Modern England,* ed. Fox (Farnham, UK: Ashgate, 2012), 1–10.
3. Thomas Harriot, *A briefe and true report of the new found land of Virginia of the commodities and of the nature and manners of the naturall inhabitants. Discouered by the English colon there seated by Sir Richard Greinuile Knight in the eere 1585* (London: By R. Robinson, 1588), B2r–B3v.
4. Ibid., E2v.
5. Thomas Harriot, *A briefe and true report of the new found land of Virginia,* introd. Pault Hulton (1590; New York: Dover, 1972), 29.
6. On the notion of a discursive "armature" of conquest, see Beatriz Pastor Bodmer, *The Armature of Conquest: Spanish Accounts of the Discovery of America, 1492–1589* (Stanford, CA: Stanford University Press, 1992). However, as pointed out in chapter 7, Eduardo Viveiros de Castro reads statements such as Harriot's at ethnographic and metaphysical face value, as an expression of Amerindian "multinaturalism" (see Viveiros de Castro, *Cannibal Metaphysics: For a Post-Structural Anthropology,* trans. and ed. Peter Skafish [Minneapolis: Univocal and the University of Minnesota Press, 2014]).
7. See Stephen Greenblatt's seminal essay "Invisible Bullets: Renaissance Authority and Its Subversion," *Glyph* 8 (1981): 40–61.
8. Kelly Wisecup, *Medical Encounters: Knowledge and Identity in Early American Literatures* (Amherst: University of Massachusetts Press, 2013), 37–65.
9. On Harriot's atomism, see Joyce Chaplin's *Subject Matter: Technology, the Body, and Science on the Anglo-American Frontier, 1500–1676* (Cambridge: Harvard University Press, 2001), 29–31, 285–86; Robert Hugh Kargon, *Atomism in England from Hariot to Newton* (Oxford: Clarendon, 1966), 24–27; Jean Jacquot, "Harriot, Hill, Warner, and the New Philosophy," in *Harriot, Renaissance Scientist,* ed. Shirley, esp. 107–8, 115; Christoph Meinel, "Early Seventeenth-Century Atomism: Theory, Epistemology, and the Insufficiency of Experiment," *Isis* 79 (1988): 68–103; B. J. Sokol, "Invisible Evidence: The Unfounded Attack on Thomas Harriot's Reputation," *DTHSOP,* no. 17 (n.d.): 22–26; Sokol, "The Problem of Assessing Thomas Hariot's *A briefe and true report* of His Discoveries in North America," *AS* 51 (1994): 14–15; Amir Alexander, "The Imperialist Space of Elizabethan Mathematics," *Studies in the History and Philosophy of Science,* 26 (1995): 575–79; Edward Rosen, "Harriot's Science, the Intellectual Background," in *Harriot, Renaissance Scientist,* ed. Shirley, 4–6; and Robert Goulding, "*Chymicorum in morem:* Refraction, Matter Theory, and Secrecy in the Harriot-Kepler Correspondence," in *Thomas Harriot and His World,* ed. Fox, 27–52.
10. Amir R. Alexander, *Geometrical Landscapes: The Voyages of Discovery and the Transformation of Mathematical Practice* (Stanford, CA, Stanford University Press, 2002), 104, 123–24.
11. Thomas Harriot qtd. in Goulding, "*Chymicorum in morem,*" 45–46.

12. Goulding, *"Chymicorum in morem,"* 46, 48.
13. Harriot, *A briefe and true report*, 25.
14. Ibid.
15. Ibid., 26.
16. Ibid.
17. Ibid., 5.
18. This terminology, however, dates only to the eighteenth century—to the bibliographer Charles d'Orléans de Rothelin. The De Brys and their colleagues in the book trade referred to the two series as "India Occidentalis" and "India Orientalis." The word "America" appears in the title beginning with volume 2, about Florida.
19. Only the first six volumes of the series were published by de Bry senior. After his death in 1598, subsequent volumes published before 1617 were issued by his two sons, Johann Theodor and Johan Israel. After 1617, Johann Theodor worked by himself on the Voyages series. After 1623, the last two volumes of the Voyages were published by Johann Theodor's son-in-law, Matthaeus Merian. For recent criticism on de Bry, see chapter 7, note 63.
20. Although it is not entirely clear how much involvement Harriot had in the De Bry edition of his *Report*, the use of the first-person plural in the captions to the engravings lead me to assume that they were written by Harriot rather than by de Bry.
21. See van Groessen, *The Representation*, 57–63.
22. See Kim Sloan, introduction to *A New World: England's First View of America*, ed. Sloan (Chapel Hill: University of North Caroline Press, 2007), 11–22; Paul Hulton, *America 1585: The Complete Drawings of John White* (Chapel Hill: University of North Carolina Press, 1984), 18; and Eric Cheyfitz, *The Poetics of Imperialism: Translation and Colonization from "The Tempest" to Tarzan* (New York: Oxford University Press, 1991), 188–98.
23. Thomas Harriot, *A briefe and true report of the new found land of Virginia of the commodities and of the nature and manners of the naturall inhabitants. Discouered by the English colon there seated by Sir Richard Greinuile Knight in the eere 1585* (Frankfurt: Theodor De Bry, 1590), XI.
24. Sabine MacCormack, "Gods, Demons, and Idols in the Andes," *Journal of the History of Ideas* 67, no. 4 (October 2006): 623.
25. See Julie Robin Solomon, "'To Know, to Fly, to Conjure': Situating Baconian Science at the Juncture of Early Modern Modes of Reading," *Renaissance Quarterly* 44 (Autumn 1991): 513–58. On the impact of Italian Hermeticism in Renaissance England, see Frances Yates, *Giordano Bruno and the Hermetic Tradition* (London: Routledge, 1964); on John Dee's Hermeticism, see Yates, *The Occult Philosophy in the Elizabethan Age* (London: Routledge, 1979); and Nicholas Clulee, *John Dee's Natural Philosophy: Between Science and Religion* (London: Routledge 1988); on the connections between Raleigh, Gilbert, and Dee, see Deborah Harkness, *John Dee's Conversations with Angels: Cabala, Alchemy, and the End of Nature* (Cambridge: Cambridge University Press, 1999), 124.

26. For a discussion of the alchemical motifs and plant symbolism in the *Primavera*, see Mirella Levi D'Ancona, *Botticelli's "Primavera": A Botanical Interpretation Including Astrology, Alchemy, and the Medici* (Florence: Olschki Editore, 1983).
27. MacCormack, "Gods, Demons," 623.
28. See Michael Gaudio's *Engraving the Savage: The New World and Techniques of Civilization* (Minneapolis: University of Minnesota Press, 2008), esp. 54–61.
29. Isidore of Seville, *The Etymologies of Isidore of Seville*, ed. Stephen Barney, W. J. Lewis, J. A. Beach, and Oliver Berghof, with the collaboration of Muriel Hall (Cambridge: Cambridge University Press, 2006), 201.
30. Stuart Clark, *Vanities of the Eye: Vision in Early Modern European Culture* (Oxford: Oxford University Press, 2007), 79.
31. This "folk" tradition of witchcraft is also implied in de Bry's depictions of the smoke of Native camp fires, as Michael Gaudio has shown (*Engraving*, 45–86).
32. *Das Wagnerbuch von 1593*, ed. Günther Mahal and Martin Ehrenfeuchter (Tübingen: A. Francke, 2005). 1:239.
33. Ibid., 1:240.
34. Ibid., 1:250.
35. See Keith Thomas, *Religion and the Decline of Magic* (1971; Oxford: Oxford University Press, 1997), 471.
36. For a discussion of Harriot's association in this circle and the accusations made against him as a mathematician, atomist, alchemist, and atheist, see Gordon Batho, "Thomas Harriot and the Northumberland Household," in *Thomas Harriot: An Elizabethan Man of Science*, ed. Robert Fox, 28–47 (Aldershot, UK: Ashgate, 2000); see also Chaplin, *Subject Matter*, 29–31; and Solomon, "To Know, to Fly, to Conjure."
37. Richard Barnes, "A Note Containing the Opinion on Christopher Marley," Harl. Ms. 6848, 185r, BL. qtd. in Chaplin, *Subject Matter*, 39.
38. Harriot, *A briefe and true report*, 27.
39. William Shakespeare, *The Tempest*, ed. Stephen Orgel (Oxford, UK: Clarendon, 1987), 2.2. For a more extensive discussion of *The Tempest* in this light, see Frances Yates, *Shakespeare's Last Plays* (London: Routledge, 1975); for a discussion of the alchemical imagery in *The Tempest* from a Jungian perspective, see Noel Cobb, *Prospero's Island: The Secret Alchemy at the Heart of "The Tempest"* (London: Coventure, 1984); for discussions of *The Tempest* in connection to New World colonialism, see Peter Hulme, *Colonial Encounters: Europe and the Native Caribbean* (New York: Methuen, 1986), 89–136; and Eric Cheyfitz, *The Poetics of Imperialism: Translation and Colonization from The Tempest to Tarzan*, expanded ed. (Philadelphia: University of Pennsylvania Press, 1997).
40. In Harriot, *A briefe and true report*, 41.
41. On Fludd, see Yates, *Giordano Bruno*, 402–407; on the Rosicrucians, see Yates, *The Rosicrucian Enlightenment* (London: Routledge, 1972).
42. Theodor de Bry, *Dritte Buch Americae, darinn Brasilia durch Johann Staden auss eigener Erfahrung in teutsch beschrieben* (Frankfurt: De Bry, 1593), n.p.

43. Ibid.
44. Ibid.
45. James I, King of England, *Daemonologie in forme of a dialogue, diuided into three bookes* (Edinburgh: Printed by Robert Walde-graue printer to the Kings Majestie, 1597), n.p.
46. Stuart Clark, *Thinking with Demons: The Idea of Witchcraft in Early Modern Europe* (Oxford, UK: Clarendon; New York: Oxford University Press, 1997), 445.
47. Not much is known about the translator, Edward Grimstone. He apparently translated various works from Spanish and French into English (see Andrew Hadfield, *Literature, Travel, and Colonial Writing in the English Renaissance, 1545–1625* [Oxford, UK: Clarendon, 1998], 105–8).
48. Joseph Mede, "A Coniecture Concerning Gog and Magog in the Revelation" (1627), in *The Works of the Pious and Profoundly-Learned Joseph Mede, BD* (London: printed by James Flesher for Richard Royston, 1664), n.p. On Mede, see also Jorge Cañizares Esguerra, *Puritan Conquistadors: Iberianizing the Atlantic* (Stanford: Stanford University Press, 2006), 94–104.
49. For a discussion of Mede's place in the evolution of an imperialist ideology in Great Britain, see David Armitage, *The Ideological Origins of the British Empire* (Cambridge: Cambridge University Press, 2000), 94–97.
50. While some Protestants identified the Antichrist with the Papacy, the Puritans, especially, also saw the English episcopacy as being infiltrated by the Kingdom of Evil (see Ernest Tuveson, *Millennium and Utopia: A Study in the Background of the Idea of Progress* [Berkeley: University of California Press, 1949], 23–70).
51. James Axtell, for example, points out that the Pequod War of 1637 was essentially a conflict between two competing and incompatible concepts of farming and ownership of land (Axtell, *The European and the Indian: Essays in the Ethnohistory of Colonial North America* [New York: Oxford University Press, 1981], 165). On John Eliot, see Richard Cogley, *John Eliot's Mission to the Indians before King Philip's War* (Cambridge: Harvard University Press, 1999).
52. John Cotton, "God's Promise to His Plantations," in *The Puritans: A Narrative Anthology,* ed. A. Heimert and A. Delbanco (Cambridge: Harvard University Press, 1985), 77. On the typological association of the Indians with the Canaanites, see also John Canup, *Out of the Wilderness: The Emergence of an American Identity in Colonial New England* (Middletown, CT: Wesleyan University Press, 1990), 79–87.
53. John Winthrop, *Winthrop Papers,* 5 vols. (Boston: Massachusetts Historical Society, 1947), 3:149
54. John Winthrop, "Reason to be Considered," in *The Puritans,* ed. A. Heimert and A. Delbanco, 73.
55. Roger Williams, "To the Reader," n.p., *A Key into the Language of America* (London: Printed by Gregory Dexter, 1643), n.p.
56. Ibid.

57. On the early modern history of the idea of the "Jewish" origin of Native Americans, see Lee Eldridge Huddleston, *Origins of the American Indians, European Concepts, 1492–1729* (Austin: University of Texas Press, 1967).
58. Samuel Purchas, *Hakluytus Posthumus, or Purchas his Pilgrims*, 20 vols. (London, 1625; Glasgow: James MacLehose & Sons, 1905–7), 19:225.
59. For a discussion of "Virginia's Verger" as a "cant of conquest," see Francis Jennings, *The Invasion of America: Indians, Colonialism, and the Cant of Conquest* (Chapel Hill: University of North Carolina Press, 1975), 78–81.
60. Purchase, *Hakluytus*, 19:231–32.
61. John Smith, *The generall historie of Virginia, New-England, and the Summer Isles with the names of the adventurers, planters, and governours from their first beginning* (London: Printed by I. D. and I. H. for Michael Sparkes, 1624), 48.
62. Ibid., 34.
63. Ibid., 38.
64. Mary Rowlandson, "The Goodness and Soveraignty of God," in *So Dreadfull a Judgment: Puritan Responses to King Philip's War, 1676–1677*, ed. Richard Slotkin and James K. Folsom (Middletown, CT: Wesleyan University Press, 1978), 326, 393.
65. Cotton Mather, *Wonders of the Invisible World*, ed. Reiner Smolinski (Lincoln: University of Nebraska Press, 2007), xi.
66. Ibid., 20.
67. Ibid., 104.
68. Ibid.
69. Ibid.
70. Ibid., x.
71. On the colonial origins of (early) modern totalitarianism, see Irene Silverblatt, *Modern Inquisitions: Peru and the Colonial Origins of the Civilized World* (Durham, NC: Duke University Press, 2004).

12. Eating Bacon

1. Francis Bacon, *The New Organon*, ed. Lisa Jardine and Michael Silverthorne (Cambridge: Cambridge University Press, 2000), 78.
2. Ibid., 77.
3. Bacon, *Of the Interpretation of Nature*, in *The Works of Francis Bacon*, new ed., ed. James Spedding, Robert Leslie Ellis, and Douglas Denon Heath, 15 vols. (Boston: Houghton, Mifflin, 1900), 6:35.
4. Ibid., 6:36.
5. Cochleus qtd. in Peter Burke, "America and the Rewriting of World History," in *America in European Consciousness, 1493–1750*, ed. Karen Ordahl Kupperman, 33–51 (Chapel Hill: University of North Carolina Press, 1995), 35. On the question of a "blunted impact," see John H. Elliott, *The Old World and the New, 1492–1650* (Cambridge: Cambridge University Press, 1970).

6. See Maria Portuondo, *Secret Science: Spanish Cosmography and the New World* (Chicago: University of Chicago Press, 2009).
7. Francisco López de Gómara, *La historia de las Indias y conquista de Mexico* (Zaragoza: Agustin Millan, 1552), Fo. Iii, fo cxii, recto.
8. Charles Whitney, *Francis Bacon and Modernity* (New Haven: Yale University Press, 1986), 11–13; see also 23–54. On the religious and prophetic contexts of Bacon's "instauration," see also Stephen A. McKnight, *The Religious Foundations of Francis Bacon's Thought* (Columbia: University of Missouri Press, 2006), 49; James Bono, *The Word of God and the Language of Man* (Madison: University of Wisconsin Press, 1995); Peter Zagorin, *Francis Bacon* (Princeton: Princeton University Press, 1998); John Briggs, "Bacon's Science and Religion," in *Cambridge Companion to Bacon*, ed. Markku Peltonen (Cambridge: Harvard University Press, 1996); Benjamin Farrington, *The Philosophy of Francis Bacon: An Essay on Its Development from 1603 to 1609, with New Translations of Fundamental Texts* (Chicago: University of Chicago Press, 1964); and Anthony Funari, *Francis Bacon and the Seventeenth-Century Intellectual Discourse* (New York: Palgrave Macmillan, 2011), 21–22; on the frontispiece of *The Great Instauration*, see John Steadman, "'Beyond Hercules: Francis Bacon and the Scientist as Hero," *Studies in the Literary Imagination* 4 (1971): 3–47.
9. Bacon, *New Atlantis*, in *Works*, 5:398.
10. Ibid., 5:384.
11. See Ralph Bauer, *The Cultural Geography of Colonial American Literatures* (Cambridge: Cambridge University Press, 2003), 4, 14–18.
12. See Bruno Latour, *Science in Action: How to Follow Scientists and Engineers through Society* (Milton Keynes: Open University Press, 1987), 215–57.
13. Bacon, *New Atlantis*, in *Works*, 5:410–11.
14. Ibid., 5:385.
15. Ibid., 5:370.
16. On the role of secrecy and censorship in *New Atlantis*, see Simon Wortham, "Censorship and the Institution of Knowledge in Bacon's *New Atlantis*," in *Francis Bacon's "New Atlantis": New Interdisciplinary Essays*, ed. Bronwen Price (Manchester: Manchester University Press, 2002), 180–98.
17. Bacon, *New Atlantis*, in *Works*, 5:411.
18. See Charles Whitney, "Merchants of Light: Science as Colonization in the *New Atlantis*," in *Francis Bacon's Legacy of Texts*, ed. William Sessions (New York: AMS, 1990), 255–68.
19. On the monarchist or absolutist politics of Baconian science, see Julie Solomon, *Objectivity in the Making: Francis Bacon and the Politics of Inquiry* (Baltimore: Johns Hopkins University Press, 1998); and Julian Martin, *Francis Bacon, the State, and the Reform of Natural Philosophy* (Cambridge: Cambridge University Press, 1992).
20. Bacon, *Gesta Grayorum*, ed. Desmond Bland (Liverpool: Liverpool University Press, 1968), 46–48.

21. Frank F. Manuel and Fritzie P. Manuel, *Utopian Thought in the Western World* (Cambridge: Harvard University Press, 1979), 244; Anthony F. C. Wallace, *The Social Context of Innovations: Bureaucrats, Families, and Heroes in the Early Industrial Revolution, as Foreseen in Bacon's* "New Atlantis" (Princeton: Princeton University Press, 1982).
22. Richard Hakluyt, *The Principal Navigations, Voyages, Traffiques & Discoveries of the English Nation,* 12 vols. (Glasgow: James McLehose and Sons, 1903), 1:xxxv.
23. On Philip's alchemical laboratories, see chapter 1, note 102.
24. See Portuondo, *Secret Science,* 61.
25. Bacon, "Of the True Greatness of Kingdoms and Estates," in *Works,* 12:183.
26. Bacon, *Of the Interpretation of Nature,* in *Works,* 6:46. As has been noted, Bacon's political and natural philosophy were likewise indebted to Machiavelli. All politics and sciences had to be harnessed for the purpose of the empowerment of the monarchical state, what Bacon called "reason of state" (see Zagorin, *Francis Bacon,* 158–59; and Martin, *Francis Bacon*).
27. On More's *Utopia,* see chapter 7 of this book. On More and Bacon, see Claire Jowitt, "'Books Will Speak Plain'? Colonialism, Jewishness and Politics in Bacon's *New Atlantis,*" in *Francis Bacon's New Atlantis: New Interdisciplinary Essays,* ed. Bronwen Price, 129–55, 132. See also Edward Surtz and J. H. Hexter, eds., *Utopia* (New Haven: Yale University Press, 1965), i–xxxii.
28. Bacon, *New Atlantis,* in *Works,* 5:395.
29. On the distinction between the fantastic, magic realism, and science fiction as literary "modes," see Amaryll Beatrice Chanady, *Magical Realism and the Fantastic: Resolved versus Unresolved Antinomy* (New York: Garland, 1985), 4–5; on the fantastic, see also Tzvetan Todorov, *Introuction à la littérature fantastique* (Paris: Editions du Seuil, 1970).
30. Bacon, *New Atlantis,* in *Works,* 5:371–72.
31. Ibid., 5:373.
32. Garcilaso de la Vega, el Inca, *Comentarios reales de los Incas,* ed. Ángel Rosenblat (Buenos Aires: Emecé, 1943), 1:272. Bacon's reference to Garcilaso's *Comentarios* can be found in "An Advertisement Touching an Holy War," in *The Works of Francis Bacon,* 10 vols. (London: Printed for C. and J. Rivington, 1819), 3:485, 489. Although parts of the *Comentarios reales* were translated by Samuel Purchas in his *Hakluytus Posthumus, Purchas his Pilgrimes,* this work was not published until 1625, which strongly suggests that Bacon had read Garcilaso's Spanish original, which had been published in two parts in 1609 and 1617. The first complete translation was published in 1685 by Sir Paul Rycaut as *The Royal Commentaries of Peru* (London: Miles Flesher/Christopher Wilkinson, 1685).
33. On Garcilaso and St. Bartholomew, see Rolena Adorno, "The Indigenous Ethnographer: The 'Indio Ladino' as Historian and Cultural Mediation," in *Implicit Understanding: Observing, Reporting, and Reflecting on the Encounters between Europeans and Other Peoples in the Early Modern Era,* ed. Stuart Schwartz, 378–402 (Cambridge: Cambridge University Press, 1994), 390. On this tradition more

broadly, see also Sabine MacCormack, *On the Wings of Time: Rome, the Incas, Spain, and Peru* (Princeton: Princeton University Press, 2007), 62; and David Brading, *The First America: The Spanish Monarchy, Creole Patriots, and the Liberal State, 1492–1867* (Cambridge: Cambridge University Press, 1993), 151, 172–74, 273–74, 365–66, 385–87.

34. See chapter 10. On the syncretism of Christian Hermeticism, see Claudio Moreschini, *Hermes Christianus: The Intermingling of Hermetic Piety and Christian Thought* (Turnhout, Belgium: Brepols, 2011).
35. Bacon, *New Atlantis*, in *Works*, 5:398–99.
36. Ibid., 5:404.
37. Ibid., 5:398.
38. On John Allin, see Donna Bilak, "Alchemy and the End Times: Revelations from the Laboratory and Library of John Allin, Purigan Alchemist," *Ambix* 60, no. 4 (2013): 390–414; on Wigglesworth and Starkey, see William Newman, *Gehennical Fire: The Lives of George Starkey: An American Alchemist in the Scientific Revolution* (Chicago: University of Chicago Press, 1994); on Fludd, see Allen Debus, *The English Paracelsians* (New York: F. Watts, 1966); on John Winthrop II, see Walter Woodward, *Prospero's America: John Winthrop, Jr., Alchemy, and the Creation of New England Culture, 1606–1676* (Chapel Hill and Williamsburg, VA: Published University of North Carolina Press for the Omohundro Institute of Early American History and Culture, 2009).
39. Karen Gordon-Grube, "Evidence of Medicinal Cannibalism in Puritan New England: 'Mummy' and Related Remedies in Edward Taylor's 'Dispensatory,'" *Early American Literature* 28, no. 3 (1993): 185.
40. On Spanish Paracelsianism, see José María López Piñero, "Paracelsus and His Work in 16th and 17th Century Spain," *Clio Medica* 8 (1973): 119–31; López Piñero, *El "Dialogus" (1589) del paracelsista Llorenç Coçar y la cátedra de medicamentos químicos de Valencia (1591)* (Valencia: Cátedra e Instituto de Historia de la Medicina, 1977); and Mar Rey Bueno, "Los paracelsistas españoles: Medicina química en la España moderna," in *Más allá de la leyenda negra: España y la revolución científica/Beyond the Black Legend: Spain and the Scientific Revolution*, ed. Victor Navarro Brotóns and William Eamon (Valencia: Instituto de Historia de la Ciencia y Documentación López Piñero), 41–55
41. Bacon, *Sylva sylvarum*, in *Works*, 4:143–500; 5:7–176; 6:223.
42. See Brian Vickers, introduction to *Occult and Scientific Mentalities in the Renaissance*, ed. Vickers (Cambridge: Cambridge University Press, 1984), esp. 13–14. On Bacon's ambivalence regarding alchemy, see Bruce Janacek, *Alchemical Belief: Occultism in the Religious Culture of Early Modern England* (University Park: Pennsylvania University Press, 2011), 75–89.
43. Francis Bacon, "The Masculine Birth of Time, or Three Books on the Interpretation of Nature," trans. Farrington, in *The Philosophy of Francis Bacon*, 66.
44. See Paolo Rossi, *Francis Bacon: From Magic to Science*, trans. Sacha Rabinovitch (Chicago: University of Chicago Press, 1968), 1–35; William Newman,

Promethean Ambitions: Alchemy and the Quest to Perfect Nature (Chicago: University of Chicago Press, 2004), 256–71; Stephen Gaukroger, *Francis Bacon and the Transformation of Early Modern Philosophy,* 175; Graham Rees, "Francis Bacon's Semi-Paracelsian Cosmology and the *Great Instauration,*" *Ambix* 22 (1975): 161–73; Rees, "Matter Theory: A Unifying Factor in Bacon's Natural Philosophy?" *Ambix* 24 (1977): 110–25; Rees, "Francis Bacon on Verticity and the Bowels of the Earth," *Ambix* 26 (1979): 202–11; Rees, "Atomism and 'Subtlety' in Francis Bacon's Philosophy," *Annals of Science* 37 (1980): 549071; Rees, "Bacon's Philosophy: Some New Sources with Special Reference to the *Abecedarium novum naturae,*" in *Francis Bacon: terminologia e fortuna nel XVII secolo,* ed. Marta Fattori (Rome: Edizioni dell'Ateneo, 1984); William Eamon, *Science and the Secrets of Nature: Books of Secrets in Medieval and Early Modern Culture* (Princeton: Princeton University Press, 1994), 286–89; and Janacek, *Alchemical Belief,* 75–89.

45. Newman, *Promethean,* 270.
46. Bacon, *Sylva sylvarum,* in *Works,* 4:221.
47. Ibid., 4:222.
48. Ibid., 4:223.
49. Ibid.
50. Ibid., 4:314–16.
51. Ibid., 5:159.
52. Ibid., 5:153.
53. Ibid., 5:161. On Bacon and mummy, see also Richard Sugg, *Mummies, Cannibals, and Vampires: The History of Corpse Medicine from the Renaissance to the the Victorians* (London: Routledge, 2016), 39–40.
54. Gaukroger, *Francis Bacon,* 175.
55. See Tara Nummedal, *Alchemy and Authority in the Holy Roman Empire* (Chicago: University of Chicago Press, 2007), 147–76.
56. On the self-promotional aspect of Paracelsus's career, see Allen Debus, "Paracelsianism and the Diffusion of the Chemical Philosophy in Early Modern Europe," in *Paracelsus: The Man and His Reputation, His Ideas and Their Transformation,* ed. Ole Peter Grell (Leiden: Brill, 1998), 225–44; and Phillip Ball, *The Devil's Doctor: Paracelsus and the World of Renaissance Magic and Science.* 1st American ed. (New York: Farrar, Straus and Giroux, 2006); on the use of salt, see Allen Debus, *Chemistry and Medical Debate* (Canton, MA: Science History Publications, 2001).
57. Francis Bacon, "The Masculine Birth of Time," 66; on Bacon's pronouncements on Arnald of Villanova, see ibid., 65; see also Bacon, *Works* 8:316.
58. On the oedipal origins of the Eucharist, see Sigmund Freud, *Totem and Taboo* (1913; London: Routledge, 2001); also Freud, *Moses and Monotheism,* trans. Katherine Jones (1939; Letchworth: Hogarth, 1939); and chapter 7 of this book.
59. For example, in a section of the *Sylva sylvarum* entitled "Experiments in Consort Touching Sulphur and Mercury, two of Paracelsus's Principles," Bacon explains that "There be two great families of things. You may term them by several names;

sulphureous and mercurial, which are the chemist's words," though he disagrees with Paracelsus's notion of salt (*sal*) as a third principle, as "it is a compound of the other two" (Bacon, *Works*, 4:331).

60. Bacon, *Sylva sylvarum*, in *Works*, 4:314–15.
61. Ibid., 4:315.
62. Bacon, "The Masculine Birth of Time," 66.
63. Bacon, *The New Organon*, 74.
64. See Rossi, *Francis Bacon*, 1–35; see also Gaukroger, *Francis Bacon*, 179.
65. *Of the Interpretation of Nature*, in *Works of Francis Bacon, Lord Chancellor of England*, a new edition by Basil Montagu, 16 vols. (London: William Pickering, 1834), 15:99. Compare *Works*, ed. Spedding, Ellis, and Heath, 6:42: "time is like a river which carrieth down things which are light and blown up, and sinketh and drowneth that which is sad and weighty."
66. Bacon, "Thoughts and Conclusion," in Farrington, *The Philosophy of Francis Bacon*, 86.
67. See Gerard Passannante, *The Lucretian Renaissance: Philology and the Afterlife of Tradition* (Chicago: University of Chicago Press, 2011), 78–119.
68. Passannante, *The Lucretian Renaissance*, 122.
69. Bacon, *Sylva sylvarum*, in *Works*, 4:331–32.
70. Ibid., 4:332–33.
71. Qtd. in Andrew Weeks, *Paracelsus: Speculative Theory and the Crisis of the Early Reformation* (Albany: State University of New York Press, 1997), 123–24.
72. Ibid.
73. Ibid.
74. Bacon, *Sylva sylvarum*, in *Works*, 4:316.
75. Ibid.
76. Bacon, *The Advancement of Learning*, in *Works*, 4:129.
77. For a discussion of Bacon's interest in the pre-Socratics, see William Sessions, "Francis Bacon and the Classics: The Discovery of Discovery," in *Francis Bacon's Legacy of Texts*, ed. William Sessions (New York: AMS, 1990), 237–54.
78. Bacon, *Of the Interpretation of Nature*, in *Works* 6:81.
79. Bacon, "The Great Instauration, Preface," in *Works*, 8:35–36.
80. Bacon, "Of Atheism," in *Works*, 12:132.
81. Bacon, "Of the Dignity and Advancement of Learning," book III, in *Works*, 8:513.
82. Bacon, "De sapientia veterum," in *Works* 12:402–13:172, 13:122.
83. Ibid., 13:122–25.
84. Newman, *Promethean Ambitions*, 262.
85. Bacon, "De sapientia veterum," in *Works*, 13:117.
86. Ibid., 13:118; my emphasis.
87. Ibid., 13:143.
88. See Carolyn Merchant, *The Death of Nature: Women, Ecology, and the Scientific Revolution* (San Francisco: Harper and Row, 1980); and Denise Albenese, *New Science, New World* (Durham: Duke University Press, 1996), 92–120.

89. Bacon, "De sapientia veterum," in *Works,* 13:144.
90. See Thomas Hofmeier, introduction to *Michael Maiers Chymisches Cabinet* (Berlin: Thurneysser, 2007), 9–72, 38.
91. Michael Maier, *Atalanta fugiens,* in *Michael Maiers Chymisches Cabinet,* 80. On de Bry's engraving of Amerindian "smoke," see chapter 4 of this book and Michael Gaudio's *Engraving the Savage: The New World and Techniques of Civilization* (Minneapolis: University of Minnesota Press, 2008), 54–61.
92. Michael Maier, *Arcana arcanissima hoc est hieroglyphica AEgyptio-Graeca vulgo necdum cognita* (London: printed by Thomas Creede, 1613), 1–55; see also Hereward Tilton, *The Quest for the Phoenix: Spiritual Alchemy and Rosicrucianism in the Work of Michael Maier (1569–1622)* (Berlin: Walter de Gruyter, 2003), 80–86; on the emblem of the Green Lion, see Betty Jo Teeter Dobbs, *The Foundations of Newton's Alchemy, or "The Hunting of the Green Lyon"* (Cambridge: Cambridge University Press, 1975).
93. Bacon, *Of the Interpretation of Nature,* in *Works* 6:28; italics in original.
94. Ibid., 6:34.
95. Ibid., 6:40.
96. On the important role that Virgil plays in Bacon's articulation of a reformed natural philosophy, see Sessions, "Francis Bacon and the Classics."
97. Bacon, *The Advancement of Learning,* in *Works* 6:188; my emphasis.
98. Bacon, *Description of the Intellectual Globe,* in *Works* 10:407.
99. See Merchant, *The Death of Nature,* 164–91; see also Merchant, "The Scientific Revolution and *The Death of Nature*," *Isis* 97 (2006): 513–33; Merchant, "The Violence of Impediments: Francis Bacon and the Origins of Experimentation," *Isis* 99 (2008): 731–60; and Merchant, "Secrets of Nature: The Bacon Debates Revisited," *Journal of the History of Ideas* 69 (2008): 147–62. For a critique of the notion that Bacon conceived of his method as one of torture, see Peter Pesic, "Proteus Rebound: Reconsidering the Torture of Nature," *Isis* 98 (2008): 304–317. While Pesic is correct in pointing out that Bacon never literally used the phrase "torture of nature"—a claim that seems to have originated with Leibniz—Merchant is doubtlessly correct in pointing to the language of violence in Bacon's conception of experimental discovery, a "violence of impediments" transformed by "art and the hand of man," as he had written in *De augmentis scientiarum.*
100. Bacon, *The Advancement of Learning,* in *Works,* 8:413.
101. On the epistemological foundations of torture and the earlier ordeal more generally, see John Langbein, *Torture and the Law of Proof: Europe and England in the Ancient Regime* (Chicago: University of Chicago Press, 1977); see also, on the connection between torture and the epistemology of discovery, Elizabeth Hanson, "Torture and Truth in Renaissance England," *Representations* 34 (Spring 1991): 53–84, esp. 54.
102. Langbein, *Torture,* 90.
103. James Spedding, Robert Ellis, and Douglas Heath, eds., *Life and Letters of Francis Bacon,* 7 vols. (London, 1868), 3:114.

104. Harvey Wheeler, "Francis Bacon's 'Verulamium': The Common-Law Template of the Modern in English Science and Culture," *Angelaki: Journal of the Theoretical Humanities* 4, no. 1 (1999): 7–26, 9, 23. See also Martin, *Francis Bacon*, esp. 72–104.
105. See Langbein, *Torture;* and Hanson, "Torture and Truth."
106. Sir Edward Coke, *The Third Part of the Institute of the Laws of England* (London: E. and R. Brooke, 1797), 34–35, qtd. in Hanson, "Torture and Truth," 53.
107. Hanson, "Torture and Truth," 65.
108. Francis Bacon, "Certain Observations Made upon a Libel Published This Present Year, 1592," in *The Letters and the Life of Francis Bacon: Including All His Occasional Works*, ed. James Spedding, 146–208 (London: Longmans, Green, 1890), 1:163.
109. Irene Silverblatt, *Modern Inquisitions: Peru and the Colonial Origins of the Civilized World* (Durham, NC: Duke University Press, 2004).
110. Bacon in *Gesta Grayorum*, 46.
111. Bacon, "The Masculine Birth of Time," 62.
112. Bacon, *The New Organon*, 100.
113. Bacon, "Naturalis et experimentalis," in *Works*, 9:371.
114. Agrippa qtd. in Rossi, *Francis Bacon*, 38.
115. Eamon, *Science*, 286–90.
116. Bacon, "De sapientia veterum," in *Works*, 13:98.
117. Ibid., 13:100.
118. Bacon, *The Interpretion of Nature*, in *Works*, 6:62.
119. Eamon, *Science*, 289.
120. Ibid., 286, 289, 288, 39, 270, 272–73, 416.
121. Bacon, *New Organon*, 100.
122. See David Asselin, "The Notion of Dominion in Genesis 1–3," *Catholic Biblical Quarterly* 16 (1954): 277–94; see also Leiss, *Dominion*, 31.
123. William Leiss, *Domination of Nature* (New York: G. Braziller, 1972), 33; see also Farrington, *The Philosophy of Francis Bacon*, esp. 51–58; and Thomas DeCosta Kaufmann, *The Mastery of Nature: Aspects of Art, Science, Humanism in the Renaissance* (Princeton: Princeton University Press, 1993), 184–94. On the history of interpretation of the biblical "dominion" mandate, see also Asselin, "The Notion of Dominion;" Keith Thomas, *Man and the Natural World: A History of the Modern Sensibility* (New York: Pantheon, 1983); Jeremy Cohen, *"Be Fertile and Increase, Fill the Earth and Master It": The Ancient and Medieval Career of a Biblical Text* (Ithaca, NY: Cornell University Press, 1989); Ronald Manahan, "A Re-Examination of the Cultural Mandate: An Analysis and Evaluation of the Dominion Materials" (PhD diss., Grace Theological Seminary, 1982); and Carolyn Merchant, *Reinventing Eden: The Fate of Nature in Western Culture* (New York: Routledge, 2003).
124. *The Vulgate*, Genesis 1:26, http://vulgate.org/ot/genesis_1.htm. Genesis 1:28 in the Vulgate does use the verb *dominare* (*benedixitque illis Deus et ait crescite et*

multiplicamini et replete terram et subjicite eam et dominamini piscibus maris et volatilibus caeli, et universis animantibus quae moventur super terram [http://vulgate.org/ot/genesis_1.htm]). But the verb simply means "to rule," without the noun's more specifically territorial connotation of "having dominion." On the crucial importance of the concept of "occupation" to British imperial ideology, see Andrew Fitzmaurice, *Sovereignty, Property and Empire, 1500–2000* (Cambridge: Cambridge University Press, 2014).

125. Bacon, "An Advertisement Touching on Holy War Political," in *Works* 13:210.
126. Peter Linebaugh and Marcus Rediker, *The Many-Headed Hydra: Sailors, Slaves, Commoners, and the Hidden History of the Revolutionary Atlantic* (Boston: Beacon, 2001), 37–40. On the crucial role that the idea of private property played in British imperial ideology, see David Armitage, *The Ideological Origins of the the British Empire* (Cambridge: Cambridge University Press, 2004), esp. 61–99.
127. Bacon, *New Organon,* 100.
128. Ibid.
129. The *OED* quotes here from H. W. Preston, *Documents Illustrating American History* (1886), 6. As William Leiss has put it, "the growing sense of command over a wider territory (the voyages of discovery and the subjugation of native peoples in the new world), and the simultaneous awareness of a greater human capacity to manipulate nature's physical and chemical processes—producing very concrete material benefits—served to rein—force this convenient rationalization for traditional forms of brutal exploitation" (see Leiss, *Domination of Nature,* xiv).
130. Francis Bacon, "Certain Considerations Touching the Plantation in Ireland," in *Letters and the Life of Francis Bacon,* 4:116.
131. Ibid., 4:117.
132. See Alan Macfarlane, *The Origins of English Individualism: The Family, Property, and Social Transformation* (Cambridge: Cambridge University Press, 1978).
133. Matthew Hale, *The Primitive Origination of Mankind* (London: pby William Godbid for William Shrowsbery, 1677), 370.
134. John Donne, *The Sermons of John Donne,* ed. George R. Potter and Evelyn M. Simpson, 10 vols. (Berkeley: University of California Press, 1953–62), 9:58.
135. See the introduction to this book.

Coda

1. Gabriel García Márquez, *Cien años de soledad,* Edición Conmemorativa (Madrid: Real Academia Española, 2007), 31–32. The English translation, here (73–74) and henceforth, is from *One Hundred Years of Solitude,* trans. Gregory Rabasa (New York: Harper and Row, 1970).
2. Ibid., 32 (English, 74).
3. See John Ochoa, *The Uses of Failure in Mexican Literature and Identity* (Austin: University of Texas Press, 2004), 83; see also Rex Clark and Oliver Lubrich, introduction to *Transatlantic Echoes: Alexander von Humboldt in World Literature,*

ed. Clark and Lubrich (New York: Berghahn, 2012), 31; and Raymond Leslie Williams, *Mario Vargas Llosa: A Life of Writing* (Austin: University of Texas Press, 2014), 138.
4. On apocalypticism in *Cien años,* see Lois Parkinson Zamora, *Writing the Apocalypse: Historical Vision in Contemporary U.S. and Latin American Fiction* (Cambridge: Cambridge University Press, 1989), 25–50. On apocalypticism is Hemispheric American literatures more generally, see also Parkinson Zamora, *The Apocalyptic Vision in America: Interdisciplinary Essays on Myth and Culture* (Bowling Green: Bowling Green University Popular Press, 1982); and Thomas Beebee, *Millennial Literatures of the Americas: 1492–2002* (Oxford: Oxford University Press, 2009).
5. García Márquez, *Cien años,* 422.
6. Gabriel García Márquez, "The Solitude of Latin America," Nobel lecture, December 8, 1982, www.nobelprize.org/nobel_prizes/literature/laureates/1982/marquez-lecture.html. For Pigafetta's account of this scene, see Antonio Pigafetta, *The First Voyage round the World, by Magellan,* trans. Henry Edward Stanley (London: Hakluyt Society, 1874), 50.
7. See Jane Robinett, *This Rough Magic: Technology in Latin American Fiction* (New York: Peter Lang, 1994); and Brian Conniff, "The Darker Side of Magical Realism: Science, Oppression, and Apocalypse in *One Hundred Years of Solitude,*" *Modern Fiction Studies* 36, no. 2 (1990): 167–79.
8. On "parody," "intertextualism," and "dialogue," see Mikhail Bakhtin, *The Dialogic Imagination,* ed. Michael Holquist, trans. Caryl Emerson and Holquist (Austin: University of Texas Press, 1981).
9. See Chester Halka, *Melchíades, Alchemy, and Narrative Theory: The Quest for Gold in "Cien años de soledad"* (Lathrup Village, MI: International Book Publishers, 1981), 3; Kathleen McNerney and John Martin, "Alchemy in *Cien años de soledad,*" *West Virginia Philological Papers* 27 (1981): 106–12; Shannin Schroeder, *Rediscovering Magical Realism in the Americas* (Westport, CT: Praeger, 2004), 39–57; and Robinett, *This Rough Magic,* 98–99.
10. García Márquez, *Cien años de soledad,* 32.
11. Charles Darwin, *Voyage of the Beagle* (London: Penguin Classics, 1989), 374. On Humboldt's influence on nineteenth-century representations of the tropics, see Nancy Leys Stepan, *Picturing Tropical Nature* (Ithaca, NY: Cornell University Press, 2001), 31–56; and Clarence Glacken, *Traces on the Rhodian Shore: Nature and Culture in Western Thought from Ancient Times to the End of the Eighteenth Century* (Berkeley: University of California Press, 1990), 655–705.
12. Bolívar qtd. in Margaret Ewalt, *Peripheral Wonders: Nature, Knowledge, and Enlightenment in the Eighteenth Century,* 191; also qtd. in Susan Gilman, "Humboldt's American Mediterranean," *American Quarterly* 66, no. 3 (September 2014): 527; and Gerard Helferich, *Humboldt's Cosmos: Alexander von Humboldt and the Latin American Journey That Changed the Way We See the World* (New York: Gotham, 2004), 303. To date, I have not been able to verify the authenticity

of this quote. On Humboldt's legacy in Latin America more broadly, and in Mexico, particularly, see Ochoa, *The Uses,* 81–110.

13. Mary Louise Pratt, *Imperial Eyes: Travel Writing and Transculturation* (London: Routledge, 1992), 124. For an earlier exploration of the connection between what has been called "Humboldtian science" and imperialism, see William H. Goetzmann, *Exploration and Empire: The Explorer and the Scientist in the American West* (1966; New York: Norton, 1979). In addition to being imperialist, Humboldt has been charged with being "derivative" by Jorge Cañizares-Esguerra in "How Derivative Was Humboldt? Microcosmic Narratives in Early Modern Spanish America and the (Other) Origins of Humboldt's Ecological Sensibilities," in *Nature, Empire, and Nation: Explorations of the History of Science in the Iberian World,* 112–28 (Stanford: Stanford University Press, 2006). For a more charitable assessment of Humboldt's writings, especially the *Views of the Cordilleras,* see his earlier *How to Write the History of the New World: Historiographies, Epistemologies, and Identities in the Eighteenth-Century Atlantic World* (Stanford: Stanford University Press, 2001), 125–29.

14. See Vera Kutzinski and Ottmar Ette, introduction to *Views of the Cordilleras and Monuments of the Indigenous Peoples of the Americas: A Critical Edition,* by Alexander von Humboldt, ed. Vera M. Kutzinski and Ottmar Ette, trans. J. Ryan Poynter (Chicago: University of of Chicago Press, 2012); on Humboldt's implicit critique of the degeneration thesis, see also Antonello Gerbi, *The Dispute of the New World: The History of a Polemic, 1750–1900,* trans. Jeremy Moyle (Pittsburgh: University of Pittsburgh Press, 1973), 405–17; and David Brading, *The First America: The Spanish Monarchy, Creole Patriots, and the Liberal State, 1492–1867* (Cambridge: Cambridge University Press, 1991), 514–34.

15. Alexander von Humboldt, *Voyage aux régions équinoxiales du nouveau continent, fait en 1799, 1800, 1801, 1802, 1803 et 1804,* 13 vols. (Paris: A la Librairie Greque-Latine-Allemande, 1816), 1:129. On the politics of Humboldt's portrait of slavery, see Vera Kutzinski and Ottmar Ette, "Inventories and Inventions: Alexander von Humboldt's Cuban Landscapes," in *Political Essay on the Island of Cuba,* by Alexander von Humboldt, ed. and trans. Kutzinski and Ette (Chicago: University of Chicago Press, 2010); also Christopher Iannini, *Fatal Revolutions: Natural History, West Indian Slavery, and the Routes of American Literature* (Chapel Hill and Colonial Williamsburg: University of North Carolina Press for the Omohundro Institute of Early American History and Culture, 2012), 281–89.

16. On the role that Humboldt's writings about New Spain may have played in the justification of annexations, see Walther Bernecker, "El mito de la riqueza Mexicana: Alejandro de Humboldt: del analista al propagandista," in *Alejandro de Humboldt: Una nueva visión del mundo,* ed. Frank Holl (Mexico City: UNAM, 2003), 95–101; Carlos Pereyra, *Humboldt en América* (Madrid: Editorial America), 193; and Martín Quirarte, *Historiografía sobre el segundo imperio de Maximiliano* (Mexico City: UNAM), 11–21.

17. See Andrea Wulf, *The Invention of Nature: Alexander von Humboldt's New World* (New York: Knopf, 2015), 88; also Vera Kutzinski, Otmar Ette, Laura Dassow Walls, eds, *Alexander von Humboldt and the Americas* (Berlin: Walter Frey, 2012); Ottmar Ette, *Alexander von Humboldt und die Globalisierung* (Frankfurt: Insel, 2009); Laura Dassow Walls, *The Passage to Cosmos: Alexander von Humboldt and the Shaping of America* (Chicago: University of Chicago Press, 2009); and Bettina Hey'l, *Das Ganze der Natur und die Differenzierung des Wissens: Alexander von Humboldt als Schriftsteller* (New York: Walter de Gruyter, 2007).
18. As Humboldt explains, the word "cosmos," which originally signified "ornament," in classical cosmography referred only to the clearly delimited "middle" region above the moon, where the stars circulate, whereas in modern times, the term came to designate the entire universe, which came to be conceptualized as boundless and to include also the innermost region, the *ouranos* (see Alexander von Humboldt, *Cosmos,* trans. E. C. Otté, 2 vols. [Baltimore: Johns Hopkins University Press, 1997], 1:69–70). On the transformation of Western conceptions of the physical world during the early nineteenth century, see Anne Marie Claire Godlewska, *Geography Unbound: French Geographic Science from Cassini to Humboldt* (Chicago: University of Chicago Press, 1999).
19. Alexander von Humboldt to David Friedländer, Madrid, April 11, 1799, in *Jugendbriefe Alexander von Humboldts,* ed. Ilse Jahn and Fritz G. Lange (Berlin: Akademie-Verlag, 1973), 657.
20. See Michael Dettelbach, "Global Physics and the Aesthetic Empire: Humboldt's Physical Portrait of the Tropics," in *Visions of Empire: Voyages, Botany, and Representations of Nature,* ed. David Philip Miller and Peter Hanns Reill, 258–92 (Cambridge: Cambridge University Press, 1996), 266.
21. See also Michael Dettelbach, "Describing the Nation: Local and Universal in Humboldt's Administrative Practice and in Late Eighteenth-Century Cameralism," in *Alexander von Humboldt and the Americas,* ed. Kutzinski, Ette, and Dassow Walls, 183–208. On the seventeenth-century precedents of this tradition (in particular Becher), see Pamela Smith, *The Business of Alchemy. Science and Culture in the Holy Roman Empire* (Princeton: Princeton University Press, 1994)
22. Alexander von Humboldt, *Versuche über die gereitzte Muskel- und Nervenfaser, nebst Vermutungen über den chemischen Process des Lebens in der Thier- und Pflanzenwelt* (Berlin: Rottmann, 1797), 1.
23. Ibid., 3–4.
24. For a list and description of the instruments the two men unloaded at Cumaná, see Humboldt, *Voyage,* 1:106–14. For an entertaining fictional account of Humboldt's preoccupation with measurement and instruments, see Daniel Kehlmann, *Measuring the World* (New York: Pantheon, 2006).
25. See Dettelbach, "Global Physics," 264.
26. Humboldt, *Voyage* 1:53–55.
27. Humboldt, *Cosmos,* 1:34.

28. Alexander von Humboldt, *Ansichten der Natur: Mit wissenschaftlichen Erläuterungen und seches Farbtafeln nach Skizzen des Autors* (Frankfurt: Eichborn, 2004), 172.
29. Humboldt, *Voyage* 2:32; my emphasis.
30. Ibid., 2:21.
31. See the introduction of this book.
32. Humboldt, *Voyage*, 2:22.
33. Humboldt, *Ansichten*, 161.
34. Ibid., 158.
35. Ibid., 160.
36. Ibid.
37. Ibid., 27.
38. Humboldt, *Voyage*, 3:19–20.
39. Ibid., 3:75.
40. Ibid.
41. Ibid.
42. See Gerbi, *Dispute*, 405–17; Brading, *First*, 514–34; and Cañizares-Esguerra, *How to Write*, 125–29.
43. See chapter 4 of this book; also Nicolás Wey-Gómez, *The Tropics of Empire: Why Columbus Sailed South to the Indies* (Cambridge: MIT Press, 2008), 64–69.
44. Humboldt, *Voyage*, 2:27
45. Ibid., 7:36.
46. Humboldt, *Cosmos*, 1:36.
47. Ibid., 1:42.
48. "Right-hand I turned, and, setting me to spy / That alien pole, beheld four stars, the same / The first men saw, and since, no living eye / Meseemed the heavens exulted in their flame / O widowed world beneath the northern Plough / For ever famished of the sight of them."
49. Humboldt, *Voyage*, 2:27.
50. See chapter 1 of this book.
51. Humboldt, *Voyage*, 2:27–28.
52. Humbodlt, *Ansichten*, 174.
53. Ibid.
54. Humboldt, *Voyage*, 2:298.
55. Ibid., 1:67.
56. Humboldt, *Cosmos*, 1:42. It should be noted here about the quote from Humboldt that the German original does not use the word "empire" (*Reich*) in this context. In turn, the English translation does not use the phrase "wissenschaftliche[r] Eroberer" (scientific conqueror), which Humboldt had earlier used in the German original, but "scientific observer" (compare *Kosmos: Entwurf einer physischen Weltbeschreibung*, 2 vols. [Stuttgart, 1845], 1:22; and *Cosmos*, 1:41). But the Baconian connection between knowledge, power, and conquest, explicitly referenced by Humboldt (*Cosmos*, 1:53), is clear.

57. Claude Lévi-Strauss, *Tristes tropiques,* trans. John Weightman and Doreen Weightman (1955; London: Jonathan Cape, 1973), 55.
58. On the notion of "purification" in modern science, and particular on Boyle's air pump, see Bruno Latour, *We Have Never Been Modern,* trans. Catherine Porter (Cambridge: Harvard University Press, 1993), 10–15; on "centers of calculation" and "immobile mobiles," see Latour, *Science in Action: How to Follow Scientists and Engineers through Society* (Milton Keynes: Open University Press, 1987), 215–57; on the notion of Humboldt as his own center of calculation, see Dettelbach, "Global Physics," 264.

Index

Abraham (patriarch), 110, 115, 198, 199, 235, 236, 456
Abraham, Lyndy, 16, 263
Abu Abdallah Muhammad XII, 108
Abu'l Hassan Ali ibn Ridwan Al-Misri, 93
Acapulco, 251
Accademia dei Lincei, 247
Ackerman Smoller, Laura, 160
Acosta, José de, 41, 149, 215, 251, 345, 360, 364, 365, 370, 386, 387, 422, 425, 428; *De natura Novi Orbis*, 255; *De promulgatione Evangelii apud Barbaros, sive De Procuranda*, 255, 262; as ethno-demonology, 422; *Historia natural y moral de las indias*, 253–64, 360, 364, 422, 428; as "old science," 371
Acts, book of, 169
Adam, 22, 29, 44, 52, 83, 90, 128, 163, 252, 276, 278, 419, 440, 451, 456, 457, 464
Adrian VI (pope), *Exponi nobis fecisti*, 211
Aeëtes (king of Colchis), 384
Ægidius Romanus (Giles of Rome), 301
Aeneas, 458, 505n34
Africa, 24, 106, 109, 175, 195, 196, 197, 198, 348, 350, 372, 407
Agamben, Giorgio, 19
Agricola, Georgius, *De re metallica*, 259
Agrippa von Nettesheim, Heinrich Cornelius, 70, 72, 187, 206, 416, 444, 445; *De incertitudine et vanitate scientiarum atque artium declamation Invective*, 463; *Three Books of Occult Philosophy*, 72
Aguilar, Jerónimo de, 233
Aguilar, Prodencio (in García Márquez's *Cien años de soledad*), 35
Aguirre, Lope de, 389
Ahab, 302
Akon, 170
Albertus Magnus, 13, 50, 79, 83, 179, 259, 324, 329, 351, 355, 372, 383, 481; *The Boke of Secretes*, 373; *De mineralibus et lapidibus*, 180; on homunculus, 332, 333, 335; on just war, 319; (Pseudo-Albertus) *Libellus de alchemia*, 333; on "natural slavery," 319; on spontaneous generation, 333

Albigensian Heresy, 50. *See also* Cathars
Albucasis (Abū al-Qāsim Khalaf ibn al-'Abbās al-Zahrāwī al-Ansari), 358
Albumazar (Abū Ma'shar), 90, 164–5; *De magnis coniunctionibus*, 164, 165, 166
Alcalá, Pedro de, *Vocabulista aravigo en letra castellana*, 214
Alcalá de Henares, University of, 54, 203, 211, 237, 253–54, 254, 291, 292, 346; Alcalá Polyglot Bible, 203
Alcántara, Pedro de, 212
alchemy, 13, 39, 40, 44, 45, 54, 61, 64, 65, 68, 69, 72, 74, 75–104, 105, 124–32, 138–39, 155, 167–83, 193, 206, 217, 219, 257, 259–62, 269, 289, 332, 333, 334–35, 337, 339, 340, 341, 350, 351, 352, 353, 354, 355, 358, 359, 360, 362, 370, 371, 374, 380, 382, 416, 430, 439, 443–44; *athanor*, 388; of conquest, 11, 25, 27, 38, 39, 485; *coniunctio*, 263, 264, 386–87; of conversion, 105–32, 378; and diabolism, 227, 416; epistemic violence of, 27, 40, 226, 262, 434, 472; and ethnography, 390; ethos, 447; Golden Fleece, 384; Golden King, 386, 388; in history of science, 71, 494n60; iconography, 339, 454; Marxian socio-economics of, 14–18, 216; mythoalchemy, 454; philosophical, 45; in Protestant early modern Europe, 73, 511n103; and pseudo-Llull, 124–32; and religion, 77–78, 513n16; spiritual, 75–77, 223; textual and philological alchemy, 449; theory of mixture, 64, 80, 94–95, 125, 126, 129, 223 (*see also* corpuscular theory of matter); in early modern Spain, 73, 510–11n102; and torture, 460; of translation, 371–78; of words, 207–9, 213–14, 217, 219, 228, 240–46; wedding, alchemical, 16, 41, 45, 77, 253, 258, 263–64, 351, 364, 381, 386, 454
Alciato, Andrea, 314; *Los emblemas*, 355
alcohol, 103–4. See also *aqua ardens*
Alexander III (pope), 200
Alexander VI (pope), 20, 21, 24, 26, 27, 41, 69, 74, 186, 192–95, 202, 207, 236, 295, 310, 331, 373, 378, 469; *Piis fidelium*, 209, 257. See also *Inter cetera*

Alexander the Great, 91, 153, 200, 201
Alexander, Amir, 403
Alexander Romance (*Historia Alexandri Magni*), 200
Alexandria, 65, 66, 70, 79, 193, 258, 272–73
Alexandrine bulls. See *Inter cetera*
Alfonsine Tables, 160, 163, 164
Alfonso VI, "the Brave" (king of León and Castile), 79
Alfonso X, "the Wise" (king of León, Castile, and Galicia), 79, 160
Algeria, 184
Al-Ghazali, Abu Hamid, 111
Algonquins, 401, 402, 409, 424
Al-Kindi (Abu Yūsuf Ya'qūb ibn 'Isḥāq aṣ-Ṣabbāḥ al-Kindī), 97, 160
Allen, Thomas, 401
Allin, John, 444
Al-Qabisi, (Abu al-Saqr Abd al-Aziz Ibn Uthman Ibn Ali al-Qabisi l-Mawsili al-Hashimi, aka Alchabitius), 164
Al-Razi, Abū Bakr Muhammad ibn Zakariyyā, 272, 355
Alsted, Johann Heinrich, 42
Altimirano, Fray Diego, 211
Amador de los Rios, José, 342
Amazon River, 374, 389
Amazons, 200, 384–85
American Jeremiad, 429
Americas, 6, 7, 8, 9, 10, 11, 12, 21, 22, 23, 24, 25, 26, 29, 40, 56, 109, 140, 149, 188, 194, 198, 203, 208, 213, 215, 218, 220, 221, 223, 228, 229, 230, 232, 237, 241, 242, 253, 254, 268, 269, 270, 274, 282, 290, 291, 292, 294, 296, 297, 346, 369, 371, 374, 378, 379, 380, 408, 412, 416, 432, 442, 469, 473, 474, 475, 477
Amerindians. See Native Americans
amity lines, 20
Ammon, 68
amplification, 85
Anahuac, 398, 399
Anaxagoras, 448
Andes, 215, 254, 259, 262, 370, 397–98
Andover, Mass., 427
Ángeles, Francisco de los (Francisco de Quiñones), 211–12, 236; "Obediencia," 236
Anglicus, Bartholomaeus; *De proprietatibus rerum,* 250
anonymous sailor, 185
Ansbach, 475
Antarctic, 251
Anthropocene, 7, 473, 488n16

anthropophagy. See cannibalism
Antichrist, 83, 85, 93, 98, 137, 138, 139, 150, 153, 154, 155, 162, 163, 164, 165, 166, 169–71, 179, 183, 257, 374, 423
Antichthones, 432
Antilles, 174, 210, 342
antimony, 371
Antipodes, 432
Aphrodite, 454
Apocalypse, of John. See John of Patmos; Pseudo-Methodius; Revelation
apocalypticism, 1, 2, 5, 29, 30, 39, 40, 54, 64, 77–104, 137, 139, 167–83, 222, 440, 483
Apollonius of Tyana, 383; *Argonautica,* 383–84
Apollo, 453–54
Apuleius, 66, 383
Aqua ardens, 103
Arabia, 148
Arabic, 12, 50, 271–72, 332
Arabs, 448
Aragon, Crown of, 98, 107, 168, 170, 171, 191, 192, 202, 267
Arcanum, 59
archetypes, 76
Argentum vivum, 100
Argonauts, 183, 370, 384
Argus, 65
Aristotle, 13, 14, 43, 49–50, 51, 81, 87, 90, 93, 100, 161, 162, 166, 179, 195, 200, 297, 313, 326, 345–46, 355, 445, 446, 448, 451; *De anima,* 315, 317, 332, 345–46; *De animalibus,* 195, 332; *De Caelo,* 261; *Eudemian Ethics,* 161; and just war, 316; *Metaphysics,* 50, 56, 318; *Meteorology,* 81, 100, 261; and "natural slavery," 315–24; *Nicomachean Ethics,* 299; *Organon,* 50; *The Parts of Animals,* 332; *Physics,* 80, 261; *Politics,* 54, 290, 306, 307, 314, 329; *Posterior Analytics,* 50; *Prior Analytics,* 50; and science, 50, 56, 318; *Topics,* 50, 55, 245
Aristotelianism, 11, 12, 13, 16, 19, 22, 26, 28, 29, 39, 43, 50–56, 57, 63, 64, 68, 71–72, 76, 79–80, 91, 95, 101, 106–7, 126, 201, 216, 217, 218, 222, 258, 267, 290, 292, 361, 430, 441, 448, 449–50, 457; *episteme, praxis, techne,* 357–58; (Scholastic) matter theory, 80, 261, 362. *See also* hylomorphism
Armenia, 106
Arnald of Villanova, and pseudo-Arnaldus, 13, 15–16, 40, 74, 84, 88, 105, 122, 125, 127, 130, 131, 138, 169–72, 179, 180, 182, 186, 196, 202,

210, 239, 264, 267, 353, 355; *De conservanda iuventute et retardanda senectute*, 97, 171; *De cymbalis ecclesiae*, 169; *Flos florum*, 99; *De humido radicali*, 97; *De tempore adventus Antichristi*, 169; *Novum lumen*, 99; *Rosarius philosophorum*, 15–16, 96–102, 125, 179, 264; *Speculum alchemiae*, 99; *Tractatus de mysterio cymbalorum*, 138, 171; *Tractatus parabolicus*, 99; homúnculos, 293, 332, 333
Artephius, 93
Arthur (king), 380
Asclepius, 65–66. See also *Corpus Hermeticum*
Asclepius, 68, 90
Ashley, Anthony, 409
Ashmole, Elias, 70, 187
Asia, 9, 106, 140, 144, 153, 162, 181, 182, 200, 201, 270, 278, 316, 337, 379, 384, 408, 432, 481
Assmann, Aleida, 59; *Geheimnis und Schleier*, 59
Assmann, Jan, 59; *Geheimnis und Schleier*, 59
astrology, 65, 68, 69, 95–96, 102, 103, 117, 126, 155, 156–67, 169, 173, 180, 193, 383, 422, 447
astronomy, 159–60, 167, 173, 373, 422, 483
Atabalipa. See Atahualpa Inca
Atahualpa Inca, 393, 395
Atalanta, 453–54
atheism, 277, 284, 335, 404, 417, 452
Athenaeus of Naucratis, 17
Athens, 130, 326
Atilius Regulus, Marcus, 285
Atlantic Ocean, 20, 22, 144, 185, 187, 195, 209, 345, 348, 379, 380, 428, 430, 438, 479, 438. See also Ocean Sea
Atlantis, 380, 433, 439
atomic bomb, 28, 267
atoms, atomism, and atomic theory, 28, 43, 44, 45, 64, 67, 77, 80, 126, 267, 268, 269, 281, 284, 326, 370, 404, 448–49, 452. See also materialism
Augustine of Hippo, 18, 28, 49, 50, 51, 62, 63, 66–67, 77, 90, 146, 161, 221, 268, 279, 280, 319, 326, 327, 373, 451; *The City of God*, 66, 90, 107, 151–52, 250, 275–76; *Confessions*, 18, 62; *De catechizandis rudibus*, 151; *De doctrina christiana*, 63, 75, 219, 250
Augustinianism, 18, 22, 39, 62, 77, 98, 111, 137, 216, 483; and just war theory, 314
Augustinians (Order), 108, 212
Aurillac (Franciscan convent), 102
Ausonio Ettore, 130–31
Australia, 5

Austria, 474, 475
autopsy and autoptic imagination, 215, 245, 568n143, 572n195
Auwera, Johann van den, 211
Averroës (Ibn Rushd), 51, 81, 355, 358; Averroism, 51, 121, 186, 198, 302
Avicenna (Ibn Sina, aka Abu Ali Sina, Pur Sina), 81, 90, 93, 97, 227, 348, 355, 358
Azores, 174, 194, 350, 379
Aztecs. See Mexica; Nahua

Babylon, 170
Bacon, Francis, 2–3, 5, 11, 33, 35, 45, 55–56, 60, 71, 88, 255, 268, 430–70; *The Advancement of Learning*, 435, 450, 452, 459, 474–75, 479, 482, 483; *An Advertisement Touching an Holy War*, 442, 466; and alchemy, 443–58; "Atalanta: or Profit," 453; "Certain Considerations touching the Plantation in Ireland," 468; *Description of the Intellectual Globe*, 459; and dominion, 462–70; and epistemic cannibalism, 446–51; *Gesta Grayorum*, 462; *Instauratio magna (The Great Instauration)*, 2–3, 45, 430, 437, 448, 474; and law, 458–62; "The Masculine Birth of Time," 462; *Maximes of the Common Law and the Elements of the Common Law*, 460; and mummies, 274, 446; *The Natural and Experimental History of the Foundation of Philosophy*, 462; *New Atlantis*, 288, 433, 434–51, 453, 458, 461–62; *New Organon*, 430, 448, 460, 462, 464; "Observations on a Libel," 461; and Oedipal complex, 447; *Of the Interpretation of Nature*, 430–31, 439, 451, 457; "Of the True Greatness of Kingdoms and Estates," 438; *Sylva sylvarum*, 445, 474; *The Wisdom of the Ancients*, 452–55, 463
Baconianism, 19, 34, 39, 42, 55–56, 439
Bacon, Roger, 40, 51, 78, 79, 84, 87–96, 98, 102, 104, 105, 125, 127 131, 139, 143, 165, 166, 167, 178, 179, 195, 201, 214, 226, 267, 340, 371, 374, 379, 401, 444, 459; *De retardatione accidentium senectutis*, 88; *Epistola de secretis operibus artis et naturae*, 88; *Opus maius*, 88, 89–90, 164, 166, 167, 201; *Opus minus*, 88, 94; *Opus tertium*, 88, 89, 95
Badiano, Juan, 247
Badianus manuscript, 61, 247
Báez Rubí, Linda, 190, 207, 214, 243
Baghdad, 165, 166
Bairo, Pietro, *Secreti medicinali*, 383

Bakhtin, Mikhail, 282, 619n8
Baldung, Hans, 414
Balearic Islands, 107, 170
balsam, 199, 273. *See also* quintessence
barbarism, 256
Barcelona, 105, 168, 191, 194, 202, 210, 341
baroque, 65, 71, 72
Barrera, Antonio, 256, 360
Bartholomew, Saint, 441, 442
Basel, 372
Basque country, 226
Bataillon, Marcel, 136
Batllori, Miguel, 24, 191
Baudot, George, 222, 225–26
Bazaluk, Oleg, 326, 327
Becher, Johann Joachim, 18, 474
Bede, 151, 153
Beheim, Martin, 209
Beltrán, Gonzalo Aguirre, 348
Bembo, Pietro, 342
Benalcázar, Sebastián, 389
Benevento, 195
Bensalem, 43–36, 434, 435, 436, 438, 453
Bentancor, Orlando, *The Matter of Empire*, 217, 257, 258, 262, 309
Benzoni, Girolamo, *Historia del Mondo Nuovo*, 420
Bergerac, Cyrano de, *States and Empires of the Moon*, 288
Berlin, 474
Bernáldez, Andrés, 172
Berrío, Antonio de, 382, 392, 394
Berthollet, Claude, 475
Beuchot, Mauricio, 214
Bayreuth, 475
bezoar stone, 354
bibles: Alcalá Polyglot Bible, 203; Geneva Bible, 465; King James Bible, 464, 465, 466, 467; Vulgate Bible, 465
Biblioteca Capitular y Colombina, 137, 140, 156, 162, 186
Biel, Gabriel, 54, 304, 312
Biggs, Noah, 2, 4, 469
Billingsley, Sir Henry, 380
Biringuccio, Vannoccio, *De la pirotechnia*, 371, 374
black bile, 161
Black Death, 54
Black Legend, 7, 34, 44, 370, 392, 419
black sun. See *sol niger*
blood: of Christ, 351; as "complexion," 94; medicine, 95, 195, 271, 276, 444; menstrual, and reproduction, 332, 334; purity, 37; and quintessence, 95, 103, 129, 195, 273. *See also* dragon's blood
Blumenberg, Hans, 62; *The Legitimacy of the Modern Age*, 62–63
Bobadilla, Francisco de, 210
boca del drago, 484
Bodenstein, Adam von, 379
Bogotá, 35, 37, 389
Bohemia, 438
Bolaños, Luis de, 238
Bolivia, 398
Bolívar, Simón, 473
Bologna, 191, 192
Bolton, Herbert Eugene, 9
Bonaventura of Iseo, 84
Bonaventure (Giovanni di Fidanza), 51, 106, 121, 227, 302, 332
Bonfil, Robert, 71
Bonfire of the Vanities, 277
Boniface VIII (pope), 74, 98, 169, 196; *Unam Sanctam*, 196
Bonpland, Aimé, 474, 474
Book of the Cow, 332
Boorstin, Daniel, 7, 9, 10
Borgia, Alfonso de (Pope Calixtus III), 193; *Inter cetera*, 196, 198, 201
Borgia, Cesare de, 192, 193
Borgia, Pedro Luis de, 193
Borgia, Rodrigo de. See Alexander VI (pope)
Bosch, Hieronymous, *The Garden of Earthly Delights*, 351
Bosporus, 168
Botticelli, Sandro, *Primavera*, 413
Bovelles, Charles de, 187, 204–5, *Epistola in vitam Raymundi Lulli*, 204
Boyarin, Jonathan, 217
Boyl, Bernardo, 209, 210, 553n102
Boyle, Robert, 17, 31–32, 33, 56, 80, 187, 274, 337, 485
Brandt, Sebastian, 153; *A Ship of Fools*, 153
Brannigan, Augustine, 8
Brazil, 270, 272, 276, 278, 282–84, 404, 419
Brendan the Navigator, 109. *See also* St. Brendan's Island
Brendecke, Arndt, 360
British Empire, 380–81
Browne, Richard, 88
Browne, Walden, 240, 250
Bruni, Leonardo, 311, 322
Bruno, Giordano, 70, 186, 206, 404, 413

Buendía, José Arcadio (in García Márquez's *Cien años de soledad*), 1–2, 34–35, 166
Bugia, 184
Burgos, 357
Burkhart, Louise, 228
Bustamente García, Jesús, 248, 250

Cabot, John, 378
Cabot, Sebastian, 374
Cádiz, 187
Cadolzburg, 85
Caduceus, 221, 351
Cajetan, Thomas, 295
Calicut, 372
Calixtus II (pope), 199
Calmecac, 246
calorimetry, 475
Calvin, John, 301; Calvinism, 45, 286, 288; *Institutes of the Christian Religion*, 304
Cambridge, 379
cameralism, 65, 72, 73, 474, 475
Campanella, Tomasso, *City of of Sun*, 288
Canaanites, 423
Canada, 5
Canary Islands, 173, 208, 251, 345, 350
Cañizares-Esguerra, Jorge, 256
cannibalism, 43, 269, 270–71, 275, 276, 278, 279–86, 290, 466, 471: alchemical, 95; cannibal heterotopias, 43, 67, 267, 269, 404; cannibal metaphysics, 43, 270, 275, 281–89, 404; cannibal science, 443–51; cannibal ventriloquism, 43, 228, 326; epistemic, 450; medicinal, 43, 271–72, 332, 444
Cano, Melchor, 218, 332
canon law, 22, 23, 25–26, 124, 196
Capaccio, 195
Cape Bojador, 196, 198
Cape Nam, 196
Cape Verde, 438
Capitulations of Santa Fe, 144, 187
Carabuco, Cross of, 442
Caracas, 475
Cardano, Girolamo, 58, 375; *De secretis*, 58; *De subtilitate libri XXI*, 376
Cárdenas, Juan de, 43, 339, 360, 361–65: alchemical theory of matter, 362–63; *Primera parte de los problemas y secretos maravillosos de las Indias*, 340, 361–65
Caribbean, 29, 34, 156, 211, 294, 375, 379, 475
Carlos II (king of Spain), 188
Carlos, Don, lord of Texcoco, 225
Carnicer, Pere, 354

Caroní River, 382
Carpini, Giovanni, 108; *History of the Mongols*, 200–201
Carro, Venancio Diego, 335
Cartagena (New Granada), 337, 350
Cartagena (Spain), 193
Casa de Contratación (House of Trade), 13, 345, 356, 360, 437
Casas, Bartolomé de las, 43, *Historia de las indias*, 171, 173, 180, 224
Casas, Christoval de las, *Vocabulario de las dos lenguas, Toscana y Castellana*, 355
Casaubon, Isaac, *De rebus sacris et ecclesiasticis exercitationes XVI*, 70
Caselles, Guillermo, 191
Castanega, Friar Martín de, *Tratado de las supersticiones y hechizerias*, 226
Castell, William, 337
Castile, 191, 210, 291
Castilla de Oro, 375
Castro, Bartolomé, 54
Catalonia, 170, 191
Cathars, 51, 108, 109. See also Albigensian Heresy
Cathay, 143, 201
Catherine of Aragon, 379
Catholic monarchs, 22, 24, 135, 136, 139, 140, 144, 145, 148, 160, 168, 171, 172, 184, 187, 191, 192, 194, 195, 300, 341, 432. See also Ferdinand (king of Aragon); Isabella (queen of Castile)
Catholicism, 6, 20, 29, 34, 42, 44, 438; Catholic Church, 54; Catholic cruelties, 419 (*see also* Black Legend); Catholic faith, 184, 188, 198, 211, 252; Catholic Liberation Theology, 292
Cavendish, Thomas, 408
Caxton, William, 112
Cecil, Sir William, 371, 390
Certeau, Michel de, 59
Cervantes, Fernando, 224–25, 226, 256
Chalcedon, Council of, 111
Chaldeans, 165
Chanca, Diego Álvarez, *Comentum novum in parabolis divi Arnaldi de Villanova*, 171
Chancas, 396
chaos, 33, 129–30, 345
Chaplin, Joyce, 403
Charles V (Holy Roman emperor), Charles I (king of Spain), 21, 24, 60, 211, 229, 238, 290, 299, 300, 311, 327, 341, 342, 375, 384; claim to universal empire, 310

Chaves, Jerónimo de, *Chronographia; o, reportorio de los tiempos*, 355, 437
chemistry, 64, 76, 475
Chennai, 201
Chesne, Josephe du, *De ortu metallorum*, 383
Chichimecs, 256
Chile, 342
Chimborazo, 476
China, 79, 108, 143, 145, 200–201, 371, 372, 373; Chinese, 256
chivalry, 40, 105, 106, 112–13
Cholula, 60
Christianity, 19, 63, 66, 70, 84, 99, 104, 105, 108, 110, 114, 117, 121, 139, 144, 153, 154, 163, 193, 196, 199, 209, 210, 218, 230, 253. *See also* Jesus Christ
Chronicles (Old Testament), 148
Chrysopoeia, 79, 96, 178, 446, 447
Cieza de León, Pedro, *Crónica del Perú*, 394
Cicero, Marcus Tullius, 50, 62, 65, 66, 205, 279, 323, 451; *De divinatione*, 161, *De inventione*, 240–41; and just war theory, 314, 327; *On Duties*, 327; pseudo-Cicero, *Ad herennium*, 241
Cinnabar, 350–51
cinnamon, 343, 354, 389
Cipango, 143
Circle of Knowledge, 430
circulation: in economics, 14, 15; *opus circulatorium*, in alchemy, 16
Clapión, Juan, 211–12, 236
Clark, Stuart, 245, 414, 422
Clavis universalis, 70
Clement, 49
Clement IV (pope), 87
Clement V (pope), *In superne preeminentia*, 196, 198
Clusius, Carolus, 337; *Rariorum aliquot stirpium per Hispanias observatarum historiae*, 350
coca, 354
cochineal, 348
Cochlaeus, Johann, 432
cocoa bean, 361
Coke, Sir Edward, 461
Colchis, 384
Colell, Antonio, 209
collective unconscious, 76
Colombia, 34, 35, 342, 475
Colón, Diego, 172
Colón, Hernando, 136, 140, 156, 157, 166–67, 172, 186; *The History of the Life and Deeds of the Admiral Don Christopher Columbus* 552–53n107
Colonna, Fabio, 247
Columbus, Christopher, 7, 8, 9, 10, 14, 20, 33, 40, 135–83, 184, 193, 201, 209, 210, 232, 278–79, 308, 339, 341, 342, 343, 370, 372, 373, 374, 378, 383, 403, 420, 430, 432, 433, 474, 477, 481, 483, 484; and alchemico-apocalyptic prophecy, 167–83; alchemy, 177–83; astrology/astronomy, 156–67; *Book of Prophecies*, 139–55, 156, 158–64, 167, 168, 172, 182; as Christ Bearer, 140–42, 158, 180, 187, 270; and cosmology, 174–75; *Diario*, 145, 157, 181; and Franciscans, 172–73; Letter from Jamaica, 135–38, 140, 141, 148, 167
Columbus, Stephen, 184, 185
Comenius, Jan, 42
compounds, 223
Conciliarism, 53, 302
Concupiscentia oculorum (lust of the eyes), 18
Condamine, Charles Marie de La, 476
Conill, Jaume, 192, 202
Coniunctio, 263, 264, 386–87
Connecticut, 70
conjunctions, 90
conquest, of America, 11, 32, 41, 42, 44, 54, 78, 199, 224, 229, 231, 232, 252, 257, 269, 327, 329, 432, 434, 462, 466; cant of (English) conquest, 370, 401, 425 (*see also* White Legend); of nature, 11, 55, 60, 269, 432, 434, 439, 484 (*see also venatio*); reformed conquest, 439; Spanish conquest, 370, 387, 419–20, 439, 462 (*see also* Black Legend); spiritual conquest, 41, 107 132, 212, 223, 234, 386, 554–55n1
Consejo de las Indias, 13, 238, 290, 291, 353, 348, 360, 438
Constance, Council of, 163, 301
Constantine I, Donation of, 23, 24, 25, 65, 216
Constantinople, 65, 154, 168, 195, 204. *See also* Istanbul
consubstantiation, 284
Conventuals (Franciscan Order), 212
conversion, 16, 18, 26, 29, 78, 81, 83, 102, 105, 107, 108, 109, 115, 116, 117–21, 123, 124, 131, 137, 139, 151, 185, 187, 188, 193, 197, 198, 199, 201, 204, 207, 208, 210, 211, 212, 213, 214, 219; *conversio*, 216, 217; hermeneutics of, 215–18, 226
convertibility, 14, 216–17
copal, 354
Córdoba, 172

Cordova, Fernando de, 192
Coronel, Antonio, 54
corpse medicine, 95, 269, 271, 275. *See also* mummies
corpuscular theory of matter, 43, 45, 78, 223, 227, 261, 362, 370, 403, 448
Corpus Hermeticum, 65, 70, 204
Corsali, Andrea, 374
Cortés, Hernando, 7, 60, 211, 251, 327, 329, 359, 389, 393; Letters to the Emperor, 211, 212, 403; as a Moses, 232–33; Second Letter, 398
Cortés, Martín, *Breve compendio la sphera y de la arte de navegar*, 373
Cortés Ramírez de Arellano, Juana, 359
Cosa, Juan de la, *Mappa Mundi*, 140
Cosín, Juan de, 210
cosmography, 159, 372–74, 432
cosmology, 9, 166, 177, 373, 391, 475, 481, 482
Costa Lima, Luiz, 56; *Control of the Imaginary*, 56
Cotton, John, 423, "God's Promise to His Plantations," 423
Council of Castile, 291
Council of the Indies. See *Consejo de las Indias*
Counter-Reformation, 38, 70, 224, 241, 254, 494
Cranston, David, 313
Cremer, Abbot, *Testamentum Cremeri*, 130
Creoles, 35, 44, 242, 361
Crockert, Pierre, 306
Crolius, Oswald, 272
Crombergers, 342
Croton lechleri, 349
crucible, 77, 81, 84–85; of the tropics, 339, 477
crucifixion, 77
crusades, 13, 39, 75, 78–104, 107, 124, 131, 140, 168, 182, 193
Cruz, Anne, 241
Cruz de la, Martín, *Libellus de medicinalibus indorum herbis* (Badianus manuscript), 247, 339
Cuauhtémoc, 212, 246
Cuba, 156, 211
Culpepper, Nicholas, 337, 444
Cumaná, 475, 478
Cummins, Tom, 238–39
Cunningham, Andrew, 78
Cupid, 452
curiosity, 18, 39, 40, 61–63, 67, 68, 77, 147, 167, 222, 251, 278, 279, 344, 384, 389–90, 434, 482, 483, 484, 505n55; curiosities, 428; in relation to the marvel and the secret, 72; theoretical curiosity, 62, 72, 74, 339. *See also* just curiosity; vain curiosity
Cusco, 254, 369, 383, 393, 395, 396
Cyprus, 198

Daedalus, 452
D'Ailly, Pierre de, 53, 143, 162–66, 167, 186, 232; *Apologetica defensio astronomice veritatis*, 162; *Secunda apologetic defensio astronomice veritatis*, 162; *Elucidarium astronomice concordie cum tehologia et hystorica veritate*, 162, 166; *Imago mundi*, 162–65, 167–68; and nominalism, 302–4; *Questio de legitimo dominio*, 303; *Tractatus de Concordia astronomice veritatis cum theologia*, 162; *Tractatus de Concordia astronomice veritatis et narrationis hystorice*, 162, 163, 168; *Tractatus de Concordia discordantium astronoorum*, 162 *Tractatus de legibus et sectis contra supersticiosos astronomos*, 162, 165, 166
Daguí, Pedro, 191; *Formalitates breves in artem Raimundi Lulli*, 192; *Ianua artis magistri Raymundi Lull*, 191, 192, 205; *Tractatus de differentia*, 192
Daniel (book of), 82, 150, 169, 173, 430, 432
Dannenfeldt, Karl, 271
Dante Alighieri (Durante di Alighiero degli Alighieri), 62; *Divine Comedy*, 62, 175, 176; *Inferno* 279; *Purgatory*, 483
Darabjerd, 271
Darien, 211
Darius (king of Persia), 91
Darwin, Charles, 472
David (king of Israel and Judah), 128, 135, 136, 148, 170, 302
De Bry, Theodor de, 45, 286–87, 404, 408–9, 425, 454–55; *The Coniuerer*, 410–11; family and printing business, 45, 408, 454; Great Voyages, 408–22; *Procession at the Obsequies of Sir Philip Sidney*, 409; *Procession of the Knights of the Garter*, 409; Small Voyages, 408
De Bry, Theodor Johann, 417, 454
Decknamen, 75, 77
Dee, John, 45, 70, 73, 187, 370, 378–81, 382, 383, 385, 388, 392, 402, 413, 417, 438; "A brief Remembraunce of Sondrye foreyne Regions," 380; and British Empire, 380–81; Euclid's *Elements*, 380; *General and Rare Memorials Pertayning to the Perfecte Arte of*

Dee, John (*continued*)
   Navigation, 380; *The Limits of the British Empire*, 380; *Monas hieroglyphica*, 380; "Of Famous and Rich Discoveries," 380
De essentiis essentiarum (Pseudo Aquinas), 259, 332
degeneration, 481
Dekkers, Johan (Tecto, Juan de), 211
Delphi, 160
Del Valle, Ivonne, 256
Democritus, 28, 43, 44, 80, 274, 289, 290, 325–26, 403, 448
demonstration, 31, 50, 55, 114, 121, 143, 145, 146, 228, 250, 251, 357, 466
Descalced Movement, 212
Descós, Arnaldo, 209
Dettelbach, Michael, 73, 474
Deule, Juan de la, 210
Deuteronomy, 328
Devil, 72, 131, 147, 221, 223, 224, 225, 227, 230, 233, 234, 235, 237, 242, 243, 252, 263, 293, 333, 334, 335, 338, 359, 377, 395, 415, 416, 417, 422, 423, 425, 426, 427, 428, 429, 484. *See also* Satan
diabolism, 10, 44, 67, 219, 221, 222, 227, 235, 252, 263, 288, 293, 331, 338, 412, 414, 415, 417, 422, 425. *See also* Devil; Satan
Díaz Hernando, 354
Díaz Balsera, Viviana, 229
Díaz del Castillo, Bernal de, 212
Diego, Juan, 248
digestion, 449–51
Diocletian, 153
Dioscorides, Pedanius, 346, 348, 355; *De materia medica*, 350
Discovery, Age of, 7, 17, 19, 25, 28, 104, 136–38, 186, 274, 430–33; doctrine (rights) of in international law, 6, 12, 21, 24, 30, 54, 296, 308, 473, 484, 487n10; "effective" discovery (occupation), 21, 380, 399, 425; hermeneutics of, 8, 25, 49–50, 54, 58, 145–47, 166, 167, 245, 433, 451, 481, 484, 501n1, 502n22; idea that America was discovered, 10, 11, 19–20, 34, 40, 49–50, 57, 59, 61, 144, 185, 267, 388–400, 472, 448n17; literature and narratives of, 11, 491n31; Northwest passage, 379, 380; paradigm and problem of, in philosophy and history of science, 5, 9, 11, 19, 27, 55–56, 482, 336, 433–32, 473, 490n27, 502n20; shock of, 12, 149, 492n38; and torture, 458–62; voyages of, 372; White Legend of English discovery of America, 370

Divine Dignities (Divine Attributes), 118–21, 126, 197, 207
Doctrina omni-insular, 22, 188, 196, 301
Doctrinas, 27, 41, 188, 198, 215, 238. *See also* Praying Towns; reduction
Dodona, 160
Dominic, Saint, 109
Dominicans, 28, 43, 50, 54, 98, 109, 111, 189–90, 211, 212, 215, 220, 224–35, 235, 294, 325; hermeneutics of conversion, 188, 201, 217, 238; and matter theory, 227–38; and rights of conquest, 295
Dominion (*dominium*): and Francis Bacon, 462–70; biblical mandate to man, 439, 464–65; legal theory of, 22, 29, 44, 465; and Francisco de Vitoria, 296–304
Doña Marina, 233
Donne, John, 187, 213, 469
Dorn, Gerhard, 72, 379
Dougal Fleming, James, 8, 58
Douglass, Gavin, 313–14
dragon fruit. *See pitaya*
dragons, 77, 337, 349, 385–86
dragon's blood (*sanguis draconis*), 44, 337, 350–51
dragon tree (*Dracaena cinnabari, Dracaena draco*), 350; iconography, 351–53, 596n41
Dragon Wonder (Pseudo-Matthew), 351
Drake, Francis, 34–35, 379, 408
Drayton, Richard, 349
Dudley, John, 372, 374
Duns Scotus, John, 51, 53, 224, 225, 304; Scotism, 189, 191–92, 202, 218
Durán, Diego, *Historia de las Indias de Nueva Espana*, 255
Dürer, Albrecht, 351

Eamon, William, 34, 60, 463
earth eating, 479–80
Earthly Paradise, 40, 151, 174, 175, 176, 177, 179, 252, 432, 483, 484
East India Company, 31
ecstasy, 138
ecstatic materialism, 40, 135, 138, 173, 374
Ecuador, 475
Eden, 178, 351
Eden, Richard, 33, 44, 343, 360, 370, 371–78; *The Arte of Nauigation*, 373; *The Decades of the New World*, 373; *A treatyse of the newe India*, 372
Edward VI (king of England), 37, 378
Egypt and Egyptians, 65, 66, 135, 154, 165, 170, 193, 231, 272, 442, 556; flight into Egypt, 351

Egyptian gold, 40, 231
El Dorado, 35–36, 44, 369, 381, 382, 383–84, 388, 391–95
Eliade, Mircea, *Forgerons et Alchimistes,* 75, 76
Elias of Cortona (Franciscan friar), 83
Elijah (Prophet), 128
Eliot, John, 423
elixir, 79, 95 99, 125, 130, 178. *See also* fifth element
Elizabeth I (queen of England), 369, 379, 380–81, 390, 413, 437, 460; as Virgin Queen, 392–93
Ellis, George Edward, 25
Empedocles, 448
empiricism, 19, 41, 64, 71, 88, 222, 226, 269, 439, 473
encomienda, 293, 293–94, 295, 325
encyclopedism, 41, 42, 111, 112, 119, 123, 205–8, 249–50, 255
England, 70, 125, 131, 373, 374
Enoch, 90
Enriquez de Ribera, Fernando (duke of Alcalá de los Gazules), 359
Ephesus, Council of, 111, 152
epicureanism, 12, 64, 65, 67, 205, 267–68, 276–82, 443, 449, 451–58, 482; Epicurus, 65, 68, 277, 279, 290, 403, 483
epilepsy, 271
epistemic mercantilism, 435
equal complexion, 93–94
equator, 174, 179, 251, 252, 375
equinoctial line. *See* equator
Erasmus, Desiderius Roterodamus, 203, 205, 302
Eremeticism, 117, 202, 216
Escalante, Bernadino de, *Discurso de la navegación que los portugueses hazen à los reinos y provincias del Oriente,* 355
Escalona, Alonso de, 353
eschatology, 62, 82, 98, 136, 138, 140, 142, 150–55, 159, 204
Escorial, San Lorenzo de el, 13, 73, 354, 438
Escorzonera, 354
Escribano, Alonso, 354
Escuela Luliana, 191
esotericism, 58, 71
Espanyol, Esperandéu, 192
Espinar, Alonso de, 211
Estudio General Luliano, 191
Ethiopia, 175
ethnocide, 254. *See also* genocide
ethno-demonology, 41, 45, 213, 215, 223, 226, 242, 248, 339, 370, 377, 406–29

ethnography, 210, 215, 223, 226, 242, 247, 253, 254, 279, 282, 370, 384, 390–91, 406–29
Eucharist, 43, 76, 270–71, 284, 447, 459
Euclid, *Elements,* 380
eudiometry, 475
Euphrates, 176
Eusebius, 151, 153
evangelism, 27, 40, 41, 42, 105, 106, 110, 111, 112, 113, 114, 115, 117, 130, 131, 141, 147, 178, 187, 188, 189, 202, 204, 207, 208, 209, 213, 214, 215, 216, 217, 220, 221, 223, 224, 228, 229, 235, 236, 238, 239, 251, 254, 254, 255, 258, 264, 296, 297, 304, 339, 351, 442
Eve, 440
exceptionalism, New World, 8, 19–28, 45, 422–29, 440, 478, 481. *See also* State of Exception
Exodus, book of, 231, 423
experimental science, 39, 40, 79, 88–96, 99, 104, 167, 214, 340, 349, 373, 379, 382, 338, 404, 405, 430, 432, 434, 435, 438, 443, 445–46, 453, 458, 475
Eymerich, Nicholas, 189; *Conservationi puritatis,* 189, 191
Ezion-Gebir, 371

Faivre, Antoine, 183
Fall, the (biblical), 29, 52, 126, 181, 269, 439, 458, 464. *See also* Original Sin
Federmann, Nikolaus, 389
Ferae bestiae, 296, 307, 308, 309, 467. *See also* Justitian I
Ferdinand IV (duke of Palatine), 419
Ferdinand (king of Aragon), 24, 26, 136, 137, 168, 171, 191, 192–93, 202, 209, 210, 294, 311, 462
Fernandes, Florestan, 285
Fernández, Rodolfo, 214
Fernández de Madrigal, Alonso (El Tostado), *Beati Alphonsi Thostati Episcopi Abulensis,* 333; *De malefic mulieribus, que vulgariter dicuntur bruxas,* 333
Fernández de Navarrete y Ximénez de Tejada, Martin, 172
Fernández de Oviedo y Valdés, Gonzalo, 44, 45, 185, 256, 339, 340, 341–46, 374–77; *Historia general delas Indias,* 342, 344; as "old science," 371; *Oviedo de la natural hystoria de las Indias (Sumario),* 341, 342, 343–45, 373
Fernando III (king of Castile), 359

Ferrari da Grado, Giamatteo, *De secretis naturae*, 202
Ficino, Marsilio, 65, 203, 277, 410, 416, 423, 444; *Corpus Hermeticum (Poimandres)*, 65, 68; *Platonic Theology*, 68, 69, 70, 186, 277
fifth element ("quintessence," *quinta essentia*), 16, 86, 94, 85, 96–104, 125, 126, 128, 129, 177, 178, 371, 449; and blood, 95, 103, 129, 195, 273; and corpse medicine, 272–74
First Twelve (Franciscans), 212, 222, 224, 228
Fitzmaurice, Andrew, 307–8
Fitzralph, William, 22, 301, 304, 465
Fixcion, 176
Flint, Valerie, 136
Flora, 178
Florence, 65, 277
Florenze, 210
Florida, la, 211, 252, 419
Flower of Michoacán, 354
Fludd, Robert, 70, 274, 383, 417, 444, 455
Focher, Fray Juan de, *Itinerarium Catholicum*, 237, 239
Fool for God (literary trope), 72, 111, 128, 139, 167
Foucault, Michel, 28–29, 440–41. *See also* heterotopia
foundry, 371
Fountain of Youth, 181
four elements, 64
Fourth Lateran Council, 107
Frampton, John, 402; *The ioyfull newes from the West Indies*, 402
France, 173, 196, 282, 284, 374, 419, 474
Francis, Saint (Francis of Assisi), 30, 83, 105, 108, 109, 121
Franciscans, 23, 29–30, 40, 41, 42, 51, 52, 54, 77–78, 105–9, 111, 131, 139, 155, 172–73, 175, 186, 189, 191, 198, 200–201, 206, 208–12, 213–15, 219, 224, 250, 274; and alchemy, 84–104, 124–32, 226–28; art and nature, 227, 333; and diabolism, 224–25, 429; hermeneutics of conversion, 226–30; historiography of, 255–56; and iconoclasm, 225; and linguistics, 239; and matter theory, 227–28; and messianic interpretation of history, 232–34, 329; and militancy, 223–25, 561n50, 562n57; and missionary ethnography, 221–22, 225–26; and natural history, 339; and nominalism, 30, 53–54, 131, 132, 224, 250, 263, 561n47; and poverty, 109, 212–16, 230–31
Franconia, 475

Frankfurt, 274, 286, 408, 409, 415
Franklin-Brown, Mary, 250–51
Freiburg, University of, 475
French, Roger, 78
Freud, Sigmund, 271
Frisch, Andrea, 287
Frobisher, Martin, 379
Frost, Cecelia, 226

Gadamer, Hans Georg, 56; *Truth and Method*, 56
Galata Tower, 168
Galen (Aelius Galenus), 93, 94, 97, 346, 347, 348, 355, 361, 445, 447
Galilei, Galileo, 55, 247
Galway, 140
Gandia (Duchy of), 193
Gans, Joachim, 401
Gante, Pedro de (Peter of Ghent), 211, 242
García de Céspedes, Andrés, *Regimiento de nauegación* 2, 4, 437
García d'Orta, *Colóquios dos simples e drogas he cousas medicinais da India*, 355–56
García Márquez, Gabriel, *Cien anos de soledad (One Hundred Years of Solitude)*, 1–2, 5, 15, 33, 34, 45, 166, 201, 471, 472, 473, 479; "The Solitude of Latin America," 471
Garcilaso de la Vega, el Inca, *Comentarios reales del los Incas*, 442
Garden of Eden. *See* Earthly Paradise
Gardiner, Edward, 337
Garibay Kintana, Ángel Maria, 249–50
Gassendi, Pierre, 268
Gaudio, Michael, 414
Gaukroger, Stephen, 63–64, 360, 446–47
Geber. *See* Jābir ibn Hayyān
Genesis, book of, 51, 128, 278, 464, 469
Geneva Bible, 465
Genghis Khan, 201
Genoa, 168, 169, 171, 186, 308, 341, 346
genocide, 498n84l, 571n185. *See also* ethnocide
Gentiles, 110, 116, 124, 148, 199
Gentili, Alberico, 205, 314
George, Patron Saint of England, 385
Gerard, John, 337; *Herbal and General History of Plants*, 350
Gerard of Cremona, 93, 272
Germany, 70, 73, 475
Gerson, Jean, 53, 162, 186, 302, 303, 304, 312, 329
Gesner, Konrad, 379

Gil, Juan, 156
Gilbert, Sir Humphrey, 379, 381, 437
Giles, Peter, 279
Giménez Fernández, Manuel, 27, 195
Ginés de Sepúlveda, Juan de. *See* Sepúlveda, Juan Ginés de
Gion, 176
Glasgow, 313
Global South, 485. *See also* Hemisphere (Southern)
Goa, 355
Gog and Magog, 153, 200
gold, 14, 15, 18, 36, 37, 40, 75, 76, 77, 78, 79, 83, 84, 85, 86, 89, 90, 91, 92, 94, 95, 100, 102, 103, 126, 131, 135, 137, 148–49, 180–82, 227, 257, 263, 309, 341, 355, 356, 359, 369, 371, 373, 375, 381, 387, 449, 450
Golden Age, 36, 355, 377, 383
Golden Fleece, 384; and alchemy, 384; Order of, 183
Golden Legend, 44, 369–400
Golem, 332
Gómez de Castro, Alvar, 210
González Echevarría, Roberto, 37
Goodrick-Clarke, Nicholas, 27, 71
Gordianus (the finder), 21
Gordon-Grube, Karen, 444
Gorricio, Gaspar, 139, 140, 143, 145, 146, 168, 172
Goulaine de Laudonniere, *L'histoire notable de la Floride, contenant les trois voyages faits en icelles par des capitaines et pilotes français*, 418
Goulding, Robert, 404
gnosis, 68
grace, 303; *gratia gratum faciens*, 303; *gratia gratis data*, 303
Grafton, Anthony, 12
Granada, 108, 144, 172
Granada, Luis de, *Ecclesiasticae rhetoricae*, 240–41
Gran Canaria, 208–9
Grand Khan, 143, 144. *See also* Genghis Khan
Great Britain, 73
Great Conjunctions, Albumasar's theory of, 165
Great Debate of Valladolid, 28, 43, 290–91, 293, 297, 310
Great Schism, 23, 162
Greece, 109, 170
Greeks, 14, 424, 456, 482
Greenblatt, Stephen, 12, 56, 136, 267, 268, 269, 326, 403; *Marvelous Possessions*, 12, 56, 136; *The Swerve*, 267, 268, 269, 326

Greene, Roland, 5
Green Lion, 77
Gregory I (the Great; pope), *Cura pastoralis*, 219
Gregory IX (pope), *Cum hora undecimal*, 217
Gregory XI (pope), 189
Grenville, Sir Richard, 401
Grimaldi, Antonio, 168
Grimstone, Edward, 422, 423, 428
Grotius, Hugo, *Mare liberum*, 21
Gruzinksi, Serge, 389
Guadalquivir River, 245
Guadalupe, Juan de, 212, 222
Guadalupe, Virgin of, 248
Guaiacum, 402
Guaman Poma de Ayala, Felipe, 442
Guanahaní, 156
Guanches, 209
Guarani, 270
Guascar. *See* Huascar Inca
Guatavita, 36
Guatemoc. *See* Cuauhtémoc
Guayacán wood, 354
Guerrero, Gonzalo, 233
Guiana, 45, 396, 382, 383, 387, 392
Guinea, 196
Guistiniani, Giovanni, 168
Gužauskytė, Evelina, 156

Habsburgs, 2, 21, 37, 44, 384; claim to universal dominion, 296; Habsburg Empire, 73, 259; monarchy, 300; mythology of *Argonautica*, 384
Haiti, 211
Hakluyt, Richard, 392, 401, 408, 409, 425; *Divers Voyages Touching the Discoverie of America*, 408; *The Principal Navigations, Voiages, Traffiques and Discoueries of the English Nation*, 408, 437–38
Hale, Matthew, *The Primitive Origination of Mankind*, 469
Harriot, Thomas, 45, 360, 383, 401–17, 424, 425; *A Brief and True Report of the newfound lande of Virginia*, 45, 401, 402–17
Harris, Benjamin, 428
Hartlib, Samuel, 42
Hartlib Circle, 42
Heidegger, Martin, 9, 56, 218, 505n27; *Being and Time*, 56, 483n23
Helmont, Jan Baptist van, 261–62

Hemisphere: Northern, 372, 376; Southern, 175, 375, 432, 485; Western, 44, 422, 423, 427–28. *See also* exceptionalism
Hemispheric American Studies, 8, 9, 10
Henry VII (king of England), 378
Henry VIII (king of England), 371, 378
Henry (prince of Portugal), 196
Henry of Segusio (Hostiensis), 22
Henry, John, 71
Heraclitus, 267, 448
Hereford *mappa mundi,* 209
Herlihy, David, 53
Herman, Susan, 37
hermeneutics: of discovery, 8, 13, 24, 25, 49, 143; philosophical, 9; of secrecy, 39, 49–74; scriptural, 49, 69, 140; scientific, 49
Hermes (Mercury), 58, 82, 221, 351, 413, 442
Hermes (Mercurius) Trismegistus, 13, 65–69, 82, 90, 179, 193, 221, 355, 383, 437, 442, 451, 556
Hermeticism, 12, 39, 41, 45, 65–70, 82, 91, 123, 158, 193, 203, 204, 205, 220, 258, 272, 407, 411, 442; Hermes Christianus, 67, 70
Hernández, Francisco, 61, 251, 339; *Historia de las plantas de Nueva Espana,* 247; *Rerum medicarum Novae Hispaniae thesaurus,* 61
Herrera, Juan de, *Tratado del cuerpo cúbico conforme a los principios de R. Llull,* 187
Herrera y Tordesillas, Antonio de, 37
Hesiod, 15, 355, 377, 452; *Theogony,* 450
Hesperia, 58, 454
Hester, John, *A hundred and fouretene experiments and cures of the famous physitian Philippus Aureolus Theophrastus Paracelsus,* 382–83
heterotopia, 28–29, 41, 278, 290, 429, 434, 440–41
Hidalgo (state), 248
Hill Scott, David, 42
Hippocrates of Kos, 97, 346, 348
Hippomenes, 454
Hiroshima, 28, 267
Hispaniola, 139, 160, 171, 174, 209, 210, 211, 237, 293, 342, 343, 345, 375
Hobbes, Thomas, 28, 31–32, 56; *Leviathan,* 28
Holy Gospel, Custody of the, 222
Holy Roman Empire, 474, 475
Holy Spirit, 67, 72, 155, 280, 422
Homer, 458
homunculus, 28, 83, 290, 293, 331, 332, 349, 373, 404, 446; *homunculus americanus,* 44, 290–336

Howard, Charles, 390
Huacas, 398
Huascar Inca, 393
Huayna Khapaq Inca, 394, 395
Hubbard, William, *A Narrative of the Troubles with the Indians,* 427
Hugh of Jabala, 200
Huitzilopochtli, 420, 428
Hulna, 199
human rights, 292
humanism, 10, 14, 23, 24, 28, 29, 30, 41, 42, 43, 55, 205, 255, 267, 311, 313–14, 340, 346, 432, 439, 482
Humboldt, Alexander von, 33, 45–46, 60, 72, 471–85; *Ansichten der Natur,* 484; *Cosmos,* 477, 478; *Examen critique de l'histoire de la geographie du nouveau continent,* 164; *Personal Narrative,* 472, 473, 478, 479, 484; and physical geography, 475, 476; *Political Essay on the Island of Cuba,* 473; and terrestrial physics, 475, 481; *Versuche über die gereitzte Muskel-und Nervenfaser,* 475; *Vue des Cordilleres et monuments des peuples indigenes de l'Amerique,* 473
Huron. *See* Wyandot
Hus, Jan, 22, 301, 304
Huygens, Christiaan, *Cosmotheoros,* 288
Hylocereus, 350
hylomorphism, 13, 43, 80, 131, 215, 218, 223, 226, 227, 258, 261, 262, 263, 268, 378
Hythlodaeus, Raphael, 279, 282

Iberian Peninsula, 29, 39, 108, 109, 168
Ichthy, 288
idolatry, 66, 201, 210, 219, 222, 225, 226, 229, 230, 231, 234, 239, 245, 247, 252, 253, 256, 290, 330, 331, 360, 412, 413, 414, 416, 420, 466
Iguaráns (in García Márquez's *Cien años de soledad*), 35
Ildefonso, Colegio de, 203
Immaculate Conception, 332
Incarnation, 22, 66, 82, 110, 191
Incas, 254, 256, 309, 369, 389, 393–94
Index librorum prohibitorum (Index of banned books), 189–90
India, 40, 79, 109, 137, 143, 145, 149, 199, 200–201, 350, 355, 372, 442, 484
Indians (Eastern), 8, 75, 140, 196, 199, 200, 201
Indians (Western). *See* Native Americans
Indies, 10, 12, 20, 24, 26, 33, 37, 70, 135, 136, 141, 156, 159, 174, 188, 209, 221, 299, 337, 442

inductivism, 2, 53, 55
Innocent VIII (pope), 26, 195, 207, 271
Inquisition, 39, 81, 109, 226, 242, 461
Inter cetera (bulls of donation), 20, 21, 22, 24–28, 41, 69, 187, 194–201, 209, 236, 257, 294, 295, 296, 310, 331, 373, 374, 378, 380, 469, 496–97n77
international law, 19, 267, 292, 326, 428
invention: of America, 10; as discovery, 9, 10, 50; of discovery, 43; Renaissance concept of, 5; in science, 33
invincible ignorance, 199, 234, 296
Ireland, 140, 381
iron, 42, 121, 122, 178, 243, 335, 340, 354, 355, 356, 357, 358, 359, 371; Iron Age, 355
Isabella (queen of Castile), 136, 173, 191, 202, 294, 461
Isabella (princess of Asturias), 171
Isaiah (prophet), 147–48, 151, 167
Isidore of Seville, 59, 326; *Etymologies*, 59, 180, 250, 414
Isis, 221
Islam, 13, 19, 51, 79, 82, 115, 144, 196, 204, 205
Isle of Cods, 377
Ismailism, 82
Isobar, 476
isotherm, 476
Israel, 135; Ten Lost Tribes of, 424
Italy, 70, 73, 267, 282, 311
Iustitium, 19
Iztaccíhuatl, 60

Jābir ibn Hayyān (Geber), 64, 81
Jackson, Andrew, 473
Jacob, Francois, 359
Jacobita, Martín, 248
Jaime I (king of Aragon), 105
Jamaica, 135, 137, 142, 156, 158, 160, 211
James I (king of England), 369, 382, 439, 460; *Daemonologie*, 422, 460
Jamestown, 425, 427
Janer, Jacob, 202, 203, 208; *Ars metaphysicalis naturalis ordinis*, 202; *Liber artis metaphysicalis*, 203
Japan, 221
Jason (Argonaut), 183, 370, 384, 386. *See also* Argonauts
Jennings, Francis, 370
Jerome, Saint, 150
Jerusalem, 130, 131, 137–38, 154, 160, 167, 168, 169; New Jerusalem, 427

Jesuits, 29, 41, 215, 220, 238, 254–55; and natural history, 339
Jesus ("Christ") of Nazareth, 65, 66, 90, 110, 128, 137, 138, 140, 141, 151, 157, 163, 189, 219, 230, 257, 442; and Dragon Wonder, 351; as homunculus, 332; as serpent, 351
Jews, 39, 71, 77, 78, 83, 84, 85, 105, 107, 108, 109, 123, 124, 145, 151, 163, 165, 199, 217, 222, 234, 456, 461
Jiménez de Cisneros, Francisco, 29, 54, 109, 188, 201–8, 209, 210, 211, 213, 224, 227, 230, 237, 241, 254–55, 346
Joachim of Fiore, 40, 41, 82–83, 130, 137–38, 139, 154–55, 163, 168, 171–72, 222; Joachimism, 82–83, 138, 154–55, 167, 168, 169, 173, 222
Johann von Paderborn, 162
John XXII (pope), 29, 179; *De crimine falsi titulus VI*, 179; *Spondent quas non Exhibent*, 81
John the Baptist, 141
John (the Evangelist), 90; Gospel of, 141, 159, 184, 351
John of Patmos, 82; Book of Revelation, 141–43, 145, 147, 148, 150, 151, 154, 173, 200, 222, 278–79, 441
John of Rupescissa, 40, 84, 102–4, 105, 125, 128, 129, 131, 138, 172, 178, 186, 202, 206, 222, 267; *Breviloquium de oneribus orbis*, 172; *De quinta essencia*, 102, 125, 129, 178, 206; *Liber lucis (Book of Light)*; 102, 103, 178
John of Saxony, 164
John of Seville (Johannes Hispalensis), 161, 164
Johnson v. M'Intosh, 6, 21, 308, 473
Johnston, Mark, 216
Jonson, Ben, 388
Joshua, 90
Juan I (king of Aragon), 191
Juan, Don (prince of Asturias), 148, 341
Juan, Jorge, 476
Juana García, 38
Judaism, 71, 77, 85, 196
Judea, 135
Judensau, 85
Julius II (pope), 26
Jung, Carl Gustav, 75–77, 388
Jupiter, 165
just curiosity (*iusta curiositas*), 19, 63, 68, 77, 279, 451, 466, 484
Justinian I, *Institutes*, 296, 307

638   Index

just war, 291, 294, 305, 306, 309, 311, 314, 319, 324–36

Kabbalism: Christian, 65, 69, 380; Jewish, 71, 83, 193, 203, 207–8, 402
Kant, Immanuel, 473
Keller, Hildegard Elizabeth, 58
Kelly, Edward, 73, 388, 413, 438
Kepler, Johannes, 403
Keymis, Lawrence, 369, 382, 383; *A Relation of the Second Voyage to Guiana*, 382
Kilian, Wolfgang, 209
Kilwardby, Robert, 50
King James Bible, 464, 465, 466, 467
King Philip's War, 427
Kings, book of, 148–49
Kircher, Athanasius, 70, 187, 220
Knight Templars, 198
Kramer, Heinrich, *Malleus maleficarum*, 225
Kronos, 450
Kuhn, Thomas, 5, 50, 72

La Concepción de Uruana, 479
Labrador Sea, 379
Lacedaemonians, 326
Lacepierre of Limoges, Pierre, 186
Lactantius, *Divine Institutes*, 65–66, 68, 268
Lafitau, Joseph-François, 220–21
Lambin, Denys, 281
Landa, Diego de, *Relación de las cosas de Yucatán*, 225
Lane, Ralph, 401
Lange, Albert 62; *History of Materialism and Criticism of Its Present Importance*, 62
Laplace, Pierre Simon, 475
Las Casas, Bartolomé de, 28, 145, 157, 220, 231, 232, 238, 262, 290–91, 294, 295, 300, 310, 311, 323, 325, 342, 378, 392, 423; *Argumentum apologiae*, 291; *Brevíssima relación*, 231, 392; *Historia de las indias*, 171, 173, 180; *De unico vocationis modo*, 224, 295
Las Navas, Francisco de, 246
Last Judgment, 126, 143, 150, 169, 268, 328
Last World Emperor, 40, 154–55, 163, 167, 169, 370, 399
Latour, Bruno, 6, 30–32, 35, 38, 39, 435, 439, 485
Laud, William, 421
Laurentian Library (Florence), 249
Lavinheta, Bernardo de, 42, 187, 205–6, 208, 240; *Explanatio compendiosaque applicatio artis Raymundi Lulli*, 42, 205–6, 240, 247

Lavoisier, Antoine, 475
law of nations (*ius gentium*), 21, 24, 289, 300, 308, 380, 425
Laws of Burgos, 294
Laws of Valladolid, 294
Lawson, Alan, 10
Lefèvre d'Étaples, Jacques, 54, 186, 203–5, 292, 314; *Corpus Hermeticum*, 204, 411; *Disputatio clerici et Raymundi Phantatici aut Phantasticus*, 203, 204; *Magia naturalis*, 204; *Mercurii Trismegisti liber de potestate et sapientia dei*, 204
Leibniz, Gottfried Wilhelm, 117, 198
Leipzig, 456
Leiss, William, 465
Le Myésier of Arras, Thomas, 186
Leo X (pope), *Alias felicis*, 211, 212, 236
Lerner, Robert, 138, 150
Léry, Jean de, 43, 283–85, 286–88, 419
Leturia, Pedro de, 26
Leucippus, 80
Lévi-Strauss, Claude, *Tristes tropiques*, 485
Libellus de medicinalibus indorum herbis (Badianus manuscript). *See* Cruz, Martin de
Libro de Conoscimiento, 175–76, 548n66
Limpieza de sangre, 37
Linnaeus, Carl, 337
Lisbon, 350
Libya, 350
lizards, 350, 351
Llull, Ramón, 13, 40, 41, 84, 88, 104, 105–32, 139, 179, 192, 202, 203, 210, 232, 235, 242, 247, 267, 355, 379, 402; *ars luliana*, 40, 106, 111, 112, 117–21, 127, 131, 202, 214, 226, 247; and legendary martyrdom and prophecy or foreknowledge of the discovery of America, 184–85, 202, 539n1, 540n2, 541n7. Works: *Arbor scientiae*, 119, 129; *Ars abbreviate praedicandi*, 122; *Ars brevis*, 111, 186, 192; *Ars combinatoria*, 187; *Ars compendiosa inveniendi veritatem*, 111, 113, 118; *Ars demonstrativa*, 111, 116; *Ars generalis ultima*, 111, 118; *Ars inventiva veritatis*, 111, 186, 203; *The Art of Contemplation*, 111, 112; *Blanquerna*, 112, 113–15, 116–17, 203, 204; *The Book of the Gentile and the Three Wise Men*, 112, 115, 123, 190, 228; *Book of Knighthood and Chivalry*, 112–13; *Book of the Lover and the Beloved*, 112, 115, 203; *Compendium logicae algazelis*, 111; *De conversione subjiecti*, 208; *Disputatio Petri clerici et Raymundi Phantastici*, 197; *Doctrina pueril*, 112, 123, 213;

Félix: or, the Book of Wonders, 112, 116, 124, 203; *Liber chaos*, 130; *Liber de acquisitione Terrae Sanctae*, 124, 198; *Liber de civitate mundi*, 124, 197, 198; *Liber de fine*, 124; *Liber super psalmum "Quicumque vult,"* 116; *Llibre del Tartar*, 116; *Quaestiones per artem demonstrativum solubiles*, 185; *Principles of Medicine*, 121–22, 208, 219, 239; *Tractatus astronomiae*, 186; *Vita coaetania*, 111–12, 203, 204
Llullism, 29, 41, 42, 69, 103, 124–32, 189–92, 196–201, 204–8, 213, 250–51, 254; in America, 208–12, 213–64, 224, 226, 228, 239, 242–45, 247, 250, 253–64, 555–56n6; llullian renaissance, 185–212, 213–14, 219, 237. *See also* Pseudo-Llull
Locke, John, 25
Lok, Michael, 379
Lombard, Peter, *Sentences*, 297, 306, 311, 312, 313, 319, 333
London, 125, 382, 413, 455
López de Gómara, Francisco, 343, 374, 378, 433; *Historia general de las Indias*, 394
López de Palacios Rubios, Juan, 22, 295
López de Velasco, Juan, 251
López Pinero, José María, 352
López Terrada, Maria Luz, 353
Lorenzo, Bartolomé, 255
Löwith, Karl, 62
Lucretius Carus, Titus, 68, 267–68, 289, 403, 449, 451, 452; *De rerum natura*, 43, 67, 68, 80, 267–69, 277, 278, 281, 284, 290
Luke (Evangelist), 141, 147, 159, 161, 184
Luther, Martin, 22, 49, 233, 301, 302, 304; Lutheranism, 300, 303
Lyon, 205
Lyubishchev, Alexander, 326

MacCormack, Sabine, 410–11
Macedonians, 438
Machiavelle, Niccoló, 325; *The Prince*, 327
Macondo, 1–2, 5, 34, 201, 471. *See also* García Márquez, Gabriel
macrocosm, 17, 19, 33, 128, 160, 179, 181, 349, 388, 444, 447
Macureguarai, 382
Madoc (prince), 380
Madras. *See* Chennai
Maffie, James, 275
Magellan, Ferdinand, 342, 372, 374, 395, 471
magic, 65, 69, 72, 182, 193, 422, 430, 447, 451–52, 463

magnetism, 57, 72, 121–22
Magus, 68, 71, 72
Maier, Michael, 177, 417, 444, 455–56; *Arcana arcanissima*, 455; *Atalanta fugiens*, 177, 417, 454–56; *De theosophia Aegyptiorum*, 456; *Symbola aureae mensae*, 556
Maillard, Olivier, 201
Maimonides (Moses ben Maimon), 202
Mair, John, 43, 54, 262, 292, 465; *Dialogus de materia theologo tractanda*, 313; and "natural slavery," 306–7, 308–10, 311–15
maize, 343
Majorca, 105–6, 115, 184, 191, 193, 208–9
Malsa, 175, 548n66
Manco Inca, 395
Mandeville, John, *Travels*, 143
Maní, 225
Manicheanism, 50, 67, 85
Manifest Destiny, 473
Manoa, 369, 394, 399
Manteo, 402
Mantua, 341
Manuel (emperor of Byzantium), 199
Manuel, Frank, 437
Manuel, Fritzie, 437
Marañon, 342
Marchena, Antonio de, 173, 234
Marchesi, Francesco, 168
Mark (Evangelist), 161, 184
Marlowe, Christopher, 417
Mars, 165
Marshall, John, 6, 12, 21, 25, 28, 308, 473, 487n10
Mar Thoma (followers of Thomas), 201
Martí, Ramón, *Pugio fidei adversus mauros et iudaeos*, 110, 242
Martínez, Juan, 394
Martyr d'Anghiera, Peter, *Decades of the New World* (*De orbo novo*), 24, 33, 45, 230, 373, 374, 377
marvel, 39, 56–57
Marx, Karl, *Das Kapital*, 14–18
Mary (Maria), 177–78, 193, 234, 332
Mary I (queen of England), 373, 379
Massachusetts, 70
materialism, 28, 43, 67, 82, 135, 268, 269, 278, 280, 448, 449. *See also* ecstatic materialism
Materia medica, 44, 61, 337, 340, 347–49
mathematics, 31, 55, 68, 88, 117, 119, 148, 160, 164, 165, 166, 167, 169, 185, 205, 206, 379, 380, 383, 401, 402, 404

Mather, Cotton, 45; *Magnalia Christi Americana*, 70; *Seasonable Discourses*, 427; *Wonders of the Invisible World*, 45, 427–29
Mather, Increase, *A Relation of the Troubles with the Indians*, 427
Matthew (Evangelist), 147, 159, 161, 184; Gospel of, 300, 351; Pseudo-Matthew, 351. *See also* Dragon Wonder
Maya, 225, 233
McGinn, Bernard, 82
Mede, Joseph, 422–23, 425, 427; "A Coniecture Concerning Gog and Magogs in the Revelations," 422–23
Medea, 384
Meder, Johann, 153
Medici, Cosimo di Giovanni de, 65
Medici, Lorenzo Pierfanceso, 277–78
Medici family, 249
medicine, 68, 96, 102, 117, 121, 206, 257, 444
Mediterranean, 15, 22, 106, 110, 116, 170, 171, 172, 316
Megasthenes, 180
Mehmed II, 168
Mehmet ibn Emir Hasan el Suudi, 343
Mela, Pomponius, *Cosmographia*, 432
melancholy, 93, 102, 161, 178. *See also* Saturn
Melanchthon, Philip, 314
Melchíades, 1–2, 30, 471–72. *See also* García Márquez, Gabriel
Melek-al-Kamil, Sultan, 108
Melgarejo, Fray Pedro, 211
Mendicants, 43, 83, 107–11, 155, 211, 215–17, 220, 222, 223, 240, 246
Mendieta, Jerónimo de, 41, 209, 225, 229–30, 232–36, 256, 429; *Historia eclesiástica Indiana*, 538n110
Mendoza, Diego de, 248
Mennens, Willem, *Aureus vellus*, 453
Merchant, Carolyn, 459
Mercury (ancient Greek god). *See* Hermes
Mercury (element), 76, 84, 100, 178, 258, 259–61, 264, 351, 362, 387, 449, 454, 475
Mercury (planet), 165
Merian, Matthäus, 454–55
Messina, 168, 197
Mestizaje, 222, 223, 389, 442; mestizo mechanism, 389, 398, 399
metallurgy, 75, 76, 79, 96, 159–61, 264, 355, 371, 383, 475
metaphor, 121–22

metaphysics, 39, 43, 51–52, 54, 55, 67, 96, 121, 131, 162, 217–18, 224–28, 232, 250, 275, 292, 311; of dominion, 296–304
meteorology, 79, 126, 131
Methodius, 153
Mētis, 60, 463, 506n44
Métraux, Alfred, 285
Mexía, Pedro de, 211, 237–38
Mexica, 221, 228, 399, 419, 428, 442. *See also* Nahua
Mexican-American War, 473
Mexico, 201, 204, 211, 212, 221, 247, 259, 342, 383, 389, 393, 398, 420, 428, 475; University of, 246, 361
microcosm, 17, 19, 28, 98, 128, 160, 179, 180, 349, 388, 444, 447, 475, 476
Milan, 341
Milesians, 15
Milhou, Alain, 136, 141, 169
millenarianism, 40, 41, 42, 82, 102, 136, 139, 150–55, 169, 483
Miller, Shannon, 390
Minima naturalia, 223, 261, 370
mining, 73, 75, 257–58, 357, 362, 371, 374, 443, 475
Miramar, Monastery of, 106
missionology, 110, 217, 228, 236, 237, 254
Mita, 254, 309, 309
Moctezuma, 393, 399
modernity, 30–31
Moerbeke, William of, 318, 322–23, 330
Moffett, Thomas, 274
Moffit Watts, Pauline, 136, 137, 166
Mohammed, 90, 164, 166
Molina, fray Alonso de, 246; *Doctrina christiana breve traduzida en lengua Mexicana*, 213–14; *Vocabulario en lengua castellana y Mexicana*, 213–14
Molina, Luis de, 218, 292
Moluccas, 342
Monardes, Nicolás, 44, 337–41, 345–54, 402; *De citris, avrantiis, ac limoniis*, 347; *De rosa et partibus ejus*, 347; *De secanda vena in pleuriti*, 347; "Diálogo del hierro," 340, 354–60; *Historia medicinal*, 337–41, 345–54, 402; as "old science," 371
monasticism, 137, 155, 216, 222, 240
money, 14
Mongol Empire, 144, 201; Mongols, 154
monism, 15
monotheism, 66

Montaigne, Michel de, 43, 281, 284, 434, 443, 449, 450; *Essays*, 281; "Of Cannibals," 45, 282–85, 434, 444, 450; "Of Coaches," 281
Montaigu, College of (University of Paris), 306, 311, 313
Montecorvino, Giovanni da, 108
Montesinos, Antonio de, 220, 293–94, 311
Montpellier, 97, 125
Montserrat, 209
moon, 56, 77, 79, 84, 126, 156, 158, 165, 363, 419
Moors, 79, 168, 170, 294
More, Thomas, 43, 230; *Utopia*, 279–81, 282, 440–41, 443
Morequito, 382
Moreschini, Claudio, 67
Morison, Samuel Eliot, *Admiral of the Ocean Sea*, 136, 158, 159
Morrison, Karl, 217
Moses, 66, 69, 90, 135, 136, 193, 232–33, 442
Motolinía. *See* Toribio de Benavente
Moyne, Jacques le, 418
Muisca, 388–89
Münster, Sebastian, 45, 182, 372; *Cosmographiae universalis*, 372
mummies, 271–74, 283, 349, 443, 446, 447. *See also* corpse medicine
Muscovy Company, 379
Muslims, 23, 26, 78, 83, 84, 85, 90, 91, 92, 106, 105, 107, 109, 114, 115, 121, 123, 124, 154, 163, 165, 169, 170, 184, 197, 198, 199, 200, 217, 234, 312, 441
mysterium (mystery), 57, 59

Nahua, 221, 225, 228, 229, 242, 246, 248, 252. *See also* Mexica
Nahuatl, 214, 226, 228, 229, 242, 247, 249, 353, 433
Napoleon Bonaparte, 474
Native Americans, 6, 8, 12, 22, 24, 25, 27, 28, 30, 32, 35, 36, 37, 42, 44, 61, 67, 83, 135, 156, 157, 158, 187, 188, 194, 209, 210, 211, 218, 220, 221, 222, 223, 234, 242, 252, 256, 262, 270, 361, 382, 388, 394, 402, 406–7, 415, 423, 429, 455; and Adam, 278; and dominion, 296–304; and ethno-demonology, 223–48, 390–91, 406–29; as Greeks, 424; as homunculi, 293, 324–36; as Israelites (Jews), 231–33, 424; and law of nations, 308; and natural law, 290; and "natural slavery," 290, 304–10, 312, 314, 324, 329, 334; phlegmatic complexion, 361; removal, 473; and slavery, 294, 310; as true men, 295

Natura, 177
natural history, 247–49, 255, 337–65, 371
natural law, 21, 25, 29, 51–53, 121, 146, 189, 190, 228, 232, 235, 290, 297, 300–302, 328, 380, 425, 439, 466
natural philosophy, 11, 13, 43, 44, 50–51, 55, 79, 131, 373, 439
"natural slavery," 28, 290, 296, 297; and Mair, 306–8; 314; and Vitoria, 304–11, 315–24
natural theology, 40, 51, 86, 106–7, 129
Naturgemälde, 476
Navarro Brotóns, Victor, 34
Navarro, Pedro de, 202
navigation, art of, 2, 117, 136, 138, 147, 159, 167, 179, 187, 231, 352, 373, 374
Navigero, Andrea, 342
Nebrija, Antonio de, 203, 239; *Lexico artis medicamentae*, 346
Neoplatonism, 12, 40, 49, 50, 65, 68, 69, 70, 72, 77, 83, 106, 117, 121, 126, 131, 138, 146, 151, 156, 159–60, 177, 186, 190, 193, 197, 203, 204, 207, 250, 254, 256, 276, 441, 447, 458
Neoterici, 302, 303, 304, 331
Neo-Thomism, 54, 220, 255, 292, 304, 306, 310, 311
Nerlich, Michael, 182–83
New England, 42, 70, 274, 423, 427–29
Newfoundland, 379
New Granada, 35
New Laws, 294, 300, 325
Newman, William, 42, 64, 73, 80, 88, 227, 332, 445, 453
New Spain, 41, 44, 215, 219, 222, 226, 236, 242, 247, 251, 353, 419, 475; as watery void, 363–66
New Testament, 49, 59, 84, 140, 141, 146, 147, 219, 280, 302, 441
Newton, Isaac, 7, 80, 187
New Zealand, 5
Nicholas V (pope), *Romanus pontifex*, 196, 199
Nicholas of Cusa, *De docta ignorantia*, 68, 186, 190
Nicholas of Lyra, *Biblia sacra cum glosa ordinaria et interlineari*, 149, 150
Nicholl, Charles, 388
Nicosia, 195, 198
Nifo, Agosto, 54, 205
Nigredo, 85. *See also* sol niger (black sun)
Niremberg, Eusebio, 70, 187, 220
Noble, David, 150
Nombre de Dios, 348

nominalism (metaphysics), 30, 43, 52–54, 131–32, 162, 205, 224, 226, 245, 250, 254, 262, 263, 306, 311, 503n15; and conquest of America, 496n73; and dominion, 300–303. See also *via moderna; Wegestreit*
North America, 342, 378, 379, 380, 381
North Carolina, 401
North Star, 251
Norton, Marcy, 347
Nottinghamshire, 371
Nubia, 175
nuclear physics, 474
Nummedal, Tara, 259, 263
Núñez de Balboa, Vasco, 211
Núñez de Herrera, Juan, 348
Nuremberg, 85, 156, 432, 553n112
Nuremberg Chronicle, 97
Nussbaum, Martha, 314

Oberman, Heiko, 53, 63
Observants (Franciscan Order), 109, 202, 212
Oceanus, 159
occult, 39, 56, 58, 71, 145, 183, 483
occult philosophy, 13, 65, 69–72, 96, 126, 206, 207–8, 349, 444, 445, 448, 458
occupation, 21, 45, 370, 399
Ocean Sea, 14, 24, 135, 144, 167, 251, 376. See also Atlantic Ocean
Ockham, William of, 51, 53, 131–32, 303, 306
Odysseus. See Ulysses
Oedipal complex, 447, 451
O'Gorman, Edmundo, 9–10, 136, 489–90n26
Oikoumene, 473
Old Testament, 49, 109, 136, 146, 147, 150–51, 257, 302, 351, 441, 451, 464
Oliver, Peter, 25
Olivi, Peter John, 230
Olmedo, Bartolomé de, 211
Olmos, Andrés de, 219–20, 225–26, 246, 247; *Arte para aprender la lengua mexicana*, 225; *Sumario*, 225; *Tratado de antiguedades mexicanas*, 225; *Tratado de hechicerias y sortilegios*, 219–20, 225, 245; *Vocabulario en lengua mexicana*, 225
Ophir, 148, 149, 373, 383
optics, 95
Oran, 202, 204
Ordás, Diego, 389
Orellana, Francisco, 389
Origen, 49
Original Sin, 143, 189, 191, 252, 278, 319, 321. See also Fall, the

Orinoco River, 174, 369, 382, 387, 389, 394, 475, 482, 484
Orosius, Paulus, 314
Orphic Theogonies, 450
Ortiz, Tomás, 220
Osiris, 193
Otomac, 479
Otomí, 242
Ottoman Turks, 65, 154, 168, 198, 200, 204, 312, 343
Otto von Freising, *Chronica sive historia de duabus civitatibus*, 200
Ouroboros, 16, 17, 351, 451
Ovando, Nicholás de, 211
Ovid (Publius Ovidius Naso), 383; *Metamorphoses*, 383, 453
Oxford University, 87, 383, 401

Pachakuti, 45, 370, 388, 396–400
Pacific Ocean, 1, 20, 438
Paden, Jeremy, 345
Padua, 54, 195
Pagden, Anthony, 256, 306
Pagel, Walter, 349
Palma de Majorca, 105, 107, 202
Palos, 172
Pan, 463
Panama, 135, 342
Pando Villarroya, José Luis de, 174
Pané, Ramón, 210, 242, 553n108; *An Account of the Antiquities of the Indians*, 552–53n107
Panuco, 252
Papal Schism, Great, 54
Papa vicarius Christi, 22, 41, 124, 188, 199, 201, 213, 235, 301
Paracelsus (Theophrastus von Hohenheim), 43, 44, 70, 72, 73, 76, 96, 128, 273–74, 278, 293, 334–35, 349, 353, 355, 379, 382–83, 444–46, 448, 449; *Astronomia magna*, 293; *De generatione rerum naturalium*, 447; *De homunculis*, 293; *De natura rerum*, 334
Paracelsianism, 72, 362, 416, 444, 447, 449
Pardo-Tomás, José, 347
Paris, 198; University of, 51, 54, 87, 98, 102, 110, 121, 132, 162, 169, 186, 191, 197, 203, 204, 205, 291, 311; National Library of, 97
Pascual, Antonio Raimundo, 185–86, 187
Passannante, Gerard, 448
Patagonia, 471
Patronado, 26
Paul (Apostle), 63, 319; Epistle to the Corinthians, 304; Epistle to the Romans, 63

Paul III (pope), *Sublimis Deus,* 295
Paul of Taranto (Pseudo-Geber), 13, 16, 64, 80, 84, 261, 352, 355, 444. See also *Summa perfectionis*
Pavia, University of, 157
Pax, Nicolás de, *Illuminati Doctoris et Martyris Raymundi Lulli,* 203
Pedrarias Dávila, Pedro, 341
Pedro IV (king of Aragon), 191
Percy, Henry, 417
Pereira, Michela, 125, 129
Pérez, Joseph, 202
Pérez, Fray Juan, 173
Pérez, Rodrigo, 210
Pérez de Ribas, Andrés, 264
Perry, Elizabeth, 241
Persia, 200, 271
Peru, 41, 201, 215, 242, 254, 309, 342, 370, 374, 387, 393, 396, 420, 442, 475
Peter, 295; epistles of, 151
peyote, 361
Phelan, James, 136, 169
Philip (the Good; king of Burgundy), 183
Philip II (king of Spain), 13, 36, 73, 187, 190, 253, 353, 354, 373, 384, 438
Philip IV (king of France), 196
Philippines, 251
Phillip Augustus II (king of France), 168
philology, 448–51
Philosophers' Egg, 95, 446
Philosophers' Stone, 16, 79, 84, 85, 99. 100, 125, 128, 130, 178–79, 263, 378, 384, 386, 388, 437, 472
Philosophical Wheel, 100
phlegmatic complexion, 361
Phoenicians, 14, 482
Picany, Blanca, 105
Picatrix, 79, 411
Piccolomini, Aeneas Sylvius (Pope Pius II); *Cosmographia pii papae,* 372; *Historia rerum ubique gestarum,* 140, 143, 162, 181; and just war theory, 314
Pico della Mirandola, Giovanni, 69–70, 171, 186, 195, 204, 207–8, 383; *Apologia tredecim questionum,* 207; *Conclusiones sive theses DCCCC,* 207; *De rerum praenotione,* 171
Picts, 409
Pigafetta, Antonio, 374, 471, 472
Pillars of Hercules, 2, 62, 179, 183, 430
Pinkus, Karen, 18
Pitaya (dragon fruit), 350

Pius II (pope). See Piccolomini, Aeneas Sylvius
Pius III (pope), 195
Pius IX (pope), 185
Pizarro, Francisco, 389, 393
Pizarro, Gonzalo, 389
Plato, 67, 68, 221, 280, 326, 327, 355, 433, 445; *Phaedrus,* 160; *Republic,* 279; *Timaeus,* 69
Platzeck, Wolfram, 206
Plautus, Caspar (Honorius Philoponus), *Nova typis transacta navgatio,* 209
Pliny, the elder (Gaius Plinius Secundus), 12, 44, 93, 180, 181, 250, 256, 313, 350; *Natural History,* 340, 344, 345, 346
Plotinus, 327; *De defectu oraculorum,* 160
pluralism (matter theory), 80, 261, 262, 263
Plutarch, 161, 451
Pocahontas, 427
Podocatharo, Lodovico, 74, 195–96
Poggio Bracciolini, Gian Francesco, 68, 267, 313
Poimandres, 65. See also *Corpus Hermeticum*
Poleur, Jean, 343
Polo, Marco, *Travels,* 143, 182, 201
polytheism, 65
Ponce de León, Juan, 211
Popocatépetl, 60
pores, 80, 81, 264, 363, 364, 370
Portugal, 20, 26, 70, 160, 372
Portuondo, Maria, 360
Potosi, 258, 374
Pou y Marti, José, 169
Powhatan, 427; Confederacy, 425
Prague, 73, 379, 438, 456
Praying Towns, 27. See also *doctrinas; reducciones*
Pre-Socratics, 28, 32, 43, 45, 67, 80, 126, 267, 290, 326, 442, 448, 449–52, 556
preemptive war, 326
Prester John, 175, 199–201, 548n66; *Epistola presbiteri Johannis,* 199, 200
Prieto, Andrés, 256, 345
Prima materia (first matter), 16, 33, 79, 100, 128, 130, 223, 228, 264, 345, 351, 478
Prisca Philosophia, 440, 556
Prisca theologia, 193
pristinum statum, 208
Proaza, Alfonso de, 203; *Carmen endecasyllabum in laudem Artis Raymundi Lulli,* 203; *Raymundi Lulij . . . De noua logica, de correllatiuis, necnon [et] de ascenso [et] descensu intellectus,* 203

projection (Jungian), 76
prophecy, 39, 45, 66, 67, 72, 77, 82–84, 135–39, 143, 144, 145–46, 169, 223, 369–70, 374; Inca prophecy, 388–400, 432
Prospero, 290, 417
Protestantism, 6, 20, 21, 34, 42, 44, 45, 73, 300, 406, 444, 457; Protestant Reformation, 54, 373, 494; and Scientific Revolution, 500n104
Proteus, 452–53, 459
Proverbs, 123, 451
Province of the Holy Cross, 211, 237
Prussia, 474, 475
Psalms, book of, 351
Pseudo-Aristotle, 89–90, 96, 126; *Meteorology*, book 4, 261. See also *Secretum secretorum*
Pseudo-Avicenna, *De anima*, 95
Pseudo-Geber. *See* Paul of Taranto; *Summa perfectionis*
Pseudo-Llull, 124–32, 139, 205–6, 213, 444; *Ars operativa medica*, 127, 206, 208, 240; *Codicillus*, 127–29; *In rhetoricam isagoge*, 190; *Liber de intentione alchimistarum*, 125, 127; *Liber lapidarii*, 125; *Liber de secretis naturae seu de quinta essencia*, 128–29; *Testamentum*, 124–29, 206, 240
Pseudo-Methodius, *Apocalypse*, 153–55, 163, 169, 173, 200, 222
psychology, 76
Ptolomy, Claudius, 160, 164, 174, 234, 306, 308, 313
Puerto Gordo, 159
Purchas, Samuel, 194, 425; *Purchas his Pilgrimes*, 343, 364; "Virginia's Verger," 425
Purgatory, Mount, 174, 178
Puritanism, 42, 70, 423
Pyrrhus, 282
Pythagoras, 448, 556

Quechua, 242, 397
Queen Elizabeth's Academy, 437
Queen's College, 371
Quetzalcoatl, 398–99, 442
quicksilver. *See* mercury
Quiñones, Francisco de. *See* Ángeles, Francisco de los
quintessence. *See* fifth element
Quintilian, Marcus Fabius, 50
Quipu, 256
Quito, 389
Quiroga, Vasco de, 238

Rabeleis, François, 282; *Pantagruel*, 314
Rábida, *Convento de Santa María de la*, 172–73, 186, 209, 234
Raleigh, Walter, 45, 360, 369–70, 380–400, 401–2, 408, 409, 413, 416, 423; *Discovery of the Beautiful Empire of Guiana*, 45, 369–70, 382–400, 408, 413; *History of the World*, 383, 384, 396
Ramírez de Fuenleal, Sebastián, 225, 246
Ramón de Penyafort, 109, 110, 111
Ramón of Toledo (archbishop), 79
Ramus, Peter, 50, 54, 445
Ramusio, Giovanni Battista: *Navigationi et viaggi*, 342, 343, 408, *Summario de la generale historia de l'Indie Occidentali*, 343
Randa, Mount, 105, 111
Rastatt, Second Congress of, 474
Ravi Mumford, Jeremy, 254
Ray, John, 247
Rayas, 20
realism (metaphysics), 43, 52–53, 54, 131, 220, 224, 228, 250, 262, 302, 503n15. See also *via antiqua*; *Wegestreit*
reconquest (*reconquista*), 26, 39, 50, 78, 79, 83, 107, 109, 145, 193, 234, 235, 293, 359, 429, 462
Recopilacion de Leyes de Indias, 188
Recusant crisis, 461
Red Cross Knight, 385
Reducción General, 215, 254
reduction, reduce, *reductio*, 237–40; definitions, English, 546n50; —, Latin, 546n50; —, Spanish 543n20; in alchemy, 14, 15, 29, 40, 41, 85, 100, 126, 130, 223, 240; in epistemology, 51, 121; as religious conversion, 27, 29, 41, 188–89, 196–98, 201, 213, 235–64; as missionary town, 238, 254, 565n111 (see also *doctrinas*; Praying Towns)
reflection, 404
Reformation (Protestant), 38, 70, 224
refraction, 403
Regiomontanus (Johannes Müller von Königsberg): *Alchmanac perpetuum*, 156; *Calendarium*, 156; *Ephemerides astrologicae*, 156
Regnans in excelsis (Pope Pius V), 461
regressus theory, 55, 465
Reizung, 45, 475, 477, 483
Relaciones geográficas, 61
Relectio (rhetorical genre), 297–98
Renaissance episteme, 432
Requirimiento, 22, 229, 295
Res/terra nullius, 6, 12, 19, 25, 143, 429, 467

Resurrection, 67, 94, 103, 275, 286
Reuchlin, Johannes, 69
Revelation, book of (Apocalypse), 138, 141–43, 150
Rey Bueno, Mar, 352
Rhazes. *See* al-Razi
rhetoric: evangelical, 207, 213–14, 240–46; deliberative, 298; demonstrative, 298; (Scholastic) judicial, 298. *See also* alchemy of words; evangelism
rhubarb, 354
Ribault, Jean, 418
Ricard, Robert, *The Spiritual Conquest of Mexico*, 213, 220, 221, 223
Richard I (the "Lionheart"; king of England), 82, 168
Río, Martín del, 349
Riohacha, 34, 35
Rivett, Sarah, 42
Roanoke Island, 401, 402; Lost Colony, 401
Robert of Anjou (king of Naples), 171
Robertson, Donald, 250
Robertson, Kellie, 62
Robles, Juan de, 210
Rodríguez de Montalvo, Garci, *Las Sergas de Esplandian*, 203
Rodríguez Freyle, Juan, *El carnero*, 35–38
Rojas, Fernando de, *La celestina*, 203
Roman Empire, 216
Roman Law, 22, 25, 380
Romanticism, 482
Rome, 130, 169, 191, 192, 194, 198, 271, 275, 282, 285, 291, 439; Romans, 438; University of, 195
Romm, James, 136
Rorty, Amélie, 314
Rosicrucians, 385, 444
Rossi, Paolo, 463
Rousseau, Jean-Jacques, 282, 482
Rovilio, Guillermo, 355
Rowlandson, Mary, *The Sovereignty and Goodness of God*, 427
Royal Office of Ordnance, 437
Royal Society of London, 2, 5, 70, 187, 427, 470
rubber tree, 343
Rubruck, William of, 108, 200
Rudolf II (king of Bohemia; Holy Roman emperor), 73, 379, 438, 455–56
Rufo Candidus of Aquitaine, Remigius, *In rhetoricam isagoge*, 206–8, 219, 239; *Oratio excemplaris*, 206
Ruhe, 46, 477, 483, 484, 485. *See also* solitude
Ruiz, Francisco, 210
Rumeu de Armas, Antonio, 172, 208
Ruscelli, Girolamo, 353
Russia, 374

Sabunde, Raimond of, 186, 190
Sahagún, Bernadino de, 41, 61, 205, 215, 217–19, 246–53, 255, 256; *Arte adivinatoria*, 248; *Florentine Codex*, 61, 213, 249; *Historia universal de las cosas de la Nueva Espana*, 218–19, 247–53, 558n22; *Libro de los Colloquios*, 228–29; *Psalmodia Christiana*, 221
Saladin, 154
Salamanca, 255; School of, 292, 295, 465; University of, 54, 167, 205, 217–18, 247, 291, 294, 295, 297, 299, 310, 311
Sale, Kirkpatrick, 136
Salem, Mass., 427; witch trials, 427
salt (in alchemy and mining), 42, 79, 127, 178, 182, 259, 260, 362, 447, 452, 454
saltpeter, 127, 178, 387
San Buenaventura, Pedro de, 248
San Gabriel, Custody of, 212, 236
San José de los Naturales, 242
San Lucar de Barrameda, 251, 345
San Marcos, University of (Lima), 254
San Salvador, 156
Sanskrit, 471
Santa Cruz de Tlatelolco, Colegio Imperial de, 204, 246–48
Santa Fe, 173
Santa Maria, 140
Santa Maria de Berrocal, convent of, 212
Santa María de Jesús, Universidad de, 246
Santa Maria de los Ángeles (friary), 211
Santiago, 234
Santo Domingo, 38, 251
Saracens. *See* Muslims
Sarmiento de Gamboa, Pedro, 395, 396; *Historia de los Incas (History of the Incas)*, 395–98
sassafras, 337, 402
Satan, 91, 143, 338, 377, 425. *See also* devil
Saturn, 102, 159–61, 164, 165, 178, 450
Saul (king of Israel and Judah), 302
Savonarola, Girolamo, 277, 278
Schedel, Hartmann, 97. See also *Nuremberg Chronicle*
Scientific Revolution: seventeenth-century, 2, 39, 42, 50, 63, 92, 247, 263, 268, 269, 274, 326, 335, 371; —, and Protestantism, 500n104; —, and Spanish imperialism, 491n33; thirteenth-century, 50

Schmitt, Carl, 19–21, 494n63
Scholasticism, 39, 40, 43, 50–55, 57, 58, 64, 67, 71, 72, 77, 179, 205, 207, 216, 258, 267, 313–14, 340, 430, 432, 448
Schongauer, Martin, 351, 352
Scott, Ridley, *1492: The Conquest of Paradise*, 136
Scotus Erigena, John, *De divisione naturae*, 111
Seaford, Richard, 15
Sebastiano da Verona, 84
Second Coming, 107, 128, 137, 138, 139, 143, 165, 183, 204, 232, 484
Second Scholastics, 217, 292, 293
secrecy, secrets, 12, 13, 18, 19, 31, 36, 37, 39, 40, 56–61, 75, 84; hermeneutics of, 49–74, 245, 460; secretary, 13, 71, 74, 195, 339, 340, 371, 383, 458, 492n40; secrets of nature, 74, 83, 90–91, 96, 179, 183, 372, 391, 441, 453, 458, 477–78, 485 (see also *venatio*); secrets of the world, 135, 147, 159, 168, 183, 374, 475
Secretum secretorum (Pseudo-Aristotle); 89–91, 95, 96, 200. See also Pseudo-Aristotle
Seex, Thomas, 371
Segovia, 291
Selye, Hans, 8
Seneca, Lucius Annaeus, *Medea*, 159, 183
Sennert, Daniel, 17
Sepúlveda, Antonio de, 36
Sepúlveda, Juan Ginés de, 205, 262, 290–291, 292, 293, 310, 314, 323, 327, 466; *Apologia*, 310; *Aristotelis de Republica Libri VIII*, 323; *De justis belli causis*, 325; *Democrates, sive de convenientia disciplinae militaris cum christiana religion dialogus*, 326; *Democrates alter*, 28, 43, 257, 290, 293, 297, 323, 324–36, 466; and just war, 326
Sequera, Fray Rodrigo de, 249, 353
Serres, Michel, 58, 267, 269
Seth, 457
Severinus, Peter (Peder Soerensen), *Idea medicinae philosophicae*, 447
Seville, 137, 171, 255, 337, 342, 345, 346, 356, 361, 394
Sgurgola, 169
Shakespeare, William, *The Tempest*, 290, 417
Sheba, queen of, 373
Sibyls, 160; sibylline tradition, 154, 169
Sicily, 168, 170
Sidney, Sir Philip, 409
Silber, Eucharius, 192

silver, 15, 36, 75, 84, 85, 92, 100, 126, 148, 180, 181, 182, 240, 254, 257, 258–59, 261, 263, 264, 355, 356, 362, 365, 381
Silverblatt, Irene, 461
Simmel, Georg, 58
Sixtus, IV (pope), 191, 192
Sloterdijk, Peter, 57
Smith, John, *General History of Virginia*, 425–27
Smith, Pamela, 18, 349
Smith, Thomas, 371
Society for Propagation of the Gospel, 31
Socrates, 160
Soderini, Pier, 276
Solamona, 435
Solinus, 93, 180
solitude, 1, 2, 46, 471, 478, 480, 483, 485. See also *Ruhe*
sol niger (black sun), 16, 27, 77, 85, 240, 351
Solomon (king), 123, 130, 148, 149, 302, 383, 442, 451
Solomon's House, 434–35, 439, 441
Song of Songs (Old Testament), 258
Soto, Domingo de, 54–55, 218, 224, 291, 323, 335, 465; *Aqui se contiene una disputa, o controversia*, 323; *Reclectio de dominio*, 295, 310
Sorbonne. See Paris, University of
South America, 1, 5, 20, 33, 34, 35, 37, 45, 46, 174, 238, 349, 369, 374, 381, 382, 388, 389, 390, 394, 395, 396, 401, 473, 478, 479, 480, 481, 485
Southern Cross (star), 251, 483–84
spagyrics, 92, 96, 178, 181–82, 214, 226, 229, 444, 449
Spain, 20, 26, 70, 73, 107, 160, 168, 171, 172, 188, 198, 209, 369, 374, 438–39
Spanish (Castilian), 170, 188, 204, 214, 228, 249, 347
Spanish Empire, 300
Sparta, 326, 439
Spenser, Edmund, 385; *Faerie Queene*, 385
Spies, Johann, *Historia von D. Johann Fausten*, 415–16
Spirituals (Franciscans), 102, 109, 155, 222
Spontaneous Generation, 332, 404
Sprenger, Jacob, *Malleus maleficarum*, 225
Staden, Hans, 287, 419
St. Agatha, 195
St. Andrews, University of, 313
Stannard, David, 136
Starkey, George, 70, 187, 444
Star of David, 77

state of exception (*Ausnahmezustand*), 14, 18, 19–20, 26, 27, 28, 29, 78, 275, 308, 461. *See also* exceptionalism
St. Brendan's Island, 209
Stearns, Raymond, *Science in the British Colonies of America*, 371
steel, 197, 358, 371
Stefan (king of Poland), 73
Stobaeus, Joannes, 70
Stoics, 28, 276, 285, 327
Strait of Magellan, 395
Strychnos, 391
Stuart dynasty, 419, 434
St. Vincent, 159
Suárez, Francisco de, 218, 292
substantial form, 79, 80, 98, 131, 218, 223
Suchten, Alexander von, 379
Sugg, Richard, 271
sulfur, 76, 84, 178, 258, 351, 358, 362, 454
Summa perfectionis (pseudo-Geber), 16, 64, 80, 92, 261, 352. *See also* Paul of Taranto
Summenhart, Conrad, 301, 304
sun, 56, 68, 77, 84, 95, 126, 156, 158, 165, 166, 180, 339, 363, 386, 419, 477
Swift, Jonathan, 282
syllogism, 50, 53
Sylvester (pope), 24
synderesis, 28, 52, 220, 312, 465
Syria, 154, 170

Tabula smaragdina, 81
Tacitus, Publius Cornelius, 58; *Germania*, 58
Taclla, 397–98
Taínos, 210, 240
Taki unquy, 398
Takua, 391
Talavera Commission, 173
Tarascan, 242
Tarragon, Council of, 98
Tarshish, 149, 373
Tartars, 154, 165, 166, 198, 199, 200–201
Tat, 68
Taylor, Edward, 274, 444
Techne, 89
Telde, Diocese of, 208
temperate zones, 480, 481, 482, 485
Templars, 198
Tenochtitlán, 211, 389, 398. *See also* Mexico
Tepepulco (Tepeapulco), 248, 249
Tequina, 375
Terra nullius. *See res/terra nullius*
Terrestrial Paradise. *See* Earthly Paradise

Testera, Jacobo de, 242
Texcoco, 211, 225
Thacher, John Boyd, *Christopher Columbus*, 158
theodicy, 315
Theophrastus, Problem XXX, 161
theosophy, 68
Thevet, André, 43, 272–73, 283, 286; *Les singularitez de la France Antarctique*, 283, 285
Third Provincial Council of Lima, 254
Thomas, Apostle, 199, 200, 201, 442
Thomas Aquinas, 19, 50, 51, 54, 80, 83, 120, 124, 189, 218, 220, 227, 268, 293, 318, 330; on homunculus, 332, 333, 373; on natural law metaphysics, 302; on slavery, 319–22; *Summa contra Gentiles*, 110; *Summa theologiae*, 19, 51–52, 54, 199, 220, 250, 259, 297, 304, 321, 332
Thomas, Keith, 315
Thomism, 28, 29, 43, 51–52, 79–81, 121, 131, 189, 190, 199, 205, 217, 220, 223, 224, 226, 227, 228, 232, 250, 254, 261, 262, 269, 293, 310, 323; art and nature, 227, 333
Thorndike, Lynn, *History of Magic and Experimental Science*, 71, 83, 88, 96, 126, 131
Thorowgood, Thomas, *Jews in America*, 424
Thoth, 65, 82, 442
Throckmorton, Elizabeth, 381
Thucydides, 28, 327; *History of the Peloponnesian War*, 326
Thule, 159, 183
Thurneyesser zum Thurn, Leonhardt, 379
Tiburtine Sibyl, 153
Tierra firme, 148, 211, 341, 342, 343, 345, 375, 379
Tiffin, Chris, 10
Tigris, 176
Timothy, 145
Tiphys, 159, 183
Titicaca, Lake, 442
Titu Cusi Yupanki, 385
Tlaxcala, 211
tobacco, 337, 343, 361
Toledo, 198, 202, 204, 341; School of Translators, 79, 160, 164, 272
Toledo, Francisco de, 215, 254, 395
Toltecs, 442
Topiawari, 382
Toral, Francisco de, 248
Tordesillas, Treaty of, 20, 21, 26, 438
Toribio de Benavente (Motolonia), 41, 224, 230–31, 232, 247, 252, 256, 429; *Historia*

Toribio de Benavente (Motolonia) (*continued*)
  de los indios de la Nueva España, 231, 245; "Letter to the Emperor Charles V," 224
Torre, Juana de la, 148
torrid zone, 54, 162, 166, 179, 251, 372, 375–76, 478, 481, 484
torture, 16, 34, 76, 84, 85, 100, 225, 258, 259, 263, 282, 285, 458–62
Tortusa, Disputation of, 217
Toscanelli, Paolo, 162
Toulouse, University of, 102, 205
Tovar, Juan de, 255
Tower of London, 381
translation, 371–78
trans-substantiation, 76, 284, 444
Trasierra, Juan de, 210
Travisari, Ambrogio, *Life of Epicurus*, 277
Trent, Council of, 190, 241, 242, 246, 253, 291
Trinidad, 174, 342, 382
Trinity, 40, 78, 84, 110, 155, 220, 221, 235
Tripoli, 170
tropics, 164, 174–81, 471, 477, 484; as analog of the alchemical crucible, 179, 181, 477; as macrocosmic crucible, 339, 387–88
Trujillo, Sebastián, *Aqui se contiene una disputa, o controversia*, 291; and Monardes's *Historia medicinal*, 354
Tuck, Richard, 205
Tullius, Servius, 93
Tunis, 106, 184, 186
Tupak Amaru Inca, 254, 395, 396
Tupinamba, 270, 279, 283, 285–88, 419
Turing, Alan, 117
typology, 69

Ullman, Father, *Buch der Heiligen Dreifaltigkeit*, 40, 78, 84–87, 101, 128, 459
Ulloa, Antonio de, 477
Ulysses, 33, 62, 279
Unay, Juan, *Libro de los grandes hechos*, 171
unicorn, 77
United Nations General Assembly, Declaration on the Rights of Indigenous Peoples, 5, 474
United States of American, 5, 473, 481
unitism (matter theory), 80, 261, 262
Uranus, 450
Urco Huaranca Inca, 396
Ursúa, Pedro de, 389
Usnea, 446

Utopianism, 20, 39, 30, 41, 92, 124, 200, 202, 204, 230, 231, 256, 279–80, 355, 370, 377, 433, 437, 440, 443

Vacuum domicilium, 25, 497n79
vain curiosity (*vana curiositas*), 18, 62–63, 67, 77, 96, 268, 466, 483
Valadés, Diego de, *Rhetorica Christiana*, 190, 237, 239, 242–45, 255, 256
Valencia, 179, 191, 192, 202
Valencia, Martín de, 206, 212, 236
Valeriano, Antonio, *Nican Mopohua*, 248
Valla, Lorenzo, 103, 326; *De voluptate*, 277, 278
Valldemossa, 106
Van Groesen, Michiel, 287
Vascosan, Michel de, 342
Vauvert, Monastery, 111
Veen, Gijsbert van, 410
Vegerano, Alonso de, 248
Venatio, 60, 390, 463
Venezuela, 342, 475
Venice, 200, 277, 342, 371
Veracruz, 212
Veragua, 148, 159
Vergil, Polydore, *De inventoribus rerum*, 55
Vermilion, 350–51
Vesalius, Andreas, 348
Vespucci, Amerigo (Vespuccian), 10, 43, 267, 276–78, 280–81, 313, 326, 343, 372, 374, 443, 483; *Mundus novus*, 10, 230, 270, 277; questionable authorship, 574–75n10; Ridolfi Fragment, 279; Soderini letter, 279
via antigua, 39, 43, 52–53, 220, 503n15. *See also* realism (metaphysics); *Wegestreit*
via moderna, 39, 52–53, 302, 503n15. *See also* nominalism (metaphysics); *Wegestreit*
Vienne, Council of, 197–98
Vigenere, Blaise de, *De igne et sale*, 452
Vilcabamba, 395, 398
Villacreces, Pedro de, 212
Vincent of Beauvais, 50
vincible ignorance, 199, 234, 296
Viracocha Inca, 396
Virgil (Publius Vergilius Maro), 58, 458; *Aeneid*, 58, 313, 458, 505–506n34
Virginia, 364, 401, 402, 409, 425–27, 491
Virgin Queen. *See* Elizabeth I
Virgin's Milk (*lac virginis*), 84, 174, 178–81, 339
Vitoria, Francisco de, 24–25, 43, 54, 218, 224, 262, 291, 296–311, 314, 324, 329, 331, 465, 466; "De indis," 295; 296–304, 306–10,

311; "On Civil Power," 301; "On the Power of the Church," 304; lectures on Aquinas's *Summa,* 304; and "natural slavery," 304–11, 315, 586–87n96
Viveiros de Castro, Eduardo, 275, 285–86
Vives, Juan Luis de, 205
void, 21, 28, 29, 44, 45, 80, 81, 264, 361, 364, 370, 403, 495n66
Vulgate Bible, 465
voluntarism, 53

Waghenaer, Lucas, *The mariners mirror,* 409
Walker Bynum, Caroline, 271
Wallace, Anthony, 437
Wanchese, 402
war, theory of, 205
Weckmann-Muñoz, Luis, 22, 188, 196, 301
Wegestreit, 52, 503n15
Welser, 389
western bat, 170, 171, 179
Wey-Gómez, Nicholás, 166
Whalley, Richard, 371
Wheeler, Harvey, 460
Whiddon, Jacob, 382
White, John, 401, 409; *The Flyer,* 409–13, 415
Whitehead, Neil, 389
White Legend, 5, 7, 34, 44, 45, 365, 370, 388–400
Whitney, Charles, 433
Wigglesworth, Michael, 444
Wilkins, John, *Discovery of a World in the Moon,* 288
William of Cremona, 301
Williams, John, *Key into the Language of America,* 424
Williamson, Arthur, 83

Willughby, Francis, 247
Winthrop, John, 423
Winthrop, John, Jr. (II), 42, 70, 444
Wisecup, Kelly, 403
witchcraft, 37, 38, 225, 226, 229, 333, 414, 415, 417, 420, 422, 427, 428, 429, 459
Witches Sabbath, 414, 459
Wittenberg Castle, 304
Wohlgemut, Michael, *Liber chronicarum,* 351
Woodward, Walter, 42
Wyandot (Huron), 220, 221
Wycliffe, John, 22, 301, 302, 304, 465

Yates, Frances, 71
yellow, 77
Yorkshire, 371
Young, J. T., 42
Young, Robert, 42
Yucatán, 225, 342
Yucca, 342
Yupanki Inca, 396–98

Zabarella, Jacopo, 54
Zacut, Abraham, *Tabule tabularum celestius motuus,* 156
Zamorra, Margarita, 136, 145
Zaragoza, Treaty of, 20, 21, 438
Zárate, Agustín, 343; *Historia del descubrimiento y conquista de las provincias del Perú,* 354–55
Zemes, 377
Ziegler, Joseph, 98, 122, 219, 239
Zion, Mount, 137, 167, 168, 170
Žižek, Slavoj, 271; *For They Know Not What They Do,* 430
Zumárraga, Fray Juan de, 204, 225, 226, 246

Writing the Early Americas

Spanning the broad chronological territory between contact and colonization through the long nineteenth century, this series publishes scholarship that amplifies, challenges, and regrounds the study of literary culture in the United States by highlighting the varied spaces, temporal periods, and forms of language of the early Americas.

www.ingramcontent.com/pod-product-compliance
Lightning Source LLC
Chambersburg PA
CBHW021412300426
44114CB00010B/465